SOUL IN
SOCIETY

SOUL IN SOCIETY

The Making and Renewal

of Social Christianity

GARY DORRIEN

FORTRESS PRESS   MINNEAPOLIS

For Sara—

Beloved daughter
who brings joy

SOUL IN SOCIETY
The Making and Renewal of Social Christianity

Copyright © 1995 Augsburg Fortress. All rights reserved. Except for brief quotations in critical articles or reviews, no part of this book may be reproduced in any manner without prior written permission from the publisher. Write to: Permissions, Augsburg Fortress, 426 S. Fifth St., Box 1209, Minneapolis, MN 55440.

Biblical quotations, unless otherwise noted, are from the Revised Standard Version of the Bible, copyright © 1946, 1952, and 1971 by the Division of Christian Education of the National Council of Churches. Used by permission.

Cover graphics: Bettmann Photos
Cover design: Brad Norr

Library of Congress Cataloging-in-Publication Data

Dorrien, Gary J.
    Soul in society : the making and renewal of social Christianity /
Gary Dorrien.
        p.   cm.
    Includes bibliographical references and index.
    ISBN 0-8006-2891-8 (alk. paper)
    1. Sociology, Christian—United States—History of doctrines—20th
century.   2. Liberalism (Religion)—United States—History of
doctrines—20th century.   3. Liberalism (Religion)—Protestant
churches—History of doctrines—20th century.   4. United States—
Church history—20th century.   I. Title.
BT738.D66   1995
261.8'0973—dc20   95-4023
                                                                    CIP

The paper used in this publication meets the minimum requirements of American National Standard for Information Sciences—Permanence of Paper for Printed Library Materials, ANSI Z329.48-1984.

Manufactured in the U.S.A.   AF 1-2891

99   98   97   96   95   1   2   3   4   5   6   7   8   9   10

Contents

Preface

Soul in Society evokes and interprets the spirit of modern social Christianity. At its best, the American religious tradition examined in this book has been rooted in the teaching and way of Jesus Christ and the proleptic reality of Christ's kingdom-bringing Spirit. It has proclaimed that Christianity has an inspiriting and regenerative social mission, and it has sought to bring the transforming power of Christian faith to social struggles for freedom, democracy, peace, and social justice. As the book's subtitle implies, my purpose in writing about modern social Christianity is to offer an interpretation of its historical and theological development and to present a normative contribution to its postmodern future.

Christian ethics in this century has been dominated by three basic forms or types of social Christian theory: social gospel progressivism, Christian realism, and liberation theology. The present work examines the origins and interrelated histories of these movements, interpreting the story of American liberal Protestantism in a way that also brings Roman Catholic, African American, feminist, environmentalist, and other voices into an increasingly pluralistic discussion. The chief distinguishing characteristic of social Christianity has been its willingness to address the intellectual, political, and moral dilemmas associated with what Ernst Troeltsch called "the modern social problem." More than any comparable religious tradition, liberal Protestantism has struggled creatively for two centuries to face up to the challenges of modern science, historical criticism, and commercial society. This book will closely examine the main lines of these struggles in modern American liberal Protestant history.

As the book's early chapters will emphasize, the social Christian project of relating Christian ethics to American society has always been riddled with difficult problems and dilemmas, some of them attributable to the racial, gender, and class privileges of its proponents. In the past generation, however, as American society has become increasingly fragmented, secular, and individualistic, as well as increasingly dominated by the interests and ethos of commercial society, the difficulties of relating Christian social teaching to the prevailing social order have greatly magnified. The triumph of a globalized and arguably uncontrollable market system militates against the realization of any form of progressive Christianity's social vision. The commercialization of the public sphere and the power of special interests to prevent social change make it difficult even to raise certain issues in the public realm. The present work will thus explore the crisis of American social Christianity in a national and world context that offers few signs of encouragement. I shall argue that in the face of its apparent defeat, however, the modern Christian vision of a just economic order is redeemable as a pluralistic, pragmatic, decentralized strategy for economic democracy. More importantly, I shall argue that a relevant and faithful social ethic can be pieced together from the pluralistic legacy of progressive social Christianity.

This inheritance is far from the triumphant social faith that a mostly white, liberal, middle-class, male Protestantism expected to pass on. "The Christian Century" has turned out very differently than its proponents envisioned. In the early years of this century, theologians such as Walter Rauschenbusch, Charles Clayton Morrison, and Shailer Mathews urged that social-gospel Christianity could become the soul of a world-embracing movement for democracy and progress. Morrison renamed his magazine *The Christian Century* to signify that social Christianity would not be a passing fashion. The social gospelers believed that their movement to recover the social meaning of Christianity was destined to absorb the energies of twentieth-century church leaders and transform the world through its idealism.

They were right about the first part. The influence of social-gospel Christianity has long outlasted its rhetoric about "Christianizing" the world. Theologians throughout this century have taken up the social-gospel project of relating Christian teaching to the problems of social justice, democracy, and peace. As a movement that sought to make American Christianity address the modern social problem, early social Christianity made an enduring achievement. Yet for all of its creativity and influence, the social-gospel movement was deeply flawed. The form of social Christianity that prevailed over it in the 1930s repeatedly denounced the idealism, optimism, and moralism of the social gospelers. A generation later, liberation theologians reclaimed much of the spirit of social-gospel Christianity against a politically conformist Christian realism, while criticizing both movements for their complicity in racial and gender oppression as well as their nationalism, provincialism, and imperialism.

The correctives only begin with this list. At the end of a century that has produced no cooperative commonwealth but instead a long list of genocidal dictatorships and wars of mass destruction, how much of the social-gospel vision of the just society can be saved or reconstructed? Were the Christian realists right to give up the idea of a democratized social order? How much of Reinhold Niebuhr's critique of Christian idealism should contemporary theologians accept as a corrective to their own idealism? Does the postmodern emphasis on race, multiculturalism, and anti-imperialism preclude the possibility or even desirability of a reconstructed common good? Can any form of Christianity be liberating to women after feminist criticism has exposed the patriarchal character of Christian scripture and tradition? Can postmodern Christianity develop a spirituality and sustainable praxis that contributes to the healing of the natural world? If Christianity no longer provides a unitive moral language for American society, is it possible to create new kinds of moral communities? Could the end of Christendom be a blessing for Christianity? This book will pursue these questions as it interprets the story of modern and postmodern social Christianity.

My scholarly debts are few but deep. I am grateful as always to my colleagues, biblical scholar Waldemar Schmeichel, ethicist Pete Gathje, and philosopher Christopher Latiolais, for their friendship and support of my work; and I am grateful to Clare and Lester Start, Robert Dewey, and editors Joy Matkowski and Lois Torvik for their careful reading of the manuscript. Without the friendship and assistance of Pam Sotherland and Laura Packard-Latiolais, my various administrative functions would be a shambles and I would be too frazzled to write anything. They are my closest friends and colleagues.

Many thanks also to Marshall D. Johnson, Director of Publishing for Fortress Press, for his support of this project, and to Michael West, an editor whose knowledge and generosity of spirit I learned to rely upon. Bob Dewey read the manuscript to an ailing John Bennett after Dr. Bennett's cataracts made him unable to read. I am especially grateful for Dr. Bennett's advice, commentary, and encouragement as I worked on the manuscript. My perspective on liberal Christianity is shaped and enriched every day by the companionship of my wife, Brenda Biggs, a Presbyterian minister who exemplifies everything that a caring and spiritually grounded pastor should be.

1 INTRODUCTION
The Good Society and the Legacy of Social Christianity

THE NOTION THAT CHRISTIANITY HAS A TRANSFORMATIVE SOCIAL MISSION is distinctly modern. Near the end of his classic work, *The Social Teaching of the Christian Churches* (1912), Ernst Troeltsch observed that modern Christianity was distinguished in Christian history by its assumption of an "entirely new" project that Aquinas or Calvin could not have imagined. The project was to make Christianity relevant to a nationalistic, capitalist, technological, and increasingly secular order. Troeltsch noted that the overwhelming force and complexity of "the modern social problem" had driven a wedge between modern Christianity and its earlier traditions. The two main social philosophies of premodern Christianity—medieval Catholicism and Calvinist/Pietist Protestantism—offered little help in alleviating what he called "all this distress which weighs on our hearts and minds like a perpetual menace."[1] Not all modern Protestant theologians after Troeltsch would regard modernity as a menace, but for most of them, as for Troeltsch, the "modern social problem" has seemed unavoidable. Christian theology embraced a new understanding of its social mission during the very period when its doctrinal basis was strongly challenged by modern science, historical criticism, and Enlightenment philosophy. The story of modern theology has thus been a distinctively social-ethical narrative.

For most of the past century, liberal Protestantism has pioneered in seeking to show what it means to face up to modernity—that is, to the social order created by Enlightenment criticism, modern science and technology, and capitalist economics. At the same time, liberal Protestantism has often dealt with the modernist challenge by accommodating the moral, religious, and social meaning of Christianity to the ethos of a secular, individualistic, market-driven culture. This book tells the story of modern Protestantism from a perspective that is

---

1. Ernst Troeltsch, *The Social Teaching of the Christian Churches*, vol. 2, trans. Olive Wyon (Louisville: Westminster/John Knox Press, 1992, c1912), 1011.

critical of its accommodationist spirit but critically affirmative of its social gospel tradition. It contributes to the future of this tradition by seeking to show how the progressive Christian vision of social and economic democracy can be redeemed in the face of its apparent defeat. More important, the book makes an argument for a social Christianity that seeks to be faithful to the distinctive kingdom-oriented ethic of the way of Christ.

To persist in struggling for the democratization of social and economic power is to hold out for a vision of the common good that is deeply rooted in North American progressive history and, especially, American liberal Christianity. Near the end of his important book on the theory of economic democracy, the eminent political theorist Robert Dahl remarks that Americans have always been torn between two conflicting visions of what a good society would be. The first is the vision of a fully realized democracy, in which democratic rights over all of society's major social and economic institutions are established. The second is the vision of a society that would provide unrestricted liberty to acquire wealth. In the first view, the right to self-government is considered superior to the right to property, and the common good is sought by democratizing social, political, and economic power. In the second view, the right to property is considered superior to the right to self-government, and the common good is sought (when it is conceptualized at all) by protecting narrowly defined property rights and by restricting the equalizing role of government.[2]

The realities of American politics are rarely as clear-cut as these ideal types; American society today uneasily conflates the two visions that Dahl describes. But if that is true, it is also true that a great deal depends on which of these visions is in the ascendancy in a given generation. As Arthur Schlesinger has noted, in each generation one of these visions does achieve predominance over the other, and when this occurs, the values and expectations of subsequent generations of Americans are shaped accordingly.[3]

There can be little argument that, for the past generation, the more individualistic or capitalist vision has been in the ascendancy in the United States. During the same period, perhaps not coincidentally, the mainline liberal Christian churches have declined in public influence and authority. Except for their witness on peace issues—especially issues pertaining to imperialism and military intervention—the mainline churches have lost much of the impact they once had on national public debates, while the religious Right has filled much of the vacuum. Notwithstanding the fact that most modern Christian theology has borne a social

---

2. Robert Dahl, *A Preface to Economic Democracy* (Berkeley: University of California Press, 1985), 163.

3. Cf. Arthur M. Schlesinger, Jr., *The Cycles of American History* (Boston: Houghton Mifflin Co., 1986), 23–48.

democratic or democratic socialist stamp, for the past century, mainline American Protestantism has generally adopted a strategy of accommodation to the dominant culture. The mainline churches have typically sought not to challenge existing relations of power but to work out an accommodation in which their role as a moral influence in society is affirmed. Faced with the advances of modern science and technology as well as the evident need to justify their own increasingly marginalized role in modern society, the mainline churches have generally refrained from challenging the structures or ethos of the dominant order in order to remain part of it. For most of the past century, mainline Christianity has focused its moral energies on the question of how to exercise power in a morally responsible way.

But mainline Protestantism has lost much of the cultural and social power it once took for granted in the United States. Moreover, the dominant order with which mainline Protestantism has historically identified is itself in crisis. The defining enemy of the past half-century has disappeared with the disintegration of Soviet communism, but this incredible historical turn has produced few celebrations. Americans no longer fear a Soviet threat, but many fear that their country is economically and culturally depleted. Many Americans worry that Japan and Germany have emerged as the victors of the Cold War, while the United States copes with the inheritance of bloated military budgets, a global network of military bases, and several decades of military-dominated scientific research. At the end of a century that began with social gospel hopes for a "cooperative commonwealth," federal and state prisons are stuffed beyond capacity, large areas of major cities are devastated seemingly beyond repair, the political system is deeply corrupted by the power of organized economic interests, economic insecurity and unemployment are rampant, and the ravages of racial hatred, ethnic tension, and injustice tear at the remaining fabric of society. The federal government's capacity to address any of these problems is severely curtailed by the globalization of modern capitalism, by the costs of maintaining a vast military system, and by the costs of an enormous federal deficit that consumes more than half of each tax dollar. At the same time, a profound crisis of meaning presses upon the elites, the middle classes, and the poor within the world's dominant capitalist societies. "We don't know where we're going," a Japanese academic told me at a conference. "We don't know the point of it anymore. My generation spent its life trying to catch up to America. We focused on economic development and dismissed everything else. Now we've surpassed America, and we can't decide what to do next, or why. Are we supposed to hold on, or keep accumulating? For what?"

In the United States, as in Japan, the answer assiduously promoted by the dominant culture is to keep accumulating. During the same period in which the influence of liberal Christianity has steeply declined, American culture has become increasingly deracinated, materialistic, and egocentric. The individualistic market has become not only the unchallenged model for economic life but the model for social and moral existence as well. The culture of seduction bombards its youthful consumers, especially, with titillating images that promote self-preoccupation and self-gratification. In this situation, American churches are compelled to restrain the egotism and antisocial forces unleashed by commercial society. Many observers within and outside Christianity contend that the church should restrict its social outreach to this effort. I shall argue that the otherwise worthy project of providing moral formation for individuals in a market-dominated culture, however, is shrunken and self-defeating when it is held to constitute the church's entire social mission. Christians are called as participants in the kingdom-bringing body of Christ to struggle for a society that is more democratic, egalitarian, ecological, caring, peaceful, and just than is the existing order. Moreover, before liberal Christianity can regain its public voice and participate in the spiritual and social transformation of American society, it must reassess its long-established acquiesence to the dominant order.

Troeltsch and the History of Christian Social Teaching

Christian theology faces this social challenge with a rich but ambiguous intellectual heritage. If mainline Christianity has lost much of its public influence, it does not face the social challenges of a new century without valuable modern traditions on which it might draw. Troeltsch's massive volumes on the history of Christian social teaching drove home the crucial differences between social Christianity and its premodern traditions. The notion that the Christian church might seek to transform society in the direction of freedom and equality was unknown in Christian history until the emergence of Christian socialism in the nineteenth century, he observed. The early Christian church had a regenerative social ethic, but it was the ethic of a marginalized eschatological community. The medieval church had a social ethic, but it was an ethic of authority and social control. The radical Anabaptist churches had a social ethic, but most of the Anabaptist churches were apocalyptic or ascetic or both. The Calvinist tradition had a world-changing social ethic, but it was turned into an apologetic for commercial society. Troeltsch was a liberal critic of socialism, but he emphasized that only with the advent of modern Christian socialism did Christianity enter the political struggle on behalf of freedom and equality:

> Christian Socialism alone has broken through these theories, and forced men
> to think out afresh the social ethic of Christianity and its relation to the actual
> changes in the social order. It has laid bare the worm-eaten condition of the
> previous conventional Christian ethic, which, at its best, offered something for
> the ethics of the family and the individual, but which, on the other hand, had

no message for social ethics save that of acceptance of all existing institutions and conditions, much to the satisfaction of all in authority.[4]

Premodern Christianity in most of its institutional forms provided much satisfaction to those in authority. If the social gospel understanding of Christianity was "neither alien nor novel," as Walter Rauschenbusch insisted, still it was only with the rise of social Christianity in England, Germany, and the United States that any part of organized Christianity proclaimed a gospel imperative to transform society. This pathbreaking tradition was more idealistic than radical. The social gospelers were progressives, not revolutionaries. Troeltsch's reformist liberalism was closer to the movement's mainstream than Rauschenbusch's socialism, and even the movement's socialist wing sought to extend American democracy rather than overthrow it. Within its religious and historical context, however, social Christianity was a radical phenomenon. The emergence of a Christianity that seriously took on the modern social problem marked a revolution in Christian social thought and experience. Troeltsch's quickly renowned account of the background to social Christianity was published five years after Rauschenbusch's electrifying *Christianity and the Social Crisis* (1907) became the manifesto of a burgeoning Christian social movement. Modern American Christianity was born in the social gospel hope that democracy was the wave of the future and that America could become the world's first genuine democracy.

Soul in Society tracks the history of this ongoing theological tradition, focusing on its liberal Protestant narrative while giving attention to figures outside liberal Protestantism who have importantly influenced its shape and direction. The book examines the connections and differences between social Christianity's three main historical/theological phases, beginning with Progressive era social gospel modernism, moving to the succeeding generation's Christian realism, and culminating in contemporary postmodern and liberationist Christianity. The question whether this last movement represents a "new liberal consensus" or the end of any possible consensus is discussed in some detail. The book gives substantive attention to such American religious thinkers as Shailer Mathews, Harry Emerson Fosdick, Justin Wroe Nixon, H. Richard Niebuhr, John Courtney Murray, Richard John Neuhaus, James H. Cone, Mary Daly, Rosemary Radford Ruether, Jacquelyn Grant, John B. Cobb Jr., James Gustafson, and Stanley Hauerwas; it gives special consideration to the writings of Charles Clayton Morrison and John C. Bennett, who importantly adapted social Christian thought to the conditions of America after the Progressive era; and it devotes extensive attention to the work and legacy of Reinhold Niebuhr, the preeminent American theologian of this century.

---

4. Troeltsch, *Social Teaching,* vol. 2, 727–28.

Rauschenbusch and the Christian Social Revolution

But the crucial figure in the book's historical narrative and religious vision is Walter Rauschenbusch. Despite his numerous exaggerations and illusions, it was Rauschenbusch who conceptualized the Christian social revolution in Christian thought, who defined its social vision, who epitomized its spiritual character, and who legitimized Christian support for radical democratic politics. Rauschenbusch was an idealist with a strong awareness of the pervasive reality of personal and social evil; he was a moralist who understood that moralism alone will never gain social justice; he was both religiously devout and deeply politicized. After Rauschenbusch, it would become commonplace for theologians to criticize the injustices of American inequality, but none matched the powerful rhetoric of *Christianity and the Social Crisis* (1907) or the detailed discussions of political economics that he offered in *Christianizing the Social Order* (1912). Though his version of the social gospel was not the dominant form of social Christianity during the heyday of liberal Protestantism, it prefigured the kind of Christianity that many contemporary liberationists and other theological progressives have reclaimed.

Niebuhr, Bennett, and Social Christianity

In the 1930s, liberal Christianity was powerfully attacked by Reinhold Niebuhr for its moral and political idealism, first in the name of Christian-Marxist realism and later without the Marxism. Much of Niebuhr's early work was principally devoted to blasting the Christian social tradition for its moralism, yet Niebuhr belonged to this tradition. Though he discarded liberal Christianity's characteristic emphasis on immanence and moral regeneration, he shared its modernist approach to Scripture and theological method; though he eventually rejected its antiwar moralism, he never doubted that Christians are morally obliged to enter the public struggle for social justice. In a generation that experienced the seeming futility of pacifism, Niebuhr gave social Christianity an alternative rhetoric, politics, and theology. His first attacks on Christian liberalism called the church to throw off its moralism in order to join the class struggle against a dying capitalist order. He later called the church to throw off its moralism to join the military struggle against fascism. He later enlisted Christian support for America's world-embracing Cold War against communism, with fewer complaints about the intractability of American Christian moralism. By the late 1940s, Niebuhr was a towering figure in American religion and politics. His dialectical realism defined for his theological generation what the "realities" of politics and ethics were. More than any other theologian of this century, he made American Christianity face the question of what it means to exercise power in a morally responsible way.

A generation after his death, Niebuhr's influence still exceeds that of any other American theologian of this century. Much of the debate in Christian ethics during the past generation has featured arguments among Niebuhr's liberal, moderate, and neoconservative followers. The present work explicates the chief arguments between these groups, giving particular attention to the important mediating work of John C. Bennett, who began his long theological career as a social gospeler, worked for many years as Niebuhr's closest collaborator, and spent the past thirty years dialoguing with various liberationist and progressive theologies. At the height of his friend's public influence in the 1950s, Bennett described his own perspective as a blend of social gospel progressivism and Niebuhrian realism. With the rise of liberation theology and the sharp decline of Niebuhr's influence in the 1960s, Bennett did not lurch to the Right with the "Niebuhrian" forerunners of neoconservatism but urged Niebuhr himself to pay heed to the new antiwar and liberationist movements. As president of Union Theological Seminary during this period, Bennett remarked on various occasions that liberation theology was reviving the social gospel tradition but in a more radical form. "More and more, I feel that this is where I came in," he would say. More than any other figure examined in this book, his writings reveal the connections between the various strands of social Christianity.

I use Bennett's attempts to respond to liberationism as a means to identify the connections between liberation theologies and earlier social Christianity. This is not an important concern to radical feminists and many other liberation theologians, however, who emphasize the break between liberationism and earlier religious perspectives. Many liberationists do not share Rauschenbusch's concern to prove that their theology is neither alien nor novel; moreover, some of the most influential feminist and African American theologians are the most radical thinkers in these movements. Liberation theologians have challenged and transformed modern Christianity by opening theology to the experiences, insights, and voices of previously silenced communities. It gives voice to the spiritualities and religious perspectives of women, people of color, and the poor and gives authority to different kinds of theological interlocutors than the "cultured despisers of religion" typically addressed by classic liberal Protestantism.

Liberation theologies seek liberation from the multidimensional evils of dependency, injustice, and oppression within and outside Christianity. For some liberationists, the purpose of liberation theology is to recover or unveil the emancipationist meaning of authentic Christianity; for others, a new emancipatory Christianity must be created that draws little from the past; for still others, Christianity in any form is intrinsically part of the problem. Radical feminist theology has especially advanced religious and ideological critiques of Christianity that reject virtually the entire inheritance of Christian teaching. I explore in this book the revolutionary challenges to Christianity posed by African

American and feminist theologies, focusing on the social meaning of Christianity and the question whether any particular beliefs are necessarily constitutive to Christian identity.

Christian theology today is deeply pluralistic, embracing religious, cultural, and ideological perspectives never imagined by Rauschenbusch or Niebuhr. In one area, however, the language and subjects of ethical discussion have changed little since Rauschenbusch's generation. Modern Christianity has long dreamed of a socioeconomic order that democratizes economic power. The social gospelers believed that the economic realm could be democratized in much the same way that American politics was already partly democratized. Niebuhr eventually gave up the social gospel vision of a cooperative commonwealth and later gave up the Marxist vision of a classless society, but he never denigrated the social gospel preoccupation with striving for economic justice. In his later career, he adopted a "vital center" liberal politics on the grounds that this New Deal–Fair Deal tradition was securing as much of the social gospel vision as was attainable in America. The later Niebuhr relativized his earlier commitment to equality, but, like his tradition, he never doubted that democracy is incompatible with severe disparities in economic condition. The progressive mainstream of Christian social thought today clings to the same vision of democratized economic power that Rauschenbusch championed, while some liberation theologians reclaim the early Niebuhr's synthesis of Christianity and Marxism. In both cases, social Christianity proclaims that some degree of equality of condition is a precondition for actual equality of opportunity.

Kaus and Civic Liberalism

In the present work I seek to retrieve and renew the social gospel vision of a democratized social order while being mindful that this social vision seems far less plausible today than it was in Rauschenbusch's time. The fact that American society has turned out very differently than the social gospelers hoped is too obvious to belabor. What is worth considering is the question whether Christians today should therefore devote themselves to redeeming the Christian social vision of a just society. Given the realities of a corporate-dominated social order, is there any point in pursuing an egalitarian politics that tries to hold back the maldistributive force of the market? Perhaps the most instructive recent response to this question has been offered by Mickey Kaus, who argues that the rise of an increasingly internationalized market economy is creating a purer, more technocratic, and more predatory form of world capitalism that cannot be democratized or even effectively reformed.

Kaus acknowledges that inequality in the United States has seriously worsened in the past decade and that the widening maldistribution of wealth is creating terrible social problems. The typical liberal response to this crisis, he observes, is to use government power to make income taxes more progressive, heighten the taxes on capital gains, and enact pro-union legislation that stops runaway shops, raises the minimum wage, and so on. But the problem is that none of these approaches effectively mitigates the maldistributive dynamics of an increasingly globalized economy. In a world market, good wages are no longer available for unskilled work, and the disparity between skilled and unskilled income is increasing. Low-skilled manufacturing jobs that once paid middle-class wages are disappearing in the United States, chiefly because corporations can make more money by exploiting cheaper labor markets in Asia, Mexico, and elsewhere. As routine production jobs move overseas, unskilled American workers are reduced to competing with each other for minimum-wage jobs in the service sector, thus deepening the maldistributive effects of deindustrialization. Drawing upon Robert Reich's analysis in *The Work of Nations,* Kaus notes that, by contrast, America's well-educated "symbolic analysts" are able to make high incomes from their work as lawyers, investment and commercial bankers, management consultants, research scientists, academics, computer programmers, and the like.[5] This class of American wage-earners is economically competitive in a high-tech world and is therefore well positioned to succeed within it. The maldistributive logic of world capitalism is compounded by what Kaus calls "the Hollywood Effect," which pays astronomical rewards to top performers in highly lucrative industries, such as the film industry.

No amount of conceivable U.S. government engineering is going to abolish the Hollywood Effect or arrest the growing gap between incomes for skilled and unskilled labor, Kaus insists. Capitalism is not only an economic system but a culture. Before capitalism went global, it was possible to keep top performers from earning the full measure of their economic value. Unions restrained the range of wage disparities, and cultural values pertaining to loyalty and trust restrained the predatory impulses of market economics. But these restraints on free enterprise are rapidly disintegrating. An increasingly internationalized labor market is destroying industrial unionism in America and shattering the cultural taboos that once restrained corporate headhunting and firm switching. "Today, if you *don't* switch employers every few years you run the risk of being branded a 'treehugger,' " Kaus remarks, adding that this phenomenon is even beginning to show up in the communitarian cultures of capitalist East Asia.[6]

The trends are indisputable and, in Kaus's estimation, too powerful for any single government to effectively resist. The internationalization of capital and

---

5. See Robert Reich, *The Work of Nations* (New York: Alfred Knopf, 1991).
6. Mickey Kaus, "For a New Equality," *The New Republic* 202 (May 7, 1990), 21; an expanded revision appears in Kaus, *The End of Equality* (New York: Basic Books, 1992), 58–77, citation on p. 65.

labor is creating a new kind of predatory capitalism that inevitably generates inequality and that obliterates cultural values and communities that get in the way. This is the social reality that American politics must address. If American progressives are to face up to the reality of global capitalism, Kaus argues, they must give up their attachment to progressive taxation and wealth redistribution. They must give up their faith in the social vision of economic democracy, which is no longer possible even in theory. What liberals must begin to comprehend is that government engineering in the economic sphere is not going to change, soften, or rechannel the maldistributive effects of world capitalism. What government can and must begin to do instead is attend to the social effects of these economic forces by circumscribing the sphere in which money matters. America needs a new equality, which Kaus calls "civic liberalism."

He draws the notion from the economic historian and Fabian socialist R. H. Tawney, who argued that the problem with inequality is not so much that some people earn more money than others, but "that some classes should be excluded from the heritage of civilization which others enjoy." This is the crucial issue for American democracy, Kaus argues. What liberalism must strive to attain is not economic equality, but social equality. The purpose of liberal politics should be "to prevent the income inequality inevitably generated by capitalism from translating into invidious social distinctions."[7] A civic liberal politics would strengthen and expand civil society, creating more opportunities for people of different classes and races to share common space, institutions, and concerns. It would counter the privatizing dynamic of commercial society and limit the social importance of money by making investments in programs that promote social equality. Toward this end, Kaus supports national health insurance and compulsory national service and calls for greater investments in community day care, infrastructure maintenance, low-cost housing, parks, and other community enterprises. He also endorses public choice in education. An American liberalism that pursued this agenda could begin to repair and reintegrate a badly fragmented society, he urges. America is unavoidably unequal but not unavoidably mean. "We can't stop the basic tides of our economy. But we can build dikes," Kaus concludes.[8] A smarter liberalism would stop chasing the social democratic illusion of economic equality. It would seek not to equalize money but to put money in its place and thereby salvage the more precious form of equality that is being lost.

This is a strong argument for a particular kind of politics of community. In its emphasis on civil society and its careful distancing from conventional liberalism and conservatism, Kaus's approach typifies the "neither Left nor Right" politics advanced by numerous communitarians in recent years. Its affirmative

---

7. Kaus, "For a New Equality," 25.
8. Ibid., 26.

side makes a compelling argument that has deep roots in the Western social democratic tradition. Kaus's invocation of Tawney is appropriate for this part of his argument in that his plea for a stronger public sphere of community life is exactly what the British Fabians had in mind when they advocated what they called "the social wage." For British social democrats such as Tawney, William Temple, Charles Gore, and Richard Titmuss, it was axiomatic that a good society must make public provisions that recognize the equal dignity and rights of all citizens. They assumed that there are certain basic social goods to which people are entitled as citizens rather than as consumers. These entitlements include health care, education, child care, and the like, which can be provided only if citizens accept their corresponding obligations to society. In Kaus's language, the Fabians affirmed that social equality is even more crucial to the life of a healthy and humane democracy than economic equality. Nothing was more important to Tawney than the flourishing of human fellowship.

But it would be difficult to find an argument more inimical to the spirit of Tawney's work than Kaus's denigration of economic equality. Tawney embraced democratic socialism because it opposed what he regarded as the two primary constitutive features of capitalism: privilege and tyranny. In his view, privilege was a function of interrelated social and economic power. It was typically a by-product of wealth converting to social power, whereas tyranny was a function of the distribution of power. Tawney viewed equality as an antidote to privilege, but against tyranny he argued for the democratization of power. Democratic socialism democratized economic and social power and thus made it possible for human fellowship to flourish. His conception of the egalitarian imperative was extreme even for a socialist. If people are to respect each other for what they are, he argued, "they must cease to respect each other for what they own." The good society would abolish the "reverence for riches" that commercial society assiduously promotes. "And human nature being what it is, in order to abolish the reverence for riches, they must make impossible the existence of a class which is important merely because it is rich," he insisted.[9]

It was plainly evident to Tawney that economic inequality and social inequality are deeply interrelated. Though he embraced the social wage as a democratic bulwark against privilege, he recognized that only marginal gains toward social equality would be possible in any society that sanctioned gross disparities in economic power. American society today offers vivid evidence for this truism. The social ravages of inequality in the United States are reflected in lift-the-drawbridge municipal arrangements, beggar-thy-neighbor tax policies, and white flight from racially integrated schools and neighborhoods. In an increasingly unequal society, the rich are able to buy their way out of dealing with others

---

9. R. H. Tawney, *Equality* (London: Allen & Unwin Ltd., 1931), 87.

while middle-class people feel increasing pressure to insulate themselves from their poor and working-class neighbors. Kaus asks, "Instead of the herculean and futile attempt to hold back money inequality, why not focus liberal political energies on reducing the importance of those inequalities by rebuilding the public sphere?"[10]

But his own description of the predatory character of global capitalism contains the answer. Kaus argues that modern capitalism is so powerful and inherently maldistributive that any form of redistributive liberal politics is doomed to failure. Having given up on "money liberalism," he wants American liberals to settle for a politics that decommodifies certain social goods. His retreat from economic justice in the name of political realism, however, ignores larger realities. His "hands-off" approach to economic power completely overlooks the environmental costs of unregulated capitalism. More pertinent to his argument, his proposal fails to be realistic about the connections between social and economic equality. Any politics that does nothing to challenge or hold back the maldistributive effects of the market in the economic sphere has little chance of holding back the destructive effects of concentrated economic power in the political and civic realms. Democracy cannot flourish or deepen in a society with a large underclass living in poverty, a widening maldistribution of income, and an extreme concentration of wealth among the rich. The growing stratification of U.S. society is eroding democracy and increasingly isolating Americans from each other. As Larry Rasmussen observes, American society "currently lives from moral fragments and community fragments only, and both are being destroyed faster than they are being replenished."[11]

In Kaus's reading, every possible strategy to arrest the growing inequality trend is doomed to failure. Progressive income taxes won't do the job, training programs will never turn most Americans into symbolic analysts, American unionism is weak and defensive, and protectionism is self-destructive. Flexible production strategies are creating highly collaborative and participatory enterprises in some fields but only for innovative workers with the requisite skills, creativity, and computer smarts. None of the standard antidotes to the inequality trend is strong enough to bring about greater equality, he argues, and some would make the problem worse.[12] Kaus concedes that a selective blend of several

---

10. Mickey Kaus, "The End of Equality?" *The New Republic* 207 (August 10, 1992), 25.

11. Larry L. Rasmussen, *Moral Fragments and Moral Community: A Proposal for Church in Society* (Minneapolis: Fortress Press, 1993), 11.

12. See Robert Kuttner, *The Economic Illusion: False Choices between Prosperity and Social Justice* (Boston: Houghton Mifflin Co., 1984); Barry Bluestone and Bennett Harrison, *The Deindustrialization of America: Plant Closings, Community Abandonment, and the Dismantling of Basic Industry* (New York: Basic Books, 1982); Michael J. Piore and Charles F. Sabel, *The Second Industrial Divide: Possibilities for Prosperity* (New York: Basic Books, 1984); Shoshana Zuboff, *In the Age of the Smart Machine: The Future of Work and Power* (New York: Basic Books, 1988).

strategies might conceivably hold back the economy's worst maldistributive effects. He rightly observes that any serious progressive strategy must combine a strong progressive income tax and a massive training program. Though he underestimates the role that a revitalized American unionism might still play in gaining democratic control over the factors of production, he rightly adds that the heart of any serious combination strategy to rescue the dream of economic justice must be some form of worker ownership or shareholding approach. Kaus doubts that this will work either, but he concedes that current experiments in cooperative ownership and other forms of shareholding hold the most promise of any progressive economic strategy.

With important modifications, this is the socioeconomic strategy for which I argue. Kaus notes some of the problems with worker ownership, especially the tendency for worker-owners to be biased toward capital-intensive investments as well as the reluctance of worker-owners "to take efficiency-enhancing steps (such as moving to another state in search of cheap raw materials) that ruthless entrepreneurs would take."[13] As I shall argue, however, the latter problem is one of the virtues of cooperative ownership, and the first problem can be dealt with by instituting tax incentives that promote full employment. Any politics that seeks to expand the cooperative sector must address these and other possible problems with worker, community, and mutual fund ownership strategies. Kaus does not pursue these issues, but if worker and social ownership strategies are to succeed, they must build upon the advantage that, as Kaus concedes, workers are typically "more creative, energetic, and responsible when they have a stake in their employer's success."[14] Cooperative strategies will never abolish the structural inegalitarian trend of higher pay for skills that Kaus describes, but they represent the best and most democratic way to gain political control over maldistributive economic forces.

Christian social ethics throughout this century has clung to the vision of a society in which true equality of opportunity is attained through the achievement of approximate social and economic equality. Kaus defends his rejection of this socioeconomic vision by emphasizing the predatory character of an increasingly internationalized market. It is time for American liberalism to stop trying to manage what cannot be controlled, he counsels. The power of the world capitalist system with all of its maldistributive dynamics exceeds the dubious reforming powers of any conceivable political coalition. National communities have negligible power to hold back the maldistributive effects of the world market. American politics cannot humanize capitalism; what it can do is provide more

---

13. Kaus, *The End of Equality,* 76.
14. Ibid., 221.

free and equal space to citizens in a society driven by economic forces that no one controls.

But the differences between societies that resist the maldistributive logic of the market and those that do not are hardly negligible. Sweden had, throughout the 1980s, a vigorous public debate over the tolerable limits of economic inequality. Swedish conservatives argued that the wage differential between corporate executives and laborers permitted by the country's solidarity wage policy should be increased to eight to one; radicals maintained that the differential should be no more than four to one. In Japan, where worker-shareholder schemes are commonplace and the ratio was sixteen to one, a serious debate over the range of acceptable income inequality also occurred. In the United States, by contrast, the ratio climbed to 145 to 1—and there was no debate. The right to attain wealth was exalted over other values. American wealth and income inequality dramatically increased in the 1980s, not merely by virtue of the maldistributive dynamics of the world market but more importantly as a by-product of specific American policies that fueled inequality. In some cases, Reaganomics broke new ground in redistributing wealth upward; in other cases, it accelerated an already-regressive trend in American policy. The Reagan administration cut the marginal tax rate for individuals from 70 percent to 28 percent, trimmed the top bracket from 70 percent to 50 percent, and capped taxes on unearned income at 50 percent. In 1978, the top rate on capital gains was cut from 49 percent to 28 percent; the Reagan Administration further reduced the capital gains rate to 20 percent, made across-the-board tax cuts that soon engendered enormous budget deficits, and gave special breaks to corporations that cut the corporate share of federal tax receipts in half.[15]

The capitalist blowout of the 1980s was a political phenomenon that exacerbated the growing gap between rich and poor. The number of people reporting incomes of more than $500,000 per year soared by 985 percent while the number of Americans living below the poverty line rose to 15.2 percent. By the end of the decade, the top fifth of the population earned more than half of the nation's income and held more than three-quarters of its wealth while the bottom fifth received barely 4 percent of its income. The richest 1 percent of Americans received income increases of 74.4 percent while the average after-tax family income of the lowest 10 percent actually *fell* by 10.5 percent. Economist Lester Thurow observed in 1986 that "we're in the midst of a real surge toward in-

---

15. Kevin Phillips, *The Politics of Rich and Poor: Wealth and the American Electorate in the Reagan Aftermath* (New York: Random House, 1990), 53, 76–79; see Donald L. Barlett and James B. Steele, *America: What Went Wrong?* (Kansas City: Andrews and McMeel, 1992), 4–7; Frederick R. Strobel, *Upward Dreams, Downward Mobility: The Economic Decline of the American Middle Class* (Lanham, Md.: Rowman & Littlefield, 1993), 30, 91–102.

equality, the economic equivalent of tectonic plate movements." Economist David Gordon noted more pointedly that "the most important story about the U.S. economy in the eighties is the economic warfare that the wealthy and powerful have been waging against the vast majority of Americans."[16]

Yet the vast majority of Americans stirred very little debate over the tolerable limits of inequality, partly because Kaus's resignation is widely shared among them. "Once we've failed to draw a line between equality and inequality, between 1 to 1 and 2 to 1, what's the basis for so self-confidently taking a stand at 8 to 1 or even 1,000 to 1?" Kaus argues.[17] But the point is not that there is anything sacred about drawing a line at eight to one or twelve to one. The point is that a serious debate over the tolerable limits of inequality is utterly necessary in the United States before the ratio reaches eight hundred to one and makes a mockery of American democracy. A progressive American Christianity that refound its public voice could begin to engender the public debate over inequality that is needed to reclaim the hopes of poor, working-class, and middle-class people for security and justice.

Social Christianity Today

For all of its illusions and mistaken judgments, social Christianity at its best has been distinguished in Christian history precisely by its willingness to confront such issues and struggle for a more just social order. If America's mainline churches have generally sought to accommodate the dominant order, modern Christianity has nonetheless sustained a vital social-ethical tradition that presses for social justice. The neoconservative theorist Michael Novak has ruefully noted that nearly all of the past century's major Christian theologians have been democratic socialists.[18] The dominance of democratic socialism within modern theology has given Novak much to oppose. I argue in this book that if this heritage presents contemporary theologians with serious difficulties, as Novak strenuously insists, it also offers them much that is worth appropriating and rethinking.

Theologians cannot proceed as if their socialist-influenced rhetoric were innocent or easily redeemed. The language of democratic socialism has become

---

16. Robert Reich, "A More Perfect State of the Union Address," *The Wall Street Journal,* January 30, 1991; Thurow and Gordon quoted in Phillips, *The Politics of Rich and Poor,* 47; income figures in Phillips, 76–79.

17. Kaus, *The End of Equality,* 13.

18. Michael Novak, "New Questions for Humanists," in *The Denigration of Capitalism: Six Points of View,* ed. Michael Novak (Washington, D.C.: American Enterprise Institute, 1979), 57; Novak, "Changing the Paradigms: The Cultural Deficiencies of Capitalism," in *Democracy and Mediating Structures: A Theological Inquiry,* ed. Michael Novak (Washington, D.C.: American Enterprise Institute, 1980), 193; Novak, *Confession of a Catholic* (New York: Harper & Row, 1983), 178–81.

severely problematic to its ethical purpose, not only because it was perverted by totalitarians decades ago but also because democratic socialism itself has traditionally embraced an ideology of centralized collectivism. The struggle for a more decentralized, democratic, and cooperative society is, to put it mildly, not aided by the burden of a rhetoric that most Americans find repulsive. Moreover, contemporary liberationist and ecofeminist movements are raising issues that cannot be merely appropriated by or added to an inherited Christian socialism but require transformations in the assumptions and theoretical frameworks of this tradition. Without investing any particular significance in the overused and undefinable term *postmodernism*, I shall take up the "postmodern" theological project of asking how much is left of modern Christianity's dominant social vision after the disestablishment of American Protestantism and the loss of any unitive source of moral value in American culture.

For those unfamiliar with the discourse tradition to which this book belongs, a cautionary note is perhaps advisable. Theology is inherently prescriptive. It can be wrong, but it cannot be neutral. In their vigorous attempts to develop and defend particular moral arguments, however, theological ethicists often appear to outsiders to be making univocal claims that they are not making. To mix theological ethics and political theory is not necessarily to assume that theology can or should sacralize any particular ideology, including one's own. I assume that to attribute divine sanction to any political ideology or position is blasphemous. The crucial dialectical task of any politically engaged theology, as Paul Tillich insisted, is to distinguish between the *obligatum religiosum* and the *reservatum religiosum*—the obligations and limits of religious engagement in political life.[19] Christianity is obliged to enter the political realm because people suffer, many of them hideously, on account of politics. If the Christian church is to take its moral teachings seriously, it must take the public implications of its moral teachings seriously. This is the *obligatum religiosum*. Any Christian concern for the common good is obliged to take up controverted political, social, and economic issues.

At the same time, Christian ethicists are obliged to take up these issues with an instructive awareness that all theological, moral, and political arguments are fallible constructions. People hear the gospel in different ways; even a sacred text does not provide infallible interpretations. To argue for a particular political ethic is not to claim that such an ethic is the only morally worthy position

---

19. See Paul Tillich, "Basic Principles of Religious Socialism," reprinted in *Political Expectation,* ed. James Luther Adams, Victor Nuovo, and Hannah Tillich (New York: Harper & Row, 1971), 60–88; Tillich, "Open Letter to Emanuel Hirsch," reprinted in *The Thought of Paul Tillich,* ed. James Luther Adams, Wilhelm Pauck, and Roger Lincoln Shinn (San Francisco: Harper & Row, 1985), 363–86.

consistent with Christianity; on the contrary, to identify any social or political position with the divine will is to commit a form of idolatry. That is, to absolutize or univocally identify the kingdom of God with any relative construction is demonic. The *reservatum religiosum* stands as a judgment on all fundamentalism, dogmatism, and religious hubris.

In Clifford Geertz's sense of the term, social Christian arguments are therefore typically "thick," weaving together descriptions, theories, analyses, and prescriptions from disparate sources. Critical theology rejects the either/or of both conservative and antireligious thinking, in which theology must either prescribe absolutes and assume a hegemonic posture over other perspectives or cease to exist. From a critical theological perspective, religion is too important in history, too constitutive in human experience, and too various in its cultural and historical forms to be consigned to absolutists or completely disregarded. To frame a theological perspective in this way is not necessarily to embrace relativism but to assume that theology is a constructive effort in which one sees only, as Paul remarks in First Corinthians, "as through a glass darkly."

The present work is perspectivist and pluralist in its assumptions, aims, and spirit but not relativist. Absolutists claim to possess universal truths that inhere in nature, reason, or divine decree and are binding, regardless of historical or cultural context. Relativists dispute that such truths exist, arguing that all truth claims can be true only with respect to the particular assumptions and contexts from which they derive. All philosophical claims are relativized by the limitations of the specific historical, cultural, and cognitive contexts out of which these claims are constructed. Perspectivism shares the relativist emphasis on historical and cultural relativity while refusing to draw the relativist conclusion that there are no universal truths. Perspectivist theologies, in particular, typically emphasize the narrative character of religious truth, arguing that religious claims should be understood fundamentally as narrative-dependent constructions of particular discourse traditions. Perspectivists generally blend historicist and confessional interpretations of religious claims and affirm that all experience, language, and reason are conditioned and limited by their derivative contexts.

The latter point obtains with special force in the case of theology because the ultimate object of Christian language transcends space and time. Because all human reason and language are products of historically conditioned experience, theological reasoning is inherently incapable of fully grasping or defining religious truths. All Christian theologies systematize mere fragments of the mysterious unconditioned reality to which they refer. The belief that an unconditioned ground of being does exist, however, distinguishes a theologically perspectivist position from a relativist position. Perspectivism relativizes the relativizers and shows that the dogma of relativism is itself a universal truth claim. Though the truth can never be adequately grasped by any theology or philosophy, it does not necessarily follow that there is no truth. As even Kierkegaard conceded in his polemic against Hegel's system, reality could be a system for God. Perspectivism takes to heart the fallible, limited, constructive character of human reasoning while rejecting the self-refuting relativist claim that there are no universal truths.

Not all perspectivist viewpoints are open-ended. Perspectivist arguments can be and often have been used in modern and postmodern theologies to protect the identity or doctrines of particular perspectives from outside criticism. In the neoorthodox theology of Karl Barth, for example, a perspectivist espousal of Christian revelation makes Christianity immune to outside historical, philosophical, and theological criticism. For Barth, Christianity is a revealed faith that bears no relationship to other world religions.[20] More recently, communitarian-narrativist theologians such as Stanley Hauerwas and William Willimon have propounded quasi-sectarian views of the church's identity and social mission on perspectivist grounds.[21] Perspectivist arguments of other kinds have been employed in liberationist theologies to assert the epistemological privilege of oppressed minorities, women, and/or Two-thirds World communities over other communities and traditions. Other forms of perspectivism (including liberationist discourses) have eschewed the language of privilege but have nonetheless emphasized difference and disconnection in making the case for a particular position.

The crucial question for these and other discourses, in my view, is whether they are open to criticism, correction, and enrichment from other perspectives. All of us are limited in our capacity to understand or appreciate the experience of anyone else, and these barriers are compounded whenever we seek to comprehend the experience of someone whose race or gender or class or nationality differs from our own. As participants in the creation of a good society, however, all of us are obliged to use all of the imagination and intelligence that we possess to challenge the limits of our understanding. The project of re-creating a democratic public begins and continues by listening—and not ceasing to listen—to the "other." In pressing the question of how to seek enrichment from other perspectives, literary theorist Mikhail Bakhtin helpfully distinguishes between what he calls the monologic and dialogic visions. The writer with monologic vision attempts to control, subordinate, and consume other voices through (or into) his or her own hegemonic voice. Writing becomes a projection of dominating power. The dialogic vision, by contrast, projects "a plurality of independent and unmerged voices and consciousnesses, a genuine polyphony of fully valid voices." Bakhtin explains that the dialogic imagination does not merge multiple

---

20. See Karl Barth, *Church Dogmatics*, vol. 1, trans. G. T. Thomson and Harold Knight (Edinburgh: T. & T. Clark, 1956), 280–325.

21. See Stanley Hauerwas and William H. Willimon, *Resident Aliens: Life in the Christian Colony* (Nashville: Abingdon Press, 1989).

voices into a single objective world illuminated by a single authorial consciousness. "Rather a plurality of consciousnesses, with equal rights and each with its own world, combine but are not merged in the unity of the event," he writes.[22]

I assume that no single tradition of political theory is sufficient as a guide to conceiving the common good or to making concrete gains toward it. This book therefore draws upon seemingly disparate theological and nonreligious sources. My political perspective blends liberal, social democratic, feminist, liberationist, and communitarian elements and is chastened by conservative criticism. The morally imperative effort to strive for freedom, equality, and ecologically sustainable development is, by necessity, guided by provisional theories and strategies. From this perspective, the essential theoretical task is to refashion various parts of a complex social inheritance into a politics that serves the common good.

My religious perspective is founded upon the way of Christ and the reality of Christ's kingdom-bringing Spirit. The social gospel is ultimately precious to me not because of its politics but because it recovers the fullness of the spiritual reality and ethic of the kingdom of Christ. In the biblical faith recovered by social Christianity, the reign of God is an immanent/eschatological reality that engenders community, peace, and justice. It is not a dispensable vestige of patriarchal religion but the heart of a liberating spiritual reality that transcends its patriarchal elements. Though I embrace much of the radical feminist critique of classical Christian theism, I do not accept the verdict that Christian kingdom language or Christianity itself is unredeemable for feminism. Rather, I argue that the spiritual reality of the resurrected Christ is the ground of a hope that sustains and transcends Christian struggles for justice and peace.

Much of this book retrieves the story of modern Christianity with limited editorial intervention, but its authorial voice becomes stronger as the narrative moves into the present. In much of chapter 6, the authorial voice simply takes over, as I try to envision how a politics of economic democracy might be reconstructed in a new century. For the sake of literary variety, I use the terms *liberal, social,* and sometimes *modern* nearly interchangeably when speaking of the modern social Christian tradition, with the understanding that liberal Christianity includes more than its social Christian current. Though I have taken the risk of bringing widely disparate voices into this interpretation of social Christianity in the United States, my account makes no claim to universality or completeness. Numerous issues, theologians, and alternative perspectives that are pertinent to the subject have been excluded, including a cluster of systematic

---

22. Mikhail Bakhtin, *Problems of Dostoevsky's Poetics,* trans. Caryl Emerson (Minneapolis: University of Minnesota Press, 1984); cf. Bakhtin, *The Dialogic Imagination,* trans. Caryl Emerson and Michael Holquist (Austin: University of Texas, 1981).

theological issues that I intend to develop in a subsequent book on theological liberalism. Neither is it my purpose to fashion a religious ethic that no one has thought of before. My concern is rather to bring the disparate voices of modern and postmodern Christian history into a conversation about what it means to follow Christ after the end of Christendom. The narrative form suits and historicizes this purpose. *Soul in Society* suggests that if Christianity no longer rules over American society, American Christians are in a better position to follow the way of Christ.

2 CHRISTIANIZING THE MODERN ORDER
The Progressivist Faith

THE CHIEF IRONY OF MODERN LIBERAL CHRISTIANITY is that during the period when its doctrinal basis was most in doubt, liberal theologians and church leaders were most determined to spread their faith throughout the world. The flagship magazine of mainline American Protestantism, *the Christian Century,* took its name from this disposition. If modern science, Enlightenment philosophy, and historical criticism had shaken the foundations of traditional Christian belief, this did not mean that modernization was necessarily destructive to Christian faith. If modern capitalism and technology were creating a social order that commodified traditional moral values and marginalized the role of religion in society, this did not mean that the churches had no important role to play in the public realm. In the closing decades of the nineteenth century, liberal proponents of "the New Theology" such as Newman Smyth, David Swing, John P. Gulliver, and Charles A. Briggs built upon the revisionist theological works of Horace Bushnell and others to lay the groundwork for a theological accommodation with modern science and historical criticism.[1] At the same time, such pioneers of social Christianity as Washington Gladden, Josiah Strong, Richard Ely, Francis

---

1. Cf. Horace Bushnell, *Views of Christian Nurture and of Subjects Adjacent Thereto* (Hartford: Edwin Hunt, 1847); Bushnell, *Nature and the Supernatural, as Together Constituting the One System of God* (New York: Charles Scribner, 1861); Newman Smyth, *The Religious Feeling* (New York: Scribner, Armstrong, and Co., 1877); Smyth, *The Orthodox Theology of To-Day* (New York: Charles Scribner's Sons, 1881); Smyth, *Old Faiths in New Light* (New York: Charles Scribner's Sons, 1879); David Swing, *Truths for Today: Spoken in the Past Winter* (Chicago: Jansen, McClurg and Co., 1874); John P. Gulliver, *Christianity and Science* (Andover, Mass.: Trustees of Andover Seminary, 1880); Charles A. Briggs, *Biblical Study: Its Principles, Methods and History* (New York: Charles Scribner's Sons, 1883); Briggs, *Whither? A Theological Question for the Times* (New York: Charles Scribner's Sons, 1889).

Peabody, and George Herron were challenging the materialism, individualism, and injustices of capitalist society in the name of Christian morality. They were also repudiating the traditional Protestant defense of American capitalism. American Protestantism would no longer present what historian Henry F. May later called a "massive, almost unbroken front in its defense of the social status quo." Liberal Christianity was invigorated during a period of intense intellectual upheaval by the rediscovery that Christianity had a social mission.[2]

By the turn of the century, the convergence of these doctrinal and social trends effected a transformation of American Protestant teaching. Henry Churchill King wrote in 1901 that "a new constructive period in theology" was apparently at hand.[3] William Newton Clarke and William Adams Brown published major textbooks that appropriated arguments from the Schleiermacher-Ritschl-Harnack tradition of German theological liberalism.[4] Brown, in particular, shared Albrecht Ritschl's grounding of religion in practical reason and his emphasis on historical revelation, as well as Adolf Harnack's identification of the "essence of Christianity" with the teachings and character of the historical Jesus. For Brown, as for the socially oriented, personalistic tradition that he represented, Christianity was the highest form of religious truth. It taught the fatherhood of God, the brotherhood of humanity, the absolute worth of the individual, an ethic of social cooperation and peace, and the kingdom of God as a historically attainable ideal.[5]

This was a believable faith. It eschewed metaphysics and fundamentalism. It appealed to practical and historical reason. Liberal Protestantism proclaimed that it was not only believable, however, but vital. It preached a creed that the whole world needed to embrace. It gave religious sanction to democratic prin-

---

2. Cf. Washington Gladden, *Applied Christianity: Moral Aspects of Social Questions* (Boston: Houghton, Mifflin and Co., 1886); Gladden, *Ruling Ideas of the Present Age* (Boston: Houghton, Mifflin and Co., 1895); Gladden, *How Much Is Left of the Old Doctrines?* (Boston: Houghton, Mifflin and Co., 1899); Josiah Strong, *Our Country* (New York: Charles Scribner's Sons, 1885); Richard Ely, *Social Aspects of Christianity* (New York: Charles Scribner's Sons, 1889); Francis G. Peabody, *Jesus Christ and the Social Question* (New York: Macmillan, 1900); George D. Herron, *The Larger Christ* (Chicago: Fleming H. Revell Co., 1891). Quotation in Henry F. May, *Protestant Churches and Industrial America* (New York: Harper & Row, 1959, c1949), 91.

3. Henry Churchill King, *Reconstruction in Theology* (New York: Macmillan, 1901), v.

4. Cf. William Newton Clarke, *An Outline of Christian Theology* (New York: Charles Scribner's Sons, 1898); William Adams Brown, *Christian Theology in Outline* (New York: Charles Scribner's Sons, 1906).

5. Brown studied under Harnack for two years in the mid-1890s and soon became a leading proponent of the Ritschl/Harnack tradition of German theological liberalism. See William Adams Brown, *The Essence of Christianity: A Study in the History of Definition* (New York: Charles Scribner's Sons, 1902).

ciples that were advancing in much of the world. With Brown's early works on the essence of liberal Christianity, the defining characteristics of America's dominant theological tradition for the next generation were established. In 1898, Brown was named Roosevelt Professor of Systematic Theology at Union Theological Seminary. By then, nearly all major chairs in theology at America's elite seminaries and divinity schools were held by liberals. Liberal Protestantism proclaimed that it was making its peace with modernity while reserving its right to criticize the social ravages of modernization.

Shailer Mathews's Reformist Progressivism

Most liberals trod lightly in the latter area. Even in the movement's social gospel wing, liberal Protestantism was usually more reformist than radical. The reformist progressivism of Shailer Mathews was more representative among social gospelers than the socialism of Walter Rauschenbusch—and even Rauschenbusch took a gradualist, reformist, resolutely democratic approach to socialism. In the writings of these two figures, however, the case for a theologically liberalized and socially transforming Christian progressivism found its most influential and compelling expressions. If Rauschenbusch was the movement's greater figure, it was Mathews who epitomized, for a subsequent generation, why liberal Christianity had moved in the wrong direction.

Both were born in the early 1860s, both were products of Baptist pietism, both graduated from seminary with their inherited evangelical-pietist beliefs largely intact, and both were crucially influenced by postseminary sabbaticals in Germany in the early 1890s. Rauschenbusch's father, August, came to the United States as a Lutheran missionary, but converted in 1850 to the stricter biblicism of the German Baptist faith. August Rauschenbusch became a church historian and taught for more than thirty years at the same seminary where his son later attained fame as America's leading social gospel theologian. Walter attended Rochester Seminary in the mid-1880s, when disputes over the legitimacy of historical criticism pitted a younger generation of scholars against the traditional orthodoxy of his father's generation. Though he accepted evolutionary theory and the conclusions of German Old Testament criticism during his student career, only after Rauschenbusch left the seminary did he embrace the liberal German theological tradition that his father had raised him to dread.

The turning point in his life occurred shortly after he began his assignment as pastor of the Second German Church (Baptist) on the border of Hell's Kitchen in New York City. Rauschenbusch arrived in New York with virtually no conception of a Christian social mission, but the grinding poverty and misery of his immigrant congregation quickly moved him to reconsider the church's mission. He was especially shaken by the malnutrition, diseases, and illiteracy of the city's children. Rauschenbusch later recalled that his awakening to the church's social mission occurred during his first month in New York, when he tried to apply the maxims of an individualistic pietism to an urban situation "and discovered that they didn't fit."[6] In reaction, he became involved in progressive politics and sought to reeducate himself not only in politics and economics but, more important, in Christian history and theology. While struggling to comprehend why the Christian churches had stripped Christianity of its prophetic social character, he underwent what he described as "a second conversion to Christ" that deepened his earlier resolve to live entirely by the teachings and spirit of Christ. Rauschenbusch's evangelical commitment to follow the way of Christ would survive all of his social and religious conversions.

This quality marked the crucial difference between liberal Christianity's evangelical and modernist tendencies. In the course of Mathews's later career, it also marked the critical difference between himself and Rauschenbusch. Mathews grew up in a secure middle-class family in Maine, where his father was a wholesale trader. He graduated from Colby College in 1884 and entered Newton Theological Institution the following fall, without any particular sense of a ministerial calling. A vague desire to teach theology brought him to seminary, but without conviction. "I had no questions to be answered and no serious doubts to be settled," he later recalled.[7] Mathews's inherited evangelicalism remained undisturbed throughout his seminary career, during which he undertook, for three months, his only experience in parish ministry. His summer pastorate convinced him not to become a pastor and not to seek ordination.

He chose instead to teach rhetoric and elocution at his alma mater. Mathews later moved to Colby's department of history and political economy after the college's eminent sociologist, Albion Small, vacated the position to become president. In 1890, lacking any graduate training in his new field, Mathews took a two-year sabbatical at the University of Berlin. Had he attended any theological lectures, he might have run into Rauschenbusch. Mathews was aware that Harnack taught at Berlin, but he was not in Germany to study theology or inclined to permit his historical training to be compromised by any personal interest in religious apologetics. Under the instruction of Hans Delbruck and Ignaz Jastrow, Mathews learned the methods of Rankeian-style objectivistic historiography. He also studied economics under Adolf Wagner and embraced Wagner's reformist, early welfare state approach to political economics. It was a formative experience. For the remainder of his intellectual career, Mathews's work would be marked

---

6. Quoted in Robert T. Handy, ed., *The Social Gospel in America* (New York: Oxford University Press, 1966), 255.

7. Shailer Mathews, *New Faith for Old: An Autobiography* (New York: Macmillan, 1936), 24.

by the influence of Wagner's ethical idealism and von Ranke's "scientific history." As Mathews later explained, the crucial lesson of his training in historiography was that one could pursue objective historical research without having to worry about its results.[8]

He returned to Colby in 1892, shortly before Small transferred to the University of Chicago to establish the country's first graduate department in sociology. Small exhorted Mathews to study sociology and promised to bring him to Chicago "as soon as it was practicable." Before it was practicable to expand the university's sociology department, however, Mathews received an offer from Ernest Burton to teach New Testament history at Chicago. He was hesitant. He had no desire to teach New Testament and was currently gearing up to teach sociology. He had already rejected an offer to teach New Testament at Newton. Burton overcame these misgivings, however, with his enthusiasm for Mathews and the university. Burton later became Chicago's president. Mathews was weary of the provinciality and isolation of Maine. He was ready to leave, and he reasoned that his training in historiography could be applied to the New Testament. "My inherited interest in religion took form in an ambition to have a part in extending its frontiers," he later explained. "A new age was in the making and religion was needed in social change."[9] He would bring his idealism and his academic training into the service of an emerging social religion.

Walter Rauschenbusch and Democratic Socialism

Rauschenbusch's path to the social gospel was more religious, more rooted in the church, and more burdened with oedipal weight. For the first five years of his parish ministry, he recognized that his "second conversion to Christ" was pushing him far beyond the vaguely liberal pietism he adopted at seminary. It was an experience of creative dislocation. While ministering to an often desperately hurting congregation and while educating himself on politics and economics, he struggled to find a theological basis for the kind of ministry that he was unexpectedly practicing. Numerous colleagues urged him to drop his preoccupation with "social work," but Rauschenbusch formed friendships with two Baptist pastors, Leighton Williams and Nathaniel Schmidt, who shared his conviction that the churches were obscuring the social character of the gospel. Rauschenbusch and his friends launched a monthly periodical, *For the Right,* that called for a social awakening in the churches. The journal never found a clear theological focus or identity, however, partly because Rauschenbusch's mind was unsettled regarding theology. He was no longer a conventional pietist,

8. Ibid., 42.
9. Ibid., 51.

but having grown up with a mortal fear of German theological liberalism, he resisted the conclusion that he was becoming a liberal. This resistance was reinforced by the social conformism of most German liberal theology. Rauschenbusch struggled with the question until 1891, when he took a leave from his parish to study English social movements and German theology.

For the Right mixed a rather muddled theological perspective with a clearer commitment to democratic socialism. Rauschenbusch's politics were strengthened by his exposure to socialist experiments in England. He was especially impressed by the achievements of Birmingham's "municipal socialism," which included a dramatically improved educational system and efficient public control of the city's water and gas systems. Rauschenbusch wrote home that American cities "should do by foresight what Birmingham did by hindsight."[10]

But his breakthrough occurred during his sabbatical in Germany. Rauschenbusch spent most of the year writing *Revolutionary Christianity,* which drew upon his pastoral experiences and his current studies in German theology, history, and sociology.[11] The book grew into a sprawling 450-page manuscript that was too disorganized and too outdated in its biblical scholarship to be worthy of publication. The process of writing it, however, was transformative for him. Rauschenbusch's growing identification with German theological liberalism was reflected in the book's evolutionary monism and its Ritschlian understanding of faith. His argument that the churches had abandoned Christianity's social mission was buttressed by his recently acquired historical knowledge. His driving theme reflected a conceptual breakthrough that marked all of his subsequent writings. He later explained:

> And then the idea of the Kingdom of God offered itself as the real solution for that problem. Here was something so big that absolutely nothing that interested me was excluded from it. Was it a matter of personal religion? Why, the Kingdom of God begins with that. The powers of the Kingdom of God well up in the individual soul; that is where they are born and that is where the starting point must necessarily be. Was it a matter of world-wide missions? Why, that is the Kingdom of God, isn't it—carrying it out to the boundaries of the earth. Was it a matter of getting justice for the working man? Is not justice a part of the Kingdom of God? Does not the Kingdom of God consist of this: that God's will shall be done on earth even as it is now in heaven? And so, wherever I

10. Quoted in Paul M. Minus, *Walter Rauschenbusch: American Reformer* (New York: Macmillan, 1988), 72.

11. Many years after Rauschenbusch's death, the text of his unpublished *Revolutionary Christianity* was misfiled at the American Baptist Historical Archives in Rochester, where it remained until it was rediscovered in the 1960s by Max Stackhouse. Stackhouse's reconstruction of the book was published under the title *The Righteousness of the Kingdom.* For his account of the text's history, see Walter Rauschenbusch, *The Righteousness of the Kingdom* (Nashville: Abingdon Press, 1968), 14–18.

touched life, there was the Kingdom of God. That was the brilliancy, the splendor of that conception—it touches everything with religion; it carries God into everything that you do, and there is nothing else that does it in the same way. [12]

This was the heart of authentic Christianity. The essence of Christianity was not a theory of atonement or even "the Fatherhood of God and the brotherhood of man" (Harnack). It was the spiritual reality of the kingdom taught by Christ and inaugurated by his resurrection. The churches no longer remembered what it meant to pray, "Thy kingdom come." Rauschenbusch had heard kingdom language throughout his life, but when its implications first washed over him, he wrote that the effect was like a revelation, as if the peak of a mountain had suddenly broken through the clouds. He wrote,

> It responded to all the old and all the new elements of my religious life. The saving of the lost, the teaching of the young, the pastoral care of the poor and frail, the quickening of starved intellects, the study of the Bible, church union, political reform, the reorganization of the industrial system, international peace—it was all covered by the one aim of the Reign of God on earth. That idea is necessarily as big as humanity, for it means the divine transformation of all human life. [13]

The kingdom was the "lost social ideal of Christendom." It could be recovered only by embracing the teachings and way of Christ. "Here was the idea and purpose that had dominated the mind of the Master himself," Rauschenbusch explained. "All his teachings center about it. His life was given to it. His death was suffered for it. When a man has once seen that in the gospels, he can never unsee it again." [14]

To see the kingdom was to perceive the world with a transformed consciousness. It was to acquire the lens through which Christian history needed to be viewed. Rauschenbusch had gone to Germany in hopes of finding a medical cure for his deafness, which he had endured for several years after a bout with Russian grippe. Though dispirited by his failure to find a cure, he returned to

---

12. Walter Rauschenbusch, "The Kingdom of God," *Cleveland's Young Men* 27 (January 9, 1913), quoted in Vernon P. Bodein, *The Social Gospel of Walter Rauschenbusch and Its Relation to Religious Education* (New Haven: Yale University Press, 1944), 7–8); reprinted in Handy, *Social Gospel in America,* 264–67. For my earlier account of Rauschenbusch's career and thought, from which parts of the present discussion are drawn, see Gary Dorrien, *Reconstructing the Common Good: Theology and the Social Order* (Maryknoll, N.Y.: Orbis, 1990), 16–47.

13. Walter Rauschenbusch, *Christianizing the Social Order* (New York: Macmillan, 1912), 93–94.

14. Quoted by C. Howard Hopkins, biographical preface to *A Gospel for the Social Awakening: Selections from the Writings of Walter Rauschenbusch,* ed. Benjamin E. Mays (New York: Association Press, 1950), 13.

America with a regenerated sense of spiritual purpose and conviction. With Williams, he resumed his community organizing in New York City and launched several new neighborhood projects, including a deaconess home and organizations for working women and men. With Williams, Schmidt, William Newton Clarke, and Josiah Strong, he formed the Brotherhood of the Kingdom, a Christian fellowship that pledged to reestablish the idea of the kingdom "in the thought of the church, and to assist in its practical realization in the life of the world." To reestablish the biblical idea of the kingdom in the life and thought of the church would require some understanding of the fate of this idea in Christian history. In 1892, Rauschenbusch offered his reading of this history in a Brotherhood pamphlet "A Conquering Idea."

His normative claim was that the biblical kingdom was a four-dimensional spiritual reality. The problem was that throughout Christian history, the churches had repeatedly reduced the kingdom to only one or two of its aspects and thus distorted its meaning. The reign of God was misrepresented most often through its identification with heaven, in which the kingdom became a merely transcendent reality. A closely related distortion was the typically Protestant reduction of the kingdom to the question of individual salvation. American Protestantism routinely reduced the organic biblical notions of the kingdom and the church to the issue of individual salvation, he observed, "because they understand nothing but individualism."[15] In Roman Catholic or hyper-Calvinist theologies, by contrast, the biblical notion of the reign of God was swallowed up by an ecclesiastical triumphalism that equated the kingdom with itself. The notion of the kingdom as the organic body of Christ was turned into an ecclesial authoritarianism that identified the kingdom with the Roman Catholic Church or with a Puritan theocracy.

Rauschenbusch allowed that all three of these historic misconceptions of the kingdom derived from some part of authentic Christianity. "Heaven is a truth; individual salvation is a truth; the church as the body of Christ is a tremendous truth," he declared. But none of these ideas, "neither singly nor combined, make up the full idea of the Kingdom of God." The reduction of the kingdom to heaven eliminated the kingdom's social dimension and thus "substituted asceticism for a revolutionary movement." This distortion of biblical faith was often sealed by reducing the present meaning of the kingdom to an individual's quest for eternal salvation. The consequence was the spiritualized egocentrism that typically passed for Christianity. Then again, the theocratic substitution of the church for the kingdom negated the church's eschatological identity and left most people in the world spiritually condemned.

---

15. Walter Rauschenbusch, "A Conquering Idea," 1892, reprinted in *Walter Rauschenbusch: Selected Writings,* ed. Winthrop S. Hudson (New York: Paulist Press, 1984), 72.

"We cannot have the Kingdom of God unless we first seize intellectually, and with the vigor of faith, the idea of the Kingdom," Rauschenbusch urged. "We need it as the basis for that work of social regeneration to which our generation has been called in the providential march of history." He conceded that his account of the church's past could be construed not only as a severe indictment but also as a strangely implausible one. It implied that the biblical idea of the kingdom had been lost for nearly nineteen centuries. Rauschenbusch pointedly recalled, however, that the Pauline doctrine of justification by faith was also lost until it was rediscovered by the sixteenth-century reformers. The social gospelers were making an analogous recovery. "Perhaps our generation is called to go back to the synoptic Christ as Luther's generation was called to go back to Paul," he ventured. "And perhaps that ideal of Christ is large enough to include in one tremendous synthesis all the terms that are crowding into the life of this second age of renaissance."[16]

The latter phrase reflected Rauschenbusch's perception that a new Reformation was brewing. The recent explosion of progressive movements dedicated to peace, democracy, economic justice, and freedom revealed that the kingdom was "moving to victory." At the same time, the churches were witnessing an explosion of millennialist religion. Rauschenbusch resisted the typical progressive tendency to write off the booming millennialist phenomenon as a know-nothing backlash. The fourth aspect of the biblical idea of the kingdom was the eschatological dimension, he explained—and the millennialists had taken hold of one end of it. "They have it in a bizarre form," he allowed, "but they have it." The characteristic millennialist focus on the fulfillment of history *in this world,* at the end of time, gave the millennialist sects a biblical sense of urgency and eschatological expectation that the mainline churches had lost. Rauschenbusch attributed the "peculiar hopefulness and vigor" of millennialist religion to its grasp of this end of the biblical faith.

He continued that the socialists held the other end. Though they did not pray "Thy kingdom come," it was the socialists, much more than the churches, who were struggling to fulfill the biblical vision of a just society. The socialist movement was struggling to bring about the kingdom of God "with God left out." The socialists grasped only a fractional part of the biblical kingdom, Rauschenbusch observed, but it was this fraction that gave their movement its distinctively religious character. Despite their antireligious posture, the socialists were becoming keepers of the biblical dream that society could be organized to meet the needs of all people.[17]

---

16. Ibid., 73.
17. Ibid., 72–74.

The social and religious project of the new Reformation was to recover the organic vision of the kingdom that had split into otherworldly, individualistic, ecclesiastical, millennialist, and socialist fragments. The kingdom was in heaven, Rauschenbusch affirmed, but it must also come to earth; while it began in the depths of human hearts, it was not meant to stay there; while the Church was "the channel through which ethical impulses pour into humanity from God," it was not identical with the kingdom; while the perfection of the kingdom was transhistorical, it was also a present reality. Because the idea of the kingdom was the key to Christ's teaching and work, "so its abandonment or misconstruction is the key to the false or one-sided conceptions of Christianity and our halting realization of it."[18] The kingdom was never to be reduced to any of its constitutive elements because the reign of God was "the sum of all divine and righteous forces on earth."[19] The Christian mission in the modern world was thus "to wed Christianity and the Social movement, infusing the power of religion with social efforts, and helping religion to find its ethical outcome in the transformation of social conditions."[20]

The manifesto for this project would not be published for another dozen years, when Rauschenbusch refashioned his Brotherhood essays and other materials into the best-selling *Christianity and the Social Crisis* (1907). Having returned to Rochester Seminary to teach church history, he was astonished when this brilliantly soaring, slashing, evocative work did not get him fired from Rochester but instead made him the most acclaimed churchman of his generation. To his surprise, he had tapped the zeitgeist. It was the high tide of American progressivism. A new generation of American Christians in a new century was prepared for his inspiriting call to build the kingdom within and outside the churches. Rauschenbusch's epochal work made only one (though highly commendatory) reference to Mathews.[21] More than anyone in the preceding decade, however, it was Mathews who laid the intellectual groundwork for the emerging social gospel movement.

Mathews and Christian Sociology

In the mid-1890s, shortly after his move to Chicago reunited him with Albion Small, Mathews wrote a series of articles for Small's *American Journal of*

---

18. Walter Rauschenbusch, "The Kingdom of God," 1893, reprinted in *Walter Rauschenbusch,* ed. Winthrop S. Hudson, 75.

19. Ibid., 76–79.

20. Quoted in Dores Robinson Sharpe, *Walter Rauschenbusch* (New York: Macmillan, 1942), 134.

21. Cf. Walter Rauschenbusch, *Christianity and the Social Crisis* (New York: Hodder & Stoughton/Macmillan, 1907), 44.

Sociology on what he called "Christian Sociology." The literature on social Christianity was already extensive; it included works by Gladden, Strong, Peabody, Ely, Herron, Lyman Abbott, William Hyde, and others.[22] The social Christian movement lacked a major study of the social significance of the teachings of Jesus, however. In Mathews's estimation, it also lacked a theological perspective that was adequately informed by the kind of sociological work that Small and Lester Ward were providing.[23] The sociological model of society as a dynamic organism became a foundational concept for Mathews. He identified, as well, with Small's reformist politics and his moral idealism. The problem was that sociology could not provide a normative warrant for either reformed politics or moral idealism. Sociology had no morally prescriptive power, and some source of socially transformative moral value needed to be found.

Mathews turned for this source to the teachings of Jesus. Here was Western society's most powerful reservoir of moral teaching, if only it could be made relevant to the needs of a new social order. Drawing on his historical training and his recent studies in sociology, he turned his articles for Small's journal into a book on the social relevance of Christian teaching. *The Social Teachings of Jesus* (1897) was the first major attempt in English to make a case for the sociopolitical significance of Jesus' teaching. Apart from Rauschenbusch's books, it was also the most influential text ever produced by the social gospel movement. The book remained in print for more than thirty years, until Mathews replaced it with a substantially revised edition, *Jesus on Social Institutions* (1928).[24]

The Social Teachings of Jesus elaborated Mathews's conception of the kingdom as an ideal social order attainable through moral effort. By the kingdom of God, he wrote, "Jesus meant an ideal (though progressively approximated) social order in which the relation of men to God is that of sons, and (therefore) to each other, that of brothers." The "brotherhood of man" was the telos of human history or, in Mathews's favorite phrase, the "goal of social evolution." Mathews ascribed to Jesus the view that the achievement of a perfect society was a "natural possibility." He commended the audacity of Jesus in assuming that the apostles would bring about the "indefinite expansion" of the kingdom. This act of faith

---

22. For an excellent discussion of late nineteenth- and early twentieth-century social Christian literature, see William R. Hutchison, *The Modernist Impulse in American Protestantism* (Durham, N.C.: Duke University Press, 1992).

23. Cf. Albion W. Small and George E. Vincent, *An Introduction to the Study of Society* (New York: American Book Company, 1894); Small, *General Sociology: An Exposition of the Main Development in Sociological Theory from Spencer to Ratzenhofer* (Chicago: University of Chicago Press, 1905); Small, *The Meaning of Social Science* (Chicago: University of Chicago Press, 1910).

24. Shailer Mathews, *The Social Teachings of Jesus* (New York: Macmillan, 1897); Mathews, *Jesus on Social Institutions* (New York: Macmillan, 1928).

was equaled, he wrote, "only by the superb optimism that saw possibilities of infinite good in humanity."[25]

The possibilities of human good would be realized when human beings accepted God's love for them, as mediated to them and inspired by the example of Jesus. People would come to love their neighbors as their brothers and sisters when, through the inspiration of Christ, they accepted God's love for themselves and others. Mathews insisted that because human beings were creatures of a loving God, the possibilities for human good were infinite. The mobilization and fulfillment of these possibilities would bring about the kingdom of God.

This rendering of Jesus' teaching soon inspired numerous imitations that were even more sentimental than Mathews's. Mathews's tone became less precious in response. His next book, *A History of New Testament Times* (1899) continued to portray early Christianity in the image of his own rather saccharine idealism, but by 1905 Mathews was prepared to acknowledge some of the differences between his faith in progress and Jesus' understanding of the kingdom.[26] *The Messianic Hope in the New Testament* acknowledged that, for Jesus, the kingdom was an eschatological reality. "Its appearance would be the result of no social evolution, but sudden, as the gift of God; men could not hasten its coming; they could only prepare for membership in it," Mathews acknowledged.[27]

For more than a decade, he had resisted Johannes Weiss's apocalyptic interpretation of the kingdom, claiming that Weiss distorted Jesus' social and ethical teachings.[28] Mathews would never accept Weiss's thoroughgoing apocalypticism, but with *The Messianic Hope* he became the first American to argue that the kingdom was primarily an eschatological reality for Jesus and for the early church. He reluctantly concluded that Weiss's historical reconstruction was basically correct. The apocalyptic sections of the Gospels were not products of later Christian redaction but reflected the heart of Jesus' own teaching. The kingdom of God was not, for Jesus, a product of "social evolution" or the goal of human idealism but an immanent future reality brought on by an unaided divine act.

25. Mathews, *Social Teachings,* 201.

26. Cf. Shailer Mathews, *A History of New Testament Times in Palestine* (New York: Macmillan, 1899).

27. Shailer Mathews, *The Messianic Hope in the New Testament* (Chicago: University of Chicago Press), 82. For helpful discussions of the importance of Mathews's work in American New Testament scholarship, see Frederick C. Grant, "Ethics and Eschatology in the Teachings of Jesus," *The Journal of Religion* 22 (October 1942), 359; and Kenneth Cauthen, "The Life and Thought of Shailer Mathews," Introduction to the Fortress Press reprint of Mathews, *Jesus on Social Institutions* (Philadelphia: Fortress Press, 1971), xlvi–liii.

28. Cf. Johannes Weiss, *Jesus' Proclamation of the Kingdom of God,* trans. D. Larrimore Holland and Richard H. Hiers (Philadelphia: Fortress Press, 1971, c1892).

This historical conclusion was troublesome not only for Mathews but also for the entire social gospel movement. By emphasizing the eschatological character of Jesus' worldview, contemporary biblical scholarship seemed to undercut the social Christian concern for social progress and justice. The debate over Christian apocalypticism heightened dramatically in 1906, with the German publication Albert Schweitzer's *The Quest of the Historical Jesus.*[29] Schweitzer affirmed Weiss's essential argument and skewered the entire European tradition of liberal Christology. With devastating polemical force, he showed that nearly all of the so-called critical studies of Jesus of the past century had projected nineteenth-century liberal values onto Jesus. In their efforts to find a historical Jesus beneath the layers of church redaction and mythology, liberal theologians had turned Jesus into an enlightened Protestant bourgeois, sometimes with mildly radical tendencies. In Schweitzer's haunting analogy, they had looked into a well for the historical Jesus and seen their own image.

Four basic responses to this crucial turn in biblical criticism were open to social gospelers and other liberal Christians. The first was a "realized eschatology" that built upon Luke 11:20, 17:20, and similar texts to claim that the kingdom had already come with Christ's incarnation. This approach informed Roman Catholic and Orthodox ecclesiologies and was importantly amplified in later Protestant theology by the eminent New Testament scholars Rudolf Bultmann and C. H. Dodd. The second was to construct a dialectic of the kingdom in which the presence of Christ in history was viewed as a foretaste or anticipation of an absolute future ordained by divine will. Numerous theologians, including Rauschenbusch in certain passages, adopted some variant of this approach. In later twentieth-century theology, figures such as Jürgen Moltmann and Wolfhart Pannenberg developed eschatological dialectics that conceived divine reality itself as the power of the future. The biblical notion of God as the eschatological presence of the future was employed, especially by Moltmann, to counteract the privatizing effect of modern existentialist and hermeneutical theologies;[30] that is, in a later theological generation, the centrality of Christianity's eschatological

---

29. Cf. Albert Schweitzer, *The Quest of the Historical Jesus: A Critical Study of Its Progress from Reimarus to Wrede,* trans. W. Montgomery (New York: Macmillan, 1968, c1906).

30. Cf. Rudolf Bultmann, *Theology of the New Testament,* 2 vols., trans. Kendrick Grobel (New York: Scribner's, 1951, 1955); Bultmann, *New Testament and Mythology,* trans. Schubert M. Ogden (Philadelphia: Fortress Press, 1984); C. H. Dodd, *The Gospel in the New Testament* (London: National Sunday School Union, 1926); *The Parables of the Kingdom* (New York: Scribner's, 1961); Jürgen Moltmann, *Theology of Hope: On the Ground and the Implications of a Christian Eschatology,* trans. James W. Leitch (London: SCM Press, 1967, c1964); Wolfhart Pannenberg, *Theology and the Kingdom of God* (Philadelphia: Westminster Press, 1969).

consciousness was viewed as the key to restoring Christianity's forward-looking, socially oriented perspective.

But Rauschenbusch's worldview was too rooted in nineteenth-century evolutionary monism and idealism for him to turn the debate over apocalyptic to his advantage. His writings generally resisted the trend in New Testament scholarship. In his reading, the parables of Jesus were protests against the worldview of late Jewish apocalypticism, rather than products of it. Rauschenbusch played up the realistic, developmental character of the Synoptic parables of the Sower, the Net, the Tares, the Mustard Seed, and Leaven. He argued that Jesus' socially oriented teachings were meant to replace the common Jewish apocalyptic understanding of the kingdom. Following the Harnack-Herrmann theory of Christian origins, Rauschenbusch thus assumed that the apocalyptic sections of the Synoptic Gospels, such as Mark 13, were retrojections of the later church's own apocalyptic worldview into the kerygmatic narratives. He explained, "It is thus exceedingly probable that the church spilled a little of the lurid colors of its own apocalypticism over the loftier conceptions of its Master."[31]

This typically liberal deprecation of apocalyptic reflected Rauschenbusch's roots in nineteenth-century German idealism, to which he clung for the rest of his life. His deeper reason for resisting the turn in New Testament scholarship, however, was that he feared that the new emphasis on apocalyptic would obscure the recent gains of social Christianity in recovering the church's social mission. He did not deny that early Christianity was suffused with an eschatological consciousness. He only—mistakenly—tried to exempt Jesus from this cultural background. Rauschenbusch acknowledged that all biblical writers made assumptions about history, society, and the world that were now outmoded. He observed that the worldview of the New Testament writers was clouded by the expectation of Christ's immanent return and by the immediate reality of Roman oppression. The writings of Paul shared these limitations of knowledge and perspective. Yet within American churches, Rauschenbusch complained, "it still passes as a clinching argument for Christian indifference to social questions that Paul never started a good government campaign."[32] The churches were clinging to the letter of the New Testament while smothering its spirit. To take the spirit of Christian social teaching seriously, Rauschenbusch implied, would require a willingness to confront the radical differences in context between the biblical and modern worlds.

This clue fueled Mathews's subsequent apologetic strategy. Rather than resort to a dialectic of the kingdom or resist the trend of New Testament scholarship, he emphasized the split between the ancient and modern worlds to heighten his

---

31. Rauschenbusch, *Christianity and the Social Crisis,* 63.
32. Ibid., 160.

case for a modernist faith. The biblical writers believed many things that were now unbelievable. Modern Christianity needed to absorb the implications of this fact. The question was how to negotiate the radical dissociation between the prescientific, mythological, apocalyptic consciousness of early Christianity and the modern rationalist consciousness.

Liberal Christianity typically dealt with this question by claiming that Christianity was primarily a way of life grounded in experience rather than a body of dogma requiring doctrinal assent. Roman Catholic modernists generally elaborated this argument in a way that was more respectful toward church tradition than their liberal Protestant counterparts. In the 1890s, Roman Catholic scholars such as Alfred Loisy and Maurice Blondel accepted modernist perspectives on Scripture, church history, and theology while claiming that the challenges posed by modernist criticism confirmed the need for an organic, authoritative, and continually developing church tradition and structure.[33] The Roman Catholic emphasis on Christianity as a historical-institutional movement was shared, in a different form, by Mathews. Protestant modernists were more inclined, however, than their Roman Catholic counterparts to appeal to a putative "heart" or "essence" of Christianity as a corrective to inherited Christian doctrine. Mathews exemplified the difference. To be a Christian, he insisted, was not to accept any particular doctrinal formulations about Christ, but to follow the way of Christ. This claim increasingly formed the basis of his approach to theology. With the publication of *The Church and the Changing Order* in 1907, he began to focus his work on the development of a liberal Christian apologetics and social theory. Over the next three decades, this project produced more than thirty volumes of theology and social theory. More than any other theologian of his time, in a career that matched the rise and decline of liberal Protestantism, Mathews elaborated the liberal modernist understanding of Christianity as a particular kind of social movement.

The "real crisis of the church" in 1907 was that it needed to define its relationship toward "formative forces" in modern society. "Will it move on indifferent to their existence, or will it cooperate with them, correct them, inspire them with its own ideals, and insure that their results shall insure a better

---

33. Cf. B.M.G. Reardon, ed., *Roman Catholic Modernism* (London: A. & C. Black, 1970); Alfred F. Loisy, *The Gospel and the Church*, trans. Christopher Home (New York: Charles Scribner's Sons, 1912, c1903); Loisy, *My Duel with the Vatican* (New York: E. P. Dutton, 1924); Loisy, *The Birth of the Christian Religion* and *The Origins of the New Testament*, single-volume edition, trans. L. P. Jacks (New Hyde Park: University Books, 1962); Maurice Blondel, *L'Action: Essai d'une critique de la vie et d'une science de la pratique* (Paris: Alcan, 1893); Blondel, *The Letter on Apologetics* and *History and Dogma,* single-volume edition, trans. Alexander Dru and Illtyd Trethowan (New York: Holt, Rinehart and Winston, 1964).

tomorrow?" he asked.[34] Mathews exhorted the church to join the modern struggle for social progress. The church's spiritual vitality was at stake in this decision in that "communion with God is possible only for the man who is living a life of supreme social service." He allowed that a progressive church would often be forced to afflict the comfortable within and outside its ranks because a contented person was "a millstone around the neck of progress."[35] The church could not afford to recycle discredited monarchical dogmas in a democratic age. At the same time, Mathews argued, America's self-satisfied cultural elites needed to understand that morality without religion had no inspiriting power.

The Church and the Changing Order sounded an evangelical note. "The history of Christian thought cannot be wholly a history of mistakes," he wrote. Liberal religion in America, which had "too often confused religion with ethical culture," needed to learn something from the failures of Unitarianism and the various ethical societies.[36] If liberal Christianity was to remain a living, growing religious movement, it had to be nourished by personal religious faith. Mathews conceded that his understanding of Christian faith was more evangelical "than that which has been considered progressive orthodoxy of the last generation." He argued that it was a mistake to view modernist criticism in purely negative terms, however, because modern science and historical criticism made it possible not only to strip away the mistaken accretions of church dogma but also to recover the spiritual essence of Christianity. The church should hold fast to Christ, he declared, as "an actual faith-compelling revelation of a God who saves from sin and death."[37] Though he would later discard the evangelical elements of his theology, Mathews insisted throughout his career that any liberal Christianity not sustained by personal religious experience would have no future.[38]

At the high tide of the social gospel movement, from 1907 to 1914, Mathews poured out a stream of evangelically tinged books that were less powerful and provocative than Rauschenbusch's writings, but also less dangerous. Rauschenbusch blasted his opponents, but Mathews's tone was unfailingly irenic. He later explained that "non-combativeness is good strategy in religion."[39] Rauschenbusch advocated socialism, but Mathews identified the social gospel with moral conversion, reform, and gradual progress. The difference between Christianity and socialism, he argued, was that socialism expected society to make good indi-

---

34. Shailer Mathews, *The Church and the Changing Order* (New York: Macmillan, 1907), 6.

35. Ibid., 100, 123.

36. Shailer Mathews, *The Gospel and the Modern Man* (New York: Macmillan, 1910), 178.

37. Ibid., 88–89.

38. Cf. Mathews, *New Faith for Old*, 294.

39. Ibid., 289.

viduals, but Christianity expected good individuals to make a good society. "Christianity assumes that it is impossible to have a good social order composed of bad men," he explained.[40] For this reason, Christianity was better suited to produce "permanent social betterment" than socialism. Socialism was too economistic in its assumptions, strategy, and spirit. It believed that a good society could be attained by creating a just socioeconomic order. Mathews observed that Christianity was more attentive to moral, intellectual, aesthetic, and religious factors. Liberal Christianity did not so much oppose socialism as insist that a good society could be created only "by producing religiously regenerate lives."[41]

For liberal Christianity, Jesus was the symbol and agent of spiritual regeneration. Mathews explained that in the religious movement that Jesus founded, "the Jesus of history became the Christ of experience."[42] *The Gospel and the Modern Man* (1910) elaborated this historical Christology, arguing that the most powerful regenerative force in Western history was the transforming spirit of Christ. "The real significance of the historical Jesus lies in the fact that in him the Spiritual Life for which humanity has searched was perfectly brought in terms of time and human relationships," Mathews asserted.[43] Because the spirit of Christ was not merely an idea but a real spiritual power, regeneration was possible for individuals and for society.

The Social Gospel (1910) propounded this theme in the book's opening sentence. "Jesus has no social gospel for bad people," Mathews declared. "His ideals presuppose goodness." These ideals bore social implications that obligated the church to promote fairness, harmony, cooperation, and peace in the public sphere. But none of these social goals was attainable without morally transformed hearts. "The teaching of Jesus is not for bad people—for those who are not possessed of a spirit like that of Jesus," Mathews instructed. "And Jesus knew this. He distinguished sharply between the world and his disciples."[44] If the world was filled with people in whom the image of God was degraded or disregarded, the work of the church was to activate human goodness by awakening people to the spirit of Christ within them.

Mathews insisted that his version of the social gospel was neither pietism nor a politicized religion. "The gospel is neither individualistic nor socialistic," he argued. "It is a message that deals primarily with human life and that seeks to transform human lives into conformity with the ideals of Jesus by bringing them into regenerating relations with God." The gospel carried social imperatives,

---

40. Mathews, *The Church and the Changing Order*, 171.
41. Ibid., 172–75.
42. Mathews, *The Gospel and the Modern Man*, 112.
43. Ibid., 111.
44. Shailer Mathews, *The Social Gospel* (New York: Macmillan, 1910), 11–13.

but it did not prescribe any particular political or economic message. "It leaves all its followers free to choose whatever particular social theory seems to them best calculated to make its principles operative," Mathews explained.[45] Politics was merely instrumental. The questions it posed for the church were never more than pragmatic. The transcendent question concerned the *way* that Christians operated in the social sphere. It concerned the Christian's spiritual identity within the social struggle for progress. Mathews warned that the Christian movement was not Christian whenever it substituted impersonal forces or strategies for faith in a personal God. "We must give Christ to the world," he exhorted. "The gospel is the power of God unto salvation to all those who believe in Jesus. It should not be complicated with questions of capital or labor. It must express itself, as we have seen, in all forms of social life, but it is not to be identified with any social theory."[46]

This was the dominant voice of liberal Christianity. To make itself relevant to a modern world, the church needed to live by the spirit of Christ, as distinguished from any particular theory of salvation or Christology or scriptural authority. What the church had to offer the struggle for social progress was not any particular theory of economics, government, or political reform, however, but the regenerative power of Christ's spirit. The social mission of the church was not to give religious sanction to any political agenda but to promote the making of a good society by spreading the cooperative, justice-demanding, peacemaking spirit of Christian faith. Though he would later dispense with the evangelical form of this appeal, Mathews continued for the rest of his career to conceptualize "the social problem" in a language of moral progress that did not threaten the ethos or interests of middle-class churches.

Rauschenbusch and the Struggle for the Kingdom

Rauschenbusch was different on both counts. He would never relinquish his emphasis on the centrality and transforming power of Christ's spirit. Neither would he endorse the comforting liberal notion that the church needed only to Christianize existing movements for social progress or "process." In Mathews's later work, the concept of the socioreligious field as a "process" took on the quality of a God term. Rauschenbusch also spoke of the kingdom in ethical terms and often equated the realization of the kingdom with the evolutionary process and the growth of democracy. He was capable of writing that if one translated "the evolutionary theories into religious faith . . . you have the doctrine of the

---

45. Ibid., 121–22.
46. Ibid., 122.

Kingdom of God."[47] He employed neo-Hegelian language in speaking of history as the "sacred workshop" of God and developed an evolutionary monist interpretation of history in which humanity "realized God" by cooperating with the work of God's immanent Spirit.[48]

The marks of philosophical and moral idealism were thus amply displayed throughout his work. Neither Rauschenbusch's theology nor his politics was ever reducible to these terms, however. For him, the Christian social movement for justice was not merely a process but a struggle. It would not be attained merely through religiously inspired good will and social progress, but also through power politics, force, and the struggle of social classes. Mathews often urged that Americans should forget about class. Rauschenbusch countered that "we must not blink the fact that idealists alone have never carried though any great social change. . . . For a definite historical victory a great truth must depend on the class which makes that truth its own and fights for it."[49] Though he often exaggerated the extent to which American politics and culture were becoming "Christianized"—and thus badly underestimated the depth of America's racial pathology—Rauschenbusch had no illusions that concentrated economic power in America could be democratized through moral effort and religious preaching. In *A Theology for the Social Gospel* (1917), he railed against the ruling class who lived "parasitic lives without any fellow-feeling for the peasants or tenants whom they were draining to pay for their leisure."[50] He had seen enough in Hell's Kitchen to know that the capitalists and absentee landlords would never relinquish their power in response to moral appeals. The struggle for social justice in America required the truth of a righteous cause and the collective solidarity of those oppressed by injustice. "If there is no such army to fight its cause, the truth will drive individuals to a comparatively fruitless martyrdom and will continue to hover over humanity as a disembodied ideal," he declared.[51]

The defining conviction of his work was announced at the outset of his manifesto for social Christianity, *Christianity and the Social Crisis:* "The essential purpose of Christianity is to transform human society into the Kingdom of God by regenerating all human relations and reconstituting them in accordance with the will of God."[52] Rauschenbusch drew primarily on the prophetic tradition and the Synoptic Gospels in assembling his argument that Scripture condemns the worship of power and the evils of injustice and oppression. For the prophets and

---

47. Rauschenbusch, *Christianizing the Social Order*, 90.

48. Ibid., 121.

49. Rauschenbusch, *Christianity and the Social Crisis*, 400–401.

50. Walter Rauschenbusch, *A Theology for the Social Gospel* (New York: Macmillan, 1917), 19.

51. Rauschenbusch, *Christianity and the Social Crisis*, 401.

52. Ibid., xiii.

for Jesus, ethical conduct was "the supreme and sufficient religious act." If the churches had distorted the social character of Christianity and thus rationalized their own power and authority, it was not too late to recover the prophetic, emancipating spirit of early Christianity. "To repent of our collective social sins, to have faith in the possibility and reality of a divine life in humanity, to submit the will to the purposes of the Kingdom of God, to permit the divine inspiration to emancipate and clarify the moral insight—this is the most intimate duty of the religious man who would help to build the coming Messianic era of mankind," he declared.[53] Those who worked to build the kingdom were creating a new kind of Christianity that was neither alien nor novel. "Their horizon is wider; their sympathy more catholic; their faith more daring." But all they were doing was recovering the radical spirit of original Christianity and translating its meaning to an industrial order.

Rauschenbusch insisted that in the socioeconomic realm, this commitment translated into democratic socialism. "The possessing classes are strong by mere possession long continued," he observed. "They control nearly all property. The law is on their side, for they have made it. They control the machinery of government and can use force under the form of law. Their self-interest makes them almost impervious to moral truth if it calls in question the sources from which they draw their income." To challenge the ruling class with mere idealism, he wrote, was to dash the finest truisms of morality "against the solid granite of human selfishness."[54] What was needed was a labor or socialist movement that would "drive a breach through the entrenchments of those opposed to it and carry the cause to victory."[55]

The cause was to democratize not only social and political power but also economic power. "As long as the working class simply attempts to better its condition somewhat and to secure a recognized standing for its class organization, it stands on the basis of the present capitalistic organization of industry," Rauschenbusch observed.[56] Trade union reformism was capable of making small gains toward justice, but it reinforced the split between America's ruling and working classes. It was this division between capital and labor itself that any serious struggle for social justice needed to abolish. Socialism was thus "the ultimate and logical outcome of the labor movement," he argued. A socialist order would abolish private control of the major means of production and thus "end the present insecurity, the physical exploitation, [and] the intellectual poverty to which the working class is now exposed even where its condition is most fa-

---

53. Ibid., 352.
54. Ibid., 400.
55. Ibid., 401.
56. Ibid., 406.

vorable."[57] A new spirit of cooperation and solidarity would be infused into a society in which workers owned the means of production and controlled the process of investment.

The role of the church within the socialist movement was to be the inspiriting and chastening soul of the movement. Rauschenbusch cautioned his fellow Christian idealists that the struggle for justice was "a war of conflicting interests." The class struggle would not be waged in the language or with the manners of middle-class idealism. "The possessing class will make concessions not in brotherly love but in fear, because it has to," he instructed. "The working class will force its demands, not merely because they are just, but because it feels it cannot do without them, and because it is strong enough to coerce."[58] The mark of Christian moral seriousness was that Christians would join the working-class side of the class struggle as Christians, but without moralistic illusions. "Christianity should enter into a working alliance with this rising class, and by its mediation secure the victory of these principles by a gradual equalization of social opportunity and power," he declared.[59]

Christianity and the Social Crisis went through six printings in its first two years and made Rauschenbusch famous. His call for a radicalized social Christian movement converted thousands of pastors, academics, and activists to the social gospel and challenged liberal Christianity to go beyond its reformist moralism. Rauschenbusch was sensitive to the criticism, raised by opponents and his closest friends, that the book failed to reveal the spiritual wellspring of his faith. His subsequent and highly popular work, *For God and the People: Prayers of the Social Awakening* (1910), filled this important gap in his self-presentation.[60] At the same time, he was sensitive to the criticism that his arguments for Christian socialism were long on moral eloquence but short on programmatic political and economic analysis. His massive work, *Christianizing the Social Order* (1912), responded to this objection and set a standard for Christian political argument that has rarely been equaled.

The claim that Christianity has a social mission was now widely accepted, he noted. The Christian social movement was transforming modern Christianity. In 1908, the newly formed Federal Council of Churches, representing thirty-three denominations, had issued a social creed that was closely modeled on the Methodist social creed of the same year. These statements called for a "living wage" in every industry, abolition of child labor, the elimination of poverty, and

---

57. Ibid., 408.

58. Ibid., 411.

59. Ibid., 414.

60. Cf. Walter Rauschenbusch, *For God and the People: Prayers of the Social Awakening* (Boston: Pilgrim Press, 1910).

a more equitable distribution of wealth.[61] Social gospelers such as Rauschenbusch, Mathews, Gladden, Strong, Frank Mason North, Charles Stelzle, Graham Taylor, and Harry F. Ward were active in the Federal Council, which functioned as a kind of laboratory for social gospel ideas that filtered into the seminaries and churches.

Christianizing the Social Order exuded the optimism of this burgeoning social movement. Rauschenbusch's earlier warnings about the inevitable harshness of the class struggle faded into the background as the prospect of a radicalized church loomed in his expectation. He rehearsed his reading of biblical and church history, arguing that the early church gradually replaced Christ's theology of the kingdom with an otherworldly theology *about* Christ. As the prophetic themes of Scripture were systematically "etherealized" by Hellenization, allegorical interpretation, and the church's attainment of political power, he explained, the heart of Christian faith was lost. "The eclipse of the Kingdom idea was an eclipse of Jesus," Rauschenbusch wrote. "We had listened too much to voices talking about him, and not enough to his own voice. Now his own thoughts in their lifelike simplicity and open-air fragrance have become a fresh religious possession, and when we listen to Jesus, we cannot help thinking about the Kingdom of God."[62]

To "Christianize" the social order was not to put Christ's name into the American Constitution or create a state religion. It was to bring society into harmony with Christian moral convictions. These teachings were not particularly distinctive, in Rauschenbusch's view. The Christian moral values of freedom, compassion, fairness, peace, sacrificial love, equality, and humility were shared by all people of good will, whether religious or not. His project was to bring society into harmony with the shared moral values of what he called "our collective conscience." To Christianize was to promote a politics of common morality. Though *Christianize* and *moralize* thus meant the same thing, Rauschenbusch argued that the former term was preferable, because *moralize* was "both vague and powerless" to most Americans. Christian moral language was not only more powerful and compelling than its secularized alternatives; in the West, it was also the source of these alternatives. Western moral languages invariably

---

61. For discussions of the American churches' social creeds, see G. Bromley Oxnam, "The Christian Challenge," in *Christian Values and Economic Life,* ed. John C. Bennett, Howard R. Bowen, William Adams Brown, Jr., and G. Bromley Oxnam (New York: Harper & Brothers, 1954), 4–8; Martin E. Marty, *Righteous Empire: The Protestant Experience in America* (New York: Dial Press, 1970), 206–9; Sidney E. Mead, *The Lively Experiment: The Shaping of Christianity in America* (New York: Harper & Row, 1963), 177–83; Robert T. Handy, *A Christian America: Protestant Hopes and Historical Realities* (New York: Oxford University Press, 1984), 149–50.

62. Rauschenbusch, *Christianizing the Social Order,* 89–90.

bore the imprint of the West's Christian heritage. Like Mathews, Rauschenbusch denied that any kind of sectarian implication should be drawn from this fact because "Christianizing means humanizing in the highest sense." Like other social gospelers, including Lyman Abbott, his writings often used *Christianize, moralize, humanize,* and *democratize* as interchangeable terms. Abbott, the editor of the influential liberal journal *The Outlook,* explained the social gospelers' defining conviction in 1906. "Democracy is not merely a political theory, it is not merely a social opinion; it is a profound religious faith," he declared. "To him who holds it, this one fundamental faith in the Fatherhood of God and in the universal brotherhood of man is the essence of democracy."[63]

The inordinately optimistic thesis of *Christianizing the Social Order* was that American society was becoming democratized in every sector apart from the economic system. The logic of democratic entitlement had already transformed American politics and education, Rauschenbusch claimed, and it was presently redefining American attitudes toward gender roles, race, and religion. In nearly every sector of American society, it was commonly assumed that only democratic forms of authority and democratic social structures were legitimate. Rauschenbusch's optimism on the culture-transforming character of American democracy caused him to underestimate the depth of American racism. Under the pressure of his concern to strengthen America's democratic culture and open its doors to German immigrants, he was not above making appeals to racial prejudice. He opposed all racially based arguments for closed immigration, but at the same time he strongly implied that German immigrants were more equal than others. In one of his fund-raising appeals for the German department at Rochester Seminary, he asked in 1905, "Are the whites of this continent so sure of their possession against the blacks of the South and the seething yellow flocks beyond the Pacific that they need no reinforcement of men of their own blood while yet it is time?" In his 1902 Rochester commencement address, he warned that Anglo-Saxons needed to join with the "princely Teutonic stock" to protect American democracy from the demands of "alien strains" arriving from other parts of the world.[64]

Rauschenbusch's early statements on immigration thus contained unmistakably racist appeals, using language that, even in its time, must be considered racially offensive. From his perspective, however, these appeals were based not so much upon racial prejudice as upon his fear that American democracy was

---

63. Ibid., 125; Abbott quoted in Jan Dawson, "The Religion of Democracy in Early Twentieth-Century America," *Journal of Church and State* 27 (1985), 48.

64. Cf. John R. Aiken, "Walter Rauschenbusch and Education for Reform," *Church History* 36 (December 1967), 459–60; Martin E. Marty, *The Irony of It All, 1893–1919,* vol. 1 of *Modern American Religion* (Chicago: University of Chicago Press, 1986), 294; Minus, *Walter Rauschenbusch,* 105.

fragile. To protect and extend America's democracy, he assumed that America needed to draw a critical mass of its immigrants from relatively democratized European cultures. Like Mathews, Rauschenbusch's writings rarely mentioned race at all; like Mathews, he assumed that racism, discrimination against women, and related social ills would be swept aside by the continued growth of democracy and social progress. Neither theologian was willing to alienate his white liberal audience with anything more than a parenthetical aside regarding racism in America. Neither of them publicly questioned the Supreme Court's 1896 *Plessy v. Ferguson* ruling that "separate but equal" segregation was consistent with the Fourteenth Amendment's guarantee of equal protection under the law. In 1900, nearly 90 percent of American blacks still lived in the South. Some of the social gospelers, notably Washington Gladden, made important contacts with black leaders through their involvement in church-sponsored efforts to support black education, such as the programs of the American Missionary Society. Relations between blacks and northern white social gospelers were for the most part limited to this context, however. Neither Mathews nor Rauschenbusch had enough acquaintance with blacks or knew enough about African American history to bring race into the purview of social Christianity. In 1912, Rauschenbusch believed that the strengthening political and cultural force of American democracy was eliminating racism and any possible excuse for it. In his America, with one crucial exception, the growing Christianization of the social order was erasing past social and cultural evils.[65]

The exception was the economic system, which Rauschenbusch called the "unregenerate section of our social order." He allowed that as individuals, most capitalists were as moral as anyone else. The problem was that the capitalist system was "a form of legalized graft" that engendered "a spirit of hardness and cruelty" in American life. "Capitalism has generated a spirit of its own which is antagonistic to the spirit of Christianity," he claimed. "The materialistic spirit of capitalism is pervading all our spiritual life and conforming our conscience to its standards."[66] He noted that the learned professions were still like islands "amid the rising tide of capitalistic profit making," but the water was rising. "As the yellow flood swirls about them and eats into their banks, the members of each profession watch it with sinking hearts," he wrote. The professional class knew in its heart that to commercialize a profession was to degrade it. In Rauschenbusch's view, the legal profession had degenerated the most. "The

---

65. For informative discussions of race and the social gospel movement, see Ralph E. Luker, *The Social Gospel in Black and White: American Racial Reform, 1885–1912* (Chapel Hill: University of North Carolina Press, 1991); and Ronald C. White, Jr., *Liberty and Justice for All: Racial Reform and the Social Gospel (1877–1925)* (New York: Harper & Row, 1990).

66. Rauschenbusch, *Christianizing the Social Order*, 315, 318.

most lucrative practice is the service of corporations, and they need the lawyer to protect their interests against the claims of the public," he explained. "The learning, the moral independence, and the public standing of the profession have suffered as it has been commercialized."[67]

The commercialization of society was not only corrupting American culture but also threatening to reverse America's democratic gains in other sectors. The concentration of undemocratic power in the economic realm impeded further progress in other sectors and thwarted even the possibility of attaining distributive social justice. It gave inordinate political power to business interests and thus undermined political democracy. To remove the economic system from democratic accountability, Rauschenbusch wrote, "means a surrender of the human point of view, a relaxing of the sense of duty, and a willingness to betray the public—if it pays."[68]

The crucial problem with capitalism was not the profit system but the autocratic power "unrestrained by democratic checks" that capitalism gave to owners and managers. For Rauschenbusch, profits were justified when they represented a fair return on one's useful labor and service. He believed that the wage system could be justified under certain conditions, such as when free land was available or a particular kind of labor was scarce. The crunch came when crowded labor markets made it possible for the entrenched power of the capitalist class to become more predatory. In the past century, control over the major means of production had dramatically shifted to a small class of owners and managers. To Rauschenbusch, this acceleration of monopoly privilege and power made economic democracy a moral imperative. Capitalism effectively negated the property rights of the working class. An American worker possessed democratic entitlements in the political sphere, Rauschenbusch noted, but in the economic sphere the same worker lacked any rights over property. A worker who toiled in a factory for forty years and contributed to the community that sustained it had no more rights over property than a medieval serf. Industrial property was too expensive for workers to own, yet most industrial property was financed by the savings of working people through their banks and insurance companies. "But therewith the money passes out of the control of the owners," Rauschenbusch wrote. "What a man deposits today may be used next week to pay Pinkertons who will do things he abominates."[69]

The chief objective of democratic socialism was to democratize the process of investment. Rauschenbusch explained that the purpose of economic democracy was not to eliminate property rights but to expand property rights under new

---

67. Ibid., 317.
68. Ibid.
69. Ibid., 343.

forms. He recalled that when British landlords owned England's legislative process, they naturally wrote their property interests into the law. In the same way, a democratized society would enact property laws that served the interests of the vast majority, for "political democracy without economic democracy is an uncashed promissory note . . . a form without substance."[70]

Rauschenbusch's socialism was a patchwork of themes from various socialist traditions that did not always fit together. Though he opposed centralized collectivism and accepted the necessity of the market in a democratic society, he often claimed at the same time that in a socialist society prices would be based entirely on service rendered.[71] He retained the utopian Marxist vision of a cooperative society while assuming—as Marx did not—that markets could not be abolished in a free society. Rauschenbusch's weakness for utopian rhetoric caused him to exaggerate the extent to which economic democracy could replace economic competition. He accepted the Marxist theories of surplus value and the class struggle, but he rejected Marx's materialistic determinism and his dismissive contempt for liberal democracy. For Rauschenbusch, the objective was not to overthrow liberal democracy but to extend the democratizing logic of liberal democracy into the economic sphere, primarily by democratizing the process of investment.

This was the programmatic heart of Rauschenbusch's socialism. For all of his idealistic rhetoric and his unassimilated borrowings from Marx, he resisted the typical socialist tendency of his time to produce "blueprints for a new humanity." He argued that *democratic* socialism would require a situationally defined mixture of cooperative and public ownership of essential industries and private ownership of small enterprises. Rauschenbusch favored cooperative ownership whenever possible, but he recognized that the mix of ownership modes in a democracy would always have to be a matter of contextual judgment. He embraced John Stuart Mill's vision of decentralized socialism as well as Mill's contention that the logic of liberal democracy leads to democratic socialism. In *Principles of Political Economy,* Mill envisioned workers "collectively owning the capital with which they carry on their operations, and working under managers elected and removable by themselves."[72] *Christianizing the Social Order* elaborated this vision of pluralistic decentralized socialism, claiming that only socialism could compete with militarism as a unifying social force in American life.

It would not be enough for liberal Christianity to point to itself as the basis for moral community in America. Rauschenbusch rejected the liberal sentiment,

---

70. Ibid., 353.
71. Ibid., 361.
72. John Stuart Mill, *Principles of Political Economy,* vol. 2 (New York: Appleton & Company, 1884), 357–59; Rauschenbusch, *Christianizing the Social Order,* 357.

epitomized by Mathews, that a renewal of public spirit in America could be generated by a liberal Christianity that supported political reform and social progress. Liberalism was not enough. It was too weak to compete with the spirit of capitalism or the spirit of nationalistic militarism. Rauschenbusch insisted that only a Christianity that pushed for socialism could hope to overcome America's assiduously reinforced egocentrism. "Capitalism has overdeveloped the selfish instincts in us all and left the capacity of devotion to larger ends shrunken and atrophied," he lamented.[73] He observed that modern Americans lifted themselves to a sense of common purpose only when they went to war. Americans gloried in their wars not because they loved violence or aspired to empire, he argued, but because war brought them their only occasion of social solidarity.

For all of his optimism about the world-historical march of democracy, Rauschenbusch thus had few illusions about America's cultural openness to economic democracy. The habits of cooperation would be hardest to learn in a culture that celebrated isolation, self-preoccupation, acquisitiveness, and will to power. In 1912, however, Rauschenbusch believed that he was witnessing the beginning of a new epoch in American life:

> It is hard enough to get four or five men to work together without serious friction. To induce a hundred or a thousand to cooperate without tyrannous coercion is a work of strategy and art. Humanity took centuries to consolidate the patriarchal family, the village commune, or the modern State. A cooperative commonwealth would join in associated work millions of people of low intelligence and education, but of strong passions and egotisms, who will have to render honest and faithful service in the main, and subordinate their passions to a higher reason and the common good, if the cooperative system is not to break down and relapse into some form of despotism. If any one thinks such an organization can be evolved by the mere propaganda of an economic doctrine or the creation of a strong party, let him take a contract to build a suspension bridge with a clothesline. But if any one thinks it is beyond the possibilities of human nature, let him rub his eyes and look around him.[74]

He insisted that this vision was not only social but also religious. *Christianizing the Social Order* contained more than four hundred pages of political economics, but Rauschenbusch described it as "a religious book from beginning to end" because the kingdom of God "means the progressive transformation of all human affairs by the thought and spirit of Christ."[75] His arguments for economic democracy were therefore, in his view, as religious as his prayers or biblical expositions. Rauschenbusch did not reduce the kingdom to his politics. "The only thing that will last and the only thing that matters is the Reign of

---

73. Rauschenbusch, *Christianizing the Social Order*, 369.
74. Ibid., 367–68.
75. Ibid., 458.

God in humanity, and the Reign of God is vaster and higher than Socialism," he declared.[76] Neither did he claim that a perfect society was attainable. He argued, rather, that the only way to find out how much of the kingdom was historically attainable was to press for its fulfillment. "We shall never have a perfect life," he wrote. "Yet we must seek it with faith. . . . At best there is always but an approximation to a perfect social order. The Kingdom of God is always but coming. But every approximation to it is worthwhile."[77]

Mathews and Foreign Policy

Liberal Protestantism typically shared the same idealism in milder forms. For Mathews, "the world" was the existing social order without Christianity. "And Jesus must and can save the world by transforming it into the Kingdom of God," he assured. "That is the very heart of the Social Gospel."[78] Though his theological perspective was moving at the time toward a more relativistic modernism, this fact did not dim Mathews's ardor for foreign missions. Like most liberal church leaders of his generation, he was deeply concerned to export what he called "the Christian movement" around the world. Liberal Christianity took the Christian commission to save the world literally, while divesting this command of its traditional soteriological meaning. Rauschenbusch often enthused that democracy, science, and Christian values were spreading throughout the world. Social Christianity was a missionary faith. The social gospelers preferred to speak of the Christian century rather than the American century, but even for them there was little difference. The rise of the United States as a world power made it possible for American Protestantism to project American democracy, science, technology, education, and religion to previously remote parts of the world. If the same capacity made it possible to project American capitalism throughout the world, the social gospelers contended that this was all the more reason to promote world missions—to counteract the destructive aspects of capitalist modernization.

"In too many cases the appearance of the missionary of God has been accompanied by the missionary of Mammon, and Western civilization with all its imperfections has appeared in Eastern lands," Mathews allowed. "The missionary, whatever his regrets, in too many cases has accepted this incursion of industrialism as a matter of course and has not been able, even if he has undertaken the task, to extend the Christian ideals into the larger forces that are reshaping

---

76. Ibid., 405.

77. Rauschenbusch, *Christianity and the Social Crisis*, 77.

78. Shailer Mathews, *The Individual and the Social Gospel* (New York: Missionary Education Movement of the United States and Canada, 1914), 68.

the social order of the entire world."[79] This was the world-historical challenge facing modern Christianity. The entire history of Christianity was a prelude to the struggle for the world now facing the Christian church. "The greatest problem which faces the world at the present time is not as to whether the Western civilization will conquer the world—that is settled," Mathews declared in 1914. "Its victory is inevitable. The real problem is whether Christianity will conquer civilization."[80]

Could liberal Protestant Christianity conquer civilization? In other words, would the spirit of democracy continue to spread throughout the world, emancipating uncounted millions from bondage and misery? Would industry and science "be filled with spiritual idealism, or will they develop a new materialism, the more dangerous because it rests upon wealth and learning?" Would new schools be organized to educate all children or to serve the interests of economic elites? Would liberal Protestantism be able to "socialize the spirit of Jesus" and thus put an end to war?[81]

These were the real questions. That the West was taking over the world was no longer arguable. The essential question was whether this incursion was to be "a blessing rather than a curse to the population of the globe."[82] Mathews conceded that an unchristianized West would make a diabolical conqueror. The church's rather daunting immediate task was to Christianize the conquering civilization at the same time that it Christianized the West's colonized subjects. Liberal Protestantism was sensitive to the charge that this self-appointed mission sacralized American imperialism. Lyman Abbott's response to the charge epitomized the self-confidence and cultural arrogance of his movement:

> It is the function of the Anglo-Saxon race to confer these gifts of civilization, through law, commerce, and education, on the uncivilized people of the world. It is said that we have no right to go to a land occupied by a barbaric people and interfere with their life. It is said that if they prefer barbarism they have a right to remain barbarians. I deny the right of a barbaric people to retain possession of any quarter of the globe. What I have already said I reaffirm: barbarism has no rights which civilization is bound to respect. Barbarians have rights which civilized people are bound to respect, but they have no right to their barbarism.[83]

Mathews typically said the same thing with nicer words. Like most liberal church leaders, he was eager to refute the charge that Christian missionaries were destroying foreign cultures and sacralizing Western imperialism. *The In-*

---

79. Ibid., 70.
80. Ibid., 66–67.
81. Ibid., 67.
82. Ibid.
83. Quoted in Handy, *A Christian America*, 109.

dividual and the Social Gospel (1914) offered his rebuttal to the missionary-bashers; it claimed that most Christian missionaries were interested in destroying only structures that supported slavery, racism, mistreatment of women and children, and injustices toward ethnic minorities. "It is Christian missionaries who are fighting the slave-trade in the midst of Africa, and it is Christian sentiment that stirred European nations to bring about its abolition," he insisted. "The militant quality of Christianity is becoming daily more evident as Christian people on the one hand better realize the purpose and social power of the gospel and on the other hand become more intelligent as regards the means by which evils can be abolished."[84]

Mathews enthused that in less than a generation, the social Christian movement had brought about a "fairly amazing" transformation of American Protestantism. Social Christianity was well suited for its world-embracing mission. He was not deeply shaken in his hopes for the world by the outbreak of the Great War. Though he campaigned against remilitarization before America entered the war, Mathews passionately supported his country's war effort after the United States intervened in Europe. He thus did not pay the price that Rauschenbusch paid for opposing the war or experience the war as the crushing blow to his idealism that Rauschenbusch felt. Mathews continued throughout and after the war to pour out optimistic books on the compatibility of social Christianity and social progress. One became a classic statement of theological modernism. Though he never acknowedged the reason or even the fact, however, even Mathews lost much of his missionary fervor during the war. The movement-oriented seize-the-day tone of his early writings faded nearly to the point of disappearing. His later books dealt less with Christianity's forward-marching progress than with the modern world's need for a progressive Christianity. Mathews continued to write about modern progress as though the war had not occurred, but his inward, apologetic turn told another story.

Liberal Protestantism supported one of its own, Woodrow Wilson, when he vowed to keep America out of war. Most liberal Protestant church leaders also vigorously supported Wilson or lapsed into silence when he took America into war. The holdouts included young Norman Thomas, who was then pastor of a mixed-ethnic Presbyterian church in East Harlem. Wilson and Thomas were both sons of Presbyterian pastors, both graduates of Princeton, and both liberal Protestants and idealists. When the churches rallied to Wilson's patriotic call, Thomas was incredulous that Christian idealism could be invoked to rationalize military intervention in Europe. "How can we accept Christ as Lord and Master and deny his spirit by sharing responsibility for the unutterable horrors of war?" he pleaded. "Even in war the church ought to stand for a form of society transcending

---

84. Mathews, *The Individual and the Social Gospel*, 76–77.

nationalism and national boundaries."[85] The spectacle of a militarized Christendom drove Thomas into the Socialist party, where he became the party's national leader for the next fifty years.

Rauschenbusch and the Great War

Thomas's favorite theologian also opposed the war and suffered for it. The prospect of a world war in Germany was traumatizing for Rauschenbusch. He feared for his relatives in Westphalia, he feared that his sons might be called to fight against them, and he feared that a world war would destroy the democratizing social progress of the past century. In the late 1890s, Rauschenbusch had celebrated America's recent victory in the Spanish-American war. His jingoistic speeches on the war claimed that America's triumph over Catholic Spain was a victory for the forces of democracy, freedom, and justice over a decaying imperial authoritarianism.[86] His most offensive remarks pertaining to race were uttered during this period. Rauschenbusch's radicalism deepened over the succeeding decade, however. He increasingly claimed that social Christianity had to oppose not only the social causes of war but war itself. With deep foreboding, he witnessed Germany's military buildup during his visits to Germany in 1907 and 1910 and spoke against the national chauvinism and greed that drove nations into war.[87] He became a near-pacifist while Germany prepared for war.

Germany was a second home to Rauschenbusch. His family heritage was German, much of his education during his preadolescent and adolescent years had been obtained in Germany, his thinking drew on German sources, and he had remained in contact with German relatives and friends. His students later recalled that the outbreak of war in August 1914 profoundly wounded him. His sparkling enthusiasm and humor vanished. He began to wear a piece of black crepe on his coat lapel and urged his American colleagues not to take sides in the war. Shortly after the war began, he countered a flood of anti-German propaganda with an article titled "Be Fair to Germany." Rauschenbusch claimed that Germany was no more militaristic than its neighbors and no more imperialist than England.[88] The following year, he publicly opposed American military sales to England; later he opposed American preparations for war. Rauschenbusch's

---

85. Quoted in Murray B. Seidler, *Norman Thomas: Respectable Rebel* (Syracuse, N.Y.: Syracuse University Press, 1961), 21.

86. Walter Rauschenbusch, Thanksgiving sermon quoted in the *Rochester Post-Express,* November 25, 1898; quoted in Minus, *Walter Rauschenbusch,* 108.

87. Cf. Rauschenbusch, *For God and the People,* 109; Minus, *Walter Rauschenbusch,* 177.

88. Walter Rauschenbusch, "Be Fair to Germany: A Plea for Open-mindedness," *The Congregationalist,* October 15, 1914.

pleas for neutrality were greeted with chilling hostility. His patriotism was ma-
ligned by numerous preachers and newspaper editors, and many of his friends
distanced themselves from him. As America's involvement in the war grew
deeper and the charges of disloyalty rang in his ears, he gradually withdrew from
the public debate over the war. He agonized over the militarization of his country
and church. "It was hard enough to combine Christianity and capitalistic business," he remarked. "Now we are asked to combine Christianity and war." He
admitted to a friend that it was "physical misery for me to get mail loaded up
with scornful and hateful letters." He wrote to Algerman Crapsey, "I am glad
I shall not live forever. I am afraid of those who want to drag our country in to
satisfy their partisan hate, or because they think universal peace will result from
the victory of the allies."[89] Though he never became an absolute pacifist, Rauschenbusch joined the pacifist Fellowship of Reconciliation in 1917 and told Dores
Sharpe that it was a delight for him to work with people who were more radical
than he was.[90]

His last two books fought off his deepening sorrow and depression. *The
Social Principles of Jesus* (1916) presented a handbook-style catechism, written
for the YMCA, on the social significance of Jesus' teaching. As a study book
for church classes, it later became Rauschenbusch's most popular work. The
book summarized the teachings of Jesus on poverty, property, compassion, violence, justice, and the kingdom of God, declaring that the kingdom "overlaps
and interpenetrates all existing organizations, raising them to a higher level when
they are good, resisting them when they are evil, quietly revolutionizing the old
social order and changing it into the new." The kingdom sometimes suffered
terrible reversals, as in the catastrophe of the current war, but Rauschenbusch
insisted that the reign of God was nevertheless always coming, even on "the
wrecks of defeat." The kingdom was only revealed in human experience in
fragments, he wrote, "but such fragmentary realizations of it as we have, alone
make life worth living."[91]

This was the tone of his final work as well. *A Theology for the Social Gospel*
was published in 1917. Three years earlier, the movement for social Christianity
had been soaring. From certain appearances, the movement was still doing very
well. The churches were filled with high-spirited, outward-looking believers who
proclaimed that they were making the world safe for democracy. One of their
own was leading America's venture in democratic globalism. Many liberal Christian leaders supported Wilson's military intervention as an example of social

---

89. Minus, *Walter Rauschenbusch,* 182; Sharpe, *Walter Rauschenbusch,* 379.

90. Quoted in Minus, *Walter Rauschenbusch,* 182.

91. Walter Rauschenbusch, *The Social Principles of Jesus* (New York: Grosset &
Dunlap, 1916), iii.

gospel idealism. For Rauschenbusch, however, the real social Christian movement was paralyzed and dispirited, if not disintegrating. It survived only on the hope that genuine social Christianity could be revived after the war was over. Rauschenbusch gave voice to this rather desperate hope. "The Great War has dwarfed and submerged all other issues, including our social problems," he acknowledged. "But in fact the war is the most acute and tremendous social problem of all."[92]

What was needed was an enlargement of the social gospel vision to deal with international issues. "Before the war the Social Gospel dealt with social classes; today it is being translated into international terms," Rauschenbusch argued. The social Christianity that was needed would address not only national inequality, injustice, and immorality but also nationalism, militarism, imperialism, and global interdependence. He conceded that the war was driving many people to abandon Christianity. He countered that those faithful souls "whose Christianity has not been ditched by the catastrophe" were demanding a Christianization of foreign policy. The ultimate cause of the war was "the same lust for easy and unearned gain" that had created national inequality and injustice. "The social problem and the war problem are fundamentally one problem, and the Social Gospel faces both," he declared. "After the War the Social Gospel will 'come back' with pent-up energy and clearer knowledge."[93]

Rauschenbusch struggled to believe this prediction in the closing years of his life, claiming that "the era of prophetic and democratic Christianity has just begun."[94] The prophet of social gospel Christianity did not live to witness the end of the catastrophe, however. Rauschenbusch became seriously ill in 1918. In March he wrote that "since 1914 the world is full of hate, and I cannot expect to be happy again in my lifetime."[95] Two months later he wrote to a friend that although his life had been physically very lonely (a reference to his deafness) and often troubled by attacks from conservatives, he was continually upheld by the spirit of Christ, which "has been to me the inexhaustible source of fresh impulse, life and courage. . . . My life would seem an empty shell if my personal religion were left out of it."[96] He died of brain cancer in July 1918, during the last weeks of the war, carrying to his death the fear that his cause was in ruins.

Liberal Protestantism was generally less inclined than Rauschenbusch to see the war as a judgment on the evils of nationalism. The president of Rochester Seminary declared in 1917 that his school was absolutely loyal to America and

---

92. Rauschenbusch, *A Theology for the Social Gospel*, 4.

93. Ibid., 4.

94. Ibid., 279.

95. Sharpe, *Walter Rauschenbusch*, 448.

96. Rauschenbusch, letter to Lemuel Call Barnes, reprinted in *Walter Rauschenbusch*, ed. Winthrop S. Hudson, 45–46.

supportive of its war effort. This announcement heightened the pressure on Rauschenbusch to endorse America's intervention. Despite intense pressure from church officials and friends to recant his neutralist position on the war, Rauschenbusch could bring himself to declare, in a statement issued from his deathbed, only that a German victory would be a "terrible calamity for the world." He desired "to see German autocracy forever overthrown," he wrote, but he could not endorse the partisan hatred, the self-righteousness, or the carnage of war, partly because he had no confidence that an Allied victory "would of itself free the world from imperialism."[97]

Mathews and the War

Liberal Protestantism generally shunned this sentiment after a liberal Protestant president took America into war. Like most liberal church leaders, Mathews had opposed military preparedness in the early years of the war. He later recalled that as president of the Federal Council of Churches, he vigorously campaigned against "anything that looked like military preparation" until Wilson stirred the "fears and passions" of America.[98] Mathews was also an active board member of the Church Peace Union, founded in 1914 by Andrew Carnegie. In the early years of his tenure as Federal Council president, he was joined by such prominent liberal church leaders as Brown, King, Gladden, Shirley Jackson Case, George Coe, and Henry Sloane Coffin in advocating American neutrality and military unpreparedness.

While opposing American military intervention, he also spurned quixotic American attempts to end the war. Mathews turned down an invitation to join Henry Ford's peace ship to Europe, and he pleaded lack of time when Secretary of State William Jennings Bryan asked him, in 1916, to join his diplomatic mission to stop the war. Bryan's apparent belief in his capacity to end the war proved to Mathews that Bryan, if not the Wilson administration, was out of touch with reality. But if Mathews could dismiss the fundamentalist Bryan, he could not resist Wilson's democratic idealism or, eventually, the patriotic appeal that Wilson drew from it. In his address to the Federal Council of Churches in 1915, Wilson instructed the leaders of liberal Protestantism that "the most vitalizing thing in the world is Christianity." Christianity was important, he explained, not because it was "a valid body of conceptions regarding God and

---

97. Cf. Minus, *Walter Rauschenbusch,* 184; Sharpe, *Walter Rauschenbusch,* 388–92.

98. Mathews, *New Faith for Old,* 197.

man, but because it is a vital body of conceptions which can be translated into life for us." The Christian mission was to change and inspire life.[99]

This was the triumphant voice of liberal Protestantism. What was crucial to Christianity was not valid doctrine, but vital living. Christian America had a mission not only to save the world for democracy but also to redeem the world with Christ's spirit. Even as Mathews and his colleagues at first resisted Wilson's efforts to remilitarize American society, they could not dispute that he was one of them. Mathews later recalled that although Wilson was reelected in 1916 because he had kept America out of the war, "clever evangelization in favor of participating in the war had its effect. Nothing is more unifying than a common hatred."[100] When America finally entered the war in April 1917, virtually all of America's liberal Protestant leaders either fell in line or fell silent. America's mission to save the world would require the defeat of the German autocracy.

Liberal Protestant leaders who publicly accepted the burden of history and national morality interpreted this burden in two ways. Figures such as Gladden and Smith; Union Seminary theologians Brown, Coffin, and Eugene Lyman; and the new president of Union, A. C. McGiffert, tried to restrain the rising American tone of self-righteousness and vengeance. They insisted that the church must have no part in glorifying war or demonizing America's enemies. Lyman was the most militant of this group in his condemnations of American jingoism. Though he described the war in 1918 as "a mighty struggle for the preservation of democracy," he also continued to characterize it as "colossally hideous . . . wholesale waste and debauchery." It was absurd to claim moral progress for a civilization that was "slaughtering or deforming its toilers by the million," he argued.[101] Liberal Protestantism was not lacking in leaders who supported American intervention only with great reluctance and with no appeal to national chauvinism.

Critical loyalism was not enough for another group of church leaders, however. Virtually all liberal Protestant leaders made a point of warning against extremism and vengeance. For a second group, however, which included Mathews, Lyman Abbott, Henry Churchill King, and Harry Emerson Fosdick, it was not enough for the church to accept Wilson's actions on lesser-evil grounds. For them, it was also the church's mission to generate moral enthusiasm for the war, partly by endorsing Wilson's crusading rhetoric. Abbott repeatedly characterized Wilson's democratic globalism as "the twentieth century crusade."[102]

---

99. Woodrow Wilson, "A New Kind of Church Life," reprinted in *Contemporary American Protestant Thought, 1900–1970,* ed. William Robert Miller (Indianapolis: Bobbs-Merrill Company, 1973), 168–69.

100. Mathews, *New Faith for Old,* 197.

101. Quoted in Hutchison, *The Modernist Impulse in American Protestantism,* 239.

102. Ibid., 238.

Fosdick later recalled that after America entered the war, "but while the spirit of the people was still limp and apathetic," he toured the country with a team of pro-war speakers that was skilled at "whipping up the enthusiasm of great audiences to get into the fight." He repentantly recalled that through this experience, "I learned how to bring down the house with out-and-out militaristic appeals." He subsequently gave stirring patriotic addresses to the troops in France and was deeply honored when an officer told him that he was worth a battalion.[103]

Mathews promoted America's war with equal vigor and without subsequent regrets. In 1908 he had become dean of Chicago's Divinity School (a position he held until 1933) while remaining a professor of historical theology. After the United States entered the war, Mathews obtained a release from his teaching duties, while continuing to function as Divinity School dean, to become executive secretary of War Savings for the state of Illinois. He and Savings Director Martin Ryerson were tremendously successful in their fund-raising efforts, selling approximately $100 million worth of wartime certificates. At the same time, Mathews gave scores of patriotic speeches around the country that passionately made the case for America's intervention in the war. He later recalled that "in the addresses which I gave from New York to California I never used such murderous eloquence as did some of my clerical friends. Patriotism is not sadism."[104]

Patriotism called for more than lesser-evil justifications, however. Mathews claimed in 1918 that there was a deep kinship between patriotism and religion. The war was making Americans remember that American liberty was more precious and more Christian than the "new god, Teutonic Efficiency," he observed. Americans had nearly forgotten their patriotic songs and rites of allegiance to their flag and nation, but these practices "are now tests of loyalty to a land that rises in splendid personality." The war was revealing that America was not only a collection of individual persons, but "a glorious super-person, possessed of virtues, power, ideals, daring, and sacrifice."[105] If the impersonal mechanisms of modern capitalism had shrouded the existence of America's soul, the war was revealing that there was, nonetheless, a soul in the social order.

Mathews condemned the American Socialist party's opposition to the war and provided a simple explanation for it. The Socialists opposed the war not on the basis of moral or political principles, he claimed, but because most of them were Germans. "Masquerading as opposition to war itself, nationalistic tendencies in Germany have reexpressed themselves among German socialists in the

---

103. Harry Emerson Fosdick, *The Living of These Days: An Autobiography* (New York: Harper & Brothers, 1956), 122; French battlefield experience recounted in Fosdick, "I Will Not Bless War!" *Christian Century* 58 (January 22, 1941), 115.

104. Mathews, *New Faith for Old*, 207.

105. Shailer Mathews, *Patriotism and Religion* (New York: Macmillan, 1918), 4.

United States," he explained. "Organized socialism in America has turned itself into anti-Americanism, condemning a war of national self-protection and pleading for peace in speech self-betrayed by its German accent." The party's loyal Socialists had therefore left the party. Mathews did not speculate on Eugene Debs's reasons for opposing the war, nor on the reasons of other non-German Socialists who also opposed it. It was enough for him that many of the Socialist party's remaining leaders were German-Americans whose pacifism was purportedly not based on socialist or pacifist commitments, but on alien nationalism. "The bolsheviki may be sincere; the German socialist is disloyal," he charged.[106]

American churches provided a telling contrast to the alien disloyalty of the war resisters. Mathews observed that the churches were needed "to strengthen the heart of the patriot in days of national trial," to free patriotism from vengeance, and to furnish "moral enthusiasm" for the war effort.[107] He noted with pride that the churches were vigorously serving America on each count. America was worthy of Christian support not only because the present war was being fought to save democracy, Mathews urged, but also because "for seventy years we have dared follow ideals which are worthy of a Christian people." He read modern American history as a narrative of freedom. The Civil War had abolished slavery; the Spanish-American war was fought to set Cuba free; America's colonization of the Philippines brought education and democracy to the Filipinos; and America had "preserved the Western Hemisphere from European spoilation."[108] This was not to deny that America was guilty of blunders and crudities, Mathews allowed; patriotism did not exclude criticism. It was to claim that America was a morally healthy nation that sought to bring greater morality, health, and democracy to the world. America's mission was "not only to make the world safe for democracy, but to make democracy safe for the world," he declared.[109] Social Christianity was committed to both regenerative causes.

Mathews never shared the subsequent remorse of friends like Fosdick for his pro-war campaigning. Though he later conceded that he was "not untouched by war psychology," he reasoned that this reaction was unavoidable under the circumstances. Germany was threatening to destroy the past century of Western social progress. "I saw in the war a conflict of two conceptions of society," he later wrote. "It was tragic that they should be forced into arms, but I hoped that the new national feelings and the misery which war caused might lead nations to see the futility of war and establish relations which would lead to international morality."[110] These "new national feelings" could energize a renewal of the social

106. Ibid., 39.
107. Ibid., 136–46.
108. Ibid., 75.
109. Ibid., 76.
110. Mathews, *New Faith for Old*, 207.

gospel movement and create a new form of international order. Mathews spent much of his later life working to redeem this hope. He was active in several peace organizations and worked especially through the Federal Council and the Church Peace Union to promote greater international cooperation and ecumenical dialogue.

Unlike their European counterparts, it was possible for American theologians like Mathews to carry on after the war much as before. The credibility of modernist theological progressivism in Europe was shattered by the war and, relatedly, by the impact of Karl Barth's theology of crisis, but no such crisis of identity or relevance immediately afflicted American Protestantism. Liberal Christianity in America was chastened but not discredited by the war. Liberal church leaders commonly admitted that they had been overly optimistic about the prospects of applying biblical social teaching to the social order, but this concession did not move them to conclude that liberal Protestantism was seriously flawed. For many, including Mathews, the war had vindicated their essential vision of America's global democratic mission. Neither were they routed from the field by an alternative theology.

They were soon confronted with a turn in American political culture for which they were less prepared, however. Wilson's campaign for an American role in the League of Nations was a quintessentially liberal Protestant cause. The vision of a new world order of mutually cooperating states had long been a staple of liberal Protestant rhetoric. The peace organizations that Mathews and other liberal Protestants had created were devoted to the strategy of collective security as an alternative to war. Wilson's postwar crusade for an American-backed League of Nations and a world court pursued their own cherished hope. His uncompromising moralism in promoting it was a symptom of its religious character and a major cause of its failure. After Wilson destroyed his health in his frenetic efforts to create an American-supported League of Nations, his unsuccessful campaign for an American role in the League fueled a resurgence of isolationist politics in America. It also chastened the remaining world-historical hopes of American Protestantism.

Liberal Protestantism trimmed its sails in response. If it was clear that the world, or even the United States, was not on the verge of being Christianized, this did not discredit the belief that the world should be Christianized or that progress toward this goal was being made. It would take longer to Christianize the social order than the prewar social gospelers had thought. Some of the social gospelers had undoubtedly gone too far in equating socialist politics with Christianity's social mission. Most of them overemphasized distributive justice and underemphasized problems pertaining to nationalism and world peace. Liberal Protestantism in the 1920s tried to make appropriate corrections—but in a culture that cared less and less what the mainline churches taught about anything.

Liberal Protestantism resisted the triumphant cult of consumption in the 1920s with little success. In the first three months of 1920, Prohibition went into effect and America's entry into the League of Nations was rejected by the Senate. The great American crusades for national morality and world democracy were over. Americans were tired of Protestant moralizing. They were tired of saving the world, tired of making America pure, and tired of the kingdom-building rhetoric of liberal Christianity. Having loosened the doctrinal ties that bound earlier generations to their communities of faith, liberal Protestantism was poorly equipped to compete with an increasingly commercialized society for the hearts of a new generation. The "return to normalcy" heralded by American politicians and embraced by many church members chastened the moral ambitions of liberal church leaders. The eminent American church historian Robert T. Handy later traced the decline of mainline Protestantism as a social force to postwar America's celebration of the consuming, egocentric, self-defining self. At the moment of American Protestantism's most ambitious political triumphs, American Protestants listened less to instruction on personal or public morality from their churches.[111]

Though they did not foresee the decline of liberal Protestantism in the 1920s, liberal church leaders such as Mathews, Fosdick, Brown, and McGiffert did perceive that their religion faced a crisis of identity and purpose. Prewar liberal Christianity was a world-embracing missionary faith. It was forward-looking and outward oriented. Liberal Protestantism after the war became less optimistic, less self-confident, and less driven to change the world. It preached to a society that increasingly rejected its world-changing idealism and resented its moralism toward alcohol and other amusements. In response, liberal church leaders became more inward-looking and reflective. They sought less to transform society than to defend their faith; they became more concerned with Christianizing modernity than with Christianizing the social order. Liberal Protestantism never renounced its commitment to creating a politics of moral community. This commitment was intrinsic to the identity of progressive Christianity. The defining project of the postwar theological generation, however, was defending the legitimacy and integrity of liberal Christian faith against the accelerating influence of secularism and fundamentalism. Such theologians as Brown, Lyman, Henry Nelson Wieman, and D. C. Macintosh contributed to this project, but the movement's major figures were Mathews and Fosdick.

Fosdick often summarized his approach to religion in the phrase "abiding experiences and changing categories." The phrase also aptly characterized Mathews's later historicist apologetics. For Mathews, theological doctrine expressed,

---

111. On the beginning of mainline Protestantism's disestablishment in the 1920s, see Handy, *A Christian America*, 185–91.

in religious form, the dominant "social mind" of a particular culture, which he defined as "a more or less general community of conscious states, processes, ideas, interests, and ambitions which to a greater or lesser degree repeats itself in the experience of individuals belonging to the group characterized by the community of consciousness."[112] He argued that Christian doctrine had been shaped thus far by seven successive social minds: the Semitic, the Greco-Roman, the imperialistic, the feudal, the nationalistic, the bourgeois, and the modern. The constructive task of theology was always to recast the meaning of Christian faith into the language and thought forms of the contemporary social mind. It followed for Mathews that theology in the modern age needed to face up to modernity. Writing near the end of the war, he cautioned against any suggestion that the war was discrediting the social goals of modernity as expressed in liberal Christianity. For all of its unspeakable horror, the war was releasing social forces that would ultimately promote social progress and democracy, he argued. The democratic modernist worldview of liberal Christianity was defeating its rivals. "Whatever sacrifice awaits us, we can with revived confidence await the outcome of that spiritual process which justifies men of courage and loyalty in expecting a nobler social order and a more complete embodiment of the ideals of the Christian religion," he declared.[113]

Mathews gave most of his remaining career to the reinterpretation and defense of what he called the modernist faith. His book *The Faith of Modernism* (1924) was one of the two defining liberal Protestant works of the 1920s; Fosdick's *Christianity and Progress* (1922) was the other. Sandwiched between these major works, not coincidentally, was J. Gresham Machen's celebrated attack on liberal Christianity, *Christianity and Liberalism* (1923). Having spent the past generation trying to transform American society and the world, liberal Christianity was forced in the 1920s to justify its existence.

Harry Emerson Fosdick

It was characteristic of both liberal and fundamentalist Christianity that the question of missions became the wedge issue in a new war for religious position. Both were missionary faiths, but fundamentalists claimed that liberal Protestant missions were humanistic and political. It was not a new charge. Thirty years before the term *fundamentalism* was invented, fundamentalists were already claiming that liberal Christianity was not Christian and that liberal theology

---

112. Shailer Mathews, "Theology and the Social Mind," *The Biblical World* 46 (October 1915), 204.

113. Shailer Mathews, *The Spiritual Interpretation of History* (Cambridge: Harvard University Press, 1917), ix.

would undermine the church's work in foreign missions. Between 1910 and 1915, an influential twelve-volume collection of fundamentalist beliefs, *The Fundamentals,* was published by the Testimony Publishing Company. More sophisticated attacks on liberal Christianity were regularly featured in theological journals published by Princeton Theological Seminary.[114] In the 1920s, this long-running battle between modern Protestantism's liberal and fundamentalist wings reached the breaking point. Fundamentalists condemned liberal theologians for endorsing evolution, embracing Enlightenment philosophy, accepting higher criticism of the Bible, and for minimizing or rejecting literal interpretations of the virgin birth of Christ, the incarnation, the atonement, the second coming of Christ, and other biblical doctrines. They charged that liberal revisionism eliminated the ultimate motivation for Christian evangelism and missions. Liberal Christianity denied or at least failed to claim that Christ was the only way to eternal salvation. The emotionally charged argument over the purpose of foreign missions brought several denominations to the brink of schism. At the height of the conflict, in 1922, Fosdick raised the specter of a fundamentalist victory.

He later recalled that "if ever a sermon failed to achieve its object, mine did."[115] Fosdick had graduated from Union Theological Seminary and entered the Baptist pastorate in 1904. His chief theological guides during his early ministry were Rauschenbusch and the Quaker philosopher Rufus Jones. He returned to Union in 1915 as a professor of practical theology and subsequently agreed, while remaining at Union, to serve as a preacher at New York City's upscale First Presbyterian Church. It was at First Presbyterian, while remaining an ordained Baptist, that he preached his controversial sermon, "Shall the Fundamentalists Win?" The sermon was a call for moderation and mutual respect between modern Protestantism's main factions. Fosdick's chief purpose was to prevent fundamentalist-modernist schisms in the existing denominations. He conceded that liberal intolerance of conservative beliefs was harmful to the church. As candidly as he could, he acknowledged that the church's conservative and modernist factions were divided over such matters as the inerrancy of Scripture, the virgin birth of Christ, and the second coming of Christ. Fosdick pleaded that there was no reason why these differences should tear the churches apart, however. What was needed in the church was not a new Reformation or a series of schisms but a spirit of cooperation that allowed different theologies to coexist within the present denominations.

Fosdick did not fudge his own theological position. He was a moderate in church politics but a liberal theologically. The defining choice of his life had not

114. Cf. *The Fundamentals: A Testimony to the Truth,* 12 vols. (Chicago: Testimony Publishing Company, 1910–1915).
115. Fosdick, *The Living of These Days,* 145.

been between liberalism and traditional Protestantism but between liberal Christianity and no faith at all. As a young man, he had realized that he could never believe in biblical inerrancy, the biblical miracle stories, supernaturalism, substitutionary atonement, or eternal damnation. The only Christian faith he could embrace was a faith that conformed to his critical reason and his moral sensibility. His unequivocal belief in the modernist imperative and his preaching eloquence made him a formidable national leader in the church's dispute over fundamentalism.

It was not a neatly two-sided dispute. Though he quickly became the church's leading figure associated with the modernist cause, Fosdick took nearly as much criticism in the mid-1920s from the religious Left as from the Right. Church radicals such as Alfred Dieffenbach, editor of the influential Unitarian *The Christian Register,* denounced him for trying to hold the churches together. Dieffenbach characteristically announced that while he could respect a consistent Roman Catholic or fundamentalist he could not respect Fosdick, who wanted to be a liberal without facing up to the implications of modernist criticism. The radicals wanted a new Reformation that would split the churches along liberal-conservative lines. For them, Fosdick was a trimmer, not a leader.[116]

But it was Fosdick who sparked the firestorm that church radicals were seeking. While attempting to make a case for conciliation, he had raised the stakes in the national struggle for the churches. As he later recalled, "I had stood in a Presbyterian pulpit and said frankly what the modernist position on some points was—the virgin birth no longer accepted as historic fact, the literal inerrancy of the Scriptures incredible, the second coming of Christ from the skies an outmoded phrasing of hope."[117] His candor set off a nationwide outburst of fundamentalist protests and rejoinders that forced many pastors to declare their positions. Though he meant to promote greater tolerance, "Shall the Fundamentalists Win?" raised the specter of a church in which the modernists would be driven out. For all of his concern about unity and fairness, Fosdick left no doubt that most of the church's intolerance came from the conservative side. The problem with fundamentalism was not so much that it professed unbelievable things, he asserted, but that it was trying to drive devout Christians out of the church. "The Fundamentalists are giving us one of the worst exhibitions of intolerance that the churches of this country have ever seen," he charged. In a world faced with "colossal problems" that required Christian attention, "the Fundamentalists propose to drive out from the Christian churches all the con-

---

116. Quoted in the *New York Times,* November 29, 1924; cited in Fosdick, *The Living of These Days,* 166.

117. Fosdick, *The Living of These Days,* 66, 146.

secrated souls who do not agree with their theory of inspiration," he observed. "What immeasurable folly!"[118]

Fosdick would soon become an example of his own warning. In the early 1920s, his national prominence in the liberal-fundamentalist debate made him a prime target for conservatives who wanted to drive religious liberals and even moderates out of the churches. *Christianity and Progress* gave them ample ammunition. Fosdick took his distance from the more crusading as well as the more secularized versions of liberal Christianity. He was neither a socialist nor a naturalist. *Christianity and Progress* elaborated this sensibility and argued that extremism never served the cause of social progress. In his often-quoted chapter on "The Perils of Progress," Fosdick argued that progressives often underestimated the power of human sin, relied too heavily on politics and "social palliatives" to solve the world's problems, and showed a radical disrespect for the wisdom of the past.[119] His view of the class struggle typified his liberal-religious outlook. Fosdick identified with the attitude of Henry George, the author of *Progress and Poverty* and apostle of "single tax" populism, who denied that he was either a friend of working people or a friend of capitalists. George explained that he was "for men; men simply as men, regardless of any accidental or superficial distinctions of race, creed, colour, class, or function or employment." This was Fosdick's liberalism, which was universalist and blind to difference. It appealed to the universal power of reason and the latent good faith in every person. "Until we can get that larger loyalty into the hearts of men, all the committees on earth cannot solve our industrial problems," he wrote.[120] His attitude toward politics epitomized the kind of liberal moralism that Reinhold Niebuhr later ferociously rejected.

The same appeal to moral feeling marked Fosdick's approach to international issues. He announced his conversion to pacifism in 1928, vowing not "to bless war again, or support it, or expect from it any valuable thing." Like Rauschenbusch, he later debated whether he should join the Society of Friends.[121] Fosdick's turn toward pacifism began shortly after the end of the Great War. By 1922 he was calling for international resistance to nationalism and, especially, the war-

---

118. Harry Emerson Fosdick, "Shall the Fundamentalists Win?" reprinted in *American Protestant Thought: The Liberal Era,* ed. William R. Hutchison (New York: Harper & Row, 1968), 170–81.

119. Harry Emerson Fosdick, *Christianity and Progress* (New York: Fleming H. Revell Company, 1922), 167–206.

120. Ibid., 119.

121. Harry Emerson Fosdick, "What the War Did to My Mind," *Christian Century* 45 (January 5, 1928), 10–11; on Fosdick's consideration of converting to the Society of Friends, see Fosdick, *The Living of These Days,* 295; on Rauschenbusch, see Minus, *Walter Rauschenbusch,* 182.

making powers of nation states. "There is hardly anything more needed now in the international situation than a multitude of people who will sit in radical judgment on the actions of their governments, so that when the governments of the world begin to talk war they will know that surely they must face the mass of people rising up to say: War? Why War?" he wrote.[122]

He allowed that good will and good politics would not be enough to resist "the strain of mob psychology and the fear of consequences" that the next call to war would inevitably generate. Any effective opposition to war would have to be founded on a deep spiritual commitment "as was Jesus' attitude: one absolute loyalty to the will of God for all mankind." Fosdick took a pass at claiming that such an attitude would purify patriotism rather than undermine it. His heart was not in this assurance, however. "But whatever be the effect upon patriotism, the Christian is committed by the Master to a prior loyalty; he is a citizen of the Kingdom of God in all the earth," he argued.[123] For Christians, loyalty to the kingdom trumped any claim made by the state. Fosdick did not waver from this conviction or from his subsequent pacifism after America entered another world war.[124]

His early writings defended the motives and the social vision of the past generation of social gospelers who had tried, however fallibly, to serve the kingdom above other loyalties. "We did not go into the ministry either for money or for fun," he recalled. "We went in because we believed in Jesus Christ and were assured that only he and his truth could medicine the sorry ills of this sick world. And now, ministers of Christ, with such a motive, we see continually some of the dearest things we work for, some of the fairest results that we achieve, going to pieces on the rocks of the business world." The economic order was, as Rauschenbusch claimed, the most unregenerate sector of American life. "You wish us to preach human brotherhood in Christ, and then we see that the one chief enemy of brotherhood between man and nations is economic strife, the root of class consciousness and war," Fosdick observed. "Everywhere that the Christian minister turns, he finds his dearest ideals and hopes entangled in the economic life. Do you ask us then under these conditions to keep our hands off? In God's name, you ask too much!"[125]

---

122. Fosdick, *Christianity and Progress,* 186.

123. Ibid., 186.

124. Cf. Fosdick, "I Will Not Bless War!" 115–18. This was the eighth in the *Christian Century*'s ten-part series in which prominent Protestant leaders announced what they would do "If America Enters the War." Fosdick explained in his closing sentence, "As for me, I am essentially a Quaker, and my convictions belong in what seems to me the great tradition of the Society of Friends." For an account of Fosdick's career during this period, see Robert M. Miller, *Harry Emerson Fosdick: Preacher, Pastor, Prophet* (New York: Oxford University Press, 1985).

125. Fosdick, *Christianity and Progress,* 113–15.

Liberal Protestantism would not cave in to the fashionable idolatry of commerce or be dissuaded from moralizing American society. Neither would it relinquish its identification of Christian ethics with the cause of social progress. Fosdick read the Bible itself as a testimony to "progressive revelation" in a progressing world. "From Sinai to Calvary—was ever a record of progressive revelation more plain or more convincing?" he asked.[126] Scripture began with Yahweh in a thunderstorm and ended with Christ saying, "God is Spirit"; it began with a tribal deity leading warriors to battle and ended with the admonition that God is love; it began with an enemy-hating monarch who commanded the slaying of the Amalekites and ended with Christ commanding, "Love your enemies and do good to those who persecute you." The biblical revelation was not a pool but a river, Fosdick explained. "The riverbed in which this stream of thought flows is stable and secure; the whole development is controlled by man's abiding spiritual need of God and God's unceasing search for man."[127]

Fosdick conceded that much of Christian history was more difficult to read as a narrative of progress. For many centuries, Christianity was turned into a system of priestcraft in which the believer's access to God "must be mediated by a priestly ritual, his forgiveness assured by a priestly declaration, his salvation sealed by a priestly sacrament." Christ's religion of freedom and grace was transmuted by a triumphant ecclesiastical power into a hierarchical religion of sacraments, ritual, and priests. Liberal Protestantism repeated and even heightened the classical Protestant strictures against ecclesiastical priestcraft. Like Rauschenbusch and Mathews, Fosdick also criticized the monarchical notion of divine reality that supported priestly religion. "The idea that God must be approached by stated ceremonies came directly from thinking of God in terms of a human monarch," he observed.[128] Fosdick drew his images of divine reality from the more "progressive" portions of Scripture and, especially, from the poetry of Tennyson, Coleridge, and Wordsworth. The idea of God as a creative, loving, personal Power informed the most developed forms of religion and fueled the most worthy alternative worldview to fundamentalism and secularism.

This rendering of the Christian faith and Fosdick's highly visible promotion of it cost him his Presbyterian pulpit in 1925. For three years, he was pilloried by the fundamentalist Right as the symbol of modernizing apostasy. Machen's attack on liberal Christianity provided the essential clue to Fosdick's notoriety. Machen argued that the problem with liberal Christianity was not only that it watered down or rejected most of the traditional tenets of Christian faith. Liberal theologians such as Mathews, Fosdick, and Brown frankly acknowledged that

126. Ibid., 209.
127. Ibid., 211–12.
128. Ibid., 219.

this was what they were doing. For this reason, Machen argued, liberal Christianity was not Christianity at all, but a new religious philosophy. The more galling problem with liberal theologians, however, was that for all of their talk about love, kindness, compassion, and good will, they were grossly insensitive and contemptuous toward the feelings of orthodox Christians. Machen observed that "they speak with disgust of those who believe 'that the blood of our Lord, shed in a substitutionary death, placates an alienated Deity and makes possible welcome for the returning sinner.' "[129] The quote was from Fosdick. Machen rebutted him with a deeply emotional claim: "Against the doctrine of the Cross they use every weapon of caricature and vilification," he charged. "Thus they pour out their scorn upon a thing so holy and so precious that in the presence of it the Christian heart melts in gratitude too deep for words. It never seems to occur to modern liberals that in deriding the Christian doctrine of the Cross, they are trampling upon human hearts."[130]

Fundamentalists were offended that Christian ministers were dismissing long-cherished Christian doctrines with apparent contempt. They were outraged that the same people had taken over the country's leading seminaries and divinity schools. Because Fosdick was a member of a noncreedal denomination, he was protected from facing heresy trials or losing his ordination. A coalition of Presbyterian fundamentalists led by William Jennings Bryan therefore campaigned for Fosdick's removal from First Presbyterian Church by demanding that he either become a Presbyterian or resign his position. Fosdick was not surprised when their petition to the church's General Assembly succeeded. He later recalled that he once heard Bryan give a spellbinding speech against evolution at Harvard. "What he said was nonsense, but the way he said it—his voice, his inflection, his sincerity—was fascinating," Fosdick recounted. "At any rate, he dominated the General Assembly in 1923."[131]

In March 1925, shortly before the Scopes trial that challenged Tennessee's state law forbidding the teaching of evolution in its public schools, Fosdick assailed Bryan in the *New York Times* for his role in the upcoming trial. Bryan defended the state's position with fundamentalist arguments that Fosdick characterized as a "gross injustice to the Bible."[132] By then, the writing was on the wall for Fosdick's preaching ministry. After two years of intense legal maneuvering to save his preaching position, he gave up and resigned from First Presbyterian. His only alternative, as a consequence of Bryan's campaign against

129. Machen's quote from Fosdick, "Shall the Fundamentalists Win?"

130. J. Gresham Machen, *Christianity and Liberalism* (New York: Macmillan, 1923), 120.

131. Fosdick, *The Living of These Days*, 147.

132. Harry Emerson Fosdick, "Evolution and Mr. Bryan," *New York Times,* March 12, 1925.

him, was to become a Presbyterian minister and immediately expose himself to heresy charges. "They call me a heretic," he observed in his farewell sermon. "Well, I am a heretic if conventional orthodoxy is the standard. I should be ashamed to live in this century and not be a heretic."[133]

Despite certain appearances, however, the fundamentalists were not winning. Fosdick became pastor of the Park Avenue Baptist Church while his liberal Baptist friend, John D. Rockefeller Jr., built and endowed the interdenominational Riverside Church. In 1931, while continuing to teach at Union, Fosdick became Riverside's first pastor, where he solidified his reputation as America's most famous and influential preacher. His success testified not only to the respectability of liberal Protestantism but also to its comfort with established power. Fosdick assured Rockefeller that, while he reserved the right to criticize business leaders, "I say far more critical things about my own realm, the ecclesiastical, than I ever dream of saying about the industrial realm." Like many liberal Protestant leaders during this period, Fosdick's preaching increasingly downplayed the issues of social privilege and economic justice. His inherited pietism took a therapeutic turn, setting the standard for a generation of psychologized liberal pastors who translated traditional Christian language into a religious language of health, aesthetic appreciation, and mutual care. Fosdick repeatedly explained that religion was an art that upheld, cultivated, and nourished "the infinite worth of human personality." It followed from this aesthetic-therapeutic premise that life itself was a work of art or, at least, that one should make one's life a work of art. Good religion promoted healthy care of the self. "Let me tell you my philosophy," Fosdick explained in 1935. "I can put it in a few words. Everyone who follows this ministry will recognize it. All my thinking starts from and comes back to it. Here it is: *the key to the understanding of all life is the value of personality.*"[134]

For Fosdick, sin was not a basic corruption of human nature or an organic social inheritance, but the victory of bad social influences and bodily impulses over the better instincts of an essentially pure self. Liberal religion brought people into an awareness of the deep goodness within themselves and mobilized their capacity to live out of this better self. "Wherever goodness, beauty, truth, love are—there is the divine," Fosdick assured. Human beings were divine to the extent that they embodied and mobilized these qualities; Jesus was uniquely divine because he embodied them fully. "The divinity of Jesus is the divinity of

---

133. Fosdick, *The Living of These Days,* 176.

134. Correspondence with Rockefeller quoted in Miller, *Harry Emerson Fosdick,* 465–66; philosophy quote in Harry Emerson Fosdick, *The Power to See It Through* (New York: Harper & Brothers, 1935), 35.

his spiritual life," he explained.[135] Divinity was not a supernatural reality but the perfection of immanent love that every person was capable of mobilizing. For Fosdick, it was the regeneration of this inner spiritual power that would create a good society. The church was a moral community that cultivated the only force that could ever morally transform society. In Fosdick's words, the church was "the point of incandescence where, regardless of denominationalism or theology, the Christian life of the community bursts into flame."[136] The mission of the church was thus to nourish the development of personality and redeem the world through the care and idealism of morally regenerated communities.

The early social gospelers had retained the pietist theme that social transformation required transformed hearts. Most of them conceived the church as a moral community that regenerated society through its access to spiritual power. Mathews had especially emphasized that only good people acting through moral communities could create a good society. Fosdick's revision of this faith prefigured the triumph of the therapeutic in modern Protestantism. Having survived a nervous breakdown in his early career, he was deeply convinced that religion must nourish emotional health. Having struggled to find a faith he could live with, he was highly attuned to the spiritual and intellectual needs of educated, upwardly mobile, mostly white Americans who yearned for religious meaning in their lives. In a society dominated by science and economics, they yearned especially for beauty. Americans were "hoodwinked and hypnotized" by the dominant notion that all truth had to be subsumed under the category of science, Fosdick wrote, "whereas art, music, poetry, love, religion can never be crowded within its limits. They belong as well to the realm of beauty."[137]

Fosdick's insistence that religion spoke the language of art rather than that of science reopened the possibility, for many of his contemporaries, of finding religious faith. He criticized the "ecclesiastical ugliness" of most Protestant worship services, calling them forms of "aesthetic starvation." If the church was going to worship at all, he claimed, it was obliged to do so with beauty, "for beauty subdues, integrates and unifies the soul, washes the spirit clean, and sends one out with a vision of the Divine, not simply believed in but made vivid. We are discovering once more that nothing in human life, least of all religion, is ever right until it is beautiful." The point was not that art and religion dispensed

---

135. Harry Emerson Fosdick, *The Hope of the World* (New York: Harper & Brothers, 1933), 103. For Fosdick's elaboration of his Christology, see Fosdick, *The Modern Use of the Bible* (New York: Macmillan, 1924), 261; for a systematic discussion of Fosdick's understanding of Christ, see Kenneth Cauthen, *The Impact of American Religious Liberalism* (New York: Harper & Row, 1962), 80–82.

136. Fosdick, *Christianity and Progress,* 233–34.

137. Harry Emerson Fosdick, *As I See Religion* (New York: Harper & Brothers, 1932), 131–32.

with truth claims, he cautioned. At their highest, art and religion were not simply beautiful but also told the truth. Neither was art (or religion) merely subjective, for "it always has been convinced that no one can know the whole of reality without seeing what the artist sees."[138] The territory of religion was the realm of spirit, personality, and beauty, which religion shared with art.

Liberal theology had begun with Friedrich Schleiermacher's romanticism. A century later, Fosdick regarded the romanticist dimension of liberal Christianity as a deeper, more central reality than its social concern. His books were filled with evocative passages from Wordsworth, Tennyson, Keats, Browning, and Shelley. In Fosdick's view, the dark side of modernity was its unrelenting de-sacralization of the world, which subjected all reality to the reductionistic imperialism of science. Modern scientism stripped human selves of their spiritual connections to the past, their communities, and the cosmos. It reduced life to dead matter and blind energy. But this philosophy could not account for the life of spirit or the existence of moral value. Religion uncovered the world of spirit behind the veil of appearances. It rescued the soul in the social order. It rejected the scientistic dogma that "mystery must give way to facts." Religion was "the appreciation of life's meaning as a whole." It did for the world's facts "what the poet's vision does for the ether waves of the sunset or a mother's love for the Bertillon measurements of a boy," Fosdick wrote. "It clothes them with radiant meanings."[139] Religion accepted the verdicts of science in science's limited sphere, but it assumed that science had little to offer to theology's true work.

Mathews and Modernism

Mathews took the opposite turn. In many respects, he and Fosdick were closely allied. Both were liberal Baptists, both were products of pietism, both viewed Christ as the embodiment of a moral ideal, both were peace activists, and both espoused a reformist idealism in politics that sought to moralize America's existing power structure from within. During the period when the liberal-fundamentalist debate was splitting the churches, Mathews and Fosdick were liberal Christianity's most prominent apologists. Both defended modernist religion as the only perspective that was both spiritually life-giving and intellectually credible. During the same period, however, Mathews became convinced that if religion was going to face up to modernity it had to take on the character and methods of modern science. He embraced the very project that Fosdick insistently rejected, which was to interpret religion according to modern scientific canons. *The Faith of*

---

138. Ibid., 136, 141.

139. Harry Emerson Fosdick, *Adventurous Religion and Other Essays* (New York: Harper & Brothers, 1926), 152–83.

Modernism (1924) offered Mathews's first and most influential defense of this approach.

"We have not yet learned how to use our new power, our new wealth, our new knowledge, our new ideals, our new freedom," he declared at the outset. Science was transforming the social order, but few people grasped the implications of its success or power. "To think of science as a merely academic matter is to forget advertising and meat-packing, oil-finding and automobile-building, radio concerts and a million other things in which the human mind has grown accustomed to think in terms of facts and inferences rather than of authority," Mathews wrote.[140] Scientific reason was giving humanity power over space, time, nature, all social systems, and all previous systems of belief. "It is a fearful thing for a civilization to be possessed of such power," he acknowledged. "Who can assure us that it will be wisely used? What hope is there of any protection against its being used for purposes of destruction? Is humanity good enough to have such power?"[141]

Mathews reported that the answer was tragic; humanity was not good enough for its power. Humanity needed to be morally transformed. Democracy and science were powerful forces for good, if rightly employed, but neither was morally regenerative. More than ever, the world needed a morally inspiriting and transforming spiritual force that could redirect humanity's use of its power. The world needed the Christian movement more than ever. But what it needed was not a Christianity that appealed to authority claims or to any other "sacred" dimension or experience removed from the realm of scrutiny. For the scientific mind, Mathews lectured, "there can be no God behind a veil too sacred to be touched." What was needed was a morally regenerative Christian movement that faced up to the challenge of scientific rationality.

Creative religion always responded to human need. In the modern world, creative religion had to respond to the needs of a science-driven society. A year after Machen's *Christianity and Liberalism,* Mathews gave his account of modern society's needs in the form of an attack on fundamentalism. "The world needs new control of nature and society and is told that the Bible is verbally inerrant," he rasped. "It needs a means of composing class strife, and is told to believe in the substitutionary atonement. It needs a spirit of love and justice and is told that love without orthodoxy will not save from hell. . . . It needs to find God in the processes of nature and is told that he who believes in evolution cannot believe in God. It needs faith in the divine presence in human affairs and is told it must accept the virgin birth of Jesus Christ."[142]

---

140. Ibid., 4, 8.
141. Shailer Mathews, *The Faith of Modernism* (New York: Macmillan, 1924), 9.
142. Ibid., 10.

Dogmatic Christianity was not only untrue but also irrelevant. It misunderstood that Christianity was not a system of doctrine but a regenerating moral and spiritual movement. "It is a community of life, not a system of philosophy or theology," Mathews wrote. "An untheological, practical, scientific age is shaping a religious and moral Christianity which has its own intellectual expression and method, its own uplift and revelation; a religion which is as intellectually tenable as it is spiritually inspiring."[143] Modernist religion, "a projection of the Christian movement into modern conditions," was the faith that could sustain moral and spiritual value in a rationalistic age.

It was futile to avoid or deflect the challenge of modernity, Mathews insisted. There were two social minds at work in modern society: "The one seeks to reassert the past; the other seeks by new methods to give efficiency."[144] All forms of dogmatic and confessional theology were examples of the former. These included all conservative theologies and also various forms of liberal theology that emphasized theological belief. In this crucial respect, he explained, most Unitarians were not modernists, but countertypes of fundamentalism. While they rejected fundamentalist beliefs, their own identity was based on the creed they did accept. Most Unitarians and radical Christians were progressive fundamentalists. In Mathews's reading, the history of Christian theology in virtually all of its forms was a history of variations on a fundamentalist project.

Modernism broke from this worldview. Modernism was not a theology, a new religion, or a new philosophical system. It was "the use of the methods of modern science to find, state and use the permanent and central values of inherited orthodoxy in meeting the needs of a modern world."[145] Modernism was not a creed, in Mathews's view, but a method. It had no confessions, it did not vote in conventions, and it did not enforce beliefs by coercion. Modernism attained beliefs only through the application of scientific method, and it relinquished its beliefs whenever they were demonstrated to be false by subsequent research. Dogmatic religion emphasized doctrinal conformity through group authority, but modernist religion began with the religious movement that gave rise to doctrine and interpreted this movement through the use of critical methodologies. "The Modernist is a critic and an historian before he is a theologian," Mathews explained. "His interest in method precedes his interest in results."[146]

The Faith of Modernism was a transitional work. It identified modernism with scientific methodology while still making evangelical claims. Mathews asserted that modernist religion emphasized the inner faith of the Christian

---

143. Ibid., 12-13.
144. Ibid., 16.
145. Ibid., 23.
146. Ibid., 31.

movement rather than Christianity's subsequent formulas. It was not a coincidence that most modernists were evangelicals, he claimed; modernist religion was truer than the church's later theologies to the spirit and purpose of Christ. Modernism was true evangelicalism because modernism focused upon Jesus himself, rather than upon the church's later dogmas about Christ. *The Faith of Modernism* thus asserted the priority of method over belief while contending that the heart of Christian belief could be recovered only by modernist methods. It sustained an unacknowledged tension between Mathews's scientific claims and his apologetic interest in upholding a particular religious perspective.[147]

Mathews was not yet prepared to concede that modernist methodologies might threaten his own perspective. Neither did he acknowedge that his modernism was another system of belief, though he ended the book with a creedal confession that began, "I believe in God, immanent in the forces and processes of nature, revealed in Jesus Christ and human history as Love."[148] While insisting that modernist religion was distinguished by its subservience to critical methodology, he assumed that nothing essential to his morally regenerative evangelical faith would be lost under modernism. Mathews allowed that, in the future, it was possible that modernist religion might flourish more bountifully in service organizations than in churches, but in either case he could not imagine a world "in which men and women will fail to associate themselves for worship and cooperation in the way of Christ."[149]

The tension between Mathews's rationalism and evangelicalism was largely dissolved in his subsequent work by his adoption of a more thoroughgoing rationalism. His essentially Newtonian conception of science provided the methodological basis for a "scientific" understanding of what he called "religious process." The modern age was not wrong in exalting scientific knowledge above other forms of knowlege or belief, he repeatedly argued. Scientific knowledge was empirical, rational, and universalistic. It explained the processes of reality, including the dynamics and character of religious development, with superior analytical power. It interpreted theological concepts as historically conditioned and determined social patterns. Mathews argued that theology erred whenever it tried to sustain the life of a social pattern beyond its time. Theological patterns varied from culture to culture and could not be translated from one social mind to another. What could be translated, however, was the function that a particular concept played in an earlier social mind or pattern.

Mathews's later work pursued this project of translation and reconstruction. Under the influence of such Chicago colleagues as Wieman, E. S. Ames, and

---

147. Ibid., 31, 34, 144. For a good discussion of Mathews's naturalistic turn, see Cauthen, *The Impact of American Religious Liberalism,* 155–66.

148. Ibid., 180.

149. Ibid., 179.

Eustace Haydon, his earlier theism was virtually replaced by a religiously tinged naturalism. The last traces of a metaphysical notion of divine reality were erased in Mathews's concluding volumes on religion as social process. *The Atonement and the Social Process* (1930) examined the successive social patterns through which the death of Christ was interpreted in Christian history. Distinguishing between the religious function of atonement theory and the various historical patterns through which this function had been conceptualized, Mathews showed that "atonement" bore different meanings as it was conceptualized in messianic, sacrificial, imperial, feudal, monarchical, and modern social patterns. Within all of these patterns, however, a connecting and religiously meaningful motif was discernible. "Whoever sees in Christianity a developing religion conditioned by and expressing social forces, finds in the doctrines of the atonement the expression of a permanent value vastly greater than the patterns in which it has been expressed," he wrote. "For all these doctrines spring from and variously express the desire to make clear that God's forgiveness does not contravene his moral order."[150]

The Growth of the Idea of God (1931) applied the same method to the ultimate object of religious language. Mathews distinguished between metaphysical and religious approaches to the idea of divine reality, explaining that metaphysics did not examine the history of religious thought but only analyzed what it stood for. Metaphysics invariably began with some presupposed notion of divine reality. "But to argue that God exists is to argue that something behind experience corresponding to an already accepted definition exists," he observed.[151] To argue that God must exist was to presuppose some particular meaning for the word *God*. But this was to beg the crucial question. The question was not whether God existed, but what God would be if God existed. Metaphysical philosophers and theologians throughout Christian history had rationalized inherited concepts of divine reality. "But neither originated the idea of God," Mathews noted. "They inherited it from some social order."[152] What needed to be studied was the historical origins of theism and the subsequent history of divine reality in social process.

Mathews portrayed the history of Western theism as the West's archetypal progress narrative, tracing God language from its roots in "primitive" religions to the rise of early monotheism, to the development of classical theism, and finally to the emergence of modern pantheist, panentheist, and naturalist con-

---

150. Shailer Mathews, *The Atonement and the Social Process* (New York: Macmillan, 1930), 165.

151. Shailer Mathews, *The Growth of the Idea of God* (New York: Macmillan, 1931), 3.

152. Ibid., 4.

ceptions of divine reality. The narrative culminated with Mathews's own scientifically driven naturalism. Modern science provided the essential normative account of the world process with which all theorists, including theologians, were obliged to begin. This account excluded all forms of supernaturalism and at least most forms of personal theism. It did not preclude a religious explanation of consciousness, however. Mathews observed that if the evolutionary process brought human beings into being, "then there must be activities within the cosmos sufficient to account for the evolution of the human species with its personal qualities. There must be personality-evolving activities in the cosmos."[153] Moreover, human consciousness could have survived the ravages of time and environment only by virtue of the perdurability of these personality-evolving activities in the cosmos. "Otherwise men, lacking the environmental elements which aided in their evolution, would perish," Mathews argued. "That is the law of life itself."[154]

The meaning of history's variously conceived ideas of God emerged from this scientific truism. "If we properly interpret the patterns in which the idea of God has been successively expressed, we see that they stand for conceptions of the personality-evolving and personally responsive activities of the universe upon which human beings depend," Mathews wrote. The word *God* signified neither the concept alone nor the activities alone. "It expresses a reality because it expresses and furthers the relation between existences."[155] The word was an instrumental notion that expressed "an experienced relationship with an objective environment, which is an element of a dynamic situation in which we are also elements."[156] Because God was a name for the personality-enhancing reality in the cosmos, Mathews allowed that it was legitimate to use such personal metaphors as Father or Almighty or Companion in speaking of divine reality. "For God is our conception, born of social experience, of the personality-evolving and personally responsive elements of our cosmic environment with which we are organically related," he explained. To believe in God was to be assured that the human struggle for a better world was aided by the cosmos's immanent life-giving force. It was to grasp that the universal life process engendered personal values, while antipersonal acts contradicted the primordial evolutionary process in which all humanity was involved. "It is hard to see how anyone can fail to feel the worth of such a basis for morals," Mathews declared. "It is realism, not legalism."[157]

---

153. Ibid., 214.
154. Ibid.
155. Ibid., 218–19.
156. Ibid., 219.
157. Ibid., 232.

But by the early 1930s, it was hard for a new generation of liberal theologians to see how Mathews could be serious. His hyperpositivist conception of science was falsified by developments in theoretical physics and rejected by theologians who charged Mathews with making science into a religion. To a generation that endured, in its youth, the horrors of the Great War and that presently confronted the social and economic ravages of the Great Depression, Mathews's rhetoric of social progress and enlightenment came to sound quainter than the biblical language of sin, redemption, and transcendence. His claims to realism were ridiculed, and his accommodationist attitude toward modern culture was disputed by theologians on both sides of an intensifying debate over neoorthodoxy. In the early and mid-1930s, the kind of moralistic politics that Mathews championed was criticized by progressives who wanted to revive the social gospel and denounced by progressives who claimed that social gospel Christianity was dying the death it deserved.

Justin Wroe Nixon

Theologians such as Justin Wroe Nixon and the founding editor of the *Christian Century,* Charles Clayton Morrison, were proponents of the former position. Nixon was a former student and colleague of Rauschenbusch's who acknowledged that the movement to Christianize the social order was in eclipse. His idea of serious social Christianity was closer to Rauschenbusch's socialism than to Mathews's reformism. Nixon's explanation for the decline of social Christianity did not emphasize the movement's tepid character or even the catastrophic effects of the Great War, however. In 1931, he recalled that the war generated a spirit of cooperation and concern for the common good that put certain issues on the public agenda for the first time. During the war, Americans seriously discussed proposals for national reconstruction, state economic planning, and economic democracy. The movement for social Christianity was derailed not so much by the war, in his view, as by America's postwar lapse into hedonism.

Nixon's major work, *The Moral Crisis in Christianity,* recalled that most Americans grew tired of cooperation and regimentation during the war. "The American people as a whole reacted from the strenuous efforts of war-time, the revival spirit of cooperation, and the numerous annoyances incident to governmental regimentation," he explained. "They were tired of 'service.' They sought to forget the war and Europe. They wanted to have their fling. Instead of 'reconstruction programs' we received as a slogan the 'deflation of labor.' Instead of national economy the greatest orgy of political corruption the nation had known for a generation began within the President's official family."[158] For Nixon,

---

158. Justin Wroe Nixon, *The Moral Crisis in Christianity* (New York: Harper & Brothers, 1931), 20–21.

the Roaring Twenties was a decade of moral corruption, consumer narcissism, and public squalor. The nation's capitalist class indulged itself and encountered little opposition from an expanding middle class. "It was a time of growing prosperity for the masses," he wrote. "And the frustrated and cynical intellectuals read Mencken and started Sinclair Lewis toward the Nobel prize. The Social Gospel went under an eclipse."[159]

Nixon allowed that the social *interpretation* of Christianity was far from dead. Social Christianity informed the church's best work throughout the world, as in the Stockholm Conference on Christian Life and Work, the British Copec movement, the work of the industrial agencies of the YMCA and YWCA, and the continuing work of the Federal Council of Churches. Social Christian teaching dominated modern theology and modern seminary curricula. As compared to the decade between 1907 and 1917, however, the expanding, forward-moving, energizing thrust of the social gospel movement had been arrested in the postwar years. Social Christianity after Rauschenbusch's death confronted an American culture that was increasingly secular, increasingly insular and commercialized, and increasingly indifferent to social justice. "Social Christians were out of a job," Nixon recalled:

> Oh, a few negroes might be lynched now and then. . . . Free speech might be suppressed. . . . The Marines might be in Nicaragua. . . . But on the whole, things were going pretty well. God was in his heaven, Calvin Coolidge was in the White House, and stocks were going up. There can be no doubt that the long period of unusual prosperity lasting from 1922 to 1929 obscured the need of any religion which had the ideal of a nobler social order than that in which Americans generally were increasing their per capita supply of this world's goods.[160]

In response to this social turn, many social gospelers gave up their hopes for social and economic democracy; others lost their faith; others retreated to academic or therapeutic substitutes for radical social action. Nixon observed that many tired radicals were finding psychiatry to be as pleasant an escape "from the problems of real life as was premillennialism in its palmiest days."[161] What was needed, he countered, was not a generation that knew the difference between neurosis and psychosis, but a renewal of social gospel idealism. What was needed was a revival of the original, prophetic, transforming spirit of social Christianity, though in a new form. He conceded that Rauschenbusch's social gospel language probably could not be revived. A recovery of Rauschenbusch's spirit was needed

---

159. Ibid., 21; cf. Nixon, *An Emerging Christian Faith* (New York: Harper & Brothers, 1930), 301–20.
160. Nixon, *The Moral Crisis in Christianity,* 26.
161. Ibid., 32–33.

and a translation of his world-transforming religion into the language and politics of a new era. The new progressive Christianity would promote equality, community, and idealism; it would make contact with other world religions and expand the boundaries of human solidarity, including interreligious solidarity. It would be life-transforming rather than an escape from life.[162] It would reject the common chauvinistic egotism of recent American life. Nixon declared:

> We are passing out of the years that the locusts have eaten, the years of Harding and Daugherty, of Fall and Sinclair, the years when Coolidge was an oracle and Mellon was a god, the years of the tired radicals and the peace of exhaustion, the years when the pilgrimage of man meant little journeys from the stock ticker to the golf course and back to the bridge game and the highball, the years when youth exchanged the bondage of laws for that of impulses, the slavery of tradition for that of convention, the tyranny of the past for that of the present, the years when there were no problems, for everyone was getting rich in the best of all possible worlds.[163]

The years of cynicism and smallness were passing. Progressive Christianity was at a crossroads. Nixon did not claim to know, in 1931, whether Christianity would become life-transforming again or an escape from life. This open question summarized the moral crisis of Christianity.

Charles Clayton Morrison

The longtime editor of the *Christian Century* endorsed Nixon's position, but contended that social Christianity's recent failings had deeper origins. Morrison observed that in certain respects the social gospel had made extraordinary gains in the past decade. The 1920s could hardly be written off as a loss for the social gospel movement. Socially oriented church agencies and mission programs had multiplied. Social theology dominated the modern theological curriculum. A generation of mainline Christian ministers had been educated in it. Morrison's major work, *The Social Gospel and the Christian Cultus* (1933) spelled out the implications of social Christianity's takeover of the mainline church establishment and the problems with its triumph.

The basic problem was that social Christianity was thus far essentially a clerical phenomenon. "The social conception of Christianity commands the sympathy, if not the adherence, of practically the entire Protestant ministry," Morrison observed. "One cannot name a northern Methodist, Baptist, or Presbyterian seminary, or a Congregational or Disciples seminary, in which the Social

---

162. Ibid., 144–45.

163. Ibid., 189–90; cf. Justin Wroe Nixon, *Protestantism's Hour of Decision* (Philadelphia: Judson Press, 1940).

Gospel is not taken for granted."[164] The Lutheran seminaries were exceptions, and Morrison allowed that distinctions had to be made among mainline seminaries in the South, but even in the southern seminaries, social Christianity was the strongest voice. Morrison believed that the triumph of social Christian thinking in the mainline Protestant churches marked a historic recovery of the original Christian spirit and hope. It was a recovery of the spirit of Jesus and thus a rediscovery of the biblical ethic of the kingdom. "When our eyes look at Jesus they do not see the Figure which Origen saw, or Augustine, or Aquinas, or Luther, or Calvin, or Wesley," he wrote. "It is our new acquaintance with him that has revolutionized our gospel and given us the gospel of the Kingdom of God which was the dominant concept and passion of his life."[165]

The idea of the kingdom was the oldest idea in Christianity and a fresh discovery. For the *church* to rediscover and claim the biblical ethic of the kingdom, however, was to create a wrenching contradiction. It was the fundamental contradiction of social Christianity. Progressive ministers, academics, and church leaders were trying to infuse the radical spirit of Christ into the church, Morrison observed. They were trying to fit the early Christian idea of the kingdom into the existing church cultus. But the existing cultus was not designed to live in the spirit of the kingdom. "When we today set the Church over against the Kingdom of God, and say, as we are accustomed to say, that the Church exists for the sake of the Kingdom and not for its own sake, we are affirming a proposition which is distinctly modern," Morrison observed. "Not that the idea of the Kingdom is modern—I repeat that it is the oldest idea in Christianity, being the concept which was paramount in the mind of Christ."[166]

The problem was that Jesus made no place in his teaching for the church. "His words throw no direct light on the relation of an organized Church to the Kingdom of which he spoke so frequently," Morrison noted. With the passing of time after Christ's death and the diminution of the early church's eschatological consciousness, the church increasingly identified the kingdom with itself. This usurpation of the kingdom idea was politicized and tragically corrupted by the church's ascension to power under Constantine. The Constantinian transmutation of a pacifist, kingdom-seeking faith into a state religion marked not only the corruption of the kingdom idea in Christianity but also the paganization of the Christian cultus—the total cultural expression of Christian faith.

This was the religious and cultural legacy that modern social Christianity was seeking to repeal. It was not a coincidence that the movement's major figures

---

164. Charles Clayton Morrison, *The Social Gospel and the Christian Cultus* (New York: Harper & Brothers, 1933), 13, 15.

165. Ibid., 4–5.

166. Ibid., 5.

were products of the Anabaptist heritage. Rauschenbusch, Mathews, Brown, Clarke, and Fosdick were all Baptists. They inherited not only their tradition's recent pietist strain but also its resistance to concentrated religious and political authority. In recent years, pastors and theologians from nearly all American denominations had similarly concluded that the biblical idea of the kingdom contradicted establishment Christianity. Morrison observed,

> In our time we are trying to restore the concept of the Kingdom to a place in our thought and purpose like that which it occupied in Christ's thought and purpose, and we find that the major problem which we confront arises from the fact that the Christian cultus, fashioned under the influence of a conception of Christianity which in modern thought has undergone profound modification, is not congenial to the social gospel. The old cultus is not adapted to the new gospel.[167]

His proof was that social Christianity was almost entirely a clerical phenomenon. "The amazing spread of the social gospel among the clergy is paralleled by its failure to make any significant progress among the laity," Morrison wrote.[168] He cited a recent interdenominational gathering of Ohio pastors at which more than six hundred ministers discussed the politics of war and economic policy. The entire range of American Protestant denominations was represented at this convocation, which declared that "we renounce completely the whole war system. We will never again sanction or participate in any war." Regarding economic policy, the Ohio pastors insisted that a good society "must necessarily be built upon the cooperative method of life." To bring about a more cooperative and equal society, they called for "a more thorough social control of economic activities to replace the anarchistic individualism which characterizes the present economic order, by means of cooperative industry, government regulation or government ownership."[169]

Morrison noted that such gatherings and resolutions were commonplace. They testified to the influence of social Christianity among many American clergy. It was equally telling, however, that very few pastors carried these resolutions back to their church pulpits. They knew that their social idealism, which was well received among other pastors, would be greeted with bewilderment, fear, and hostility in their congregations. "These men regard the reconstruction of the social order as of the very essence of the Christian gospel," Morrison observed. "But they find it impossible to introduce into their pulpits and their parish work anything more than the faintest suggestion of the social idealism which burns in their hearts."[170]

---

167. Ibid., 5–6.
168. Ibid., 20.
169. Ibid., 17–20.
170. Ibid., 20.

The triumph of social Christianity in the seminaries was turning out pastors who shared little in common with most of their parishioners. "With a continual stream of young life charged with social idealism and conceiving of religion in terms of the Kingdom of God—with such a stream of young life pouring from the seminaries into the pulpits and parishes of all our denominations, the future of the church is promising indeed," Morrison wrote. This was his first reaction. On reflection, he feared that a storm was gathering in the churches. "The fact of such progress is encouraging," he noted. "But it is also perilous. I confess that I look upon it with grave anxiety."[171] What happened to the young pastor who quickly learned to keep his social idealism to himself? Did he become disillusioned, or cynical, or frustrated, or dishonest, or self-deceitful? Did he seek a different outlet for his idealism or renounce the idealism that brought him into the ministry?

Morrison observed that all of these reactions were amply displayed among contemporary clergy. "The dominant influence which has entered into the training of the church's professional leadership is practically irrelevant to the actual situation in which a minister finds himself when he becomes the pastor of a church," he wrote. "The result is that great numbers of our most earnest and competent men awake with a rude shock to find that their parish ministry affords them no adequate outlet for their most cherished ambition."[172] Their efforts to relate the ethic of the kingdom to contemporary social and political issues were commonly felt to be intrusive, meddling, and unreligious. Parishioners felt that the pastor should stick to his job, which was to provide inspiration and comfort for troubled hearts. The church's clerical ranks increasingly consisted of pastors who wanted to infuse the old cultus with the kingdom ethic, but most churchgoers presupposed the old cultus's distinctions between what was religious and what was not.

"We have here the making of a spiritual tragedy," Morrison warned.[173] A gulf was opening between pastors and laity, and both sides knew it. The gulf was widening with each seminary graduating class that entered the ministry. It was creating suspicion and resentment in the churches. This phenomenon was related to, but distinct from, the church's earlier controversies over historical criticism and evolution. The earlier controversies had been painful but were never threatening to the church's fundamental identity or existence. "There were tension and misgiving while the thing was being done, and though the church was badly

---

171. Ibid., 21.

172. Ibid., 23. For a similar account of the situation in American mainline Protestant churches, see Reinhold Niebuhr, "The Radical Minister and His Church," *Radical Religion* 2 (Winter 1936), 25–27.

173. Morrison, *The Social Gospel and the Christian Cultus*, 25.

shaken it was not shaken to its foundations," Morrison recalled. "Time only was required in which the educational process might work and a gradual adjustment come about."[174]

But social Christianity was a more revolutionary challenge to the churches. It was not an intellectual dispute to be settled among academics but a challenge to the entire ethos of Christendom and "the whole structure and procedure of the economic order." It would require a remaking of the church as radical as the Protestant Reformation. "The cultus we now have is the expression of another conception of Christianity than the social conception," Morrison wrote. "Can social Christianity be grafted upon it? Or must there be a radical remaking of the Christian cultus?"[175]

The church's cultus included its liturgy of worship, its theology, its organizational structure, and its ethical standards. In Morrison's view, the problem with the social gospel was that it was almost entirely a preacher's gospel, confined cultically to the sermon. "It has not been the church's gospel," he observed. "The laity have little share in it. They do not know how central and dominant it is in the thinking of their ministers. They get only enough of it to be irritated by it."[176] The upshot was that social Christianity did not seem religious. Confined to the sermon, its preaching on social justice seemed to the laity to be a secular diversion. "He is preaching politics, they say, or science, or economics, or internationalism; we want our preacher to talk about religion!"[177]

Morrison sympathized with this reaction. The laity were right; the typical discourse of social Christianity was secular. It talked politics from the pulpit. What was needed was to make social Christianity religious. "And to make it religious it must be given an organic place in the liturgy of communal worship, so that it shall not be merely the individual utterance of a preacher but the confessional utterance of the worshiping congregation itself," he argued.[178] Social preaching typically failed to carry religious power because it was mere preaching. It was not grounded or incorporated in the other dimensions of the church's cultus. Many pastors read Rauschenbusch only as source material for sermons. But this was not nearly enough, Morrison urged. Social Christianity needed to appropriate not only Rauschenbusch's sermon material, but his systematic theology, his interest in hymnody, his deep concern with prayer, his desire for new

---

174. Ibid.,, 27.

175. Ibid., 28. For Morrison's subsequent elaborations of his theology of the kingdom and of the need for a new ecumenical Reformation, see Charles Clayton Morrison, *What Is Christianity?* (Chicago: Willett, Clark & Company, 1940), 108–42; and Morrison, *The Unfinished Reformation* (New York: Harper & Brothers, 1953), 186–217.

176. Morrison, *The Social Gospel and the Christian Cultus,* 42.

177. Ibid., 44.

178. Ibid.

liturgical forms, his commitment to the democratization of church structures, and his vision of the church as a transforming moral community. Rauschenbusch understood that a kingdom-oriented church would require a transfigured cultus. "His hopeful eyes saw new hymns, new prayers, new denominational activities expressive of social idealism as signs of the awakening of the whole church," Morrison recalled.[179] More than any other modern figure, Rauschenbusch embodied the kind of cultus-transforming spirit that modern Christianity needed.

Morrison acknowledged the irony in this claim. To argue that Christianity needed a new kingdom-oriented cultus was to emphasize the importance of the priestly function. He pointed to Rauschenbusch as the exemplar of the prophetic *and* priestly faith that was needed. But Rauschenbusch's writings were filled with hostility for priestly faith. He repeatedly contrasted the ethical, justice-making character of prophetic religion to the enervating, corrupting ceremonialism of priestly religion. Like Mathews, he used the word *priestcraft* only as an epithet. More stridently than Mathews, he regarded Roman Catholic and Orthodox sacramentalism as a priestly paganization of Christianity's original prophetic character. As Morrison recalled, Rauschenbusch saw the priest only "as the champion and defender of a decadent church, who used the principle of authority to create for himself a privileged position as the sole dispenser of grace."[180] Against the ritualism and authoritarianism of priestcraft, Rauschenbusch upheld the prophetic commitment to freedom, justice, unmediated grace, and immediacy.

But Rauschenbusch was also a priest, Morrison observed. His *Theology of the Social Gospel* was a priestly work more than a prophetic work. His prayers and his hymn collections were priestly efforts. Rauschenbusch failed to see these efforts as priestly work because he failed to recognize the constructive aspect of priestly religion. In Morrison's estimation, social Christianity was currently paying a heavy price for this typically Protestant prejudice. "The entire cultus must be transformed under the social imperative if a socialization of theology is to become acceptable," he claimed. The doors to all four sides of the church's cultus had to be thrown open "if civilization is ever to be brought within hailing distance of the Kingdom of God."[181]

Fosdick's often-quoted sermon against nationalism, "Christianity's Supreme Rival," went to the heart of the matter. Fosdick claimed that the early Christians were persecuted by the Roman Empire not on account of their religion but because they put Christ first and refused to acknowledge the supreme authority of the state. Morrison observed that this was almost right. The early church was per-

---

179. Ibid., 101.
180. Ibid., 102.
181. Ibid., 242.

secuted for holding the kingdom above any claims of the state. Fosdick's error was in thinking of religion as a personal matter of the inner spiritual life. He claimed that the state did not persecute Christians on account of their religion because he identified religion with personal faith. By this reasoning, the early church's refusal to worship the emperor was an external application of religion. "This is the usual evangelical way of saying it," Morrison noted. "But an exactly accurate statement must say that their refusal to worship the emperor *was* their religion."[182] To recover *this* religion would require a break from Constantinianism, a new cultus, and a commitment to live in the kingdom of Christ.

"The Christian faith was originally and should be today embodied in a fellowship which stands over against the secular order—over against the state, and the economic order and all institutions and conventions of 'this world,' " Morrison concluded. The social Christianity of Mathews and Fosdick was too tame and domesticated. It found its niche in the prevailing social order too easily. It preached not only a Christ of culture but also a Christ of the dominant culture. The culture-transforming Christianity that was needed would live more danger-ously and with deeper spiritual conviction. It would renounce its "comfortable terms with the political state" and its "comfortable terms with the new economic order."[183] It would generate autonomous moral communities that changed the world through their spiritual power, rather than through their alliances with prevailing political and economic powers.

Coming from a pillar of the liberal Protestant establishment, this was an extraordinary indictment of liberal Protestantism's spiritual weakness and its accommodation to the dominant order. It called the church to renounce its power, its privileges, its cultural prestige, and its apologies for capitalism, imperialism, and militarism. It called the church to seek the kingdom by renouncing the established church. It disowned the very religious establishment that Morrison's magazine represented and served. The *Christian Century* had begun as a liberal Disciples of Christ journal called the *Christian Oracle*. The magazine moved from Des Moines to Chicago in 1888 and twelve years later, during the ascendancy of liberal Protestantism's world-embracing social hopes, was renamed the *Chris-tian Century*. Morrison had served for sixteen years as a Disciples pastor when, in 1908, he bought the journal for a bargain-basement fifteen hundred dollars. In the next ten years, during the heyday of the social gospel movement, he transformed the magazine from a Disciples house organ into the major journal of mainline American Protestantism. The *Christian Century* became the leading voice of American liberal Christianity. The magazine was officially declared "undenominational" in 1918, and by the early 1920s virtually all of the church's

---

182. Ibid., 243.
183. Ibid., 251, 244.

intellectual leaders, including such Morrison recruits as Fosdick, Charles Gilkey, Harry F. Ward, and Francis McConnell, were writing for it.[184]

Like Morrison, most of the early *Century* regulars were social gospelers with forceful, opinionated writing styles. Like Morrison, many of them were preoccupied after the war with the pacifist issue. Morrison's attention in the early 1920s was chiefly absorbed by his campaign to "outlaw" war through the enactment of what later became, in 1928, the Kellogg-Briand Pact. He repeatedly editorialized on the church's moral imperative to undermine the war-making powers of the state. At the same time, he was committed to making the magazine a forum for all areas of Christian social and personal concern. He sought promising writers who could address a variety of issues in his style and with his general perspective. In 1922, he found the fire hydrant of religious and political opinions that he was seeking when Reinhold Niebuhr began to write for the *Century*.

Reinhold Niebuhr and the *Christian Century*

Niebuhr was then a young pastor at Detroit's Bethel Evangelical Church, having graduated from Yale Divinity School in 1915. His father, Gustav, was a German Evangelical Synod pastor who read Harnack, supported Teddy Roosevelt, and studied the Bible in Hebrew and Greek. His pietist faith and his powerful intellectual energy deeply influenced his four children, three of whom became seminary professors. Reinhold was his favorite. Like his father, Reinhold entered the ministry "with a few thoughts and a tremendous urge to express myself."[185] At Bethel church, he vigorously supported America's intervention in the war and subsequently witnessed the explosive rise of the automobile industry. Niebuhr spent more time on the church and college lecture circuit than at his parish, however. He was a spellbinding orator, combining a highly charged intellectual message with a constantly animated, whirling, gesticulating speaking style. His work for the church's War Welfare Commission and his charismatic performances at church and college conferences gained him a national reputation in Protestant circles before he began to write for the *Century*.

By the time that he came to Morrison's attention, Niebuhr was also moving toward Morrison's pacifism. His enthusiasm for Wilson's world-saving rhetoric was quickly chastened after the war by the vengeful tone of the Paris Peace

---

184. On Morrison and the origins of the *Christian Century,* see William E. Tucker and Lester G. McAllister, *Journey in Faith: A History of the Christian Church (Disciples of Christ)* (St. Louis: Bethany Press, 1975), 328; D. Newell Williams, ed., *A Case Study of Mainstream Protestantism: The Disciples' Relation to American Culture, 1880–1989* (Grand Rapids: Eerdmans, 1991), 129–30.

185. Niebuhr letter to Will Scarlett, 1960, quoted in Richard Wightman Fox, *Reinhold Niebuhr: A Biography* (New York: Pantheon Books, 1985), 294.

Conference. Niebuhr had hoped that an Allied victory would be a victory for world democracy, reconciliation, and open markets. The object of the war was not to humiliate or destroy Germany, he reasoned, but to bring Germany into the family of liberal democratic nations. He did not doubt that this was Wilson's view of the war. The spectacle of Wilson making concession after concession to French and English demands for reparations gave Niebuhr second thoughts on the war, however. He was disgusted by the Versailles Treaty. The loss of his idealistic reasons for supporting the war made him open to Morrison's vigorous antimilitarism.

In 1923, Niebuhr took a European tour with a group of ministers, academics, and others led by Sherwood Eddy. The group attended lectures in England and met with British intellectuals and Labour party leaders. Many of their discussions focused on France's reported cruel mistreatment of Germans in the occupied Ruhr Valley. Niebuhr already resented France's attitude toward his ancestral homeland; the stories about French abuses in the Ruhr drove him to see for himself whether the stories were exaggerated. Accompanied by Kirby Page and Will Scarlett, he journeyed to the Ruhr and witnessed what he called "the closest thing to hell I have ever seen." For three days, he listened to blood-curdling stories about atrocities and sexual assaults committed by the occupying French forces. He saw severely malnourished German children at the Red Cross centers and families separated by barbed wire. The atrocity stories, the atmosphere of hate, and the starving children drove him across a line. Niebuhr lost not only his idealistic reasons for supporting war, but all of his reasons. "This is as good a time as any to make up my mind that I am done with the war business," he wrote in his diary.[186]

His published report on the Ruhr occupation made no mention of his pacifist resolution, which was a private matter. Publicly, Niebuhr was more concerned that a revival of American isolationism would cause America to turn its back on the European situation. He urged that America needed to use its diplomatic muscle to prevent a catastrophe in Germany. Niebuhr's determination not to support militarism or war never drove him to any kind of isolationism. He struggled for the next decade to be a pacifist while arguing for an aggressively internationalist foreign policy and while fearing, as he wrote in the *Century,* that "the principle of nonresistance is too ideal for a sinful human world."[187]

Most of Niebuhr's early writings for the *Century* did not bear his name because Morrison paid him only for unsigned editorials. His numerous editorials for the magazine were never hard to pick out, however. Niebuhr honed his

---

186. Niebuhr diary entry quoted in Fox, *Reinhold Niebuhr,* 78.
187. Reinhold Niebuhr, "Wanted: A Christian Morality," *Christian Century* 40 (February 15, 1923), 202; cited in Fox, *Reinhold Niebuhr,* 79.

distinctively dialectical, aggressive, ironic writing style while filling the *Century* with editorials, articles, and reviews on national and world events. Morrison could never get enough of them. "Just send them in," he urged in 1923, "and as many as possible, and as often as possible. You have the right touch."[188]

Morrison saw in Niebuhr the figure who might redefine the meaning of social Christianity for a postwar generation. Niebuhr's social perspective at the time was strongly influenced by his friendship with Detroit's Episcopal bishop, Charles Williams, and by his participation in the Fellowship for a Christian Social Order (FCSO), a national organization of liberal Christians founded in 1921 by Eddy and Page. The FCSO was an educational association concerned with developing a Christian approach to the problems of industrial capitalism. It was formed at a time when a critical mass of Christian progressives was beginning to move toward Rauschenbusch's view of the class struggle and away from the dominant liberal view, represented by Mathews and Fosdick, that the church should be a moral mediator between—or above—the struggle between labor and capital. In 1922 Niebuhr and Williams founded FCSO's Detroit branch, which embraced a pro-labor politics without advocating socialism. The following year, Williams died of a heart attack, leaving a stunned Niebuhr with the sense that it was his mission to complete his mentor's work. He wrote in his diary, "Nowhere have I seen a personality more luminous with the Christ spirit than in this bishop who was also a prophet." He wrote to Williams's diocese, "Your diocese has lost a great bishop, but the church universal has lost infinitely more; it has lost a prophet who had the courage to challenge the complacency of a very self-righteous civilization."[189]

At Williams's urging, Niebuhr had begun to study Rauschenbusch for the first time. His writings over the succeeding decade tried to express the implications of his admiration for Williams and his ambivalence toward Rauschenbusch. He wrote in 1923, "There is no Christian basis to modern industry. It is based upon a purely naturalistic conception of life and cynically defies every spiritual appreciation of human beings. Christianity has had nothing to do with the organization of industrial civilization. It ought therefore to have no pride in it."[190] This sentiment hardened to an increasingly radical politics throughout the 1920s, culminating with Niebuhr's entry into the Socialist party in 1929.

Niebuhr thus increasingly adopted Rauschenbusch's politics but not his style. Though he joined the Socialist movement as a Christian, Niebuhr downplayed Rauschenbusch's language of the kingdom and his call to follow the way of

---

188. Quoted in Charles C. Brown, *Niebuhr and His Age: Reinhold Niebuhr's Prophetic Role in the Twentieth Century* (Philadelphia: Trinity Press, 1992), 25.

189. Fox, *Reinhold Niebuhr,* 76.

190. Niebuhr, "Wanted: A Christian Morality," 202.

Christ. Though he tried to be a pacifist and even served as national executive council chair of the Fellowship of Reconciliation, Niebuhr repeatedly criticized his fellow pacifists for their naivete, their moralism, and their faith in universal reason. His collected articles of this period, *Does Civilization Need Religion?* proclaimed that he still had a "robust" faith in human possibilities despite the fact that all "immediate evidences" contradicted this faith. The book called for a fusion of reason and religiously inspired good will to solve modern civilization's social problems while complaining that religious liberalism overestimated human virtue. He warned that powerful economic interests would not relinquish their power without a struggle, yet closed the book with a call for "religiously inspired moral idealism." Niebuhr struggled to affirm his liberal idealism in the late 1920s while repeatedly criticizing its creed, its manners, its sentimentality, and its politics.[191]

Like virtually all liberal Protestant leaders, Niebuhr supported Prohibition, but he blasted the *Christian Century* for giving inordinate importance to the issue. In 1928, Morrison opposed Herbert Hoover's foreign policy and his anti-labor politics, but he supported Hoover over Al Smith in the presidential election because of Smith's opposition to Prohibition. For Morrison, antimilitarism and Prohibition were the heart of progressive Christian politics. To give up on Prohibition was to forsake the social gospel project of morally transforming American society. Though Hoover's politics were repugnant to social Christians in many respects, and though Smith's politics were much closer to liberal Christianity's social agenda, Smith appeared to the *Century* to be morally tone-deaf. He cared nothing about the politics of moral community. He was a Catholic who dealt with the politically delicate problems of religion by ignoring religious concerns. His secular, instrumentalist, amoral approach to politics would never create a good society.

Niebuhr was not voting for Smith, either; he supported Norman Thomas's Socialist ticket. He could not abide the spectacle of the *Christian Century* supporting Hoover, however. He had always stoutly supported Prohibition and still did, but if Prohibition could be saved only by swallowing Right-wing economic policies and imperialist adventures in Latin America, he argued, then Prohibition would have to be sacrificed. As usual, liberal Protestantism was too moralistic. Morrison's combination of quasi-pacifism and Prohibition was sadly typical of liberal Protestantism even at its best. Niebuhr insisted that if liberal Protestantism was going to be truly progressive, it had to begin to give higher priority to economic justice than to moral purity. In the present context, this meant giving

---

191. Cf. Reinhold Niebuhr, "A Critique of Pacifism," *Atlantic* 139 (May 1927), 640–41; Niebuhr, *Does Civilization Need Religion? A Study in the Social Resources and Limitations of Religion in Modern Life* (New York: Macmillan, 1927), 207–38.

support to a wet, Catholic, Democratic political operator over a dry, Protestant, Republican conservative.[192]

Though he pushed hard for socialism, Rauschenbusch never joined the Socialist party, mainly because he disliked its assaults on bourgeois morality and its frequent hostility to religion. He also feared that secular state socialism would rationalize new forms of dictatorial state authority. Hoover's victory over Smith moved Niebuhr to dispense with the same misgivings, however. As a seminarian and former pastor, Norman Thomas had been inspired by Rauschenbusch's writings. His ascension to the top of the Socialist party made it possible for Christian socialists like Niebuhr to join the party. Niebuhr also joined Thomas's League for Industrial Democracy, the leftist New York Teachers' Union, the Fellowship of Reconciliation, and Paul Douglas's League for Independent Political Action. Having moved to Union Theological Seminary in 1928 to teach social ethics, Niebuhr missed few opportunities to enmesh himself in radical politics. In 1930, along with Eddy, Page, and John C. Bennett, he created the radical Fellowship of Socialist Christians (FSC), which became Niebuhr's primary organizational outlet. They were joined by such figures as Roswell Barnes, Buell Gallagher, Francis Henson, and Frank Wilson and, shortly afterward, by Paul Tillich and Eduard Heimann. The leading figures of a new theological generation stopped using progressive euphemisms for socialism and called for the abolition of private industrial property.

Niebuhr believed that his radical turn took him far beyond the boundaries of liberal Christianity. Even at its best, in the writings of Mathews, Fosdick, and Morrison, liberal Protestantism was too moralistic, too enamored with modern progress, and too trusting in its hope for a community of love. The problem was not simply that liberal Protestantism reduced politics to moral striving; the problem was also that liberal Protestantism typically reduced religion to moral striving and personal faith. Fosdick added aesthetic appeals and Mathews appealed to the authority of science, but these were poor substitutes for prophetic Christianity. Niebuhr's rather patronizing review of Fosdick's *Adventurous Religion* set the tone for a new generation of self-styled Christian realists. Though Fosdick had done important work in fighting the rise of fundamentalism, Niebuhr conceded, his claim to being adventurous was belied by his failure to challenge the injustices of modern capitalism. Like liberal Protestantism itself, Fosdick had failed to challenge "the fundamental immoralities of modern civilization, its immoral nationalism, its lust for power, and its accentuated greed."[193]

---

192. Reinhold Niebuhr, "Governor Smith's Liberalism," *Christian Century* 45 (September 13, 1928), 1107–8.

193. Reinhold Niebuhr, "How Adventurous Is Dr. Fosdick?" *Christian Century* 44 (January 6, 1927), 17–18.

The end of a theological era was marked five years later, in 1932, by the publication of Niebuhr's *Moral Man and Immoral Society.* For two generations, Christian thinkers had joined with other progressive intellectuals and activists in seeking to build an organic moral community that would replace the heartless, impersonal mechanisms of modern capitalism. The social gospelers declared that the project of building a cooperative commonwealth would bring about the kingdom of God. In the early 1930s, Morrison and Nixon called the church to reclaim the social gospel's kingdom-seeking idealism. A larger group of social Christians conceived the reign of God in more traditional, transcendent terms, while nonetheless committing themselves to the creation of a moral common-wealth in America. *Moral Man and Immoral Society* blasted this religious and political project with stunning force. It skewered the defining faith not only of Niebuhr's obvious liberal opponents, such as Mathews and Fosdick, but also of radical and liberal Christians who, until the day before, had been his close associates. They included such progressive Christians as Morrison, Eddy, Page, Gilkey, Thomas, Ward, and John Haynes Holmes. The book's aggressive sarcasm toward Christian moralism moved Gilkey to declare to his family that Niebuhr had gone insane.[194] The *Christian Century* and other liberal journals were slightly more guarded, but vigorously chastised Niebuhr for his cynicism, his defeatism, and his purportedly less-than-Christian morality.

For a younger theological generation that no longer believed the world was getting better, Niebuhr's book marked a turning point. The age of religious idealism had passed, and with it had passed the politics of moral community. Less than a year after the book's publication, Bennett declared that Niebuhr defined reality for a new generation. "The most important fact about contem-porary American theology is the disintegration of liberalism," he announced.[195] The church's social mission was not to nurture personality or bring about the cooperative kingdom but to promote attainable gains toward justice in a brutal, power-grabbing world. Liberal Christianity was nothing without its moralized politics, and Niebuhr shredded its morality and politics. Though it was severely criticized in the liberal Christian press, the reputation of *Moral Man and Immoral Society* heightened throughout the succeeding decade as the rise of Nazi fascism made Niebuhr's dark vision seem prophetic. By 1939, Hitler's brutal militarism and his pact with Stalin made Niebuhr's cynicism seem understated. For a theological generation that witnessed the Great War in its youth and the rise of

---

194. Quoted in Langdon Gilkey, "Reinhold Niebuhr as Political Theologian," in *Reinhold Niebuhr and the Issues of Our Time,* ed. Richard Harries (Grand Rapids: Eerdmans, 1986), 182. Gilkey recalled that his father later changed his estimate of Niebuhr's book.

195. John C. Bennett, "After Liberalism—What?" *Christian Century* 50 (November 8, 1933), 1403.

fascist and communist totalitarianism afterward, it was Niebuhr's apocalyptic realism that made sense of the world. The humanistic religion of their professors was an echo from a lost world.

The kind of religion that Christian realism advocated in its place seemed like a reactionary throwback to liberals like Mathews. In his closing years, Mathews was deeply saddened by the rise of a theological generation that disdained his reformism, his moral idealism, his scientific naturalism, and his belief in progress:

> One of the surprises of life is the reappearance in a younger generation of questions which an older generation supposed it had answered or at least comfortably neglected. In religion as in politics and business it is hard to capitalize experience. Instead of learning how to use parental experience to avoid duplicating parental mistakes a new generation apparently wishes to recapitulate foolishness before making new moral adventures.[196]

Mathews never doubted that the war had been necessary or even that America's participation in it served the cause of democracy and progress. When he sought to explain the apparent disintegration of his generation's religious and social achievements, however, he had no doubt that the war was to blame. He explained in 1936:

> The natural course of all reconstructive processes has been disarranged by the Great War and those who are now entering middle age have grown up in an age of disillusionment and struggle. Their confidence in democracy has been rudely shaken. The inability of individuals to withstand group pressure has induced among some theologians an almost psychopathic attitude of pessimism and the elevation of crisis above process. It is no accident that such a feeling should originate on the continent of Europe, or that it should reappear among those who have reached maturity in the midst of the rapid changes in the United States. I cannot believe that such a mood is either healthy or conducive to religious faith. It is more akin to the eschatology of a subject Jewish people and savors too much of defeatism and distrust of intelligently implemented love. One might almost describe it as premillenarian liberalism.[197]

Thus did liberal Christian moralism concede its defeat to a theological generation that exalted crisis, pessimism, and power over love and cooperation. The "premillenarian" label aptly described the widening gulf between liberal Christians who called themselves liberals and liberal Christians who called themselves realists. Christian realism would reconfigure the modern meaning of Christianity with the kingdom left out.

---

196. Mathews, *New Faith for Old,* 219.
197. Ibid., 298.

3 CHRISTIAN REALISM
The Niebuhrian Turn

FOR MOST OF HIS EXTRAORDINARY CAREER, the greatest figure in modern American liberal theology never tired of expressing his disdain for modern American liberalism. In the 1920s, Reinhold Niebuhr preached a conventionally progressive mixture of liberal theology, pacifism, and political reformism while complaining that liberal Christianity was too soft to confront the evils of the world. He called for moral efforts to redeem American society while warning that morality had little power. He joined the pacifist Fellowship of Reconciliation while bristling at the moralistic idealism and, often, the effeminate manners of his pacifist colleagues.

Niebuhr as Socialist

In the early 1930s, these awkwardly mixed feelings and the terrible human wreckage of the Great Depression drove Niebuhr to a sterner creed. *Moral Man and Immoral Society* (1932) delivered the message. In the autumn months that preceded the book's publication, Niebuhr ran for Congress on the Socialist party ticket and told New Yorkers that only socialism could save Western civilization. Norman Thomas headed the party's national ticket, but, as Thomas only vaguely comprehended, Niebuhr was moving to a kind of radicalism that made Thomas's socialism seem tame by comparison. A month after Niebuhr won only 4 percent of the vote, his searing assault on modern political and religious liberalism was published.

The book's tone was icy, aggressive, and eerily omniscient. It marked the end of Niebuhr's calls to build the kingdom of God. It ridiculed the moral idealism that had fueled liberal Christianity for the past half-century. It argued that while individuals were occasionally capable of altruism or self-transcendence, human groups never willingly subordinated their interests to the interests of others.

Morality was for individuals. If individuals occasionally overcame their inevitable egotism in acts of compassion or love, there was no evidence that human groups ever overcame the power of self-interest and collective egotism that sustained their existence. Liberal Christianity's attempts to moralize society were thus not only futile but also stupid.

"Stupid" became Niebuhr's favorite epithet. Because liberal moralists failed to recognize the brutal character of human groups and the resistance of all groups to moral suasion, he argued, they were virtually always driven to "unrealistic and confused political thought." Secular liberals appealed to reason, and Christian liberals typically appealed to love in their struggles for a just society, but both strategies were hopelessly inadequate. *Moral Man and Immoral Society* reflected Niebuhr's anger at the human ravages of the Depression and his frustration with America's aversion to socialism. The book was milder than an article that Niebuhr published the same summer, which proclaimed that "it will be practically impossible to secure social change in America without the use of very considerable violence." *Moral Man and Immoral Society* drew back from such posturing, but it repudiated any kind of progressive politics that failed to recognize that politics was about struggling for power.[1]

Niebuhr thus repudiated pacifism and embraced a Christian variant of Marxism. From Marxism he obtained not only an explanation for the impending collapse of bourgeois civilization but also an antidote to liberal Christianity's pious moralism. For many years afterward, he charged that America's liberal churches were capitulating to the culture of modernity and thereby reducing Christianity to sentimental banalities. "Liberal Christian literature abounds in the monotonous reiteration of the pious hope that people might be good and loving," he claimed. Shailer Mathews was a favorite target. Niebuhr ridiculed Mathews's "strikingly naive" idealism, which called Christians to be "champions of the underprivileged" without giving moral sanction to the underprivileged themselves to fight for their interests.[2] For Niebuhr, Mathews's work epitomized the stupidity of liberal moralism. In the 1930s, Niebuhr's bromides against Christian liberalism and its secular variants were fueled by a Marxist insistence on the centrality of the class struggle and the futility of reformist politics.

A decade later, Niebuhr relinquished his Marxism but retained his disdain for liberalism. Having drawn his earlier realism about politics and moral reformism from Marxist theory, he now criticized liberal moralism in the language

1. Reinhold Niebuhr, *Moral Man and Immoral Society: A Study in Ethics and Politics* (New York: Charles Scribner's Sons, 1947, c1932), xx; Niebuhr, "Catastrophe or Social Control?" *Harper's* 165 (June 1932), 118.

2. Reinhold Niebuhr, *An Interpretation of Christian Ethics* (San Francisco: Harper & Row, 1963, c1935), 105–8.

of classical Christian theology. He later explained, "Even while imagining myself to be preaching the Gospel, I had really experimented with many modern alternatives to Christian faith, until one by one they proved unavailing."[3] The conviction that survived each of these conversions, however, was that liberal Christianity and Deweyan secular liberalism were too feminized, too moralistic, and too attached to the myth of progress to confront the evils of the world. The theology of modern liberal Christianity, he declared in 1940, "is little more than eighteenth-century rationalism and optimism, compounded with a little perfectionism, derived from the sanctificationist illusions of sectarian Christianity."[4] Liberal Christianity was not only too moralistic to play a serious role in the political sphere; it was also too naive about human nature to deserve to be called Christianity. Liberal Christian moralism consumed Christianity itself in its misguided pursuit of innocence.

The latter point was elaborated in Niebuhr's magnum opus, *The Nature and Destiny of Man*. Liberal Christianity usually made some effort "to maintain some contact with the traditional faith by affirming simply that Jesus was a very, very, very good man," Niebuhr wrote. The problem was that, having reduced Christianity to its own delicate moral sensibility, liberal Protestantism could not rule out the possibility that a better person than Jesus might appear in the future, "in which case the loyalty of the faithful would be transferred to him."[5] For all of its talk about social relevance, about Christianizing the social order, and about following the way of Christ, liberal Christianity was politically irrelevant and barely Christian at all. Having resolved to make Christianity relevant to the modern age, liberal Christian theologians were succeeding only in reducing the profound mythic truths of Christianity to the saccharine sentimentality of modernity's "children of light."

Thus did Niebuhr describe his own group. If he disliked and repeatedly attacked liberal Christianity, he was nonetheless part of it. Having begun his pastoral career as a social gospel liberal, he never completely broke from the tradition that first fired his imagination and idealism. Niebuhr never doubted that the church in America should be a force for social justice and democracy. His fundamental identification with theological liberalism was underscored by his persistent emphasis on the mythical character of Christian doctrine. Though he credited theological conservatism with preserving a more realistic estimate of human nature than liberal theology, and though he increasingly resorted to clas-

---

3. Reinhold Niebuhr, "Ten Years That Shook My World," *Christian Century* 56 (April 26, 1939), 546.

4. Reinhold Niebuhr, "Christian Moralism in America," *Radical Religion* 5 (1940), 19.

5. Reinhold Niebuhr, *The Nature and Destiny of Man: A Christian Interpretation* vol. 1, *Human Nature* (New York: Scribner's, 1949, c1941), 146.

sical Christian language about original sin and salvation in developing his position, theological conservatism was never an option for Niebuhr on fundamental
questions of authority, belief, or interpretation.

   An Interpretation of Christian Ethics (1935) spelled out his reasons. In
Niebuhr's estimation, conservative Christianity was untenable "partly because
its religious truths are still embedded in an outmoded science and partly because
its morality is expressed in dogmatic and authoritarian moral codes." Conservative
Christianity fossilized the orthodox formulas and thought forms of earlier historical periods and thus turned a living historical faith into a kind of ancestor
worship. Niebuhr claimed that if the conservative churches had not petrified such
dogmas as the inerrancy of Scripture and the historicity of the Bible's creation
accounts into literal objects of faith, such articles "would otherwise have long
since fallen prey to the beneficent dissolutions of the processes of nature and
history."[6] Fundamentalism endured only on the strength of a determined intellectual and, especially, scientific know-nothingism. Conservative theologies were
fundamentally marked by their insistence on taking mythical teachings literally.
As Niebuhr frequently noted in the decades preceding Vatican Council II, this
insistence characterized not only Protestant evangelicals and fundamentalists but
also most contemporary Roman Catholic theology.[7]

   Niebuhr's alternative was that Christian mythical teaching should be taken
seriously but not literally. "It is the genius of true myth to suggest the dimension
of depth in reality and to point to a realm of essence which transcends the surface
of history, on which the cause-effect sequences, discovered and analyzed by
science, occur," he explained.[8] Science dealt with the surfaces of nature and
history. It broke isolated objects of inquiry into their smallest possible constitutive
parts in order to gain maximum control over them. In its effort to bring coherence
to its radically subdivided and pluriform world, Niebuhr observed, science was
always strongly disposed to propound an overly mechanistic view of reality. One
by-product of this predisposition was that, as scientific knowledge increased,
religious reasoning lost any claim to utility or intellectual credibility.

   In Niebuhr's understanding, however, religious myth belonged to a different
realm of existence than the realm of empirical causality on which scientific
explanation operated. His thinking was crucially influenced by Paul Tillich, who
fled Nazi Germany in 1933 and, on Niebuhr's initiative, joined Niebuhr at Union
Theological Seminary. Tillich's emphasis on myth and his view of religion as

---

   6. Niebuhr, *An Interpretation of Christian Ethics,* 2.
   7. Cf. Reinhold Niebuhr, "Reply to Interpretation and Criticism," in *Reinhold Niebuhr: His Religious, Social, and Political Thought,* ed. Charles W. Kegley and Robert
W. Bretall (New York: Macmillan, 1956), 443–46.
   8. Niebuhr, *An Interpretation of Christian Ethics,* 7.

the dimension of depth in life were amply reproduced in Niebuhr's writings of the mid-1930s. For Niebuhr, as for Tillich, religious myth did not challenge a properly chastened science that eschewed mechanistic philosophy and that recognized its own unprovable assumptions. Religious myth pointed, rather, to a deeper realm, "the ultimate ground of existence and its ultimate fulfilment." With Tillich and Nikolai Berdyaev, Niebuhr viewed myth as a product of human spirituality that symbolically expressed human experiences of supernatural power or presence in the natural realm. Because religious myths pointed to the ultimate ground of existence, most religious mythologies presented transhistorical accounts of creation and redemption. "But since myth cannot speak of the transhistorical without using symbols and events in history as its form of expression, it invariably falsifies the facts of history, as seen by science, to state its truth," Niebuhr explained.[9] The Christian doctrines of the divine creator, the fall, and the incarnation were central examples of myths that needed to be taken seriously but not literally.

Niebuhr argued that the myth of God as creator was not a scientific postulate but a religious image that portrayed God's organic relation to the world as well as God's distinction from the world. In the Jewish-Christian myth of the divine creator, God's being was constitutive of all reality while not being exhausted by it. This teaching was intelligible only if one accepted at the outset that it was a mythical construction. Niebuhr observed that Christian teaching about the incarnation made similar claims about the double nature of Christ. If taken literally, these claims were absurd; if the Christian myth of the incarnation was interpreted as myth, it was religiously deep in meaning.

The myth of the fall was Niebuhr's bellwether example of what was at stake in the interpretation of Christian mythical teachings, however. For him, the strength of conservative Christianity was that it took the biblical myth of the fall literally and thus took with utter seriousness the biblical notion that human nature is thoroughly corrupted by sin. The crippling weakness of conservative Christianity was that it conceived the fall as a literal event and thus defended the historicity of a mythical account that lacked any historical foundation. Conservative Christianity refused to acknowledge that the fundamental myths of Christianity were myths. By refusing to deal with the implications of historical and scientific criticism, conservative Christianity discredited itself and provoked unnecessary conflicts with the social and natural sciences. Conservative theologies fortunately retained a correct insistence on the fallen or corrupted state of nature, including the human condition, but they based this doctrinal claim on discredited literalistic interpretations of Scriptural texts.

---

9. Ibid.

The problem with liberal Christianity, by contrast, was that it did not take the defining myths of Christian faith seriously enough. Having dispensed with a literalistic interpretation of the fall, for example, liberal Christianity quickly degenerated into a culture religion that failed to take the underlying meaning of the myth with any seriousness at all. In the Scriptural story of the fall, Adam and Eve brought sin into a sinless world by defying the command of a jealous God not to eat the fruit of the tree of knowledge. In liberal Christianity, Niebuhr observed, the effort to overcome literalism, anthropomorphism, and supernaturalism produced a theology that reduced the meaning of this story to an expression of the fears of primitive people toward higher powers. Having repudiated a mistaken appropriation of religious myth, liberal Christianity typically proceeded to discard the myth of the fall altogether. The Enlightenment myth of progress displaced a primitive myth about the jealousy of a divine tribal monarch.

It was precisely the scriptural myth of the fall, however, that expressed what was crucially lacking in liberal Christianity. The biblical image of a jealous creator was not a primitive anthropomorphism but a mythical depiction of the human situation. The root of human evil, Niebuhr argued, was the human pretension of being God. As creatures made in the image of God, human beings possessed capacities for self-transcendence that enabled them to become aware of their finite existence in distinction from, though constitutive with, God's infinite existence. The same awareness moved human beings, however, to attempt to overcome their finiteness by becoming infinite, like God. This was Adam's sin. In its most fundamental and its most developed forms, Niebuhr observed, evil was always a good that imagined itself to be better than it was. The driving force of evil was egotism, which was always wrapped in self-deceit and deceit of others. The biblical myth of the fall was thus not a dispensable relic of primitive fear and superstition "but a revelation of a tragic reality of life." The truth of the myth was attested by every page of human history. The Enlightenment myth of progress and human perfectibility embraced by liberal Christianity was a pitiful substitute for the biblical myth.[10]

Liberal theology could retrieve the serious meaning of the fall, Niebuhr claimed, only by retrieving the true meaning of the classical Christian doctrine of original sin. This could not be accomplished by refurbishing any literalistic theory of inherited corruption. Niebuhr disavowed not only any interpretation of the fall as an account of the origin of evil but also any theory that conceptualized original sin as a biologically transmitted evil. He pointedly rejected Augustine's theory that original sin was transmitted through lust in the act of procreation.[11]

---

10. Ibid., 54; Cf. Niebuhr, *The Nature and Destiny of Man* 1:265–80.

11. Cf. Niebuhr, *An Interpretation of Christian Ethics,* 55; *Faith and History: A Comparison of Christian and Modern Views of History* (New York: Scribner's, 1949), 120–23; and *The Self and the Dramas of History* (New York: Scribner's, 1955), 12–19.

The classical Pauline-Augustinian doctrines of original sin were self-defeating because they destroyed the basis for moral responsibility that Christian morality required. If original sin was an inherited corruption, then human beings lacked the freedom to choose not to sin and thus could not be held morally responsible for being in sin.

The true meaning of original sin was existential, not biological. The reality of original sin was attested by history, Niebuhr explained, but it was not itself historical. Just as the myth of the fall was a description of the nature of evil rather than an account of the origin of evil, so the reality of original sin was an inevitable fact of human existence but not an inherited corruption of existence. The human capacity for self-transcendence made original sin inevitable. Though original sin was a reality "in every moment of existence," it had no history. Niebuhr's major work *The Nature and Destiny of Man* built a massive theological edifice on the implications of this paradoxical truism. The defining truism of Christian ethics was that sin was an inevitable existential corruption for which human beings were morally responsible.[12]

If original sin had no history, Niebuhr was nonetheless acutely mindful of the history of the doctrine of original sin. He acknowledged that the doctrine had often been employed to rationalize injustice, oppression, and status quo politics. In the 1930s, after renouncing his own earlier social gospel progressivism and pacifism, Niebuhr tried to show that radical politics and a theological emphasis on human sin were compatible. If politics was about struggling for power, and radical politics was about struggling for a just redistribution of power, it followed that religion could serve the cause of justice only if it took a realistic attitude toward power, interest, and evil. As he observed in 1933:

> Classical religion has always spoken rather unequivocally of the depravity of human nature, a conclusion at which it arrived by looking at human nature from the perspective of the divine. It is one of the strange phenomena of our culture that an optimistic estimate of human nature has been made the basis of theistic theologies. Next to the futility of liberalism we may set down the inevitability of facism as a practical certainty in every Western nation.[13]

Niebuhr's most explicitly Marxist work, *Reflections on the End of an Era* (1934), expanded this twofold theme with apocalyptic fervor. Throughout its entire brief reign, he observed, modern capitalism had been attended by an attitude of unqualified optimism. The philosophers of modernity had dreamed of progress "almost until the hour of its dissolution." But the ravages of capitalist egotism now confronted modernity's apologists with the deepest and most un-

---

12. Cf. Niebuhr, *The Nature and Destiny of Man* 1:178–86.

13. Reinhold Niebuhr, "After Capitalism—What?" *The World Tomorrow* 16 (March 1, 1933), 204.

pleasant truths about themselves. "The wise men of our era did not realize at all that mind is the servant of impulse before it becomes its master and that the first effect of mind upon impulse is to make man more deadly in his lusts than the brute," he explained. If the brute in the forest lived by robbing and destroying other life, there was, at least, a form of harmony in the primitive struggle for survival, because each species survived. In the struggle for survival organized by commercial society, however, human self-consciousness and egotism transmuted "the brute's will-to-survive into the human will-to-power." Niebuhr conceded that capitalism did not create economic imperialism; every powerful nation was naturally driven into imperialism by its will to live. But capitalism did dramatically heighten the imperialism of the major powers and intensified their competition "to exploit the backward portions of the world." In his view, the Great War was fought, in part, to establish imperial rights to exploit Africa.

Modern capitalism was thus driven by its distinctive will to power to create its own peculiarly insidious forms of imperialism. The problem with capitalism was not a defect in the system or the egotism of individuals who profited from it, but the system itself. "The sickness from which modern civilization suffers is organic and constitutional," Niebuhr declared. "It is not due to an incidental defect in the mechanism of production or distribution but to the very character of the social system. . . . Private ownership means social power; and the unequal distribution of social power leads automatically to inequality and injustice."[14]

Niebuhr assumed that capitalism would never generate the degree of mass consumption that mass production required. He assumed that the concentration of economic ownership under capitalism ensured a severe maldistribution of wealth. For only a brief period of its history, he observed, it had been possible to think that the massive disparities of wealth created under capitalism would not engender social anarchy and disintegration. This period was over. Modern capitalism had created economic development of a kind, but at the expense of vulnerable masses in the dominant countries and in the nonindustrialized world. Capitalist society was now disintegrating on the contradictions of a system that required, but could not accommodate, continually expanding markets. "The technique of providing markets for both surplus products and surplus capital by lending surplus capital to permit the purchase of surplus goods has run its course in both English and American imperialism in less than a century," he declared. "Capitalism in short can exist only by attempting to universalize itself but it can live healthily only as long as it fails to do so."[15]

Liberalism and capitalism were finished. No amount of reformist tinkering could stop the world historical drift toward fascism. The only way to avert a

---

14. Reinhold Niebuhr, *Reflections on the End of an Era* (New York: Scribner's, 1934), 17–26.

15. Ibid., 27–28.

fascist takeover of the entire Western world, Niebuhr claimed, was for the West to turn to socialism. In 1930, he founded the Fellowship of Socialist Christians as a vehicle for his increasingly radical politics. Three years later, shortly before the inauguration of Franklin Roosevelt, Niebuhr announced that capitalism was dying the death it deserved. Capitalism was dying because it was "a contracting economy which is unable to support the necessities of an industrial system that requires mass production for its maintenance, and because it disturbs the relations of an international economic system with the anarchy of nationalistic politics." It deserved to die because it was unable to justly distribute the wealth created by modern technology. "There is nothing in history to support the thesis that a dominant class ever yields its position or privileges in society because its rule has been convicted of ineptness or injustices," he contended. "Those who still regard this as possible are rationalists and moralists who have only a slight understanding of the stubborn inertia and blindness of collective egoism."[16]

Reflections on the End of an Era elaborated Niebuhr's certainties about where history was going. Reformists like Roosevelt were kidding themselves. There was no third way. The chief tragedy of modern life was that modern technology made intranational cooperation and international reciprocity absolutely necessary, but capitalism made justice and cooperation impossible. Injustice, exploitation, and imperialism were not by-products of capitalist modernization but constitutive in the structure of capitalism itself. The ravages of capitalist injustice would therefore never be removed by moral effort, political reformism, or even the recognition that capitalism was destroying modern civilization. "If the social injustice which makes modern capitalism untenable is actually rooted in the very nature of capitalism it is not likely that capitalism will be converted to justice by logical and historical proof that social inequality will destroy it," Niebuhr asserted.[17] What was needed was a socialist revolution in which the church played a challenging, inspiriting, and chastening role.

Liberal Christianity was too soft on both political and theological counts to sponsor this project. "In my opinion adequate spiritual guidance can come only through a more radical political orientation and more conservative religious convictions than are comprehended in the culture of our era," he declared. Liberal Protestantism was too moralistic and too middle class to challenge existing relations of power. The transformative Christianity that was needed would be instructed by Marxism without capitulating to it. "If Christianity is to survive this era of social disintegration and social rebuilding, and is not to be absorbed in or annihilated by the secularized religion of Marxism it must come to terms

---

16. Niebuhr, "After Capitalism—What?" 203.
17. Niebuhr, *Reflections on the End of an Era*, 30.

with the insights of Marxist mythology," Niebuhr instructed.[18] Marx's theory of
the class struggle and his critique of the capitalist modes of production and
distribution were more valuable than all of the preachings of moral reformers.
Like liberal Christianity, however, Marxism typically betrayed its moral project
into an illusion, "for it believes that a kingdom of pure love can be established
in history and that its vindictive justice will be transmuted into pure justice." In
its own way—which Niebuhr somewhat misconstrued with his references to
morality and pure love—Marxism was as naive and utopian as liberal Christianity.
Marxism and liberal Christianity both failed to sustain the dialectic tension
between spirit and nature. To collapse the tension between the demands of spirit
and the impulses of nature was to open the door to authoritarian hubris. It was
to cover the impulses of nature with "the moral prestige of the spiritual" and
thus secure moral immunity for a regime or position that operated without moral
restraint. Thus did Marxism easily degenerate into a bad religion.[19]

Niebuhr's blasts against liberal Christian moralism drew ample fire in return.
The guardians of liberal Christianity responded to his torrent of books and articles
in the mid-1930s with a pained, bewildered, and sometimes furious counterattack.
The *Christian Century* lambasted the cynicism and "unrelieved pessimism" of
Moral Man and Immoral Society and claimed that "to call the book fully Christian
is to travesty the heart of Jesus's message to the world." Thomas and John Haynes
Holmes both criticized the book's "defeatism," while Francis Pickens Miller,
Yale theologian Robert Calhoun, and Union theologian Henry Van Dusen all
complained that Niebuhr's theology relinquished any notion of a divine presence
or power that could be socially transformative. According to the liberals, Niebuhr
ignored the teachings of Jesus, he had no theology of the church or the kingdom,
and he abandoned any faith that God's active presence in the world could be
socially regenerative.[20]

Reflections on the End of an Era drove this liberal counterattack to a climax.
Though Niebuhr's closing words on the experience of grace were appreciatively
noted by Morrison and Van Dusen, most liberals found the book an insulting
and equally cynical sequel to *Moral Man and Immoral Society*. To many of them,
the book was a slightly Christianized apology for Marxist politics, revolutionism,
and apocalypticism. To the Gandhian pacifist Holmes, it was not even slightly

---

18. Ibid., 135; cf. Reinhold Niebuhr, "Is Religion Counter-Revolutionary?" *Radical
Religion* 1 (Autumn 1935), 14–20.

19. Niebuhr, *Reflections on the End of an Era*, 136.

20. For reviews of *Moral Man and Immoral Society*, see Theodore Hume in *Christian
Century* 50 (January 4, 1933), 18; Norman Thomas in *The World Tomorrow* 15 (December
14, 1932), 565, 567; and John Haynes Holmes in *Herald Tribune Books*, January 8,
1933, 13. Reviews and correspondence cited in Richard Wightman Fox, *Reinhold Niebuhr:
A Biography* (New York: Pantheon Books, 1985), 142–43.

Christian. Holmes repeated the typical liberal criticisms of Niebuhr, repudiating Niebuhr's "growing dogmatism of temper, his flat repudiation of idealism, his cynical contempt for the morally minded, his pessimistic abandonment of the world to its own unregenerate devices, and his desperate flight to the unrealities of theological illusion." But the stock rejoinders weren't enough. Niebuhr had already withstood these charges. He repeatedly dismissed the heart of Christian faith while expecting people not to dismiss his claim to being a Christian. For Holmes, this was the crucial point, which he drove home with a vicious attack on Niebuhr's realism and faith. "It is clear enough that Jesus' serene trust in human nature, his stern acclaim of the moral law, his utter reliance upon spiritual forces, his sunny optimism, his radiant passion, would all have seemed a little ridiculous to Niebuhr," Holmes declared. "The latter would not have opposed the Man of Galilee, but he certainly would have despised him. And with what relief he would have turned to the 'cynical and realistic' Pilate. Pilate as the man of the hour!"

This attack on Niebuhr's personal faith cut him deeply. Holmes was ridiculing his claim to a faithful relationship with Christ. After Niebuhr protested against the "monstrous" unfairness of Holmes's assault, Holmes replied that he still counted Niebuhr as a friend. He explained that there was no reason why he and Niebuhr could not remain friends; the problem was only that Niebuhr was experiencing a shattering and pitiful "disintegration, confusion, and breakdown." His recent writings sadly revealed a "tragic instance of intellectual and spiritual bankruptcy" that Holmes was seeking, in friendship, to name correctly.[21]

With ample justification, Niebuhr told his real friends that he despised Holmes. The episode confirmed his feeling, however, that his next work needed to spell out his conception of emancipatory religion and, especially, his understanding of the teaching of Jesus. This feeling was assiduously reinforced by Van Dusen and by Niebuhr's brother, Yale theologian H. Richard Niebuhr, who urged him to stifle his politics and develop a deeper theological position. *An Interpretation of Christian Ethics* was Niebuhr's response. Though he later dissociated himself from the rigidly schematic dualism of this work, the book's fundamental attempt to clear a path between the backward dogmatism of conservative Christianity and the moralistic sentimentality of liberal Christianity remained at the center of his thought. *An Interpretation of Christian Ethics* never defined its key terms, it made inconsistent assertions about the relationships

---

21. John Haynes Holmes, "Reinhold Niebuhr's Philosophy of Despair," *Herald Tribune Books,* March 18, 1934, 7. For discussion of Holmes's correspondence with Niebuhr, see Fox, *Reinhold Niebuhr,* 153. For Holmes's subsequent declaration of his opposition to American intervention in World War II, see Holmes, "If War Comes, I Will Not Support It," *Christian Century* 57 (December 11, 1940), 1546–49.

between love and law, and it exaggerated the qualitative dichotomy between the private realm (in which love is the highest value) and the public realm (in which justice is the highest value). In subsequent years, when Niebuhr was pressed on these points, he conceded that the book contained numerous confusions and mistakes. It was a beginning attempt to define his theological realism. He refused to defend the book's exaggerated dualism or its claim that love transcended law in the objective sphere.[22]

Niebuhr's driving concern was never to elaborate a systematic theory on these questions, however. In the mid-1930s, his overriding concerns were to challenge the liberal ethos of America's cultural elites, to make the case for a socialist revolution, and to provide an alternative religious basis for radical politics. Having rejected the liberal belief in the inevitability of progress, he lurched to an equally extreme belief in the near inevitability of catastrophe. Only the socialist hope stood between a disintegrating West and fascism.

Niehbuhr as Antifascist

The liberal churches were slow to absorb the fascist threat to their survival. Niebuhr was fascinated and repelled by the spectacle of American church leaders who clung to their pacifism and their moralistic slogans while fascism advanced in Europe. Having served as a national leader of the pacifist Fellowship of Reconciliation during the 1920s and early 1930s, he was well acquainted with the moral sensibility that he now sought to discredit. As he observed in his 1934 announcement, "Why I Leave the F.O.R.," pacifists constituted "a kind of Quaker conventicle" in American Christianity. This was code for saying that most of the church's pacifists were middle-class moralists who prized their own purity over justice.

But the Quaker approach would attain neither moral purity nor justice. This was the crucial point. "Recognizing, as liberal Christianity does not, that the world of politics is full of demonic forces, we have chosen on the whole to support the devil of vengeance against the devil of hypocrisy," Niebuhr announced. He would support Marxist vengeance, knowing there was a devil in it, rather than allow the devil of hypocrisy to avoid conflict and preserve the status quo. Niebuhr allowed that he respected those "who try to have no traffic with devils at all." The problem was that those who refused to take sides made themselves accomplices to injustice and potential accomplices to greater oppression and genocide. Moral purity was an illusion. "In so far as we are radical

---

22. Cf. Niebuhr, "Reply to Interpretation and Criticism," 434–35; Paul Ramsey, "Love and Law," in *Reinhold Niebuhr: His Religious, Social, and Political Thought*, 80–123.

Christians we must find a more solid ground for the combination of radicalism and Christianity than the creed of pacifism supplied," he declared. Pacifism was too consumed with virtue to challenge anything, much less to make gains toward justice.

These were political arguments, however. Niebuhr's resignation from the FOR elaborated his reasons for believing that pacifism did not serve the struggle for justice. He did not challenge the constellation of religious assumptions that typically fueled Christian pacifist commitment. But this was the deepest source of liberal Christian conviction. Prominent Christian leaders such as Morrison, Fosdick, Holmes, Walter Russell Bowie, George A. Buttrick, Georgia Harkness, Kirby Page, John Nevin Sayre, Edmund Chaffee, and Richard Roberts embraced pacifism primarily on religious grounds. Their images of Christ, their conceptions of the way of Christ, and their understandings of the teaching of Jesus shaped their consideration of the moral choices available to them.

Niebuhr surmised that most mainline church members did not share the pacifism of their leaders. In the mid-1930s, however, virtually all of America's mainline Protestant churches officially declared that they would never support another war. Between 1934 and 1936, "the war business" was unequivocally renounced by the Disciples of Christ, the Episcopal Church, the Northern Baptist Convention, the General Council of Congregational and Christian Churches, both of the major Presbyterian churches, and both of the major Methodist Episcopal churches. The Southern Methodists were typical, declaring in 1935 that war making belonged "to the jungle period of human development" and that there was "not one single defensible argument" to justify Christian participation in war. The following year, the Northern Methodists agreed that warfare was "utterly destructive," that it was "the greatest social sin of modern times," and that going to war was a denial of Christ. The church therefore declared "that the Methodist Episcopal Church as an institution does not endorse, support or propose to participate in war." Niebuhr's break from Christian pacifism thus occurred at the moment of its dramatic ascendancy in American life. The specter of American Christendom actually embracing pacifism was startling and unsettling to Niebuhr. His resignation from the FOR spelled out his political reasons for spurning the Christian zeitgeist. He understood that his political arguments were not nearly enough to meet the challenge of antiwar Christianity, however. Any serious challenge to liberal Christianity's pacifistic ethos would have to challenge prevailing understandings of the teaching and way of Christ.[23]

---

23. Reinhold Niebuhr, "Why I Leave the F.O.R.," *Christian Century* 51 (January 3, 1934); reprinted in Reinhold Niebuhr, *Love and Justice: Selections from the Shorter Writings of Reinhold Niebuhr,* ed. D. B. Robertson (Louisville: Westminster/John Knox, 1992, c1957), 254–59; Methodist church statements quoted in Kirby Page, *Must We Go to War?* (New York: Farrar and Rinehart, 1937), 182–86.

Niebuhr turned to this task in *An Interpretation of Christian Ethics*. The book made a frontal assault on liberal Christianity's defining conviction that the teachings of Jesus were socially relevant. On one crucial point, Niebuhr allowed, Christian liberals such as Mathews had grasped the character of Jesus' teaching. Mathews argued that Jesus' teaching was not about getting justice, but about giving it. His mistake was in claiming that a relevant social ethic could be derived from Jesus' ethic of love perfectionism. "The ethic of Jesus does not deal at all with the immediate moral problem of every human life—the problem of arranging some kind of armistice between various contending factions and forces," Niebuhr declared. "It has nothing to say about the relativities of politics and economics, nor of the necessary balances of power which exist and must exist in even the most intimate social relationships."[24] The teachings of Jesus were counsels of perfection, not prescriptions for social order or justice. They had nothing to say about how a good society might be organized. They lacked any horizontal point of reference and any hint of prudential calculation. The points of reference in Jesus' teaching were always vertical, defining the moral ideal for individuals in their vertical relationship to God. Jesus called his followers to forgive because God forgives; he called them to love their enemies because God's love is impartial. He did not teach that enmity could be transmuted into friendship by returning evil with love. He did not teach his followers that it was their mission to redeem the world through their care or moral effort. These Gandhian admonitions were being read into the teaching of Jesus by liberal Christianity.

Niebuhr conceded that the pacifism of the historic peace churches and religious orders could be justified on biblical grounds. The Franciscans, the Mennonites, the Amish, the Brethren, and similar groups accepted the love perfectionism of Jesus' ethic in a literal way—and withdrew from active involvement in the public sphere. These communities grasped the vertical orientation of Jesus' teaching and tried to organize their entire lives in accord with its literal meaning. Niebuhr allowed that under these essentially sectarian circumstances some practical teaching might be derived from the teachings of Jesus. Resistance to violence would be forbidden. Rewards for work or service would be eschewed. Resentment toward those guilty of abuse or mistreatment would be forbidden. Love of enemies would be commanded. Niebuhr drove the point home. The love perfectionism of Jesus was a relevant impossibility for each individual in his or her life before God. No part of Jesus' ethic, however, could be seriously (or at least directly) applied to the problems of social relationships in a fallen world, outside the confines of countercultural sects.

The peace of the world in a fallen world could not be gained by following or appealing to the way of Christ. Neither could it be gained by turning the

---

24. Niebuhr, *An Interpretation of Christian Ethics*, 23, 105.

perfectionism of Jesus into a social ethic. Peace movements did not bring peace. Most peace movements were led, Niebuhr observed, by middle-class professionals whose social and economic privileges were made possible by the unacknowledged struggles and violence of others. The insertion of a perfectionistic ethic into public political discussions often imperiled the interests of justice.

Christian realism knew that the peace of the world was gained neither by moral absolutism nor by political idealism. Augustine's maxim capsulized the wisdom of Christian realism: The peace of the world is gained by strife. Niebuhr conceded that the teachings of Jesus might be employed to develop the negative or critical side of a Christian social ethic. The teachings of Jesus defined a perfectionistic ideal that judged all forms of social order or rule. Because he offered no guidance on how to hold the world in check until the coming of the kingdom, however, no realistic ethic could be drawn from Jesus' teaching. The central problem of politics was the problem of justice, which was always the problem of how to gain, sustain, and defend a relative balance of power. "The very essence of politics is the achievement of justice through equilibria of power," Niebuhr argued. "A balance of power is not conflict; but a tension between opposing forces underlies it. Where there is tension there is potential conflict, and where there is conflict there is potential violence. A responsible relationship to the political order, therefore, makes an unqualified disavowal of violence impossible."

This was the point on which liberal Christianity had been thrown into hopeless confusion. "It was impossible for the Church to escape the fact of coercion or to deny its necessity," Niebuhr explained. "Yet it felt that the Christian gospel demanded uncoerced co-operation. It therefore contented itself, as a rule, with the regretful acceptance of the fact and necessity of coercion, but expressed the hope that the Christian gospel would soon permeate the whole of society to such a degree that coercion in the realm of politics and economics would no longer be necessary." Mathews was his prime example. The past two decades had added nothing to Mathews's comprehension, Niebuhr incredulously observed. Mathews was still contrasting the gospel ethic of cooperation, peace, and love to the politics of revolutionary coercion. He was still claiming that Christianity was committed to a "moral process" of regeneration rather than any economic philosophy. Niebuhr acidly summarized this understanding of Christian faith: "Christianity, in other words, is interpreted as the preaching of a moral ideal, which men do not follow, but which they ought to."[25]

The illusions of soft utopians and the violence spawned by hard utopians framed Niebuhr's depiction of the necessary struggle for justice. He repeatedly blasted the soft utopianism of Mathews, John Dewey, and other liberals, "who

---

25. Ibid., 106–7, 116.

imagine that the egoism of individuals is being progressively checked by the development of rationality or the growth of a religiously inspired goodwill."[26] *Moral Man and Immoral Society* ridiculed the liberal faith that "with a little more time, a little more adequate moral and social pedagogy and a generally higher development of human intelligence, our social problems will approach solution."[27] Soft utopianism was soft because it failed to accept the inevitability of collective egotism and the necessity of using violence to make gains toward social justice. Because they refused to recognize the brutal character of all social relationships and the violence that permeated all forms of political rule, liberals confused and often impeded the historical struggle for justice, despite their glowing words of tribute to it.

The hard utopians renounced these illusions. Marxism was instructively realistic about the inevitability and necessity of violence, Niebuhr observed. Marxism clung to its own illusion, however, which was that communism was bringing about the end of history. In the mythology of modern orthodox Marxism, the Soviet state was the incarnation of the absolute. To a critical mind, Niebuhr observed, this element of Marxist faith had no more credibility than Dewey's willful faith in progress. Niebuhr was far more respectful toward the Marxist illusion than toward Dewey's rationalism, however. The closing sentences of *Moral Man and Immoral Society* explained his reasoning. While Soviet utopianism was indeed mistaken, Niebuhr argued, it was, nevertheless, "a very valuable illusion for the moment; for justice cannot be approximated if the hope of its perfect realization does not generate a sublime madness in the soul." Niebuhr conceded that the sublime madness of communist utopianism was dangerous because it promoted terrible fanaticisms. Hard utopianism needed to be brought under the control of reason. At the same time, however, Niebuhr hoped "that reason will not destroy it before its work is done."[28] Communist utopianism had important work to do in advancing the world-embracing struggle for justice.

Niebuhr began to grasp in the mid-1930s that communist utopianism was not a harmless illusion. The consolidation of Stalin's dictatorship gradually disabused Niebuhr from his hope that the Soviet regime could be liberalized. He remarked in 1935, "Here lies the root of Marxian utopianism and all the nonsense connected with it. The state will wither away!" But in the Soviet Union, this utopian faith was maintained through the repressive force of an increasingly powerful state. "I once thought such a faith to be a harmless illusion," he recalled. "But now I see that its net result is to endow a group of oligarchs with the religious sanctity which primitive priest-kings once held."[29] This realization later

---

26. Niebuhr, *Moral Man and Immoral Society,* xii.
27. Ibid., xiii.
28. Ibid., 276–77.
29. Reinhold Niebuhr, "Religion and Marxism," *Modern Monthly* 8 (February 1935), 714.

evolved into a principled anticommunist politics. For most of the decade, however, Niebuhr continued to defend the Soviet revolution's "progressive" gains and continued to dispute the common American attitude toward "communist violence." In Niebuhr's view, communism was dangerous not because it promoted or engendered violence, but because its understanding of the social problem was mistaken. The fundamental communist mistake was to assume that political democracy was merely an instrument of class rule. The fact that modern democracy grew out of the bourgeois revolutions did not necessarily mean that democracy was simply a ruse to control the masses. "The fact is that democratic principles and traditions are an important check upon the economic oligarchy, even though the money power is usually able to bend democracy to its uses," he wrote.[30]

Niebuhr did not doubt that democracy was overmatched in America and Europe by the power of what he called "the financial oligarchs." He nonetheless insisted that democratic political power offered at least some kind of check on economic power. His proof for the reality of democratic power was that, wherever the rule of the capitalist class was imperiled by democratic demands, the capitalists always sought to abrogate democracy. A telling example of this reaction was the current spectacle in Germany. What made fascism so deeply ominous, Niebuhr observed, was that it promoted a radical and absolute cynicism toward democratic institutions.

Liberal idealism was no match for the cynical evils of fascism or for the enormous savageries of Stalinism or capitalism. This untiring refrain filled Niebuhr's writings throughout the 1930s and early 1940s. Terrible things were happening in the world, yet liberals like Mathews and Dewey claimed to believe that reason and good will could solve the world's problems. Niebuhr summarized the tenets of this faith, in 1936, in a polemic that revealed his exasperation with its persistence. Liberals apparently believed, he wrote:

a. That injustice is caused by ignorance and will yield to education and greater intelligence

b. That civilization is becoming gradually more moral and that it is a sin to challenge either the inevitability or the efficacy of gradualness

c. That the character of individuals rather than social systems and arrangements is the guarantee of justice in society

d. That appeals to love, justice, good will, and brotherhood are bound to be efficacious in the end. If they have not been so to date, we must have more appeals to love, justice, good will, and brotherhood

e. That goodness makes for happiness and that the increasing knowledge of this fact will overcome human selfishness and greed

---

30. Niebuhr, *An Interpretation of Christian Ethics,* 117.

f. That wars are stupid and can therefore be caused only by people who are more stupid than those who recognize the stupidity of war

That such a faith could survive the terrors of the twentieth century was, to Niebuhr, a continual source of astonishment. He poured out an unceasing torrent of words to refute it. Liberalism was a form of blindness, he claimed. It was blind to "the perennial source of conflict between life and life, the inevitable tragedy of human existence, the irreducible irrationality of human behavior and the tortuous character of human history."[31] He repeatedly chastised Dewey, in particular, for purveying such nonsense. For more than twenty years, however, despite their considerable differences in temperament and philosophy, Dewey and Niebuhr shared the same politics. Both believed that authentic democracy required democratic socialism. Both believed that existing democratic gains could be saved only by extending democracy into the economic system. Both believed that only democratic socialism could achieve social justice, which Niebuhr defined as "a tolerable equilibrium of economic power." Both used the rhetoric of progress to claim that socialism was the next logical step for history to take. "Socialism is the logical next step in a technical society, just as certainly as capitalism was a logical first step," Niebuhr explained in 1936. "First private enterprise developed vast social progress. Then history proved that the private possession of these social processes is incompatible with the necessities of a technical age." For Niebuhr, as for Dewey, modern civilization thus faced the choice between retrogression or progress.[32]

By this reckoning, fascism was not a genuine historical alternative but "a frantic effort to escape the logic of history by returning to the primitive." Whatever victories it might win, it could produce only "pathological perversities" with no staying power. The real choice was between retrogression or socialism. "Socialism means the next step forward," Niebuhr argued. "That next step is the elimination of the specific causes of anarchy in our present society. The basic specific cause of anarchy and injustice is the disproportion of social power which arises from the private possession of social process."[33] For him, as for Dewey, social ownership of the means of production was "a minimal requirement of social health in a technical age."[34]

---

31. Reinhold Niebuhr, "The Blindness of Liberalism," *Radical Religion* 1 (Autumn 1936), 4.

32. Reinhold Niebuhr, "The Idea of Progress and Socialism," *Radical Religion* 1 (Spring 1936), 28. Niebuhr's "tolerable equilibrium" phrase appeared frequently in his writings, as in Niebuhr, "Ten Years That Shook My World," 545.

33. Ibid.

34. Reinhold Niebuhr, "The Creed of Modern Christian Socialists," *Radical Religion* 3 (Spring 1938), 16.

The metaphors of health and sickness recurred throughout Niebuhr's writings to describe America's social choice. He described socialism as "a primary requisite of social health" and repeatedly ridiculed Roosevelt's New Deal for its mistaken attempts to save a dying patient. It was not only obvious that capitalism was destroying itself, he insisted; it was also axiomatic that capitalism had to be destroyed lest it reduce the Western democracies to barbarism. Niebuhr continued to scorn the New Deal after it became apparent that capitalism was not disintegrating after all.[35] He assumed that socialism meant state socialism. While insisting that only socialism could save Western civilization, Niebuhr never undertook a sustained discussion or analysis of socialist economics. His penetrating reflections on the immorality and egotism of ruling groups were not applied to his own solution for modern society's ailments. Though state socialism would invest immense political and economic power in the hands of a self-interested, technocratic planning elite, Niebuhr did not reflect upon the implications of his social analysis for democratic state socialism. He assumed that history would either move forward to socialism or backward to a relatively unregulated capitalism.

This explained his attitude toward capitalism, which was dogmatic. Throughout the 1930s and early 1940s, Niebuhr's writings on capitalism assumed that without a socialist revolution, capitalist economic rationality defined reality. He thus repeatedly warned that Roosevelt's budget deficits were ruining any chance of an economic recovery. These warnings were issued throughout Roosevelt's first term, in the face of a New Deal economic program that reduced national unemployment from 25 percent to 14 percent and despite the fact that only once—in 1936—did Roosevelt's budget deficit exceed $4 billion. Niebuhr assumed that the serious choice was between nationalizing the means of production and balancing the federal budget. He therefore urged Roosevelt to raise taxes during the recession of 1937 and 1938—a move that would have exacerbated the recession and undercut Roosevelt's employment efforts. As it was, Roosevelt's anxiety about his administration's budget deficits caused him to reduce spending on employment in 1937—and helped to send the unemployment rate soaring to 19 percent the following year. Roosevelt was never committed enough to a Keynesian, social investment approach to generate a full economic recovery in the 1930s. By 1940, seven years after he took office, his employment programs had reduced unemployment only to 14.5 percent.[36]

---

35. For helpful discussions of Niebuhr's thinking during this period, see Arthur M. Schlesinger, Jr., "Reinhold Niebuhr's Role in Political Thought," in *Reinhold Niebuhr: His Religious, Social, and Political Thought*, 140; and John C. Bennett, "Reinhold Niebuhr's Social Ethics," in *Reinhold Niebuhr: His Religious, Social, and Political Thought*, 73.

36. Cf. William E. Leuchtenburg, *Franklin D. Roosevelt and the New Deal, 1932–1940* (New York: Harper & Row, 1963), 167–196, 326–348.

Niebuhr regarded even Roosevelt's cautious economic interventionism as futile and potentially dangerous, however. Though he maintained that radicals had to defend the New Deal "wherever it is under attack from reactionary critics," he was equally insistent that Roosevelt's deficit spending was a form of insulin, "which wards off dissolution without giving the patient health." The New Dealers were quacks who were forced to perpetuate "the fiction that government spending is a temporary measure," he charged. "This quackery must be recognized and exposed."[37] No long-range good would come from Roosevelt's "whirligig reform." There was no point in trying to reform capitalism. Capitalism was not to be played with or improved. It could only be accepted on its own terms or abolished. "If that man could only make up his mind to cross the Rubicon!" Niebuhr wrote of Roosevelt in 1938. "A better metaphor is that he is like Lot's wife. Let him beware lest he turn into a pillar of salt."[38] The metaphors captured Niebuhr's either/or schematism. As Arthur Schlesinger later remarked, however, it was not Roosevelt's task to cross the Rubicon, but to navigate his nation's way up the Rubicon.

Despite his scorn for Roosevelt's reformism, Niebuhr began voting for Roosevelt in 1936. He later explained that nothing could be more obvious than "that socialism must come in America through some other instrument than the Socialist Party." He regarded the emergence of a genuine farmer-labor party as one of the "inevitabilities of American politics" but warned that it might take another four to eight years to organize a national party.[39] In the meantime, the Democrats offered the only pragmatic choice for progressives. Though he agreed with his Socialist party comrade Norman Thomas that the New Deal was carrying out the Socialists' platform on a stretcher, Niebuhr held his nose and voted for Roosevelt because, unlike the Socialist party, Roosevelt was making actual gains toward social justice. In 1939, while insisting that Roosevelt's reforms were mere palliatives for a dying patient, he urged his readers to support the "genuine gains" of the New Deal, especially the Wagner Act. By the fall of 1941, he began to concede that Roosevelt's reforms were more than palliatives, allowing that "social justice will depend increasingly upon taxation schedules in the coming years." A few months later he retreated further from his Marxist either/or, declaring that taxation schedules "will have more to do with the kind of justice we achieve in our society than any other single factor." Niebuhr continued to

---

37. Reinhold Niebuhr, "New Deal Medicine," *Radical Religion* 4 (Spring 1939), 1–2.

38. Reinhold Niebuhr, "Roosevelt's Merry-Go-Round," *Radical Religion* 3 (Spring 1938), 4. Schlesinger comment in Schlesinger, "Reinhold Niebuhr's Role in Political Thought," 142.

39. Reinhold Niebuhr, "The Socialist Campaign," *Christianity and Society* 5 (Summer 1940), 4.

insist on the necessity of a socialist alternative long after he got used to voting for Roosevelt, however. In 1943, he explained that while he had given up much of his Marxism, it remained "quite obvious that these forms of 'private' property which represent primarily social power, and the most potent social power of our day at that, cannot remain in private hands. The socialization of such power is a *sine qua non* of social justice."[40] Niebuhr thus supported the semi-Keynesian policies of the New Deal while insisting that they represented a holding action on inexorable social forces. In the long run, he still believed, history would move either forward to socialism or backward to a purer capitalist barbarism. Though his writings in the early 1940s increasingly conceded that Roosevelt's liberalism was attaining some measure of genuine political control over the economy, it was only near the end of Roosevelt's life—after the Second World War took care of America's unemployment problem—that Niebuhr gave up his Marxist either/or.

It was Roosevelt's foreign policy in the years preceding the war that pressed Niebuhr into his first major reconsideration. Though he repeatedly denounced America's liberal intelligentsia for failing to face the bitter imperatives of international power politics, Niebuhr himself was slow to concede the necessity of Roosevelt's rearmament campaign against fascism. In 1937 he condemned Roosevelt's naval buildup as a "sinister" evil, declaring that "this Roosevelt navalism must be resisted at all costs."[41] The following year, he wailed that Roosevelt's billion-dollar defense budget "cries to heaven as the worst piece of militarism in modern history." He protested that the United States and England were drifting "into the worst possible foreign policy." These were rather strong accusations at a time when Europe and the United States were confronted with the rise of a heavily militarized Nazi movement in Germany, but Niebuhr spelled out the implication of his charge. Roosevelt's billion-dollar naval campaign was "the most unjustified piece of military expansion in a world full of such madness," he pronounced.[42]

---

40. Reinhold Niebuhr, "Crisis in Washington," *Radical Religion* 4 (Spring 1939), 9; Niebuhr, "Taxation and the Defense Economy," *Christianity and Society* 6 (Fall 1941), 5; Niebuhr, "Better Government Than We Deserve," *Christianity and Society* 7 (Spring 1942), 10; Niebuhr, postscript to A. T. Mollegen, "The Common Convictions of the Fellowship of Socialist Christians: A Suggested Statement as the Basis for Discussion," *Christianity and Society* 8 (Spring 1943), 28.
41. Reinhold Niebuhr, "Brief Comments," *Radical Religion* 3 (Winter 1937), 7.
42. Reinhold Niebuhr, "Brief Notes," *Radical Religion* 3 (Spring 1938), 7. For Niebuhr's pre-Munich assessments of the European situation and his arguments for collective security through a strengthened League of Nations, see Reinhold Niebuhr, "Notes on the World Crises," *Radical Religion* 1 (Autumn 1935), 6–9; Niebuhr, "Pacifism and Sanctions: A Symposium," *Radical Religion* 1 (Winter 1936), 27–30; Niebuhr, "Catholicism and Anarchism in Spain," *Radical Religion* 2 (Spring 1937), 25–28; Niebuhr, "European Impressions," *Radical Religion* 2 (Autumn 1937), 31–33.

Roosevelt's defensive military buildup was thus more evil than Hitler's crazed militarism. In his desperation to avoid war, Niebuhr counseled that the only justifiable American policy was to refuse to prepare for war. He assumed that collective security was the only realistic alternative to war. Though he did not advocate American enrollment in the League of Nations, he urged that the United States should enact neutrality legislation and voluntarily support League sanctions. He regarded the world's preparations for war and, in particular, Roosevelt's militarism as a repeat of the madness that triggered the Great War. Niebuhr clung to this analogy until the 1939 Munich crisis, which extinguished his hope that the League could prevent another world war. He perceived that the Munich accords merely whetted Hitler's appetite for conquest and fed his contempt for international law. In his words, "Munich represented a tremendous shift in the balance of power in Europe . . . it reduced France to impotence . . . it opened the gates to a German expansion in the whole of Europe . . . it isolated Russia . . . and it changed the whole course of European history." Niebuhr could no longer deny that Hitler was determined to conquer Europe. The following year, he confessed that Roosevelt "anticipated the perils in which we now stand more clearly than anyone else." In the light of recent events, he wrote, Roosevelt's military buildup had "proved to be conservative rather than hysterical." American socialists had been wrong to oppose Roosevelt and grievously wrong to condemn his rearmament campaign. The kind of idealistic isolationism that Thomas was still defending "plays into the hands of reactionary appeasement and . . . fails completely to understand the kind of peril which our civilization confronts." It was time to get serious. Though Niebuhr often found Roosevelt too cunning and devious for his own good, he urged that there could be no question, in 1940, about which presidential candidate the Christian Left should support.[43]

Niebuhr's Gifford Lectures were delivered at Edinburgh in the spring and fall of 1939, at the height of his alarm that liberal moralism and weakness were paving the way to fascism. *The Nature and Destiny of Man* elaborated his contention that the alternatives to a Christian view of human nature were false and dehumanizing. The Christian doctrine of sin was a desperately needed corrective to all variants of modern humanism-optimism and cynicism-nihilism. As Europe prepared for war, Niebuhr observed that "the fateful consequence in contemporary political life of Hobbes's cynicism and Nietzsche's nihilism are everywhere apparent."[44] His implicit theme in the Gifford Lectures was that modern European culture lacked the moral and intellectual resources to resist

---

43. Reinhold Niebuhr, "The London Times and the Crisis," *Radical Religion* 4 (Winter 1938–1939), 32; Niebuhr, "Willkie and Roosevelt," *Christianity and Society* 5 (Fall 1940), 5, 7.

44. Niebuhr, *The Nature and Destiny of Man* 1:25.

modern cynicism, nihilism, militarism, and will to power. Modern alternatives to Christianity were incapable of generating the realistic, reformist, spiritually powered defense of European civilization that was needed to save Europe from fascist barbarism.

The Nature and Destiny of Man generally took the high road, refraining from commenting upon the current threat to European civilization. At the same time that his Gifford Lectures were making a magisterial case for the relevance of a Christian vision, however, Niebuhr poured out a barrage of articles that dealt, often polemically, with the politics of rearmament, war, and spiritual dignity. He warned that democracy's inherent defects as a form of government "and the blindness of liberalism as the culture of democracy combine to make democracy almost defenseless against the concentrated fury which the totalitarian powers are unleashing."[45] Niebuhr praised Roosevelt for grasping the reality of the fascist threat to democratic civilization. The problem in 1940 was that America wanted to look the other way. America's liberal culture was unwilling to face the brutal threat to its own freedom, much less the freedom of other nations, posed by Hitler's militarism. Though American democracy desperately needed the inspiriting, challenging, morally formative faith that only a realistic Christianity could provide, American church leaders were perversely unwilling to meet the need.

In Niebuhr's view, the churches of America were sinking to a new low of moral insensitivity and cowardice. Pacifists like Morrison and Fosdick were covering America's fearfulness with a religious glow, claiming that staying out of Europe was the most Christian response to the war. "In the burst of hysterical self-righteousness which now consumes the energies of the American churches, it has not yet occurred to the Christian moralists than an attitude which is dictated or influenced by the neutrality of a nation in which those churches live, may be just as dubious from the standpoint of the 'example and teachings of Christ' as the identification of war with the Christian ethic," he wrote. Faced with a suffering world in which the victims of fascist slavery cried out for rescue, Niebuhr bitterly observed, American church leaders were identifying the Christian gospel with the slogan, "Keep America Out of the War."[46]

The *Christian Century* was leading this chorus with "hysterical" self-righteousness, in Niebuhr's estimation. Under the pressure of its obsession with

---

45. Reinhold Niebuhr, *Christianity and Power Politics* (New York: Scribner's, 1940; reprinted by Archon Books, 1969), 71.

46. Niebuhr, "Christian Moralism in America," 16–17; Niebuhr, *Christianity and Power Politics,* 33. For Niebuhr's defense of his attack on the self-righteousness of Christian pacifists, see Niebuhr, "An Open Letter," *Christianity and Society* 5 (Summer 1940), 30–33. Morrison's writings on the war were subsequently published in Charles Clayton Morrison, *The Christian and the War* (Chicago: Willett, Clark & Company, 1942).

keeping America out of the war, the *Century* was opposing Roosevelt's reelection (after supporting him in 1936) and warning that Roosevelt's political machine, his appeal to the poor and working classes, his militarism, and his charisma added up to fascism. According to Morrison, the American "road to fascism" was being paved by Roosevelt "even more smoothly than the road by which Mussolini and Hitler came to power." In May 1940, Morrison editorialized that it was not too late for America to convene a conference of neutral countries to formulate terms for an armistice. By the following month, he was not above pleading that it was too late for America to join the war. Hitler would either be stopped by the forces presently arrayed against him, the *Century* editorialized, "or he will not be stopped." Niebuhr responded that Morrison's conference proposal was "fatuous" and his foreign policy "completely perverse and inept." The *Century*'s isolationism was a "shocking revelation of the disposition of Americans to close their eyes to the magnitude of the tragedy which has engulfed Europe," he declared.

Niebuhr understood that Morrison and most liberal Christian leaders were not absolute pacifists. Morrison regarded himself as a pragmatic peacemaker. But in 1940 these distinctions had become irrelevant. If liberal Christianity could not rouse itself to fight against Nazi tyranny, it would never fight any evil aggressor:

> Most of our pacifism springs from an unholy compound of gospel perfectionism and bourgeois utopianism, the latter having had its rise in eighteenth century rationalism. This kind of pacifism is not content with martyrdom and with political irresponsibility. It is always fashioning political alternatives to the tragic business of resisting tyranny and establishing justice by coercion. However it twists and turns, this alternative is revealed upon close inspection to be nothing more than capitulation to tyranny. Now capitulation to tyranny in the name of non-resistant perfection may be very noble for the individual. But it becomes rather ignoble when the idealist suggests that others besides himself shall be sold into slavery and shall groan under the tyrant's heel.

The moral imperative of any authentically social Christianity was to fight the fascist menace, he implored, "lest we deliver the last ramparts of civilization into the hands of the new barbarians."[47]

In the name of gospel idealism, The *Christian Century* was advocating connivance with tyranny and preaching that slavery was better than war. To a "very, very sick" civilization that needed an inspiriting call to arms, liberal

---

47. Unsigned editorial, "No Third Term!" *Christian Century* 57 (October 16, 1940), 1273; unsigned editorial, "Defending Democracy," *Christian Century* 57 (June 5, 1940); Reinhold Niebuhr, "To Prevent the Triumph of an Intolerable Tyranny," *Christian Century* 57 (December 18, 1940), 1580; Cf. Niebuhr, "Editorial Notes," *Christianity and Society* 5 (Spring 1940), 10.

Protestantism preached weakness and purity. Niebuhr observed that it was nearly a universal dogma of American Christianity "that any kind of peace is better than war." In the present case, the terms of peace would require concessions to a tyrannical regime "which has destroyed freedom, is seeking to extinguish the Christian religion, debases its subjects to robots who have no opinion and judgment of their own, threatens the Jews of Europe with complete annihilation and all the nations of Europe with subordination under the imperial dominion of a 'master race.' " The appeasing moralism of America's dominant liberal culture was thus making the world safe for fascism. "It imagines that there is no conflict of interest which cannot be adjudicated," Niebuhr remarked. "It does not understand what it means to meet a resolute foe who is intent upon either your annihilation or enslavement."[48]

Morrison replied that he was not the one who was confused. For all of Niebuhr's words about liberal Christianity's moral confusion, its contortions, and its distortion of Christian teaching, it was he who twisted and distorted the gospel into a creed that killed for democracy. Niebuhr ascribed a moral meaning to Christianity that had nothing to do with the way or spirit of Christ. The terrible sin of liberal Christianity, by contrast, was to remain faithful to the gospel that Niebuhr had once embraced. Though he still considered Niebuhr his friend, Morrison decried the "flat repudiation of idealism" that filled Niebuhr's recent writings. What Niebuhr called realism was an abandonment of the world "to its unregenerate devices." The latter phrase marked the end of Morrison's relationship with his protégé. Niebuhr wrote to Morrison that their friendship was over. "Friendship does not exist by fiat but lives in life and deeds," he declared. "You can get no moral advantage of me by generously claiming to be my friend when I say a friendship is ended. This whole business of covering up ugly realities with words is of no avail." The defining conflict "between your side and mine," he told Morrison, was a symbol of the world's tragic conflict. "But you cannot admit being in it; for if you did where would your nice warless world be, which you are trying to preserve."[49]

The break with Morrison confirmed Niebuhr's resolution to create an alternative to the *Christian Century*. Mainline Protestantism needed a journal that spurned Morrison's moralism and denounced the pervasive liberal Christian sentiment that anything was better than war. *Christianity and Crisis* was Niebuhr's response to this need. Launched in February 1941, the journal featured an impressive roster of sponsors, including Bennett, Eddy, Will Scarlett, Henry Sloane Coffin, William Adams Brown, John R. Mott, and Francis McConnell, but in

---

48. Niebuhr, *Christianity and Power Politics*, 44, 68.
49. Morrison quoted in Harvey Cox, "Theology, Politics, and Friendship," *Christianity and Crisis* 46 (February 3, 1986), 16; Fox, *Reinhold Niebuhr*, 196.

its early years *Christianity and Crisis* was unmistakably a vehicle for Niebuhr's religious politics. The magazine's format was cloned after the *Christian Century,* but its editorial line called for a revolt against the *Century*'s isolationism. With the founding of *Christianity and Crisis,* Niebuhr signaled his seriousness about creating a realignment in American liberal Protestantism. His other journal was too radical and politicized to get a hearing among most pastors and church leaders. *Radical Religion* was renamed *Christianity and Society* in 1940, but Niebuhr understood that a socialist journal under any name could gain only a very limited readership. Though he kept the FSC and its journal alive, he turned his attention in 1941 to *Christianity and Crisis,* the *Nation,* and the newly formed Union for Democratic Action (UDA).

Niebuhr and Realpolitik

The UDA was a labor-socialist caucus composed mostly of New York social democrats and Marxists who were disgusted by the Socialist party's isolationism. Though he was already scrambling to find sponsors for *Christianity and Crisis,* Niebuhr took on the same task for the UDA, partly because his Christian friends were only one segment of the progressive interventionist movement that he envisioned. Theologians such as Henry Sloane Coffin and Henry Van Dusen were important to *Christianity and Crisis* and to Niebuhr's efforts to create a realistic form of social Christianity. At the same time, their opposition to Niebuhr's pro-labor politics confirmed his desire to create a labor-socialist movement that was internationalist, interventionist, and realistic about the role of force in the struggle for justice. With help from several unions and the *Nation* magazine, Niebuhr organized and became national chair of the UDA, which attracted such union leaders as Lewis Corey, Murray Gross, George Counts, A. Philip Randolph, and Franz Daniel. If it was not the genuine national-scale farmer-labor party that Niebuhr still hoped for, the UDA was, at least, a serious attempt to bring progressive intellectuals, activists, and unionists into a common struggle for justice and democracy. Niebuhr's conception of what this would mean was accepted by the UDA's leadership. It meant that the traditional socialist denigration of religion was out. It meant that communists would be excluded from membership. Above all in 1941, it meant that American progressives would exhort their nation to face up to its world-embracing struggle against fascism.

Niebuhr's writings of this period pounded on these themes. He noted that Marxism had once provided a powerful antidote to bourgeois moralism, but under the enervating influence of a dominant bourgeois culture, even Western Marxists were going soft. American progressivism of all kinds, both secular and religious, was indulging in a massive display of self-deception and cowardice. He warned that the consequences of American appeasement would cross the ocean. "If Hitler conquers Europe and penetrates into South America (which he may well do without much military effort) we would be forced to compete in the world with a slave economy, with an economy which would combine the efficiency of the modern machine with the low labor prices of slavery," Niebuhr wrote. His immense frustration with the pervasive influence of modern liberalism drove him to doubt whether world democracy would survive or whether it even deserved to survive. "The fact is that moralistic illusions of our liberal culture have been so great and its will-to-power has been so seriously enervated by a confused pacifism, in which Christian perfectionism and bourgeois love of ease have been curiously compounded, that our democratic world does not really deserve to survive," he declared.[50] The future of democratic civilization hung on the question whether American and European democrats would stir up their courage in the West's final hour.

Regardless of whether his country was at war or between wars, Niebuhr was rarely insensitive to the sins of nationalistic hubris, chauvinism, or jingoism. The United States had barely entered the war against Japan when he began to complain that American Christianity's pro-war pronouncements were nearly as insufferable as its earlier isolationism. "Many of the sermons which now justify the war will be as hard to bear as the previous ones which proved that it was our 'Christian' duty to stay out," he warned. From thousands of pulpits, American pastors were already proclaiming that the war had to be fought to secure a new international order in which war would be abolished. Niebuhr retorted that Japan's attack changed nothing in the moral content of the situation. "If the defeat of Japan can contribute to the building of a better international order, we ought to have declared war upon her and not waited for the attack," he argued. But if it was important not to fight with Japan for the sake of building a new international order, America should have refrained from striking back.

Niebuhr allowed that Americans needed the gospel's idealism to be saved from cynicism and complacency. At the same time, however, whether in peace or at war, Americans also needed Christianity's realism to be saved from sentimentality. For Americans, the dangers of a "perverse sentimentality" were always more potent, in his view—even in wartime—than the perils of cynicism.[51] American Christianity could go to war only if the war promised to bring about international harmony and peace. But this was not what war was about. Niebuhr struggled throughout the war to teach the church this lesson while maintaining

---

50. Reinhold Niebuhr, "Notes," *Christianity and Society* 5 (Autumn 1940), 12–13; Niebuhr, *Christianity and Power Politics,* 91, 47.

51. Reinhold Niebuhr, "Editorial Notes," *Christianity and Society* 7 (Winter 1941–1942), 9; Niebuhr "sentimentality" quote in Schlesinger, "Reinhold Niebuhr's Role in Political Thought," 144–45. Cf. Niebuhr, "Politics and the Christian Ethic," *Christianity and Society* 5 (Spring 1940), 24–28.

a balance between realism and idealism. He opposed America's insistence on an unconditional German surrender, argued against the Allied obliteration bombings of German cities, and worked to defeat the Morgenthau plan to make postwar Germany a greatly weakened power. Niebuhr equivocated on whether the atomic bombings of Hiroshima and Nagasaki were necessary, but at the end of the war he urged an organizational meeting of the World Council of Churches to adopt a policy of forgiveness toward the defeated Axis powers.

The pivotal works of Niebuhr's career, which were written during this period, elaborated his realist-leaning dialectic of idealism and realism. *The Nature and Destiny of Man* developed a theological understanding of human consciousness, guilt, sin, redemption, and history. His succeeding major work elaborated the dialectic of idealism and realism in explicitly political terms, presenting Niebuhr's theory of democracy. *The Children of Light and the Children of Darkness* (1944) contrasted the moral idealism of modern democracy's "children of light" to the moral cynicism of the fascist and Stalinist "children of darkness." Modern liberal democracy, in his reading, was largely a product of the idealism, individualism, and rationalism of its children of light, from John Locke to Adam Smith to Thomas Jefferson to John Dewey. Despite its considerable ideological diversity, Niebuhr argued, the liberal democratic tradition nearly always reproduced the dream of social harmony "to be achieved by a cool prudence and a calculating reason." This was the defining faith that united liberals, libertarians, social democrats, and other children of light.

Niebuhr countered that the central claims and hopes of this faith had been refuted by the "actual facts of social history." The central historical fact was that the static class struggle of feudal society had been transformed, under capitalism, into open warfare. Marxism was based on this truism. "Marxism was the social creed and the social cry of those classes who knew by their miseries that the creed of the liberal optimist was a snare and a delusion," Niebuhr wrote.[52] Marxist realism thus shredded the liberal pieties and conceits of bourgeois culture. Marxism exposed the stupidity of the liberal children of light. If Marxist philosophy was itself seriously mistaken, Niebuhr argued, it was not flawed in the way that liberals always claimed. The problem with Marxism was not that it promoted moral cynicism. As a critique of the ravages of capitalism and the illusions of liberal democracy, Marxism built upon the central facts of social history. This was not moral cynicism, but realism. To Niebuhr, the problem with Marxism was that it was not nearly cynical enough. Marxism was realistic only in its critique of capitalism; as a prescriptive social philosophy, it was utterly

---

52. Reinhold Niebuhr, *The Children of Light and the Children of Darkness: A Vindication of Democracy and a Critique of Its Traditional Defense* (New York: Scribner's, 1944), 31.

utopian. It had no constructive theory of the state and no conception of the necessity of coercion and violence under communist conditions. Marx actually believed that unequal power would be destroyed under a communist revolution. He actually believed that no state would be necessary under communism, in that all states were dictatorships. The same belief was echoed in Lenin's *Toward the Seizure of Power,* which declared that "all need for force will vanish" under communism, "since people will grow accustomed to observing the elementary conditions of social existence without force and without subjection."[53]

This was hardly the creed of a moral cynic, Niebuhr observed. While Marxism promoted a "provisional cynicism" toward the existing order, Marxist philosophy was ultimately a sentimental creed. Like their liberal enemies, Marxists were children of light who believed that conflict, power, violence, and coercion could be eliminated in a transformed society. "Their provisional cynicism does not even save them from the usual stupidity, nor from the fate, of other stupid children of light," Niebuhr wrote. This fate was to have their creed become the vehicle by which certain children of darkness imposed their demonic cynicism on captive populations.

The latter theme was downplayed in *The Children of Light and the Children of Darkness,* while the Soviet Union was America's wartime ally. It was not a new theme for Niebuhr, however. Though he could still write in 1937 that the Soviet revolution was "full of promise for mankind," he was chastened the same year when Thomas and Eugene Lyons both returned from the Soviet Union to report that Stalin's regime was a totalitarian police state that viciously persecuted all dissenters. Niebuhr's comrades in the democratic socialist Left compiled an extensive literature in the late 1930s that documented Stalin's crimes and condemned the tyrannical structure of his regime. Their reports were fiercely condemned by many liberals and fellow-traveling pro-communists, some of whom were Niebuhr's friends. By 1939, it was clear to Niebuhr which of his friends were right. "I feel genuinely sorry for my friends who seem to be under a spiritual necessity to deny obvious facts about Russian tyranny," he wrote. "The Marxian misunderstanding of man has contributed to the development of a tyranny in Russia which almost, though not quite, rivals fascist tyranny."[54] *The Children of Light and the Children of Darkness* was mild by comparison. Niebuhr remarked that Stalin's relationship to Marxism would probably be viewed in the future as

---

53. Ibid., 32.

54. Niebuhr quoted in John C. Bennett, "Tillich and the 'Fellowship of Socialist Christians,' " *North American Paul Tillich Society Newsletter* 16 (October 1990), 3; Eugene Lyons, *Assignment in Utopia* (New York: Harcourt, Brace and Company, 1937). On Thomas's anticommunism, see Gary Dorrien, *The Democratic Socialist Vision* (Totowa, N.J.: Rowman & Littlefield, 1986), 57–58, 64–68. Niebuhr statements on Soviet tyranny quoted from Niebuhr, "Ten Years That Shook My World," 543.

analogous to Napoleon's relationship to eighteenth-century liberalism. He was disinclined to view America's antifascist ally in a harsher light. Niebuhr would point a much harsher light on Soviet brutality, however, as soon as the war was over.[55]

Despite its brevity and its muddled discussions of communism, *The Children of Light and the Children of Darkness* was a major work. It expounded the dialectic of idealism and realism on which Niebuhr's subsequent writings were based. The children of darkness were wise because they understood the power of self-interest; they were evil because they recognized no law beyond themselves. The children of light were virtuous because they accepted the existence and authority of a law beyond their own will, but they were foolish because they underestimated the power of self-will. For Niebuhr, the mission of Christian realism was to create a new democratic culture that would unite realist wisdom and idealist virtue. Most modern arguments for democracy conceived it as the political system that people deserved on account of their human rights, their innate goodness, or both, he observed. This conception of democracy as the political system befitting human dignity was a typical product of liberal idealism. It was also a grave mistake. "The excessively optimistic estimates of human nature and human history with which the democratic credo has been historically associated are a source of peril to democratic society; for contemporary experience is refuting this optimism and there is danger that it will seem to refute the democratic ideal as well," Niebuhr wrote.[56]

Modern democracy needed a more realistic intellectual basis for the sake of its justification and its survival. This need inspired Niebuhr's most famous epigram: "Man's capacity for justice makes democracy possible; but man's inclination to injustice makes democracy necessary."[57] Niebuhr did not deny that the human capacity for fairness was often moved by genuine feelings of compassion and solidarity, but to him it was evident that all such feelings were mixed in human nature with more selfish motives. The crucial point was that democracy was necessary because virtually everyone was selfish. Because human beings were so easily corrupted by the attainment of power, Niebuhr argued, democracy was necessary as a restraint on greed and the human proclivity to dominate others. The common good was promoted not so much by appeals to morality and good will as by restraining the abuse of unequal power, especially through policies that democratized power.

---

55. Niebuhr, *The Children of Light and the Children of Darkness,* 33. For Niebuhr's later reflections on communism, see Reinhold Niebuhr, *Christian Realism and Political Problems* (New York: Scribner's, 1953), 33–42; and *Pious and Secular America* (New York: Scribner's, 1958), 39–60.

56. Niebuhr, *The Children of Light and the Children of Darkness*, x.

57. Ibid., xi.

This included economic power. Niebuhr acknowledged that in a commercial society, economic power overmatched other forms of social and political power. He further observed that in the United States the maldistribution of power in the economic realm far outstripped existing disparities of power in other realms. Rauschenbusch's social gospel theme still obtained: Without economic democracy, political democracy in America was an uncashed promissory note. In 1939 Niebuhr had written that the chief problem with liberalism was that it was "unable to move toward the economic democracy which is required to maintain its political democracy."[58] In 1944 Niebuhr still believed that Marxism was correct in emphasizing the "social character of industrial property" in opposition to the bourgeois insistence on its individual character.[59] In a technical age, a "tolerable equilibrium of economic power" required the socialization of property. He was still a socialist because he still believed that only socialism could democratize the base of American economic power.

The Children of Light and the Children of Darkness expressed Niebuhr's first doubts about the efficacy of industrial socialization, however. "Though Marxism is nearer to the truth than liberalism on the property issue, the socialization of property as proposed in Marxism is too single a solution of the problem," he wrote.[60] Liberalism regarded all individual power, including economic power, as limited and primarily defensive. Marxism correctly insisted on the social character of economic power, but failed to recognize the dangers of socialized power. In their contrasting ways, liberalism and Marxism both failed to recognize that property was a form of power that could be used, in either its individual or social forms, to promote a particular interest against the common good. Marxism claimed that socialization would eliminate the maldistribution of economic power under capitalism. It failed to comprehend, Niebuhr wrote, "that even universalized property may become the instrument of particular interest."[61]

Marxism thus failed to anticipate the rise of a self-interested new class of revolutionary oligarchs who would rule over the still disenfranchised masses in the name of their revolution. "Nowhere in Marxist thought is the combination of political and economic power in the hands of this oligarchy understood," Niebuhr observed. He did not regard this failing as a refutation of democratic socialism. If Marxism identified economic power too absolutely with private ownership, this mistake was not inherent in socialism. If Marxism failed to anticipate or comprehend the phenomenon of socialist dictatorship, not all dem-

---

58. Walter Rauschenbusch, *Christianizing the Social Order* (New York: Macmillan, 1919, c1912), 353; Niebuhr, "Ten Years That Shook My World," 545.
59. Niebuhr, *The Children of Light and the Children of Darkness*, 104.
60. Ibid., 106.
61. Ibid., 110.

ocratic socialists shared this failing. The social conditions that produced Marxism still cried out for democratic socialism. "Since economic power, as every other form of social power, is a defensive force when possessed in moderation and a temptation to injustice when it is great enough to give the agent power over others, it would seem that its widest and most equitable distribution would make for the highest degree of justice," he concluded.[62]

"It would seem" was a signal, however. By the mid-1940s, Niebuhr was holding onto democratic socialism more from desire than conviction. He regarded economic democracy as essential to social justice, but he was no longer certain that economic democracy was attainable. In 1947, the Fellowship of Socialist Christians changed its name to Frontier Fellowship. Niebuhr explained, "We continue to be socialists in the sense that we believe that the capitalist order of society stands under divine judgment and that there is no justice in modern technical society without a completely pragmatic attitude toward the institution of property. It must be socialized wherever it is of such a character that it makes for injustice through inordinate centralization."[63]

Niebuhr never retracted his view that social justice required greater gains toward economic democracy. He still believed that concentrated economic power in America overmatched American democracy. He still believed that only a more democratized economic sector could secure and deepen America's democratic gains. He was no longer certain that democratic socialism was attainable, however, and he no longer believed that Roosevelt's "whirligig reformism" was a mere palliative. Having conceived political economy as a choice between free market capitalism and state socialism, Niebuhr tried to defend a chastened democratic socialism stripped of its Marxist illusions. He still equated socialization with nationalization, however, and in the late 1940s he began to suggest that the New Deal–Fair Deal tradition might be creating the elusive third-way alternative he had previously dismissed as illusory.

Niebuhr's retreat from socialism was accelerated by the fact that he regarded democratic socialism as a system different in kind, rather than merely different in degree, from liberal capitalism. Having identified socialism with nationalization, he finally stopped calling himself a socialist in the late 1940s. Because decentralized economic democracy was not a serious possibility, the only serious alternative was a politics of the welfare state. Niebuhr edged steadily closer to this conclusion in the late 1940s. He worried that Truman was inadequate for the task and commented that "the common people of America returned a rather little man, not quite adequate for the job, to the White House rather than risk

---

62. Ibid., 113–14.
63. Reinhold Niebuhr, "Frontier Fellowship," *Christianity and Society* 13 (Autumn 1948), 4.

the dangerous joy ride of free enterprise which the Republican party promised the nation." Niebuhr still believed that the essential political task was "to distribute economic power and so to bring the undistributed centers of power under democratic control that the highest justice may be achieved." The question was how to bring about the highest possible degree of distributive justice. It was a pragmatic question. Niebuhr was already deeply embroiled in national Democratic party politics. In 1947, he folded the UDA into a new organization dominated by establishment liberals, the Americans for Democratic Action (ADA). Niebuhr's association with the ADA brought him into close contact with various prominent New Dealers and Congress of Industrial Organizations (CIO) officials, as well as journalists such as Joseph Alsop and Marquis Childs and politicians like Hubert Humphrey and Claude Pepper. These associations and his increasingly pragmatic mind-set brought him to the edge of Schlesinger's "vital center" politics. Niebuhr suggested in 1949, "There is a bare possibility that the kind of pragmatic political program which has been elaborated under the 'New Deal' and the 'Fair Deal' may prove to be a better answer to the problems of justice in a technical age than its critics of either right or left had assumed."[64]

This "possibility" became a truism for Niebuhr in the early 1950s, though he accepted it with little enthusiasm. His somewhat reluctant endorsement of welfare state capitalism tamed his passion for economic justice and his rhetoric about it. Following his lead, Frontier Fellowship changed its name in 1951 to Christian Action and reduced its economic plank to a vague political exhortation "to maintain a high and stable level of economic activity, avoiding inflation and depression." This was compatible with almost any conceivable Democratic or even Republican economic policy. The following year, Niebuhr explained that he no longer thought in terms of general positions regarding capitalism and socialism. He no longer viewed the question of economic justice in ideological terms but was now concerned only with "the effect of this or that policy in this or that situation; how well does this particular constellation of power satisfy the requirements of justice and of freedom?"[65] Niebuhr was testy with those, including the *Christian Century,* who worried that his politics were veering toward a middle-of-the-road conformism. The middle ground did not have to be a "dead center," he replied; throughout the world, the struggle for the middle ground was a fight for democracy. If the American situation was less desperate than

---

64. Reinhold Niebuhr, "Plutocracy and World Responsibilities," *Christianity and Society* 14 (Autumn 1949), 7–8. For Niebuhr's account of the formation and politics of Americans for Democratic Action, see Reinhold Niebuhr, "The Organization of the Liberal Movement," *Christianity and Society* 12 (Spring 1947), 8–10.

65. Reinhold Niebuhr and others, "Christian Action Statement of Purpose," *Christianity and Crisis* 11 (October 1, 1951), 126; Niebuhr, "The Anomaly of European Socialism," *Yale Review* 42 (December 1952), 166–67.

elsewhere in the world, the essential struggle in American politics was not different from other countries. It was to nurture and defend democracy. For Americans in the present world situation, to fight for democracy was to oppose communism militantly and to support greater democratic gains at home. For the remainder of his career, Niebuhr's writings emphasized these issues while playing down issues pertaining to political economy. He occasionally noted that capitalism had failed to solve the economic problem "short of war preparations," but he was no longer prepared to make much of the system's shortcomings.[66] He did not so much embrace welfare state capitalism as conclude that there was no serious alternative to it.

Though he aligned himself with a triumphant vital center liberalism at the moment of its greatest prestige, Niebuhr's sensitivity to irony, paradox, and injustice saved him from the excesses of American triumphalism. In a period when celebrations of American power, American democracy, and American prosperity became commonplace in American culture, he did not join the American celebrants. Niebuhr's acute sensitivity to the pitfalls of individual and collective pride made him an effective critic of America's chief conceits. He supported the Cold War while speaking out against McCarthyism and other forms of reactionary anticommunism. He repeatedly cataloged the evils of communism and called for a militant American resistance to communism without indulging American conceits about the righteousness of American society.

The irony of America's situation, he wrote in 1952, was that America could not be virtuous in its role as a world superpower "if we were really as innocent as we pretend to be."[67] In his view, America's long-cultivated myth of innocence made the United States the most reluctant major empire in world history. This predisposition carried certain moral advantages, including the lack of a classic imperial power lust. But America's illusions about its own righteousness were also dangerous to a world in which the United States was now a great power, Niebuhr warned. "We have been so deluded by the concept of our innocency

---

66. Reinhold Niebuhr, "Superfluous Advice," *Christianity and Society* 17 (Winter 1951–1952), 4–5; Niebuhr's "war preparations" quote cited in Richard Wightman Fox, "Niebuhr's World and Ours," in *Reinhold Niebuhr Today,* ed. Richard John Neuhaus (Grand Rapids: Eerdmans, 1989), 4. For Niebuhr's defense of Christian Action's liberal pragmatic politics, on the occasion of the organization's termination, see Niebuhr, "Farewell," *Christianity and Society* 21 (Summer 1956), 3–4. Commenting on the organization's various incarnations and its slow road to a vital center politics, Niebuhr remarked, "We ought always to have realized that even a very mild socialism would be irrelevant to the American political scene. The fluid class structure of the American society failed to provide the class resentments which furnish the socialist cause with its primary motive power."

67. Reinhold Niebuhr, *The Irony of American History* (New York: Scribner's, 1952), 23.

that we are ill prepared to deal with the temptations of power which now assail us," he observed.[68] Faced with the world-historical task of impeding the advance of Soviet communism, the United States was morally obliged to renounce its self-image of innocence.

To protect itself and its allies from communist aggression, the United States was morally required to become morally guilty through its acceptance of the burdens of empire. Niebuhr unfortunately gave little attention to the Third World and thus failed to appreciate Third World perspectives on America's perceived historical burden.[69] From his perspective, the crucial symbol of America's imperial burden was the problem of nuclear deterrence. The moral burden of possessing atomic weapons could not be renounced without imperiling the survival of the free world, he argued. Yet if these weapons were ever used (again), Americans would be covered with a terrible guilt. "We might insure our survival in a world in which it might be better not to be alive," Niebuhr wrote. "Thus the moral predicament in which all human striving is involved has been raised to a final pitch for a culture and for a nation which thought it an easy matter to distinguish between justice and injustice and believed itself to be peculiarly innocent."[70]

If innocence was an illusion, so was the commonplace American notion that American society already fulfilled the limits of attainable justice. Niebuhr generally failed to give the struggle for racial justice in America the priority it deserved. His books discussed racial prejudice and conflict only parenthetically, and for most of his later career his attention was absorbed more by the challenges of the Cold War than by America's racial problems. His shorter writings, however, did contain numerous forcefully written critiques of the ravages of American racism. He repeatedly noted that America's racial history of enslavement and oppression contradicted American claims to innocence. He recognized that the reality of pervasive racial injustice in America refuted the claim that America was a just society and impeded every effort to make American society juster.

To believe in one's racial superiority was to ignore the conditioned character of one's life and culture and to pretend that one's color, creed, or culture represented the final good, he observed. "This is a pathetic and dangerous fallacy, but it is one in which almost all men are involved in varying degrees," Niebuhr wrote in 1948. It could not be cured by social engineering, though government policies to prohibit racial discrimination and promote racial injustice were necessary. "The mitigation of racial and cultural pride is finally a religious problem

---

68. Ibid., 38.

69. Cf. M. M. Thomas, "A Third World View of Christian Realism," *Christianity and Crisis* 46 (February 3, 1986), 8–10.

70. Niebuhr, *The Irony of American History*, 39.

in the sense that each man, and each race and culture, must become religiously aware of the sin of self-worship, which is the final form of human evil and of which racial self-worship is the most vivid example," he argued. "Religious humility, as well as rational enlightenment, must contribute to the elimination of this terrible evil of racial pride."[71]

Niebuhr thus conceded that America's racial situation was an exception to his overall assessment of America's social situation. "We have regarded both liberty and equality as more easily realizable than they are," he wrote in 1957. "But we have realized them beyond the dreams of any European nation. We failed catastrophically only on one point—in our relation to the Negro race." But the American dilemma over race was "on the way of being resolved," he claimed, pointing to the Supreme Court's recent insistence on equality as a criterion of justice. With the Court's 1954 decision barring racial discrimination in public schools, Niebuhr proclaimed that "at last the seeming sentimentality of the preamble of our Declaration of Independence—the declaration that 'all men are created equal'—has assumed political reality and relevance."[72] If America's racial legacy was a singular blot on its otherwise uniquely successful venture in building a just society, Niebuhr believed that, even in this area, his country was beginning to fulfill the promise of its founding creed.

This left only the socialist critique. Niebuhr never disputed that America's claims to being a just society could also be challenged on distributive economic grounds. Throughout his later career, he advocated Left-Keynesian economic policies to raise the condition of the poor and fulfill the essential economic preconditions of equal opportunity. He frequently noted that economic power was not the only form of social power in American society, but he allowed that economic power remained the most fundamental and determinative form of power. Niebuhr gave virtually no sustained attention to economic issues in his later career, however. Though he frequently discussed the socioeconomic failures of Marxism, he gave only slight and usually parenthetical attention to economic policy questions in the last twenty-five years of his life.

The chief reason was that he believed that American politics had successfully outstripped the power of "the social creed which characterizes a commercial society." As Niebuhr explained in *The Irony of American History*, American policymakers over the past generation had developed a pragmatic approach to political economy "which would do credit to Edmund Burke, the great exponent

---

71. Reinhold Niebuhr, "The Sin of Racial Prejudice," *The Messenger* 13 (February 3, 1948); reprinted in *A Reinhold Niebuhr Reader: Selected Essays, Articles, and Book Reviews*, ed. Charles C. Brown (Philadelphia: Trinity Press, 1992), 71. Cf. Niebuhr, "The Mounting Racial Crisis," in *A Reinhold Niebuhr Reader*, 108–10.

72. Niebuhr, *Pious and Secular America*, 76.

of the wisdom of historical experience as opposed to the abstract rationalism of the French Revolution."[73] Though the principles of a hypercapitalist social creed continued to "dominate our theory," he conceded, the great achievement of the New Deal was to establish a substantial degree of social justice in America in the face of this creed.[74]

"We have equilibrated power," Niebuhr claimed. "We have attained a certain equilibrium in economic society itself by setting organized power against organized power. When that did not suffice we used the more broadly based political power to redress disproportions and disbalances in economic society."[75] Niebuhr was greatly impressed by what he called the "fluidity of the American class structure" and by the emerging American structure of countervailing labor, capitalist, and governmental power. In the economic sphere, the liberal reformers had been vindicated. The effective way to establish economic justice in America was not to eliminate private ownership but to develop countervailing forms of economic power. Because property was not the only determinant of social power or even the only determinate of economic power, it could not be the only source of injustice. Niebuhr's comparative silence on economic issues was reinforced by his belief that the welfare state was equalizing the various sources of domestic social power. Welfare state capitalism was attaining as much of the democratic socialist ideal of social justice as appeared to be attainable.

Niebuhr did not believe that justice was actually attainable under liberal capitalism or under any other socioeconomic system. The struggle for justice was never finished, not because a balance of power was impossible to achieve but because sin corrupted every gain toward perfect justice. Every gain toward justice contained the seeds of injustice within itself and thus reflected the dialectical mixture of good and evil motives that fueled even the most well-meaning human act. It followed for Niebuhr that the common good was therefore to be sought not by appealing to good will or to moral ideals of fairness or justice, but primarily by restraining human egotism through a democratic balance-of-power politics. In a just society, government would not so much attempt to meet the needs of the poor as attempt to ensure that the poor had enough power to meet their own needs. In his estimation, America's welfare state was succeeding in this task—even under a Republican administration—because it sanctioned economic freedom under the interventionist governance of a democratic state.

Niebuhr's realism thus became, in the 1950s, a form of apologetics for the status quo. He believed that the American welfare state was creating as much of a just society as one could realistically expect to attain. He believed that

---

73. Niebuhr, *The Irony of American History,* 89.
74. Ibid., 108.
75. Ibid., 101.

current efforts to promote racial integration were beginning to overcome the entrenched evils of American racism. Under the pressure of his concern to thwart the spread of communism, he gave comparatively short shrift to the challenges of America's socioeconomic and racial problems. He feared that Americans were too impatient and immature to endure the hardships of what John F. Kennedy later called "a long twilight struggle, year in and year out" to defeat world communism. Throughout the 1950s, despite a stroke that left him with greatly diminished energy, Niebuhr labored with considerable success to mobilize liberal and church support for a policy of vigorous anticommunist containment. Through his books and articles, his speaking tours, his consultations with government officials, and his participation in Americans for Democratic Action and other organizations, he worked assiduously to establish bipartisan support for an anticommunist foreign policy.

The Niebuhr later revered by neoconservatives was the Niebuhr of this period, whose highly masculine rhetoric of power, duality, and realism promoted an aggressive anticommunist politics. When neoconservatives later claimed that they became conservatives only because "real" liberalism no longer existed, it was Niebuhr, above all, whom they invoked as the prototype of real liberalism. Real liberalism was not the feminized progressivism of Jane Addams, Eleanor Roosevelt, George McGovern, and most liberal church leaders. Real liberalism did not blur the line between private and public spheres, or imagine that conflict and violence could be eliminated, or struggle for justice on the basis of moral appeals. Real liberalism would never proclaim that the personal was the political or that cooperation could replace competition. Most importantly, real liberalism would never shrink from fighting against communism, which Niebuhr defined in 1953 as "an organized evil which spreads terror and cruelty throughout the world and confronts us everywhere with faceless men who are immune to every form of moral and political suasion." Through his realistic insistence on the pervasiveness of sin, the inevitability of conflict, the limits of political action, and the necessity of a militarized anticommunism, Niebuhr defined and epitomized, for neoconservatives, the kind of liberalism that was still needed. This rendering of Niebuhr's work and career was reinforced by Christian Leftists who viewed Niebuhr chiefly as the figure who turned American Christian ethics into a form of Cold War apologetics. In John Swomley's typical indictment, Niebuhr provided "the religious rationale for the military foreign policy that created the contemporary American empire and the policy of global intervention culminating in the war in Vietnam."[76]

---

76. Cf. Michael Novak, "Needing Niebuhr Again," *Commentary* 54 (September 1972), 52–61; Novak, "Reinhold Niebuhr: Model for Neoconservatives," *Christian Century* 103 (January 22, 1986), 71; James Nuechterlein, "The Feminization of the American

Niebuhr's postwar writings provided ample proof texts for these essentialist readings of his work. The chief effect of his writing and sermonizing in the 1950s was to wed American Protestantism to America's anticommunist struggle for the world. Christian realism became fundamentally a form of Cold War politics. In Niebuhr's own understanding of his work, however, Christian realism was never a fixed system or ideology, but a dynamic orientation that responded to social challenges of the moment. In the early 1950s, while America was convulsed over McCarthyism and FBI agents dug for incriminating details about Niebuhr's radical past, Niebuhr portrayed "communism" as a devouring totalitarian monolith committed to world domination. Like many of his liberal ADA friends, especially Bennett and Schlesinger, Niebuhr detested Joseph McCarthy and was determined not to allow him to monopolize the anticommunist issue. In the early 1950s, under the pressure of his concern to prove that ADA liberals were not soft on communism, Niebuhr demonized communists and implicitly condoned parts of McCarthy's campaign to smoke communists out of American government, education, and religion. Niebuhr strongly supported the government's execution of the Rosenbergs for stealing atomic secrets and, in a 1953 article for *Look* magazine, he carelessly and mistakenly claimed that McCarthy's assistant, J. B. Matthews, had accurately identified more than a dozen pro-communist fellow travelers in the churches.

Niebuhr later apologized for these excesses. Even at the height of his anticommunist fervor, however—which lasted until McCarthy self-destructed in 1954—he was never the kind of anticommunist who insisted that America must fight anticommunist wars around the world. Unlike many professional anticommunists, he did not back away from attacking McCarthy's viciousness or from denouncing the militaristic hubris of conservatives who wanted to "roll back the Soviet empire." He opposed the kind of anticommunism that conceived the Cold War primarily in military terms. Niebuhr's writings on the Cold War emphasized, rather, that Soviet communism needed to be understood and resisted primarily as a religious phenomenon. As he explained in his 1953 essay "Why Is Communism So Evil?" the evil of communism flowed "from a combination of political and 'spiritual' factors, which prove that the combination of power and pride is responsible for turning the illusory dreams of yesterday into the present nightmare, which disturbs the ease of millions of men in our generation." The following

---

Left," *Commentary* 84 (November 1987), 43–47. Niebuhr quote in Reinhold Niebuhr, *Christian Realism and Political Problems* (New York, Scribner's, 1953), 34; Swomley quote in John M. Swomley, Jr., *American Empire: The Political Ethics of Twentieth Century Conquest* (London: Macmillan, 1970), 34. For a similar critique of Niebuhr's legacy, see Bill Kellermann, "Apologist of Power: The Long Shadow of Reinhold Niebuhr's Christian Realism," *Sojourners* 16 (March 1987), 15–20.

year he phrased the matter more pointedly, in a statement that capsulized his perception of the Cold War: "We are embattled with a foe who embodies all the evils of a demonic religion," Niebuhr wrote. "We will probably be at sword's point with this foe for generations to come."[77]

This view of Soviet communism as a perverted religion shaped Niebuhr's understanding of how the Cold War should be waged. It would be a tragic mistake, he argued in 1952, to conceive and oppose communism as another form of Nazism. "Nazism was a morally cynical creed which defied every norm of justice," he observed. But communism was a "morally utopian creed" that was devoted to the establishment of a new universal order "rather than to the supremacy of a race or nation." Unlike the Nazi creed, communism was not malevolent in its intention, but this fact made communism more dangerous to the world than fascism had ever been. The moral utopianism of communist faith gave communism a universal appeal in the Third World that fascist racism never had. For the same reason, communism was capable of creating greater and longer-lasting evils in the world than fascism. This truism could be understood, Niebuhr argued, only "if it is realized how much more plausible and dangerous the corruption of the good can be in human history than explicit evil." It followed for him that the recent emergence of the world communist threat could be compared, not to the Nazi menace—which could be frontally attacked—but only to the rise of militant Islam in the high Middle Ages.[78]

The analogy was religiously objectionable but politically and strategically revealing. The mistakes of the Crusaders needed to be taken into account in figuring out how to fight off communism. What was needed was not a crusading mentality that tried to wipe out a deeply entrenched, universalistic world religion. Niebuhr recalled that the Islamic power disintegrated not from external pressure by its enemies but primarily from its inner contradictions and corruptions. The sultan of Turkey was ultimately unable to sustain his double role as spiritual leader of the Islamic world and head of the Turkish state. "Stalin has this same double role in the world of communist religion," Niebuhr observed. He predicted that Soviet communism would eventually disintegrate, whether led by Stalin or a successor, under the strain of the same structural contradictions.

Like his friend and political associate George Kennan, Niebuhr believed that the Soviet regime would eventually self-destruct on the contradictions and failures of its unworkable system. The purpose of containment strategy was to

77. Reinhold Niebuhr, "Communism and the Protestant Clergy," *Look* 17 (November 17, 1953), 37; *Christian Realism and Political Problems,* 42; and "The Peril of Complacency in Our Nation," *Christianity and Crisis* 14 (February 8, 1954), 1.

78. Reinhold Niebuhr, *The Irony of American History* (New York: Scribner's, 1952), 128.

keep enough diplomatic and military pressure on the Soviets to accelerate the implosion of the Soviet state. Kennan was the putative architect of American containment strategy but, like Niebuhr, an opponent of heavily militarized approaches to anticommunism. In 1947, he argued that if the United States kept the pressure on for perhaps ten to fifteen years and showed itself to be a more attractive alternative, the monolithic discipline of the governing Soviet party could be undermined. "And if disunity were ever to seize and paralyze the Party, the chaos and weakness of Russian society would be revealed in forms beyond description," he wrote. "Soviet Russia might be changed overnight from one of the strongest to one of the weakest and most pitiable of national societies."[79]

Niebuhr's early formulations of this belief were less eerily prophetic than Kennan's, but prescient nonetheless. He argued in 1952 that militaristic anti-communists misunderstood the nature of the enemy. "If we fully understand the deep springs which feed the illusions of this religion, the nature of the social resentments which nourish them and the realities of life which must ultimately refute them, we might acquire the necessary patience to wait out the long run of history while we take such measures as are necessary to combat the more immediate perils," he wrote. Soviet communism was an evil, conspiratorial, universalist religion that would eventually self-destruct if the West maintained a self-respecting and patient strategy of containment.[80]

The emergence of a more pragmatic Soviet regime in the late 1950s moved Niebuhr to reconsider both ends of this argument. In 1958, faced with the apparent success of Soviet economic reconstruction and the Soviet Union's unarguable achievements in science, technology, and military expansion, Niebuhr began to doubt that Soviet communism was incapable of sustaining itself indefinitely. At the same time, he began to question the inevitability of the Cold War. If he was no longer certain that communism would eventually self-destruct, he also no longer believed that a state of warfare between the two superpowers was inevitable or sensible. In 1958, "as a kind of trial balloon to initiate discussion," Niebuhr's coeditor and closest colleague, John C. Bennett, proposed that America should give up its "perpetual official moral diatribe" against world communism. "We should accept the fact that communism is here to stay in at least two great countries, that in them it is a massive human experiment which will have its chance," Bennett urged. The communist turn was irreversible but not unchangeable.

To the surprise of many, Niebuhr was moving to the same view. He endorsed the thrust of Bennett's editorial with a declaration of his own. The fate of the

---

79. X [George F. Kennan], "The Sources of Soviet Conduct," *Foreign Affairs* 25 (July 1947), 579–80.

80. Niebuhr, *The Irony of American History,* 129.

world "depends upon our capacity to leaven the lump of our own orthodox conceptions of an changeable Communist orthodoxy," he asserted. Though the communists still officially believed that the logic of history assured their eventual triumph, Niebuhr insisted that "we had better, for the sake of the world, recognize that this belief is not tantamount to a policy of plotting for world domination by any possible means." Soviet communism was not an immutable monolith, an overpowering enemy, a world-threatening conspiracy, or an enemy with which America could not learn to coexist. The following year, in *The Structure of Nations and Empires,* Niebuhr made a case for American-Soviet coexistence, urging that foreign policy realism in the current world situtation required greater flexibility in America's attitude toward the Soviet government. What was needed, he wrote, was "a less rigid and self-righteous attitude toward the power realities of the world and a more hopeful attitude toward the possibilities of internal development in the Russian despotism."[81]

Christian realists conducted a lively debate in the late 1950s over these inherently arguable questions of interpretation and strategy. Many of Niebuhr's associates disputed his arguments for coexistence and his insistence that communism was capable of making internal reforms. Some of them clung to his earlier belief that Soviet communism was an evil but self-destructive religion that had to be waited out; others claimed that both positions were too passive. Niebuhr's turn toward coexistence was influenced by Kennan, who maintained his belief that the Soviet system was inherently unstable while also urging a policy of coexistence. Kennan and Niebuhr both worried throughout the 1950s that "containment" was acquiring an overly militarized meaning in American policy, that American policymakers often overestimated Soviet political, economic, and military strength, and that policymakers such as John Foster Dulles were mythologizing the Cold War into a holy war.

The latter development was especially troubling to Niebuhr in that his own writings were often quoted to support America's hardening Cold War mythology. It was deeply frustrating to Niebuhr that America's most famous self-described Christian realist advocated massive nuclear retaliation and made unctuous pronouncements about the Cold War as a struggle between good and evil. Dulles had come into national prominence during World War II, when he chaired the Federal Council of Churches' Commission for a Just and Durable Peace. He and Niebuhr had worked together (unsuccessfully) to urge the fledgling World Council

---

81. John C. Bennett, "A Condition for Coexistence," *Christianity and Crisis* 18 (April 28, 1958), 53–54; Reinhold Niebuhr, "Uneasy Peace or Catastrophe," *Christianity and Crisis* 18 (April 28, 1958), 54–55; and *The Structure of Nations and Empires: A Study of Recurring Patterns and Problems of the Political Order in Relation to the Unique Problems of the Nuclear Age* (New York: Charles Scribner's Sons, 1959), 282.

of Churches to adopt a policy of forgiveness toward the defeated Axis powers. Dulles's performance as secretary of state in the Eisenhower administration forced Niebuhr to rethink what Cold War realism should mean, however. Though Dulles was adept at quoting Niebuhr, Niebuhr felt that Dulles overmoralized the Cold War and relied too much on the threat of retaliatory nuclear force. The latter failing caused Dulles to ignore immediate challenges to international stability, especially the 1956 Suez crisis. In Niebuhr's view, realism did not indulge in nuclear brinkmanship, mythologize the Cold War, or adopt an arrogant disregard for the configurations of power among smaller countries. It did not use the nuclear threat as a substitute for aggressive, imaginative, persistent diplomacy. In the mid-1950s, partly in reaction to the undesirable connotations that "Christian realism" was acquiring, Niebuhr began to dissociate himself from his own contributions to Cold War mythology. He told friends that Eisenhower and Dulles were too stupid to be entrusted with America's fate. Niebuhr's associates were divided in their assessment of Dulles's management of the Cold War. Some did not share Niebuhr's fervently partisan dislike for Republicans. On the morning after Eisenhower's election to the presidency in 1952, an acutely distressed Niebuhr told his daughter Elisabeth, "You poor girl, you've never lived under a Republican administration, you don't know how terrible this thing is going to be." In the succeeding years, Dulles's simultaneously threatening and passive approach to foreign affairs confirmed Niebuhr's feelings for Republicans.

The Niebuhrians never doubted that they could manage world affairs better than Dulles. For all of their disagreements with Dulles and each other over foreign policy, however, no single issue during Eisenhower's administrations provoked lasting divisions within Niebuhr's circle or even between them and the Republican establishment. The Niebuhrians had few substantive disagreements with each other in the 1950s over pressing foreign policy decisions. The strength of America's basic foreign policy consensus was signified by their agreement as to how containment should be interpreted. Like most of his political associates, including Schlesinger, Kennan, Bennett, Hans Morgenthau, Kenneth W. Thompson, and Paul Ramsey, Niebuhr supported America's intervention in Korea and its policy of nuclear deterrence. The Soviet invasion of Hungary in 1956 confirmed his belief that the United States had no other choice regarding nuclear policy. Nuclear disarmament was impossible, he wrote, because the Soviets would accept only an agreement that drove America out of Europe. These conclusions were generally shared by American church leaders and academics in the 1950s, not least because of Niebuhr's towering influence over contemporary Christian ethics.[82]

---

82. Niebuhr's reaction to the 1952 election quoted in Elisabeth Sifton, "Remembering Reinhold Niebuhr," *World Policy Journal* 10 (Spring 1993), 87; quote on the necessity

Christian realism became far more difficult to define in the turbulence of the succeeding decade, however. Not long after they celebrated the election of a kindred spirit to the presidency, Niebuhr's extended group of religious and secular associates began to splinter on both strategic and tactical issues. John F. Kennedy and several of his advisors, especially McGeorge Bundy, openly admired Niebuhr's work and paid frequent tribute to him as the theorist who had shown how to combine Christianity with political realism. Several of Niebuhr's associates, including Schlesinger and Paul Nitze, became important figures in the Kennedy administration. For his part, Niebuhr supported Kennedy and praised his warnings about the burdens of power, while harboring misgivings about Kennedy's depth and, especially, his personal morality. Kennedy's maneuvers against Cuba subsequently gave him deeper misgivings. Niebuhr denounced the Bay of Pigs fiasco and Kennedy's subsequent embargo on Cuban products. Kennedy's militaristic anticommunism "has enabled Castro to blame all his economic problems on [us]," he argued. "It has aroused the latent anti-Yankee resentment and fear of our power throughout the Hemisphere."[83] The ascension of a Niebuhr-quoting liberal-realist-anticommunist to the presidency gave Niebuhr particular occasion to question America's use of its power in the world.

The Berlin crisis heightened Niebuhr's doubts about the meaning of realism in his country's foreign policy. The Soviets walled off East Berlin in 1961 and forced Kennedy to decide whether the wall should be allowed to stand. American policymakers feared that destroying the wall might spark a Soviet nuclear or conventional force attack. Niebuhr and Bennett agreed that if the Soviets launched a nuclear attack, America would have to reciprocate. The question was whether the United States should respond to a conventional force attack with nuclear weapons.

In 1950, Niebuhr and Bennett had defended America's right to use nuclear weapons in a first strike to destroy invading Russian tanks. In 1961, faced with a situation that brought the nuclear superpowers into a possible nuclear exchange, they reconsidered their position on the morality of nuclear deterrence. Bennett took the lead. He noted that American ethicists had written very little in the past

---

of the nuclear deterrent in Reinhold Niebuhr, "Our Moral Dilemma," *The Messenger* (November 5, 1957), 5. For Kennan's explanation of the development of his view on the Cold War, see George F. Kennan, *The Nuclear Delusion: Soviet-American Relations in the Atomic Age* (New York: Pantheon Books, 1982), ix–xxx. For an important account of Niebuhr's role in forging a Cold War foreign policy consensus, see Walter LaFeber, *America, Russia and the Cold War, 1945–1966* (New York: John Wiley & Sons, 1967). I am grateful to John C. Bennett for his insights and recollections regarding this period of Niebuhr's career: author's interview with Bennett, January 2, 1993.

83. Reinhold Niebuhr, "Drama on the Cuban Stage," *New Leader* 38 (March 5, 1962), 11.

decade about the possibility that America could be driven to incinerate much of the planet. He attributed this ethical silence to a widespread fatalism that assumed that there were no genuine moral choices to be made in the nuclear arena. Since the obliteration bombings of World War II, he noted, most American Christian ethicists had accepted the premise that moral questions had to be subordinated to strategic questions during war. This assumption was widely identified with Niebuhrian realism, but Bennett questioned the premise and its morally fatalistic consequences. Christian realism had to begin to address the moral dilemmas of American nuclear policy. "The idea of nuclear retaliation raises moral problems that have not been given enough attention," he urged. It was one thing to grant the moral legitimacy of nuclear weapons as a deterrent, but this principle did not necessarily sanction any particular doctrine about retaliation, first use, countervalue warfare, or the use of tactical weapons. Bennett offered an opening proposal. "For us to attack the cities of Russia would be a great atrocity," he asserted. "No moral commitment can oblige us to perpetrate such an atrocity. But it would be almost as evil a deed to take the step that might initially involve the use of tactical nuclear weapons, knowing that it would be almost sure to result in the total conflict in which we would be both the destroyers and the destroyed."

This critique of tactical first use pushed Christian realism into new territory, but Niebuhr's response to Bennett quickly surpassed Bennett's formulation. "The first use of the nuclear weapon is morally abhorrent and must be resisted," he announced. Niebuhr doubted that a democratic society could survive a nuclear triumph. "Could a civilization loaded with this monstrous guilt have enough moral health to survive?" he asked. Without reflecting on the fact that American democracy had already "survived" Hiroshima and Nagasaki, he left the question hanging. The following year, Niebuhr declared that it could be time "to take some risks for peace comparable to our ever more dangerous risks in the game of deterrence." The United States needed to adopt a more flexible position on disarmament, he urged. It could begin by taking certain unilateral initiatives, such as dropping America's unrealistic insistence on foolproof inspection.[84]

The Niebuhr-Bennett shift on nuclear policy set off a round of position taking among Niebuhrians. Paul Ramsey argued that only conventional weapons could be used in retaliation; Paul Tillich supported the Niebuhr-Bennett arguments against nuclear first use while defending the moral right to retaliate with tactical weapons against a tactical attack; Hans Morgenthau declared "without qualification" that no resort to nuclear weapons could ever be morally justified; Norman

---

84. John C. Bennett and Reinhold Niebuhr, "The Nuclear Dilemma: A Discussion," *Christianity and Crisis* 21 (November 13, 1961), 200–202; Niebuhr, "Logical Consistency and the Nuclear Dilemma," *Christianity and Crisis* 22 (April 2, 1962), 48.

Gottwald contended that nuclear weapons could be morally used but only against military targets. Other Niebuhrians expressed their stunned disbelief that Niebuhr was sanctioning any form of this debate. "If we declare we shall not use thermonuclear weapons except in the ultimate defense, we have assisted the Soviet Union in plotting a campaign of expansion and imperialism," Kenneth W. Thompson warned. "I would prefer the moralist to master a strategy of restraint, silence where policy dictates, and self-discipline rather than merely to protest with all right-thinking men the grave hazards of the nuclear age." Carl Mayer went further than Thompson, claiming that the Niebuhr-Bennett opposition to first use and the targeting of cities would increase the danger of a nuclear war. The only way to peace, he reminded the realists, was full preparation for war. "It seems that the days of what came to be known as Christian realism are about over in America," Mayer lamented. "But it is somewhat ironical that the very magazine that used to be the staunchest champion of such a realism should today, in the matter of the most crucial political problem of the age, espouse views that hardly differ from those of *The Christian Century.*" Though Niebuhr continued to claim that nuclear deterrence was preserving the world's peace, his new positions on the morality of deterrence undermined the force of nuclear realist doctrine and, by extension, made it more difficult to define or defend a policy of anticommunist containment. Niebuhr conceded in response to his critics that his position was inconsistent but explained that he was driven to it by his fear that the current balance of terror was unsustainable.[85]

Niebuhr against the War in Vietnam

The deeper split between Niebuhrians was yet to come. For more than twenty years, since the Chinese revolution, Niebuhr had consistently opposed American intervention in Asian civil wars. He supported U.S. intervention in Korea because the Korean War was launched by a Soviet-backed invasion. The war in Vietnam seemed to present a special case, however, because it was both a civil war and a Soviet proxy war. Niebuhr agonized in the early 1960s about America's proper role in Vietnam. He subscribed to the reigning domino theory, which claimed

---

85. Paul Ramsey, "Dream and Reality in Deterrence and Defense," *Christianity and Crisis* 21 (December 25, 1961), 228–32; Paul Tillich, "The Nuclear Dilemma: A Discussion," *Christianity and Crisis* 21 (November 13, 1961), 203–4; Hans J. Morgenthau, "The Nuclear Discussion: Continued," *Christianity and Crisis* 21 (December 11, 1961), 223; Norman K. Gottwald, "Moral and Strategic Reflections on the Nuclear Dilemma," *Christianity and Crisis* 21 (January 8, 1962), 239–42; Kenneth W. Thompson, "The Nuclear Dilemma: A Discussion," *Christianity and Crisis* 21 (November 13, 1961), 203; Carl Mayer, "Moral Issues in the Nuclear Dilemma," *Christianity and Crisis* 22 (March 19, 1962), 38.

that communists would conquer all of Southeast Asia if America withdrew from Vietnam. At the same time, he was aware that the American-backed Diem regime in South Vietnam was a repressive dictatorship. The moral choices were deeply ambiguous to Niebuhr. He spent much of his time in the early 1960s reminding his secularized Kennedy-group followers that Christian realism had a moral dimension. He feared that too many highly placed and self-styled Niebuhrians were reducing realism to amoral manipulation. During Kennedy's administration, Niebuhr waffled on Vietnam, not anticipating that Vietnam would become the acid test of America's moral realism, and of his.

Lyndon Johnson awarded Niebuhr the Medal of Freedom, the nation's highest civilian honor, in 1964. Niebuhr supported Johnson's reelection the same year, partly because Johnson promised not to escalate America's involvement in Vietnam. When Johnson sent the Marines into the Dominican Republic the following year, Niebuhr strongly opposed the invasion, arguing that force could only be creative—and not resented by its purported beneficiaries—when it was the "tool of a legitimate authority in the community." The Dominican invasion badly failed this test, in his view. At the same time, while Johnson massively escalated America's presence in Vietnam, Niebuhr tried to find a third way. He believed that the war was unwinnable, but the prospect of losing Vietnam to communism prevented him from joining the early antiwar opposition. He therefore proposed that Johnson should persuade Thailand to offer asylum to all of the region's anticommunist warriors "and then defend this asylum with massive military power." This bizarre plan revealed not only Niebuhr's ignorance of Southeast Asian culture and politics, but also the strength of his nationalistic concern that the United States needed to convince other nations of its superior military might.[86]

At the outset of the following year, Niebuhr was still exhorting Johnson to "take a stand" in Thailand, but in the succeeding weeks he began to face up to reality in Vietnam. As America's involvement in Vietnam deepened and Niebuhr's friend Vice President Hubert Humphrey vigorously defended American policy in Vietnam, Niebuhr became increasingly forthright in his opposition to the war. He argued that it was a mistake to make Vietnam an object of anticommunist containment, "when we are in fact dealing with the nationalism of a small nation of Asia." The carnage and futility of the war were sickening to him. He criticized America's use of chemical weapons and argued that bombing North Vietnam was useless. "We are making South Vietnam into an American colony by transmuting a civil war into one in which Americans fight Asians," he objected in 1966. "By escalating the war we are physically ruining an unhappy nation in

---

86. Reinhold Niebuhr, "Caribbean Blunder," *Christianity and Crisis* 25 (May 31, 1965), 113–14; Niebuhr, "Consensus at the Price of Flexibility," *New Leader* 41 (September 27, 1965), 20.

the process of 'saving' it." The following year he called for an American withdrawal from Vietnam and appealed in the *New York Times* for a public outcry
"against these horrendous policies." He decried America's intervention in Vietnam as an example of the "illusion of American omnipotence" and told friends
that he was frightened by his lack of patriotism. "For the first time I fear I am
ashamed of our beloved nation," he confessed.[87]

If Niebuhr was surprised to find himself among the war protesters, the
spectacle was shocking, bewildering, and sometimes infuriating to many of his
colleagues and former students. Ramsey spoke for them when he lamented that,
in the political climate of the 1960s, "even Reinhold Niebuhr signs petitions and
editorials as if Reinhold Niebuhr never existed."[88] The real Niebuhr would not
have supported unilateral disarmament initiatives or opposed the war in Vietnam,
Ramsey suggested. But in the 1960s Niebuhr was deeply chastened by his
country's "illusion of omnipotence" and its too cynical lesser-evilism. He believed that a mistaken commitment to literal worldwide anticommunist containment was making America commit indefensible evils in the world. In 1969,
Niebuhr confirmed that he had followed Kennan in shifting away from a containment strategy "to the partnership of the two superpowers for the prevention
of a nuclear war." Like Kennan, he disavowed "any simple containment of
Communism." Later the same year, while images of America's incineration of
Vietnam burned in his mind, Niebuhr revealed that his reassessment of America's
role in the world was taking a radical turn.

> I must now ruefully change that decade-ago opinion of mine in regard to Barth's
> neutralism. While I do not share his sneer at the "fleshpots of Germany and
> America," I must admit that our wealth makes our religious anti-Communism
> particularly odious. Perhaps there is not so much to choose between Communist
> and anti-Communist fanaticism, particularly when the latter, combined with our
> wealth, has caused us to stumble into the most pointless, costly, and bloody
> war in our history.[89]

---

87. Reinhold Niebuhr, "The Peace Offensive," *Christianity and Crisis* 25 (January
24, 1966), 301; Niebuhr, "Escalation Objective," *New York Times* March 14, 1967;
Niebuhr, Foreword to *Martin Luther King, Jr., John C. Bennett, Henry Steele Commager,
Abraham Heschel Speak on the War in Vietnam* (New York: Clergy and Laymen Concerned
about Vietnam, 1967), 3; closing quote in Fox, *Reinhold Niebuhr,* 285.

88. Paul Ramsey, "How Shall Counter-Insurgency War Be Conducted Justly?" Paper
presented at American Society of Christian Ethics Meeting, January 21–22, 1966; re-
printed in Ramsey, *The Just War: Force and Political Responsibility* (Lanham, Md.:
University Press of America, 1983, c1968), 458. For Bennett's response, see John C.
Bennett, "From Supporter of War in 1941 to Critic in 1966," *Christianity and Crisis* 26
(February 21, 1966), 13–14.

89. Ronald H. Stone, "An Interview with Reinhold Niebuhr," *Christianity and Crisis*
29 (March 17, 1969), 48–49; Reinhold Niebuhr, "Toward New Intra-Christian En-
deavors," *Christian Century* 86 (December 31, 1969), 1662–63.

Schlesinger later explained that as the Cold War developed, "Niebuhr grew increasingly alarmed over the delusions generated by excessive American power."[90] The critic of group egotism increasingly recognized that his own country had become a reactionary world power through its arrogance of power.

The later Niebuhr also reconsidered the religious meaning of Christian realism, especially regarding his relationship to theological liberalism. He remarked on several occasions that his attempts to refurbish the classical Christian rhetoric of original sin had been mistaken. "I made a rather unpardonable pedagogical error in *The Nature and Destiny of Man,*" he wrote. "My theological preoccupation prompted me to define the persistence and universality of man's self-regard as 'original sin.' This was historically and symbolically correct. But my pedagogical error consisted in seeking to challenge modern optimism with the theological doctrine which was anathema to modern culture."[91] Niebuhr still believed that original sin was Christianity's only empirically verified doctrine, but he regretted that his major writings reveled in a "proud and heedless" disregard for the effect of his rhetoric. He had believed that he could rehabilitate the church's ancient language about sin, partly because he denied the historicity of the Bible's creation myths and rejected Augustine's theory of the transmission of sin through procreation. "But these labors of modern interpretation of traditional religious symbol proved vain," he concluded. "The reaction to my 'realism' taught me much about the use of traditional symbols."[92] He learned that no matter how vehemently he criticized religious conservatives, he could not retrieve the language of premodern Christianity without appearing to endorse a regressive authoritarianism.

Niebuhr took this problem very seriously, partly because he shared the prevailing liberal assumption about modern theology's primary reference group. He put the matter plainly in his intellectual autobiography. "My avocational interest as a kind of circuit rider in the colleges and universities has prompted an interest in the defense and justification of the Christian faith in a secular age, particularly among what Schleiermacher called Christianity's 'cultured despisers,' " he explained. This apologetic burden was taken to peculiar lengths in Niebuhr's work. Like Mathews and Fosdick, Niebuhr assumed that theologians in a secularized modern culture were required to address modern skepticism and indifference to religion. In the modernist social and intellectual context, theology had to take an apologetic form. It accepted and addressed the objections of those

---

90. Quoted in Matthew Berke, "The Disputed Legacy of Reinhold Niebuhr," *First Things* 27 (November 1992), 39.

91. Reinhold Niebuhr, *Man's Nature and His Communities: Essays on the Dynamics and Enigmas of Man's Personal and Social Existence* (New York: Scribner's, 1965), 23.

92. Ibid., 24.

who considered themselves too sophisticated to be religious. If Niebuhr was brutally dismissive toward much of the literature in this theological tradition, he was nonetheless part of it. He rejected the appeals to progress, idealism, aesthetics, spiritual therapy, and scientific theism that liberal theologians variously offered up, but his own desire to justify Christian commitment to its cultured despisers was no less consuming. In Niebuhr's case, the crucial despisers were nonreligious academics who shared his politics. His considerable success in speaking to them was signaled by the fact that some of his followers, including Morton White, called themselves "atheists for Niebuhr."

Niebuhr took their reactions to his work to heart. Some were among his closest friends. In his last substantive work, *Man's Nature and His Communities,* Niebuhr observed that it was their criticism that affected him most deeply in his later career. He recalled that he was particularly chastened by the reactions of political philosophers to *The Nature and Destiny of Man;* they applauded his discussions of human nature but rejected his theological presuppositions. Niebuhr's later works took their objections to heart. Though he was always adept at writing in a secular idiom—his numerous articles for the *Nation* rarely used religious language—Niebuhr's major works in his earlier career were explicitly religious. He did not attempt to make his arguments more palatable to a secular audience by downplaying his religious assumptions or motivation. His later writings clearly took this secularizing turn, however, as in such books as *The Structure of Nations and Empires* (1959), *Man's Nature and His Communities* (1965), and *The Democratic Experience* (1969). *Man's Nature and His Communities* reworked Niebuhr's familiar arguments about realism, politics, and human nature into secular language, resorting to what Niebuhr called "more sober symbols" of analysis. Niebuhr's closing works were written in the language of secular political philosophy, not because he discarded his religious worldview but because he was still reaching for a greater impact on America's nonreligious academic audience. Bennett observed that Niebuhr's chief concern throughout his career was to influence the direction of American government. In his last years, Niebuhr reasoned that American theologians would get no hearing at all, and thus have no influence on secular audiences, without making similar adjustments.[93]

This shift in tactics was related to a deeper change in Niebuhr's attitude toward modern liberalism. For more than thirty years, with a tone of utter certainty

---

93. Reinhold Niebuhr, "Intellectual Autobiography," in Kegley and Bretall, *Reinhold Niebuhr: His Religious, Social, and Political Thought,* 3; on the "atheists for Niebuhr" phenomenon, see Perry Miller, "The Influence of Reinhold Niebuhr," *Reporter* 18 (May 1, 1958), 40; Niebuhr, *Man's Nature and His Communities,* 24; Bennett quote in Harold R. Landon, ed., *Reinhold Niebuhr: A Prophetic Voice in Our Time* (Greenwich, Conn.: Seabury Press, 1962), 88.

and disgust, he skewered liberal Christianity for its purported simplemindedness, moralism, idealism, and sentimentality. In his characterization, liberal Christianity reduced creation to an evolutionary concept, reduced God to the process of evolution, reduced sin to a "provisional inertia of impulses," and reduced Christ to a symbol of history.[94] In 1956, however, the liberal theologian Daniel Day Williams called Niebuhr to account for this characterization. "What liberalism is he looking at?" Williams asked. "Hegel cannot be reduced to these dimensions. Neither can Rauschenbusch. Williams observed that Niebuhr could not have been thinking of his teacher, D. C. Macintosh, when he penned his customary attacks on Christian liberalism. Neither could he have been thinking of Macintosh's liberal colleagues at Yale, Eugene Lyman and Robert Calhoun, nor of such figures as Josiah Royce or William Ernst Hocking. But these were America's major theological exponents of liberal Christianity, Williams implied. Niebuhr specialized in demolishing a caricature. He never confronted liberal Protestantism at its best. The figures he skewered were extremists or lightweights or both.[95]

This offensive was an example of the tactic it criticized. Williams did not recognize his own liberalism in the idealistic progressivism that Niebuhr attacked. Liberal Christianity was a richer tapestry than Niebuhr ever allowed. To seal his own polemical victory, however, Williams dismissed Niebuhr's polemical targets as figures unworthy of attention. He claimed that Niebuhr ignored liberal Protestantism's major exponents. But Mathews was hardly a minor figure. Neither were Fosdick and Morrison, the eminent bishops Francis McConnell and G. Bromley Oxnam, nor such academics as Shirley Jackson Case, Harry F. Ward, or Gerald Birney Smith, all of whom Niebuhr skewered for their moralistic idealism. Niebuhr admired McConnell, yet pronounced that the writings of this great soul revealed "the final bankruptcy of the liberal Christian approach to politics."[96] None of the Yale theologians on Williams's list compared to Mathews in influence, productivity, or stature; none of them had anywhere near the impact on the making of liberal Protestantism that Fosdick and Morrison exerted. Moreover, the intellectual heavyweights on Williams's list—Royce and Hocking—were philosophers, not theologians. The liberalism that Niebuhr attacked was the dominant, though not the only mode of modern liberal Protestant thought.

The younger Niebuhr would have issued this reply to Williams, arguing that he took on a pervasive religious and cultural disposition while other liberal

---

94. Reinhold Niebuhr, "Coherence, Incoherence, and Christian Faith," *Journal of Religion* 31 (July 1951), 162; cited in Daniel Day Williams, "Niebuhr and Liberalism," in *Reinhold Niebuhr: His Religious, Social, and Political Thought,* 196.

95. Williams, "Niebuhr and Liberalism," 196.

96. Niebuhr, *An Interpretation of Christian Ethics,* 110.

academics like Macintosh and Williams wrote more cautiously for each other. But by the mid-1950s, Niebuhr no longer wanted this fight. He admired Royce and Hocking, and he respected Williams. If they were liberals, so was he. The publication of Russell Kirk's *The Conservative Mind* had recently forced him to redefine his relationship to liberalism and conservatism. Niebuhr's fondness for Edmund Burke and his praise for the tragic view of human nature espoused by conservatives had led many observers to believe that he was becoming a conservative. Kirk's enlistment of Burke as an apologist for inequality and conformity forced Niebuhr to clarify his position. He distinguished between Kirk's traditional conservatism, which defended hierarchy, inequality, and undemocratic authority, and traditional liberalism, which was committed to social justice but lacked a realistic understanding of the realities of sin, power, and interest. His own perspective, Niebuhr explained, was a realistic liberalism that grasped the limiting reality of human egotism but that nonetheless pushed for the fullest possible attainment of democracy and distributive justice.[97]

Williams's challenge drove Niebuhr to elaborate this delineation. "When Professor Williams names names I am embarrassed," he admitted. Niebuhr conceded that his repeated characterizations of modern liberalism were too sweeping and categorical, that he overidentified liberalism with certain currents in American politics and philosophy (especially Deweyan philosophy), and that he overgeneralized the connection between liberalism and historical optimism.[98] In Niebuhr's usage, "liberalism" was a faith that trusted in the virtue of rational individuals and the fact of historical progress. Much of American liberalism— especially Deweyan progressivism and the more spiritually uprooted remnants of social gospel Christianity—fit this definition. In the late 1950s, however, Niebuhr began to admit that liberal Christianity was a richer, more diverse, and more realistic tradition than his numerous writings about it claimed. His own work was nothing if not a type of liberal Christianity. "When I find neo-orthodoxy turning into sterile orthodoxy or a new Scholasticism, I find that I am a liberal at heart, and that many of my broadsides against liberalism were indiscriminate," he wrote in 1960. "On the whole I regret the polemical animus of my theological and political activities and am now inclined to become much more empirical, judging each situation and movement in terms of its actual fruits."[99]

Niebuhr's later writings were written in this spirit. He confessed that his articles and major works contained "rather violent, and sometimes extravagant"

---

97. Cf. Russell Kirk, *The Conservative Mind: From Burke to Eliot* (Chicago: Henry Regnery, 1987, c1953); Reinhold Niebuhr, "Liberalism and Conservatism," *Christianity and Society* 20 (Winter 1954–1955), 3–4.

98. Niebuhr, "Reply to Interpretation and Criticism," 441–42.

99. Reinhold Niebuhr, "The Quality of Our Lives," *Christian Century* 77 (May 11, 1960), 568.

assaults on the character and ethos of modern liberalism. Much of his work heaped ridicule on liberal Christians who, if misguided, were still people who shared his fundamental religious and social values. Like him, they conceived religion as a power or energy for social struggle. Niebuhr's last writings tried to redress certain effects of his attacks on liberal Christianity. He had never meant to give comfort to reactionaries. He had never meant to bolster conservative views on theology or politics. He had never meant to provide a warrant for conservative illiberalism, elitism, dogmatism, or opposition to social justice. His writings were frequently used for these purposes, however.

Niebuhr set the matter straight in *Man's Nature and His Communities*. The guiding principle of his mature life, he declared, was that "a realist conception of human nature should be made the servant of an ethic of progressive justice and should not be made into a bastion of conservatism, particularly a conservatism which defends unjust privileges."[100] Authentic Christian realism opposed the maldistribution of social and economic power that conservatives defended. Niebuhr confessed that his repeated attacks on liberal Christianity revealed "some radical contradictions in my attitudes" before he reached the point, in later life, when intellectual clarity became possible. For all of its grievous errors and illusions, liberal Christianity was the faith that understood the mystery of human existence in terms that were credible and spiritually moving to him. It was also a faith that endorsed and promoted his own ethic of progressive justice. The recent erosion of liberal Protestantism's social influence filled him with regret. Having spent his life trying to refortify liberal Protestantism, he was saddened in his closing years to witness the decline of the liberal Protestant churches, colleges, and ecumenical institutions that had made his public career and his influence possible.

Niebuhr as Theologian

Niebuhr's stature among the giants of modern theology was anomalous. Unlike other major Christian theologians of his generation, he gave no attention to technical questions concerning theological method, hermeneutics, language, or exegesis. Niebuhr did not believe in the historicity of Christ's resurrection, but his writings failed to offer any alternative account of Christianity's Easter faith. Neither did his writings develop a theology of the Trinity or the incarnation, or even use trinitarian or incarnational language. He did not develop a theology of the Holy Spirit or the church. The great Christian themes of regeneration, sanctification, and the church as the body of Christ thus had little place in his work.

---

100. Niebuhr, *Man's Nature and His Communities*, 21–25.

Except as a transcendent ideal that stands in judgment over history, Niebuhr gave even less sanction to the doctrine of the kingdom. Though his one systematic work, *The Nature and Destiny of Man,* contained a moving section on "The Kingdom of God and the Struggle for Justice," his discussion gave little attention to the kingdom theme and made no effort to develop a theology of the kingdom. Niebuhr's subsequent writings denigrated the effect of the kingdom idea in Christian theology and eschewed the biblical conception of the church as the kingdom-prefiguring body of Christ. For Niebuhr, the biblical notion of the kingdom as an inbreaking spiritual and historical reality was a mistaken relic of early Christianity that Christian realism needed to avoid. Near the end of his life, he pressed the point on young Wolfhart Pannenberg, whose new theology of the kingdom was beginning to attract attention. Niebuhr had read some of Pannenberg's work and, upon meeting him, told him forthrightly that he was making a terrible mistake. Any appeal to the biblical language or idea of the kingdom was bound to produce disasters, he lectured. Niebuhr understood that Pannenberg's theology generally avoided politics, but this did not matter. The social gospelers had provided the last proof that anyone should need that the kingdom idea was a loser, he claimed. It made Rauschenbusch incorrigibly naive in his attempts to relate Christianity to politics. "I am almost grateful for the act of mercy that he died before seeing what the war had done to the world," Niebuhr told Pannenberg. "It would have broken his heart." He declared that if he could do it, he would eliminate even the language of the kingdom from the Christian story.[101]

Niebuhrian realism took its instruction not from the biblical language of the kingdom or the church or the Spirit, or from classical Christianity's theology of the Trinity or the incarnation, but from the biblical themes of sin, prophesy, the sovereignty of God, the cross, and divine grace. Niebuhr heavily relied upon the notions of myth and symbol to build a theological foundation out of these themes, but he conspicuously failed to justify or define the meanings of these slippery notions in his thought. Emil Brunner pressed the question in his contribution to Niebuhr's festschrift. After noting that Niebuhr customarily urged Christians to take their myths seriously as living symbolizations of Christian experience, Brunner asked, "But what kind of reality lies hidden beneath these symbols? . . . To what extent there stands behind Niebuhr's 'eschatological symbols' a *reality,* and what kind of reality—or whether perhaps these eschatological symbols are merely 'regulative principles' in the Kantian sense—these

---

101. Cf. Niebuhr, *The Nature and Destiny of Man* 2:244–86; discussion by Richard John Neuhaus in *Reinhold Niebuhr Today,* 108; Neuhaus, "Wolfhart Pannenberg: Profile of a Theologian," Introduction to Pannenberg, *Theology and the Kingdom of God* (Philadelphia: Westminster Press, 1969), 31–32.

are questions on which we should like to have him make a definitive pro-nouncement." Niebuhr repeatedly waved off these questions throughout his ca-reer, however, explaining that he was not a theologian, but a social ethicist.[102]

Niebuhr's considerable deficiencies as a theologian thus opened his theo-logical ethics to criticism from various perspectives. His lack of a theology of regeneration was scored by Christian pacifists such as Morrison and John Howard Yoder, who claimed that Niebuhr propounded a sociological rather than a biblical understanding of the church. His lack of a theology of the church was similarly criticized from various standpoints for failing to distinguish the dynamics of Christian fellowship from the dynamics of other groups. His legendary disinterest in nature epitomized, for a subsequent generation of ecologically conscious theologians, the anthropocentric arrogance of Christian theism. His orthodoxy was questioned by those who affirmed traditional understandings of the incar-nation, the resurrection of Christ, and the triune nature of divine reality. For those who sought to blunt the force of Niebuhr's social teaching, his failure to justify his theological arguments offered ample opportunities for criticism or dismissal.

Niebuhr unfortunately invited this kind of criticism by his penchant for attacking other figures at their weakest point. His teaching style and his writing were typically polemical. Hargie Likins later recounted that, during his time as Niebuhr's student, "A number of us commented on his tendency to pick the weakest point in an individual's thought, then demolish it brilliantly and grin like a little kid. I especially remember his doing so with Freud."[103] Niebuhr's last graduate assistant, Ronald Stone, similarly recalled that Niebuhr's lectures on Western intellectual history generally "resembled a demolition derby so that he could get on to his theological perspective."[104] Niebuhr annoyed and infuriated more than a few scholars over the decades with his characteristically negative use of dialectic. This trait marked not only his political writing, but much of his systematic theological work. Rather than a systematic argument, *The Nature and Destiny of Man* resembled a shooting gallery in which Niebuhr one-sidedly portrayed and shot down various Greek, Renaissance, and other rationalist phi-losophers to clear the field for his Christian realist alternative. Unlike Tillich, whose dialectics sympathetically drew upon and synthesized differing perspec-tives, Niebuhr typically considered other positions in order to blast them. His

---

102. Emil Brunner, "Some Remarks on Reinhold Niebuhr's Work as a Christian Thinker," in *Reinhold Niebuhr: His Religious, Social, and Political Thought,* ed. Kegley and Bretall. In the same volume, see Niebuhr, "Intellectual Autobiography," 3; and "Reply to Interpretation and Criticism," 439.

103. Quoted in Ronald H. Stone, *Professor Reinhold Niebuhr: A Mentor to the Twentieth Century* (Louisville: Westminster/John Knox Press, 1992), 78.

104. Ibid., 78.

dialectic did not seek to synthesize the strongest parts of other positions, but negated them at their worst.

Yet he was the most important Christian ethicist and the most influential American theologian of the twentieth century. Niebuhr's unparalleled energy and brilliance made him the single modern Christian ethicist whom subsequent theologians cannot avoid. More than any modern theologian, he set the terms of Christian ethical debate and shaped the character of American theological discussion. He effected a transformation of American theological consciousness. Tillich later recalled that this transformation occurred with the same suddenness and force as the thunderbolt that had shattered German theology a half-generation earlier. In the German case, the opening for Karl Barth's massive assault on German theological liberalism was created by the ravages of the Great War. The liberal bourgeois theology that dominated German universities for several decades "simply disappeared under the tremendous impact of the Barthian theology," Tillich recalled. He continued: "When I remember what happened here, it was similarly astonishing. When I came [to America in 1933], everybody asked only one question—whatever was discussed theologically—namely the question, 'What do you think about pacifism?' "

Tillich was hesitant in this social climate to address the question because he was a newcomer to America and not a pacifist. It was Niebuhr, he recounted, who transformed the social context in which American theology was produced. "This disappeared after Reinie made his tremendous attack," he recalled. "I believe it was absolutely necessary, and I tried to support him as much as I could in my lectures and early writings; but he was the man who changed the climate in an almost sudden way."[105] In subsequent years, Niebuhr often reminded his students that this was the decisive background to his thought and career. "When I came here [to Union], this was absolutely a paradise of Social Gospel liberalism," he told them.[106] He recalled in 1960: "It was in full swing when I arrived at the Seminary in 1928. The Social Gospel was creative in redeeming American Protestantism from an arid Calvinistic or pietistic individualism. But it was defective in identifying the Christian faith with a mild socialism and a less mild pacifism all encased in an overall utopianism."[107]

It was Niebuhr who made liberal Christianity confront the harshest realities of egotism, power, interest, and violence. He often obscured the crucial difference between his theology and the social gospel by claiming that the social gospelers

105. Paul Tillich, "Sin and Grace in the Theology of Reinhold Niebuhr," in Landon, ed., *Reinhold Niebuhr: A Prophetic Voice in Our Time*, 32–33.

106. Quoted in Charles C. Brown, *Niebuhr and His Age: Reinhold Niebuhr's Prophetic Role in the Twentieth Century* (Philadelphia: Trinity Press International, 1992), 37.

107. Reinhold Niebuhr, "Professor's Column," *Union Seminary Tower,* May 1960, 3; quoted in Stone, *Professor Reinhold Niebuhr,* 84.

"didn't believe in sin."[108] This polemical exaggeration undoubtedly owed something to the fact that Niebuhr never seriously acquainted himself with Rauschenbusch's work. Niebuhr's originality as a theological interpreter of the reality of evil did not lay in his emphasis on the power or ravages of evil; Rauschenbusch's work was equally emphatic in this area. Moreover, Rauschenbusch emphasized the reality of a solidaristic transmission of evil much more than Niebuhr. It was Rauschenbusch (building upon Ritschl's theology) who developed a doctrine of the kingdom of evil to explain the pervasive and seemingly intractable reality of social evil.[109]

For Rauschenbusch, sin was a nihilating, organic reality in human nature and history that was reproduced through socialization as cruelty, perversity, racism, ethnic feuds, nationalism, sexual abuse, drug addiction, and the like. "When negroes are hunted from a Northern city like beasts, or when a Southern city degrades the whole nation by turning the savage inhumanity of a mob into a public festivity, we are continuing to sin because our fathers created the conditions of sin by the African slave trade and by the unearned wealth they gathered from slave laborers for generations," he wrote.[110] The social reality of the kingdom of evil was, for Rauschenbusch, a profound truth that liberal progressive theologies and traditional orthodox theologies typically trivialized. His solidaristic concept of the kingdom of evil offered a deeper and more compelling explanation of the persistence of certain social evils, especially racism, than Niebuhr's focus on the sin of pride. That human beings are implicated in the historical evils of their ancestors was, for Rauschenbusch, a truism that only social gospel theology seriously addressed.

The problem for Niebuhr was that social gospel Christianity in the generation following Rauschenbusch's death did not seriously address or even recognize the kingdom of evil. The social gospelers of Niebuhr's time adopted Rauschenbusch's idealism about the struggle for social justice, but eschewed his realism about the evils within and without that opposed that struggle. Niebuhr often claimed that Rauschenbusch's (purportedly) reformist and moralistic conception of the class struggle was much less realistic than his own. Here again, the claim was misleading. Rauschenbusch's writings contained numerous accounts of the class struggle that Niebuhr might have written in his Marxist phase. Though he clearly preferred to argue for democratic socialism on moral grounds, Rauschenbusch insisted without equivocation that "we must not blink the fact that idealists alone

108. Niebuhr, "Intellectual Autobiography," 13.

109. Walter Rauschenbusch, *A Theology for the Social Gospel* (New York: Macmillan, 1917), 69–94; see Albrecht Ritschl, *The Christian Doctrine of Justification and Reconciliation,* trans. by H. R. Macaulay and A. B. Macaulay (Edinburgh: T. & T. Clark, 1902), 327–50.

110. Ibid., 79.

have never carried through any great social change. . . . For a definite historical victory a great truth must depend on the class which makes that truth its own and fights for it."[111] He argued that the class struggle was a war of conflicting interests in which the working class would forcefully pursue its demands, not merely because these demands were just, but also because organized workers would be strong enough to get their way.[112] In crucial respects, Rauschenbusch was closer to Niebuhr than to the social gospel moralism that Niebuhr later repudiated.

What did separate Niebuhr in the 1930s from Rauschenbusch's social gospel faith was Niebuhr's dialectic of sin. For all of his insistence on the nihilating power of the kingdom of evil, Rauschenbusch never doubted that the kingdom of God was a stronger force not only beyond history, but within it. The divine kingdom was prefigured in the life of the church as the body of Christ and as a sign of true community. Rauschenbusch assumed that the reign of God would never be fully realized in history, but he also assumed that the church's vocation was to work at building the divine kingdom. The church would never build a perfect order, he wrote, yet the church was obliged to seek it with faith. The kingdom would never be fully disclosed in history, "but every approximation to it is worthwhile."[113]

This was the spirit of the social gospel. Though Rauschenbusch emphasized that the kingdom of evil was solidaristic and accumulative, and though he recognized that the kingdom of evil afflicted all human hearts and all social orders, he nonetheless conceived evil as an enemy that could be impeded and even defeated by the good. The social imperative of the social gospel was that Christians were to "moralize" or "Christianize" the social order through moral, political, and spiritual efforts that diminished the force of evil in the world. His writings did not shrink from distinguishing between the "regenerate" and "unregenerate" sectors of the social order or from describing the struggle for social justice as a fight between the "forces of righteousness" and the "forces of evil." Rauschenbusch even believed that regenerated social institutions could have redeeming effects on individuals.

This was the mind-set that Niebuhr's dialectic of sin tore apart. Niebuhr was only comprehensible in the light of his social gospel background. His assumption that the church must underwrite a politics of social justice was a social gospel assumption. Though he never undertook a serious study of Rauschenbusch's writings, Niebuhr spent his entire life reacting to the legacy of Rauschenbusch's

---

111. Walter Rauschenbusch, *Christianity and the Social Crisis* (New York: Macmillan, 1907), 400–401.

112. Ibid., 411.

113. Ibid., 420–21.

movement—mostly in opposition. His claim that the teaching of Jesus had no direct social relevance except as an impossible ideal would have horrified Rauschenbusch. His unrelenting attacks on liberal Christianity would have struck Rauschenbusch as morally wrong and politically perverse. Niebuhr thunderously rejected Rauschenbusch's belief that democratized collectivities could have redeeming effects on individuals; for Niebuhr, society was inevitably immoral. Not long after *Moral Man and Immoral Society* vigorously elaborated this conviction, Niebuhr decided that the notion of "moral man" was a social gospel illusion, as well. The latter insight went to the heart of the argument within social Christianity and generated Niebuhr's most important contribution to the Christian social tradition. This was his discovery that good and evil are not merely opposing forces, but are inevitably mixed together in human nature and history.

Niebuhr expounded this perception in his critique of Freud. The popularity of Freud's psychology was partly attributable, in Niebuhr's view, to Freud's realism about the tragic aspects of human nature and society. For intellectuals who no longer believed in the Enlightenment myth of human progress, Freud's postulation of a death instinct that competed with eros for control over self and society was compelling. Niebuhr conceded that Freud's dualistic account of the struggle between eros and death marked an advance over rationalistic psychologies of the recent past. For Freud, the work of eros was to bind together "single human individuals, then families, then tribes, races, nations, into one great unity, that of humanity." Culture and civilization were products of the work of eros, which "shared its rule over the earth" with the death instinct—the nihilating power that destroyed culture and civilization. Freud concluded:

> And now, it seems to me, the meaning of the evolution of culture is no longer a riddle to us. It must present to us the struggle between Eros and Death, between the instincts of life and the instincts of destruction, as it works itself out in the human species. This struggle is what all life consists of essentially and so the evolution of civilization may be described as the struggle of the human species for existence. And it is this battle of Titans that our nurses and governesses try to compose with their lullaby song of Heaven.[114]

This was how modern secular intellectuals dealt with evil when history forced them to confront it. Niebuhr gave short shrift to Freud's understanding of evil, however. "These supposedly profound words, which pretentiously offer a clue to the meaning of 'the evolution of culture,' throw little light on the actual human situation," he asserted. Niebuhr conceded that Freud's idea of a mysterious

---

114. Sigmund Freud, *Civilization and Its Discontents*, trans. by James Strachey (New York: W. W. Norton, 1961, c1930), 102–3; quoted in Niebuhr, *An Interpretation of Christian Ethics*, 59.

inner conflict between a distinct death impulse and the life impulse had the virtue "of calling attention to the dynamic character of evil in the world." But only psychopaths acted out of a pure love of destruction, Niebuhr noted. Among animals and most people, the death instinct served the life impulse. People killed to save their own lives, the lives of their loved ones, or to protect the communities and social orders created by eros. The problem with Freudian theory was not with Freud's postulation of a death instinct, but with his dualistic understanding of it.

The same confusion marred even the most realistic forms of social gospel liberalism. The death instinct was more than a nihilating power that competed with or struggled against the life impulse. The death instinct was inextricably bound up with the life impulse. For this reason, Niebuhr argued, evil was always constitutive in the good. No human act, no matter how loving or seemingly innocent, was devoid of egotism. Purity of any kind was an illusion. A realistic understanding of sin would therefore not be merely a dialectic of two forces held in tension, but a dialectic of interpenetration. Good and evil were always part of each other.

Niebuhr conceded that the implications of his dialectic for politics were "morbidly pessimistic to moderns." The chief implication was that any gain toward a good end simultaneously created greater opportunities for evil. Every movement that engendered greater democracy, equality, freedom, or community also engendered new opportunities to create tyranny, squalor, or anarchy. Every effort to make the public sphere more humane heightened the possibility of producing unintended evil consequences. Democratic gains increased the possibilities for greater numbers of people to do evil things. Movements for political reform or transformation were thus most dangerous when they were oblivious to or claimed to be innocent of the harmful possibilities they created. "The conclusion most abhorrent to the modern mood is that the possibilities of evil grow with the possibilities of good, and that human history is therefore not so much a chronicle of the progressive victory of the good over evil, of cosmos over chaos, as the story of an ever-increasing cosmos, creating ever-increasing possibilities of chaos," Niebuhr concluded.[115] Christian realism was distinguished by its acceptance of this truism. Greater justice would be gained and maintained not from the efforts of those who believed in progress, but from the morally committed efforts of people who knew that progress was an illusion.

Religiously, Christian realism appealed to what Niebuhr called "the vertical dimension in human life," which revealed "the ultimate possibilities of good and the depths of evil in it." The relevance of an impossible ethical ideal—the law of love—was that it reminded Christians that there was an ideal, even if

---

115. Niebuhr, *An Interpretation of Christian Ethics*, 59–60.

sin made the ideal unattainable. For Niebuhr, the cross was the ultimate symbol of this most fundamental Christian truth. "The message of the Son of God who dies upon the cross, of a God who transcends history and is yet in history, who condemns and judges sin and yet suffers with and for the sinner, this message is the truth about life," he declared.[116] Niebuhr gave little attention to the cross as salvation from sin, except in this sense. For him, the cross revealed the deepest mythic truth of Christianity, which was that Christ took on the suffering of the world in order to redeem it through his fellow-suffering love. The cross was thus the ultimate symbol of sacrificial love, in which Christ redeemed suffering not by abolishing it, but by sharing the condition of those who suffer. For Niebuhr, Christ's law of love was the orienting reality that directs Christian behavior, as far as possible, toward this compassionate moral ideal.

In the sociopolitical sphere, Christian realism repeated Max Weber's distinction between the ethics of conscience and the ethics of responsibility. Niebuhr's later work reformulated his earlier dichotomy between the ethics of love absolutism and political responsibility, but the assertion of an essential distinction between these realms remained fundamental to his ethical perspective. Realism negotiated between the ideal and the actual. For Niebuhr, the task of a responsible political ethic informed by the love absolutism of Christianity was to pursue the highest attainable social good, which is justice. In his early career, Niebuhr equated justice with equality, arguing that equality is the only regulative principle of justice. *An Interpretation of Ethics* referred to both freedom and equality as principles of justice, but Niebuhr gave clear preeminence and regulative significance to equality. In 1938 he was still arguing that only equality has regulative force as a principle of justice, but Niebuhr's disenchantment with Marxism moved him in the early 1940s to adopt a more pluralistic understanding of justice. The second volume of *The Nature and Destiny of Man* still gave priority to equality but asserted that liberty and order are also regulative principles of justice. This shift away from a strongly distributivist idea of justice accelerated after Niebuhr gave up on socialism. His various writings on justice in the 1950s did not give priority to equality; they repeatedly referred to liberty, order, and equality as equally regulative principles of justice. The later Niebuhr sometimes implied that liberty is more important than order and equality, but on other occasions he used *justice* and *balance of power* as virtually interchangeable terms.[117]

---

116. Reinhold Niebuhr, *Beyond Tragedy: Essays on the Christian Interpretation of History* (New York: Charles Scribner's Sons, 1937), 20–21.

117. See Reinhold Niebuhr, "Christian Faith and the Common Life," in *Christian Faith and the Common Life,* ed. Nils Ehrenstrom, M. G. Dibelius, et al. (Chicago: Willett, Clark & Co., 1938), 85; *An Interpretation of Christian Ethics,* 132–36; *The Nature and Destiny of Man* 2:255–56; "The Limits of Liberty," *The Nation* 154 (January 24, 1942), 86–88; *Faith and History: A Comparison of Christian and Modern Views of History* (New York: Scribner's, 1949), 189; and "Christian Faith and Social Action," and "Liberty and Equality" in Niebuhr, *Faith and Politics,* ed. Ronald Stone (New York: George Braziller, 1968), 131, 186–92.

The vague, inherently slippery, and sometimes inconsistent character of Niebuhr's discussions of justice have given rise to conflicting interpretations of his ethics. Interpreters such as Dennis McCann and Karen Lebacqz emphasize the dispositional character of Niebuhr's ethic, arguing that it provides few criteria for distinguishing between just and unjust uses of power. Most interpreters agree that Niebuhr's ethic is largely dispositional, but some, especially James Gustafson and Robin Lovin, argue that McCann exaggerates the intuitive character of Niebuhr's ethical thought. Their reading is endorsed by Harlan Beckley, who, while acknowledging the dispositional character of Niebuhr's ethic, emphasizes that Niebuhr made use of middle axioms to discern the possibilities of justice in negotiating between the ideal and the actual. Merle Longwood takes this argument further, claiming that while Niebuhr did not develop his canons of justice into a systematized theory of justice, the makings of a workable theory can be derived from his work. The debate among Niebuhr's interpreters is itself dispositional, often revealing as much about the agendas of contemporary theologians as about Niebuhr. It is not so much a debate about whether Niebuhr's ethic was dispositional, but to what degree. McCann and Lebacqz recognize that Niebuhr employed the principles of liberty, order, and equality as middle axioms in his ethical reasoning. Their contention is not that Niebuhr's ethic was purely dispositional but that his conception of the principles of justice was never clear enough to yield adequate criteria for distinguishing between moral and immoral uses of power. For Gustafson, Lovin, and Longwood, however, Niebuhr's ethic provides at least an outline of a Christian dialectic that, arguably, given its distinctive character, should not be compared to more rationalized theoretical models of justice.[118]

What cannot be disputed is that the debate is fueled by the unsystematic character of Niebuhr's discussions of justice and by the—arguably necessary—relativity of his conception of justice. For Niebuhr, justice was a relational term that had no meaning apart from the provisional meaning given to it through its dependence on love. The rules of justice were "applications of the law of love

---

118. See Dennis P. McCann, *Christian Realism and Liberation Theology: Practical Theologies in Creative Conflict* (Maryknoll, N.Y.: Orbis Books, 1980), 80–93, 103; Karen Lebacqz, *Six Theories of Justice* (Minneapolis: Augsburg Press, 1986), 83–99; James Gustafson, "Theology in the Service of Ethics: An Interpretation of Reinhold Niebuhr's Theological Ethics," in *Reinhold Niebuhr and the Issues of Our Time,* ed. Richard Harries (Grand Rapids: Eerdmans, 1986), 24–45, comment on McCann on 45; Harlan Beckley, *Passion for Justice: Retrieving the Legacies of Walter Rauschenbusch, John A. Ryan, and Reinhold Niebuhr* (Louisville: Westminster/John Knox Press, 1992), 312–43; Merle Longwood, "Niebuhr and a Theory of Justice," *Dialog* 14 (Fall 1975), 253–62; Robin Lovin *Reinhold Niebuhr and Christian Realism* (Cambridge: Cambridge University Press, 1995), 198–234.

and do not have independence from it," he argued.[119] Justice was an application of the law of love to the sociopolitical sphere. It was regulated by such middle axioms as freedom, equality, and order (or balance of power), but the concrete meaning of justice in any given situation could not be taken directly from these principles. The meaning of justice could be determined only in the interaction of love and situation, through the mediation of the principles of freedom, equality, and order.

To object that Niebuhr did not provide a normative theory of justice was therefore not, for him, to make an appropriate criticism. Christian realism dealt with proximate problems, seeking always to bring about a greater balance of power and further gains in freedom and equality. The task of theological ethics was not to construct a normative theoretical account of the nature of justice, but to bring the intuitive and pragmatic insights of prophetic Christianity to bear on pressing social problems. Christian realism was more concerned with immediate obstacles to freedom and equality than with the relationships between freedom and equality in a just society. More important, Niebuhrian realism privileged intuitive discernment over method because it was fundamentally a love ethic. Niebuhr insisted that only love empowered by divine grace could prevent the struggle for justice from degenerating into a war among interests. Without the formative and redeeming power of love in historical struggles for justice, he explained, "the frictions and tensions of a balance of power would become intolerable."[120]

Christian realism did not claim to resolve the tension between the love ethic ideal and the responsibilities of power. It did not resolve the fundamental paradox of Christian morality, but embraced it. Niebuhr's ethic begins and ends with the paradox that Christians must assume moral responsibility for the consequences of their acts, while taking moral inspiration and guidance from a consequence-disregarding ethic of love. As Beckley observes, "A fully adequate conception of justice requires acts of love that disregard consequences, because the consequences of such uncalculating acts are necessary to preserve and extend justice." Yet Niebuhr believed that the consequences of acting from heedless love are only rarely beneficial. "Their consequences are normally disastrous for a reasonably just balance of power," Beckley explains. The upshot is that Niebuhr was left "with a consequentialist justification for occasional sacrificial actions performed only by agents who could ignore consequences."[121]

Niebuhr concluded that no conceivable theory of justice could map out general rules for how a consequence-disregarding sacrificial ethic should inspire

---

119. Niebuhr, "Reply to Interpretation and Criticism," 435.

120. Niebuhr, "Why the Christian Church Is Not Pacifist," 116. See Niebuhr, *An Interpretation of Christian Ethics*, 62–83.

121. Beckley, *Passion for Justice*, 322–23.

particular justice-bearing consequences. For him, love was an indispensable but inherently paradoxical source for obtaining justice. Love is a generative and formative force in struggling for justice, but at the same time love reminds us that every gain toward justice is corrupt. Because he conceived justice as a strategy for approximating an impossible ethical ideal, Niebuhr was left with only provisional and highly intuitive judgments about what justice required. His strategy used mediating principles of justice to discern how power might be wielded in a morally responsible way, but Niebuhr pointedly refrained from elaborating the regulative functions of these principles. His ethic emphasized, instead, the deeper paradox built into any attempt to take the Christian love ethic seriously in a fallen world.

His work thus offered remarkably little vision of what a good society should look like. Niebuhr's discussions of justice equated it with an approximate balance of power, but his own dialectic of sin revealed why distributive justice does not necessarily lead to a good society. Any politics that merely redistributes power is likely to produce an evil balance of power. Niebuhr's ethic offered a prophetic criticism of inequality, a warning about the limits of political solutions, an outline of a tridimensional understanding of justice, an appeal to the redemptive power of heedless love, and a witness to the ever-gracious providence of a sovereign God. As Bennett acknowledged, however, it did not offer a positive vision of a good society. "I think you get at Niebuhr negatively so much better than you do positively," Bennett remarked in 1961. "That's the reason that there's lack of vision in a way, lack of a positive vision. It's the criticism of inequality that's more obvious than the actual vision of what an equal world would be like."[122]

Niebuhrian realism eschewed the utopian dimension of Christian faith and spurned the biblical language of the kingdom in its theology and its political ethics. Niebuhr thus rejected any Christian social vision that sought or required transformations in America's existing social institutions, conditions, or attitudes. This was the "Christianizing" messianism that had to be given up. His work offered support for gradual changes in America's status quo, but, having discarded the grammar of the kingdom, he opposed theological perspectives that radically challenged the ethos or social arrangements of American society. Though he supported the causes of racial integration and racial justice in America, he frequently urged civil rights leaders to be more patient in their demands. Niebuhr tended to view the African American struggle for justice in America not from the perspectives of oppressed blacks but from a dominant white liberal perspective that viewed black demands for justice as divisive. Thus, as Preston Williams

---

122. From 1961 colloquium discussion of Niebuhr reprinted in Landon, ed., *Reinhold Niebuhr: A Prophetic Voice in Our Time,* 92–93.

later recalled, "When Martin Luther King was moving, Reinhold Niebuhr was saying, 'Too fast, too fast.' "[123]

Niebuhr's relationship to feminism bore similar problems. His wife, Ursula, was a distinguished scholar and professor at Barnard College. More than most theologians of his time, Niebuhr was outspoken in his support of equal rights for women. In 1944, he observed that the right of women "to explore and develop their capacities beyond the family function, was unduly restricted in all previous societies." He acknowledged that the "wisdom of the past" that opposed women's freedom in the name of protecting the family was usually marked by the "taint of ideology." "The male oligarchy used fixed principles of natural law to preserve its privileges and powers against a new emergent in history," he wrote.

Niebuhr's allusion to the "wisdom" of patriarchal ideology was not only ironic, however. His "balanced" approach to feminism claimed that modern feminism "came into history with some help from the errors of an inorganic and libertarian conception of the family and of an abstract rationalism which defied the facts of nature." The relevant fact of nature was that mothers were biologically more intimately related to their children than fathers were. "This fact limits the vocational freedom of women; for it makes motherhood a more exclusive vocation than fatherhood, which is indeed no more than an avocation," he asserted. Because motherhood was a vocation grounded in nature, but fatherhood was not, it was not unreasonable for patriarchal apologists of the past to oppose women's freedom to protect the organic integrity of the family. That is, antifeminist ideology was not merely ideological. Rather, the wisdom of the past "recognized the hazard to family life in the freedom of women."

The latter truth was emphasized, not without ideological cunning, in premodern Western societies to the exclusion of women's rights. By contrast, early feminism rode the wave of modernity's antiorganic, anticommunity, libertarian protest against the pre-Enlightenment past, emphasizing women's rights over women's obligations. In Niebuhr's view, the volatile question of the meaning of justice in family life was typically framed, in public discussion, by these two extreme, ideologically driven perspectives. The ideal solution to the challenge of modern feminism, he argued, would be to create a society that balanced female rights and female obligations. Niebuhr believed, in 1944, that American society had fortunately achieved such a balance. The ideal balance between women's rights and family obligations "was finally acknowledged in our society, partly because the bourgeois community had lost some of its appreciation of the organic integrity of the family."[124]

---

123. Cf. Herbert O. Edwards, "Niebuhr, 'Realism' and Civil Rights in America," *Christianity and Crisis* 46 (February 1986), 12–15. Williams quote from a seminar class at Harvard Divinity School, 1975.

124. Niebuhr, *The Children of Light and the Children of Darkness*, 76–77.

This was a progressive argument in its time. To Niebuhr, it was a mark of America's success in creating a just society that American society had found approximately the right balance between women's rights and natural female obligations. His insistence that women were uniquely obliged to preserve the "organic integrity" of family life, however, was a product of the same tradition he rightly called "male ideology." Niebuhr evaluated modern feminism not from a feminist perspective but from the perspective of a privileged white liberal male. The few references that he made to feminism in his vast corpus of writings typically implied that feminism in American society had already gone as far as it should go. This belief was reinforced not only by Niebuhr's assumption that mothers owed deeper obligations to their families than fathers but also by his later tendency to portray the United States as a just society that had already "equilibrated power" and emancipated women.

Reinhold and H. Richard Niebuhr

Though Niebuhr's emphasis on realism and evil often moved observers to categorize him as a neoorthodox theologian, he remained a theological liberal. His brother, H. Richard Niebuhr, perceived that he attacked liberal Protestantism so insistently because he remained a liberal Protestant. In the mid-1930s, while Reinhold ridiculed liberal Christianity for its moralistic idealism, Richard tried to dissuade him from his abiding attachment to liberal religion. The liberal outcry against *Moral Man and Immoral Society* gave Richard the opportunity to convert his brother. "I have no defense of idealism to offer," he assured Reinhold, distinguishing himself from Reinhold's liberal critics. "I hate it with all my heart as an expression of our original sin." But the problem with his brother's assault on liberalism was that it retained liberal assumptions about religion and politics. Richard explained:

> I think the liberal religion is thoroughly bad. It is a first-aid to hypocrisy. It is the exaltation of goodwill, moral idealism. It worships the God whose qualities are "the human qualities raised to the nth degree," and I don't expect as much help from this religion as you do. It is sentimental and romantic. Has it ever struck you that you read religion through the mystics and ascetics? You scarcely think of Paul, Augustine, Luther, Calvin. You're speaking of humanistic religion so far as I can see. You come close to breaking with it at times but you don't quite do it. [125]

It seemed to Richard that his brother was ready to break with liberal Christianity but could never quite do it. He had not, and never would, renounce the

---

125. Letter from H. Richard Niebuhr to Reinhold Niebuhr, January 1933, quoted in Fox, *Reinhold Niebuhr,* 145.

liberal view of religion as power for the social struggle. He would not give up his liberal view of religion as the dimension of depth in life that was conceptualized and expressed through myth. Neither would he give up the liberal view that good religion had to be involved in the social struggle for justice and freedom. Reinhold could never accept his brother's verdict that "we want to be saviors of civilization and simply bring down new destruction." Richard was wrong to claim that political activism "is the cancer of our modern life." He was doubly wrong in his prediction that Reinhold was "about ready to break with that activism." Richard's arguments on these themes were nonstarters. Though the social gospel had gone to seed, Reinhold could never renounce the social gospel's command to make the world a better place.

Richard's appeal to the Augustinian-Lutheran tradition was another matter, however. It was a reminder of family roots. Reinhold was already sprinkling his books with Pauline quotes on sin. He was already quoting Augustine that the peace of the world is gained by strife. Though he continued to use Marxist arguments throughout the decade, he was already looking, in 1933, for an alternative language for Christian realism. He curtailed his active involvement in the Socialist party and set out on the intellectual course that produced, in 1939, *The Nature and Destiny of Man*. His father had lived and preached the faith of Paul, Augustine, Luther, and Calvin. As a young man, Niebuhr had left his father's provincial Midwestern world behind to conquer the expansive, modern world of liberal Protestantism. In the mid-1930s, aided by his brother's appeals to the faith in which they were raised, he created the massive theological synthesis that reshaped American liberal theology for more than a generation. He wedded liberal activist religion to an Augustinian theological worldview.

Niebuhr's subsequent model of the self owed more to his Augustinian heritage than to his acquired liberal sources. *The Nature and Destiny of Man* brilliantly dissected the dilemmas of the isolated egotistical male. Whether he was conscious of it or not, this creature's life was driven by his struggle with the sin of pride. In refusing to accept his dependence, he pretended to be adequate unto himself and thus put himself in the place of God. It was in his nature to keep others at a distance, to make himself the center of the universe, to seek power over others, and, ultimately, to challenge the authority of God. For Niebuhr, following Augustine and Calvin, hubris was always the primary form of human sin. It followed from this understanding of the human predicament that salvation meant salvation from egocentrism and will to power. Christianity was a religion that delivered isolated selves from their pride and self-absorption by defeating their self-will. As Niebuhr explained, Christianity was "a religion of revelation in which a holy and loving God is revealed to man as the source and end of all finite existence against whom the self-will of man is shattered and his pride abased."[126] The

---

126. Niebuhr, *The Nature and Destiny of Man* 1:201.

solution to "man's" egotism was an all-powerful, all-knowing, self-sufficient deity whose grace, alone, could humiliate and redeem human conceit.

This understanding of the human situation and the Christian response to it was surely an insightful and penetrating description of something. It was possibly a revealing description of the experience and religious struggle of a highly ambitious, attention-seeking, but repentant theologian.[127] It was undoubtedly an acutely discerning description of the predicament of self-centered, power-seeking, and hierarchically minded men. But was it a description of the universal human predicament, as Niebuhr claimed? Was it so obviously superior to liberal Christian understandings of the self? Did this account describe the situation of people, especially women, who are not aggressive, who do not keep people at a distance, and who are not self-centered? Did it describe the sins of women who sacrificed their careers for the sake of their husbands and children? In particular, did it describe the situation of Ursula Niebuhr, who gave up her position at Barnard to take care of her husband after his stroke? Were hubris and will to power the primary moral failings of everyone that Niebuhr knew? Or were they merely the primary moral failings of those he considered important?

To question Niebuhr's model of the self on feminist grounds is not necessarily to reject Niebuhr's account, which drew upon a rich heritage of Christian thought. Feminist criticism includes a multiplicity of perspectives on the theory and politics of women's empowerment, some of which draw upon Niebuhr's theological

---

127. For interpretations of Niebuhr's life and career that emphasize his aggressive ambition, see Fox's biography; John Murray Cuddihy's *No Offense: Civil Religion and Protestant Taste* (New York: Seabury Press, 1978); and Cuddihy's discussion in *Reinhold Niebuhr Today*. In Cuddihy's version of Niebuhr's life, Niebuhr was a young preacher from the provinces who was terrified of not making it in the big city. His ambition finally brought him to New York, where his spellbinding sermons on sin and collapsing civilizations made him a great success. "He used a few prooftexts on sin as a kind of disedifying discourse to hold people who wouldn't be held by positive thinking," Cuddihy explains. "What he knew was this message and these texts. He broke in, and he was ambitious. He was somewhat ashamed of the gospel, but he was also ashamed of the opponents of the gospel." The Fox and Cuddihy portraits of "Reinie on the make" undoubtedly shed light on Niebuhr's lifelong preoccupation with the pitfalls of egotism and self-will. In Cuddihy's version, however, Niebuhr was essentially a self-promoting opportunist who did not so much believe in Christianity as use it. This interpretation grossly exaggerates Niebuhr's opportunism and fails to capture anything of the devout Christian theist who wrote deeply moving prayers, who was extraordinarily generous to his students, and who gave his time and care to virtually everyone who approached him. Fox, also, exaggerates Niebuhr's supposed incapacity to sustain close friendships. Though it is true, as Fox documents, that Niebuhr never had enough time to satisfy especially demanding friends like Waldo Frank, part of the reason was surely that he gave so much time to the numerous friends and acquaintances who sought his attention. Cf. Cuddihy's discussion in *Reinhold Niebuhr Today*, 125–26; and Cuddihy, *No Offense*, 31–47.

anthropology. From nearly any feminist perspective, however, Niebuhr's account of the egocentric self was primarily a true description of power-seeking males.[128] The understandings of divine reality and redemption that derived from this anthropology shared the same limitations in perspective. Niebuhr's conception of his work, his assumptions about the public and private spheres, his style of argument, and his theology were prototypically masculine. His writings were filled with hypermasculine images that pictured life as a conflict among aggressive egotists. His language about divine reality generally portrayed God as a sovereign ruler whose holiness and power abased human pride. His conceptions of the private and public realms shared the paternalistic assumptions of vital-center welfare state liberalism.[129] Niebuhr presupposed that the private realm of home, family, friends, and religion was the sphere in which moral values were generated and sustained. As Richard Wightman Fox has observed, Niebuhr assumed that the paternally governed family was the bedrock of cultural order and the place where true human fulfillment was attainable.[130]

These assumptions about the nurturing and value-creating functions of the private realm provided the basis for Niebuhr to justify the secularity, competitiveness, and comparative valuelessness of the public realm. It was not the business of the public sphere to nurture identity or instill values. The business of the public sphere was to maintain order and ensure individual opportunity, including economic opportunity. To be sure, certain values were appropriate to the public sphere, but these were instrumental values that served society's quest for justice. If the private realm was the sphere of true fulfillment, the public (male) realm was the sphere in which society's harsher business was to be managed. Like the liberalism of his time, Niebuhr assumed that the paternalistic state had to be the guarantor of justice in modern society. If the struggle for justice in America was impeded by maldistributed wealth, unemployment, racial discrimination, or lack of available health care, it was the state's responsibility to redistribute wealth (or at least income), invest in job creation and training, outlaw racial discrimination, and provide health insurance. For the liberalism of Niebuhr's time, the state was viewed as a friend, if not a benevolent father.

---

128. See Barbara Hilkert Andolsen, Christine E. Gudorf, and Mary D. Pellauer, eds., *Women's Consciousness, Women's Conscience: A Reader in Feminist Ethics* (San Francisco: Harper & Row, 1987); Judith Plaskow, *Sex, Sin and Grace: Women's Experience and the Theologies of Reinhold Niebuhr and Paul Tillich* (Lanham, Md.: University Press of America, 1980); Judith Vaughan, *Sociality, Ethics and Social Change: A Critical Appraisal of Reinhold Niebuhr's Ethics in the Light of Rosemary Ruether's Works* (Lanham, Md.: University Press of America, 1983); Daphne Hampson, "Reinhold Niebuhr on Sin: A Critique," in *Reinhold Niebuhr and the Issues of Our Time*, 46–60.

129. Cf. Arthur M. Schlesinger, Jr., *The Vital Center: The Politics of Freedom* (Boston: Houghton Mifflin, 1949).

130. Fox, "Niebuhr's World and Ours," 5.

Niebuhr's disgust with any kind of softness or sentimentality in the public sphere was amply displayed throughout his career. Fox observes that when Niebuhr was a young man, "what annoyed him most of all about liberal Protestantism was its effeminate, namby-pamby faith in goodness and love." In the course of writing his flawed, but generally outstanding biography of Niebuhr, Fox discovered that Niebuhr was unable to form close friendships with certain peers who sought his friendship. He had particular difficulty with liberal church leaders because "they took too much time, they were passive, they were decorous, they were implicitly feminizing."[131] Fox overgeneralizes the claim that Niebuhr was too busy saving the world to sustain close friendships. Niebuhr made numerous friendships with less demanding students and colleagues, as well as very close friendships with Bennett, Will Scarlett, Sherwood Eddy, June Bingham, and others. Fox is correct, however, that Niebuhr clearly subordinated the cultivation of friendships to his public career of speaking, teaching, and writing. He was a loving father and husband, but spent most of his weekends on the lecture circuit. His life was not so much a web of relationships as a hierarchy of causes and commitments. To a paternalistic Protestant culture that worried about its creeping softness, he offered a powerful, self-assured, and vigorously masculine voice.

It is not a voice that would find much place, much less a dominant place, in postmodern academic or liberal Christian culture. Contemporary liberationist movements have produced discourses and codes of manners that Niebuhr could not have imagined. It is difficult to imagine Niebuhr, in turn, functioning in a culture that became, in a few years, so different from his own. Whether he would have adapted his worldview and style to contemporary feminism, multiculturalism, and postmodernism is unknowable. He undoubtedly would have found much within these movements sadly similar to the progressivist idealisms he once denounced. Though it no longer towers over the field, Niebuhr's work remains indispensable to any social Christian ethic that seeks to be realistic about the limitations of politics, religious idealism, and human nature. His attentiveness to irony and paradox, his insistence on the inevitability of collective egotism, and his sensitivity to the complex ambiguities inherent in all human choices have made permanent contributions to Christian thought. Any attempt to rethink or renew the social Christian tradition must deal with the legacy of its most important critic and advocate.

If it is axiomatic that social Christianity must absorb the truths of Niebuhr's theological vision, however, it is equally clear that his attempt to make Christianity speak the language of modern political realism reduced the Christian reality to domesticated modern American dimensions. Niebuhr's reformulation of the moral

---

131. Ibid., 8.

meaning of Christianity was influenced as much by his religious skepticism as by the shifts in his political views. In both respects, his version of the Christian mystery codified the religious worldview of an American nationalist and self-described "unbelieving believer." Niebuhr's politics and his religious faith were deeply compromised by his understanding of what it meant to be realistic. His disregard for the language of the kingdom contained the essential clue. The "reality" in Niebuhr's Christian realism was the world of human striving, conflict, and sin over which God ruled as sovereign Lord. When Niebuhr invoked the authority of "reality" for Christian realism, he did not refer to the reality of Christ's resurrection or the Spirit's transforming power. The presence of the kingdom inaugurated by Christ and vivified by the Spirit was not a reality that shaped his ethical thought. Niebuhr believed in the sovereignty of a Creator God of history and the redeeming power of divine love mediated through the cross of Christ. For him, Christ's death on the cross symbolized the impossible possibility of love as the standard for human relations. The cross symbolized the paradoxical reality of a love within history that transcends "the sinful rivalries of ego with ego."[132] These beliefs importantly distinguished him from the atheists for Niebuhr, but his worldview was otherwise no more supernaturalist or kingdom-oriented than that of his atheist friends. He was not prepared to cut against the grain of America's reality or oppose a real American interest in the name of Christian truth. If his formulation of the Christian faith claimed little enough for some of his followers to remain in the church, for many others it claimed too little to convey the Christian spiritual reality or its hope for the world.

---

132. Niebuhr, *The Nature and Destiny of Man* 2:72–73. For Niebuhr's discussion of the cross as the symbol of "impossible possible" love, see Niebuhr, *Beyond Tragedy: Essays on the Christian Interpretation of History*, 20–21.

4 REALISMS IN CONFLICT
Disputing the "New Liberal Consensus"

ONE YEAR AFTER REINHOLD NIEBUHR DIED, Michael Novak wrote that it seemed like ten. The Niebuhr-quoting realists who came to power in 1960 had created a catastrophe in Vietnam and fueled an explosion of new social movements that challenged the legitimacy and morality of America's dominant order. The voices of a new political generation denounced Niebuhr's vital-center liberalism for its accommodation to the dominant order and, especially, for its role in buttressing America's Cold War foreign policy. The cultural revolutions of the 1960s produced not only an antiwar movement and a radicalized civil rights movement but also new social movements committed to women's rights, feminism, sexual liberation, Black Power, environmentalism, antimilitarism, and economic redistribution. At the moment that Novak reflected on the disappearing legacy of Niebuhr's work, an idealistic politician straight out of the Methodist social gospel tradition was the Democratic party's presidential candidate.

Novak had been a prominent figure in the New Left and antiwar movements; he had even worked for George McGovern's presidential campaign. He was beginning to feel misgivings about America's countercultural movement and particularly about his role within it, however. He knew for certain that he could no longer stomach the moralistic rhetoric or tone of modern liberalism. McGovern's idealistic whining had put him over the edge. More than he realized at the time, Novak was turning to the political Right. Like the formerly Leftist editor of *Commentary* magazine, Norman Podhoretz, he was turning against the same movements for feminism, environmentalism, antimilitarism, and economic democracy that he had recently supported. In the first stage of his conversion to neoconservatism, he turned to Niebuhr as the symbol of the kind of liberalism he could still accept. His article for *Commentary*, "Needing Niebuhr Again," contended that in the aftermath of the 1960s, Niebuhr was needed more than ever. But he despaired that Niebuhr's lessons for American liberalism and even

American liberal Christianity had already been forgotten. "The new moralism we see all around us is all too like the old moralism, against which Niebuhr directed the central energies of his life," Novak wrote. "In many ways it is as if he had lived and worked in vain."[1]

In his prime Niebuhr advised government officials, appeared on the cover of *Time* magazine, attracted a large following of religious and secular admirers, and dominated his field to the point where, as Alan Geyer later recalled, he seemed "an omnipresent figure in theology and ethics."[2] In his closing years his work was widely ignored because it epitomized a rejected past. The foremost theorist of international politics in Niebuhr's generation, Hans Morgenthau, once remarked that he regarded Niebuhr as "the greatest living political philosopher of America, perhaps the only creative political philosopher since Calhoun."[3] Niebuhr received similar accolades from Arthur Schlesinger Jr., Hubert Humphrey, George Kennan, Henry Van Dusen, and many others during the last years of his life, while he witnessed the emergence of a theological generation that seemed to share none of the assumptions or spirit of his work. Union Seminary theologian Tom Driver contended in 1968 that Niebuhr's work was "essentially defensive or conservative." Christian realism defended the Western liberal tradition on which its own intelligibility was based, Driver observed. It tried to preserve and extend justice by restraining self-interest. "The question now is whether that defensiveness can be combined with a sufficient degree of historical creativity," he argued.[4] For him, Christian realism was too defensive and too compromised by its association with established power to offer the generative historical vision that was needed.

Princeton theologian Richard Shaull propounded a liberationist variant of this critique, arguing that Niebuhr's Christian realist paradigm needed to be replaced by an alternative theology drawn especially from the experiences of Third World, black American, and other marginalized Christian communities.[5]

---

1. Michael Novak, "Needing Niebuhr Again," *Commentary* 54 (September 1972), 52.

2. Alan Geyer, quoted in symposium on "Christian Realism: Retrospect and Prospect," *Christianity and Crisis* 28 (August 5, 1968), 178.

3. Hans J. Morgenthau, "The Influence of Reinhold Niebuhr in American Political Life and Thought," in *Reinhold Niebuhr: A Prophetic Voice in Our Time*, ed. Harold R. Landon (Greenwich, Conn.: Seabury Press, 1962), 109.

4. Tom Driver, "Christian Realism: Retrospect and Prospect," 179.

5. Richard Shaull participated in the 1968 *Christianity and Crisis* symposium on Christian realism, along with Geyer, Driver, John C. Bennett, Harvey Cox, and Roger Shinn. For his subsequent elaboration of a North American liberationist perspective, see Shaull, "Christian Faith as Scandal in a Technocratic World," in *New Theology*, No. 6, ed. Martin E. Marty and Dean G. Peerman (New York: Macmillan Company, 1969); and Shaull, *Heralds of a New Reformation: The Poor of South and North America* (Maryknoll, N.Y.: Orbis Books, 1984).

Shaull was a former Niebuhrian whose conversion to liberation theology had occurred during his Latin American missionary experience. His critique of Christian realism was amplified with heightened polemical force by Latin American liberationists such as Rubem Alves, who argued that "realism is functional to the system, contributes to its preservation and gives it ideological and theological justification." In his view, so-called Christian realism was essentially an ideology of the dominant social order. "Realism has not yet recognized that it is an American ideology and yet proceeds to pass universal judgment over the other 'regional' theologies," he claimed.[6]

John C. Bennett

Liberation theology gave notice that the reign of Christian realism was over. In theology no less than in politics, the zeitgeist is often a vengeful spirit. John C. Bennett had witnessed a similar phenomenon in his early career. In 1936, he observed that each intellectual generation typically criticized its predecessors beyond all fairness while exaggerating the novelty of its own wisdom. Though he was firmly identified with the Niebuhrian challenge to liberal Christianity, Bennett acknowledged that the Niebuhrians often treated this tradition unjustly in their determination to supplant it.[7] For the next half-century, Bennett's own work would only rarely be guilty of this fault. He defended a Christian social ethic that closely resembled Niebuhr's realism without duplicating Niebuhr's exaggerations or his stigmatizing attacks on liberalism. In the 1960s, when a new radicalism debunked the purported illusions, cynicism, conservatism, and outdatedness of Christian realism, it was Bennett who defined most helpfully what Christian realism had been and how it needed to be revised.

Henry Van Dusen later recalled that the defining characteristics of Bennett's career were foreshadowed during his student years in the late 1920s at Union Seminary. As Bennett's theological mentor, Van Dusen was impressed by Bennett's "intellectual preeminence, outgoing if shy friendliness, and, above all, bold and determined dedication to unconventional reform."[8] When Niebuhr arrived at Union in 1928, Van Dusen recommended Bennett to him as a younger

---

6. Rubem A. Alves, "Christian Realism: Ideology of the Establishment," *Christianity and Crisis* 33 (September 17, 1973), 176.

7. John C. Bennett, "The Social Interpretation of Christianity," in *The Church through Half a Century: Essays in Honor of William Adams Brown,* ed. Samuel Cavert and Henry Van Dusen (New York: Charles Scribner's Sons, 1936), 113.

8. Henry Pitney Van Dusen, Preface to *Theology and Church in Times of Change: Essays in Honor of John Coleman Bennett,* ed. Edward LeRoy Long, Jr., and Robert T. Handy (Philadelphia: Westminster Press, 1970), 9.

colleague "uncommonly endowed with wisdom and common sense."[9] Thus did a lifelong friendship and intellectual partnership begin. Bennett's reforming spirit and disciplined intelligence would mark all of his work in a career closely intertwined with Niebuhr's.

His first book laid much of the groundwork for an argument that he elaborated throughout his career. *Social Salvation* (1935) presented Christian realism as a corrective variant of social gospel liberalism. "Social salvation belongs to the heart of Christian thought," Bennett declared at the outset, explaining that his work was to be understood as "a theological preface to social action."[10] It was not necessary to choose between Rauschenbusch and Niebuhr, though Bennett clearly preferred Niebuhr. His explication of realist social thought drew on Rauschenbusch's theories of the kingdom of evil and the class struggle, while toning down Rauschenbusch's teaching on the kingdom of God. "A few years ago it was all so clear," he recalled, somewhat wistfully. "The Social Gospel was regarded as a rediscovery of the original gospel of Jesus. Its charter was the teaching of Jesus concerning the Kingdom of God. The social task of the Christian was to apply the principles of Jesus to the social order. The Christian who believed in the Social Gospel faced the future with a clear sense of direction and with the confidence that the authority of Jesus was behind him."[11]

But these certainties had disintegrated in the past generation. Bennett observed that contemporary biblical scholarship was confused and deeply split over the interpretation of the New Testament's kingdom language. Neither was it possible to identify the teaching or Spirit of Christ with any particular social movement. The absolute love ethic of Jesus was "far removed from anything which is now possible in the world," Bennett argued. It was not directly relevant to the social world in which modern Christians were called to live out their faith. "Glib talk about applying the principles of Jesus has become unreal," he asserted. "We can no longer speak of a 'Christian' social order. The best that we can hope to achieve in this world will involve a compromise with the ideal of Jesus." To concede the point was not to deny Christianity but only to give up a rather recent and idealistic version of it. "It has never been characteristic of Christianity to think that the Christian ideal could be fully embodied in human life," Bennett observed. "Rather has it been taught that man never loses the status of sinner; at best he becomes a forgiven sinner. Realism about the stubbornness of human evil is no strange heresy but is in line with the main trends of historic Christianity."[12]

---

9. Reinhold Niebuhr, "John Coleman Bennett: Theologian, Churchman and Educator," in Long and Handy, *Theology and Church in Times of Change,* 234–35.

10. John C. Bennett, *Social Salvation: A Religious Approach to the Problems of Social Change* (New York: Charles Scribner's Sons, 1935), vii.

11. Ibid., 69.

12. Ibid., 81.

The latter theme echoed Niebuhr's recent discussion of classical Christian realism in *Reflections on the End of an Era*. Niebuhrian realism recovered the prudential wisdom of the classical Christian cultus. Bennett did not dispute the Rauschenbusch-Morrison account of how the consolidation of the classical Christian cultus eclipsed the kingdom idea in early Christianity. Like Niebuhr, he disputed only the supposition that true Christianity was concerned with bringing about the reign of God. The kingdom was more elusive, more difficult to define, and ultimately more transcendent than the social gospelers believed.

Yet the main thrust of social gospel theology and ethics was right, in Bennett's view. The social gospel was neither alien nor novel but "an inevitable development of the teachings of Jesus." It recovered Jesus' compassion for the poor and his passion for justice. "If we are to have his concern for the real welfare of persons we must take whatever measures are necessary to overcome the evils which crush persons now," Bennett wrote. Just as Jesus was deeply concerned with the problems of bread and economic distribution, so was the church commanded to care about distributive justice. In the social and political context of first-century Palestine, political solutions to the problem of justice were unimaginable. The distributive economic problem in the early church's social context could only be addressed through personal giving.

Modern Christians tried to follow Christ in a crucially different context. "Today the problem of bread cannot be solved without a new economic system," Bennett urged. "Our integrity as Christians depends upon our efforts to overcome the injustice which is the other side of our own privileges."[13] The social gospel insistence on this point was correct. Here, as they claimed, the social gospelers had recovered the spirit of original Christianity. The question of social compassion was not a secondary or dispensable aspect of Christianity but the moral heart of Christian faith. Jesus' parable of the Last Judgment focused upon it. "Did not Jesus separate the sheep and the goats on the basis of their attitude toward the economic needs of others?" Bennett wrote. "While the earlier Social Gospel may have been wrong in identifying the Kingdom of God with a new social order, entrance into the Kingdom does depend in our time upon the struggle to remove the obstacles to human welfare in history."

Whether Christians should speak of "building the kingdom" was ultimately irrelevant. The social gospelers had taken hold of the essential obligation, which was to live out, as far as possible, the moral and spiritual meaning of the kingdom faith. The reign of God was always coming. "Whether it is to be gradual or a series of crises God will not do our work for us," Bennett instructed. "The catastrophes about which we talk so much with rather academic detachment will have no virtue in themselves, for unless we do our part they will mean punishment

---

13. Ibid., 90–91.

without redemption for the countless souls who are in their way." Authentic Christianity accepted the moral burden of the church's role in bringing about social salvation.[14]

Bennett was careful not to identify the gospel with any system of political economy, including democratic socialism. The economic question was a practical issue, not a dogmatic one. He was emphatic about the revolutionary truth of the social gospel movement, however. The social gospelers had transformed American Protestantism, in his view; they had brought the church to its true form. "It is no exaggeration to say that until the last generation the prevailing social ethic in the Church has never contemplated radical social change to be brought about by human effort in co-operation with divine forces in society," he noted.[15] It was the Christian socialist mainstream of the social gospel movement that revolutionized modern Christianity. Bennett cited Ernst Troeltsch's famous account of this transformation, which documented that modern social Christianity alone had "laid bare the worm-eaten condition of the previous conventional Christian ethic" to discover and live out the social meaning of Christianity.[16] If the social gospelers took their kingdom rhetoric too literally and invested too much faith in progress, these were small faults, in Bennett's view, by comparison to the revolutionary achievements of the Christian social movement.

Christian realism built upon this achievement while eschewing the illusions, optimism, near pantheism, and pacifism of the social gospel tradition. Christian realism was dedicated to social salvation without enshrining any particular ideology with divine sanction. It denounced the ravages of the existing system without prescribing any alternative system as a *Christian* solution. It distinguished more clearly than the social gospelers between dogmatic and practical issues. Bennett's practical judgment in the mid-1930s was that capitalism was plainly not working and that some form of democratic socialism would better serve the common good. "In other words," he explained, "it seems clear that a more just society, in which poverty and insecurity are abolished and in which there is more co-operation for the common good, is entirely possible, and that it is the present system which has turned out to be impractical."[17]

Social Salvation bore the distinguishing marks of Bennett's subsequent work. It identified with Niebuhr's perspective while avoiding Niebuhr's polemical spirit; it adopted Niebuhr's theological anthropology while eschewing Niebuhr's characterization of Christian teaching as mythical; it criticized social gospel optimism

---

14. Ibid., 91.

15. Ibid., 105.

16. Ernst Troeltsch, *The Social Teaching of the Christian Churches,* vol. 2 (Louisville: Westminster/John Knox Press, 1992, c1931, German 1912), 728; quoted in Bennett, *Social Salvation,* 106.

17. Bennett, *Social Salvation,* 133.

while identifying with the social gospel movement; it made an ethical case for Bennett's progressive politics without reducing Christianity to this commitment. Bennett's subsequent writings similarly echoed Niebuhr's evolving theological and political positions without dissociating himself from his liberal Christian heritage. "I still believe that we cannot afford to depart far from the spirit and the method of liberalism," Bennett declared in 1939. He rejected "the tirades against theological liberalism which have become commonplaces of current discussion." The liberalism in which he was raised was unrecognizable in the fashionable attacks upon it, and he wanted no part of an illiberal Christianity. Bennett was equally clear as to what separated him from the tradition of Mathews, Rauschenbusch, and Morrison, however. "The sense that there is no social choice, especially in international relations, which is not intolerably evil, is the thing that haunts me constantly," he confessed.[18] Christian realism sought to maximize the possibilities for good, but with the tragic awareness that the possibilities for evil expanded with the good.

Bennett's major work, which was written during the Second World War, elaborated his conception of social evil. *Christian Realism* observed that the horrors of the war were driving many people to speculate about the existence of superhuman forces of evil. Bennett sympathized with the sentiment but countered that it was neither necessary nor socially desirable to revive the ancient Christian idea of supernatural evil. The nearly apocalyptic evils of the twentieth century could be accounted for, in his view, by taking into account the ravages of human egotism, the vicious circles of hatred and fear inherited from the past, the culture-shattering pace of modern social change, the power madness of overly powerful modern rulers, the ease with which ordinary patriotism was manipulated into nationalistic hatred and cruelty, and the destructive capabilities of modern technology. These were the means by which ordinary people committed extraordinary evil, Bennett argued. "If we ascribe our plight to superhuman devils, we shall either neglect our real enemies or yield to the spirit of fatalism."[19] Christian realism recognized the pervasive and indistinguishable character of social evil without giving in to it, mythologizing it, or making it an excuse for social indifference or injustice.

Bennett's major work also joined Niebuhr in his campaign to prepare and energize Americans for their anticipated participation in the war. Bennett believed that Niebuhr's interpretation of the teachings of Jesus exaggerated the theme of love perfectionism and thus unfortunately reduced Jesus' love ethic to the realm

---

18. John C. Bennett, "A Changed Liberal—But Still a Liberal," *Christian Century* 56 (February 8, 1939), 179.

19. John C. Bennett, *Christian Realism* (New York: Charles Scribner's Sons, 1952), 33.

of intimate personal relations. Niebuhr's account went too far in stripping Jesus' teaching of its social meaning, but in Bennett's view Niebuhr's rendering of the moral problem of violence and coercion was essentially correct. "Jesus was sufficiently influenced by the apocalyptic thinking of his time to be able to concentrate upon the Kingdom of God in absolute terms to the neglect of the immediate political consequences of his choices," Bennett judged. But this mindset was not an option for most of Jesus' modern followers, and thus the New Testament's moral pronouncements were not laws that later followers were compelled to apply mechanically to their situation. For example, he explained, "When violence is already in progress and the question at issue is not that of violence or no violence but whether one side is to be able to dictate to the other terms of surrender, then those who are responsible for public policy may be obliged to continue to use force to prevent such a result."[20]

Bennett allowed that Quakers, Mennonites, and other Christian pacifists could claim to be following the true way of Christ. For those Christians who were committed to the attainment and protection of gains toward social justice, however, and who therefore took responsibility for public policy, the moral choices were more complex. "No nation as a nation can be expected to have the moral discipline to live according to the pacifist faith, paying the price of the cross rather than defending itself or preparing to defend itself," he observed.[21]

Few Christian pacifists would deny this, however. For most of them, the issue was not the plausibility of the state's claims but whether the way of the cross could ever sanction participation in war. The question was not whether the state could morally justify its resort to defensive or protective violence but whether a Christ-following church could take part in war. Bennett had a Niebuhrian answer to this question in its immediate American context. "I do not believe that pacifists, especially in America, face the problem that arises when they themselves do not bear the brunt of the suffering to which their policy of non-violence may contribute," he wrote. Though American pacifists spoke often about the way of the cross, they were not the ones whom European and Japanese facism was crucifying. Bennett acknowledged that some American pacifists undoubtedly would divert the world's suffering to themselves if they could do so. But the crucial point was that no such way was open to them. They could not suffer in place of the actual victims of fascism. "When there is no redemptive way of the cross open to Christians in a situation, it is important for them not to disguise their responsibility for the increase of the sufferings of others by the use of words that suggest falsely that they are the ones who suffer," Bennett argued.[22]

---

20. Ibid., 102.
21. Ibid., 104.
22. Ibid., 108.

Like Niebuhr, Bennett remembered with shame how American churches sacralized the last war. Unlike Niebuhr, he did not castigate the churches for their role in nourishing a deep revulsion for war in the succeeding generation. Until recently, Bennett had fully shared in this revulsion. He did not demean its moral impulse or its religious warrant. He hoped that the past generation of Christian antiwar feeling would play a constructive and constraining role in the churches if America went to war again. "The disillusionment about war which has been so pervasive may have led many to a moral indifferentism concerning the issues involved in this war, but there is genuine moral insight in that disillusionment which must not be lost," he asserted. Abraham Lincoln's attitude toward war was his model. Lincoln waged a tragically necessary war without hubris or bad faith. He pressed on to victory in a just war without assuming that his side was righteous or that God was on his side. Bennett declared that this was "the only attitude—other than the position of the pacifist—which has any right in the Christian church."[23]

Bennett's idealism moved him to hope for the emergence of a national progressive coalition that would realign America's political party system. In the absence of such a movement, he drifted with Niebuhr toward Roosevelt's liberal pragmatism. In 1939 he remarked, "It is uncomfortable to have no political movement in which one can have much faith, and to be left with the bare hope that out of the New Deal and the new political consciousness of labor a coherent progressive movement may come into existence."[24] Like Niebuhr, he increasingly resigned himself to the conclusion that New Deal reformism marked the limits of progressive politics in America. It was futile to hold out hope for an American version of the British Labour party. Democratic socialism was not so wild a dream in England, he explained, but America's individualism, its comparatively weaker democratic traditions, and its antipathy for trade unionism nullified any serious hope for American economic democracy. In the early 1950s, Bennett concluded that American Christianity should therefore press for "an experimental modification of capitalism to meet particular needs" rather than challenge the capitalist system at its center.[25] Like Niebuhr, Bennett was chastened by the fact that even the mildest economic reformism in America had to contend with the opposition of most churchgoing Protestants. Though it was not especially difficult to enlist mainline Protestant support for initiatives pertaining to world peace-making, better race relations, and ecumenical cooperation, Protestant leaders

---

23. Ibid., 110.

24. Bennett, "A Changed Liberal," 181.

25. John C. Bennett, "Christian Ethics in Economic Life," in *Christian Values and Economic Life,* ed. John C. Bennett, Howard R. Bowen, William Adams Brown, Jr., and G. Bromley Oxnam (New York: Harper & Brothers, 1954), 213.

met stiff resistance when they encouraged greater support for trade unionism. The Federal Council of Churches had pounded on this wall without effect for several decades. "This situation reflects a persistent problem within Protestantism," Bennett conceded. "Local churches do reflect the interests and the opinions of those economic groups that are dominant among their members. They do not often bring to their members a distinctively Christian social ethic that counteracts the influence of prevailing opinion in the community."[26] Bennett's rather modest conception of what was politically realistic in the 1950s was informed by his awareness that American Protestantism's upwardly mobile laity still did not accept the New Deal.

More than Niebuhr, Bennett was deeply involved in the church's institutional life and work, becoming America's leading participant in the international ecumenical movement. He played active roles in the 1937 Oxford Conference, in the 1948 founding convention of the World Council of Churches (WCC) at Amsterdam, and in subsequent WCC assemblies at Evanston (1954), New Delhi (1961), and Uppsala (1968), as well as at the 1966 WCC-sponsored World Conference on Church and Society in Geneva. For two decades, he led the WCC's Department of Church and Society and shaped much of the social witness of world ecumenical Christianity. His concern with the church's institutional life also motivated him to accept numerous administrative tasks at Union Seminary. Bennett taught at Auburn Seminary and Pacific School of Religion before returning to the Union faculty in 1943 as a professor of theology and ethics. In 1955 he succeeded Niebuhr as dean of the faculty at Union, in 1960 he was appointed to the newly established Reinhold Niebuhr Professorship of Social Ethics at Union, and in 1963 he assumed the presidency of Union, which he served until his formal retirement in 1970.

More than any figure of his time, Bennett shaped and was persistently engaged with the project of making mainline Christianity relevant to the modern world. More than any other figure, he embodied connections between the social gospel and realist Christianity. In 1959, he noted that while he was "a grateful product of the Social Gospel," he had often criticized the social gospel tradition "for its uncritical optimism, for its lack of theological depth, [and] for its tendency to identify the gospel and the church with particular social programs and social systems."[27] Christian realism at the end of the 1950s retracted none of these criticisms. A realist corrective to social gospel idealism had been necessary. Bennett worried that whenever it was stripped of its social gospel roots, however,

---

26. John C. Bennett, "Christian Ethics and Forms of Economic Power," in Bennett, et al., *Christian Values and Economic Life,* 238.

27. John C. Bennett, "How My Mind Has Changed," *Christian Century* 76 (December 23, 1959), 1501.

so-called Christian realism appeared to be cynical and conservative. He knew from his circle of colleagues that many self-described Christian realists did not share Niebuhr's social gospel past, his passion for social justice, or his increasing dissatisfaction with Cold War orthodoxy.

The differences between their realism and Niebuhr's would break open in the next decade. Niebuhr's rejection of monolithic cold warriorism, his call for a policy of Soviet-American coexistence, and his reconsideration of American nuclear policy drove the first wedge between Right and Left Niebuhrians. In each case, his reconsiderations were prompted or influenced by a position taken by Bennett. In 1959, shortly before Christian realism began to be pilloried for its ties to the corporate-military establishment, Bennett urged that the realist deflation of Christian idealism was a long-completed project. The pressing threat to existing American Protestantism did not come from idealistic currents within it but from a "loss of the radical sense of social responsibility which the Social Gospel brought to American Protestantism." A one-sided Niebuhrian corrective had gone too far, as Niebuhr himself recognized. It was wrong for the churches to be complacent in a country where blacks were still denied basic rights as citizens. It was wrong for churches to sacralize the American way when the American way showed so little care for the poor, the vulnerable, and the common good. Though he had once embraced the welfare state as a realistic alternative to democratic socialism, Bennett declared that the untended social ravages of the past decade had convinced him that defending the welfare state was not enough:

> Today I am convinced that our country is handicapped by the fact that there has been so little of the socialist impulse in our tradition. We seem singularly unable to do well those things that cannot be done for profit and which depend upon the initiative of the state or of the community working through the state; we adhere to the half-conscious dogma that those things which can only be done effectively by the community are in some way on a lower level than those which are effectively done for profit by individuals and private groups. This assumption is the source of the great American inhibition which prevents us from ever doing enough toward education, toward urban renewal and housing, toward making medical care available to all families without bankrupting them.[28]

It seemed to Bennett that the very concept of a public good was dropping out of American political discourse and consciousness. He exhorted American church leaders to challenge their country's ideologically sanctioned preoccupation with private interests. "I am appalled by the degree to which our great nation is rendered almost helpless to solve many of its urgent problems because of the individualistic dogma which it has inherited from an earlier period," he declared.

---

28. Ibid., 1501–2.

While conceding that theologians should not prescribe economic policies on Christian grounds, Bennett asserted that they were obliged to oppose the reigning "unchristian individualistic ideology" that sanctioned public disregard for the common good. America celebrated its growing private wealth while ignoring its deepening public poverty. American prosperity was growing alongside under-funded schools, inadequate health care, worsening air and water pollution, a deteriorating infrastructure, and a worsening polarization between the prospering and working classes. For Christian realism in the 1960s, Bennett argued, these were the defining realities.

Christian Realism in a New Era

He continued to assume that America was obliged to repel communist advances in the world. Realism toward Soviet power continued to require vigilant resis-tance, patience, and counterforce. Bennett also believed that "a considerable change of emphasis" was needed in American foreign policy, however. America needed to abandon its "generalized hostility toward communism as a monolithic and unchanging adversary."[29] It needed to become more pragmatic and less self-righteous in its approach to the Soviet Union. It needed to face up to its own mounting public squalor. And it needed to renounce the reactionary policies in the Third World that made the United States the world's foremost counterrevolutionary power.

The last point touched a nerve among Christian realists. In 1966, while serving as president of Union Seminary and while becoming increasingly iden-tified with the antiwar opposition to America's intervention in Vietnam, Bennett served as the chief organizer and cochairman of the WCC-sponsored World Conference on Church and Society in Geneva. Except for the WCC assemblies, this was one of the most influential and broadly representative ecumenical con-ferences of the modern era, bringing together 410 Protestant and Orthodox delegates from around the world. Under Bennett's careful guidance the conference addressed the Vietnam War and adopted a resolution, written chiefly by Bennett, that censured America's intervention in Vietnam:

> We would suggest that the churches have a special obligation to question con-tinually the wisdom and rightness of the present Vietnam policies of the bel-ligerents. The massive and growing American military presence in Vietnam and the long-continued bombing of villages in the South and of targets a few miles from cities in the North cannot be justified. . . . In view of the dangers created by this situation, we urge that all hostilities and military activity be stopped and that the conditions be created for the peaceful settlement of the Vietnam

29. John C. Bennett, "Beyond Frozen Positions in the Cold War," *Christianity and Crisis* 24 (January 11, 1965), 269.

problem through the United Nations, or the participants in the Geneva Conference, or other international agencies.[30]

This rather mild declaration ignited a firestorm in American Christendom. Bennett was careful to prevent the Geneva Conference from calling for immediate American withdrawal from Vietnam, but his role in producing an international Christian denunciation of American policy in Vietnam was nonetheless deeply offensive to many Americans. Their feelings were expressed by a conservative Niebuhrian who did not like the conference's tone, its procedures, or its resolutions. On Bennett's initiative, Paul Ramsey had been invited to the conference as a nonvoting member. In his account of the conference, Ramsey bitterly criticized Bennett and other church leaders for their presumption in taking specific stands on controversial issues. *Who Speaks for the Church?* decried the influence of the churches' "social action curia" that produced such spectacles as the Geneva Conference. "By and large, the American participants, composed too largely of the social action curias, clergymen and academics, brilliant youth one rarely met at the Methodist Youth Fellowship, and with no Christian laymen whose vocation it is actually to share in policymaking executive leadership in the aspired responsible society, did not come to startling new awareness," Ramsey reported. "By and large, they saw or thought they saw their own reflections in the mirror."[31]

Ramsey saved his heaviest fire for the conference's resolution on Vietnam. Bennett criticized America's terrorizing and indiscriminate destruction of Vietnamese villages, culture, and infrastructure. To these moral objections, Ramsey replied that "no one ever said that the military destruction taking place in the South is contributing anything positive to political stability or to solving the problems which have produced a revolutionary situation in that country." This was a counterrevolutionary war, not a construction project or relief mission. The object of the war was to smash the Vietcong, which inevitably required horrific violence and destruction. The question was not whether American intervention required massive destructive force but whether the United States was able and willing to prevent a communist takeover of South Vietnam. This was the real issue, which a smattering of church leaders with moral qualms about "excessive destruction" was hardly competent to address. Said Ramsey:

> The real determiners of United States policy have to estimate the *degree* of danger of escalation into world conflict; and, having done so, they have to compare this with the danger of world conflict if some other course of action is taken or if there is no military action at all in South Vietnam or in the rest of Southeast Asia. Doubtless this depends on the political picture one has of

30. Quoted in Paul Ramsey, *Who Speaks for the Church? A Critique of the 1966 Geneva Conference on Church and Society* (Nashville: Abingdon Press, 1967), 84.
    31. Ibid., 100.

the world, but what accredits the churchmen's picture against that of the government's as a justifying reason?[32]

Ramsey urged that the ecumenical movement had more important and appropriate work to do. He was not opposed to the ecumenical movement itself, like "those conservatives and right-wingers who on every occasion attack the NCC and WCC irrationally and indiscriminately."[33] His attack was more discriminating. The churches did not need an ecumenical movement that took positions on divisive social and political issues, in his view. What was needed was an ecumenical movement that strove to attain a consensus on crucial theological foundations before it issued statements of any kind on controversial issues.

Bennett's reply was characteristically respectful and discriminating. He agreed with Ramsey that the churches and ecumenical agencies should focus most of their pronouncements on areas where some kind of consensus was possible. The effort to attain agreements on fundamental theological issues was central to the life and purpose of the ecumenical movement. It would be a grave mistake for the ecumenical movement to abandon this effort and replace it with pronouncements on every social issue. Bennett cautioned that in a "highly pluralistic theological situation," however, it was extremely difficult, if not impossible, to obtain ecumenical agreements on fundamental theological beliefs. It was much more difficult to attain agreements on certain doctrinal issues than upon certain pressing social issues, but Ramsey's approach would have prevented the churches from addressing any controversial social problem. "Ramsey wants to wait until there is a position in the church that is beyond significant debate, but this would involve a strong inhibition against speaking at all about specific decisions," Bennett observed. Ramsey's prescription stripped the church of its prophetic mission and nullified any culture-forming role for the church in the public square. He vehemently criticized *Christianity and Crisis* for opposing Barry Goldwater's candidacy in the 1964 presidential election, but Bennett retorted that Goldwater's candidacy cried out for liberal Christian opposition. Goldwater's campaign took reactionary positions on domestic and foreign policy issues that were irreconcilable with mainline Christian concerns for justice, freedom, and peace. "It would have been a scandal if no agencies of the church had called attention to this situation," Bennett argued.[34]

But the pressing issue was Vietnam. Bennett conceded that there were few political issues on which the churches were compelled to take a specific stand, and he believed that even then, as with Vietnam, it was usually possible to leave

---

32. Ibid., 90.

33. Ibid., 21.

34. John C. Bennett, "A Critique of Paul Ramsey," *Christianity and Crisis* 27 (October 30, 1967), 247.

room for several policy options. In the present case, he did not believe that church leaders should insist on immediate American withdrawal from Vietnam. What he did believe was that the tragedy of Vietnam had been forced upon American churches in a way that required them to make assessments, draw lines, and speak out. This was undeniably a subjective judgment, and Bennett pressed it subjectively. "I am concerned about the cumulative effect of the bombing of many villages, the saturation bombing with napalm of large areas of jungle because of the suspicion that they contain Vietcong, and I have never understood why these things worry Mr. Ramsey so little," he wrote.[35]

By then, the Niebuhrians were deeply split. Ramsey spoke for an assortment of Right-leaning Niebuhrians who maintained Niebuhr's Cold War politics of the early 1950s and were confounded by Niebuhr's recent positions on U.S.–Soviet relations, nuclear policy, and Vietnam. Ramsey's perplexity toward Niebuhr was attributable, in Bennett's view, to his blindness to the conflicts between Christian morality and American power politics. "Why does he never say anything in criticism of the American stance in the world today?" Bennett implored. "He gives the impression that there is no conflict between the Christian perspective and the American stance in the world."[36] Ramsey countered that Bennett, Niebuhr, Roger Shinn, and other *Christianity and Crisis* regulars were obliterating Christian realism. He traced the downfall of Christian realism to the early 1960s, when *Christianity and Crisis* began to search for a "new liberal consensus" in social ethics. "Christian realism is to be found in the sound articulations of the early Niebuhr in *The Nature and Destiny of Man* or in those of the late Niebuhr in *The Structure of Nations and Empires,*" he instructed. "It is missing from the genial, quasi-pacifist pragmatism of many of his disciples today."[37] The disintegration of Christian realism was certified by the fact, he complained, that even Niebuhr was signing petitions and editorials as if Niebuhr had never existed.[38] "Reinhold Niebuhr himself can be quoted in support of the liberal consensus!" he exclaimed with incredulity. The spectacle of Niebuhr making alliances with old-style liberals, progressives, and antiwar protesters marked the occasion, as Ramsey put it, to say, "Farewell to Christian Realism."[39]

The hardline Cold War Niebuhrians repeatedly invoked Niebuhr's response to fascism to support their own interventionist position on Vietnam, but Bennett

---

35. Ibid., 248.

36. Ibid., 249.

37. Paul Ramsey, "Farewell to Christian Realism," 1966; reprinted in Ramsey, *The Just War: Force and Political Responsibility* (Lanham, Md.: University Press of America, 1983, c1968), 487.

38. Paul Ramsey, "How Shall Counter-Insurgency War Be Conducted Justly?" 1966; reprinted in Ramsey, *The Just War,* 458.

39. Cf. Ramsey, "Farewell to Christian Realism," 479–88.

and Niebuhr insistently replied that the analogy between the Nazi threat and the present Vietnamese crisis was spurious. The Munich analogy was false because communism was not primarily a military threat, as Nazism had been, and because the Asian situation was far more complicated than the European situation in World War II had been. Bennett remarked, "Those who speak with most conviction in favor of our Vietnam policy seem to us to be blind to many intangible factors in the Asian situation that could cause military successes to lead to political and moral defeats."[40] Ramsey's blast against the Geneva Conference moved Bennett to summarize his own perspective on what Christian realism meant in the late 1960s:

> I think that the basic theological and ethical teaching in the church should encourage a critical attitude toward the following elements in the US stance: the hangover of capitalist ideology that causes us to drag our feet in relation to socialistic experiments abroad; our absolutistic, crusading anti-Communism in relation to Asia and Latin America; a counter-revolutionary bias that seems unwilling to allow nations in Asia and Latin America to have their own experiments with a revolution; a habit of over-stressing military solutions because we are competent in this field and have the hardware but do not understand the people in some other cultures enough to grasp the political aspect of their struggles; tendencies of a more idealistic sort that mask illusions, especially the tendency to assume that if we try hard enough we will compensate for all the evil that we do by producing a democratic or quasi-democratic solution.[41]

This agenda marked a change in the consciousness and perspective of Christian realism. The moral underside of American anticommunism in the Third World had only rarely been a Christian realist theme. Bennett's emphasis on curtailing American imperialism in the Third World came from his revulsion toward the Vietnam War and from his desire to redefine Christian realism. Though he and Niebuhr had occasionally criticized aspects of American imperialism in the past, their realism pertaining to the national interest, the struggle for power, and the limitations of morality had provided a highly nationalistic framework for their moral and political analyses. America's maneuvers in the Third World were typically assessed not from the perspectives of those affected by American policy but by a method that sought to establish America's genuine national interest in the situation and the moral conflicts this interest presented for American policymakers. American Christian realism addressed the question of how to exercise national power in a morally responsible way, while assuming that any nation's foreign policy reflected the demands of its economic and security interests. Christian realism combined Christian moral concern with a nationalistic

---

40. John C. Bennett, "From Supporter of War in 1941 to Critic in 1966," *Christianity and Crisis* 26 (February 21, 1966), 14.

41. Bennett, "A Critique of Paul Ramsey," 249.

realism in politics. It tried to tame the excesses of American presumption while assuming that American foreign policy would be shaped decisively not by moral or ideological concerns but by some conception of America's national interest.

This was the realism that Ramsey, Kenneth W. Thompson, Carl Mayer, Ernest Lefever, and other Right-leaning Niebuhrians still defended. It was also the approach defended by Arthur Schlesinger Jr., Hans Morgenthau, and other Niebuhrians who shared Niebuhr's current perspectives on the Cold War and the Vietnamese situation. As Ramsey explained, it was an approach that "nudged Christians toward the need to assist in preserving the equilibrium of political power while 'that man in Washington' did the same for the nation as a whole." Ramsey believed that in his "sober" moments, Niebuhr still understood that "this nation has inherited both power and responsibility in imperial proportions." Christian realism in its heyday absorbed the meaning of this truism. "This means simply that we are one of the nations that has the power significantly to influence events beyond our borders," Ramsey explained. "Whether we do or don't, we *do*. There is need for more, not less, Christian realism in our premises. It is the premises the Church is 'competent' to affect. The decisions of political prudence upon those premises are another matter."[42]

Authentic Christian realism accepted the burdens of American power in a new generation. As Ramsey perceived, however, many Niebuhrian realists no longer viewed America's imperial inheritance as a moral responsibility. Confronted with the Vietnam debacle and an explosion of domestic and international dissent against American imperialism, they began to claim that American Christian realism was too provincial, too nationalistic, and too inclined to justify American capitalism, militarism, and anticommunism. The Niebuhrian revisionists included Bennett, Roger Shinn, Ronald Stone, Robert McAfee Brown, and Charles West. The problem with Christian realism was not with its realistic approach to politics and human nature, they claimed, but with its exclusionary Euro-American purview. Christian realism made pronouncements on the limitations and realities of world politics without listening to the voices of non-Western, nonwhite peoples affected by American politics. Bennett's participation in the World Council of Churches and, especially, his discussions with Third World Christians at the Geneva Conference convinced him that American Christian realism needed to be opened to non-American perspectives on world politics.

Nearly half of the conference's members had come from churches in Asia, Africa, and Latin America. Bennett later recalled that it was a transforming experience for him to spend two weeks discussing world events with Third World Christians who did not share his language or assumptions. He referred to it afterwards as "the Geneva experience." "American churchmen who have had

---

42. Ramsey, "A Farewell to Christian Realism," 488.

the Geneva experience need not take over any other country's ideology, but they may gain some freedom from our own," he advised. "A succession of experiences of this type should enable the American churches to provide some corrective for the vision of the magistrates who now control our destinies."[43]

This was the break point for Christian realism. Niebuhr's followers were split among several factions on various social and theological issues, and a significant Right-Left division had emerged on issues pertaining to anticommunist resistance. Bennett's response to these debates opened Christian realism to a deeper internal critique, however. To call for a more open-ended, multiculturalist corrective to Niebuhr's Euro-American framework was to challenge Christian realism at a deeper level than the running disagreements over national policy. Bennett was by no means a radical proponent of bringing Christian realism into dialogue with liberation theology. He was already considerably outflanked by such Niebuhrian colleagues as Shaull and M. M. Thomas in bringing liberationist critiques to bear on the assumptions and ideology of Christian realism. Former students of Niebuhr such as Robert McAfee Brown and Beverly Harrison would later move in similar directions, entering into liberationist paradigms that Bennett continued to regard as "other."[44]

Bennett was often moved to remind his more radical friends that realism was an antiutopian impulse. It opposed not only the facile optimism of moralistic progressives but also the world-changing idealism that informed much of the tougher-sounding liberationist rhetoric. "Nothing has happened to refute the realistic analysis of the stubbornness of evil in society or the tragic side of history," he cautioned in 1968. "No return to a pre-Niebuhrian optimism is possible."[45] For all of his qualifications and Niebuhrian dialectics, however, it was Bennett who argued most persistently that Christian realism was not a Cold War ideology but a form of social Christianity that was open to new challenges and perspectives. Christian realism employed "middle axioms" that were always provisional in character, but through which the meaning of Christian faith in a given context could be expressed. That is, Christian realism used prescriptive maxims that were normative for a given time but were not indefinitely or universally applicable. "Christian realism grew up in response to European situations so far as foreign policy is concerned," Bennett recalled. "Today we need to encourage forces for radical change, especially in Latin America where our tendency is the opposite." The tendency of Niebuhrian realism was to focus on

---

43. Bennett, "A Critique of Paul Ramsey," 249.

44. Cf. Robert McAfee Brown, *Theology in a New Key: Responding to Liberation Themes* (Philadelphia: Westminster Press, 1978); Beverly Wildung Harrison, *Making the Connections: Essays in Feminist Social Ethics* (Boston: Beacon Press, 1985).

45. Bennett quoted in "Christian Realism: Retrospect and Prospect," 176.

how American power could be used to promote democracy and justice in the world, he noted. But in a new era, "I think that we should be realistic about the limits of American power or the possibility of our power to do more harm than good when we try to police the world."[46]

He later conceded that Christian realism was not a "self-sufficient" or self-contained theological perspective. "It is a corrective theology that at its best incorporated some of the spirit and the dynamism of the Social Gospel and the Christian Socialism of the Niebuhr of *Moral Man and Immoral Society* for which it was a corrective," he explained. "Without the continuing influence of these sources, latter-day Christian realism often is the North American ideology that Rubem Alves finds it to be."[47] What was needed was a theology that affirmed that "the powerless victims of injustice must gain power," Bennett urged. He recalled that during its most creative period, this theme was highly familiar to Christian realism. It resounded throughout *Moral Man and Immoral Society* and Bennett's *Social Salvation*. In recent years, liberation theology had given a new voice to this project. The major work of Bennett's later career, *The Radical Imperative*, elaborated his conviction that the best impulses of Christian realism could be recovered through a serious engagement with liberationist criticism.

"I see the need to transform the use of American power in the world," he declared at the outset. "This would involve abandonment of the role of the United States as guardian of the *status quo* for the sake of our economic interests, of being the habitual opponent of revolutions abroad, of being the great power that is the special friend of cruel rightist tyrannies in the interest either of 'anti-Communism' or of maintaining stability as the value of highest priority."[48] Bennett acknowledged that his anti-imperialist agenda marked a return to an earlier mode of Christian realism. "I recognize in myself a too bland acceptance of national trends in the 1940s and 1950s," he confessed. "The fact that there was considerable harmony between my ethical convictions and the policies of the United States Government during the Second World War and during the early years of the cold war contributed to this, as did my tendency to be overly optimistic about the effects of the 'mixed economy.'"[49] *The Radical Imperative* was thus closer to the spirit of *Social Salvation* than Bennett's other works.

To make itself realistic to a new situation, Christian realism had to be more ecumenical in spirit and more willing to learn from Latin American, African American, and feminist theologies. "So long as I assumed that my church, the

---

46. Ibid., 176.

47. John C. Bennett, "Continuing the Discussion: Liberation Theology and Christian Realism," *Christianity and Crisis* 33 (October 15, 1973), 197.

48. John C. Bennett, *The Radical Imperative: From Theology to Social Ethics* (Philadelphia: Westminster Press, 1975), 7–8.

49. Ibid., 9–10.

church to which I looked for inspiration and guidance, was limited to worldwide Protestantism, my church was sadly truncated," Bennett admitted. "This was actually true of me until the late 1950s, and I doubt if I was exceptionally bigoted in such matters."[50] Like Niebuhr and nearly all liberal Protestant leaders, Bennett viewed the Catholic church for most of his career as a reactionary monolith that prohibited self-criticism and opposed modern democracy, science, and liberal culture. Like Niebuhr, he developed a positive interest in Catholicism only after he began to comprehend, in the 1950s, that Catholic scholars such as Jacques Maritain and John Courtney Murray were developing theories of modern democracy and religious freedom that drew upon distinctively Roman Catholic sources. The emergence of modernizing theological tendencies and the Catholic church's distinctive capacity to sustain organic communities of memory drove Bennett to rethink his inherited anti-Catholicism. The reforms of the Second Vatican Council accelerated this reappraisal. In his role as Union Seminary president, Bennett became a major proponent of Protestant-Catholic dialogue and ecumenical cooperation. He conceded that for many Catholics, the tradition-changing decrees of Vatican Council II brought about "debilitating confusion and something close to a loss of religious identity." These reactions needed to be understood as "the natural consequences of drastic changes, especially of the movement away from authoritarianism and exclusivism."[51] Bennett was hopeful that a somewhat scaled-down but revitalized Catholic church would emerge from its present disputes over authority, moral teaching, and holy orders, however, and he looked forward to the social guidance and inspiration that a revitalized Catholicism might offer to the non-Catholic world.

Liberation Theologies

The Radical Imperative gave more sustained attention to the challenge of liberation theologies. The book was written at the high point of academic and church interest in the new radical theologies emerging from feminist, African American, and Latin American perspectives. The classic texts of liberation theology were published between 1969 and 1973: James H. Cone's *Black Theology and Black Power* and *A Black Theology of Liberation* appeared in 1969 and 1970; Rosemary Radford Ruether's *Liberation Theology* was published in 1972, a year before the appearance of Mary Daly's *Beyond God the Father* and the English edition of Gustavo Gutiérrez's manifesto, *A Theology of Liberation*.[52] These radical state-

---

50. Ibid., 91.

51. Ibid., 94.

52. Cf. James H. Cone, *Black Theology and Black Power* (New York: Seabury Press, 1969); Cone, *A Black Theology of Liberation* (Philadelphia: J. B. Lippincott Co., 1970);

ments were the most influential theological works of the period. Bennett ignored Daly, who was already moving toward a post-Christian feminism, but *The Radical Imperative* otherwise responded to the radical challenges of liberationist criticism.

Bennett admitted that he had only recently begun to appreciate the importance of feminist theology. Ruether's assertion that the oppression of women was "undoubtedly the oldest form of oppression in human history" was the kind of claim that he had only lately begun to take seriously:[53]

> If I had read that statement five years ago, I would have doubted its validity. I would have thought the word "oppression" an overstatement for a phenomenon considered so universal. I was too much impressed by the privileges enjoyed by middle-class and upper-class women, and by the informal and indirect forms of power often exercised by them, and by the fact that so many women seemed satisfied with their condition. Today I am more impressed by the extraordinary burden of an imposed status of inferiority and subjection from which women have suffered through the ages and by the injustices and the indignities from which they still suffer even after they have won many rights and opportunities formerly denied them.[54]

He was chastened by the feminist exposure of the deep misogyny of Jerome, Augustine, Aquinas, and other church fathers. He was further chastened by feminist critiques of the chauvinism of Luther, Calvin, and other Protestant reformers and by the antifeminism of even most social gospelers.

Bennett recalled that although Rauschenbusch supported women's suffrage, his endorsement of the suffrage movement was grudging at best, largely because of his certainty that a woman's proper social role was to be a wife and mother "in a family consecrated by the presence of quite a few children."[55] Rauschenbusch gave no encouragement to women, including his daughters, who aspired to other careers. Like the liberal church tradition to which he belonged, Rauschenbusch labored to make the biblical witness credible to modern people, but he did not cringe at the Pauline injunctions that the head of a woman was her husband or that women should keep silent in church. Bennett noted that modern Christians often laughed out loud when such passages were read in public or

---

Rosemary Radford Ruether, *Liberation Theology: Human Hope Confronts Christian History and American Power* (New York: Paulist/Newman Press, 1972); Mary Daly, *Beyond God the Father: Toward a Philosophy of Women's Liberation* (Boston: Beacon Press, 1973); Gustavo Gutiérrez, *A Theology of Liberation: History, Politics and Salvation,* trans. and ed. Caridad Inda and John Eagleson (Maryknoll, N.Y.: Orbis Books, 1973).

53. Ruether, *Liberation Theology,* 95; quoted in Bennett, *The Radical Imperative,* 109.

54. Bennett, *The Radical Imperative,* 109.

55. Ibid., 115. For an account of the social gospel's Victorian cultural background, see Janet Forsythe Fishburn, *The Fatherhood of God and the Victorian Family: The Social Gospel in America* (Philadelphia: Fortress Press, 1981).

even in church. He highlighted the importance of such implicitly antipatriarchal Pauline texts as Galatians 3:28 and 1 Corinthians 7:4, but acknowledged that the explicit scriptural basis for a critique of patriarchy was thin. Part of the modern radical imperative was to reinterpret Christian theology for a culture influenced by feminist criticism. The imperative was accentuated for Bennett by the laughing responses to Pauline instruction. "How long have congregations laughed at the reading of Holy Scripture?" he asked. "For how many centuries have the assumptions of those passages been so conveyed to congregations that they have taken their truth for granted?"[56]

The questions answered themselves. Feminist criticism posed a revolutionary challenge to modern Christianity. A new epoch in Christian history had arrived for which there were no precedents and few resources. The predominant images and language of Christian Scripture, tradition, theology, and liturgy were suddenly judged to be crucial components of an identity-forming cultural system that demeaned women and gave religious sanction to patriarchy. Christian teaching sacralized father-ruling conceptions of creation, nature, ontology, history, authority, and social roles. Bennett remarked that he knew many women "who feel that everything about the worship of the church leaves them out and they wonder if they can take it much longer."[57] Many others had already left the church. This was the most pressing liberationist challenge to liberal American Christendom, in his view, partly because it was the liberationist movement closest to the liberal white churches.

Bennett observed that the black American experience was more remote to liberal Protestantism. It was true, as Cone had recently asserted, that no white theologian had ever taken the oppression of African Americans as a point of departure for American theological reflection. But the truth was worse than this, Bennett noted, because until the civil rights movement of the 1950s, white American church leaders paid virtually no attention to the oppression of African Americans. The social gospelers rarely mentioned race at all, except to worry that too many non-Anglo-Saxons were getting into America. The famous social creed adopted by the Federal Council of Churches in 1908 presented an impressive list of economic demands but never mentioned race. In 1932, after four years of deliberation, the Federal Council expanded the creed to seventeen articles, thirteen of which dealt with economic objectives. The remaining articles called for the repudiation of war, negotiated settlements to all disputes, just treatment of offenders, protection of civil liberties, and finally "Justice, opportunity and equal rights for all; mutual goodwill and cooperation among racial, economic

---

56. Bennett, *The Radical Imperative*, 112.
57. Ibid., 118.

and religious groups."[58] The forefunner to the National Council of Churches thus tucked a single fleeting reference to racial justice into its elaboration of "The Social Ideals of the Churches."

Christian realism largely shared this failing, as Bennett acknowledged. *Social Salvation* enumerated the "many social evils that had priority for me in 1935," but the legacy of slavery, racial hatred, and racial injustice was not among them. African American liberationism was a product of *this* historical narrative, which was invisible in white liberal theologies. Like all liberation theologies, black liberationism did not begin with abstract doctrines inherited from the past or taken from authority but with the suffering experiences of oppressed people. African American theology explicated the meaning of Christian faith not from some purported universalistic standpoint but self-consciously from the perspective of black experience. As Cone explained, it embraced the historic African American identification with the biblical exodus narrative and emphasized the biblical image of God as "the God of the oppressed, involved in their history, liberating them from bondage."[59]

Bennett voiced several misgivings about Cone's elaboration of this perspective. He worried that Cone was too dismissive toward Christian teaching on nonviolence, that Cone's inflammatory rhetoric seemed to promote black racism, and that Cone was not open to internal or external criticism. When he wrote sentences such as "What we need is the destruction of whiteness, which is the source of human misery in the world," Bennett worried that Cone was indulging a "passionate self-righteousness" that exempted itself from criticism and distorted the victim's own spirit. These were only cautionary notes, however. Bennett acknowledged that Cone's seeming provincialism and self-righteousness were probably strategically motivated to make white people "feel the lash of his rhetoric against whiteness as such." When Cone wrote that it was impossible to think of Christ as nonblack in the twentieth century, Bennett surmised that he was using "black" as a metaphor for all oppressed people. In this event, his theology elaborated the biblical notion that Christ was present especially in the sufferings of the poor, the weak, and the oppressed. While he disputed Cone's operative assumption that racism was monolithic and unchanging, he affirmed the biblical thrust of Cone's theology and called attention to the justice of his critique. "This is a racist culture," Bennett wrote. "Racism is embedded in institutions as varied as racially slanted intelligence tests, the habits of police, and practices in the sale of real estate. The deposit of centuries of an imposed state of inferiority has left its mark on what black people expect for themselves and on what white

58. Ibid., 121.
59. Cone, *A Black Theology of Liberation,* 19.

people expect of them."[60] In this situation, black liberation required Black Power, but liberation was unattainable if Black Power was isolated. Black liberation needed progressive white allies, Bennett argued, but his strategic concern with Cone's work was that Cone left no room for alliances.

Latin American liberationism, being farther away, proved easier to embrace. Bennett warmly praised Gutiérrez's work for its biblical grounding, its theological learning, its emphasis on experience, its critique of economic modernization strategies, and its deep concern for the sufferings of the Latin American poor. He reported that it was Gutiérrez who first convinced him that the economic development strategies devised for Latin Americans in the United States and Europe had fostered economic, political, and cultural dependency in Latin America and hopelessly locked Latin Americans into cycles of debt, structural poverty, and deeper misery. Bennett praised Gutiérrez's selective appropriation of Marxism, which viewed the class struggle as a fact and class neutrality as an illusion without reproducing the dogmatic shibboleths of orthodox Marxism. He respectfully explicated Gutiérrez's notion of institutionalized violence, which distinguished between overt forms of repressive and revolutionary violence and the more structural, systemic forms of violence that permeated Latin American societies.

In his appropriation of Marxism and his discussion of violence, Bennett observed, Gutiérrez was developing a social perspective that closely resembled Niebuhr's approach in *Moral Man and Immoral Society.* This comparison brought out Bennett's two misgivings about Gutiérrez's liberationism. The first was that he offered no discussion of how counterrevolutionary violence against oppressive power could be morally controlled. The second was that Gutiérrez's rhetoric was unabashedly utopian. *A Theology of Liberation* resounded with the utopian assurance that a new society and "a new kind of man" were coming into being.[61] Bennett granted that political revolutions required revolutions in human consciousness. His concern was that liberation theology could sacralize new forms of political and religious tyranny under the mandate of revolutionary transformation. "My question is the familiar question of Christian realism, the question as to how soon new forms of egoism will appear which will distort the new structures," he explained.[62] But Bennett was generally confident that Gutiérrez understood the dangers of absolutizing any political movement or of underestimating the pervasiveness of human sin, including revolutionary egotism. Gu-

---

60. Bennett, *The Radical Imperative,* 126–29.

61. See especially Gutiérrez's chapters on "Liberation and Salvation" (chapter 9) and "The Church: Sacrament of History" (chapter 12) for his discussions of "Faith and the New Humanity" and "The Christian Community and the New Society."

62. Bennett, *The Radical Imperative,* 140.

tiérrez pointedly ruled out any "Christian ideology of political action or a political-religious messianism." His writings gave evidence of a Niebuhrlike awareness of the inevitable ambiguity of politics. In the form represented by Gutiérrez, Latin American liberationism was a powerful and compelling form of social Christianity that Bennett hoped would inspire a revival of progressive Christian commitment in the United States.

Could Christian realism stretch this far? For Bennett, the progressive theology that was needed would keep a realistic grip on the morally ambiguous character of all human striving while taking inspiration, correction, and instruction from the recent explosion of liberation theologies. It would operate out of the tradition of modern liberal theology while subjecting this tradition to liberationist criticism. It would be deeply ecumenical in spirit, drawing Protestant, Catholic, and Orthodox theologies into a dialogue that diminished long-standing barriers to mutual recognition and cooperation. It would resist utopian ideologies while keeping alive the Christian socialist vision of a democratized social order. It would recognize that politics was a struggle for power while seeking to maximize the regenerative power of nonviolence, cooperation, and ecumenical dialogue. It would thus create the "new liberal consensus" in mainline Christianity that Ramsey had foreseen and decried.

Having identified with a quite different form of Christian realism, it was dispiriting for Ramsey and other Right-leaning Niebuhrians to witness the forging of alliances between realist and various progressive and liberationist currents. By the mid-1960s, *Christianity and Crisis* was entirely alien to the conservative Niebuhrians. The magazine embraced liberationist causes and opened new discussions on feminist, ecological, and economic ethics. In the mid-1970s, while Bennett was writing *The Radical Imperative,* such important American Protestant theologians as Robert McAfee Brown, Harvey Cox, Paul Lehmann, Gayraud S. Wilmore, Langdon Gilkey, Letty Russell, J. Philip Wogaman, Beverly Wildung Harrison, Preston Williams, and Alan Geyer contibuted to this renewal of progressive Christian thought, often in dialogue with such Catholic scholars as Ruether, Leslie Dewart, Gregory Baum, David Tracy, and Daniel Maguire.[63] North American efforts to revive and redefine Christian socialism were impor-

---

63. Cf. Paul Lehmann, *The Transfiguration of Politics* (New York: Harper & Row, 1975); Langdon Gilkey, *Reaping the Whirlwind: A Christian Interpretation of History* (New York: Seabury Press, 1976); Gayraud S. Wilmore, *Black Religion and Black Radicalism* (Garden City, N.Y.: Doubleday, 1972); Letty M. Russell, *Human Liberation in a Feminist Perspective—A Theology* (Philadelphia: Westminster Press, 1974); J. Philip Wogaman, *A Christian Method of Moral Judgment* (Philadelphia: Westminster Press, 1976); Leslie Dewart, *The Future of Belief: Theism in a World Come of Age* (New York: Herder and Herder, 1966); Gregory Baum, *Religion and Alienation: A Theological Reading of Sociology* (New York: Paulist Press, 1975).

tantly aided by the writings of German theologians Jürgen Moltmann, Johannes Metz, and Dorothee Soelle, as well as by such Latin American liberationists as Gutiérrez, Juan Luis Segundo, José Míguez Bonino, Leonardo Boff, Enrique Dussel, and José Comblin.[64] At the same time, the rise of the environmentalist movement produced new ecological theologies that criticized liberal theology for its anthropocentrism and its capitulation to market economics.

Liberal Protestantism had always taken pride in its critical spirit, its tolerance, and its comparative openness to new challenges. Modern liberal Protestantism at its best was distinguished by its intellectual creativity and social idealism. This self-image was developed in a religious and academic culture in which the predominance of a liberal Protestant worldview could be assumed, however. For all of their celebrations of freedom, democracy, and pluralism, the social gospelers never questioned that America was and needed to remain a Protestant nation. If the cultural hegemony of Protestantism in American life was beginning to erode, the social gospelers never doubted that it needed to be restored and strengthened, albeit in a new form. Long after liberal Protestantism relinquished the dream and the rhetoric of Christianizing America, liberal Protestant leaders continued to assume that America belonged to them. Like most of his white male Protestant colleagues, who held virtually all of America's prestigious academic positions in religion, Niebuhr routinely invoked the "we" of American Protestantism interchangeably with the "we" of America. For mainline Protestantism, there was little need to distinguish between Protestant and American obligations in determining whatever needed to be redeemed or restored or created. America was a Protestant project that other groups were invited to join, provided that they accepted the authority and governing ethos of America's Anglo-Saxon–Germanic Protestant culture.

With the rise of social movements and the acceleration of socioeconomic trends that directly challenged American Protestantism's cultural authority, liberal Protestant theology was thrown into a new situation. The disestablishment of mainline Protestantism was effected partly through the erosion of its membership base and largely through the rise of new social, religious, and economic forces that eroded liberal Protestantism's cultural power. Having jettisoned much of its

---

64. Cf. Jürgen Moltmann, *The Crucified God: The Cross of Christ as the Foundation and Criticism of Christian Theology*, trans. R. A. Wilson and John Bowden (New York: Harper & Row, 1974); Johann Baptist Metz, *The Emergent Church: The Future of Christianity in a Postbourgeois World*, trans. Peter Mann (New York: Crossroad Company, 1981); Dorothee Sölle, *Beyond Mere Dialogue: On Being Christian and Socialist* (Detroit: Christians for Socialism in the United States, 1978); José Míguez Bonino, *Doing Theology in a Revolutionary Situation*, ed. William Lazareth (Philadelphia: Fortress Press, 1975); Juan Luis Segundo, *The Liberation of Theology*, trans. John Drury (Maryknoll, N.Y.: Orbis Books, 1976).

traditional teaching regarding eternal damnation, scriptural authority, and morality, liberal Protestantism found it increasingly difficult to sustain the interest
or religious loyalty of its children. Having accommodated themselves so thoroughly to the ethos of modern culture and commercial society, mainline churches
were in a poor position to resist the deracinating, desacralizing, and commodifying
effects of consumer culture. The displacement of mainline Protestantism was
further accelerated by the expansion of pluralizing social trends that included
not only the growth of Roman Catholic and non-Christian religious communities
in America but also the proliferation of therapeutic and other highly individualistic
forms of spiritual expression.

The liberal Protestant theology in the 1970s tried to cope with all of these cultural
revolutions. The religion departments of American church-related colleges, having previously featured curricula dominated by the giants of modern Protestant
theology, struggled to adjust to the implications of ecumenism, feminism, religious pluralism, and the apparent decline of the mainline churches. The decentering of mainline Protestantism fueled a heightened awareness of world religious
pluralism and engendered new approaches to comparative religion, theologies
of world religions, and interreligious dialogue. As much as any academic discipline in American higher education, religious studies became deeply pluralized
in the 1970s and 1980s. The most influential survey of Christian theology during
this period was appropriately titled *The Shattered Spectrum.*[65]

The shattering of liberal theology's governing assumptions about its social
position and universal character brought to an end the modern era of theological
giants. In the past generation, no theologian has attained the public or professional
recognition that theologians such as Barth, Niebuhr, Tillich, and Emil Brunner
received earlier in this century. The crucial reason for this diminution of theology's
public influence is not that there are no theologians whose work compares to
that of Barth or Tillich. Theologians such as Wolfhart Pannenberg, Thomas F.
Torrance, and Eberhard Jüngel continue to produce large-scale theological dogmatics in the style of Barth, Brunner, and Tillich, but their works receive comparatively little attention.[66] The crucial difference is that theology has become
too deeply pluralized to exalt or privilege the works of system-building synthe-
sizers. Liberal Protestantism no longer speaks from on high and no longer looks

---

65. Cf. Lonnie Kliever, *The Shattered Spectrum: A Survey of Contemporary Theology*
(Atlanta: John Knox Press, 1981).

66. Cf. Wolfhart Pannenberg, *Systematic Theology,* vol. 1, trans. Geoffrey W.
Bromiley (Grand Rapids: Eerdmans, 1991); Pannenberg, *Anthropology in Theological
Perspective,* trans. Matthew J. O'Connell (Philadelphia: Westminster Press, 1985); Eber-
hard Jüngel, *God as the Mystery of the World: On the Foundation of the Theology of the
Crucified One in the Dispute between Theism and Atheism,* trans. Darrell L. Guder (Grand
Rapids: Eerdmans, 1983).

for a single compelling voice. It does not seek a grand synthesis of liberal, liberationist, realist, process, feminist, ecological, and other theologies. It rarely bridges even the gulf between university-oriented "public" theologies and church-oriented confessional theologies. The most important of the older-style German dogmatic theologians, Jürgen Moltmann, eschews the scholastic style of his teachers and offers a progressive Protestant theology that supports democratic socialism, environmentalism, feminism, and near pacifism.[67] The most widely read and perhaps most influential American liberal Protestant theologian of this generation, Harvey Cox, goes further than Moltmann in attempting to find a new identity for liberal Protestantism through his dialogues with alternative religious traditions and perspectives.[68] While Moltmann remains essentially a biblical theologian, Cox is a cultural theologian who seeks to develop a multi-cultural, postmodern approach to liberation theology. His numerous books pursue dialogues with popular religious traditions and progressive social movements in various world religions, seeking always to develop deeper mutual understanding and cooperation among religious traditions.

Michael Novak and the Christian Realist Right

If the dimensions of postmodern theological pluralization were not fully evident in the mid-1970s, the implications of this transformation in social, political, and religious consciousness were sufficiently evident to produce a backlash. The decentering postmodern turn in theology was vehemently resisted not only by liberal Protestants, who were losing power, but also by conservative Catholics, evangelicals, neoorthodox theologians, and others who also opposed the relativistic implications of postmodern pluralism. More than a decade later, a national academic and media furor over multiculturalism belatedly raised certain aspects of this cultural shift for debate. Long before the American media made multiculturalism a national controversy, however, a reaction against the decentering relativism implicit within the pluralization of religious studies began to take shape within modern theology. In systematic theology, this countertrend took numerous forms. Barthian theologians such as Robert Jenson and Thomas F. Torrance and Barthian evangelicals such as Donald Bloesch called for a return to a Word-oriented neoorthodoxy or orthodoxy. Neo-Barthians such as Hans Frei and George

---

67. Cf. Jürgen Moltmann, *On Human Dignity: Political Theology and Ethics,* trans. M. Douglas Meeks (Philadelphia: Fortress Press, 1984); and *Creating a Just Future: The Politics of Peace and the Ethics of Creation in a Threatened World* (Philadelphia: Trinity Press International, 1989).

68. Cf. Harvey Cox, *Religion in the Secular City: Toward a Postmodern Theology* (New York: Simon & Schuster, 1984); and *Many Mansions: A Christian's Encounter with Other Faiths* (Boston: Beacon Press, 1988).

Lindbeck argued that with the breakup of liberal modernist foundations, a Barthian type of theological hermeneutics could support a narrativist neoorthodox religious identity. Former liberals such as Thomas Oden and Carl Braaten converted to more traditional forms of confessional orthodoxy, arguing that narrativist approaches conceded too much to relativism. In the Roman Catholic church, analogous reactions against postmodernism and liberation theology were led by such figures as the eminent Swiss theologian Hans Urs Von Balthasar and the Vatican's Joseph Cardinal Ratzinger.[69]

These systematic theologies provided crucial support for social theologians and ethicists who also opposed the trend toward radical politics, multiculturalist pluralism, and postmodernism in theology. In theology as in American politics, neoconservatism emerged in the early 1970s as a protest against the various social movements associated with the peace movement and counterculture radicalism. Among neoconservative social theologians, however, a different figure emerged as the symbol of what needed to be recovered in Christian theology. Neoconservatives rarely appealed to Barth, who was a political radical, or even to Brunner, who never retracted his hostile assessment of capitalism. For those former Christian liberals and leftists who turned politically to the Right in the 1970s, the galvanizing figure was Reinhold Niebuhr. For Novak, Richard John Neuhaus, Robert Benne, Dennis McCann, James Nuechterlein, and other neoconservatives, it was Niebuhr—or their version of him—who symbolized what had been lost in postmodern Christianity and what needed to be recovered.

Novak was the first to voice this sentiment, in the same year that he turned toward neoconservatism. "Not long ago, Niebuhr towered over Christian political thinkers in the land," he recalled in 1972. "Now the new Movement—of moralism, hope, vision, and radical analysis—appears to have tumbled that once lofty tower, or far more sadly, to have wandered past it into a desert." It was Niebuhr who explained that America "suffered from a kind of secularized religion" in which the nation regarded itself as a kind of church, "a movement

---

69. See the chapters by Braaten and Jenson in *Christian Dogmatics* (2 vols.), ed. Carl E. Braaten and Robert W. Jenson (Philadelphia: Fortress Press, 1984); Thomas C. Oden, *After Modernity . . . What? Agenda for Theology* (Grand Rapids: Academie Books, 1990), revised edition of *Agenda for Theology: Recovering Christian Roots* (San Francisco: Harper & Row, 1979); Donald G. Bloesch, *Essentials of Evangelical Theology,* 2 vols. (New York: Harper & Row, 1978); Hans Urs Von Balthasar, *The Von Balthasar Reader,* ed. Medard Kehl and Werner Loser, trans. Robert J. Daly and Fred Lawrence (New York: Crossroad, 1985); Joseph Ratzinger, *Introduction to Christianity,* trans. J. R. Foster (New York: Herder and Herder, 1970). For works that survey the field and make, respectively, neo-Barthian and evangelical contributions to it, see George A. Lindbeck, *The Nature of Doctrine: Religion and Theology in a Postliberal Age* (Philadelphia: Westminster Press, 1984); and Clark H. Pinnock, *Tracking the Maze: Finding Our Way through Modern Theology from an Evangelical Perspective* (San Francisco: Harper & Row, 1990).

of social goodness," Novak remarked. America's dream of the greening of America was its "most ineradicable national fantasy." But politics was not a morality play; politics was tragedy. This was Niebuhr's most valuable and now sadly neglected lesson to American idealists. "He unmasked many of the moral pretensions of America by ripping to shreds traditional religio-ideological interpretations of American destiny," Novak argued. It was Niebuhr who made a generation of American moralists pay attention to "issues of power and interest— he refused to leave to Machiavelli the things of Machiavelli."[70]

This was the Niebuhr that was needed again. Novak implied that the dovish liberal-turning Niebuhr of the 1960s was not the real Niebuhr. "It would have been marvelous to have had him at the height of his powers during the turbulence of the 1960s," he remarked, but alas, Niebuhr had always defined himself through his engagement with public events, and in his last years he was too ill to make the effort. "Had Niebuhr been well, he might have shown the way on three issues in particular," Novak suggested. These issues were "black liberation, the politics of the Third World, and the new moralism."[71] But Niebuhr's failing health prevented him from taking on the idealisms of a new generation, while his closest associates scrambled to accommodate Christian realism to them. The new idealists were reintroducing "personalist moral discourse into political matters" and embracing an unsupportable sense of guilt over white racism, Novak claimed. Their abandonment of Niebuhrian realism was epitomized by their slogan that "the personal is the political."

Niebuhr's generation of Christian leftists had rejected every form of moralism, from the sentimentality of liberal Christianity to the self-righteous cold warriorism of John Foster Dulles, but a new generation of Christian progressives proclaimed that personal virtue was central to good politics. Novak acknowledged that this sentiment was deeply rooted in American Protestant history. It was also, in his view, not only politically dangerous but also morally corrupting and self-deceiving. A new Christian realism was needed to unmask the pretensions and bad politics of the 1960s generation. For neoconservative Christians, the exemplary figure was the aggressively masculine, militantly anticommunist Niebuhr of the 1940s and 1950s, who explained the pathology of 1960s progressivism before it existed.

The chief conceit of the 1960s generation was that a new generation of newly educated academics, government planners, and other professionals could make the world a better place. Following David Bazelon and the American socialist Michael Harrington, Novak invoked a concept with a colorful history in Marxist thought to describe this new generational power bloc, referring to it

70. Novak, "Needing Niebuhr Again," 52–54.
71. Ibid., 57.

as the New Class. The distinguishing mark of the New Class was that it sought to gain status and power not through economic productivity but through organizational position. The New Class was not out to accumulate capital but to attain managerial power. As Novak observed, Harrington had recently appealed to the defining conceit of the New Class in his vision of an emerging "conscience constituency" in American politics. Harrington noted that the postwar baby-boomers were presently entering the professional middle class in unprecedented numbers, having earned their degrees during the crowning years of the civil rights movement and the horror of America's war in Vietnam. Having received a distinctive cultural education, they were predisposed toward racial justice, peace, and anti-imperialism. Harrington wanted to recruit them to his brand of progressive politics. Because the New Class was predisposed toward social planning, he argued, it was in a position to forge alliances with working-class and poor people—or to become their sophisticated enemy. The New Class could become the "conscience constituency" of American society, using its education to create a good society, or it could become a self-interested socioeconomic class that sought to protect its own new privileges. Harrington worried about Yuppie politics before it had a name. He pushed hard for the former choice, however, arguing that the 1960s generation was uniquely suited to create an American social democratic and anti-imperialist politics.[72]

Novak's response was deflating. "This attribution of 'conscience' to a po-litical class shocks a Niebuhrian," he reported. Harrington was right to call the new generation of academics, policymakers, bureaucrats, journalists, and other professionals a New Class. He was right to observe that this New Class was generally liberal in its politics and that it was composed largely of people who were predisposed toward government planning. What was shocking was to hear a Marxist blather on about the 1960s generation as a moral force in American politics. Niebuhr's most elementary lesson, which was partly cribbed from Marx, was being forgotten. Reason and morality were the servants of interest. It was true that the New Class liked to think of itself in morally virtuous terms, Novak observed: "The New Class covers its political campaigns—in 1968 as in 1972, in the civil-rights movement and in the anti-war movement—with an aura of morality so thick it would make the righteous Anglo-Saxons of a century ago envious."[73] The problem was that the New Class concealed its lust for power and its class interests under the cloak of its righteousness.

---

72. Michael Harrington, *Toward a Democratic Left: A Radical Program for a New Majority* (New York: Macmillan Company, 1968), 289–91. For Bazelon's elaboration of the New Class idea, see David T. Bazelon, *Power in America: The Politics of the New Class* (New York: New American Library, 1967).

73. Novak, "Needing Niebuhr Again," 60.

Novak did not dispute that two of the New Class's chief causes—the civil rights and antiwar movements—were morally justified. What was problematic about even these commitments, however, was that their moral righteousness prevented young progressives from acknowledging or even noticing what they were gaining from their moral poses. The New Class denounced "the System" and proclaimed its alienation from commercial society, for example, but its own desire for status and power was served by the growth of an activist federal government. In the name of compassion, fairness, and equality, the New Class was creating an increasingly administered society that provided well-paying, ego-gratifying jobs for New Class liberals. The New Class also had special psychic interests, in Novak's view. "It somehow feels it must exorcise its complicity in various social evils: white racism, militarism, imperialism, male chauvinism, consumerism, affluence. Acute discomfort at moral accusations distorts the vision of this class and makes it politically volatile," Novak wrote. "A desire to escape ambiguity and to be thoroughly good is an ambivalent political resource, as American history amply reveals."[74]

This desire to be good was often imposed, moreover, at the expense of others. The New Class supported school busing, for example, but sent its own children to private schools. Novak drew out the Niebuhrian irony. "It is high irony, of a sort Niebuhr would have savored, that the New Class in finding his realism 'dated' has conveniently overlooked precisely his most central theme: that claims on the part of groups to represent 'conscience,' 'morality,' and 'principle' must be exposed for what they are: disguises for naked power and raw interest," Novak remarked. The fundamental Niebuhrian maxim was to beware of the children of light. In dismissing Niebuhr, the New Class was returning to the Christian moralism that Niebuhr thoroughly refuted, while the official spokesmen for Christian realism sought not to be left out. For Novak, it was not Christian realism to tell poor people, as Harvey Cox advised, to have a confidence in the morality of their cause "not too complicated by strictures that warn against its possible defilement." Neither was it Christian realism to indulge white racial guilt, as Bennett was doing in his claim that white racism was "a deeper cultural sickness than we realized in the early '60s."[75]

The neoconservatives renounced this unsupportable moral burden and the confused idealism that imposed it. For most of them, the process of converting to neoconservatism required an extended and often traumatic reconsideration of their core beliefs, their socialization, their friendships, and their religious and political affiliations. Novak aptly remarked that a neoconservative was "a person

---

74. Ibid., 61.
75. See comments by Cox and Bennett in "Christian Realism: Retrospect and Prospect."

of the left who has become critical of the left." The essential characteristics of neoconservatism, in his assessment, were "(1) an initial sympathy for socialist, social democratic and anticapitalist points of view; and (2) a criticism of these points of view."[76] For most neoconservative theologians, the journey from the first to the second point affected not only their politics but, more deeply, the way they understood Christianity. Novak noted more than once that virtually all of the major twentieth-century theologians had been democratic socialists.[77] Like most neoconservative theologians, his early career and his religious outlook were rooted in this tradition. In the mid-1970s, while struggling to overcome his religiously nurtured idealism, he reasoned that the lack of a single example of democratic socialism in the world revealed something about the worthiness of democratic socialism even as an ideal. If the struggle to attain the ideal always failed, then democratic socialism was unworthy of the hopes invested in it by the past century of Christian theologians. Novak later recalled that this conclusion was at first profoundly disorienting and disillusioning to him. For several years, he was afraid to write about it or even discuss it with his wife and friends. "It wasn't until the mid-'70s that I became able to think of the issue in empirical terms at all," he recalled. "My religious background and my lack of background in economics made it difficult for me to keep the actual comparative factors in focus."[78] He was able to break from his Christian socialist past only after he adopted an alternative intellectual tradition and ideology. His alternative was the Anglo-Scottish–American Whig tradition and its ideology of "democratic capitalism."

The Lutheran neoconservative Robert Benne made a similar pilgrimage. At the outset of his major work, *The Ethic of Democratic Capitalism* (1981), Benne observed that while most American economists endorsed free-market capitalism on both economic and ethical grounds, most Christian social ethicists were strongly critical of capitalism on both grounds. "The mainstream of Christian social ethics leads toward outright condemnation of democratic capitalism and a passionate hope for an ideal democratic socialism," he noted. This was his own tradition. In his early career, he adopted a Christian socialist perspective that blended Niebuhrian themes with the economic theories of John Kenneth Galbraith. But throughout the 1970s, Benne increasingly doubted that Christian

76. Michael Novak, "Reinhold Niebuhr: Model for Neoconservatives," *Christian Century* 103 (January 22, 1986), 69.

77. Cf. Michael Novak, "New Questions for Humanists," in *The Denigration of Capitalism: Six Points of View,* ed. Michael Novak (Washington, D.C.: American Enterprise Institute, 1979), 57; Novak, "Changing the Paradigms: The Cultural Deficiencies of Capitalism," in *Democracy and Mediating Structures: A Theological Inquiry,* ed. Michael Novak (Washington, D.C.: American Enterprise Institute, 1980), 193.

78. Michael Novak, interview with author, March 20, 1990.

ethicists knew what they were talking about. He began to take more economic instruction from neoclassical economists than from Galbraith or from mainstream Christian social ethicists.[79]

The problem was that he was a Christian ethicist. He lived and worked in professional, intellectual, and religious contexts in which some form of the democratic socialist vision was utterly dominant. Benne observed that the conservative wing of modern Christian ethics was maintained by Left-liberal welfare state apologists who embraced Galbraith's mildly socialist analysis of the American industrial state. In his assessment, the Christian realists held the middle ground. "Those who carry forward the legacy of Niebuhr and Tillich—the Shaulls, Bennetts, and Browns—carry forward a vision of democratic socialism supplanting a decadent capitalism," he explained. He observed that even a mild and cautious realist like J. Philip Wogaman ultimately opted for democratic socialism "as the embodiment of Christian ethical hope." Moreover, in Benne's reading, the realists were now outnumbered by an ascending Left wing composed of the various strands of liberation theology. The liberationist wing included not only liberation theologians but also the program agencies of the World Council of Churches and the National Council of Churches. "Marxist thought has become the major tool of economic analysis and prescription for Christian liberation theology and ethics," he argued.[80]

Benne was candid about how this situation affected him personally. "This unhappy situation creates a good deal of pain in my life," he reported. He shared enough of the spirit of modern theology to want to be critical of modern commercial society. "But I share enough of the viewpoint of the mainstream of the American economics establishment to arrive at quite a different interpretation of the American economy than that of the ethics establishment," he wrote. "I find that many of the judgments of the ethics establishment are imposed simplistically upon ambiguous and complex economic phenomena and their 'prophetic insights' are often misguided."[81] For him, the socialist myth was understandable, even sympathetic as an attempt to combine modernity with the Christian hope for moral community, but it was misguided nonetheless. As a never attained but still powerful ideal, it functioned in modern Christian ethics as a religious myth or, more precisely, as the modern metaphor for the kingdom ideal. Benne's alternative to social Christianity's kingdom mythologizing was the existing American order,

---

79. Robert Benne, *The Ethic of Democratic Capitalism: A Moral Reassessment* (Philadelphia: Fortress Press, 1981), 2–3.

80. Ibid., 4.

81. Ibid., 5.

which he called, following Novak, democratic capitalism.[82] In his view, Niebuhrian realism (properly understood) led to an acceptance of the structure and
ethos of America's existing socioeconomic order.

This argument was elaborated most importantly by Novak. Borrowing from
Daniel Bell's tripartite model of modern liberal democratic societies, Novak
argued that modern democratic capitalism is a threefold social system consisting
of a particular kind of political order, culture, and economy. Democratic capitalism arose "when a polity constituted as a democratic republic, with inbuilt
checks and balances, and with auxiliary precautions to protect personal and
minority rights against their usurpation by majorities, is added to a capitalist
economy," he explained. "The latter is constituted by laws, customs and institutions that promote the creation of new wealth through invention, discovery
and enterprise."[83] For Novak, democratic capitalism was not merely an ideal
social system, but a spiritual achievement. Unlike most intellectuals, including
such neoconservatives as Irving Kristol, Peter Berger, and Paul Johnson, he
insisted that capitalism should not be conceived as a set of technical and instrumental arrangements. Responding to Bell's typical assertion that capitalism "is
simply instrumental and rational, and creates no values of its own," Novak
countered that this was exactly the problem with most accounts of the capitalist
revolution. Virtually all intellectuals, including many neoconservatives, thought
that capitalism had no spiritual basis. This mistake prevented them from grasping
the essence of capitalism. "It is simply not true that capitalism 'creates no values
of its own,' " Novak argued. "Capitalism is intrinsically related to some core
values—to liberty in the sense of self-discipline, to invention, creativity, and
cooperation, the root of the corporation; to work, savings, investment in the
future; to self-reliance, etc."[84]

Like most intellectuals, Bell misunderstood capitalism because he missed
its spiritual basis. "He misses the underlying spiritual power of democratic
capitalism and its capacities for self-renewal," Novak asserted. "He conceives
of it in too purely instrumental terms, neglecting to note the disciplines it teaches,

---

82. Benne mistakenly asserted that the phrase "democratic capitalism" was originated
by Novak. For an account of the origins of the rhetoric and ideology of "democratic
capitalism" in nineteenth-century American Whiggery, see Louis Hartz, *The Liberal
Tradition in America: An Interpretation of American Political Thought since the Revolution*
(New York: Harcourt Brace Jovanovich, 1955), 110–12.

83. Michael Novak, letter to *New Oxford Review* 55 (July/August 1988); cf. Novak,
"Defining the U.S. System," *Washington Times,* April 28, 1989; Daniel Bell, *The Cultural
Contradictions of Capitalism* (New York: Basic Books, 1978).

84. Michael Novak, "Class, Culture and Society" (review of *The Winding Passage:
Essays and Sociological Journeys, 1960–1980,* by Daniel Bell), *Commentary* 72 (July
1981), 72.

the moral abuses it is designed to prevent, and the virtues it uniquely elicits."[85] The crucial and transformative dimension of democratic capitalism was its realm of spirit. But even many neoconservatives missed the "powerfully self-transforming, creative, and inventive spirit" of capitalism, Novak lamented. His work would correct this pervasive mistake. *The Spirit of Democratic Capitalism* (1982) elaborated Novak's discovery of "spiritual resources in democratic capitalism I had long repressed in myself."[86] *Toward a Theology of the Corporation* (1981) claimed that multinational corporations "mirror the presense of God" in seven sacramental ways and evoked a "sense of communal religious vocation in economic activism." By virtue of their communal-religious character and their independence from the state, Novak asserted, corporations "offer metaphors for grace, a kind of insight into God's ways in history."[87] *The Catholic Ethic and the Spirit of Capitalism* (1993) continued that capitalism was not merely productive, virtue-producing, and spiritually true, but also provided a universal standard "to which cultures must measure up." Democratic capitalism set the standard by which all world cultures, political systems, and economies should be judged. The relativistic notion that capitalism was "just a set of technical arrangements" was utterly falsified by the experiences of recent American immigrants, Novak concluded, who found capitalism to be "more attractive morally, psychologically, and spiritually than the existing alternatives."[88]

Though he spent much of his career criticizing the social democratic thrust of most American Catholic and Protestant social teaching, Novak was greatly cheered by the publication of Pope John Paul II's 1991 encyclical, *Centesimus Annus*, which made a stronger endorsement of market economics than any previous papal statement.[89] With Neuhaus and George Weigel, he enthused that the pope's warm words for capitalist economics marked a breakthrough in Catholic teaching that American Catholic social theory needed to absorb.[90] With apparent justification, American Catholic neoconservatives boasted that their writings on capitalism were taken seriously at the Vatican and were influencing the devel-

---

85. Ibid., 72. For an extensive examination of the history and theory of American neoconservatism, see Gary Dorrien, *The Neoconservative Mind: Politics, Culture and the War of Ideology* (Philadelphia: Temple University Press, 1993).

86. Michael Novak, *The Spirit of Democratic Capitalism* (New York: American Enterprise Institute/Simon & Schuster, 1982), 26.

87. Michael Novak, *Toward a Theology of the Corporation* (Washington, D.C.: American Enterprise Institute, 1981), 41–43.

88. Michael Novak, *The Catholic Ethic and the Spirit of Capitalism* (New York: Free Press, 1993), 226.

89. Cf. John Paul II, *Centesimus Annus* (Wash., D.C.: Catholic News Svce., 1991).

90. Michael Novak, "A Papal 'Yes' to Capitalism," *Forbes* 147 (May 27, 1991), 182–83.

opment of Catholic social teaching. Their belief in the universal and spiritual truth of capitalist ideology was bolstered by the readiness of the church's universal teaching office to praise the superiority of modern capitalism, albeit with far more carefully hedged and equivocating formulations than those produced by neoconservatives.[91]

As a political-intellectual movement, neoconservatism originated in the late 1960s as a reaction against the anti-Americanism of the New Left and the ascendancy of a seemingly radicalized liberalism in the Democratic party. Neoconservatives were repelled by the McGovern presidential candidacy in 1972, which epitomized the spirit of a new, feminized, idealistic, and antiwar liberalism in American politics. Though they initially disputed that they had become conservatives at all, the neoconservative label stuck to them, mainly because they went on to objectively align themselves with the politics and institutions of America's conservative establishment. Neoconservatism was not merely a defense of capitalist economics but an intellectual movement that promoted militant anticommunism, a minimal welfare state, the rule of traditional elites, a return to traditional cultural values, and a politics of opposition to New Class liberalism.

The movement's Christian theological wing embraced all of these causes on political and religious grounds. Within American conservatism, neoconservatism was distinctive for its ethnic quotient. More than half of the movement's prominent intellectual leaders were Jews, while several of its most prominent Christian advocates were Catholics. Just as the "new liberal moralism" in America was no longer dominated by liberal Protestants, so was American conservatism no longer monopolized by the WASP establishment. Jews and Catholics were both secure enough in their Americanism and positioned securely enough in the dominant order to criticize their country as well as defend it from ungrateful critics. American assimilation and ecumenism had advanced far enough by the 1970s that Jews and Roman Catholics could invoke Niebuhr's authority to assail a liberal Protestant culture they found to be too idealistic and too accommodating to feminism, gay rights, and multiculturalism.

Neoconservatives and Access to Power

In the closing years of the Cold War, neoconservatives pressed for an American military buildup and aggressive military interventions in Central America. Within months of Ronald Reagan's inauguration, they founded the Institute for Religion and Democracy, which organized religious support for Reagan's foreign policy agenda and assiduously criticized the mainline Protestant and Catholic churches

---

91. Cf. Novak, *The Catholic Ethic and the Spirit of Capitalism*, 114–43; Richard John Neuhaus, *Doing Well and Doing Good: The Challenge to the Christian Capitalist* (New York: Doubleday, 1992), 48–49.

for promoting liberation theology, the nuclear freeze initiative, and the Central American sanctuary movement.[92] Neoconservatives such as Novak, Neuhaus, George Weigel, Ernest Lefever, and John Cooper appealed to Niebuhr's anticommunism in making their case for an aggressive anticommunist militancy.[93] The rise of New Class moralism was creating utopian idealisms that Niebuhr never imagined but for which his realism was the crucial antidote. Novak declared, "Niebuhr is needed because so many uncritically accept the oppressed of the Third World as a messianic force, attribute Third World poverty to U.S. exploitation, discount the military threat posed for the West by an armed force greater than Hitler's, and resume again the attacks of the 1930s on 'concentrations of economic power' in the multinational corporations."[94]

Neoconservatism was defined in the 1970s and 1980s chiefly by its militant anticommunism. Though most neoconservatives also emphasized the importance of what they called "waging culture wars" against feminism and other cultural radicalisms, their movement was preoccupied with the Soviet threat during the closing years of the Cold War. It was primarily on the basis of their anticommunism that neoconservatives secured numerous positions in the Reagan and Bush administrations and sustained highly effective coalitions with paleoconservative, New Right, and other conservative forces. In the 1980s, while increasingly straining from various tensions with their conservative allies, neoconservatives developed an elaborate infrastructure of institutes, think tanks, journals, and consulting firms, often by drawing support from Old Right foundations. Their alliances with Old Right organizations and foundations were viable as long as America was externally threatened by a conspiratorial Soviet enemy.

With the disintegration of the Soviet threat, the conservative coalition quickly unraveled. American conservatism splintered for a host of cultural and ideological reasons that I have analyzed elsewhere.[95] In the present context, the pertinent

92. For representative documents published by the Institute on Religion and Democracy, see *Christianity and Democracy*, 1981; *The Catholic Church in El Salvador*, 1981; *Christianity, Democracy and the Churches Today*, 1982; *A Time for Candor: Mainline Churches and Radical Social Witness*, 1983; and *Sanctuary: Challenge to the Churches*, 1986; all booklets edited and published by the Institute on Religion and Democracy, Washington, D.C.

93. Cf. Richard John Neuhaus, "Toeing the Line at the Cutting Edge," *Worldview* 20 (June 1977), 14–22; reprinted as *The World Council of Churches and Radical Chic* (Washington, D.C.: Ethics and Public Policy Center, December 1977); and Rael Jean Isaac and Erich Isaac, *Sanctifying Revolution: Mainline Churchmen Turn Radical*, Ethics and Public Policy Reprint (Washington, D.C.: Ethics and Public Policy Center, May 1981). Novak quote in Novak, *The Spirit of Democratic Capitalism*, 315–32.

94. Novak, *The Spirit of Democratic Capitalism*, 332.

95. Cf. Dorrien, *The Neoconservative Mind*, 323–96.

disagreement among neoconservatives centers on the question whether American foreign policy should continue to be formulated in ideological terms. For many neoconservatives, the dissolution of Soviet communism marks the moment to stop quoting Niebuhr on the wisdom of foreign policy realism. Joshua Muravchik, Ben Wattenberg, Midge Decter, A. M. Rosenthal, and numerous others proclaim that the time has come for a rebirth of Woodrow Wilson's world-embracing democratic idealism. With the death of communism, realism is no longer enough. The purpose of American foreign policy should not be merely to promote America's national interest, as realists claim, but to export American democracy around the world. "Democratic globalism" is the positive side of anticommunism. If democratic globalism was a liberal Protestant fantasy in its first incarnation, it is now reclaimed, in the twentieth-century's closing decade, by an intellectual-political movement that is neither liberal nor (for the most part) Protestant. For most neoconservatives, the foreign policy worthy of American idealism and power is to aggressively promote the expansion of American democracy throughout the world. Just as the communist threat required America to adopt an ideological world mission for the past half-century, the challenges of a postcommunist world now require America to adopt a new mission and a new creed, borrowed from the generation that last attempted to remake the world in America's image. For those who believe in the superiority of American democracy, neoconservatives argue, it is morally imperative to fight for the extension and success of the democratic idea. Americans owe it to others to help them share in the opportunities and privileges of American-style democracy.[96]

Novak and Neuhaus share this Wilsonian sentiment, though in milder forms than some neoconservatives. Both avoid the crusading rhetoric of Muravchik's "democratic idealism" and Wattenberg's "pro-democracy unipolarism." For them, the heart of the neoconservative project is no longer in the foreign policy field, but in the interrelated areas of culture and economics. Democratic capitalism requires not only a particular kind of free-market economy, but a particular kind of culture. Whether American culture meets the need of American capitalism is a troubling question for Novak. His writings work both sides of the neoconservative debate over culture. Like Berger, he frequently celebrates the popularity and influence of American culture around the world, enthusing that much of the world is wearing American blue jeans, listening to American music, and learning to speak English. American cultural values are triumphant throughout the world,

---

96. Cf. Joshua Muravchik, *Exporting Democracy: Fulfilling America's Destiny* (Washington, D.C.: American Enterprise Institute, 1991); Gregory A. Fossedal, *The Democratic Imperative: Exporting the American Revolution* (New York: Basic Books, 1989); Ben J. Wattenberg, *The First Universal Nation: Leading Indicators and Ideas about the Surge of America in the 1990s* (New York: Free Press, 1991); Charles Krauthammer, "The Unipolar Moment," *Foreign Affairs* 70 (1991): 22–33.

he exults. He does not share the disdain of America's intellectual class for the decadent mediocrity and consumerism of American middle-class culture. This is the intellectual snobbery that he gave up when he became a neoconservative.

But on other occasions Novak condemns the same culture for its nihilism and vulgarity. Reflecting on the power of commercial advertising and the dominant values of the commercial media, he writes that "we are beseiged by ideas, ideals, and solicitations that on reflection we find morally repulsive."[97] He reports that he and his wife have long felt "that the world of the media was a tidal wave, which we could hardly hold back by ourselves. We have long felt under seige, even in our own home. . . . Our own public moral culture, formed preeminently by television, cinema, and music, is a disgrace to the human race."[98]

For Novak, the key to this contradiction is that the Left controls the commanding heights of American culture. The shortcomings of American moral culture are not attributable to the nature of capitalism or the character of commercial society, he insists, but are direct consequences of the fact that "the Left still owns the heights of American culture."[99] America's social ills are not to be blamed on the corrupting effects of commercial society, but upon the New Class liberals who shape American culture. The problem is that the New Class controls the media, the universities, and the churches, resulting in the debasement of America's moral culture and institutions. In the wake of the dissolution of the Soviet enemy, many neoconservatives argue that it is time to bring the struggle home. Neoconservative religion seeks to regenerate American society by waging a struggle for America's soul against the knowledge class of liberal academics, clergy, and media stars.

Neuhaus pursues this project with particular zeal. He agrees with Novak that the sickness of American culture is mainly attributable to the conceits of the elite communications media, the afterglow of 1960s radicalism in the universities, and the persistence of radical progressivism "in the little worlds of liberal religion."[100] He repeatedly criticizes the influence of feminism in American universities and liberal churches, claiming that feminist ideology is hostile to intellectual freedom and incompatible with Christian faith. Neuhaus concedes that there is such a thing as "legitimate" feminism, which restricts itself to the pursuit of fair treatment and equal opportunity in the public realm. He observes that nearly all feminist theologians are more radical and ideological than this,

---

97. Novak, "Changing the Paradigms," 199.

98. Michael Novak, "The Revolt against Our Public Culture," *National Review* 36 (May 4, 1984), 48.

99. Michael Novak, "The Left Still Owns American Culture," *Forbes* 145 (March 5, 1990), 118.

100. Richard John Neuhaus, "Notes on the Culture Wars," *First Things* 9 (January 1991), 61.

however. In his reading, virtually all contemporary feminist theologians employ some version of ideological gender analysis in which gender is viewed as a fundamental organizing variable in social structure, culture, and personal life. Gender feminism analyzes society and culture by focusing upon the system of male domination made possible by men's control over women's sexuality, reproduction, personal and family life, and social roles. As Neuhaus explains, expanding upon Christina Sommers's critique of feminist theory, gender feminists claim "that our entire social and cultural order is skewed by the 'hegemony' of a patriarchal/sex/gender system that is designed to oppress and exploit women."[101]

Neuhaus concedes nothing to gender feminists, whose ideology, in his accounting, requires "relentless civil war against the democratic polity itself." Unlike the nonideological proponents of equal opportunity for women, who proceed by rational argument and do not regard gender or patriarchy as important analytical variables, gender feminists reject rationality as an instrument of male hegemony. For them, so-called rationality is driven by male will to power. In Neuhaus's telling, gender feminism is contemptuous toward most women, who are supposedly "possessed of a slave mentality that makes them collaborators with their male masters in opposing the struggle for feminist analysis." Gender feminism is thus defined by "radicalized gnostic elites" who despise the vast majority of women as much as they hate men.[102]

Neuhaus finds this radicalized gnosticism to be virtually inherent in feminist theology. The "keystone of feminist theology," in his reading, is the dogma that unfairness is systemic in Christianity. The unfairness dogma dismisses all reformist efforts to ensure better treatment for women that fail to challenge the patriarchal character of traditional Christianity. "Feminist theology may be expressed in 'moderate' or 'radical' forms, but the enterprise itself is inherently radical," Neuhaus argues. He claims that the radical lesbian feminism of Episcopal theologian Carter Heyward is symptomatic of the conclusion to which feminist theology is inevitably driven. For Heyward, the Christian doctrine of atonement represents "the sadomasochism of Christian teaching at its most transparent." For Neuhaus, it also marks the point of absolute dissociation between genuine Christianity and any kind of feminist ideology. "The lesbian feminist voice of unremitting rage, to which Carter Heyward and others would give expression, is, as claimed, the vanguard of feminist theology; and that theology is, as claimed, determinedly radical," he writes. "That is to say, it is radical in its rejection of historic Christianity."[103] For Neuhaus, as for Novak, religious feminism exposes

---

101. Richard John Neuhaus, "Feminism and Feminism," *First Things* 24 (June/July 1992), 66.

102. Ibid., 66–67.

103. Richard John Neuhaus, "The Feminist Faith," *First Things* 2 (April 1990), 61.

the animating essence of feminist ideology, which is a gnostic rage against sexual difference.

"The rage of feminists is partly to be explained by the weakness of the males they encounter," Novak instructs. "Men find it more difficult to stand up to the fury of a woman than to any other thing on earth; nothing so tests their manhood." In his view, the church's current problems with feminist criticism are traceable to the fact that (male) church leaders are failing the test. Because church leaders are failing to repudiate the inane absurdities of feminist theologians, he argues, modern Christianity finds itself besieged by self-hating feminists who demand a world made over. In his reading, feminism is ultimately a declaration of war against nature, experience, and tradition. The feminist revolution is not progressive, humane, or even radical, but total. "That is why the hatred they manifest is so unbelievably intense," he explains.[104]

Feminism is thus the ultimate flight from Niebuhrian realism about human nature. The feminist rage against difference is rationalized by the nihilistic doctrine that human nature does not exist. Like Richard Rorty, Neuhaus observes, feminists proclaim that socialization "goes all the way down." Much more than Rorty, however, feminists and other radicals have a deep vested interest in the claim that socialization is totally determinative. Rorty's maxim gives ballast to the feminist crusade to "break the disciplines" in the universities and replace traditional academic disciplines with women's studies, black studies, peace studies, and the like. In other words, academic feminists seek to turn the universities into indoctrination centers in which their orthodoxies are immune from criticism. "Black studies, Chicano studies, Marxist studies, gay and lesbian studies—all claim to possess a 'cognitively privileged truth' that enables them to critique everyone while being critiqued by no one," Neuhaus asserts. As Sommers alleges, feminism and its allied academic movements are therefore not academic disciplines at all, but religions, and bad religions at that. "When the university gets rid of religion, it does not end up with nothing to believe in but with a multitude of belief systems—most of them wildly incoherent and very, very angry," Neuhaus asserts.[105]

In the 1980s, the spectacle of a rising gay rights movement diverted Neuhaus's attention somewhat from the ravages of feminism. In his view, the gay rights movement is developing into a fourth institutional home for the adversary culture. "Moving beyond the three enclaves of countercultural shelter, homosexual ac-

---

104. Michael Novak, "Woman Church Is Not Mother Church," *Catholicism in Crisis* 2 (February 1984), 20–21; cf. Novak, *Confession of a Catholic* (San Francisco: Harper & Row, 1983), 193–98.

105. Richard John Neuhaus, "The Feminist Revelation," *First Things* 18 (December 1991), 56–58.

tivism is a growing factor in our politics, especially in urban politics," he warns. It is also unprecedented in American cultural history. "The homosexual movement is inherently and of necessity fundamental in its challenge," Neuhaus argues. "Unlike feminism, it cannot settle for adjustments in the relationships between women and men within the institution of the family. The organized homosexual cause has no choice but to be at war with those relationships and with that institution." In the past, he recalls, homosexuals kept their condition to themselves or hoped to find social tolerance for their deviation from an unquestioned moral norm. But in the social climate created by the gay rights movement, "to 'come out of the closet' is to declare war on the norm." Gay rights activism is therefore, in his view, the most radical assault on traditional morality yet produced by the adversary culture.

Unlike his critique of feminism, which at least grants legitimacy to "non-ideological" reforms that eliminate discrimination against women, Neuhaus disputes that the gay rights movement has any legitimate basis. He recalls that gay rights activism began in the early 1970s, when it "hitched a ride with the civil rights cause." In a social climate in which everyone claimed victim status, he remarks, homosexuals made superficially plausible claims that they are discriminated against in their attempts to secure suitable housing and employment. They established new organizations and later campaigned for gay rights bills across the country, seeking protection from discrimination in America's housing and employment markets. Neuhaus notes that religious opposition to gay rights legislation was largely confined to fundamentalist, Roman Catholic, and Orthodox Jewish organizations. "The late Paul Ramsey of Princeton was among the few in mainstream Protestantism who argued publicly that such gay rights bills were a ruse," he recalls. Ramsey contended that gay rights activism was not meant to remedy an injustice but to redefine the meaning of justice. That is, Neuhaus explains, the purpose of the gay rights movement is not to rectify some imagined injustice, but "to 'redefine' family out of existence."[106]

"Gay rights" is thus about cultural subversion rather than justice. Most gay rights gays are well-educated professionals with no dependents, Neuhaus observes. They possess extraordinary advantages over others in their discretionary time and income. "Were homosexuals the victims of discrimination, one would have expected an upsurge of housing and job complaints after the passage of gay rights bills," he argues. "In fact, this has not happened. The gay rights bills were important for a quite different reason. They were a critically important wedge, opening the way to additional steps in relativizing the social and moral status of heterosexuality and the family." That Ramsey was right about the

---

106. Neuhaus, "Notes on the Culture Wars," 61.

phoniness of "gay rights" is now obvious, he concludes, "to all who have eyes to see."[107]

The ultimate tragedy of this cultural episode, Neuhaus contends, is that the price for the ravages of feminism and gay rights will be paid most by those least able to withstand it. Professional-class people can afford to send their children to schools that do not subject students to sex education and gay rights propaganda. The children of the underclass are a captive audience, however. "They have no choice," Neuhaus explains. "They have to go to the schools that everybody else has abandoned. They are the ones who are left. They are the guinea pigs of the cultural revolutionaries who have been rejected by the larger culture." Their fate is to have teachers who sneer at the myth of Ozzie and Harriet families.

Neuhaus allows that there are countertrends to this depressing litany of social decline. In the economic sphere, the American and world trend is strongly supportive of free market capitalism; even American intellectuals are beginning to absorb that socialism is dead. In the political sphere, American policy debates moved considerably to the Right in the 1980s, as the symbol of far-Right and supposedly unelectable Republicanism became an enormously popular president. "In the economic and political spheres, there are heartening signs of something like a turn toward sanity," he observes. In the cultural sphere, the situation is more complicated. This is the front for neoconservatism, which faces formidable opposition, but which has time on its side. As Neuhaus explains, "What used to be the mainstream churches are drying up; the media, however reluctantly and erratically, adjust to their markets; and tenured professors will one day die, making room for a generation that is not prepared to spend its years in the afterglow of youthful radicalisms." The redemptive forces of nature and the business cycle offer reason to be hopeful about the future. The only hopeless situation is the situation of the poor, Neuhaus argues, whose children will remain cultural captives. Their situation is unique, not because they are victimized by racial or economic injustice, but because they are "the victims of the cultural revolutionaries from whom the larger society has turned away in disgust."[108]

Neoconservatives claim to speak for the "larger society" whose values and interests are demeaned by the New Class adversary culture. Their writings rarely find anything wrong with American society that cannot be blamed on the hypocrisy or subversion of the putative New Class. They charge that cultural radicals in the universities, churches, and media are poisoning the minds of American youth and destroying the cultural foundations on which American freedom and prosperity depend. While they inveigh against the spiral of divorce, drug ad-

---

107. Ibid., 62; cf. Neuhaus, "Homosexuality and the Churches," *First Things* 3 (May 1990), 64–70.
108. Neuhaus, "Notes on the Culture Wars," 63.

diction, hopelessness, and social decay in American society, however, neoconservatives give a free ride to commercial interests that relentlessly manipulate baser human instincts. They carefully ignore the social and cultural effects of corporate elites that assiduously promote self-absorption, materialism, immediate gratification, and preoccupation with sex. In the name of defending traditional cultural values, they routinely condemn educators and clergy for subverting American culture while ignoring the far more influential and subversive impact that commercial society makes by turning labor and nature into commodities.

This contradiction at the heart of neoconservatism and the vindictive rhetoric that neoconservatives frequently employ have convinced many Christian ethicists that it is pointless to argue with neoconservatives. Bennett's assessment of neoconservatism speaks for many theologians. "I think that neoconservatism is one of the worst movements in this country in my time," he declares. "Those people are from my point of view wrong about everything. They were right in opposing Soviet communism but if their feelings about our policy had controlled our policy we might well have had the ultimate nuclear war. In their celebration of capitalism they show little concern for the large sections of our people who have been neglected."[109]

He regards the purported connection between neoconservatism and Niebuhr as an absurd neoconservative conceit. "The only thing that Reinhold Niebuhr and the neoconservatives have in common is the word realism," he contends. "The way they go on against feminism and environmentalism and gay rights—it's unbelievable. Their anti-feminism, especially, is horrible. This has nothing to do with Reinie or with how we understood Christian realism. I try not to take their meanness personally, but when they bring Reinie into it, that's more than I can take." For Bennett, the genuine tradition of Niebuhrian realism is a liberal project that presses in new ways to fulfill Niebuhr's fundamental commitment to progressive social justice. It is represented today, not by neoconservatives, but by such progressive Christian realists as Ronald Stone, Roger Shinn, Larry Rasmussen, Alan Geyer, Jean Bethke Elshtain, Charles West, and Kermit Johnson.[110]

As an argument that dismisses the neoconservative claim to Niebuhr's legacy, Bennett's protest is undoubtedly justified. His judgment is widely shared among many Christian ethicists who have less reason to defend Niebuhr's name or legacy. The widespread tendency among Christian ethicists to dismiss neoconservatism itself as reactionary or mean-spirited, however, underestimates the intellectual, moral, and political seriousness of neoconservatism as a force in American society and religion. If the break between liberal Christianity and

---

109. Bennett, letter to author, December 10, 1992.
110. Bennett, interview with author, January 2, 1993.

Niebuhr's wayward followers is too embittered to sustain a serious dialogue, this does not mean that liberal Christianity has nothing to learn from neoconservative criticism. If liberals are people who cannot take their own side in an argument, the saying applies with particular force to liberal Christianity. The importance given to pluralism, empathy, and diversity in liberal Christianity often impedes its proponents from taking positions that might offend anyone or create controversy. In a culture in which the liberal churches command little esteem, the predisposition to retreat to mere niceness is reinforced.

By contrast, neoconservatives repeatedly take the risk of giving offense to a secular culture on issues pertaining to personal morality and responsibility that liberal Christianity implicitly cedes to the religious Right. While the mainline churches mostly maintain an embarrassed silence over the media's disregard for religion, neoconservatives attack the media's antireligious biases. While liberal Protestantism maintains its long-ingrained accommodation to the dominant culture, neoconservatives assail the decadence of a culture that fails to engender moral habits associated with hard work, productivity, personal responsibility, and deferred gratification. Because they are rightly repulsed by the crudeness and authoritarianism of the religious Right, progressive theologians have difficulty absorbing the possibility that any social criticism from this source could be instructive. That the religious Right has anything to teach liberal Christianity is a bitter proposition. More than a few theologians dismiss neoconservatism as an intellectualized form of Moral Majority politics. They are also quick to charge neoconservatives with opportunism. Neoconservatives fueled these suspicions in the 1980s through their alliances with the fundamentalist Right and their apologies for corporate capitalism.

But neoconservatives also express the resentments of fundamentalists and other religious conservatives in ways that liberal church leaders and theologians need to hear. Particularly instructive to the renewal of Christian social theory has been the neoconservative emphasis on re-creating the public sphere. Neoconservatives such as Novak, Weigel, Max Stackhouse, Dennis McCann, and James Nuechterlein have made important contributions to this discussion, but the crucial figure in the debate over "God in public" has been Neuhaus. It is Neuhaus who explained to mainline Protestants in the 1980s that the rise of a politicized religious Right was a variation on the old liberal Protestant dream of Christianizing America, and it is Neuhaus who has tried to explain to the fundamentalist Right that its most reviled humanist bogeyman, John Dewey, is an important guide to the re-creation of a vital American public sphere.

Neuhaus and the Catholic Moment

Neuhaus interprets the history of modern American Protestantism as a rise and fall narrative centering on the Protestant vision of a Christian America. As he explains in *The Naked Public Square* (1984), the modern liberal Protestant mission to Christianize America and the world is rooted in an older American Protestantism that regarded "America" and "civilization" as interchangeable terms. America was not a nation of tribes who happened to live here; America was the redeemer nation that broke away from the decadence of the Old World to create a new world and a new future. "The key participants were Protestant Christianity, civilization, and America," Neuhaus recounts. "Protestant Christianity produced civilization, and America carried the promise of both."[111] The innovation of the social gospel was to politicize American Protestantism's cultural self-assurance and exhort the church to extend the blessings of American Christian democracy to the rest of the world.

Progressivist Christianity was not fazed by the fact that historical criticism and modern science were undermining the credibility of traditional Christian doctrine. The social gospelers believed that they had recovered the heart of original Christianity, which was to transform society into the kingdom of God. The world-changing rhetoric of the social gospel had to be toned down after the Great War, Neuhaus recalls, but liberal Protestantism was able to maintain its confidence as long as the Protestantism-America-civilization trinity remained credible. Mainline Protestantism accommodated itself to the needs and character of American civilization and sought to make a contribution to America's progress. "In the world of ideas and the shaping of culture, Protestantism felt it was no longer needed or wanted," Neuhaus explains. "Its hope, again, was to be of some use, to make a contribution, on terms set by others."[112]

But this was a strategy with diminishing returns. By the end of the Progressive era, the problem for liberal Protestantism was not merely that it was too compromised to be culturally formative. The problem was also that mainline church leaders accelerated the erosion of their faith by setting their sights too low. Neuhaus refrains from making the point, but his judgment applies to Niebuhr as much as to the progressive church leaders he criticizes. "The demoralization of the mainline is due in large part to the success of a too limited goal," he observes. "Since the 1930s the social mission of mainline Protestantism has been to advance—albeit with 'a sense of uneasiness and guilt'—the programs and fortunes of the left wing of the Democratic party." Just as the Church of England was once derided for being "the Tory party at prayer," Neuhaus remarks that mainline American church leaders in the 1980s prayed "for the second coming of a George McGovern, assuming that FDR was no longer available."[113]

---

111. Richard John Neuhaus, *The Naked Public Square: Religion and Democracy in America* (Grand Rapids: Eerdmans, 1984), 214.
112. Ibid., 215.
113. Ibid., 231.

Liberal Protestantism was thus reduced to little favors for liberal Democrats. If mainline Protestantism deserved better than this, Neuhaus implies, the cold fact remains that it worked itself out of a job:

> The happy convergence on which mainline Protestantism counted has not worked out. By the end of the last century its leaders had pledged their lives, their fortunes, and their sacred honor to the enlightened leadership of the nation. But the pledge was not reciprocated. By the middle of this century the nation's cultural elite began to make it quite explicit: the complete Christian common-wealth was not on, at least not the "Christian" part; the "redeemer nation" would make it on its own without reference to the Redeemer. Mainline Protestantism was barely thanked for its help in bringing the society to the point of secular self-sufficiency. It had succeeded in making itself dispensable. It would be permitted to tag along on the continuing journey, to help out with odd jobs and, for old times' sake, to offer an invocation when appropriate, but it must not make a nuisance of itself.[114]

This loss of status and relevance contains the essential clue to the alienation of most liberal church leaders, Neuhaus argues. Many church leaders have rebelled against the American enterprise because the terms of their remaining prestige are unacceptably demeaning. Neuhaus recognizes the feeling but offers no sympathy for it:

> When the bearers have lost confidence in the tradition they bear, then that tradition must be ridiculed, lest it be suspected that it has in fact been betrayed. The trinity of Christianity-America-civilization may have been naive and dis-credited, but probably no more so than the current bureaucratized obeisance to the trinity of Christianity–third world–revolutionary justice. They may both be instances of backstopping Christian truth by demonstrating its utility to some other end, but at least the first version engaged American Christians "where they live" and resulted in more than memos for a revolution, the noise of prophetic assemblies, and pervasive feelings of failure and guilt.[115]

Mainline Protestantism is too religiously enervated and too engulfed in the "miasma of guilty laceration" to provide the culture-transforming faith that is needed. What is needed is a serious, realistic, confident, and religiously uncom-promised Christianity that dares to make unlikely ecumenical alliances. Neuhaus observes that liberal Protestant leaders could never imagine themselves joining forces with Christians in the religious Right, whom they perceive to be hopelessly reactionary. He is more hopeful that American Catholicism might seize the moment. In the mid-1980s he proclaimed that "the Catholic moment" in Amer-ican life was arriving or, at least, that it should arrive. "By virtue of numbers, of a rich tradition of social and political theory, and of Vatican II's theological

---

114. Ibid., 242–43.
115. Ibid., 237.

internalization of the democratic idea, Catholics are uniquely posed to propose the American proposition anew," he claimed.[116]

Neuhaus warned in 1984 that the moment could be missed. An earlier moment was missed in 1960 because President Kennedy's chief religious concern was to convince American voters that he was not a serious Catholic. It could be missed again, a generation later, if American Catholicism succumbed to the same relativizing and accommodating pressures that were destroying mainline Protestantism. It would definitely be missed if American Catholic leaders did not begin to resist strenuously the poisoning effects of liberation theologies, he warned. And it could also be missed if American Catholicism failed to make selective alliances with Protestant fundamentalism. "For these and other reasons, Catholicism may miss its moment, prematurely embracing the mainline's sense of guilt and unease, finding satisfactions in having failed at a task it never got around to attempting," he argued.[117] Neuhaus subsequently elaborated his hopes for the Catholic moment at book length and shortly afterward, in 1990, converted from Lutheranism to the Catholic church.

He recognizes that his vision of a realigned social Christianity appears implausible, which explains his emphasis on the connection between the social gospel and the religious Right. The religious Right's vision of a Christian America is rooted in the history of mainline Protestantism. Neuhaus observes:

> The need for culturally formative religion cannot be met today by a revival of mainline Protestant hegemony. We do well to remember, however, that the vision of today's moral majoritarians was in large part lifted from the mainline. Its notion of Christian America is not peculiarly fundamentalist and it is most certainly not "unAmerican." The estranged cousins have come back decked out in the family wardrobe. It is always embarrassing to be confronted by the ideals of our younger and more vital days.[118]

The religious politics of modern fundamentalism are thus neither alien nor novel. If culture-forming biblical religion is to play a role in re-creating American democracy, Neuhaus argues, what is needed is a Christian movement that affirms the interests and claims the truths of the religious Right.

This argument has surprising Deweyan credentials. In the 1920s, when progressive intellectuals routinely denigrated fundamentalist leaders such as William Jennings Bryan and their followers, Dewey insisted that liberal contempt for fundamentalists was not progressive. As Neuhaus recalls, Dewey argued that Bryan was, to be sure, a mediocrity, but that he was also "a typical democratic figure." This connection between mediocrity and democracy was crucial, Dewey

---

116. Ibid., 262.

117. Ibid. Cf. *Idem, The Catholic Moment: The Paradox of the Church in the Postmodern World* (San Francisco: Harper & Row, 1987).

118. Ibid., 220.

instructed, because "democracy by nature puts a premium on mediocrity." The critical point for Dewey was that Bryan's form of mediocrity was constitutive to any democratic experiment that progressives had in mind. American evangelicals comprised not only the heart of any conceivable mass movement in American politics, Dewey noted, but also much of the best in American public life. "These people form the backbone of philanthropic social interest, of social reform through political action, of pacifism, of popular education," Dewey observed. "They embody and express the spirit of kindly good will towards classes which are at an economic disadvantage and towards other nations, especially when the latter show any disposition towards a republican form of government."[119] It was the "church-going classes" that elected Lincoln and supported FDR and opposed aggregations of wealth in America. Evangelical Protestantism was the middle of every American political movement.

Neuhaus concedes that Dewey's description of the conservative Protestantism of his time "would seem to bear little resemblance to the moral majoritarians of today." The new religious Right is not well known for its social reformism, its pacifism, or its compassion for the poor. But Neuhaus suggests that the two fundamentalisms are more alike than it seems; after all, contemporary fundamentalism comes from the same middle America that Dewey's church-going classes came from. "If today its expression seems reactionary, anti-democratic, and mean-spirited, that is because it is exploited by leaders of such negative dispositions," he argues. McCarthyism provides an instructive analogy. Many decent Americans gave Joseph McCarthy the benefit of the doubt because many liberal intellectuals, politicians, and church leaders showed nothing but contempt for popular American doubts about U.S. policy. Elite contempt for popular feelings in the 1950s played into the hands of a demagogue who exploited popular resentments. The same thing has happened in American religion, Neuhaus contends, partly because mainline Protestant leaders have failed to heed the warnings of John Dewey.

A powerful grassroots mass movement of politicized Christians has arisen that does not view itself as having entered into a social contract for the adjudication of interests. The religious Right has no interest in a politics in which disinterested individuals stripped of any connection to a past, a community, or a faith make bargains for justice. To them, justice is not the end of a bargain or a work of human imagination, but participation in a transcendent good. They are determined to talk about God in the public square. In the name of religious truth, Neuhaus observes, they are determined to challenge the modern state that gives liberal American reasons for permitting abortion and pornography. When they enter the public square, they challenge the meaning-bestowing powers of the mostly secular

---

119. Ibid., 178.

elites who rule over it. They challenge the modern dichotomy between fact and value. They reject the liberal doctrine that the public arena must adjudicate interests but not morality. If the religious Right is often dangerously reactionary in its politicized religion, Neuhaus allows, it nonetheless exposes the central vulnerability of a social contract liberalism dominated by secular elites. The Moral Majoritarians may have the wrong answers, but they at least raise the right questions.

They picture Dewey as the high priest of American secular humanism—the despiser of "religious superstition" who ruined the public schools with his "progressive" subversion of American common sense. Neuhaus concedes that this line on Dewey is mainly right; Dewey "got an awful lot of things quite wrong," he notes, especially with regard to religion. But if Dewey's secular prejudices distorted his understanding of biblical religion, he at least understood that the American democratic experiment is an experiment. "He knew that it is an experiment that cannot be sustained without a public philosophy, and that such a public philosophy must be grounded in moral truth," Neuhaus observes. Like other public philosophers such as Niebuhr, Walter Lippmann, and John Courtney Murray, Dewey perceived that the truths on which America's democratic experiment are founded have to be rediscovered in every generation. In the spirit of this social mission, Neuhaus describes his own work as an attempt to advance "a religiously grounded public philosophy for the democratic experiment in freedom and virtue."[120]

This experiment takes no religious lessons from Dewey. Though he realized that Americans need a common faith that can nurture and shape their experiment in democracy, Dewey claimed to believe that secular humanism could stand in for religion. He sought to replace biblical religion with a humanistic "common faith" that was, unfortunately, neither common nor adequate but merely the provincial worldview of a secular liberal elite. But Dewey had the right project, Neuhaus argues, which was to rediscover the truths of American democracy. "Dewey's great mistake was to think that he could break those truths away from their necessary and continuing dependence upon biblical religion," he contends. "He lived in a time when the best and the brightest were miseducated to believe that traditional religion was simply beyond the pale of plausibility for the truly enlightened." But the cultural hegemony of this rationalist dogma is no longer secure. "Indeed it is collapsing all around us," Neuhaus concludes.[121] What is needed is a common American faith that sustains liberal democracy by virtue of its true commonality and wisdom.

---

120. Richard John Neuhaus, "The Real John Dewey," *First Things* 19 (January 1992), 54.

121. Ibid., 55.

Like Niebuhr, Neuhaus assumes that the liberal Christian project of Christianizing America is impossible. America will never be a moral community or a community of moral communities; social conflict is too endemic in human nature, too intrinsic in the struggle for power, and too inevitable in modern mass society to ever bring about the triumph of moral cooperation. Unlike Niebuhr, however, Neuhaus does emphatically claim that a new moral consensus based on biblical religion is possible to achieve. Niebuhr was ambiguous on the question. He occasionally implied that a common moral language rooted in biblical religion was necessary if American society was going to hold together. More often he implied that it would be enough for the churches to hold the secular realm accountable on fundamental issues pertaining to morality and justice. In both cases, Niebuhr's explicit teaching was that the churches need to be separate from the secular sphere while remaining active within it, challenging the state to meet a higher moral standard than the achievement of stability. The secular sphere needs to be protected from religious domination but also instructed and challenged by religious teaching. That America might ever achieve a more substantive moral consensus than this was a hope that Niebuhr entertained but did not defend. The watchwords of Niebuhrian realism were irony, paradox, ambiguity, and tension. Niebuhr was willing to live with a secular-religious tension.

This is not enough for Neuhaus, who begins his constructive argument by distinguishing his position from Moral Majoritarianism. Neuhaus argues that while the fundamentalist Right is crucial to any conceivable Christian movement that might transform American culture, it operates in a way that negates any constructive impact that religion might make to this mission. The fundamentalist movement is part of the solution, but the fundamentalist approach is not, chiefly because the Christian Right regards its defining beliefs as immune to public criticism. Fundamentalists want to change society on the basis of their religious beliefs, but they are unwilling to permit these beliefs to be publicly debated. By attempting to change the public sphere on the basis of a private belief system that cannot be publicly questioned, Neuhaus observes, the Moral Majoritarians guarantee that their political victories will never represent anything more than the triumph of one interest group over others. More important, they guarantee that their movement will not contribute to the creation or strengthening of an American moral consensus but will only weaken the basis of that consensus by politicizing their private beliefs.

This is not public philosophy. As Neuhaus observes, any consensus-building public discourse worthy of the name must withstand the scrutiny of public criticism and debate. The fundamentalist approach is indefensible. It proceeds not on the basis of persuasion, but coercion. It tries to impose religious teachings on outsiders on the basis of a bare authority claim. Politicized fundamentalism is therefore not only alien to democracy, but hostile to it. At the same time,

Neuhaus argues, it is a mistake to take this lesson too far, as he believes that Novak does. Novak claims that American democracy maintains a sense of transcendent accountability by preserving an empty shrine at the center of the social order. He observes that while American religious leaders often seek a public social role, American democratic capitalism provides a role for them that "is neither in command nor at the center." In American democracy, Novak contends, respect for the transcendence of God and the freedom of individual conscience are served by a "reverential emptiness" at the heart of society rather than by "a socially imposed vision of the good."[122]

Neuhaus counters that this is an overreaction to the problem of cultural pluralism. Novak's empty shrine is too similar to the naked public square. Novak speaks against the imposition or public enforcement of virtue but fails to recognize that effective moral discourse in the public realm is not necessarily coercive. "Democratic persuasion, not emptiness, is the alternative to coercion," Neuhaus contends. Moreover, the sense of transcendence that marks America's experiment with democracy is not without content, but derives from a particular tradition. "Both historically and in present sociological fact, it is religiously specific, it refers to the Judeo-Christian tradition," Neuhaus argues.[123] The only moral consensus that Americans might ever conceivably achieve would derive from this tradition. What is needed is a social philosophy that could mend the rupture "between public policy and moral sentiment."

Biblical religion is thus the only possible basis for a common American faith. Neuhaus cautions against the notion that the remedy for the naked public square is naked public religion, however. This is the fundamentalist mistake. The Christian Right tries to moralize the public sphere with naked appeals to religious authority. Neuhaus counters that the Christian social philosophy that is needed would develop a mediating language through which ultimate religious truths could be related to penultimate political issues. "In our several traditions there are rich conceptual resources for the development of such a mediating language—whether concepts be called natural law, common grace, general revelation, or the order of creation," he observes. "Such a civil engagement of secular and religious forces could produce a new public philosophy to sustain this American experiment in liberal democracy." He does not claim that it is possible to create a social philosophy that everyone accepts or that will not provoke disagreements. The existence of a common faith might provoke more disagreements than the lack of one. "But at least we would know what we are disagreeing about, namely, different accounts of the transcendent good by which we might order our life together," Neuhaus explains. Against those who claim

---

122. Novak, *The Spirit of Democratic Capitalism,* 68–69.
123. Neuhaus, *The Naked Public Square,* 121.

that good democracies evade the question of the good, he insists that democracy "becomes a political community worthy of moral actors only when we engage the question of the good."[124]

The democratic experiment in America thus requires a religiously inspired communitarian faith that grounds American public life in a never completed search for the transcendent good. Neuhaus urges that the process of creating a common social philosophy could begin to repair the moral ravages of modernity. It could also create the only brake on state power that has any chance of succeeding in America. For Neuhaus, this is the chief political function of the culture-forming Christianity that is needed. In Christian teaching, all nations and authorities stand under the judgment of God. In American society, Neuhaus contends, only the force of this biblical teaching is capable of keeping the state in its place. The biblical notion of divine transcendence relativizes the claims of all other authorities and orders the world under a sacred canopy. Contrary to the prejudices of America's culture-dominating secular elites, however, biblical religion also sanctions a pluralism of social authorities and institutions. Neuhaus observes that it is not biblical religion but the power lust of the modern leviathan that threatens to destroy pluralism. Without an "agreed-upon authority that is higher than the community itself," the modern state will continue to assume ever greater authority over all lesser authorities.[125] It follows for Neuhaus that a healthy pluralism of various social authorities and mediating institutions can be safeguarded only through the creation of a publicly sanctioned religious faith.

Neuhaus supports this conclusion by observing that there "are no areligious moral traditions of public, or at least of democratic, force in American life." This is not to claim that there is no other source of moral value in American life or that religion is reducible to morality; it is to claim that in the United States, religion and morality are necessarily conjoined. "Religion in our popular life is the morality-bearing part of culture, and in that sense the heart of culture," Neuhaus explains. Biblical religion is thus the single viable source of resistance to the continued self-aggrandizement of the state. "Of all the institutions in society, only religion can invoke against the state a transcendent authority and have its invocation seconded by 'the people' to whom a democratic state is presumably accountable," he observes.[126] It is also the only means by which a substantive notion of virtue can be insinuated into the naked public square. With

---

124. Richard John Neuhaus, "Nihilism without the Abyss: Law, Rights and Transcendent Good," paper delivered at 1985 conference on Religion and Law at Catholic University Law School, cited in Stanley Hauerwas, "A Christian Critique of Christian America," in *Community in America: The Challenge of Habits of the Heart,* ed. Charles H. Reynolds and Ralph V. Norman (Berkeley: University of California Press, 1988), 257.

125. Neuhaus, *The Naked Public Square,* 76.

126. Ibid., 154–55.

the disintegration of mainline liberal Protestantism, it is up to a new coalition of public-minded Christians to moralize the public sphere. "What is required today is a reformist vision of public policies that will empower people to take charge of their lives in their freely chosen communities of allegiance and mutual aid," he urges.[127] In America, this vision will have to be fired primarily by religious communities.

This is an estimable project. It makes a distinctive and original case for a common faith. It draws upon aspects of social gospel Christianity, Deweyan democracy, and secular communitarian theory while rejecting the liberalizing and secularizing dimensions of these perspectives. It presents withering attacks on the weakness of mainline Protestantism and the disregard for religion shown by America's elite media. It makes a compelling critique of the deterioriation of moral discourse in the public square and a powerful appeal for the renewal of persuasive moral discourse. The emphasis on public persuasion is surely the best alternative to authoritarian coercion and to the secularist dogma that the public square has to be naked in a democracy. The most telling critique of Neuhaus's argument is available in his own account of American culture, however. His prescription is culturally and politically viable only if it is true, as he insists, that America is not a secular society. Neuhaus claims that the image of America as a secular society is a myth invented by academics and media pundits who think that their self-descriptions describe America. But most Americans believe in God, he observes. When asked why certain practices are morally right or wrong, most Americans make no resort to liberal theory but refer to biblical or religious teaching. Their operative moral framework is covenantal, not social contractual. "The proposition that America is a secular society is contrary to sociological fact," he insists.[128]

But if belief in God is pervasive in American society, Neuhaus's own account illustrates why most American religion is poorly suited to support a serious public faith of any kind. Most Americans may believe in God, but this affirmation does not lead most of them to make serious commitments to any community of faith or distinctively Christian ethic. Modern American religion abounds with prescriptions to help anxious consumers get in touch with their feelings, relinquish negative thoughts, and rediscover the child within themselves. As Neuhaus observes, even most fundamentalist churches no longer dispute the presuppositions of commercial society or its secular culture, but content themselves "with offering religiously coated pills for the promotion of health and happiness." American fundamentalism no longer challenges the ethos of commercial society,

---

127. Richard John Neuhaus, "Robert Bellah and Social Democracy," *First Things* 7 (November 1990), 62.

128. Neuhaus, *The Naked Public Square,* 113.

as William Jennings Bryan did, but seeks to make individuals "whole" within it. Having set upon the goal of becoming successful and respectable in American society, fundamentalist preachers increasingly turn the gospel into a therapeutic balm for the anxieties of overstressed souls, finding impressive markets for their ministrations.

In this regard they are following the example of mainline Protestantism, for which the triumph of the therapeutic is an old story. Liberal Protestantism has long made its living from its capacity to bring comfort, healing, and inspiration to troubled professional class achievers. Faced with a social order that increasingly doubted whether it needed religion, at a time when psychoanalytic therapy was beginning to pose as a substitute for religion, the mainline churches countered with their own forms of therapeutic relief. Instead of building communities of virtue that could inform public discourse, Neuhaus explains, mainline Protestantism "acquiesced in being relegated to the private sphere where it did a thriving business in 'meeting the needs' of individuals for spiritual and other satisfactions."[129] Though he does not press the point, modern American Catholicism is hardly immune from the same ethos of narcissism. American religious culture in virtually all of its nonsectarian denominational forms is deeply infused, not with the outward-looking spirit of biblical religion, but with various kinds of individualistic New Age spiritualities.

Richard Wightman Fox notes the irony. Neuhaus claims that American Christianity is capable of generating the culture-transforming common faith that is needed. He claims that the chief obstacles to the renewal of an American moral consensus are an ever-expanding state and the machinations of New Class knowledge elites who call the United States a secular society. "But his own book suggests that the problem lies much deeper: in an embedded ideology of self-absorption that has dominated American culture for several generations," Fox observes.[130] Having noted the modern American religious preoccupation with self-cultivation, it is unconvincing for Neuhaus to claim that American churches are capable of forging the culture-transforming consensus that social gospel Christianity in its heyday could not achieve.

The deeper irony is constitutive in Neuhaus's neoconservatism. Neuhaus rails against the pervasive degeneration of America's biblical faith into various forms of therapeutic self-absorption. He criticizes the role of an expanding state in turning American citizens increasingly into passive, self-preoccupied consumers. But he writes virtually nothing about the chief cause of the cultural retro-

---

129. Ibid., 142.

130. Richard Wightman Fox, "The Liberal Ethic and the Spirit of Protestantism," in *Community in America: The Challenge of Habits of the Heart,* ed. Reynolds and Norman, 245.

gression that he decries. As Fox observes, "Astonishingly, Neuhaus never suspects that the business community in general and the advertising industry, in particular, have played any part in undermining the idea of transcendent authority."[131] But it is commercial society that uproots traditional cultural values pertaining to self-sacrifice, deferred gratification, and the importance of self-transcending loyalties. It is not the church or the state that bombards youthful consumers with titillating images designed to promote consumption and self-absorption. It is commercial society that assiduously encourages narcissistic self-indulgence, reduces social values to commodities, and reduces the complexities of moral discernment in the public arena to the test of economic rationality. The commercial culture of seduction promotes not only materialism and egocentrism but, ultimately, nihilism with unrelenting persistence. Its image of the good life is not a vision of the common good but the life of self-gratification, self-pre-occupation, and material success unceasingly paraded in the mass media. Having aligned himself with a political movement that celebrates the superiority of capitalism over all possible alternatives, however, Neuhaus cannot bring himself to consider that the cultural situation he decries has economic causes.

Neoconservatives sometimes reply that American Christianity should try to restrain the egotism and antisocial forces unleashed by commercial society. For Neuhaus, the church is also obliged to assume "the culture-forming task of constructing a religiously informed public philosophy for the American experiment in ordered liberty."[132] He and Novak both believe that modern American Catholicism is particularly suited for this project. Modern Catholicism is unique in its size, its power, its deep historical rootage, and its capacity to generate a Christian social philosophy. Unlike any other Christian tradition excepting Calvinism, modern Catholicism is modern in its spirit, theologically orthodox, and favorably disposed toward the task of creating a Christian social philosophy. More than the Calvinist churches, American Catholicism is socially and institutionally equipped to renew the American experiment in democracy. Neuhaus converted to Catholicism on the strength of these convictions. In his view, though every theological generation struggles with a new "crisis" in the church, the church's crisis is always the crisis of unbelief. He believes that under the leadership of Pope John Paul II, modern Catholicism is withstanding the acids of modernity more faithfully and courageously than the various Protestant churches. "John Paul is far ahead of those Christians, including many Roman Catholics, who are only now learning to accommodate the faith to a debased modernity that history is fast leaving behind," he asserts. "It is said that John XXIII opened the windows

---

131. Ibid.
132. Neuhaus, *The Catholic Moment,* 283.

of the Church to the modern world. John Paul has entered the modern world to help open the windows of the modern world to the worlds of which it is part."[133]

Neuhaus thus found a home in the pope's social and theological conservatism. The church that he embraces is more deeply torn by disputes over legitimacy, authority, feminism, moral teaching, and distributive justice than his version of it reflects, however. The feminist revolt against male privilege that neoconservatives persistently demean is deeply rooted in modern Catholicism. If the Vatican's orthodoxy offers Neuhaus a refuge from what he calls "the captivities of the mainline," it is not evident to many Catholic theologians that their church is avoiding or solving the problems that afflict modern Protestantism. Neither is Neuhaus's enthusiasm for a common social philosophy rooted in conservative Christianity widely shared by either Catholic or Protestant theologians. The passing of modernism is not producing new universal creeds but a heightened emphasis on particularity, difference, and diversity. Neuhaus is right that there is nothing necessarily progressive about the postmodern emphasis on cultural diversity and difference, but he is seriously mistaken to think that conservative Christianity can shape a new moral consensus in the face of America's increasing cultural diversity. If his warnings against postmodern relativism and tribalism are often justified, his polemical attacks on feminism, multiculturalism, gay rights, and virtually any form of liberal or progressive politics make him an especially unlikely architect of the common faith that he seeks. His attacks on progressive Christianity confirm rather that a common social vision is unattainable. A common faith is unreachable even among Niebuhrians.

Neuhaus's epitaphs for liberal Protestantism are wounding but premature. It is unarguably true, as neoconservatives repeatedly announce, that mainline Protestantism has irretrievably lost its hegemonic power in American culture. It is also undoubtedly true, as is frequently charged, that the mainline churches have undermined their religious and cultural authority by failing to uphold clear prescriptive teachings. Niebuhr's description of himself as "an unbelieving believer" captures the ambiguity of liberal Protestantism's struggle with modernity. Liberal theology does not claim to possess an infallible foundation. It claims that religious certainty is never the possession of any tradition, but always an illusion. This is not the religion that many people seek. For them, liberal Protestantism is too relativistic in its theology and often too idealistic in its politics. In its Niebuhrian form, it is too enamored with irony, paradox, and ambiguity and too comfortable with the language of myth.

Liberal Protestantism at the end of the American century is obliged to take these objections seriously. The assurance that liberal Protestantism is a spent force, however, is willfully exaggerated, reflecting the hopes of its disillusioned

---

133. Ibid., 284.

orphans. For millions of Americans, Fosdick's choice describes themselves. The choice is not between liberal and conservative Christianity but between a progressive Christian faith and no religion at all. For most of them, the church is a spiritual home, a community of fellowship, and the place where they live out their idealism. Though American churches increasingly cater to the therapeutic demands of consumers who want to work on themselves, the churches nonetheless remain distinctive for their capacity to inspire loyalty, community, and a sense of transcendent good. No other institution in American life rivals the churches' capacity to inspire community or mobilize community efforts to address immediate social needs.

If the cultural dethronement of liberal Protestantism is no longer a matter of argument, the question of its future identity and social mission is vigorously contested. For some, the loss of dominating cultural power is a source of sadness or regret or recrimination. For some, it is a blessing. Having lost its hegemonic status and many of its social privileges, liberal Protestantism is at least potentially liberated from its alliance with established power. It is free to define itself without feeling beholden to the dominant order. It is free to explicate the moral meaning of Christianity while relinquishing the moral burdens of empire. It is free to reassess the viability of its long-held socioeconomic vision without bearing the self-assigned responsibility to "uphold Christian civilization" or establish a new hegemonic morality. It is free to preach a gospel that is not for everyone and doesn't claim that it is. Liberal Christianity in a postmodern age is free to transmute the heritage of a century-long tradition into new forms, believing that Christianity can be transformative without being chauvinistic.

5 DE-CENTERING VOICES
| Pluralization and
| the Liberationist
| Revolutions

Charles Clayton Morrison and Ecumenism

IN 1948, CHARLES CLAYTON MORRISON PUBLISHED A ROUSING MANIFESTO for a resurgent ecumenical Protestantism under the title *Can Protestantism Win America?* Though he insisted that it was not too late to win America, Morrison did not spare his Protestant readers any unsettling news. His opening pages claimed that Protestantism was waging a failing struggle with Roman Catholicism and secularism for hegemony over America's cultural and spiritual life. To say that Protestantism, Catholicism, and secularism were competing for America's soul was not to ascribe "any dark or illegitimate purpose" to any of these social forces, he assured. It was only to recognize that each force rightly proclaimed its convictions "and that each is incompatible with the other two."[1]

The latter words marked the boundary of Morrison's ecumenism. The mark of any serious faith was that it tried to win converts, he claimed, for "the missionary spirit is of its essence." But liberal Protestantism no longer had a missionary spirit or tried to win converts. Morrison observed that numerous Protestant denominations had "entirely lost their evangelistic vigor."[2] Liberal Protestantism liked to pretend that it was not in competition with Catholicism and an increasingly secular culture. It eschewed evangelism and generally treated religion as a matter more of taste than of truth. It was too sentimental, too mannered, too compromised by its accommodation to modern culture, and too soaked in relativism to proselytize the masses. But these traits were bearing bad consequences not only for Protestantism but for America, partly because neither Catholicism nor secularism was constrained by self-doubt or self-censorship.

---

1. Charles Clayton Morrison, *Can Protestantism Win America?* (New York: Harper & Brothers, 1948), 1.
2. Ibid., 4.

Secularism had no soul at all, and in Morrison's view, American Catholicism was still essentially antimodern, antidemocratic, and theologically fundamentalist.

The trend in modern Protestantism was to search for common ground with the Catholic church, but Morrison claimed that this was a futile pursuit. Protestantism and Catholicism held "radically different conceptions of the Christian religion," he insisted. "Whatever points of apparent similarity exist between them are vitiated by the irresponsible power system that Catholicism is when it is seen whole." Catholicism sanctioned hierarchy, dogmatism, and authoritarianism, while modern Protestantism sanctioned freedom and democracy. It was inconceivable to Morrison that America might have become a democracy if it had been settled by Roman Catholic pioneers. Neither was it conceivable that modern Protestant ecumenism might find constructive commonalities with the Catholic church. "Protestantism cannot cooperate ecclesiastically with a dictatorship," he declared. "It must make a clear-cut decision to accept its task of winning America to Christ without any illusion that it has a collaborator in Roman Catholicism."[3]

Mainline Protestantism was clearly indulging this illusion. In the name of promoting greater ecumenical understanding, cooperation, and communion, Morrison complained, liberal church leaders were minimizing the importance of their own core beliefs. This strategy was a loser. It would never help to modernize Catholicism, and it would never win America. Morrison warned that modern Protestantism was afflicted with an even deeper and more complicated illusion than its ecumenical sentimentality, however. The most threatening rival to the Protestant faith in America was not Catholicism but America's ascending secular culture. Though American Catholicism was a growing faith, the mainline Protestant churches were losing members not to Catholicism but to secularism. For Morrison, this was the ultimate proof that the liberal Protestant attempt to accommodate modern culture was mistaken:

> The assumption that modern culture has been moving toward a Christian goal has been the undoing of Protestantism. It has weakened its will and confused its faith. Too long has Protestantism stood in awe of modern culture. Its sense of mission has been obfuscated by the messianic pretensions of science, by the prestige of public education, and by the benefits which technology and an ever enlarging state paternalism were conferring upon the people.

Like the secularists who controlled America's mass media and wrote its textbooks, Protestant church leaders hailed all of this as progress, Morrison noted. The loss of mainline Protestantism's "militant vitality" was traceable to its sycophantic relationship to modern culture. "It is an amazing fact that for

---

3. Ibid., 85–87.

three generations Protestantism stood in awe of this secular culture which we now see in catastrophic ruin," he remarked. "It yielded to it with half its heart, and was thereby rendered incapable of giving wholehearted expression to the Christian faith. It has been afraid to stand up to modern culture, expose its pretensions and proclaim its own gospel."[4]

American Protestantism was afraid to confront modern culture because American Protestants were half persuaded by its pretensions. This fear took two predominant forms, in Morrison's view. The first was the strategy of cultural withdrawal favored by evangelical and fundamentalist Protestants. Conservative Protestantism typically protected its identity by shielding itself and its teachings from public criticism. It thus preserved the comforts of a defensive, inward-looking, and overtly fearful religion. "In a kind of cloistered isolation, conservatism has been running on the momentum of the Christian tradition, rather than on the perennial dynamics of the Christian faith," Morrison explained. American evangelicalism lived off the memory of premodern orthodoxy without adding anything to it.

The other main reaction to modernity was the strategy of appeasement adopted by liberal Protestantism. Liberal Protestantism typically did not seek to transform modern culture with a dynamic Christian faith but allowed modern culture to redefine the faith's meaning. For the past half-century, liberal Protestant leaders typically assumed that Christianity was cluttered with tradition, while modern culture represented progress. Modern Protestantism sought to get on the right side of history by identifying the kingdom ethic of original Christianity with the ideology of progress proclaimed by a secularizing modern culture. The chief effect of this strategy was to accelerate the secularizing trend in American society, Morrison argued. Liberal Christian moralism did not provide an alternative to secularism but assimilated itself into an increasingly secular order. This strategy purchased undoubted respectability and security for the mainline churches, but at a high price. "The attempt to appease this culture by giving so much of Christianity away to moralism and secularism was sure to find a ready response in certain areas of a mentality produced by secularized education," Morrison noted. "But this form of 'adjusted Christianity' has been conspicuously sterile. It has lacked power and the sense of urgency that belongs to the Christian faith. It has rested in its negations. It had no dynamic of its own."[5] If the conservative churches were backward and authoritarian, they at least kept alive the notion that Christianity is true. Liberal Protestantism was decadent by comparison.

---

4. Ibid., 87.
5. Ibid., 89.

The Protestant problem was not a matter of numbers, since in 1948 American Protestants still outnumbered Catholics by two to one. Mainline church participation was at a record high in America and would continue to climb for another decade. The problem was qualitative and relative. Did mainline Protestantism possess enough spiritual depth and solidarity to triumph over secularism and Catholicism? Was Protestantism advancing in relation to these competing social forces? Morrison's answers were sharply negative. In his view, mainline Protestantism was losing ground to its rival forces, especially to secularism, because it was spiritually enervated, theologically weak, and institutionally compromised. "In its present state it is no match for the secularism which it confronts," he judged. Yet he insisted that it was not too late for liberal Protestantism to win America.

The fact that American Protestantism had little competitive history was part of its problem. Until recently, the Protestant churches had dominated American culture with little outside competition. They had not been forced to "win" America in Morrison's sense of the term because they assumed that America was already culturally Protestant. In an increasingly pluralized America, however, the Protestant churches were now paying the price for their earlier self-assurance. American Protestantism was forced to compete for cultural and spiritual influence that it previously assumed was its birthright. The problem that this development presented for mainline Protestantism was compounded by its acquired liberalism. To win the struggle for America's soul, modern Protestantism would have to renounce its embarrassed denial that it was competing to win anything. It would have to give up not only its inherited ease but also its liberal qualms about converting people. It would have to become acquainted with the language of competition, evangelism, conversion, and victory. In Morrison's vision, the resurgent Protestantism that was needed would be militant, united, and theologically purified. His prescription was less radical in its politics than *The Social Gospel and the Christian Cultus* had been but more ambitious in its ecumenical agenda.

Morrison urged that a fractured denominational Protestantism would never win America. "Modern Protestantism is the heir of the factionalism, the contentiousness, the theological egotism in which its denominations had their origin," he observed. It was thus incapable of bearing the spiritual richness of Christianity. As long as the various Protestant denominations maintained themselves as separate churches, Morrison insisted, the dream of an ecumenical Protestantism and the dream of a renewed Protestant America were both unattainable.

> The denominational mind is necessarily narrow, provincial, shortsighted, detached from the total reality. It cannot rise to the eminence from which alone the whole American scene may be envisaged. Its loyalties are inevitably less than ecumenical. The full richness of the Christian faith can therefore find no adequate expression in the "broken lights" of Protestant denominationalism.

And the inherent power of the Christian faith can find no adequate implementation for itself in these autonomous and ecclesiastically insulated "churches."[6]

What was needed was an ecumenical movement that brushed away unnecessary theological differences and sought to create a united Protestant church. Morrison observed that the spiritual imperative of a united church "has not become a substantive part of Protestant thinking. It hovers over Protestantism and haunts it, but it has not been seized upon with conviction." To seize the ecumenical vision with conviction would be to liberate Protestantism from its ghettoizing traditions. It would allow modern Protestantism to forge a new unity based only upon devotion to Christ.

Morrison's theological proposal was disarmingly simple. He argued that the doctrinal edifices separating Protestant denominations from each other were all products of a historical egotism and factionalism that modern Christianity needed to disavow. The churches' disagreements over the sacraments or church polity were not worth the divisions they created in the Christian body. Having inherited a factional legacy, Morrison observed, the conscience of modern Protestantism was still relatively undeveloped regarding the unity that Christians owed to each other in Christ. But there were signs that such a conscience was beginning to emerge. "The old, brittle spirit of divisiveness is waning in the more enlightened areas of Protestantism," he remarked. Dogmatic and ecclesiological differences were increasingly viewed as less important than the church's desired unity in Christ. In Morrison's view, devotion to Christ as Lord was the only basis that ecumenical Christianity needed or could sustain. The sovereign authority of Christ was the only principle that could hold ecumenical Christianity together. "Everything else—I say it sweepingly—*everything else*—Bible, creed, sacraments, tradition, 'ancient order of things'—is divisive, sectarian, hopeless, when it is held without being referred to Christ for his judgment upon it," he declared.[7]

He allowed that this was not how most Protestants defined themselves. The Reformation principle of *sola scriptura* was burned into the consciousness of virtually every Protestant church. With the partial exception of Anglicanism, every Protestant church claimed that its teachings and identity were derived uniquely from the Bible. The notion of Protestantism as a "religion of the book" was axiomatic to most Protestants. In Morrison's view, it was also a terrible mistake:

Each denomination has historically held its interpretation of the Bible as the standard of loyalty to the Bible itself, and any serious departure from this standard on the part of its members, ministers or churches has been regarded as heresy and visited with the appropriate penalty. Its interpretation was regarded

6. Ibid., 97.
7. Ibid., 178.

as identical with the Bible—it *was* the Bible. Thus Protestantism has proliferated an astonishing litter of miniature papal infallibilities, each based upon the essential principle in the papacy against which Protestantism had revolted.[8]

By investing the Bible with a legal authority that equaled or exceeded the authority of Christ, Morrison argued, historic Protestantism made the Bible an idol that rationalized Protestant sectarianism. Protestant biblicism created a paper pope under the assumption that some authority other than Christ was necessary. But this assumption was mistaken. The Bible could become the "infinitely precious book" that Protestantism claimed it to be only if it was relieved of "the false authority which Protestant sectarianism has attributed to it." Moreover, Protestantism could attain its long-sought spiritual power and unity only if it relinquished all of its authorities, traditions, and familiar securities in order to follow Christ.

This was the vibrant, freedom-loving faith that could still win America. If liberal Protestants really believed in their faith, why should they not evangelize others to it? If they possessed the only credible and progressive religious alternative to the soul-killing emptiness of secularism, how could they not try to convert America to their faith, before it was too late? The imperative to Christianize America had not changed. For all of his criticism of liberal Protestantism, Morrison never doubted that only the liberal Protestant churches could save America's soul. For all of his ecumenical vision and idealism, he spurned the increasingly common notion that ecumenism should extend to Catholics and Jews. Any Protestant ecumenism that extended beyond Protestantism was a form of appeasement. "The idea that these three religious faiths are fundamentally alike is simply not true," he asserted. "The Jews and the Catholics may derive some practical profit from the prevalence of this sentimentalism among Protestants, but those Protestants who yield to it only bring injury to their own faith."[9] Morrison felt that Protestantism and Judaism were far closer to each other than either religion was to Catholicism, but Judaism was, nonetheless, a rival religion. For liberal Protestantism to give itself away to either faith was to abandon Christianity. Modern Protestantism was deficient not because it had anything to learn from Catholicism, evangelicalism, Orthodoxy, or Judaism, but because it wasn't true to itself.

Can Protestantism Win America? was an echo from a lost world. Morrison accepted that religious diversity in America was inevitable, but he did not regard pluralism as a virtue. Like other liberals of his generation, he was more concerned about the erosion of Protestant authority in America than about the rights of minorities. For him, as for G. K. Chesterton, America was "the nation with the

---

8. Ibid., 147.
9. Ibid., 93.

soul of a church." Like other social gospelers who witnessed the second half of the twentieth century, he feared that the increasing pluralization of America was destroying America's soul. Morrison, Luther Weigle, William Bower, F. Ernest Johnson, and other Protestant leaders repeatedly protested that in the name of protecting the rights of America's expanding minorities, American lawmakers were infringing the majority's right to maintain a common American faith.

For the last generation of Christianizing liberal Protestants, the public school was the crucial medium through which new generations could be initiated into the common faith. It was through the public school that Americans of all backgrounds learned the values and traditions of the American democratic experiment, which was a Protestant project. Morrison and his colleagues therefore opposed state aid for parochial schools and denounced the trend of court rulings and school board decisions that disallowed various religious practices, programs, and Bible studies in the public schools. In the wake of the Supreme Court's ruling in the 1948 McCollum case, which disallowed a church-affiliated released-time program in Champaign, Illinois, that made use of public school property, the guardians of liberal Protestantism took their last major stand. The chief interdenominational agency of mainline Protestantism, the International Council of Religious Education, reminded Americans in a strongly written statement that their country's historic experiment in freedom was incomprehensible apart from its faith in "the God of the Old and New Testaments." This faith was "embodied in our laws, documents, and institutions," the church leaders observed. For each generation of Americans, it was a civic and moral duty to retell the story of America's democratic experiment and renew the religiously grounded virtues that made this experiment succeed.

This duty carried crucial implications for the public schools. "We expect that the schools will expose our children to this point of view," the church leaders instructed. But it was not enough to expose American youths to a Protestant understanding of their history. The church leaders also expected public schools "to teach this common religious tradition as the only adequate basis for the life of the school and the personal lives of teachers, students, and citizens in a free and responsible democracy." There was nothing in American law or tradition, after all, that prevented public schools "from making provision for the religious interpretation of life."[10]

If American Protestantism provided "the only adequate basis" for the American experiment in freedom and democracy, it was imperative for America's schools to inculcate a watered-down common version of this faith to its children,

---

10. Cited by Nevin C. Harner, "A Protestant Educator's View," in *American Education and Religion,* ed. F. Ernest Johnson (New York: Institute for Religious and Social Studies, 1952), 88.

especially those from non-Protestant backgrounds. America's memory and hope were embodied in its common faith. As Robert Lynn later explained, Morrison's generation regarded America's public faith as constitutive of its inner history. To lose this faith was to sever any connection to the inner life source of America's past. "When an individual loses touch with his hopes and memories, he risks the danger of amnesia and eventual self-destruction," Lynn explained. "So does the public that neglects the renewal of its faith."[11] The pluralization and secularization of American society were thus threatening to produce an America that was not only not Christian but also not really American.

Morrison accepted that a "common" hegemonic faith in twentieth-century America would have to be short on substance. Though the question was often debated in the *Christian Century,* liberal church leaders never reached a consensus on how much of their own faith could be read into the common faith that supported American politics and culture. Some of them uneasily endorsed President Eisenhower's appeals to a vague American pietism in which religion was declared to be critically important to the health of American society, while the kind of religion was irrelevant. Most of them judged, however, that the narcoticizing religiosity promoted by Eisenhower was too superficial to play any seriously culture-renewing social role. The patriotic culture religion that oozed from American television sets in the 1950s was not the socially regenerative public faith sought by the old social gospelers but, rather, its ultimate trivialization.

If the decline of American Protestantism was signaled by the degeneration of its public faith, it was confirmed during the same period by the rise of a common cultural awareness that white Anglo-Saxon Protestants constituted one American ethnic group among others. This was a novel development in American consciousness. Before the emergence of the term *WASP* in the mid-1950s, many Jews and Catholics routinely referred to white Protestants as "the Americans." With the shift in consciousness signaled by the increasing tendency to view this group as one ethnic entity among others, Morrison's dream of a victorious Protestantism became an object of ridicule. Lynn observed that WASPs themselves often invoked the term, "sometimes as a form of self-mockery, occasionally as a confession of guilt, and almost inevitably, whether intended or not, as expressive of a new historical self-consciousness." The upshot in any case was that WASPs could no longer assume a majority status or "the exclusive possession of national identity," Lynn remarked. The "bland unconsciousness" of Protestant America was no longer possible.[12]

---

11. Robert W. Lynn, "The Eclipse of a Public: Protestant Reflections on Religion and Public Education, 1940–1968," in *Theology and Church in Times of Change: Essays in Honor of John Coleman Bennett,* ed. Edward LeRoy Long, Jr., and Robert T. Handy (Philadelphia: Westminster Press, 1970), 198.

12. Ibid., 200.

John Courtney Murray and the American Proposition

A new religious situation had come to pass that liberal Protestantism was poorly equipped to fathom or accept. The liberal Protestant vision of a common public faith was a vision of religious unity, but the American reality was an accelerating religious diversity within a rapidly secularizing culture. The specter of a growing and culturally powerful American Catholicism vividly exemplified the trend. In the same year that John Kennedy was elected to the presidency—after assuring Americans that he would not take instructions from the Vatican—another prominent Roman Catholic published a groundbreaking assessment of the American experiment. In his book *We Hold These Truths* (1960), Jesuit theologian John Courtney Murray explored the religious and political meaning of "the American Proposition"—a phrase he used nearly interchangeably with the "public consensus" or "public philosophy" of America. With the publication of this epochal work, liberal American Protestantism took instruction on the religious implications of American pluralist democracy.

Murray noted that the American Proposition was aptly summarized in the opening assertion of Thomas Jefferson's Declaration of Independence, which testified to the existence of certain universal truths. These truths were "the basis and inspiration of the American project, this constitutional commonwealth," Murray argued. The American experiment proposed that "certain unalienable rights" endowed by God were self-evidently real and universal. It claimed that all "men" were created equal and that all possessed the rights to life, liberty, and the pursuit of happiness. Murray contended that this faith was defensible only as a form of natural law argument, but his more pressing and influential argument focused on the religious implications of the right to liberty posited by the American Proposition. As he explained,

> The American Proposition makes a particular claim upon the reflective attention of the Catholic in so far as it contains a doctrine and a project in the matter of the "pluralist society," as we seem to have agreed to call it. The term might have many meanings. By pluralism here I mean the coexistence within the one political community of groups who hold divergent and incompatible views with regard to religious questions—those ultimate questions that concern the nature and destiny of man within a universe that stands under the reign of God. Pluralism therefore implies disagreement and dissension within the community. But it also implies a community within which there must be agreement and consensus. There is no small political problem here. If society is to be at all a rational process, some set of principles must motivate the general participation of all religious groups, despite their dissensions, in the oneness of the community. On the other hand, these common principles must not hinder the maintenance by each group of its own different identity. The problem of pluralism is, of course, practical; as a project, its "working out" is an exercise in civic virtue. But the problem is also theoretical; its solution is an exercise in political in-

telligence that will lay down, as the basis for the "working out," some sort of doctrine.[13]

We Hold These Truths offered a Catholic version of this doctrine. Murray conceded that "the fact of America" posed new problems for what he called "the universal Church"—that is, the Roman Catholic church. "The Catholic community faces the task of making itself intellectually aware of the conditions of its own coexistence within the American pluralistic scene," he observed. Catholicism existed in America under circumstances that were unique in the church's history. But the point of Murray's inquiry was to pursue the meaning of the church's American existence "not in the horizontal dimension of history but in the vertical dimension of theory."[14]

The most pressing theoretical problem for modern American Catholicism was the question of how to interpret the First Amendment. Murray noted that Catholics were frequently asked if they really believed in the amendment's first two provisions. The question was often meant to provoke embarrassment, but Murray insisted that there was nothing for Catholics to be embarrassed about because the American Constitution was not an object of faith. The Constitution prescribed law, not dogma. It contained articles of civil peace that Americans were required to observe, not articles of faith that they were required to believe. Among those who tried to invest the Constitution with religious or dogmatic authority, Murray observed, three conflicting groups dominated the debate. The first group claimed that the Constitution prescribed certain distinctly Protestant religious or cultural teachings rooted in free-church Puritanism. The second group, which was rooted in the tradition of early American deism and rationalism, claimed that the Constitution reflected the worldview of Enlightenment secular liberalism. The third group, which Murray called "the secularizing Protestants," tried to bridge the differences between America's Puritan and rationalist traditions. The secularizing Protestants accommodated their religious faith to the norms of American secular culture, bringing about "a coincidence of religious and secular-liberal concepts of freedom."[15]

Murray had little interest in mediating these arguments. He merely observed that all three traditions were deeply rooted in American history, all of them viewed the Constitution as a collection not only of laws but also of dogmas requiring "religious" assent, each of them contradicted the other two, and all three were wrong in their assumption that the Constitution was some kind of creed. If Americans were required to believe in the First Amendment in the way

---

13. John Courtney Murray, *We Hold These Truths: Catholic Reflections on the American Proposition* (New York: Sheed and Ward, 1960), ix–x.

14. Ibid., 27-28.

15. Ibid., 49.

that Christians assented to the Nicene Creed, the unavoidable implication was that the Constitution contained a religious test. In that case, Murray argued, "the Federal Republic has suddenly become a voluntary fellowship of believers either in some sort of free-church Protestantism or in the tenets of a naturalistic humanism. The notion is preposterous. The United States is a good place to live in; many have found it even a sort of secular sanctuary. But it is not a church, whether high, low, or broad. It is simply a civil community, whose unity is purely political." Put differently, the United States was a pluralistic republic that could never sanction the insinuation of any religious teaching into its law. Any attempt to read religious teaching into American law was "prima facie illegitimate and absurd," Murray declared.[16]

The United States was not only pluralistic in its political and legal philosophy but also increasingly pluralistic in what Murray called its "religio-social structure." Because American society was becoming increasingly pluralized, he argued, it was imperative for Americans to begin to accept, in a deeper way, the values enshrined in the American Proposition. With the rise of Catholic power in the United States, the American acceptance of diversity implied in the Declaration of Independence was being tested. Murray's prime example was the public school system:

> From a socio-religious point of view, American society has assumed a new pluralist structure, notably different from the structure it exhibited a century ago when the public school system had its beginnings. America's new self-understanding—its understanding of the new structure of its religious pluralism—has invalidated four concepts of the public school that have been entertained. I mean the concept of the public school as (a) vaguely Protestant or (b) purely secular in its atmosphere. I also mean the concept of the public school as the vehicle (a) for the inculcation of "democracy" as a quasi-religious ideology, or (b) for the transmission of spiritual and moral values in some non-sectarian sense.

All of these notions were deeply rooted in American experience, and all of them violated the spirit of the American Proposition, in Murray's view. America's dominant Protestant and secular ideologies were outmoded in a pluralistic society that increasingly outstripped its Protestant heritage. "None of these four concepts fit with the present facts of American life," he declared. "American society is neither vaguely Protestant nor purely secular. The religion of America is not 'democracy,' nor is it some generalized faith in 'values.' Religion in America has a form, a precisely defined form, a pluralistically structured form. This is the fact."[17]

---

16. Ibid., 54.
17. Ibid., 144.

This was the fundamental fact. To accept the fact of religious pluralism was to accept its subversive implications. But in this crucial respect, Murray argued, American society was stuck in a political and cultural pattern that could no longer be justified. American educators and political leaders continued to regard the public school as the only educational institution entitled to receive public support, while church schools were barred from receiving public support. But this dual pattern was a product of nineteenth-century American Protestantism, Murray argued: "It is a relic of the past, surviving in the present on the momentum of ideas and social facts that time itself has left behind."

Murray did not claim that the segregationist pattern of American public education could be readily changed. He counseled that the construction and implementation of a pattern appropriate to a pluralistic society would require generations of work. If the solution to the problem would be difficult to attain, however, it was nonetheless imperative for American educators, politicians, and religious leaders to begin the work of social reconstruction. In the existing system, religion was segregated "in the concrete pluralist sense" from the public schools, while religious schools were segregated from public aid. Having recently grappled with the evils of "separate but equal" racial discrimination, Murray argued, it was now time for America to address the immorality of religious discrimination.

The notion that public aid should be denied to any school that teaches a particular religion was a violation of the moral canon of distributive justice, in Murray's view. This long-standing American prejudice had never passed the test of morality and was now politically indefensible as well. "The principle of distributive justice would require that a proportionately just measure of public support should be available to such schools as serve the public cause of popular education, whether these schools be specifically religious in their affiliation and orientation, or not," Murray argued. He expected America to address this social task with the same "dynamism of change" and openness to new moral challenges that characterized its pursuit of other democratizing reforms. "I mean a growth in moral insight, assisted by a realistic grasp of socio-religious reality," he wrote. America would face the institutional implications of its religious pluralism when Americans became converted to a deeper moral understanding of what it meant to live in a pluralist democracy.[18]

The first liberal Protestant leader to endorse the main thrust of this argument was John C. Bennett. In 1958, well before the reforms of Vatican II engendered a new spirit of cooperation and fraternity between Catholics and mainline Protestants, Bennett appealed to Protestant leaders to rethink their opposition to parochial school aid. He noted that parochial schools throughout the country assumed much of America's educational burden and helped public school systems

---

18. Ibid., 146.

save money but were denied public assistance even for such "fringe benefits" as transportation, health services, lunch programs, and textbooks. In Bennett's view, it was unjust to penalize Catholics for maintaining their own schools. He endorsed the Catholic view that it was unfair for Catholics to bear a "double burden of expense" for education.[19] At the same time, he cautioned that a juster and more pluralistic approach to education would have to guard against any erosion in the state's support for public education. A juster approach would require higher public investment in education and support for time-sharing, aid for fringe benefits, and other pluralizing reforms.

Several years later, after the Supreme Court disallowed the Lord's Prayer and Bible reading in public schools and after Vatican II inspired a new ecumenical spirit between American Catholics and Protestants, many mainline Protestant leaders relinquished their hardline opposition to parochial school aid. In 1965, they supported a legislative compromise that widened public entitlements for students in nonpublic schools.[20] The work of pluralizing American politics and culture would take generations, as Murray predicted. In the case of the education issue, the slippery politics of parochial school aid remains unresolved, and the complexity of the issue has only intensified in subsequent decades as other religious and cultural groups make similar claims. In each case, however, as Murray insisted, the American challenge is not simply to create a more pluralistic politics but to accept the implications of cultural diversity on deeper levels of personal, moral, and imaginative awareness.

When Bennett published *The Radical Imperative* in 1975, his discussion of modern Catholicism reflected the extraordinary advances in ecumenical understanding that the previous decade of dialogue and cooperation had achieved. Bennett's tone was friendly and familiar, with barely a trace of the defensiveness, uneasiness or distrust that had marked liberal Protestant attitudes in the pre-Vatican II past.[21] In the 1960s, Bennett was showered with honorary doctorates from Catholic universities eager to pay tribute to his ecumenical efforts. By the early 1970s, it was not unusual for theological students to assume that modern Protestant and Catholic theologians were engaged in a common enterprise. The modernizing reforms of Vatican II made it possible for Catholics to employ the same critical methodologies used by Protestant scholars without facing eccle-

---

19. John C. Bennett, *Christians and the State* (New York: Charles Scribner's Sons, 1958), 248.

20. Cf. Editorial, "New Opportunity for Education," *Christianity and Crisis* 25 (March 8, 1965), 31; "Symposium: Religion in the Public Schools," *Religious Education* 59 (November/December 1964), 443–72; discussion in Lynn, "The Eclipse of a Public," 204–6.

21. Cf. John C. Bennett, *The Radical Imperative: From Theology to Social Ethics* (Philadelphia: Westminster Press, 1975), 91–94.

siastical censure. Catholics made immediate contributions to ecumenical, biblical, historical, ethical, and systematic theological studies that pre-Vatican II Catholicism could not have sanctioned. Vatican II's legitimation of historical criticism, its endorsement of Murray's approach to church and state issues, and its warm words for Protestant "separated brethren" laid the groundwork for a new, more cooperative, and genuinely dialogical relationship between modern Catholic and various Protestant churches. Catholic scholars such as George McRae, Raymond Brown, and David Tracy were appointed to important theological chairs, respectively, at Harvard Divinity School, Union Theological Seminary, and the University of Chicago Divinity School. The writings of such major Catholic theologians as Karl Rahner, Bernard Lonergan, Hans Küng, and Edward Schillebeeckx were increasingly studied at liberal Protestant seminaries and divinity schools, while Catholic theologians such as Leslie Dewart, Johannes Metz, and Gregory Baum made important ecumenical contributions to the renewal of Christian social theology.

Barely a decade after the closing session of Vatican II, the sense of Catholics as "other" was greatly diminished at most of America's leading liberal Protestant seminaries. As a Catholic student at Harvard and Union during this period, I rarely felt excluded from the community's discourse or history. Most of my Catholic friends shared this perception. Though the theological curricula at both institutions were still heavily dominated by the writings of liberal Protestant scholars, we accepted that modern critical theology thus far had been predominantly a liberal Protestant story. At the same time, it was equally clear that the era of liberal Protestant domination in theology was ending. Catholic students had little reason to feel excluded, as *Catholics,* from the content or direction of contemporary theological discussion. Confessional differences were no longer crucially determinative factors in biblical scholarship, historical theology, or social ethics. Though the nature and structure of authority in Catholicism set definite limits to the growing convergence between modern Catholic and Protestant theologies, the trend toward convergence was nonetheless real enough for Protestants like Bennett to seek inspiration and enlightenment from modern Catholicism.

If the growth of Catholic power subverted the American Protestant establishment, as Morrison warned, modern Catholicism also came to terms with Americanism in ways that Morrison had deemed impossible. Ecumenical dialogues of the 1960s and 1970s vindicated the ecumenical dreams of liberal Protestants that Morrison had chastised. To the surprise of its older-generation anti-Catholic proponents, liberal Protestantism was shaken more deeply in this period by movements rooted partly in its own churches than by any outside competing church. Having braced for a struggle with an alien Catholic rival, liberal Protestantism was challenged instead by the eruption of repressed voices belonging to people of color, women, and other minorities. Having paid little attention to the struggles of women and minorities in its own churches, mainline Christianity was confronted with decentering feminist, racial, and cultural claims that neither Morrison nor Murray had imagined.

James H. Cone and Black Theology

Liberal Protestantism took a warranted pride in its connections to the civil rights movement and the ministries of most civil rights leaders, especially Martin Luther King Jr. Though many civil rights leaders were products of the black church tradition, many of them were also, like King, closely tied to liberal Protestantism by virtue of their seminary education, their church affiliations, and their theology. King repeatedly noted that Rauschenbusch, Niebuhr, and Paul Tillich were the foremost influences on his theological worldview. His social ethics blended Rauschenbusch's social gospel idealism with Niebuhr's realism about human nature and the limitations of politics, while his understandings of divine reality and the relationships between love, power, and justice were decisively influenced by Tillich. His appeal to the color-blind promise of the American dream and his rhetoric of national moral regeneration were deeply rooted in his distinctive blend of liberal Protestant theology, progressive American political philosophy, and the cultural ethos of black Christianity. With powerful moral force, King called America to fulfill the egalitarian promise of the American Proposition and thus challenged American liberal Protestantism to redeem its own tradition. Though he never found the breadth or depth of support from mainline Protestantism that the civil rights movement deserved, he spoke a language and called for the realization of moral and political ideals that liberal Protestants could hardly fail to recognize. Though he was always, above all, an exemplar of the black church tradition, he also exemplified the best of the liberal Protestant tradition.

But for a new generation of black Christians, many of them influenced by the Black Power movement, this was precisely the problem with King's legacy. He epitomized a white progressive ideal. His theology built upon white middle-class liberal sources that were alien to many black Americans. His rhetoric was too moralistic for radical black Christians such as James H. Cone, a young and soon-prominent theologian to whom Malcolm X was a more authentic and in-spiriting figure. King and Malcolm both went to prison, but King went for noble moral reasons; both men were religious, but King preached a Gandhian way-of-Christ pacifism; both called for a transformation of America's political and economic systems, but nobody was more middle class than King. On each point, Malcolm X's hard-core street-life background, his militancy, and his racial politics made him a more compelling model to Cone.

King's movement preached a liberal theology that claimed that race should not matter, but for Cone what was needed was an emancipatory black Christian vision that emphasized black pride, identity, and power. What was needed was a black theology of liberation. King's murder in 1968 confirmed for Cone not only the evil of white America but also the insufficiency of King's social strategy. "By the summer of that year, I had so much anger pent up in me that I had to let it out or be destroyed by it," he later recalled. Cone's anger was fueled not only by the murders of King and Malcolm X, and other black leaders, but also by his personal encounters with racism and by his identification with the victims of America's slave ships and auction blocks. "Because of these experiences, I promised myself that I would never again make a political or theological compromise with racism," he explained. "Racism is a deadly disease that must be resisted by any means necessary. Never again would I ever expect white racists to do right in relation to the black community."[22] In later years, Cone credited King as an important source for black theology and emphasized that King was much more radical than popular American iconography suggested. At the outset of Cone's intellectual career, however, before "black theology" or "liberation theology" had names, it was Black Power radicalism that fueled his rereading of the biblical faith.

Black theology would liberate African American Christianity from its dependence on white liberal, evangelical, and charismatic forms of Christianity. It would make black Christianity speak in its own voice. Cone later vowed that black theology would also correct the various Marxist, racist, black nationalist, and even black Christian put-downs of the African American Christian tradition. The latter imperative became clear to Cone only after the publication of his first book, however. *Black Theology and Black Power* (1969) sharply attacked the black churches for their political, ecclesiological, and religious conservatism. With blistering polemical force, Cone assailed the established white and black churches while calling for a merger of prophetic black Christianity and Black Power radicalism. The book's repudiation of black church authoritarianism carried the marks of Cone's recent decision to leave the African Methodist Episcopal church (AME), which had spurned his requests for a teaching position and prevented him from exercising any influence in the church as a theologian.

---

22. James H. Cone, *My Soul Looks Back* (Maryknoll, N.Y.: Orbis Books, 1986, c1982), 46–47; cf. Martin Luther King, Jr., *Stride toward Freedom: The Montgomery Story* (New York: Harper & Row, 1958), 91; King, "Pilgrimage to Nonviolence," *Christian Century* 77 (April 13, 1960), 439; King, *Where Do We Go from Here? Chaos or Community?* (New York: Harper & Row, 1967). For Cone's discussion of the dialectic of King's American dream and Malcolm X's American nightmare, see James H. Cone, *Martin & Malcolm & America: A Dream or a Nightmare* (Maryknoll, N.Y.: Orbis Books, 1991).

Cone joined the United Methodist church, but with the publication of *Black Theology and Black Power* his attack on the established churches and his espousal of a nationalist Black Power politics drew him to the attention of several black nationalist and revolutionary groups, including the Congress of African People (CAP) led by Amiri Baraka (LeRoi Jones). Having left the AME church, Cone was looking for a political-religious home. He soon realized that he would not find one among the existing black nationalist or revolutionary groups, however; all of them categorically repudiated the black churches and biblical Christianity. They repeated the Marxist denigration of black religion with arrogant certainty. To them, black Christianity was inevitably reactionary; it bore no emancipating promise and preserved nothing worth preserving. It was rather a particularly demeaning and oppressive vestige of slavery that consoled the victims of racism in their oppression and reconciled them to it. These were creedal certainties to the Black Power nationalists and revolutionaries, but Cone belonged to another community of faith. He could not join a revolution that excluded his parents, even if this meant that he had to back away from some of the black nationalist claims of his first book. He determined that if black Christianity was to find its own prophetic voice, it would have to correct the various put-downs that ridiculed the black church from all sides. Black Christianity would have to explicate the revolutionary meaning of a potentially liberating but largely repressed tradition.

Cone regarded prophetic black Christianity as more than a black church tradition; it included the histories and experiences of blacks in all Christian churches. He affirmed that the black church tradition was central to black Christianity and its liberating promise, however—which made it imperative for black theology to address the contention of Joseph R. Washington Jr.'s often-cited work, *Black Religion* (1964). In Washington's influential reading, the black church tradition was an historically contingent cultural phenomenon. It was not rooted in a distinctive religious identity, and it had never developed a distinctively black Christian theological foundation. Rather, black Christianity was merely the organizational form that African American Christians had been driven to adopt in a racially segregated society. It reflected the sociocultural necessities of a bygone era. Because the black churches had no legitimizing religious foundation, Washington argued, it was appropriate to question whether they should continue to exist. In Washington's view, the time had come for them to dissolve into America's established white-dominated churches.

Cone accepted part of this prescription for himself while rejecting its larger claims. He joined the United Methodist church while defending the integrity of the black church tradition. Whether one joined a black- or white-dominated church was a matter of individual discernment, he argued. The black churches would remain for those who could best live out their faith within them. For Cone, the crucial issue raised by Washington was not whether blacks should belong to one denomination or another, but whether black Christians in any confessional context could lay claim to a distinctive theological identity and tradition. *A Black Theology of Liberation* (1970) sought to provide an affirmative answer by refashioning themes from the black church tradition into a new theological perspective: liberation theology. In his original version of it, black liberation theology was deeply militant and accusatory. It scared most of its white readers and prompted even a sympathetic white observer like Bennett to treat black liberationism with a more strained and defensive attitude than he adopted toward other liberation theologies. In Bennett's reading, black theology spoke in only one voice, and it was plainly a voice of rage. Cone later recalled that during this period he regarded virtually all white theology as "a racist, theological justification of the status quo." He was contemptuous of white theologians for refusing to acknowledge their racism and for failing to confess their complicity in the structural perpetuation of racism. "I could barely contain my rage whenever I read their books or found myself in their presence," he later recalled. "They were so condescending and arrogant in the way they talked about black theology, always communicating the impression that it was not genuine theology, because it was too emotional and anti-intellectual."[23]

For most white liberal theologians, black theology was not theology at all because it did not address the "proper" subject matter of theology—"namely, the rational justification of religious belief in a scientific and technological world that has no use for God." *A Black Theology of Liberation* observed that Christian theological liberalism was preoccupied with the question of how to justify religious belief in a scientific age. The agenda of liberal theology was set by skeptics and atheists. It sought to establish credible grounds for belief in divine reality in the face of scientific and philosophical criticism. "But most blacks never heard of Aristotle, Anselm, Descartes, or Kant, and they do not care about the interrelationship of theology and philosophy," Cone countered. "Unless God's revelation is related to black liberation, blacks must reject it. The Barthians [and liberal theologians] have confused God-talk with white-talk, and thus have failed to see that there is no real speech about God except in relationship to the liberation of the oppressed."[24]

This distinctly liberationist argument soon gained wide currency through the explosion of Latin American, African American, and feminist liberation theologies in the 1970s. The claim was original to Cone, however. *A Black Theology*

23. Joseph R. Washington, Jr., *Black Religion* (Boston: Beacon Press, 1964); Bennett, *The Radical Imperative*, 119–31; James H. Cone, "Preface to the 1986 Edition," in *A Black Theology of Liberation*, ed. James H. Cone (Maryknoll, N.Y.: Orbis Books, Twentieth Anniversary Edition 1990, c1970), xiv.

24. Cone, *A Black Theology of Liberation*, 83.

of Liberation proclaimed that the God of genuinely Christian theology took sides with the oppressed and was revealed through their struggle for freedom. Liberation was not a by-product of religious experience but the very essence of divine activity in the world. Cone conceded that this understanding of God as a partisan liberating power was not unknown in liberal theology because it was a primary biblical theme. He insisted that white theology in all of its liberal, Barthian, and conservative forms was incapable of embracing the meaning of this biblical teaching, however. "White religionists are not capable of perceiving the blackness of God, because their satanic whiteness is a denial of the very essence of divinity," he claimed. "That is why whites are finding and will continue to find the black experience a disturbing reality."

To assert that God is black was to accept the biblical teaching that "the essence of the nature of God is to be found in the concept of liberation." To be black was to be oppressed; to know God was to experience God's saving power in the struggles of the oppressed. In racist America, Christ could not be white, Cone argued, because white is the color of the oppressors. The liberator of the oppressed could only share the condition and color of those who are oppressed. It followed for Cone that "those who want to know who God is and what God is doing must know who black persons are and what they are doing." The point was not to join the war on poverty or present other white liberal sin offerings, Cone instructed, but to "become black with God" through the experience of joining the oppressed in their struggle for freedom. Cone doubted that this was possible for white people. "They do not really want to lose their precious white identity, as if it is worth saving," he explained. For black theology, it was imperative not to get caught up in the problem of saving white oppressors but to proclaim the gospel as a message of emancipation for those oppressed by white Americans. "God comes to us in God's blackness, which is wholly unlike whiteness," Cone wrote. "To receive God's revelation is to become black with God by joining God in the work of liberation."[25]

This project required an unflinching willingness to proclaim the truth as it appeared from a black liberationist standpoint. As Pascal observed, truth on one side of the mountain is often falsehood on the other. Black liberation theology affirmed the truths of black experience without regard for liberal anxieties about black anger or violence. Shortly after Cone assumed his teaching position at Union Theological Seminary, during Bennett's tenure as seminary president, Bennett called Cone into his office to ask if he literally believed that the white church was the antichrist. Cone respectfully confirmed that this was exactly what he believed. He was not spinning metaphors. "But why did you choose to teach

---

25. Ibid. 64–66. On the same theme, see James H. Cone, *Black Theology and Black Power* (New York: Seabury Press, 1969).

at Union if you mean it literally?" Bennett implored. Cone responded, "John, my father cut billets and logs for a living, and I work at Union. And as long as I have to support my family, I might as well do it here. Living in a racist society, every black person has to assume that his job may not meet all the requirements for which he or she may have been called." It was hardly the assuring response that the paragon of white liberal Christianity was seeking. Though he was always careful to invoke a biblical warrant for his theological claims, Cone's criterion of truthfulness was ultimately whether a particular claim or argument served the cause of black liberation. "What we need is the divine love as expressed in black power, which is the power of blacks to destroy their oppressors, here and now, by any means at their disposal," he asserted. "Unless God is participating in this holy activity, we must reject God's love."[26]

The echoes of Malcolm X thus resounded throughout Cone's early and subsequent writings. Though he later revised several key aspects of his theology in response to criticisms from black theologians, Cone's commitment to a Malcolm X–like Black Power perspective has remained central to his work. His theology is devoted to promoting the interests and empowerment of oppressed people of color, especially African Americans. Toward this end, he repeatedly cautions that all theologies are limited, perspectival, and ideological. Theological claims are never truly universal and always reflect the cultural and political biases of their proponents. What makes black liberation theology distinctive is that it faces up to this truism. Black theology does not claim to appropriate the entire inheritance of classical Christian teaching. It does not make universalist claims or, in Cone's version, accept traditional Christian teaching pertaining to suffering or divine universality. Black theology explicates the perspectives and spiritual experiences of oppressed black Christians in their struggle for liberation, Cone explains. It accepts as religiously true only those beliefs that advance this struggle. It identifies with the biblical theme of a divinely chosen people and finds its own history prefigured in the Exodus narrative of deliverance from slavery, but it rejects the exilic, postexilic, and New Testament themes pertaining to redemptive suffering. The notion that Christians are to follow the way of Christ to the cross has no rightful place in a black theology, Cone insists, because God has chosen blacks "not for redemptive suffering but for freedom. Black people are not elected to be Yahweh's suffering people." It follows for Cone that black theology can be falsified only if it can be shown that it does not advance the biblically sanctioned cause of black liberation.

Does Cone's theology meet this test? In the 1970s, several black theologians and religious scholars began to argue that it does not. Though he became the

---

26. Discussion with Bennett recounted in Cone, *My Soul Looks Back,* 73; closing quote in Cone, *A Black Theology of Liberation,* 70.

dominant figure in American black theology, Cone's work was widely criticized among African American scholars for its narrow racial focus, its overdependence on the theologies of Paul Tillich and Karl Barth, its politicization of Christian teaching, and its neglect of African American history and culture. In ways that reflected their considerably variant religious perspectives, figures such as Gayraud S. Wilmore, Charles Long, Carleton Lee, and Cecil Cone argued for a black religious perspective that was rooted in the literature and religious forms of African American culture. Wilmore and Cecil Cone contended that Cone's theology was too politicized to offer a viable religious vision for black Americans. Wilmore and Long further believed that Cone's work was too church-oriented to provide an emancipatory social vision. For them, black religious thought was a deeper, richer, and older tradition than black Christian theology. They urged Cone to pay attention to the difference.[27] Other observers criticized Cone's disregard for feminism, his exclusive focus on the oppression of American blacks, and his failure to address economic factors. Some noted the irony that, while Cone criticized King's dependence on white liberal theology, his own writings were filled with quotations from Tillich and Barth. Bennett worried that Cone's Black Power perspectivism was self-righteous and that it claimed immunity from public criticism. Radical feminist Mary Daly declared that Cone's outlook was deeply patriarchal and that his strategy of liberation, while transcending religion as a crutch, "tends to settle for being religion as a gun."[28]

These were serious criticisms, unlike the stream of abuse that Cone received from critics such as Andrew Greeley, who condemned Cone's "Nazi mentality" and his "hatred for white people." Having learned from Malcolm X not to take white criticism seriously, Cone dismissed most criticisms of his work:

> White theologians wanted me to debate with them about the question of whether "black theology" was real theology, using their criteria to decide the issue. With clever theological sophistication, white theologians defined the discipline of theology in the light of the problem of the unbeliever (i.e., the question of the relationship of faith and reason) and thus unrelated to the problem of slavery and racism. Using a white definition of theology, I knew there was no way I

---

27. Cf. Charles Long, "Perspectives for a Study of Afro-American Religion in the United States," *History of Religion* 11 (August 1971), 54–66; Long, "Structural Similarities and Dissimilarities in Black and African Theologies," *Journal of Religious Thought* 32 (Fall/Winter 1975), 9–24; Gayraud S. Wilmore, *Black Religion and Black Radicalism* (Garden City, N.Y.: Doubleday, 1972); Cecil Cone, *Identity Crisis in Black Theology* (Nashville: African Methodist Episcopal Church, 1975); James H. Cone, "Epilogue: An Interpretation of the Debate among Black Theologians," in *Black Theology: A Documentary History*, vol. 1, 1966–1979, ed. James H. Cone and Gayraud S. Wilmore (Maryknoll, N.Y.: Orbis Books, 1993), 425–39.

28. Bennett, *The Radical Imperative,* 126–28; Mary Daly, *Beyond God the Father: Toward a Philosophy of Women's Liberation* (Boston: Beacon Press, 1985, c1973), 25.

could win the debate. And even if I had managed to give a "good" account of myself, what difference would that have made for the liberation of poor blacks?[29]

But Cone could not dismiss the reactions of Wilmore, Long, and Cecil Cone to his work or reject the criticisms of black feminist or "womanist" writers. Though he sharply repudiated black theologians such as Preston Williams, Major Jones, and J. Deotis Roberts when they tried to combat racism with appeals to universal rationality or Christian reconciliation, the objections of his cultural critics belonged to a different category.[30] They did not appeal to the context-transcending power of universal moral reason, as Williams and Jones did, or call for a religiously inspired reconciliation between blacks and whites, as Roberts did, but rather called for a deeper black religious grounding in African American slave narratives, tales, sermons, and music. Their own theological positions ranged from Long's antitheological history of religions culturalism to Wilmore's nontheological Christian culturalism to Cecil Cone's theology of African theism, but all agreed that Cone's liberationism was too dependent on white Christian theology and Black Power radicalism. What was needed was neither a reassertion of King's moralistic universalism nor a translation of Black Power politics into Christian theology, but a new common language of black religion that was rooted in the traditions of African American culture.[31]

Despite the considerable differences between them regarding religious belief and method, Cone's cultural critics convinced him that black theology needed to do more than translate Malcolm X's revolutionary black nationalism into Christian language. "I was embarrassed by this critique, because no one had been more critical of white theology than I," he later recalled. "To find out from my black colleagues that I was still held captive by the same system that I was criticizing was a bitter pill to swallow. What then was I to do? Deny the obvious or give up in despair?" Cone did neither, but set out to deepen the historical

---

29. Cone, "Preface to the 1986 Edition," xiii.

30. James H. Cone, *God of the Oppressed* (San Francisco: HarperCollins, 1975), 203–6. Cf. Preston N. Williams, "James Cone and the Problem of a Black Ethic," *Harvard Theological Review* 65 (October 1972), 483–84; Major Jones, *Christian Ethics for Black Theology* (Nashville: Abingdon Press, 1974); J. Deotis Roberts, *Liberation and Reconciliation: A Black Theology* (Philadelphia: Westminster Press, 1971); Roberts, *A Black Political Theology* (Philadelphia: Westminster Press, 1974).

31. Charles Long, "Perspectives for a Study of Afro-American Religion in the U.S.," *History of Religions* 11 (August 1971), 54–66; Long, "Structural Similarities and Dissimilarities in Black and African Theologies," *Journal of Religious Thought,* 33 (Fall/ Winter 1975), 9–24; Gayraud S. Wilmore, *Black Religion and Black Radicalism* (Garden City, N.Y.: Anchor Books, 1972); Cecil W. Cone, *The Identity Crisis in Black Theology* (Nashville: African Methodist Episcopal Church, 1975); Cecil W. Cone; "The Black Religious Experience," *Journal of the Interdenominational Theological Center* 2 (Spring 1975), 137–39.

and cultural basis of his theology. "Since I was absolutely sure that I was right about liberation being the central motif of the gospel and one of the most creative elements of black religion, what I needed to do was to rethink the content and shape of black theology in that light," he explained. *The Spirituals and the Blues* (1972) presented his first attempt to establish a deeper cultural grounding for his work, explicating the religious meaning of the African American spirituals and blues tradition.[32]

His subsequent major work offered a more systematic synthesis of black theology's biblical and cultural wellsprings. *God of the Oppressed* (1975) mixed Cone's narrativist reading of the biblical tradition and his characteristic emphasis on political struggle with richly evocative discussions of African American history, culture, and church life. Cone identified the story of black liberation with the biblical story of salvation, arguing that black theology's assertion of a single narrative line from Scripture to liberation theology did not represent a movement from human need to divine reality but reflected the movement of God's revelation to humanity. The book retained Cone's commitment to a Barthian revelational positivism in which theology always begins with the revealed Word rather than with human questions or projections, but Cone's deepening immersion in African American history was already pushing him to a more thoroughly culturalist perspectivism in theological method.

His neoorthodoxy had been chosen largely by default. Cone explained that when he first began to develop a theology of black Christianity, he was familiar with only three basic theological perspectives. These were the Protestant neoorthodox, liberal, and conservative theologies taught in European and North American seminaries. On the one hand, in his assessment, liberal theology's devotion to historical and scientific criticism negated too much of traditional Christian teaching to provide a groundwork for black theology. "Black church people would not respond enthusiastically to the historical-critical approach to the Bible, and especially the historical Jesus," he explained. On the other hand, he was repelled by the fundamentalism and outright racism that he found in conservative theologies. As he saw it, this left only the neoorthodox approach, which preserved the classical Protestant devotion to biblical authority and the divinity of Christ without lapsing into fundamentalism. Barthian neoorthodoxy insisted upon the primacy of the Word of God, but did not identify the words of Scripture with God's Word. For Barth, the words of Scripture and the words of biblical preaching were forms of God's Word only as witnesses to the revealed Word of God, which is Jesus Christ. In his early writings, Cone insisted that only Barthian neoorthodoxy provided an appropriate theological framework for the articulation of

---

32. Cone, *My Soul Looks Back,* 60–61; Cone, *The Spirituals and the Blues* (Maryknoll, N.Y.: Orbis Books, 1991, c1972).

black Christian experience. Like black Christianity, Barthian neoorthodoxy was not interested in religion, but in Jesus Christ; for both perspectives, Christianity was not a religion, but the revelation of divine truth. Barthian revelational positivism thus upheld traditional Protestant affirmations about Christ, biblical authority, and biblical preaching in a way that uniquely affirmed the central elements of black American religion.[33]

God of the Oppressed repeated these assertions while uneasily holding the revelationist and culturalist approaches in tension. Only a few pages after he affirmed that theology must begin with the revealed Word rather than human words, Cone also insisted that "we cannot test the truth of the black story by using intellectual categories that were not created from black experience itself. Instead we must immerse ourselves in the existence of the people, feeling their hurts and pain, and listening to their testimony that Jesus is present with them." African American religion is only comprehensible in the light of black America's struggle for freedom, he argued. "Unless the interpreter of black religion is willing to suspend his a priori definitions of reality, and open himself to another reality found in the social existence of black people, then his comments about the truth or untruth of black religion become merely an academic exercise which tell us far more about his subjective interests than about the religious life of black people," Cone declared. The Word of God is not a theological proposition, but a divine call to freedom. Black theology did not claim to embrace universal religious truths but regarded truth itself as an always-particular project of freedom waged against various forms of nonfreedom.

The assertion that religious truths are not propositional was a Barthian argument, but Cone's emphasis on black experience and the contextual character of Christian truth increasingly dissociated his approach from Barth's revelationism. In Cone's narrativist understanding of religion, the truths of religion are the stories that shape the identities of black communities and empower their struggle for liberation. Christian truths are revealed whenever oppressed people open themselves to the identity-transforming narratives of Scripture. The marks of biblical religion are therefore revolutionary and solidaristic. Biblical truths do not sacralize oppression or accommodate the dominant powers or reduce religion to personal salvation or healing. Biblical religion inspires oppressed people to become liberated from the bondage of ignorance, fear, inertia, and oppression. To understand the Bible is to view the world from this perspective, which explains, for Cone, why the scriptural message virtually always eludes white people. "Because the values of white culture are antithetical to biblical revelation, it is impossible to be white (culturally speaking) and also think biblically," he wrote. "Biblical thinking is *liberated* thought, i.e., thinking that is not entrapped by

---

33. Cone, *My Soul Looks Back,* 82–83.

social categories of the dominant culture." Biblical thinking is always driven by the liberating interest of the oppressed. "Any other starting point is a contradiction of the social a priori of the Scripture," he concluded.[34]

Cone's commitment to the liberating interest of the oppressed has opened his thought to further influences and critiques. The traces of his Barthian theological training have become thinner as he turns more deeply to what he calls "the black sources in James Cone."[35] Moreover, his silence on political economics has been challenged by various Christian socialists and Third World liberationists, who press the question whether black theology wants a new economic system or merely a bigger slice of the American capitalist pie. Cone concedes that his early writings evaded the question, but his encounters with Third World liberationists and his friendship with Cornel West have moved him to explore the possibilities of a democratic socialist alternative to capitalism. In the late 1970s, having concluded that his Black Power–Christian framework was too limited to address fundamental issues pertaining to economic power, Cone began to assert "that the black church cannot remain silent regarding socialism, because such silence will be interpreted by our Third World brothers and sisters as support for the capitalistic system which exploits the poor all over this earth."[36]

Black theology needed to establish its solidarity with Third World liberationist movements but could not do so without seriously addressing economic and ideological issues that Cone was predisposed to avoid. Moreover, the liberating interest of the oppressed in the United States also cried out for a stronger economic analysis. Cone's writings on political economy have never moved beyond his exhortatory appeals to embrace democratic socialism, but his later insistence on the importance of political economy has nonetheless marked an important departure in black liberation theology. He calls black churches to "take a stand against capitalism and for democratic socialism, for Karl Marx and against Adam Smith, for the poor in all colors and against the rich of all colors, for the workers and against the corporations." It is clear that American blacks "must begin to think of a radical and total reconstruction of this society from its material, economic base," he declares. Though his call for a democratic socialist alternative implicitly raises the question of the need for a new multiracial political movement, Cone customarily directs his challenge to the leaders of established black liberal

---

34. Cone, *God of the Oppressed*, 97, 124.

35. Cone, *My Soul Looks Back*, 60. Cf. James H. Cone, "The Gospel and the Liberation of the Poor: How My Mind Has Changed," *Christian Century* 98 (February 18, 1981), 162–66.

36. James H. Cone, *The Black Church and Marxism: What Do They Have to Say to Each Other?"* (New York: Institute for Democratic Socialism, 1980), 4. On Cone's encounters with Third World Christian socialism, see Cone, "Black Theology and Third World Theologies," *Chicago Theological Seminary Register* 73 (Winter 1983), 3–12.

organizations. "Why are there no genuinely radical and independent voices coming from our leaders today?" he asked in 1980:

Why do they pose alternatives that exist only within capitalism, a system which offers no hope for the masses of blacks? Personally I like Andy Young, NAACP, Urban League, SCLC, Jesse Jackson and our black elected officials, and I do not wish to minimize the hard work and devotion they have given on our behalf. The same is true for our ministers and theologians of the gospel. But what I find missing in what they propose are genuinely new visions of the social order.

Cone suggested that a blend of Marxist criticism and prophetic black religion might provide the emancipatory vision that was needed. "Together black religion and marxist philosophy may show us the way to build a completely new society," he wrote.[37]

These were critical, but hopeful words. Cone believed that the dominant civil rights organizations and most black churches were politically compromised, ineffectual, and timid, but he still believed in 1980 that popular black religion could become a transformative political force in American society. Partly by virtue of his participation in the National Committee of Black Churchman (NCBC), which he led during the 1970s, he envisioned a politically radicalized church that would embrace the prophetic, revolutionary spirit of black liberation theology. The NCBC worked throughout the 1970s to advance this religious vision, but its effort to promote liberation theology in the black churches achieved little success.

The contrasts with Latin American liberationism are telling. As a product of black church Christianity, black theology is more deeply rooted in an indigenous religious tradition than Latin American liberationism. Though it is often strongly critical of the black churches, black theology is nourished by the spiritual and cultural traditions of black American religion. Latin American liberationism has little to compare to this religious and cultural wellspring. Gutiérrez and other Latin American liberationists have found few resources in Latin American Christian history for their religious project. Gutiérrez appeals to the example of Bartolome de Las Casas, the sixteenth-century bishop who gave up his colonial estates to work with the Peruvian Indians and struggle for their cause, but Latin American Catholicism offers few such figures who can be said to prefigure liberation theology. Most Latin American liberationists belong to the church that sacralized Latin America's oppressive governments and social structures. Theologians such as Gutiérrez are thus driven to a more radically rejectionist attitude toward their church's past than African American liberationists typically adopt toward their tradition.

---

37. Cone, "The Black Church and Marxism," 9–10.

But the pervasive presence and immense cultural power of Catholicism in Latin America also give Latin American liberationist movements crucial advantages over African American liberationism. Latin American liberationism (in its dominant Catholic forms) has developed within a culturally dominant religious structure. Latin American liberation theology challenges the authoritarianism and reactionary politics of Latin America's dominant religious power from within. It has been able to create hundreds of thousands of decentralized Christian base communities partly because it is a subversive force within a powerful church. African American liberationism has none of these factors working for it, however. Black theology has sought to radicalize America's black churches, but these churches have little power in American society, and theologians such as Cone are compromised by their desire not to undercut whatever power these churches sustain. The liberationist project of subversion is more ambiguous in African American contexts than in Latin America. Latin American liberationism has spawned a vast base community movement and other social movements, but nothing like these movements has come from black theology. Though Latin American liberationists have been forced to spend much of their time defending their orthodoxy, they are able to say that liberation theology is the product of a genuine social movement. Latin American liberationism explicates the spirituality and moral struggles of the base community movement. By contrast, black theology remains almost entirely a concern of black academics. In 1980, Cone was still hopeful that black theology could engender a new, more inspiriting, and powerful form of social activism in American churches, but in subsequent years he has not disputed the verdict—voiced especially by Wilmore—that the effort to convert the black churches to black liberation theology has failed.

Wilmore cites various reasons for this situation, including a lack of financial resources and infrastructure, the rise of conservative evangelicalism, the de-radicalization of the Black Muslim faith after the death of Elijah Muhammed, and, in the 1980s, the triumph of Right-wing Republicanism in American politics. "In the 1960s Malcolm helped us radicalize the black church by exposing its servile accommodation and pushing its clergy more and more toward an explicit black nationalism," Wilmore recalls. "What we have instead is the rising prosperity of the black middle class, the ineptitude of the older civil rights organizations, and the somnolence of mainstream African American Christianity." The last problem, especially, has encouraged Muslim leaders to believe "that the time is ripe for the successful proselytization of the entire black community in the United States," Wilmore observes.[38]

---

38. Gayraud Wilmore, "A Revolution Unfulfilled, but Not Invalidated," *A Black Theology of Liberation,* ed. James H. Cone, Twentieth Anniversary Edition, 1990, 154.

For Wilmore and Cone, the failure of black theology as a social movement is symptomatic of black America's deeper crisis of spirit and cultural disintegration. Wilmore points to the disorganization of black labor, the "almost complete breakdown of the family," the ravages of drug addiction, and the trivialization of black culture as "signs of deculturation, demoralization, and the alienation of a confused black middle class from its traditional role in the vanguard of the race." He notes that many church leaders have responded to this cultural crisis by retreating to their "stained-glass foxholes," which usually means devoting themselves to "preaching, raising money, and jockeying for ecclesiastical offices."[39] Yet he and Cone cling to the conviction that black liberation theology is still the most promising and viable form of progressive religion in the United States. Black theology alone links the liberating message of biblical faith to a radical politics that is both race and class conscious. While liberal Christianity offers "effete religiosity in conspiracy with a triumphalistic secularism," black theology keeps alive the biblical vision of a just society. Wilmore notes that black theology is also belatedly developing a liberationist politics that addresses gender oppression. Like Cone, he invests much of his hope for the renewal of black theology in the emergence of womanist criticism.[40]

For many years, feminist critics of Cone's work exhorted him to acknowledge that sexism is a form of oppression that liberation theology must address. Cone's response was adamantly negative. "When I began writing about black theology, the problem of sexism was not part of my theological consciousness," he later recalled. "When it was raised by others, I rejected it as a joke or as an intrusion upon the legitimate struggle of black people to eliminate racism."[41] As a youth raised in Arkansas, he had feared to be in the presence of a white woman, "because her word alone could get a person lynched, legally electrocuted, or confined to prison for life." Years later, as a black theologian, it seemed to him that the feminist movement and its rhetoric of violation presented yet another white ruse to distract attention from the ravages of racism. The feminist preoccupation with rape struck him as a throwback to the racist fear-mongering of his youth, when fourteen-year-old Emmett Till could be lynched for whistling at a white woman. When white women insisted that they were degraded by male chauvinism and the social systems created by male dominance, Cone thought their complaints were frivolous at best. "Unfortunately, my early reflection on women's liberation was so competely controlled by black males' fears that I

---

39. Ibid., 155–56.
40. Cf. Ibid., 160; James H. Cone, "Introduction," in *Black Theology*, vol. 1, ed. James H. Cone and Gayraud Wilmore, 279–83; Cone, "Introduction," in *Black Theology*, vol. 2, ed. James H. Cone and Gayraud Wilmore, 257–64.
41. Cone, *My Soul Looks Back*, 115–16.

could not think straight regarding the complexity of the problem," he later recalled. "It was easy for me to say that if white women are oppressed by their men, it is not the fault of black men. We black men certainly are not oppressing white women."[42]

But the arguments of his feminist colleagues and students were too familiar, too similar, and too painful to ignore. Teaching at Union Seminary, Cone encountered numerous white feminists who forced him to recognize the parallels between racist and sexist injustice. More importantly, he was chastened by the claims of black women that sexism is a serious problem among blacks, as well.

> Black women's silence began to end at Union and other places, because black men misused their silence by refusing to even consider that sexism was a real problem in the black community. Black men continued to claim that "black women have always been free." As I listened to black women articulate their pain, and as I observed the insensitive responses of black men, it became existentially clear to me that sexism was a black problem too.

This realization drove Cone to confess his complicity and the complicity of black Christianity in the perpetuation of injustice toward women. In recent years, he and Wilmore have called attention to the routine mistreatment and ridicule inflicted on churchwomen and have warned that black church leaders are replicating the sins of white racists through their chauvinism. "Most of us have not even thought about the unique suffering of black women," Cone confessed in 1982. "We have not allowed ourselves to be taught by black women so that our theological reflections can more adequately reflect the whole black community." Black theology speaks for black churches that are 75 percent female, but led entirely by males. "I do not see how we can keep our credibility as 'liberation' theologians and remain so unliberated in our dealing with the question of sexism," Cone declared. "Nearly all black theologians have either ignored sexism completely or have made such irrelevant comments on it that silence would have been preferable."[43] He later pressed the point more sharply: "If we black male theologians do not take seriously the need to incorporate into our theology a critique of our sexist practices in the black community, then we have no right to complain when white theologians snub black theology."[44]

Cone's subsequent writings have expressed support for black feminism, though without incorporating feminist arguments into his theological vision. As Delores Williams observes, Cone's work continues to draw inspiration and wisdom from Malcolm X, W.E.B. DuBois, and Martin Luther King Jr., without bringing women's voices into the conversation. "Not a single woman is named,

---

42. Ibid., 116–17.
43. Ibid., 118–22.
44. Cone, "Preface to the 1986 Edition," xvi.

quoted, or given credit for contributing to the transformations Cone says he has made in his thought and style in the last twenty years," she notes.[45] Cone endorses the legitimacy of feminist criticism but does not incorporate black feminist or womanist themes into his constructive work. He opposes the injustices to women exposed by feminist criticism without adopting a feminist perspective on gender as a category of analysis.

If his support for women's liberation thus falls short of taking feminist criticism fully to heart, the trajectory of his career nonetheless demonstrates the utter seriousness and honesty with which he applies the liberationist test to his work. Having begun with a blend of Barthian neoorthodox theology and Black Power politics, Cone's theology has grown into a multistranded liberationist perspective that outstrips, without negating, its origins in black revolutionary nationalism. Without accepting the strictures of Long and Wilmore against church-oriented theologies, Cone embraces their fundamental claim that an emancipatory black Christianity has to be grounded in the history and culture of black American religion. Without accepting the claims of many feminists that biblical religion is too patriarchal to support a truly liberating theology, Cone throws the weight of his influence and moral authority into ridding the church of sexism.

Though Bennett had worried that he was not open to criticism, Cone has revised his position in response to criticism more readily than any other major theologian of his generation. Though black theology has not inspired the popular following that Latin American liberationism engendered, it has inspired a new generation of black Christian intellectuals to find a third way between King's Christian liberalism and Malcolm X's Muslim radicalism. Black scholars such as West, Dwight Hopkins, Robert Franklin, Jacquelyn Grant, Michael Dyson, Katie Cannon, Cain Felder, Renita Weems, Clarice Martin, Thomas Hoyt, and Toinette Eugene were importantly influenced in the 1970s and 1980s by the emergence of a multistranded black liberationist theological tradition. The existence of black American liberationism also provides a bracing test of white liberal Christian seriousness. Though liberation theology is inherently controversial in North American churches, it is nonetheless comparatively safe for a white liberal theological establishment to support liberation theology in Latin America. Liberal Protestant and Catholic seminaries readily incorporated Latin American theologies into their curricula in the 1970s and 1980s, while liberal Protestant and Catholic churches supported the sanctuary movement, opposed U.S. foreign policy in Latin America, and mobilized other forms of concrete support for Latin American liberationist movements.[46]

---

45. Delores S. Williams, "James Cone's Liberation: Twenty Years Later," in *A Black Theology of Liberation*, Twentieth Anniversary Edition, ed. James H. Cone, 191.

46. Cf. Renny Golden and Michael McConnell, *Sanctuary: The New Underground*

But black theology hits closer to home. It questions the progressive self-image of liberal American Christianity and criticizes the hypocrisy and injustice of white liberal attitudes toward race. Liberal Christianity is more comfortable with the pieties of race-blind liberalism than with the realities of American racial politics described by black theologians. Liberal theologians prefer to deal with race by invoking King's ideal that race should not matter. If race should not matter, they reason, then it is mistaken to confer significance upon race as a category of analysis. To speak of "white theology" or "black theology" is to reinforce racial thinking, but the goal of a good society is to abolish it. Though nearly everyone claims to oppose any argument that implicitly or explicitly ascribes an ontological meaning to race, liberals worry that black theology's racial rhetoric implicitly ontologizes race and thus provides a rationale for reverse racism.

With the exception of Albert Cleage, however—the black nationalist theologian who does argue that it is religiously necessary for blacks to believe that the historical Jesus was black—black theologians deny that race is ontologically meaningful. For them, race is a social fiction that whites have manipulated to rationalize immense social evils. Black liberationists use terms such as *blackness* and *whiteness* as cultural signifiers. In Cone's lexicon, *black* and *white* are terms with cultural but not metaphysical meanings. They can be used as metaphors for the dialectic of oppression but do not signify different kinds of human beings. Though his rhetoric often frightens white interpreters into mistaken readings, and though he does deny that white people are capable of understanding Scripture or the black experience, Cone always stops short of attributing qualities of being to race. Black soul cannot be learned, he explains, but comes from "the totality of black experience, the experience of carving out an existence in a society that says you do not belong." His work and the writings of other black theologians give instructive accounts of this experience, providing important perspectives for white American Christians on their country, their churches, and themselves.[47]

Railroad (Maryknoll, N.Y.: Orbis Books, 1986); Paul Burks, "This Is Sanctuary: A Reformation in Our Time," in *Churches in Struggle: Liberation Theologies and Social Change in North America,* ed. William K. Tabb (New York: Monthly Review Press, 1986), 291–300; William Sloane Coffin, "Sanctuary for Refugees and Ourselves," *Christianity and Crisis* 43 (March 18, 1985), 75–76; Robert McAfee Brown, "Liberation Theology: Paralyzing Threat or Creative Challenge?" in *Mission Trends No. 4: Liberation Theologies in North America and Europe,* ed. Gerald H. Anderson and Thomas F. Stransky (New York: Paulist Press, 1979), 3–24; Richard Shaull, *Heralds of a New Reformation: The Poor of South and North America* (Maryknoll, N.Y.: Orbis Books, 1984).

47. Albert B. Cleage, Jr., *The Black Messiah* (New York: Sheed and Ward, 1969); Cleage, *Black Christian Nationalism* (New York: William Morrow and Co., 1972); Cone, *A Black Theology of Liberation,* 25.

These perspectives have been generally received as unwelcome news. Though black theologians have attained numerous positions at highly regarded universities and seminaries, black liberationism as a theological and/or ecclesial movement faltered in the late 1970s and further declined in the succeeding decade, partly as a consequence of its strained relationship to the ecumenical establishment. The effort to promote black theology in the black churches has always been hampered by the highly politicized character of Cone's work and by the seemingly unorthodox arguments advanced by Cone, Wilmore, Long, and others. The movement's early momentum was flattened by the reactionary turn in American national politics and the related ascendancy of the fundamentalist Right, which made effective appeals to the cultural conservatism of many black church leaders.

Black theology was stymied during the same period, however, by its troubled relationship with the National Council of Churches and the mainline Protestant denominations, which generally favor moderate and conservative black church leaders over the NCBC liberationists. At a critical period of the NCBC's organizational life, the National Council of Churches and the Consultation on Church Union funded numerous traditional black church caucuses while avoiding liberationist groups. During the same period, ecumenical Protestantism made race a lower-priority concern on its agenda than in the 1960s and early 1970s. For those who had tried to build a genuine North American liberation theology movement, the spectacle of a U.S. ecumenical establishment that supported liberation theology in Latin America but not in the United States was bitterly disillusioning, though hardly inexplicable. Black theology was too close to mainline church leaders to seem innocent or nonthreatening, especially during a period when ecumenical Protestantism was itself beseiged by attacks from the political and religious Right.[48]

At the same time, unlike feminist theology, black theology is too alien to the experience or culture of mainline church leaders to sustain a high-priority status on the ecumenical agenda. Black theology is too radical for the liberal churches, despite the fact that it is theologically more orthodox and traditional than most feminist theologies. Black theology in its milder forms gives African American accents to social gospel, Christian realist, and evangelical theologies. In the tradition of Martin Luther King Jr., it typically blends liberal Protestant theology with the ethos of the black church. In its more radical forms, black theology is still firmly grounded in the language and thought forms of biblical religion. Though Cone has increasingly distanced himself from the Barthian revelationism of his early work, his theology continues to be shaped by scriptural narrative and the saving claims of Christ. As James Evans explains, black theology

---

48. Cf. Wilmore, "A Revolution Unfulfilled, but Not Invalidated," 152–53.

characteristically makes six basic theological affirmations, all of which are grounded in Scripture and embodied in the black church tradition. Black theology typically affirms that the content of divine revelation is liberation, that Scripture is the primary record of this revelation, that the God revealed by Scripture takes the side of the oppressed, that the zenith of God's self-disclosure is the mediating and liberating life of Jesus Christ, that Christ's identification with the oppressed creates a distinctive community of faith, and that this community prefigures the "last shall be first" spirit of the immanent kingdom.[49]

Most black theology is Christ-centered and kingdom-oriented. It takes no interest in a religious perspective that displaces the liberating work of Christ with some metaphysical, cultural, or feminist construct. With notable exceptions, black theology is the product of a tradition founded upon the liberating work of Christ. The movement's major founders, such as James Cone, Wilmore, Roberts, and Cecil Cone, are either rooted in or in solidarity with the black church tradition. The same identification with the Christ-centered tradition of black church Christianity obtains with such second-generation scholars as West, Felder, Franklin, Hopkins, Dyson, Hoyt, and Vincent Wimbush.[50] The tie between black feminism and the Christ-centered black church tradition is more strained, but even here, most womanist theologians declare their loyalty to "black women's Jesus."

Womanist Theology

Womanism is the name given by black feminists to a spiritual sensibility distinctive to women of color. For some black feminist theologians, Alice Walker's description of a unique black women's spirituality provides a more compelling departure for theological reflection than the male-dominated black church tradition. In her landmark volume of womanist prose, *In Search of Our Mothers' Gardens,* and in her acclaimed novel, *The Color Purple,* Walker depicts "womanish" black women as "outrageous, audacious, courageous, and willful" lovers of life, enjoyment, and themselves. A womanist prefers women, but can also love men; she is not a separatist "except for health"; she is committed "to the survival and wholeness of entire people, male and female." She is a universalist by temperament and a feminist, though a feminist with a particular depth of

---

49. James H. Evans, Jr., *We Have Been Believers: An African-American Systematic Theology* (Minneapolis: Fortress Press, 1992), 9.

50. Cf. Cornel West, *Prophesy Deliverance! An Afro-American Revolutionary Christianity* (Philadelphia: Westminster Press, 1982); Cain H. Felder, *Troubling Biblical Waters: Race, Class, and Family* (Maryknoll, N.Y.: Orbis Books, 1989); Robert Michael Franklin, *Liberating Visions: Human Fulfillment and Social Justice in African-American Thought* (Minneapolis: Fortress Press, 1990); Dwight N. Hopkins, *Black Theology USA and South Africa: Politics, Culture, and Liberation* (Maryknoll, N.Y.: Orbis Books, 1989).

background and character. As Walker explains, "womanist is to feminist as purple to lavender."[51]

Walker's work is inspiriting to many black feminists who seek not merely to feminize black theology or colorize feminist theology, but to develop their own distinctive theological voices. Through Walker's influence, they emphasize the theme of survival as much as liberation; like Walker, they insist that gender, race, and class are interconnected variables not reducible to any hierarchical ordering. Yet even black feminist theology typically operates within the mainstream of Christian doctrine and in close connection with the black church tradition. For most black feminist theologians, Walker's womanist spirituality is not an alternative religion but a discerning framework through which they reflect upon the meaning of their spiritual existence within and outside the church. Theologians such as Williams, Grant, Cannon, Weems, Eugene, Kelly Brown Douglas, and Cheryl Townsend Gilkes are all influenced by Walker's account of womanism and also committed to Christianity.[52]

If womanist theology understands Jesus Christ from a distinctive spiritual perspective, it is nonetheless, like black theology generally, firmly grounded in a tradition that looks to Jesus as healer, liberator, friend, and Lord. Grant's *White Women's Christ and Black Women's Jesus* (1989) spells out the main features of womanist Christology. In her account, womanist theology eschews the hierarchical reductionisms of other liberation theologies. Womanism refuses to be drawn into reductionist debates about whether racial or gender oppression is more fundamental. Black feminism reflects the experiences of black women, for whom racial, sexist, and economic oppression are not separable categories but aspects of a corporate tridimensional social reality. "Black women must do

51. Alice Walker, *In Search of Our Mothers' Gardens: Womanist Prose* (San Diego: Harcourt Brace Jovanovich, 1983), xi–xii; Walker, *The Color Purple* (San Diego: Harcourt Brace Jovanovich, 1982).

52. Cf. Delores S. Williams, "The Color of Feminism: Or Speaking the Black Woman's Tongue," *Journal of Religious Thought* 43 (Spring/Summer 1986), 42–58; Williams, "Womanist Theology: Black Women's Voices," in *Black Theology*, vol. 2, ed. James H. Cone and Gayraud Wilmore, 265–72; Katie G. Cannon, *Black Womanist Ethics* (Atlanta: Scholars Press, 1988); Kelly Delaine Brown-Douglass, "Womanist Theology: What Is Its Relationship to Black Theology?" in *Black Theology*, vol. 2, ed. James H. Cone and Gayraud Wilmore, 290–99; Cheryl Townsend Gilkes, "The Role of Women in the Sanctified Church," *Journal of Religious Thought* 43 (Spring/Summer 1986), 24–41; Renita Weems, *Just a Sister Away: A Womanist Vision of Women's Relationships in the Bible* (San Diego: Lura Media, 1988); Toinette M. Eugene, "While Love Is Unfashionable: Ethical Implications of Black Spirituality and Sexuality," in *Women's Consciousness, Women's Conscience: A Reader in Feminist Ethics,* ed. Barbara Hilkert Andolsen, Christine E. Gudorf, and Mary D. Pellauer (San Francisco: Harper & Row, 1987), 121–41.

theology out of their tri-dimensional experience of racism/sexism/classism," Grant asserts. "To ignore any aspect of this experience is to deny the holistic and integrated reality of Black womanhood. When Black women say that God is on the side of the oppressed, we mean that God is in solidarity with the struggles of those on the under side of humanity."[53]

Womanist theology issues a "challenge of the darker sister" to white feminism, charging that most feminist theology is both racist and culturally white. The dominant feminist theologies may be drawn from women's experience, Grant observes, but the referent is virtually always white women's experience. "White women's experience and Black women's experience are not the same," she declares. "Indeed all experiences are unique to some degree. But in this case the difference is so radical that it may be said that White women and Black women are in completely different realms." In her view, the ravages of slavery and segregation have created an abyss between black and white women that make feminist solidarity language absurd. Grant remarks, "When we read narratives of slaves and ex-slaves, current 'sisterhood' rhetoric appears simply as one of two possibilities: (1) a crude joke, or (2) the conciliatory rhetoric of an advantaged class and race."[54] Having grasped the threefold dimensions of their oppression, womanists are not appeased by the endorsements or guilt offerings of privileged "allies."

"A womanist is one who has developed survival strategies in spite of the oppression of her race and sex in order to save her family and her people," Grant asserts.[55] Survival and redemptive suffering are thus deeper themes in womanist theology than liberation because the concrete need to survive is more pressing than any hope for transformation. Grant explains that the impulse to survive defines the significance of Jesus for womanist theology. For womanism, Jesus is the divine cosufferer who identifies with blacks in their suffering and empowers them to survive it. "For Christian Black women in the past, Jesus was their central frame of reference," Grant recalls. "They identified with Jesus because they believed that Jesus identified with them. As Jesus was persecuted and made to suffer undeservedly, so were they. His suffering culminated in the crucifixion. Their crucifixion included rape, and babies being sold." Womanist theology honors the memory of black Christianity and embraces its defining commitment to Christ as divine cosufferer and redeemer. As Douglas observes, "To assert the Blackness of Christ reflects Black women's commitment to their families and communities, as maintained by a social-political analysis of wholeness." In

---

53. Jacquelyn Grant, *White Women's Christ and Black Women's Jesus: Feminist Christology and Womanist Response* (Atlanta: Scholars Press, 1989), 209.

54. Ibid., 195–96.

55. Ibid., 205.

her view, womanist theology thus helps black women see themselves in the image of the suffering Christ.[56]

Yet womanist theology also holds fast to the hope for liberation that black Christianity equates with Christ's resurrection. "The condition of Black people today reflects the cross of Jesus," Grant remarks. "Yet the resurrection brings the hope that liberation from oppression is immanent. The resurrected Black Christ signifies this hope." Douglas confirms that life and wholeness are the primary signs of the presence of "the womanist Black Christ." Womanist theology develops spiritual, sexual, and communal aspects of black Christianity that black theology has neglected. Douglas asserts that the liberating black Christ must liberate humanity not only from racism, classism, and sexism but also from heterosexist discrimination against gays and lesbians.[57] Despite all of its points of tension and disagreement with earlier black liberation theologies, however, womanism typically affirms its solidarity with black theology through its fundamental insistence on the emancipating power of the cosuffering and resurrected black Christ. For womanist theology, as for Cone, Christ is black not because black people need him to be black, but because "Christ *really* enters into our world where the poor, the despised, and the black are, disclosing that he is with them, enduring their humiliation and pain and transforming oppressed slaves into liberated servants."[58] Christ is black because he truly became one with the oppressed in their suffering, Cone explains; he is Lord because his resurrection both symbolizes and literally empowers the project of freedom, which is liberation.

Mary Daly and Feminist Theology

If black theologians conceive Christianity in ways that make many white Christians feel excluded, black theologians nonetheless seek to recover a true Christian identity. For them, the problem is not authentic (liberating) Christianity but the various historical perversions of it. Black theology in its various liberal, radical, and womanist forms constantly presses white liberal Christians to question whether they are following Christ or merely subscribing to a decadent culture-religion bearing Christ's name. Whether white feminist theology can press the same question on feminist grounds, however, is a far more controverted issue that challenges Christian doctrine more radically and affects American churches more directly than black theology.

---

56. Ibid., 213; Kelly Brown Douglas, *The Black Christ* (Maryknoll, N.Y.: Orbis Books, 1994), 107.

57. Grant, *White Women's Christ and Black Women's Jesus,* 216; Douglas, *The Black Christ,* 109–10.

58. Cone, *God of the Oppressed,* 136.

Black theology has a history; like the social gospelers and Latin American liberationists, black theologians appeal to a true Christian faith that needs to be recovered. If the problem is historical, then historical solutions to it are conceivable, and a history of witnesses to genuine Christianity can be identified. This kind of strategy is problematic for feminists, however. Though some feminist theologians, notably Rosemary Radford Ruether and Letty Russell, make appeals to a true essence or liberating tradition within historical Christianity to support their theological positions, many others reject the search for a usable past as contrary to feminism. Feminists dispute not only whether feminism is compatible with any appeal to a male savior but also whether Christian tradition has anything to offer as a source or ground for feminism. More than other kinds of liberationist religion, white feminist theology inevitably raises the question whether its fundamental impulse is inimical to Christianity itself.

Bennett avoided the question in *The Radical Imperative,* partly to avoid giving sanction to any reactionary claim that Christianity and feminism are incompatible. The question had already been pressed in Mary Daly's impassioned assault on Christian patriarchy, however. *Beyond God the Father* (1973) rejected the liberal feminist project of reforming Christianity. Liberal feminism tries to minimize or eliminate the patriarchal cast of traditional Christian language, thought, and liturgy, but Daly argued that feminist liberation requires deeper critiques of Christianity and new forms of language and community. She remarked that if liberal feminists carried out their program of depatriarchalizing the entire Bible, it might be possible to salvage enough material for a little pamphlet. She later revised this estimate downward. *Beyond God the Father* named the crucial problem that would mark her subsequent intellectual-spiritual project. "Women have had the power of *naming* stolen from us," she observed. "We have not been free to use our own power to name ourselves, the world, or God." The Genesis story of Adam's naming the animals and the woman symbolized women's condition of exclusion and oppression. "To exist humanly is to name the self, the world, and God," Daly asserted. "The 'method' of the evolving spiritual consciousness of women is nothing less than this beginning to speak humanly— a reclaiming of the right to name. The liberation of language is rooted in the liberation of ourselves."[59]

Beyond God the Father explained that language is an identity-forming agency that creates reality and participates in it. The project of liberating language would require more than a program of depatriarchalization; it would require a transformation of consciousness out of which new discourses would emerge. Before feminist liberation could engender the "real leap in human evolution" that is needed, however, feminists had to castrate the phallocentric value systems that

---

59. Daly, *Beyond God the Father,* 8.

patriarchy has imposed and dispel the power of patriarchy over the minds and hearts of its victims. This repudiation of patriarchy, Daly asserted, amounted to "a kind of *exorcism* that essentially must be done by women, who are in a position to experience the demonic destructiveness of the super-phallic society in our own being."[60]

Daly's early writings cataloged the ways in which biblical religion taught women to hate themselves, to defer to men, to feel guilty for the evils of the world, and to keep silent. The myth of the fall was a chief example. Liberal theology generally affirmed that the Genesis story of the fall was mythical while attempting to derive some existential or ontological meaning from it. Niebuhr's maxim that biblical myths should be taken seriously but not literally was typical. The meaning that liberal theologians typically took from the myth of the fall was that it symbolized the universal human condition of alienation or estrangement. The biblical myth had little meaning of any kind for male-female relations.

But the fall had a more serious meaning for women, Daly observed:

> The myth has projected a malignant image of the male-female relationship and of the "nature" of women that is still deeply embedded in the modern psyche. It is not adequate for theologians simply to intellectualize and generalize the alleged content of the myth as an expression of a universal state of alienation. Indeed this approach is intellectually bankrupt and demonic. It amounts merely to abandoning the use of explicitly sexist theological imagery while failing to acknowledge its still persistent impact upon society.

The silence of liberal theology about the destructiveness of biblical teaching was demonic because it conveyed the message that sexual oppression was not at issue and not a problem. It took several thousand years for theologians to notice the "hoax of cosmic proportions" that Hebrew mythology had perpetrated, Daly noted. For thousands of years, theologians managed not to notice the absurdity of portraying men as the givers of life while blaming women for the world's evil. "Having at last noticed the incongruity, theologians have dismissed it from their attention," she wrote. "Few have even barely begun to glimpse the significance of the tragedy of sexual injustice that was inadvertently 'revealed' by the story of the Fall."[61]

The story of the fall was fundamentally a myth of feminine evil that supported "the entire structure of phallic Christian ideology," Daly claimed. It amounted to a case of "cosmic false naming" because it metamorphosized the viewpoint of women-hating men into God's viewpoint. *Beyond God the Father* stopped short of claiming that Christianity is inherently oppressive or that male evil is unredeemable. Daly's feminism was not yet explicitly post-Christian. To describe

---

60. Ibid., 10.
61. Ibid., 45–46.

the integrity of be-ing toward which a real leap in human evolution would move, she invoked the notion of androgyny, an ideal that combined female and male elements and implied that certain aspects of maleness might be worth redeeming. Daly later discarded the notion as a "semantic abomination" and declared that Christianity is intrinsically hostile to women.

Beyond God the Father was thus a transitional work, but one that prefigured Daly's movement toward radical separatism. To be liberated is to break free from all phallic morality, she argued, including every existing form of Christianity. Daly noted that it was not yet possible to develop a liberating feminist ethics because women were not yet free enough to think out of their own experience. *Beyond God the Father* stopped short of claiming that no imagined form of Christianity is compatible with women's liberation. It did claim, however, that "the final cause" in life, the "cause of causes," is to liberate repressed female energy "by the qualitative leap of courage in the face of patriarchy."[62] Nietzsche's vision of a transvaluated morality was being reclaimed by feminist visionaries who comprehended—as the misogynist Nietzsche did not—why patriarchal morality is sickly, hypocritical, demeaning, and life-killing.[63]

Beyond God the Father conceived divine reality as intransitive verb or dynamic be-ing not requiring an object. Liberating feminism indwells the metamorphic power of words and female energy, Daly exulted; it imagines ultimate-intimate reality as verb, as movement. In her subsequent work, Daly often uses Goddess language, but her project is not simply to replace the oppressive God language of patriarchal religion with older mythologies. She warns that if feminism is not truly radicalized by the metamorphic force of dynamic be-ing, it will ultimately reduce the Goddess to a suffocating static symbol that barely improves upon patriarchal theism. To merely substitute Goddess for God is like trying to reform Christianity. Liberal theology tries to accommodate feminist criticism by eliminating patriarchal God language, while most Goddess theologies employ feminist criticism to perform a transsexual operation on the patriarchal God. Both strategies are futile and life-killing, Daly urges. "A transsexed patriarchal god is still patriarchal and will function (at least in subliminal or subterranean ways) to serve the interests of the fathers, for such a symbol is external to the experienced reality of women and nature," she explains.[64]

The recent emergence of liberal feminist Christianity is a closely related but more pathetic mistake, in her judgment. Feminist Christianity is a contradiction in terms. Feminism is about reclaiming women's elemental powers, but Chris-

---

62. Ibid., 189.

63. Ibid., 102.

64. Mary Daly, "Original Re-Introduction," preface to the 1985 edition of *Beyond God the Father,* xviii.

tianity seeks to extinguish female power and spirit. Daly argues that liberal feminist Christianity is a ruse that many self-deceived women are adopting to obscure the difference. They include the dramatically increasing number of female ministers and priests. Having crushed the ancient Goddess traditions, Christianity in its modern liberal forms is now prepared to accommodate carefully modulated female energies. The existence of feminist Christianity testifies to the spiritual and cultural power of a reawakened female consciousness, but it functions only to retard and extinguish this spiritual awakening. "Since christian priests function as reversers of the biophilic work of Pagan priestesses, reducing religion to a static state, female christian priests would seem to be in the unfortunate condition of imitation reversers, serving dead symbols and serving these up to starving congregations of bamboozled believers who are doubly tricked by this incorporation of females into the processions of priestly predators," she explains.[65]

Feminist Christianity tries to modify the terms on which women are reconciled to the father, but radical feminism is not interested in reconciliation with the father. Radical feminism seeks rather to affirm "our original birth, our original movement, surge of living." To affirm the original surge of life is to remember a female self not constrained by "the prevailing religion of the entire planet," which is patriarchy. As Daly explains in *Gyn/Ecology: The Metaethics of Radical Feminism,* radical feminism is a revolt against every male-produced religion and ideology:

> All of the so-called religions legitimating patriarchy are mere sects subsumed under its vast umbrella/canopy. They are essentially similar, despite the variations. All—from buddhism and hinduism to islam, judaism, christianity, to secular derivatives such as freudianism, jungianism, marxism, and maoism— are infrastructures of the edifice of patriarchy. All are erected as parts of the male's shelter against anomie. And the symbolic message of all the sects of the religion which is patriarchy is this: Women are the dreaded anomie.[66]

In Daly's vision, feminist liberation creates the preconditions of a new feminist ethic. *Gyn/Ecology* explains that like all male-produced religions and ideologies, Christianity is a form of phallicism that symbolically and literally compels worship of maleness. It seeks to control and literally extinguish female spirit. In her subsequent writings, especially *Pure Lust: Elemental Feminist Philosophy* and *Outercourse,* Daly seeks to break free from every form of phallic morality and reawaken female spirit/be-ing. Her life-affirming philosophy of dynamic be-ing carries Nietzschean echoes, but her ventures into what she calls "the Realm of the Wild" produce highly un-Nietzschean celebrations of "Re-

---

65. Ibid., xviii.
66. Mary Daly, *Gyn/Ecology: The Metaethics of Radical Feminism* (Boston: Beacon Press, 1990, c1978), 39.

volting Hags" and "Spinning Crones." To lust for happiness, Daly exults, is to live "a life of activity, of Unfolding spiritual, intellectual, sensory, physical, e-motional potency." Liberated soothsayers see through the society of godfather, son, and company, she declares. "Beyond this, Crones sense astonishing yet perfectly sensible synchronicities—or Syn-Crone-icities. Spinning Crones who have Lived through earthquakes, tornadoes, tidal waves, parching sojourns in deserts of the spirit, are stronger than before; Norns know our Hour is arriving."[67]

This is a powerful, lyrical, and soaring spiritual vision. It describes the spiritual experiences of many women in metaphorical language that mixes Goddess traditions, the patterns of gnostic dualism, and Daly's imaginative leaps into uncharted cronespace. It renames the world in ways that are deeply moving to many readers. Daly's prominence in contemporary theology is attributable not only to the passionate energy and brilliance of her writing but also to her inspired capacity to open new worlds of experience to her readers. For many, she is the premier theorist of a shared experience of awakening "from the patriarchal state of sleeping death" to a state of spiritual ecstasy. For many others who do not share the condition of gender oppression or the liberating ecstasy of "spooking, sparking and spinning," her writings evoke genuine excitement at the possibility of a life-enhancing spirituality untouched by patriarchal ideology. Like the gnostic movements that early Christianity variously struggled against and accommodated, her work is spiritually powerful because it offers a religious vision of deliverance from a hostile world. Radical spiritual feminism promises total transformation to its converts, while shunning the critical methodologies of unconverted observers. Daly's later writings, especially her autobiographical *Outercourse: The Be-Dazzling Voyage* (1992), abound with remarkably uncritical accounts of her experiences with auras and other occult phenomena. If the world is ruled by forces that conspire against the female spirit, emancipation from that world is available to women who remember the secret wisdom of the dismembered Goddess.

Daly's "Be-Dazzling Voyage" through what she calls "the Four Spiral Galaxies" has thus engendered an emphatically separatist spirituality that speaks the language of the occult. In *Gyn/Ecology,* she addresses the issue of separatism by noting that many women remain uncomfortable with the label antimale. This discomfort drives some women to distinguish between being antipatriarchal and antimale, she notes. To Daly, however, the distinction is a fearful self-deception. "The courage to be logical—the courage to name—would require that we admit

---

67. Daly, "Original Re-Introduction," xi–xii. For works that elaborate this "Realm of the Wild" rhetoric and vision, see Mary Daly, *Pure Lust: Elemental Feminist Philosophy* (Boston: Beacon Press, 1984); and Daly, *Outercourse: The Bedazzling Voyage* (San Francisco: HarperCollins, 1992).

to ourselves that males and males only are the originators, planners, controllers, and legitimators of patriarchy," she observes. "Patriarchy is the homeland of males; it is Father Land; and men are its agents." It is men who rape and terrorize women all over the world. What men call "civilization" is a misogynistic conspiracy "in which men collectively victimize women, attacking us as personifications of their own paranoid fears, as The Enemy." What men call "culture" is the culture of rape, genocide, and war that supports male "civilization." Radical feminism is therefore "absolutely Anti-androcrat, A-mazingly Anti-male, Furiously and Finally Female."[68]

Just as the most prominent figure in black liberation theology is its most radical major proponent, so has the language and agenda of religious feminism been influenced most importantly by its most radical theorist. In the latter case, however, liberation means emancipation from any form of Christianity or Judaism. Feminist theorists such as Naomi Goldenberg, Carol P. Christ, Susan Griffin, Starhawk, Daphne Hampson, Charlene Spretnak, and Zsuzsanna E. Budapest embrace this conclusion—sometimes without Daly's separatism—in the hope of re-creating new-old forms of woman-identified spirituality.[69] For those who embrace radical feminist criticism but stop short of opting for spiritual utopianism, the prominence of Daly-type feminism makes it necessary to explain why radical feminists go too far. Christian feminists define themselves partly by their relationship to Daly's work. Ruether speaks for many of them in declaring that while radical feminism is attractive in many respects, it is nonetheless mistaken on religious and political grounds.

Ruether observes that in Daly's work, "the history of women becomes a trail of crucifixions, with males as the evil archons of an anticosmos where women are entrapped." Seeking "an alternative land within their inner selves," radical feminists engender a new language of inner transformation that breaks

---

68. Daly, *Gyn/Ecology*, 28–29.

69. Cf. Naomi R. Goldenberg, *The Changing of the Gods: Feminism and the End of Traditional Religions* (Boston: Beacon Press, 1979); Carol P. Christ, "Rethinking Theology and Nature," in *Weaving the Visions: New Patterns in Feminist Spirituality*, ed. Judith Plaskow and Carol P. Christ (San Francisco: Harper & Row, 1989), 314–25; Carol P. Christ, *Laughter of Aphrodite: Reflections on a Journey to the Goddess* (San Francisco: Harper & Row, 1987); Susan Griffin, *Woman and Nature* (San Francisco: Harper & Row, 1978); Starhawk, *Dreaming the Dark* (Boston: Beacon Press, 1982); Charlene Spretnak, ed., *The Politics of Women's Spirituality: Essays on the Rise of Spiritual Power within the Feminist Movement* (New York: Anchor Books, 1982); Zsuzsanna E. Budapest, *The Holy Book of Women's Mysteries*, vols. 1 and 2 (Los Angeles: Susan B. Anthony Cove No. 1, 1979, 1980); Carol P. Christ and Judith Plaskow, *Womanspirit Rising: A Feminist Reader in Religion* (New York: Harper & Row, 1979); Irene Diamond and Gloria Feman Orenstein, eds., *Reweaving the World: The Emergence of Ecofeminism* (San Francisco: Sierra Club Books, 1990).

apart the dominant language of patriarchy. "They escape together through the holes rent in the fabric of patriarchal ideology into a separate and higher realm of female interiority," Ruether notes. Daly's radical feminism thus replicates the spiritual dualism of ancient Gnosticism, except that in her version, as Ruether remarks, feminism is built "on the dualism of a transcendent spirit world of femaleness over against the deceitful anticosmos of masculinity."[70]

Rosemary Radford Ruether

Ruether embraces much of the radical feminist critique of the ravages of male domination, but she argues that radical feminism goes too far when it embraces a separatist vision that dehumanizes men. Separatism reverses the logic of misogynistic patriarchy, treating women as normative humanity and males as defective humans. But this strategy is no more liberating or life-affirming than its enemy because it projects moral responsibility for all of the world's evils onto an alien group. "Such enemy-making of men would ultimately subvert the whole dream of a women's culture based on mutuality and altruism," Ruether asserts. "The very process of projecting the negative part of their own psychic potential onto males, and failing to own these themselves, would tend to make such women's groups fanatical caricatures of that which they hate." To dehumanize the other is ultimately to dehumanize oneself, since, as Ruether observes, "one duplicates evil-making in the very effort to escape from it once and for all, by projecting it on the 'alien' group."[71]

Ruether's influential alternative to radical feminism combines a program of hermeneutical retrieval with a democratic socialist and environmentalist politics. Her feminist vision blends elements of liberal, socialist, and radical feminism and is supported by her appropriation of prophetic Christianity. Ruether embraces the liberal feminist doctrine of a common human nature and its derivative principle of equal rights for all people, while criticizing liberal feminism for its merely reformist politics and its preoccupation with securing equal opportunity rights. In her view, liberal feminism impedes the struggle for equality whenever its fixation with attaining equal opportunity laws ignores the social structures that prevent working-class, minority, and poor women from taking advantage of their formal rights. Liberal feminism is not enough, but the liberal doctrine of equal rights is nonetheless the foundation of any progressive feminism.

Building upon Zillah Eisenstein's thesis in *The Radical Future of Liberal Feminism*, Ruether argues that the liberal feminist pursuit of social equality is

---

70. Rosemary Radford Ruether, *Sexism and God-Talk: Toward a Feminist Theology* (Boston: Beacon Press, 1983), 229–30.

71. Ibid., 231; on Daly's gynocentric dualism, see Ruether, *Gaia and God: An Ecofeminist Theology of Earth Healing* (San Francisco: HarperCollins, 1992), 147–48.

unattainable on liberal terms. Liberal feminism advocates federally funded child care, parental leaves of absence, flextime, work sharing, and comparable worth, but shies away from demanding structural socioeconomic changes that would make this agenda viable. Liberal feminist demands for equality contain redistributive implications that outstrip the limitations of liberal feminism's own reformist politics.[72] Lacking a class perspective, it typically becomes a vehicle for the career ambitions of middle- and upper-class women. Liberal feminism is embraced by credentialed professional-class women who seek for themselves the same rights and opportunities enjoyed by men of their class and who therefore hire working-class domestic workers to do their "women's work" for them. "This is then touted as the fulfillment of the promise of liberal feminism, although actually the economic position of the white upper middle class is being reinforced against women and men of lower classes and races," Ruether notes. "The glitter of feminist 'equality,' as displayed in *Cosmopolitan* and *Ms.,* both eludes and insults the majority of women who recognize that its 'promise' is not for them."[73]

Socialist feminism seeks to break down the hierarchies of race and class that liberal feminism leaves unchallenged. Bourgeois society mythologizes the special place assigned to members of the "weaker sex" whose economic standing permits them to choose not to enter the labor market. By contrast, most working-class and middle-class women are forced to work for wages while struggling at the same time to manage their households. Socialist feminism addresses both forms of bondage by struggling for a social transformation that restores women's economic autonomy in new forms. Under a socialist order, male and female workers would become owners of the means of production; their rights as citizens would be expanded to include rights over industrial property. Socialism promises economic freedom to women by making them owners of the enterprises they work for and by socializing key aspects of "women's sphere" domestic work. Without a socialist transformation of the structure of economic power, the civil rights that liberal feminists struggle to attain will remain class privileges.

Ruether acknowledges that democratic socialism remains little more than a utopian vision and that even in theory democratic socialism does not have a satisfactory answer to the problem of women's economic inequality. In seeking to relieve women of their extra burden of domestic work, the socialist impulse is to collectivize kitchens, laundries, housecleaning, and housing. Radical socialists such as Shulamith Firestone go further, arguing that even women's role as childbearers must be alleviated by developing a collectivized technology of

---

72. Cf. Zillah R. Eisenstein, *The Radical Future of Liberal Feminism* (New York: Longman, 1981).

73. Ruether, *Sexism and God-Talk,* 222.

test tube fertilization and mechanical wombs. Without taking the feminist revolution this far, Firestone insists, women will never achieve equality with men.[74]

But socialism has its own history of tyranny, enslavement, and oppression to answer for, and Ruether suggests that Firestone's social engineering may represent the ultimate enslavement of humanity in the name of women's liberation. "If collectivism means state control, then an abolition of the home would be the total alienation of one's life to institutions external to one's own control and governed by a managerial elite," she observes. "In the name of the liberation of women, we would hand over the remnants of that self-employed and autonomous sphere of life where we own and control our own means of production— our reproductive organs, our kitchens, and so on."[75]

Like liberalism, state socialism operates from the unstated androcentric assumption that the male work role is normative. Liberalism and socialism both seek to incorporate women into the male-dominated public order, whether by securing equal rights for women or by liberating women from economic dependence. Neither ideology challenges the primacy of the male work role itself but assumes that liberation for women requires women's integration into the domain of male-dominated careers and public power. Socialist feminism has to be more creative and culturally radical than either of these traditions, Ruether asserts. It must affirm the traditional socialist emphasis on class while rejecting its impulse to centralize social ownership and authority. State socialism claims to restore ownership of the means of production to the people, but its collectivistic politics empowers a ruling class of managers and political hacks rather than the people. Ruether's socialist feminism is thus closer in spirit to the communal or utopian socialist tradition than to state socialism. As she explains:

> In contrast to state socialism, communitarian or utopian socialism has understood socialism as the communalization of work on the base of a communal family. The split between home and work, women's work and men's work, is overcome by reintegrating them in a community that both raises children collectively and owns and manages its own means of production.[76]

Her vision of socialist feminism is community-oriented and participatory; it decentralizes ownership and authority while seeking to create a society that values cooperation, community, and the common good over material success or power. "Feminism needs to ask whether, instead of making the male sphere the human

---

74. Shulamith Firestone, *The Dialectic of Sex: The Case for Feminist Revolution* (New York: William Morrow and Co., 1970), 183–224.

75. Ruether, *Sexism and God-Talk,* 226.

76. Ibid., 227; for Ruether's earlier reflections on this theme, see Rosemary Radford Ruether, *New Woman, New Earth: Sexist Ideologies and Human Liberation* (New York: Seabury Press, 1975).

norm and attempting to assimilate women into it, it is not necessary to move in the opposite direction," Ruether urges. "Should we not take the creation and sustaining of human life as the center and reintegrate alienated maleness into it?"[77] Socialist feminism seeks to make men more involved in their families while deconstructing the androcentric mythology of the workplace as society's locus of meaning and importance.

Though Ruether rejects much of the spirit of radical feminism, it is in this respect that her feminism appropriates the radical perspective. Radical feminism understands that there is something deeper than equal opportunity or distributive justice at stake in the modern rebirth of feminist consciousness. It insists that gender oppression is the fundamental historical form of enslavement and that liberation from gender oppression requires not merely a new politics, but a new spirituality. If patriarchy subordinates women's bodies, sexuality, and reproductivity to male ownership and control, radical feminism liberates women from patriarchal laws and social roles. If patriarchy makes women emotionally dependent upon controlling males, radical feminism liberates women from maleness itself. Radical feminism is not merely radical, but revolutionary; it is a revolution of consciousness.

Ruether eschews the separatist spirit of radical feminism while accepting its insistence that feminism is not reducible to any kind of politics. She rejects the radical feminist tendency to view gender oppression as more fundamental or important than other forms of oppression, but she affirms that gender must be regarded as a fundamental organizing variable in social structure, culture, and personal life. Any feminism that fails to understand and attack patriarchy as a social system will also fail to liberate women from the shackles of male domination. Her theology thus seeks to integrate the liberal concern with equal rights, the socialist commitment to distributive justice, and the radical emphasis on gender feminism. Though each of these perspectives is deficient as a system, she argues, each is necessary, authentic, and generative to the extent that it remains open to the liberating capacities of other perspectives.

Ruether draws religious support for this project from her interpretation of prophetic Christianity. Like most liberation theologians, she contends that liberation is the heart and chief theme of biblical faith. In her view, the same "prophetic-liberating tradition" that inspired earlier liberation movements can be extended to support the struggles of women for liberation. While conceding that the Bible is deeply patriarchal in its assumptions and worldview, she attacks the evils of sexist injustice by appealing to the Bible's passion for freedom and social justice. "Feminism, in claiming the prophetic-liberating tradition of Biblical faith as a norm through which to criticize the Bible, does not choose an

---

77. Ruether, *Sexism and God-Talk*, 228.

arbitrary or marginal idea in the Bible," she observes. "It chooses a tradition that can be fairly claimed, on the basis of generally accepted Biblical scholarship, to be the central tradition, the tradition by which Biblical faith constantly criticizes and renews itself and its own vision." Though the feminist challenge is newer and more radical than other forms of prophetic criticism, there is nothing new about applying prophetic criticism to the Christian tradition, nor is there any justifiable reason to continue to exclude women from the prophetic norm. Ruether explains, "By including women in the prophetic norm, feminism sees what male prophetic thought generally had not seen: that once the prophetic norm is asserted to be central to Biblical faith, then patriarchy can no longer be maintained as authoritative."[78]

The prophetic-liberating tradition proclaims God's favor for the oppressed; it criticizes the dominant systems and holders of power, it proclaims the vision of a coming new age of peace and justice, and it criticizes religious ideologies that sacralize an unjust social order. It also contains intimations of an alternative social order founded upon the principles of freedom, equality, cooperation, and sustainable development. The echoes of Rauschenbusch are strong in Ruether's insistence that feminist theology is radical but deeply Christian. "Feminist theology is not asserting unprecedented ideas; rather it is rediscovering the prophetic context and content of Biblical faith itself when it defines the prophetic-liberating tradition as norm," she asserts.[79] Like other liberation theologies, feminist theology thus strips away the layers of ideology and misunderstanding that previously concealed Christianity's liberating content. More deeply, feminist theology exposes the meaning of Christianity's liberating content to those who are most oppressed among the oppressed. "Feminist theology makes explicit what was overlooked in male advocacy of the poor and oppressed, namely, *women* of the oppressed," Ruether explains. The explicit biblical critique of hierarchy is thus deepened to become, in contemporary Christianity, a critique of patriarchy. Feminist theology deepens and transforms Christianity's liberating-prophetic tradition "to include what was not included: women."[80]

This is a major voice in contemporary Christian feminism. Ruether's rendering of Christianity's usable past is variously disputed by feminist theologians such as Letty Russell, Beverly Harrison, Carter Heyward, Susan Brooks Thistlethwaite, Delores Williams, Anne Carr, Mary E. Hunt, Sharon Welch, Jac-

---

78. Ibid., 23–24.

79. Ibid., 31; cf. Rosemary Radford Ruether, "Feminist Theology and Spirituality," in *Christian Feminism: Visions of a New Humanity,* ed. Judith L. Weidman (New York: Harper & Row, 1984), 15–16.

80. Ruether, *Sexism and God-Talk,* 32; cf. Rosemary Radford Ruether, *Liberation Theology: Human Hope Confronts Christian History and American Power* (New York: Paulist/Newman Press, 1972).

queline Grant, Rebecca Chopp, and Elisabeth Schüssler Fiorenza, yet, like Ruether, all of these thinkers seek to bring feminist and Christian claims together through an appeal to a liberating narrative or principle.[81] While she rejects Ruether's particular project of hermeneutical retrieval, for example, Schüssler Fiorenza makes a similar appeal to the emancipating power of a Christian past. In dissociating her approach from Ruether's, she claims that Ruether presents an idealized picture of prophetic Christianity that overlooks this tradition's oppressive androcentric elements. Rather than subject prophetic religion to historical and ideological criticism, Schüssler Fiorenza argues, Ruether appeals to it as an interpretive pattern abstracted from biblical history. She therefore gives insufficient attention to the patriarchal character of biblical prophecy and its repression of Goddess religion. In Schüssler Fiorenza's reading, Ruether "simply postulates that as a social-critical tradition the prophetic traditions can be used in the interest of feminism." Schüssler Fiorenza does not doubt that prophetic Christianity can be used to promote feminism, but she is doubtful that feminist theology "can transform this social-critical androcentric tradition into a feminist liberating tradition and use it to its own ends."[82]

"Its own ends" trumps any religious apologetic or warrant. In her eagerness to claim a biblical warrant for Christian feminism, Schüssler Fiorenza argues, Ruether downplays the oppressive patriarchal character of biblical thought. Just because the Bible promotes "freedom" and "social justice" does not mean that Scripture implicitly supports feminism. Patriarchal religion has a social conscience but not necessarily a conscience that supports feminism. For Schüssler Fiorenza, as for several other feminists who share Ruether's general approach, Ruether takes too little from radical feminism in this regard. She assumes too easily that the androcentric bias of biblical religion is dispensable. But the biblical tradition regarded women as property, it suppressed Goddess worship among Israelite women, it sacralized the destruction of the Goddess religions, and it analogized the relationship between Yahweh and Israel as between a man and his wife/dependent virgin/unfaithful harlot. The "prophetic-liberating tradition" of biblical religion is deeply marked by these traditions, Schüssler Fiorenza

---

81. Cf. Letty M. Russell, *Human Liberation in a Feminist Perspective: A Theology* (Philadelphia: Westminster Press, 1974); Beverly Harrison, *Making the Connections: Essays in Feminist Social Ethics,* Carol S. Robb, ed. (Boston: Beacon Press, 1985); Carter Heyward, *Our Passion for Justice* (New York: Pilgrim Press, 1984); Mary E. Hunt, *Fierce Tenderness: A Feminist Theology of Friendship* (New York: Crossroad, 1992); Sharon Welch, *Communities of Resistance and Solidarity: A Feminist Theology of Liberation* (Maryknoll, N.Y.: Orbis Books, 1985); Susan Brooks Thistlethwaite, *Sex, Race, and God: Christian Feminism in Black and White* (New York: Crossroad, 1989).

82. Elisabeth Schüssler Fiorenza, *In Memory of Her: A Feminist Theological Reconstruction of Christian Origins* (New York: Crossroad, 1988, c1983), 17.

observes. It is thus a mistake, in her view, for feminist theologians to assume "that the revelatory 'surplus' of the social-critical prophet tradition is a feminist liberating one."[83]

She counters that the heart of the feminist spiritual quest is "the quest for women's power, freedom, and independence." Schüssler Fiorenza is doubtful that any appeal to a purportedly liberating tradition of the Christian past can actually be empowering to feminist women. Ruether's hermeneutical approach amounts to a neoorthodox attempt to rescue biblical religion from its feminist critics, but what is needed is to develop "a feminist historical hermeneutics that could incorporate Wicca's feminist spiritual quest for women's power."[84] An authentically feminist hermeneutic would read Scripture in a way that makes it a source and symbol for women's power, independence, and freedom. It would not claim that the true or essential meaning of Scripture is concealed in a prophetic-liberating tradition that is at least implicitly hospitable to feminism. It would rather engender a sense of solidarity with early Christian women who struggled against patriarchy.

"We participate in the same struggle as our biblical foresisters against the oppression of patriarchy and for survival and freedom from it," Schüssler Fiorenza argues. "We share the same liberating visions and commitments as our biblical foremothers." The point of a feminist hermeneutic is not to inspire empathy or identification with early Christian women in their struggles, "but to continue *our* struggle in solidarity with them." By rediscovering the memory of early Christian women's struggle against male supremacy, feminist scholarship encourages feminists "in historical solidarity with them to commit ourselves to the continuing struggle against patriarchy in society and church."[85] Schüssler Fiorenza's major work *In Memory of Her* (1983) proclaims more than once that "our heritage is our power."[86] By deconstructing the androcentric bias under which Scripture was written, she argues, it is possible to discern not only the struggles of early Christian women for equality in the church but also traces of the early church's egalitarian and inclusive practices. The point is not so much that "true original Christianity" was implicitly feminist, but that Christian feminism preserved the memory of early Christian women who struggled to be free in a world dominated by men. To affirm a radical feminist identity while remaining in the

---

83. Ibid., 18.

84. Ibid., 19; cf. Elisabeth Schüssler Fiorenza, *Discipleship of Equals: A Critical Feminist Ekklesia-logy of Liberation* (New York: Crossroad, 1993), 53–79.

85. Elisabeth Schüssler Fiorenza, *Bread Not Stone: The Challenge of Feminist Biblical Interpretation* (Boston: Beacon Press, 1984), 115.

86. The statement is quoted from the poet Judy Chicago. On the same theme, see Elisabeth Schüssler Fiorenza, *But She Said: Feminist Practices of Biblical Interpretation* (Boston: Beacon Press, 1992).

Christian church is to challenge the injustice of Christian patriarchy, to promote female power, and to preserve the memory of earlier women of spirit.

Ruether and Schüssler Fiorenza are both Roman Catholics, but both teach at liberal Protestant institutions. Their influence is perhaps stronger within liberal Protestantism and the secularized world of academic religious studies than within the Catholic church, but for many Catholic theologians as well, Ruether and Schüssler Fiorenza define what it means to take feminist criticism seriously. What it means is that Christian commitment can be justified on feminist grounds only if it promotes the freedom and empowerment of women. The critical principle of feminist theology is a liberationist axiom. Ruether and Schüssler Fiorenza both adopt a stronger form of the liberationist principle than most Latin American or African American liberationists, however. For them, as for many academic feminist theologians, feminism is not compatible with any normative understanding of the lordship of Christ or the sovereignty of God. As Daphne Hampson observes, Ruether's theology equates Christian truth with her political-ecological understanding of liberation without remainder. "One is hard pressed to see how hers is a theology, as opposed to simply a political agenda for the liberation of people," Hampson argues. "In fact, if one reads her work carefully, one notices that she never speaks of God, but rather of people's concept of God, which may lead them on in their striving for justice."[87]

The same critique applies with stronger force to Schüssler Fiorenza's theology. Ruether's "golden thread" approach to Scripture and Christian tradition at least appeals to a major biblical theme. As she observes, the theme of liberation is hardly marginal to the Bible. But Schüssler Fiorenza disputes Ruether's assurance that a feminist theological agenda can be read into prophetic Christianity. Rather than claim a biblical warrant for feminism on liberationist grounds, Schüssler Fiorenza begins with a feminist commitment that needs no support from biblical religion. What feminism does need from the past, she urges, are examples of women struggling against male domination. Christian feminists draw strength for their fight against patriarchy from the examples of early Christian women. They remain Christians partly to remain faithful to the memory of earlier Christian dissenters and partly because they recognize that to abandon Christianity is to cop out. "Western women are not able to discard completely and forget our personal, cultural or religious Christian history," Schüssler Fiorenza explains. "We will either transform it into a new liberating future or continue to be subject to its tyranny whether we recognize its power or not."[88] In this view, feminists can fight the power of Christian patriarchy more effectively within the church than by renouncing their ties to the church.

---

87. Daphne Hampson, *Theology and Feminism* (Oxford: Basil Blackwell, 1990), 29.
88. Ibid., 35.

Hampson finds both claims highly dubious. She argues that the historical and cultural differences between modern middle-class women and first-century women are too great to allow any meaningful comparison between them. "To be asked to see myself as one in solidarity with first-century women strains my credibility," she observes. "It is then not immediately apparent why 'our heritage is our power': we are in a radically different situation, with different problems and different options."[89] Schüssler Fiorenza's pragmatic argument also seems overwrought to Hampson. Is it really true that the Christian myth is still a powerful identity-forming force in Western culture? Is Christianity still so powerful that feminists are required to transform it from within? Hampson replies that Schüssler Fiorenza's thesis is not only untrue but also a counsel of despair. Western women today are not so trapped. Most of them know little or nothing about their biblical heritage, nor are they significantly shaped by biblical teaching.

Moreover, Hampson argues, the fact that many feminists explicitly reject Christianity is not harmful to feminism. Schüssler Fiorenza's rationale for her Christian feminist project is weak and confused, if not unbelievable. "Surely one does not spend one's life as a biblical scholar reinterpreting the tradition because that is all that can be done in view of the fact that, like it or not, we live within this trajectory?" Hampson asks. To recommend a life of engagement with Christianity on these grounds seems pitiful to her. While Schüssler Fiorenza's scholarship may be rewarding to readers with a historical or religious interest in her subject, her apologetic arguments hang a heavy burden on a very thin line.

In her attempt to discredit the religious and intellectual integrity of Christian feminism, Hampson exaggerates the purportedly nonreligious, overpoliticized character of feminist theology. Yet her critique does identify a critical problem with certain influential forms of feminist theology as *Christian* theology. The problem was underscored by a panel discussion featuring Ruether and Schüssler Fiorenza at the 1991 American Academy of Religion annual meeting in Kansas City. In a lecture-discussion session ostensibly devoted to feminist perspectives on the quest of the historical Jesus, Ruether and Schüssler Fiorenza made only a few glancing references to Jesus. They were pressed by several questioners to explain, however, why they thought the assigned topic was important or not important. Specifically, they were asked if feminist theology had any stake in the historical Jesus debate. Beyond their claim that the Jesus movement engendered certain ethical and political convictions that feminism embraced, was there any substantive religious reason for feminists to affirm Christianity? More pointedly, one questioner asked, was it possible for feminist theology to answer this question by confessing faith in Christ's incarnation or resurrection? Could feminist

---

89. Ibid., 34.

theology sanction a Christian identity that hinged upon a confession of faith in the lordship of Christ?

It happened that Hampson was seated next to me. As Ruether and Schüssler Fiorenza fudged their way through the earlier questions, Hampson muttered, "So what?" and "They're begging the question!" The last question brought out a clearer response, however. Though Ruether's writings often refer to Jesus as "liberator," she and Schüssler Fiorenza both shook their heads and denied that feminist Christianity could be based upon faith claims about the divinity of Christ. For them, Christianity was usable only as a particular kind of ethical-political-communal movement that, in Ruether's words, "discards hierarchical caste privilege and speaks on behalf of the lowly." In *Theology and Feminism,* Hampson identifies the crucial problem with this approach. "The whole *raison d'être* of that early Christian community was that it believed certain things of Christ—at the very least, that it was he whom God had raised from the dead," she observes. "Indeed one's own reason for looking to this community was presumably that, as a Christian, one needed oneself to make some reference to Christ." The communities of women with whom Schüssler Fiorenza declares her solidarity existed only because they believed certain things about Christ. Without their faith in Christ's redeeming death and resurrection, there was no cause for a Jesus movement and no need for Christian feminism. Hampson observes that Schüssler Fiorenza's writings rarely mention Christ, however. "Like it or not then, one is forced to confront the questions which Schüssler Fiorenza, through her strategy, seeks to avoid," she remarks. "Is it possible for feminists to be Christians, when Christ is a male figure?"[90]

The question is crucial, though Hampson wrongly suggests that most Christian feminists avoid the subject of Christ. Ruether's work emphasizes that Jesus proclaimed the immanence of the reign of God and the vindication of the poor and oppressed: "His ability to speak as liberator does not reside in his maleness but in the fact that he has renounced this system of domination and seeks to embody in his person the new humanity of service and mutual empowerment," she argues. Rebecca Chopp's feminist "hermeneutics of marginality" similarly gives close attention to Jesus as the symbol of freedom and herald of a new aeon.[91] Heyward confesses that she "could no more pretend that the Jesus-figure, indeed the Jesus of the Kerygma, is unimportant to me than I could deny the significance of my parents and my past in the shaping of my future."[92] The

90. Ruether quote in Ruether, *Sexism and God-Talk,* 137; Hampson quotes in Hampson, *Theology and Feminism,* 34.

91. Ruether, *Sexism and God-Talk,* 137; Rebecca S. Chopp, *The Power to Speak: Feminism, Language, God* (New York: Crossroad, 1991, c1989), 40–70.

92. Carter Heyward, *The Redemption of God: A Theology of Mutual Relation* (Washington, D.C.: University Press of America, 1982), 196.

problem for Christian feminism is not so much that Jesus was male, but that Christianity proclaims his divinity. As Heyward explains, Christian feminism can affirm Jesus as a brother and confess an attraction to him on narrativist or ethical grounds, but confessions of Christ's divinity are another matter. Jesus should be remembered, she argues, but not revered. "I do not find it helpful to think of Jesus as Lord," she remarks. "I may call him 'Christ,' but it is not because he was divine, different from us, in any superhuman or supernatural way, but rather because he was exactly human, like us."[93] The Jesus of history–Christ of faith distinction is crucial to her insistence on ruling out any confession of faith *in* Christ. The centrality of Christ in Christianity "has resulted from a mis-conception of Jesus as a divine person rather than as a human being who knew and lived God," she argues. For her, as for many Christian feminists, "Jesus matters only if he was fully, and only, human."[94]

Heyward's relational theology claims that redemption is attainable only through human relationships. Rita Nakashima Brock similarly contends that whatever is truly christological, "that is, truly revealing of divine incarnation and salvific power in human life, must reside in connectedness and not in single individuals." Brock rejects any theology that focuses on Jesus or makes Jesus a hero figure. She argues that the "healing center of Christianity" is the reality of erotic relational power, which Jesus neither brings into being nor controls, but which he experienced through his involvement in a "community of mutual liberation." Neither is the saving reality of erotic power dependent upon Christ's resurrection. "The relational nature of erotic power is as true during Jesus' life as it is after his death," she explains. "He neither reveals it nor embodies it, but he participates in its revelation and embodiment." Brock therefore interprets "Christ" to mean "Christa/Community," the communal process by which healing erotic power is made manifest. For her, as for many Christian feminists, it is axiomatic that feminist theology must be not only antipatriarchal but also anti-supernaturalist, rejecting all unilateralist understandings of power.[95]

For many feminist theologians, any notion of divine reality that conceives divine power as transcendent is incompatible with feminism. A God whose being transcends the processes of nature, history, and community cannot be a power that liberates female spirit, but only a being that enslaves its overpowered subjects. Radical Christian feminists reject the power-over theism of classical Christianity and the spirituality of domination that derives from it. The fact that Jesus was

---

93. Carter Heyward, unpublished sermon quoted in Grant, *White Women's Christ and Black Women's Jesus,* 187.

94. Heyward, *The Redemption of God,* 31–32.

95. Rita Nakashima Brock, *Journeys by Heart: A Christology of Erotic Power* (New York: Crossroad, 1993), 52, 66.

male considerably heightens the need to remythologize divine power. As Heyward explains, radical Christian feminism can accept Jesus as a brother if he had only one nature, which was only human. To attribute a divine nature to Jesus is problematic, however, because it bonds the divine nature to the human nature of a man. The maleness of Jesus is not a problem for feminism if Jesus was only human; but if Jesus was also divine, his maleness is threatening to feminism. Feminism is about the liberation of female spirit and power, but the Christian doctrine of the incarnation presents "the image of the invisible God" (Col. 1:15) in male form.

Hampson aptly summarizes the problem. "The feminist problem is that one cannot simply speak of the one nature without the other. Inescapably, if one is to have a Christology, one must bring the two natures together, and herein lies the problem," she explains. Whether one adopts a "high" or "low" Christology, starts from above or below, or distinguishes sharply between the Jesus of history and the Christ of faith is finally irrelevant. All Christologies are left with the same problem. "The problem is that this divine Christ is, in the second of his two natures, the human person Jesus, who is male," Hampson observes.[96]

Christianity affirms the uniqueness of Christ, whether in a high or low Christology, but authentic feminism is incompatible with Christology of any kind, in her view, because Christology unavoidably links divine power to maleness. As a religious feminist, Hampson agrees with Christian feminists who disavow the doctrine of Christ's divine nature, but she insists that they are wrong to call themselves Christians. Christian feminism dithers in a halfway house that is neither Christian nor sufficiently feminist, in her view. Feminism is a revolutionary challenge to Christianity. It is not fundamentally a demand for women's equality in a male-dominated world; it is a different view of the world. Hampson argues that conservatives are right to warn that feminism represents a more radical challenge to Christianity than other critiques, "for the feminist challenge strikes at the heart of Christianity."[97]

Hampson longs for a feminist theology that breaks free from Christianity yet is deeply religious and theological. In her reading, however, the dominant feminist theologies are making bad bargains at both ends. They disavow fundamental Christian teaching but fail to break free from Christianity. At the same time, they seek to "transform" Christianity with theologies that are highly politicized and not very religious. This trait is a failing that feminist theology shares with modern liberal theology in general, she remarks:

> What strikes me then about much modern theology—and this is not least true
> of feminist theology—is how profoundly secular it is. It is as though theology

---

96. Hampson, *Theology and Feminism*, 59.
97. Ibid., 1.

has lost its moorings. In the case of feminist theology, what seems to have replaced talk of God is largely talk of women's experience. Thus Elisabeth Schüssler Fiorenza tells us of the community of women in the early church, celebrating their courage in adversity and their egalitarian politics. Rosemary Ruether looks to alternative traditions within the Christian heritage, suggesting that here we may find communities, the knowledge of which will empower us. Mary Daly advocates the self-realization of women and the overcoming of oppression in a new age.[98]

Throughout the literature of Christian and radical feminist theology, she concludes, one finds remarkably little discussion of divine reality.

Women-Church

The evolution of the Women-Church movement in the United States bears out some of Hampson's argument. Women-Church began in the early 1980s as an offshoot of radical Catholic feminism, but its national conferences in 1983, 1987, and 1993 increasingly shed its Catholic past. The 1993 conference in Albuquerque featured more than thirty varieties of Sunday morning services, including Goddess worship, an Indian pipe ceremony, Sufi dancing, a Holocaust remembrance, a Quaker meeting, and various feminist liturgies, but not a Catholic mass. Having begun as a movement in which Catholic feminists created a space for themselves while remaining linked to the Catholic church, Women-Church has increasingly become a multitendency network of feminists with highly ambiguous connections to Christianity of any kind. One of the movement's chief organizers and theologians, Mary E. Hunt, contends that it would be a mistake for Women-Church to renounce its historical ties to Christianity. At the same time, she affirms, the movement's increasingly pluralized and post-Christian direction makes it necessary "to beg the question of Jesus."

Hunt insists that this posture is not problematic for religious feminists "because women's infinite creativity and cleverness permit us to be many things at once." Her own trajectory reflects the ambiguous identity but clearer direction of the Women-Church movement. "The church I come from—and I emphasize from—is the Roman Catholic church," she states. The Catholic feminist and writer Jane Redmont comments more ruefully that although she is a longtime activist in Women-Church, "I am also someone for whom Jesus is important and I have noticed that Jesus isn't there much anymore."[99] Women-Church is clearly moving in a direction that will require it to beg more than the question

---

98. Ibid., 170.

99. Hunt quoted in Peter Steinfels, "Women's Group Recasts Religion in Its Own Image," *New York Times,* April 21, 1993, A12; Redmont quoted in Steinfels, "Catholic Feminists Ask, Can We Remain Catholic?" *New York Times,* April 16, 1993, A9.

of Jesus. If the movement reflects the intellectual and religious incoherence that Hampson criticizes, it also increasingly shows signs of developing into the post-Christian religious feminist movement that she seeks.

Religious feminism is a richer tapestry than its post-Christian and radical threads, however. Thousands of women serve as pastors in mainline churches and more than half of today's students at liberal Protestant seminaries are women. For many or perhaps most of them, the notion that following Christ is "disempowering" or "enslaving" is contrary to experience. Many feminists do not find that their spiritual freedom is diminished by confessing the uniqueness, centrality, or lordship of Christ; the greater threat to them is the possibility of losing their faith in Christ. Many feminists have had to overcome the attribution of religious significance to Jesus' maleness by reactionaries who want to exclude women from priestly ministry. It is a disquieting experience for them to see feminist theologians repeating the same argument.

Theologians such as Patricia Wilson-Kastner and Elizabeth A. Johnson argue for the compatibility of feminism and Christianity in ways that better reflect the blend of feminist Christianity preached in mainline churches today. An Episcopal priest, Wilson-Kastner contends in *Faith, Feminism, and the Christ* (1983) that the significance of Christ's incarnation is related to his humanity, not to his maleness. "Christ is not simply the new male person, but one who shows all persons how to live. As a human he shows us what human self-possession and self-giving are," she asserts. Her theology affirms the unique incarnation of Jesus while refusing to limit Christ to Jesus. "Jesus became flesh so as to show forth the love of God among us, a love which is not merely an expression of good will, but the power of an energy which is the heart, core, and cohesive force of the universe," she explains. If the living Christ is more than the historical Jesus, this does not mean that there is any ground for Christology apart from the incarnation, crucifixion, and resurrection of Jesus. Her Logos-cosmology seeks to overcome, like radical feminism, the ravages of dualism and alienation, but Wilson-Kastner appeals to the healing power of God's redeeming all-inclusive love in Christ. "In the crucifixion of Christ the dualisms and negativity that feminism seeks to overcome have been conquered," she argues. "Through the resurrection the whole is healed and is being healed. Through the dynamic life of the risen Christ, the varied beings of the cosmos gather into one living whole in God, in which all that is good, beautiful, and true is nurtured and grows in the unending life of God."[100]

Wilson-Kastner embraces the classical Christian affirmation that the unity of divinity and humanity in Christ makes it possible for God to take on the

---

100. Patricia Wilson-Kastner, *Faith, Feminism, and the Christ* (Philadelphia: Fortress Press, 1983), 90, 91, 115.

suffering of the world in order to redeem it. In the death of Christ, she affirms, God accepts "the fragmented human condition into the divine life for healing, and the humanity of Christ gathers into himself all the forces of alienation and destruction active in his own death." The brokenness of the world is gathered up in Christ's redeeming death, and the eschatological reality of God's triumph over alienation is prefigured in Christ's resurrection. Everything converges in Christ, "and in his person and activity everything finds wholeness and meaning." Wilson-Kastner acknowledges that many people do not find this vision of Christ meaningful, credible, or liberating. Her concern is not so much to convince them otherwise as to show that Christian faith *is* compatible with feminism; the notion that one cannot embrace feminism and follow Christ is mistaken. "The figure of Christ remains our central symbol: one of inclusiveness, healing, and living unity, which fulfills the expectation of feminism," she observes. If Christianity frequently does not present a liberating, inclusive, kingdom-bringing Christ to the world, the fault is not with Christ: "Rather, the church's own lack of fidelity and vision has allowed it to be used by others, and itself to use Christ, as a sacred justification for social, political, economic, and religious repression."[101]

Building on her knowledge of the patristic tradition and the theology of Jürgen Moltmann, Wilson-Kastner urges that a redeveloped trinitarian theology instructed by feminist criticism is needed to express the relational nature of divine reality.[102] In her reading, the monarchical image of God that feminist critics rightly attack is the product of a patriarchal Christian tradition that has prized unopposed power-over and that has herefore failed to sustain a trinitarian understanding of divine reality. The same thesis is elaborated in Elizabeth A. Johnson's richly textured study of the triune, relational, suffering mystery of divine reality, *She Who Is: The Mystery of God in Feminist Theological Discourse* (1992). For Johnson, as for Wilson-Kastner, the key point of coherence between Christian theology and feminist criticism is the relational character of ultimate reality. Johnson explains,

> At the deepest core of reality is a mystery of personal connectedness that constitutes the very livingness of God. The category of relation thus serves as a heuristic tool for bringing to light not just the mutuality of trinitarian persons but the very nature of the holy mystery of God herself. Divine unity exists as an intrinsic *koinonia* of love, love freely blazing forth, love not just as a divine attitude, affect, or property but as God's very nature.[103]

---

101. Ibid., 100, 116.

102. For Moltmann's theology of the Trinity, see Jürgen Moltmann, *The Trinity and the Kingdom of God: The Doctrine of God* (New York: Harper & Row, 1981).

103. Elizabeth A. Johnson, *She Who Is: The Mystery of God in Feminist Theological Discourse* (New York: Crossroad, 1992), 228.

Like the biblical wisdom tradition, which uses the female metaphor Sophia to signify divine wisdom, Johnson uses feminine metaphors to personify God's creative, indwelling, relational wisdom. In her view, the problem of Christian theism is that God has been traditionally portrayed as a unipersonal monarch who rules over the world commanding obedience. Similarly, the problem of Christology is that for much of Christian tradition, Christ has been portrayed as the imperial ruler or reigning king of glory who sustains the earthly rule of the patriarchal head of the family, empire, and church. The subversive, liberating Jesus who renounced power and identified with the oppressed is thus turned into an icon of the solitary ruling male ego. Feminist criticism deconstructs the oppressive mythology of the imperial Christ. Johnson argues that the maleness of Jesus is a problem, however, only for a church that uses it to justify unequal male power. In a just church, the maleness of Jesus would not be an issue but merely one aspect of Jesus' historical contingency along with his race, ethnicity, language, and Galilean roots.

As a Roman Catholic advocate of women's ordination, Johnson is sensitive to the claim that Christ's incarnation establishes a special affinity or even identity between maleness and divinity. The teaching office of the Vatican employs this argument in its case against women's ordination.[104] Johnson observes that in order to sustain their claim that men enjoy a closer identification with Christ on account of their "natural resemblance" to him, opponents of women's ordination have been forced to implicitly overthrow the doctrine of Christ's dual nature established at Chalcedon (451). The Council of Chalcedon proclaimed that no mixing occurred between the human and divine natures of Christ. Despite the orthodox teaching that in Christ's dual nature each nature keeps its own properties, however, Johnson observes that the androcentric imagination nevertheless "occasions a certain leakage of Jesus' human maleness into the divine nature, so that maleness appears to be of the essence of the God made known in Christ."[105]

Drawing upon the rich classical language about God as spirit, sophia, Word, and mother/father, Johnson counters with a feminist reconstruction of the classical Christian doctrine of God's immanent triune being:

> This language is not a literal description of the inner being of God who is in any event beyond human understanding. It is a pointer to holy mystery in trust that God really is the compassionate, liberating God encountered through Jesus in the Spirit. It is language which affirms that what is experienced in Christian faith really is of God; that what we are involved with is nothing other than saving divine mystery. At rock bottom it is the language of hope. No one has ever seen God, but thanks to the experience unleashed through Jesus in the

104. Cf. Congregation for the Doctrine of the Faith, "Declaration on the Question of the Admission of Women to the Ministerial Priesthood," *Origins* 6 (February 3, 1977).
105. Johnson, *She Who Is,* 152.

Spirit we hope, walking by faith not by sight, that the livingness of God is with us and for us as renewing, liberating hope.[106]

Johnson's work exemplifies how a Christian theological engagement with feminism can bring about a richer and truer understanding of Christian faith. In her work, the full range of Christianity's theological and spiritual resources are used to refashion the inner and social meaning of Christianity in light of feminist criticism. The result is a project of theological retrieval that expresses and illumines the faith embraced by thousands of feminist women and men. It expresses the spirituality of a church that sees God's Spirit at work in the emancipation of female spirit. It illumines the personal and communal experience of "the Spirit's universal quickening and liberating presence, the living memory of Wisdom's particular path in the history of Jesus, and inconceivable Holy Wisdom herself who brings forth and orients the universe." Human language is never adequate in describing the burning, ever-gracious mystery that it signifies, Johnson acknowledges, "but a more inclusive way of speaking can come about that bears the ancient wisdom with a new justice."[107] Her work epitomizes the possibility that Christian theology might emerge from its encounter with feminism with a deeper, more authentic, and spiritually more powerful faith.

By calling Christianity to hear the voices of women and men previously excluded from the naming process, liberation theologies open the church to deeper understandings of what it means to follow Christ. Harnack once remarked that the heart of Christianity is both simple and exhaustive, for it is "Jesus Christ and his Gospel."[108] Liberal Protestantism has produced numerous alternatives to this perspective, but its mainstream has long upheld that Christianity is centered in the incarnation and way of Christ. Morrison gave voice to this conviction in calling for an ecumenical movement that relativized every Christian doctrine and tradition except devotion to Christ. A generation later, at the end of a theological career at Union Theological Seminary that spanned nearly forty years, Henry Van Dusen observed that liberal Christianity was not only Christ-centered, but "the most determinedly Christocentric theology in Christian history."[109] He conceded that modern Protestant history was littered with failed alternatives and that liberal Protestantism had often invoked a Christ of its imagination. The point, however, was that liberal Protestantism was always strongest, most faithful, and truest when it held fast to the Lordship and teaching of Christ:

---

106. Ibid., 200.

107. Ibid., 273.

108. Adolf von Harnack, *What Is Christianity?* trans. Thomas B. Saunders (New York: G. P. Putnam's Sons, 1901), 10.

109. Henry P. Van Dusen, *The Vindication of Liberal Theology: A Tract for the Times* (New York: Charles Scribner's Sons, 1963), 41.

If Liberal Theology holds validity, it is precisely because its interpretation of Jesus Christ is most fully adequate, most true to authentic Christian Faith. By the same token, Liberal Theology's enduring significance rests upon the decision whether it offers just another among the Christologies of the Christian centuries *or* whether in fact it declares the most genuinely "orthodox" Christology in Christian history, *and* whether that understanding and interpretation of Jesus Christ can be "credible and convincing" to intelligent, informed, honest minds of today.[110]

Van Dusen was too chastened by the failures of liberal Protestantism to call for a renewal of world-changing social gospel idealism. He did not share Rauschenbusch's radical politics or his enthusiasm for Christianizing America. He did not invoke the kingdom ideal with the fervor of Rauschenbusch or Morrison. Like Rauschenbusch and Morrison, however, he believed that liberal Protestantism was uniquely suited to throw off Christianity's various biblical and ecclesiastical authoritarianisms without reducing Christianity to culture religion or moralism. What was needed was a Christianity that followed the liberating Christ faithfully in freedom. Van Dusen's understanding of divine reality was strongly trinitarian, but the central focus of his work, like that of his tradition, was upon "the mind and especially the faith of Jesus."[111] If Barthian neoorthodoxy put the transcendent and ineffable mystery of God at the center, liberal Protestantism put the face of Christ at the center. It invoked Paul's testimony that the God who commanded light to shine out of darkness "has shone in our hearts to give the light of the knowledge of the glory of God in the face of Christ" (2 Cor. 4:6). Liberal Christianity took on the slippery, always fallible project of finding the true Christ among the welter of clues, notions, and biblical statements about him. Van Dusen explained, "Through those imperfect records, Jesus ever afresh lays constraint upon his Movement in the world, holding it more or less true to his mind and faith, and impelling it to new advances for fulfillment of his purposes."[112]

This is the spiritual center of liberal Protestant social Christianity, which continually asks what it means to follow Christ in the modern world. In the past generation, liberal Protestantism has taken guidance and inspiration especially from liberation theology in seeking to discern what it means to follow Christ. It has thus increasingly learned to look for Christ in the faces of the poor, forgotten,

---

110. Ibid., 45–46.

111. For Van Dusen's trinitarian theology, see Henry P. Van Dusen, *Spirit, Son and Father: Christian Faith in the Light of the Holy Spirit* (New York: Charles Scribner's Sons, 1958), 89–177; quote from Van Dusen, *The Vindication of Liberal Theology,* 93.

112. Van Dusen, *The Vindication of Liberal Theology,* 148; for Van Dusen's social theology, see Henry P. Van Dusen, *God in These Times* (New York: Charles Scribner's Sons, 1935).

mistreated, silenced, and oppressed. To see the face of Christ in those who have had no power to shape history or name the world is to find the true Christ in a way that subverts the middle-class world of liberal theology. Liberation theology's various pluralizing and subversive currents strip liberal Protestantism of its remaining pretensions but in a way that recovers its vitalizing center. As Gutiérrez remarks, the Christian religion has been tied for most of its history to a culture, the Western culture; to a race, the white race; to a sex, the male sex; and to a class, the ruling class. Its history has therefore been written mostly by the hands of white, Western, privileged males. Liberation theology opens liberal Christianity to other memories of Christ, including, in Gutiérrez's words, "the memory of Christ in every person who is humbled, thirsty, hungry, in prison, present in the despised races, in the exploited classes."[113] If liberationist concerns drive many people to reject Christianity, liberation theology recovers for many others the social Christian memory of Christ the liberator.

---

113. Gustavo Gutiérrez, "Freedom and Salvation: A Political Problem," in *Liberation and Change,* ed. Ronald Stone (Atlanta: John Knox Press, 1977), 92; cf. Matthew 25:31–46.

6 FAILURE OF A DREAM?
Economic Democracy and the Economics of Nature

THEOLOGIANS HAVE DREAMED FOR MOST OF THE PAST CENTURY of a transformed economic order. In the Progressive era, American social gospelers such as Shailer Mathews and Francis Peabody were repelled by the socialist movement's emphasis on class conflict and its antireligious polemics, but they believed more ardently than most socialists that Americans were capable of building a cooperative, equitable, community-oriented society. Their writings proclaimed that with enough religiously inspired good will and devotion to the common good, Americans could build the cooperative commonwealth that biblical teaching idealized.

Democratic Socialism and Christian Realists

American Christianity's greatest figure during this period reminded his liberal followers that idealists alone have never carried through any important social change. Walter Rauschenbusch's socialism was based on his realism about the class struggle. The "great truth" of democratic socialism could only be won by an organized proletarian class "which makes that truth its own and fights for it," he declared. Rauschenbusch regarded socialism as "the ultimate and logical outcome of the labor movement" because only socialism promised to extend the democratizing logic of liberal democracy to the economic system. Though he adopted much of the rhetoric of Marxist socialism, his programmatic vision sought not to abolish the market system but to establish democratic control over the economy.[1]

A half-generation after his death, nearly every major Protestant theologian in Europe and America shared his view of the need to find an alternative to capitalism. Rauschenbusch's broadsides against the unfairness, spiritlessness,

---

1. Walter Rauschenbusch, *Christianity and the Social Crisis* (New York: Hodder & Stoughton/Macmillan, 1907), 400–401, 408.

and antidemocratic character of modern capitalism were heightened in the 1930s by such major Protestant thinkers as Karl Barth, Emil Brunner, Paul Tillich, Reinhold Niebuhr, John C. Bennett, William Temple, and Charles Raven. The Swiss Reformed neoorthodox Brunner was the most conservative figure in this group, yet even Brunner condemned capitalism with unequivocal scorn. Christian socialists typically shared Marx's appreciation of the productive capacities of capitalism; like Marx, Rauschenbusch argued that capitalist financial accumulation and industrialization were necessary preconditions for the creation of a desirable social order. For Brunner, however, modern capitalism was not a prelude to anything except moral and social catastrophe. Modern capitalism, he instructed in *The Divine Imperative,* "is that system in which all that we can see to be the meaning of the economic order from the point of view of faith is being denied: in which, therefore, it is made almost impossible for the individual to realize, in any way through his economic activity, the service of God and his neighbor. This system is contrary to the spirit of service; it is debased and irresponsible; indeed we may go further and say it is irresponsibility developed into a system."[2]

Capitalism was too unredeemably debased to be reconciled with any authentic form of Christianity, in the estimation of modern Christianity's most conservative major theologian. Brunner shared little of liberal Protestantism's social optimism, very little of its immanental spirituality, and none of its optimism about human nature, but for him it was axiomatic, as it was for liberal Protestantism, that the capitalist devotion to individual self-interest and private property was hostile to Christian teaching. During the same period, the major figure in modern Anglicanism, William Temple, turned these commonplace critiques into an economic program. In the 1920s and 1930s, while writing numerous books on Christian philosophy, theology, and spirituality, Temple also became an important advocate and theorist of democratic socialism. In 1941, shortly before his enthronement as archbishop of Canterbury, he proposed that an excess profits tax could be enacted to create worker- and community-controlled enterprises.[3] The following year, in *Christianity and the Social Order,* he developed a critique of capitalism that drew upon natural law theory. While production naturally existed for consumption, he argued, modern capitalism reversed the natural order of things by making consumption dependent upon production and production dependent upon finance. Like such Catholic theorists as Heinrich Pesch, Oswald von Nell-Bruening, and John A. Ryan, Temple thus drew upon natural law distinctions in formulating his social ethic, while going far beyond existing Catholic moral

---

2. Emil Brunner, *The Divine Imperative,* trans. Olive Wyon (Philadelphia: Westminster Press, 1947, c1932), 423.

3. William Temple, *The Hope of a New World* (New York: Macmillan, 1941), 54–59.

theory in developing his critique of capitalism. His alternative called for subordination of profits to the end of fellowship, withering capital investment, mutual export trade, economic democracy, a socialized monetary system, and the social use of land.[4] "It is important to remember that the class-war was not first proclaimed as a crusade by Marx and Engels; it was first announced as a fact by Adam Smith," he observed. "Nothing can securely end it except the acquisition by Labour of a share in the control of industry. Capital gets its dividends; Labour gets its wages; there is no reason why Capital should also get control and Labour have no share in it."[5] Like his friend the economic historian R. H. Tawney, Temple conceived democratic socialism as the form of political economy most consistent with Christian ethics and the democratizing logic of liberal democracy.

In Temple's lifetime, Niebuhrian realism promoted a hard-core Marxist version of this faith. *Moral Man and Immoral Society* was not a rejection of the Christian socialist economic vision but a repudiation of its typically moralistic character. Niebuhr wanted to base Christian socialism on his conflation of biblical and Marxist political realism. Though his commitment to realist-pragmatic politics later moved him to relinquish socialism, Niebuhr remained a partisan of the democratic Left for the rest of his life. He never denied that maldistributed economic power was a social evil that undermined political democracy, but in his later career he concluded that America's emerging welfare state was fulfilling as much of the democratic socialist dream as could be attained. His Left/Keynesian political economics defined for his theological generation what it meant to apply the prophetic criterion of distributive justice to real-life American politics.

The emergence of German political theologies, feminism, black theologies, and Third World liberation theologies in the 1960s re-established, in new forms, the primacy of democratic socialist discourses in modern theology. For the past generation, most modern and postmodern Christian theologians have operated, as Michael Novak complains, within a democratic socialist horizon. The most influential Protestant theologian of the past thirty years, Jürgen Moltmann, argues that democratic socialism is the historical form that Christian hope must take, "given the present poverty of capitalism and its democracies as well as socialism and its dictatorial governments."[6] The doyen of Latin American liberation theology, Gustavo Gutiérrez, proclaims that Christian theology today must speak "of social revolution, not reform; of liberation, not development; of socialism, not modernization of the prevailing system."[7] The Argentine liberationist, José

---

4. William Temple, *Christianity and the Social Order* (Middlesex: Penguin Books, 1942), 77–96.

5. Ibid., 96.

6. Jürgen Moltmann, *On Human Dignity: Political Theology and Ethics,* trans. M. Douglas Meeks (Philadelphia: Fortress Press, 1984), 174.

7. Gustavo Gutiérrez, *The Power of the Poor in History: Selected Writings,* trans. Robert R. Barr (Maryknoll, N.Y.: Orbis Books, 1983), 45.

Míguez Bonino, urges that while socialism must not be identified with the divine kingdom, socialist praxis is "really and continually related" to the kingdom and thus "concretely defines my Christian obedience in the world."[8]

African American and feminist theologians have made substantial contributions to modern and postmodern Christian socialism. Cornel West, James Cone, Michael Dyson, and others advocate democratic socialism as an insufficient but necessary element of any emancipationist praxis. The liberation theology that is needed, West contends, would include Marxist, feminist, Garveyist, ecological, and antimilitarist elements. Its economic system would feature state-owned industries of basic producer goods, decentralized worker-controlled enterprises, consumer and producer cooperatives, small businesses run by self-employed entrepreneurs, and other self-employed artists, writers, and workers. "Just as I believe that the Christian faith in the modern world—given its allegiance to democracy and individuality—requires resistance to race-based and gender-based hierarchies, so I believe that it demands opposition to class-based social hierarchies," West explains.[9]

Rosemary Radford Ruether concurs that the goal of Christian social ethics must include "a democratic socialist society that dismantles sexist and class hierarchies, that restores ownership and management of work to the base communities of workers themselves, who then create networks of economic and political relationships." Ruether further envisions an organic, communitarian society in which the processes of child nurturing, education, work, and culture are integrated to permit men and women to share the responsibilities of homemaking and caring for children. She further envisions an ecological society "in which human and non-human ecological systems have been integrated into harmonious and mutually supportive, rather than antagonistic, relations."[10] Her social vision thus becomes more explicitly utopian with each further-reaching description of a cooperative, feminist, ecological society. Because the entire vision can be fulfilled only by alternative communities characterized by high levels of intentionality (and high rates of burnout), Ruether subscribes to a "mosaic" strategy that views movements for social justice, feminism, economic democracy, peace, and ecology as prefigurative pieces of an unrealized collective vision. Her work is distinguished by its sustained effort to integrate the multiplicity of democratic socialist, feminist, and environmentalist perspectives.

---

8. José Míguez Bonino, "For Life and against Death: A Theology That Takes Sides," in *Theologians in Transition,* ed. James M. Wall (New York: Crossroad, 1981), 176.

9. Cornel West, "Harrington's Socialist Vision," *Christianity and Crisis* 43 (December 12, 1983), 484–85; and *Prophetic Fragments* (Grand Rapids: Eerdmans, 1988), 134–35.

10. Rosemary R. Ruether, *Sexism and God-Talk: Toward a Feminist Theology* (Boston: Beacon Press, 1983), 232–33.

This imperative to make progressive Christianity more open to diverse perspectives and problematics has heightened its disputes over the meaning of socialism. Moltmann criticizes Latin American liberationists for underemphasizing the necessity of democracy, while Latin American liberationists criticize Moltmann's social democratic socialism for being too middle class and reformist. West and Cone argue that traditional Christian socialism is too economistic, too reformist, and much too racially and culturally homogeneous to provide the emancipatory vision that is needed. Ruether and other feminists reject the androcentric language and worldviews that pervade traditional Christian socialism. Ecological theologians such as John B. Cobb Jr. and Sallie McFague contend that Christian socialism is too anthropocentric and too accepting of the capitalist drive for unsustainable economic growth. Debates over these issues have preoccupied Christian social ethics for much of the past generation.

But the moral or political worthiness of democratic socialism itself has only rarely been the focus of debate. The dividing question in progressive theology has not been the worthiness or viability of democratic socialism, but the kind of democratic socialism that is needed. As Trutz Rendtorff observes, the vision of a community bound by ties of cooperative and mutual service rather than the competitive market resonates deeply in Christian hearts.[11] The strength of this predisposition is confirmed in the writings of theologians who rarely address socioeconomic issues at all. The prominent Roman Catholic theologian David Tracy, while generally avoiding political discussions, contends that some form of Frankfurt School Marxism or democratic socialism is needed as an alternative to state socialism and late capitalism. McFague also generally avoids socioeconomic issues but observes that "some forms of socialism" best reflect her organic understanding of the political order and her commitment to care for the poor, the vulnerable, and the afflicted.[12] The question for these theologians has not been socialism, but the kind of socialism that promotes freedom, equality, community, and ecology. More vigorously than Tracy or McFague, the project of renewing Christian socialism has been embraced by such important contemporary theologians as Harvey Cox, Gregory Baum, Leonardo Boff, Robert McAfee Brown, Beverly Harrison, Kenneth Leech, Johannes Metz, Arthur McGovern, Delores Williams, Ronald Preston, Dorothee Soelle, Franklin Gam-

---

11. Quoted in David Heim, "The Church in Capitalism," *Christian Century* 109 (November 11, 1992), 1019.

12. David Tracy, *The Analogical Imagination: Christian Theology and the Culture of Pluralism* (New York: Crossroad, 1981), 37–38, n. 36; Sallie McFague, *Models of God: Theology for an Ecological, Nuclear Age* (Philadelphia: Fortress Press, 1987), 122, 177.

well, J. Philip Wogaman, Gibson Winter, Daniel Maguire, and Joe Holland.[13] Moreover, the same essential vision of democratized power is propounded in milder forms by numerous liberal theologians who generally avoid the language of socialism, including David Hollenbach, Letty Russell, Larry Rasmussen, M. Douglass Meeks, Douglas Sturm, Preston Williams, Harlan Beckley, Alan Geyer, Warren Copeland, and Robin Lovin.[14]

The democratic socialist vision of a cooperative democratic commonwealth has thus defined at least part of the Christian moral vision for most liberal or progressive theologians of the past century. Moreover, Christian socialists have typically opposed the overcentralizing tendency of most social democratic parties in Europe and the United States. For many years, the central policy proposal of most social democratic or democratic socialist parties in Europe and the United States called for centralized government ownership of the major means of industrial production. The need for a top-down, state economic planning apparatus was assumed. The "socialism" in democratic socialism was an ideology of centralized collectivism. Socialism meant economic nationalization, political centralization, and what the British Fabians called the rationalization of society. Fabian socialism proclaimed that every act of collectivization marked progress toward the desired "socialist" order of rationalized economic planning.

Like the Syndicalist traditions with which it was often allied, Christian socialism typically resisted this overcentralizing ideology. Anglican socialism was rooted in the pre-Marxist cooperativism of F. D. Maurice, Charles Kingsley,

---

13. Cf. especially Gregory Baum, *The Social Imperative: Essays on the Critical Issues That Confront the Christian Churches* (New York: Paulist Press, 1979); Harvey Cox, *Religion in the Secular City: Toward a Postmodern Theology* (New York: Simon & Schuster, 1984); Robert McAfee Brown, *Theology in a New Key: Responding to Liberation Themes* (Philadelphia: Westminster Press, 1978); Beverly W. Harrison, *Making the Connections: Essays in Feminist Social Ethics* (Boston: Beacon Press, 1985); Arthur McGovern, *Marxism: An American Christian Perspective* (Maryknoll, N.Y.: Orbis Books, 1980); Dorothee Sölle, *Beyond Mere Dialogue: On Being Christian and Socialist* (Detroit: Christians for Socialism in the United States, 1978); Franklin I. Gamwell, "Democracy, Capitalism, and Economic Growth," in *Economic Life: Process Interpretations and Critical Responses,* ed. W. Widick Schroeder and Franklin I. Gamwell (Chicago: Center for the Scientific Study of Religion, 1988), 223–50; J. Philip Wogaman, "Socialism's Obituary Is Premature," *Christian Century* 107 (May 30/June 6, 1990), 570–72.

14. Cf. especially David Hollenbach, *Justice, Peace, & Human Rights: American Catholic Ethics in a Pluralistic Context* (New York: Crossroad, 1988); Letty M. Russell, *Human Liberation in a Feminist Perspective—A Theology* (Philadelphia: Westminster Press, 1974); Larry Rasmussen, *Moral Fragments and Moral Community: A Proposal for Church in Society* (Minneapolis: Fortress Press, 1993); Douglas Sturm, *Community and Alienation: Essays on Process Thought and Public Life* (Notre Dame, Ind.: University of Notre Dame, 1988); Warren R. Copeland, *Economic Justice: The Social Ethics of U.S. Economic Policy* (Nashville: Abingdon Press, 1988).

and John Ludlow.[15] The cooperativist economic democracy of Temple, Raven, Tawney, and Charles Gore was continuous with this tradition, which sought to create decentralized forms of socialization. The social gospel progressivism of Rauschenbusch and Justin Wroe Nixon similarly favored cooperativist strategies over state socialism. Tillich's socialism bore a closer relationship to Marxism than most Christian socialism, but even Tillich assumed that the pricing system and market discipline of a market economy were necessary for democratic socialism.[16] Christian socialists rarely failed to oppose what Tillich called "the bureaucratization of the economy." Because Christian socialism predated state socialist currents that eventually dominated most social democratic and democratic socialist parties, figures like Rauschenbusch and Temple justifiably claimed that their vision of social and economic democracy deserved to be called socialism. A similar insistence on claiming the democratic socialist mantle has marked most Christian social ethical writing in the second half of the twentieth century.

Neoconservatism and Christian Ethics

That modern Christian theology has borne a mostly social democratic or democratic socialist stamp is thus a truism. But at the end of a century that began with ringing social Christian hopes for a new "cooperative commonwealth," how much is left of modern Christianity's dominant social vision? How much of the vision of a democratized social order can be saved or reconstructed in a political culture in which "socialism" mostly conjures up repulsive images of state authoritarianism? Were the Christian realists right to finally reject democratic socialism? How is it possible to reclaim the Christian social vision of democratized economic power at a time when corporate capitalism has globalized?

Neoconservative ethicist Robert Benne contends that the time has come for Christian ethicists to break from their social democratic–democratic socialist heritage. "I believe that Christian ethicists should rather turn their attention to the possibilities for justice within liberal capitalism," he writes.[17] His call is echoed with greater ardor in the "Postcommunist Manifesto" authored by Max

---

15. Cf. Gilbert C. Binyon, *The Christian Socialist Movement in England* (London: SPCK, 1931); Maurice B. Reckitt, *Maurice to Temple: A Century of the Social Movement in the Church of England* (London: Faber and Faber, 1947).

16. Cf. Paul Tillich, *The Socialist Decision* (New York: Harper & Row, 1977, c1933), 160; Tillich, "Basic Principles of Religious Socialism," reprinted in *Political Expectation*, ed. James Luther Adams, Victor Nuovo, and Hannah Tillich (New York: Harper & Row, 1971), 78–82.

17. Robert Benne, review of Gary Dorrien, *Reconstructing the Common Good*, in *Christian Century* 108 (February 27, 1991), 239–40.

Stackhouse and Dennis McCann, which proclaims that the death of communism bears unavoidable implications for Christian social ethics. Stackhouse and McCann observe that "the Protestant Social Gospel, early Christian realism, much neoorthodoxy, many forms of Catholic modernism, the modern ecumenical drive for racial and social inclusiveness, and contemporary liberation theories all held that democracy, human rights and socialism were the marks of the coming kingdom." But liberal Christianity has been wrong about socialism, they assert. "The future will not bring what contemporary theology said it would and should."[18] In their view, the verdict of history has come down not only against the communist mistake but against even the forms of democratic socialism that militantly opposed communism. Socialism is dead, and with its death lies the end of liberal Christianity's attempt to give it a human face.

For neoconservatives, the project that remains for Christian social ethics is to apply the chastening lessons of Niebuhrian realism to the economic order. Neoconservatives such as Novak disavow the Christian social project of breaking down existing concentrations of economic power. Though Niebuhr failed to press his political realism into a critique of social democratic economics, Novak explains, neoconservatism completes this essential Niebuhrian task by breaking entirely with the social Christian tradition of economic democracy. "Niebuhr did not give much attention to economic issues," Novak observes. "Precisely in Niebuhr's neglect, I found my own vocation. Surely, I thought, the next generation of Niebuhrians ought to push some of Niebuhr's deeper insights into the one major area he neglected."[19]

Novak's assumption of this neglected task has drawn him deeply into the American political Right, where, in the 1980s, he became a Reagan supporter and a chief mythologist of American capitalism. To apply Niebuhr's realism to the economic realm, he claims, is to relinquish the social Christian dream of democratizing economic power. Neoconservative realism insists that the values and legitimizing principles of democracy are pertinent only to the political sphere. To face up to modernity is to exclude democratic tests of legitimacy, equality, and accountability from the economic realm. Realism emphasizes wealth creation and, for the most part, allows the market to take care of distribution. It accepts that economic power is not to be subjected to democratic tests. It accepts the hegemony of corporate monopoly capitalism. It accepts the outcomes of free market economics, which include America's existing maldistribution of wealth.

---

18. Max L. Stackhouse and Dennis P. McCann, "Public Theology after the Collapse of Socialism: A Postcommunist Manifesto," *Christian Century* 108 (January 16, 1991), 1, 44–47.

19. Michael Novak, "Father of Neoconservatives: Reinhold Niebuhr," *National Review* 44 (May 11, 1992), 39–42.

In the wake of the dissolution of the only serious alternative to capitalist society, neoconservatives argue, it is time for modern Christianity to face up to modernity in the economic realm.[20]

Having insisted for decades that their vision of social and economic democracy has nothing to do with communism, however, it would be strange indeed if Christian ethicists concluded that the dissolution of communism somehow discredits their long-held social vision. The ravages of imperialism, structural dependency, maldistribution of wealth, and environmental destruction are no less devastating with the triumph of capitalism. The demise of the perverted form of socialism that once competed with capitalist democracy for world power has done little to alleviate the conditions that originally gave rise to Christian socialism. Christian ethicists have pressed the case for social and economic democracy for the past century because their commitments to distributive justice and their resistance to the all-commodifying logic of capitalism compelled them to seek an alternative to capitalist democracy. To call this entire project a mistake is to resign social Christianity to a status quo politics that sacralizes the privileges of the wellborn and the fortunate. It is to pretend that concentrations of economic power can be ignored without undermining political democracy and without doing harm to the poor and vulnerable.

Yet the Christian socialist tradition has been flawed in crucial respects. For most of the past century and especially in recent years, much of the literature on Christian socialism has featured a dreamy utopian air that only vaguely defines its subject and only rarely addresses the political and economic problems associated with economic democracy. Theologians have typically endorsed or promoted economic democracy with virtually no consideration of the economic problems or trade-offs that social democratic strategies present. Few modern or postmodern theologians have taken on the questions of economic efficiency, organization, or growth; few of them have even matched Rauschenbusch's attempts to discuss the economics or structure of cooperative ownership. By failing to describe the kind of socialism that they endorse, many Christian ethicists have left the mistaken impression that Christianity is compatible with any kind of socialism. Gutiérrez repeatedly calls liberationism a socialist project, for example, declaring that the political goal of liberation theology must be to create a society "in which private ownership of the means of production is eliminated." He explains that a just society can be created "only by installing a political power

---

20. Cf. Michael Novak, *The Spirit of Democratic Capitalism* (New York: American Enterprise Institute/Simon & Schuster, 1982); Peter L. Berger, *The Capitalist Revolution: Fifty Propositions about Prosperity, Equality and Liberty* (New York: Basic Books, 1986); Richard J. Neuhaus, *Doing Well and Doing Good: The Challenge to the Christian Capitalist* (New York: Doubleday, 1992).

at the service of the great popular majorities," but his writings never penetrate beyond these scattered slogans about "eliminating the private appropriation of wealth" to describe the kind of socialism that liberation theology seeks to create. Though he is quite precise in describing the ideologies and social systems that he opposes, Gutiérrez resorts to vague slogans in describing the alternative that liberation theology promotes. Like most liberationists, he thus fails to discuss the relationship between democracy and socialism, to explain how the mistakes of communist revolutions can be avoided, to distinguish between different types of socialism, or to address the problems associated with creating socialist economies in poor, largely preindustrialized societies. Like Marx, his writings on political economy are consumed with his critique of capitalism. The parallel should be instructive, for it was precisely Marx's vagueness and utopianism with regard to the socialist alternative that allowed generations of totalitarians to call themselves Marxists.[21]

Christian socialists have typically sought to avoid this mistake by dissociating themselves from nondemocratic socialist traditions. From Rauschenbusch to Moltmann, the major theologians of liberal Christian socialism have insisted that democracy is the heart of socialism. They have argued that there is no democracy without democratized economic power and no socialism without democracy. The failures and horrors of communism have nothing to do with progressive Christianity, they have claimed, because Christian socialism is grounded in a profoundly different political tradition than communism. Christian socialism seeks to fulfill the democratizing promise of liberal democracy. It does not seek to obliterate liberal democracy but to retrieve, renew, and extend the liberal democratic revolution.

But the problem of Christian socialism is deeper than the problem of demonstrating its commitment to democracy. At the end of a century in which tens of millions have died in prison camps, killing fields, and torture chambers in the name of building socialism, the word *socialism* has acquired powerfully repugnant associations. It is no longer the name of an innocent ideal. In much of the world, *socialism* is synonymous with totalitarian brutality, terror, bureaucratic stagnation, economic backwardness, and moral squalor. In its democratic forms, socialism has its own history of overcentralizing state collectivism. Its most benign face is the overcentralized Swedish welfare state, which finances its elaborately paternalistic government from a diminishing economic base. Wherever they have attained power, social democratic parties have promoted greater equality, civil liberty, and social insurance, but nearly always with a high degree of centralized government bureaucracy. Wherever it has sought power, democratic socialism has lost the radical communitarian-utopian spirit that fueled the Chris-

---

21. Gutiérrez, *The Power of the Poor in History*, 37–38, 45–46.

tian socialist, syndicalist, and even social democratic movements of the early twentieth century. Under these historical circumstances, it is crucially important, but not enough, for Christian socialists to explain that their socialism is democratic.

This dilemma was anticipated by Temple in the 1930s and early 1940s. Though he produced some of the most creative and programmatic Christian socialist thinking of this century, Temple generally avoided the rhetoric of socialism. He worried that "socialism" was already indelibly associated with Left-authoritarian politics, partly because democratic socialist economic strategies were often difficult to distinguish from authoritarian socialism. Temple opposed state socialism while appreciating that, for most people, socialism meant economic nationalization. He therefore eschewed the language of socialism in making his case for decentralized economic democracy. As he explained in *Christianity and the Social Order,* he fervently hoped that all Christians might accept his arguments for economic democracy. He knew that few Christians outside the trade unions and the political Left would ever embrace socialism, however. Temple was not interested in bolstering a suspect ideology with the prestige of Christian faith. His concern was to elucidate what it meant to follow Christ in the modern world. He appropriated guild socialist ideas in his constructive effort to discern the prophetic meaning of Christianity in the modern world, but he never reduced the gospel's transcendent meaning to his politics or attempted to turn Christianity into an endorsement of socialism. For him, socialist ideology was a barrier to the modern Christian project of democratizing social and economic power. He vigorously promoted economic democracy as a Christian ethical project while eschewing the progressive Christian tendency to sacralize socialist ideology.[22]

The difference is crucial. Progressive Christianity is not unavoidably beholden to the dubious ideology of socialism, but it is necessarily beholden to the claims of distributive social justice. In the name of fulfilling their commitment to social justice, however, theologians have repeatedly tried to redeem the language of socialism long after "socialism" acquired unredeemable connotations. As Temple feared, the upshot is that theologians have often confused much of modern Christianity's social teaching and undercut its moral influence.[23] Moreover, the problem is symptomatic of a larger failure of imagination and independence in progressive theology. For much of modern Christian thought, socialist

---

22. Temple, *Christianity and the Social Order,* 101.

23. For my own earlier grapplings with this problem, which employed the language of democratic socialism while seeking a suitable alternative to it, see Gary J. Dorrien, *The Democratic Socialist Vision* (Totowa, N.J.: Rowman & Littlefield, 1986), 15; Dorrien, *Reconstructing the Common Good: Theology and the Social Order* (Maryknoll, N.Y.: Orbis Books, 1992), vii.

theory has provided a seemingly indispensable conceptual framework and vocabulary. The socialist rhetoric of freedom, community, solidarity, and equality has energized the social vision of Anglican socialism, the American social gospel, German religious socialism, Christian realism, German theologies of hope, Third World liberation theologies, African American liberationism, feminist theology, and various ecumenical and progressive theologies. Progressive Christianity and democratic socialism arose at the same time and often together, sharing similar impulses and moral commitments. But at the end of a century in which "socialism" conjures up, at best, the image of an overextended, paternalistic welfare state, how much is left of modern Christianity's long-cherished dream of economic democracy?

Market Socialism and Economic Democracy

Many progressive theorists point to some version of Oscar Lange's market socialist model. In the 1930s, Lange tried to show that market mechanisms and incentives could be integrated into socialist theory. He argued that a large state sector could coexist with, and benefit from, the pricing and market discipline of a private sector of small enterprises. In his proposal, state planners would simulate and be instructed by the private sector's pricing system. The crucial problem with this scheme, however, is that it retained a highly centralized and collectivist conception of the role of the state. Though he granted a larger role for the market than traditional state socialism does, Lange still had centralized planners trying to replicate the innumerable and enormously complex pricing decisions of markets—a task exceeding the competence, time constraints, and knowledge of any conceivable planning board. Langean-style blueprints for "market socialism" invariably founder on this fundamental problem.[24] Though a considerable degree of state planning is inevitable in any industrial or postindustrial society—especially in economic markets where long-term planning is imperative—the purpose of economic democracy should be not to expand the role of state intervention but to democratize the base of economic power. If social Christianity is to reclaim its long-held vision of economic democracy, I believe that it must turn not to a Langean-type command model but to the kind of decentralized mixed-model strategy promoted by Temple.

Progressive Christianity has long propounded a particular form of postmodernism in which liberal democracy is viewed as an unfinished project in need of a democratic transformation. In this perspective, the common project for America's various progressive social movements is to expand the modern

---

24. Cf. Oskar Lange and F. M. Taylor, *On the Economic Theory of Socialism* (New York: McGraw-Hill, 1964, c1931).

democratic revolution by democratizing social and economic power. In a post-modern social context, however, it is not enough for this project to focus on either workplace or electoral issues. The effort to democratize power must take place not only at the point of production (as in Marxism) or in the electoral arena (as in liberalism) but also in the postindustrial community or "living place" where people struggle to attain sufficient health care, child care, housing, a clean environment, and healthy neighborhoods. It is a project that requires a feminist, multicultural, ecological, and anti-imperialist consciousness that liberal Protestantism lacked in the lifetimes of Rauschenbusch and Tillich. Liberationist and ecological critiques have raised issues that cannot be merely appropriated by or added to an inherited progressive Christianity, but which require transformations in the assumptions and theoretical frameworks of this tradition.

At the same time, I believe it is grievously mistaken to think that any serious challenge to existing relations of power can ignore the factors of production. There is a pronounced tendency in contemporary postmodern, feminist, and multiculturalist criticism to emphasize cultural and political issues while avoiding any discussion of economic alternatives. The reasons for this preference are far from mysterious. The internationalization of capital, the brutal assaults on trade unionism, the failures of democratic socialism, and the ascendancy of hyper-capitalist economic doctrines in recent years have discouraged progressive theorists from focusing on issues pertaining to economic distribution or power. Cultural theory is more manageable and rewarding than the seemingly hopeless problem of inequality. But to concede defeat in the economic area is to surrender on virtually every political and cultural front. Those who control the terms, amounts, and direction of credit largely determine the kind of society that others live in. The question of who controls the process of investment is therefore hardly less pressing, crucial, or determinative at the end of the twentieth century than it was in Rauschenbusch's time. As progressive Christianity has long insisted, gains toward social and economic democracy are needed for the same reason that political democracy is necessary: to restrain the abuse of unequal power.

If Christian ethicists have appropriately insisted that democracy has an economic dimension, however, they have only rarely addressed the political and economic trade-offs that their vaguely socialist prescriptions require. Just as there are serious problems with organizing and maintaining political democracy, there are equally serious problems with economic democracy. Democratically controlled capital is less mobile than corporate capital, and the return on democratically controlled capital tends to be lower than that in corporations because worker-controlled enterprises are more committed to keeping low-return firms in operation. Producer cooperatives are therefore often not well suited to compete in international markets with fast-moving, hierarchical capitalist enterprises. Moreover, cooperative enterprises require cooperative, egalitarian cultural values and habits that cut against the grain of America's dominant cultural traditions. In an American context, any strategy to break down the prevailing concentration of economic power must confront not only certain economic trade-offs but also forbidding political and cultural barriers.

The case for a democratized economic order is based upon more than a moral commitment to social justice, however. There is substantial evidence that economic losses caused by worker participation can be offset by gains in productivity made possible by it. People often work harder and more efficiently when they have a stake in the company. Moreover, the tremendous upsurge in runaway plants and economic deindustrialization over the past twenty years in the United States has created new interest in worker ownership. Experiments with various kinds of worker ownership have dramatically increased as a response to the problems of capital flight, runaway shops, bureaucratic waste in the managerial sector, and industrial decline. In the Progressive era, when theologians such as Rauschenbusch and Temple made the case for economic democracy, there were few examples of cooperative ownership or decentralized social ownership to which they could point. But today there are thousands of worker-owned firms in the United States, and, though they have been characteristically slow in rising to the challenge, several American unions have begun to bargain for worker ownership, worker control over pension funds, and worker management rights. These developments are not yet, but have the potential to become, the building blocks of a genuine movement for economic democracy.[25]

The most instructive example of integrated cooperative ownership surely, is the Mondragon cooperatives in the Basque region of Spain. In the 1950s a Catholic priest, José Maria Arizmendi, inspired a group of students to launch a cooperative stove factory (Ulgor) that quickly grew into a complex of foundries incorporated as agricultural cooperatives. Mondragon has since grown into a highly successful and diversified network of worker-owned enterprises that are democratically managed on the basis of cooperative membership. Between 1966 and 1975, sales rose from $47 million to $336 million, and in the 1980s Mondragon became Spain's largest exporter of durable goods. In more than forty years, this network has witnessed only two closings. The Mondragon cooperatives employ more than 100,000 workers in an integrated complex of more than 125

25. Cf. Len Krimerman and Frank Lindenfeld, *When Workers Decide: Workplace Democracy Takes Root in America* (Philadelphia: New Society Publishers, 1991); Eileen McCarthy and Corey Rosen, *Employee Ownership in the Grocery Industry* (Oakland: National Center for Employee Ownership, 1987); Corey Rosen, Katherine Klein, and Karen Young, *Employee Ownership in America: The Equity Solution* (Lexington, Mass.: Lexington Books, 1986); Michael Quarrey, Joseph Raphael Blasi, and Corey Rosen, *Taking Stock: Employee Ownership at Work* (Cambridge, Mass.: Ballinger Publishing, 1986).

financial, industrial, and service companies in a wide range of economic sectors, including robots and mass transit. Mondragon contains more than seventy-five industrial firms, an agricultural cooperative, five schools, a technical college, and a central bank—the Caja Laboral Popular—which is half-owned by its own employees and half-owned by other cooperatives. Founded in a church basement in 1958, the Caja Laboral Popular has $2 billion in assets and specializes in making loans to cooperative firms and providing industry-specific consulting assistance. Each Mondragon worker-owner holds one share of voting stock, and profits are distributed in the form of additions to a capital account on which 6 percent interest is paid annually. Seventy percent of annual profits are distributed to worker-owners on the basis of salary scale and seniority, 10 percent are donated to charity, and the remaining 20 percent are reinvested. Because the network's worker-owners cannot withdraw money from their capital accounts until they retire, Mondragon is able to make long-term investments in expansion, diversification, research and development, and reinvestment from its accumulated capital stock.[26]

The Mondragon complex consistently outperforms comparable capitalist enterprises throughout Europe, demonstrating that worker empowerment and cooperation can be turned into economic advantages. Mondragon began as an attempt to apply Arizmendi's Catholic personalist social doctrine to the local economy of a community steeped in Catholic social teaching and strengthened by a common ethnic heritage. The network's origins and early success were undoubtedly aided by its cultural, religious, and ideological roots. Researchers have repeatedly found that neither culture nor ideology is crucial to Mondragon's continued success, however. As George Benello remarks, "The secret of Mondragon is not ideological, but organizational: it is 'how to' knowledge that makes it work." Mondragon succeeds primarily not because it trades upon the peculiarities of Basque culture but because it has learned how to trade upon the advantages wrought by worker empowerment and cooperation.[27]

26. On Mondragon, see H. Thomas and Chris Logan, *Mondragon: An Economic Analysis* (London: Allen and Unwin, 1982); William Foote Whyte and Kathleen King Whyte, *Making Mondragon: The Growth and Dynamics of the Worker Cooperative Complex* (Ithaca, N.Y.: ILR Press NYSSILR, 1988); K. Bradley and A. Gelb, *Cooperation at Work: The Mondragon Experience* (London: Heinemann Educational Books, 1983); R. Oakeshott, *The Case for Workers' Co-ops* (London: Routledge and Kegan Paul, 1978); Terry Mollner, *Mondragon: A Third Way* (Shutesbury, Mass.: Trusteeship Institute, 1984).

27. Quoted in Len Krimerman and Frank Lindenfeld, "Contemporary Workplace Democracy in the United States: Taking Stock of an Emerging Movement," *Socialism and Democracy* 11 (September 1990), 117; cf. Joyce Rothschild and J. Allen Whitt, *The Cooperative Workplace: Potentials and Dilemmas of Organizational Democracy and Participation* (Cambridge: Cambridge University Press, 1989).

Cooperative Enterprises in the United States

The skills, habits, and kinds of knowledge acquired by the Mondragon cooperatives are requisite for any viable movement for democratized economic power. In the United States, the massive deindustrialization of America's manufacturing base and the steep decline of American unions have driven many unions and other associations of workers and activists to acquire the requisite practical knowledge to organize worker-controlled firms. In 1980 there were fewer than two hundred cooperative enterprises in the United States. These included some significant experiments in worker ownership, including a network of sixteen highly productive plywood mills in the U.S. Pacific Northwest, but for the most part cooperative ventures in the United States were small, isolated, and restricted to a handful of economic sectors. American proponents of economic democracy were told that worker and community ownership might be fine in Northern Europe or Spain, but it would never work in the United States. American culture was too individualistic and competitive for cooperative strategies to work.

With the pressure of the deindustrialization trend and the losses in union membership, however, numerous American unions have begun to face up to the essential task of organized labor in an internationalized economy. Unions and other worker associations are increasingly trading wage restraint for worker ownership or, more ambitiously, for greater worker control over investment and enterprise management. Though most American unions still do not devote significant resources or energies to worker takeover strategies, thousands of firms have converted to worker ownership in recent years. Today there are more than twelve thousand worker- and community-controlled enterprises in the United States, which include not only small producer cooperatives but also very large enterprises such as the United Parcel Service, Republic Engineered Steels, Avis, America West Airlines, Publix Supermarkets, Chicago Northwestern Railroad, and Northwestern Steel and Wire. The best known of these enterprises—UPS— is renowned for its low rates, efficiency, and high employee morale. Founded by James E. Casey, who declared that the company would be "owned by its managers and managed by its owners," UPS is owned by fifteen thousand of its managers and supervisors. It features a generous annual bonus plan and an employee stock option plan through which former UPS clerks and drivers retire as millionaires.

The trend toward worker ownership in the United States has thus far made only small gains toward democratizing American economic power. Most employee ownership plans in the United States offer shares without voting rights, most of them assure that employees will be kept in a minority ownership position, very few of them provide educational opportunities to help worker-owners develop management skills, and virtually none offers a program to build solidarity or help worker-owners build links with other cooperative enterprises or raise awareness of economic democracy issues. Most American experiments in worker ownership remain deeply American. They offer stock ownership to workers while preventing workers from obtaining managerial control or economic coordination. They promote worker ownership while stifling any movement for economic democracy. The practice of instituting worker ownership without facilitating democratic control or solidarity thus thwarts the development of the practical skills, knowledge, awareness, and cultural ethos that economic democracy requires. American unions have reinforced these shortcomings by failing to press for workplace democracy and by failing to encourage workers to become more adaptable.[28]

With all of its limitations, however, the recent movement toward worker ownership in the United States has created several thousand employee-owned firms and more than a thousand worker-controlled firms. Employee stock ownership plans now cover more than 10 percent of the American workforce. Many firms are currently working toward greater labor-management cooperation, including such enterprises as Farmland Industries, Agway, Land O'Lakes, Ocean Spray Cranberries, Sunkist, Weirton Steel, Seymour Specialty Steel, O & O Supermarkets, Republic Container, Republic Cable, North American Rayon, Antioch Publishing, Austin Engineering, Burns & McDonnell Engineering, M. W. Carr & Company, Irontown Iron, Gore Associates, Norcal, Scully-Jones Company, TDI Industries, Walnut Acres, and White Pine Copper. If the American experience of worker ownership has thus far produced very little coordination or solidarity among groups of worker-owners, it has at least demonstrated that American worker-managed cooperatives can be highly productive and competitive in world markets.

Moreover, the existence of democratically controlled enterprises such as Weirton Steel and Agway has begun to create a crucial base of experts and consultants with experience in cooperative management techniques. Industrywide unions such as the United Steel Workers and the Amalgamated Clothing and Textile Workers have promoted worker ownership and helped to establish the AFL-CIO Employee Partnership Fund, which provides capital for union-led conversions to worker ownership. Organizations such as the Midwest Center for Labor Research, the Northeast Ohio Employee Ownership Center, and the Industrial Cooperative Association have facilitated worker buyouts and developed sector-specific expertise in cooperative management that was unavailable to earlier generations of American cooperatives.[29]

---

28. Cf. Joseph R. Blasi, *Employee Ownership: Revolution or Ripoff?* (New York: Harper Business, 1988), 189–219.

29. Cf. Krimerman and Lindenfeld, "Contemporary Workplace Democracy," 113–26; Blasi, *Employee Ownership,* 189–251; Thomas H. Naylor, "Redefining Corporate Motivation, Swedish Style," *Christian Century* 107 (May 30/June 6, 1990), 566–70.

For any firm that moves to cooperative management, much less any movement that seeks to expand the cooperative sector, the problem of defining the right of effective control is a crucial issue. Rather than allow their members to sell out to the highest bidder and take their capital gains, most cooperatives require members to sell out to the company. This policy guards against any reversion to traditional investor ownership, but in cooperatives where share prices range up to $90,000, younger workers are often excluded. The narrow form of economic democracy is often good for cooperatives—which use high borrowing fees to discourage less-motivated workers—but it does little to democratize the base of economic power. To serve the cause of distributive justice, any politics of economic democracy must do more than empower highly motivated or fortunate workers who are prepared to buy into high-priced cooperatives. Most cooperatives operate on the traditional principle that those who own a company's capital have the right to control the company. In other words, property rights determine the right of effective control. On this principle, workers must be the primary investors in a firm in order to control it. In the United States, however, cooperative firms are generally forced to operate without government assistance and often without adequate advice or financing from banks. The upshot is double jeopardy. Because cooperatives generally presuppose a traditional theory of property rights and because they typically do not receive outside financing, they often operate from a severely restricted financial base; that is, cooperative firms are often undercapitalized as the price of workers' control. The narrow form of economic democracy thus continues to measure human value in terms of exchange value, while heightening the economic risks that cooperative worker-owners are obliged to assume.

The wider form of economic democracy, by contrast, is a strategy not only to empower wage earners but also to empower those who do not earn wages: homemakers, the disabled, welfare families, retirees, the unemployed. It includes socially owned firms in which the right of control is established on the basis of membership rights.[30] Worker ownership of stock is an important but, by itself, insufficient basis for economic democracy, first because pure worker ownership often prevents cooperatives from accumulating a sufficient capital base, and second because the idea of social and economic democracy is to organize society for the sake of the common good, not just for the sake of wage earners. Economic

---

30. On the concept of membership rights, see Ota Sik, *For a Humane Economic Democracy,* trans. Fred Eidlin and William Graf (New York: Praeger, 1985). Sik proposes that worker-owned capital could be owned collectively and that all workers could become members of internal democratically managed "assets management" and "enterprise management" associations. See also the working paper of Ann Arbor Democratic Socialists of America, "Toward a Cooperative Commonwealth" (Ann Arbor, Mich.: Ann Arbor DSA, 1983).

democracy in its wider form therefore features not only worker-owned cooperatives but also various forms of mutual fund or public bank social ownership that entail significant democratically determined public control of investment and decision making. Cooperative, community-oriented strategies expand the base of social and economic power principally by expanding the cooperative and mutual fund sectors. The objective is not to eliminate property rights but to expand property rights under new forms. The mix could include national development banks, cooperative banks, employee stock ownership plans, mutual fund enterprises, community land trusts, and regional planning agencies that guide investments into locally defined areas of need, such as housing, soft-energy hardware, infrastructure maintenance, and mass transit.

The crucial task for any large-scale project in economic democracy would be to construct an appropriate mix of cooperative and mutual fund forms of ownership. There are serious reasons why a politics of merely expanding the cooperative sector is not enough. Because they prohibit nonworking shareholders, cooperatives generally attract less outside financing than capitalist firms; because they are committed to keeping low-return firms in operation, cooperatives tend to stay in business long after they become unable to pay competitive wages; because cooperatives are committed to particular communities, cooperative capital and labor are less mobile than corporate capital and labor; because they maximize net income per worker rather than profits, cooperatives tend to favor capital-intensive investments over job creation; because cooperative worker-owners often have all of their savings invested in a single enterprise, they are often disinclined to invest in risk-taking innovations. All of these problems can be mitigated to some extent with productivity-enhancing tax incentives and regulations, but all of them also reflect trade-offs inherent in any cooperative strategy. The same trade-offs inhere in any serious strategy to pursue environmentally sustainable development. In a world in which the pursuit of unlimited economic growth has brought about the prospect of ecological disaster, economic democracy must aim to create alternatives not only to the capitalist modes of production and distribution but also to the capitalist fantasy of unlimited growth. The kind of economic development that does not harm the earth's environment will require a dramatically expanded cooperative sector consisting of worker-owned firms that are rooted in communities, committed to survival, and prepared to accept lower returns.

But it will also require more than a strategy of expanding the cooperative sector. Worker ownership increases economic risks to workers, and it privileges workers in more profitable sectors. Moreover, worker-owners in successful firms are often biased toward capital-intensive (rather than job-creating) investments because they do not want to dilute their profits-per-existing-worker ratios. Cooperatives thus tend to be slower than capitalist firms to expand employment when increasing demand makes job creation possible. The problem of capitalization can be mitigated to some extent by instituting internal capital accounts—such as Mondragon's retirement accounts—that facilitate reinvestment of savings and enable worker-owners to plan for the long term. Tax incentives and regulations promoting job expansion, reinvestment, innovation, and bank lending to cooperatives can also help cooperative firms succeed. It can no longer be doubted that cooperative approaches can succeed, even by capitalist standards of success.

But the most successful experiment in cooperative ownership reveals why other forms of decentralized democratic control are needed. Mondragon succeeds because it imposes fairly high borrowing fees upon its new members; workers have to buy their way into the cooperatives. As noted, this approach excludes less driven, less risk-taking members. It is capable of producing highly successful cooperative enterprises, but it addresses only a part of the problem of distributive justice. To address the distributive problem by universalizing the cooperative approach would negate a crucial source of Mondragon's success because a universal Mondragon would be unable to impose high entry fees. If everyone had to belong to a Mondragon-style cooperative, many of them would fail, and then the state would be forced back into its familiar capitalist role of socializing the economy's losses. Economic democracy requires a government that supports cooperative initiatives, but economic democracy cannot succeed by requiring workers to join them.

Mutual Funds and the Meidner Plan

The trend in contemporary economic democracy theory is therefore toward mutual fund (or public bank) models of decentralized social ownership. Mutual fund models typically establish competing holding companies in which ownership of productive capital is vested. The holding companies lend capital to enterprises at market rates of interest and otherwise control the process of investment, including decision-making power to initiate new cooperatives and shut down unprofitable enterprises. The holding companies are generally owned by equity shareholders, the state, or other cooperatives. The most extensive project undertaken in this area thus far has been the Meidner plan in Sweden. Rudolf Meidner is a pioneering economist in the field of collective capital sharing and control whose proposal, in modified form, was enacted in 1982 by the Social Democratic government in Sweden. The plan called for an annual 20 percent tax on major company profits to be paid in the form of stock to eight regional mutual funds. The funds are controlled by worker, consumer, and government representatives. As their proportion of stock ownership grows, these groups are collectively entitled to representation on company boards. Voting rights of the employee shares are jointly held by locals and branch funds. In the compromise form of the plan enacted by the Swedish government, a 40 percent ceiling was placed on the amount of stock that the eight funds in total could own of any single firm. Even in this form, however, the Meidner plan could, if resumed, render effective control over profitable firms in Sweden to the worker and public organizations.[31]

Because the funds represent part of workers' compensation, the Meidner plan contains a built-in system of wage restraints and also facilitates a new form of capital formation. It requires no program of nationalization, and investors still seek the highest rate of return. Like most mutual fund models, it separates risk in production from entrepreneurial risk, assigning production risks to worker-managed enterprises and entrepreneurial risks to the holding companies. The overriding importance of the mutual fund model, however, is that it offers a way beyond the welfare state, by expanding the base of economic power, while saving the social and political gains of liberalism. It establishes democratic control over the process of investment without resorting to overcentralized state planning. It promotes economic democracy while checking the growth of both private and public economic power. In Sweden, the move toward economic democracy has to some extent replaced the previous Social Democratic emphasis upon continually expanding the welfare state. The fate of the mutual fund model in Sweden is clearly tied to the fate of the Social Democratic party. The charter for the original Meidner plan expired in 1990 and the Social Democrats lost the succeeding election, largely because the country's economic power was eroded by the financial demands of its extensive welfare state. The future of economic democracy in Sweden depends in part upon whether the Social Democrats choose to emphasize economic efficiency and distribution of power rather than the politics of expanding the welfare state.

In highly variable forms, though nearly always in ways that decentralize power as much as possible, theorists such as Severyn Bruyn, Thomas Weisskopf, David Winter, Peter Abell, Raymond Plant, Alec Nove, Saul Estrin, David Belkin, David Miller, John Roemer, Robert Dahl, and Radoslav Selucky have elaborated models of economic democracy that emphasize mutual fund strategies.[32] The distinct advantage of mutual fund ownership is that it diversifies

---

31. Cf. Rudolf Meidner, "A Swedish Union Proposal for Collective Capital Sharing," in *Eurosocialism and America: Political Economy for the 1980s,* ed. Nancy Lieber (Philadelphia: Temple University Press, 1982); Meidner, *Employee Investment Funds: An Approach to Collective Capital Formation* (London: George Allen & Unwin, 1978); Jonas Pontusson, "Radicalization and Retreat in Swedish Social Democracy," *New Left Review* 165 (September/October 1987), 5–33.

32. See especially Alec Nove, *The Economics of Feasible Socialism* (London: Allen & Unwin, 1983); Nove, *Socialism, Economics, and Development* (London: Allen & Unwin, 1986); David Miller, *Market, State and Community: Theoretical Foundations of*

forms of risk sharing and thus promotes greater efficiency by forcing firms to be financially accountable to a broad range of investors. It would be a mistake to turn the mutual fund model into the next progressive blueprint, however. As Belkin observes, the blueprint mentality is part of the problem. It was a mistake for democratic socialists of the past to equate socialization with nationalization; it was a mistake to reject production for profit; it was wrong to think that state planners could replicate the complex pricing decisions of markets; later on, it was a mistake to think that worker-owned cooperatives could organize an economy not linked by markets.

Today it would be wrong to replace earlier socialist blueprints with a singular mutual fund or social ownership model. From a democratic perspective, the crucial problem with the mutual fund model is that it weakens workers' power at the firm level and increases the power of those agents who invest collectively owned social capital. In some mutual fund models, notably Estrin's, the holding companies would be required to bear considerable capital risks while allowing their client firm managements to make critical decisions affecting these risks *and* without being eligible to share in the profits. In every model, mutual fund social ownership theory presents difficult trade-offs between the needs of the holding companies and the rights of worker-managed enterprises. To the extent that the holding companies are granted supervisory control over their client enterprises, worker control is diminished; to the extent that the holding companies are kept in a weak position, the crucial advantages of the mutual fund model are traded off as the client enterprises essentially become cooperatives.

Mutual fund models have been created in the first place because worker-owned firms are often deficient in the entrepreneurial field. As Estrin observes, conflicts of interest between the worker-members and profitability can cause cooperatives to be "insufficiently attuned to market signals." The case for opting toward a strong mutual fund model rests heavily on this concern. It is arguable that even the mutual fund approach is too decentralized to be feasible in certain markets, however. Most social market theorists place as much control as possible in human-scale organizations in which the distance between management and workers is minimized. This "politically correct" preference could seriously restrict, however, the scale and types of markets in which democratically controlled

Market Socialism (Oxford: Clarendon Press, 1990); John Roemer, "Market Socialism: A Blueprint," *Dissent* 38 (Fall 1991), 562–69; David Belkin, "Vision Long, Sights Narrow: After the False Dawn of Socialist Economics," *Socialist Forum* 18 (Fall 1991); Radoslav Selucky, *Marxism, Socialism, and Freedom* (London: Macmillan, 1979); and Julian Le Grand and Saul Estrin, eds., *Market Socialism* (Oxford: Oxford University Press, 1989). The last text contains valuable articles by Estrin, Le Grand, David Miller, Raymond Plant, David Winter, and Peter Abell.

enterprises might be able to compete with aggressive, integrated, large-scale capitalist corporations.[33]

The upshot of these problems is not that progressive Christianity should therefore abandon its dream of democratizing economic power but that no single scheme to redistribute power should be universalized. I believe that Estrin's model of circular ownership and control offers the best solution to the fundamental issue of control. In this model, which resembles the "second-degree" cooperatives of Mondragon, cooperative firms would become shareholders in the holding companies themselves, thus minimizing the trade-offs between democratic control and efficiency posed by noncircular models. It would be deeply mistaken to enshrine this particular model or any model as the next object of faith, however. Rauschenbusch believed that a combination of state and cooperative ownership would create a good society; Temple developed a type of guild socialism that featured a Meidner-like plan for creating worker-controlled collective capital funds; Niebuhr and Bennett supported a blend of syndicalist and nationalization programs until they gave up on socialism; many other modern theologians have promoted "socialism" without describing what it is. If the latter approach is too vague and evasive for the progressive Christianity that is needed, neither should Christian ethicists embrace any particular model or mixture of models as the next sign of the kingdom. It would be seriously misguided to claim that all capitalist firms should be turned into cooperative or mutual fund enterprises. It would be equally mistaken to claim that new democratized enterprises must follow a pure Mondragon or Meidner model.

Decentralized, economic democracy must be a project built from the ground up, piece by piece, opening new choices, creating more democracy, seeking to build a new economic order that is more egalitarian, more cooperative, and more ecological than the existing order. It is a project that breaks from the universalizing logic of state socialism. The tests of its efficacy are pragmatic. To impose something like a universal Mondragon on a capitalist society would require coercion over workers who do not want to belong to cooperatives. Today in the Pacific Northwest, some plywood workers choose employment in conventional firms over membership in the plywood cooperatives. No political economy worth building would force them into a different choice.

The issue of choice, however, is the key to the alternative that progressive Christianity has long sought. A politics that expands the cooperative and mutual fund sectors could give workers important new choices. As Belkin observes, the

---

33. See Belkin, "Vision Long, Sights Narrow," 8–10; and Belkin and Joanne Barkan's reply to Roemer's "Market Socialism" in *Dissent* 38 (Fall 1991), 569–72; Estrin quote in Estrin, "Workers' Co-operatives: Their Merits and Their Limitations," and in Le Grand and Estrin, eds., *Market Socialism,* 190.

central conceit of neoclassical economics could be turned into a reality if meaningful choices were created. The neoclassical conceit is that capitalism does not exploit anyone because labor employs capital as much as capital employs labor. But in the real world, it is virtually always the owners of capital, and not the owners of labor, who organize the factors of production. To expand the cooperative, mutual fund and other social market sectors would give choices to workers that neoclassical theory promises but does not deliver. It would also begin to create a political culture that is more democratic, egalitarian, cooperative, and ecologically conscious than the one we have now.[34]

Social market strategies offer a third way between the systems of the competitive market and the state. Under capitalism, businesses are not structured to be fully accountable to their constituencies and surrounding communities; they are not self-regulating or chartered to operate in the public interest. Capitalist enterprises are driven by the laws of the competitive market to maximize profit while leaving the social and environmental ravages of market economics to the state. It is government that is left with the task of regulating or coping with environmental destruction, corporate monopolies, consumer exploitation, unemployment, cycles of inflation and recession, speculation, corporate debt, and maldistributed wealth. These regulatory tasks of the modern state are added to the state's fundamental responsibilities in the areas of national defense, protection of property and civil rights, infrastructure maintenance, education, and other social needs.

The modern state has grown enormously in response to these impossibly complex and virtually endless demands upon it. American political rhetoric regularly castigates the bureaucratic inefficiency, pettiness, and arrogance of government, but the growth of America's unregulated market economy has made the growth of a regulatory federal government necessary. In the 1980s, after the Reagan administration made good on part of its antigovernment campaign rhetoric by abolishing numerous federal programs and regulations, a less-regulated corporate sector responded with an orgy of corporate mergers, stock market speculation, greenmail, and soaring business debt. The antigovernment excesses of the Reagan-Bush era produced a tripled national debt, unprecedented trade deficits, a $500 billion bank scandal, a worsening deterioration of America's cities and infrastructure, and a massive redistribution of wealth to the rich. These

---

34. Cf. John Roemer, *Free to Lose: An Introduction to Marxist Economic Philosophy* (Cambridge, Mass.: Harvard University Press, 1988); Richard Norman, *Free and Equal: A Philosophical Examination of Political Values* (Oxford: Oxford University Press, 1987); John Baker, *Arguing for Equality* (London: Verso, 1987); G. A. Cohen, "Are Freedom and Equality Compatible?" in *Alternatives to Capitalism,* ed. Jon Elster and Karl Ove Moene (Cambridge: Cambridge University Press, 1989), 113–26; Irving Howe, "Socialism and Liberalism: Articles of Conciliation?" *Dissent* 24 (Winter 1977), 22–35.

excesses provided a political opening in the 1990s for a return to a stronger government-regulated politics. Bill Clinton's election was founded primarily on his promises to make government work again to revive economic growth, provide universal health care, and make a market society more equitable.

American politics revolves primarily around the question of the extent to which the state should regulate the economy. Arthur M. Schlesinger Jr. has observed that the narrative line of modern American political history can be conceptualized as a struggle between the politics of private interest and public purpose. In Schlesinger's reading, the competition between America's private interest and public purpose impulses has dominated American politics in alternate thirty-year cycles for at least the past century.[35] Whatever the merits of his theory of historical cycles, his focus on the private interest–public purpose argument is certainly merited, as is his observation that liberal Christianity has long supported a welfare state politics that views the state as a potentially constructive force for social justice.

If America's mainline churches have generally supported liberal Democrats since the New Deal, however, the more progressive stream of mainline Christianity and its dominant tradition in modern Christian ethics have pressed for a society in which private power itself is democratized. Social market strategies pursue the latter objective by creating alternatives to the state and market systems. While accepting that both the state and market perform indispensable functions in a dynamic society, social market strategies seek to expand and create new social sectors that belong to neither the competitive market nor the regulative state systems. Producer cooperatives take labor out of the market by removing corporate shares from the stock market and maintaining local worker ownership; community land trusts take land out of the market and place it under local democratic controls to serve the economic or cultural needs of communities; community finance corporations take democratic control over capital to finance cooperative firms, make investments in areas of social need, and fight the redlining policies of conventional banks.[36]

The purpose of expanding the social market sphere is not only to create alternatives to the state and market systems, but to change the ways that governments and markets operate. Cooperative and mutual fund organizations are subversive enterprises; whenever they succeed, they challenge the mythos of modern capitalism. They prove that there are viable democratic alternatives to a corporate capitalist system that organizes business enterprises like dictatorships

---

35. Arthur M. Schlesinger, Jr., *The Cycles of American History* (New York: Simon & Schuster, 1984).

36. Cf. Severyn T. Bruyn, *A Future for the American Economy: The Social Market* (Stanford: Stanford University Press, 1991).

and takes economic control away from communities. At the same time, social market strategies challenge the modern liberal notion that the state should function primarily as an economy-regulating agency. Social market theorists such as the Catholic sociologist Severyn Bruyn contend that the state should be less involved in regulating the economy and more involved in facilitating economic self-regulation and accountability. As Bruyn remarks, "The state's primary role should not be to govern corporations but to promote incentives for them to provide their own systems of social justice and equity."[37]

In this vision, the state would seek to guide the economy toward greater self-regulation, partly by providing incentives for corporations to become more accountable to shareholders and more responsive to the social and economic needs of local communities. It would provide incentives for trade unions to develop self-monitering systems that promote environmental protection, product safety, and other public interests. "This means encouraging the development of social audits as well as financial audits, and making it easier for banks, mutual funds, and pension funds to practice social investment without impairing their ability to invest prudently on behalf of their beneficiaries," Bruyn explains. "The market becomes a system of exchange in which firms cooperate as well as compete to advance their own interests in the context of the public interest."[38] Social market strategies thus seek to create systems of exchange that promote corporate decentralization and worker ownership in place of markets that foster corporate monopoly, domination, and disregard for the personal, community, and environmental costs of market economics.

To struggle for such an order is not to presume that social market strategies would work on a large scale if they were imposed next year on a political culture unprepared for them. The social vision of economic democracy cannot be imposed or transplanted at all. It can only take shape over the course of several decades, as hard-won social gains and the cultivation of cooperative habits and knowledge build the groundwork for a better society. Such a project does not call for large-scale investments in any particular economic model; it does not rest upon illusions about human nature; it does not envision or require a transformed humanity. Niebuhr's epigrammatic justification of democracy will suffice for economic democracy: The human capacity for justice makes democracy possible, but the human inclination to injustice makes democracy necessary. Niebuhr did not deny that the human capacity for fairness is often moved by genuine feelings of compassion and solidarity, but to him it was evident that all such feelings are

---

37. Severyn T. Bruyn, "Beyond the Market and the State," in *Beyond the Market and the State: New Directions in Community Development,* ed. Severyn Bruyn and James Meehan (Philadelphia: Temple University Press, 1987), 7.

38. Ibid.

mixed in human nature with more selfish motives. The crucial point was that democracy is necessary precisely because virtually everyone is selfish. Because human beings are so easily corrupted by the attainment of power, Niebuhr argued, democracy is necessary as a restraint on greed and the human proclivity to dominate others.

By the time he wrote the book that elaborated this argument, Niebuhr was no longer inclined to press the argument as a case for economic democracy. *The Children of Light and the Children of Darkness* was written in 1944, several years after Niebuhr gave up on Marxism and only a few years before he formally rejected Christian socialism. During these few years, when he tentatively held out for a socialism stripped of its Marxist illusions, he did not explore the possibilities of a politics that democratized and decentralized economic power. For Niebuhr, socialism meant economic nationalization, state economic planning, and production for use. To him, there were only three serious possibilities: free market capitalism, state socialism, and New Deal liberalism. Throughout the 1930s, while America's welfare state was being constructed, Niebuhr ridiculed and denounced it with unqualified contempt. A decade later, having renounced his Marxism, he made his peace with Roosevelt's liberal reformism and accepted the liberal dichotomy between politics and economics. Realism compared liberal capitalism not with a fantasized democratic socialist alternative but with existing historical alternatives.

This conclusion remains a serious possibility for Christian ethics. Whether it is the only possibility depends largely on the viability of decentralized, social market alternatives that Niebuhr never considered. It is crucial to bear in mind that economic democracy does not seek merely to make capitalism more equitable. If it is true that cooperative enterprises are not well suited to compete with centralized capitalist corporations in certain world markets, it cannot be repeated too often that economic democracy seeks a different kind of economic development than capitalism has produced. The kind of economic development that sustains the world's ecology will require an economic perspective that views environmental destruction not as an "externality" but as a violation of a sacred trust.

Ecotheology

Liberal Christianity has been a notably anthropocentric tradition. From its biblical heritage, it inherited the assumption that human beings are especially privileged over other species. From its Enlightenment heritage, it routinely assumed that Christianity was defensible only as a form of religious humanism. By taking what liberal theologians themselves called "the anthropocentric turn" away from religious orthodoxy, modern Christianity intensified the traditional Christian view that humanity is the center of history and the apex of creation. With few exceptions, even among most of those who identified with some form of neoorthodoxy, modern theologians have taken human experience and need as the measure of religious value. From Schleiermacher to Mathews to Gordon Kaufman, modern theologians have theorized on the humanity-centered human search for meaning, coherence, social justice, and salvation. The human drama of salvation has trumped other claims, including the claims of an imperiled natural world.

Most of liberal Christianity's major theologians have evinced little conception or awareness of nature at all. For Rauschenbusch and Mathews, the project of modern Christianity was to Christianize society by overcoming the individualistic limitations of Protestant pietism, either through a prophetic understanding of Christianity's revolutionary social character (Rauschenbusch) or through a commitment to religiously sanctioned social progress or "process" (Mathews). For both, the dialectic of self and society was all-consuming. Fosdick was more sensitive to nature than either Rauschenbusch or Mathews, but his appropriation of Romanticist poetry and his evocations of nature consciousness were motivated by therapeutic and pastoral concerns. For Fosdick, nature was a source of religious edification; the mystery and beauty of the natural world brought the self into contact with the religious source of its own nature. In the face of a soul-killing culture that believed mainly in exchange value, the mystery of nature bore witness to the reality of spirit. Like his tradition, however, Fosdick never doubted that progressive religion had to be focused on human need and experience. Nature consciousness was a source for the edification of the only species of meaning-seeking creatures.

For all of his denunciations of liberal Christian moralism, Reinhold Niebuhr's conceptions of nature and religion were thoroughly in the liberal modernist mold. For him, as for liberal Christianity, religion was an energizing power that served human needs and dictated human responsibilities. As his brother, H. Richard, plaintively observed, for Reinhold "nature" meant human nature; for Richard it meant rain, grass, stars, and glands. Reinhold Niebuhr thought in terms of the absolute and the relative; for him God was a transcendent judge who made human responsibility possible by giving humanity the freedom to defy God's absolute goodness. But for Richard Niebuhr, God was "not so much the absolute, as he is the determining dynamic." Richard rejected his brother's human-centered moralization of Christianity for the same reasons that he rejected liberal Christianity. Reinhold regarded religion as a power, but Richard countered that "for religion itself religion is no power, but that to which religion is directed, God . . . I think the liberal religion is thoroughly bad." Richard admitted that his

rejection of the liberal view of religion drove him into a deep contradiction—
"the acute dilemma of my life"—because he did believe that striving for power
was evil. He was an absolutist when it came to the question of renouncing power.
He thus agreed with Christian pacifists about the evils of violence and power
worship, while rejecting the liberal Christian belief that religion could be a power
for good.[39]

But liberal Christianity was nothing without its belief that religion could be
a power for good. For Reinhold Niebuhr, as for his tradition, religion was a
human construct, grounded in human moral and religious strivings, made possible
by humanity's unique capacities for transcendence, good, and evil. Like most
liberal theologians, he assumed that only human beings were intrinsically valuable. To the extent that he reflected at all upon nature beyond human nature,
he regarded the natural world as the servant of human need and gratification.
An anthropocentric approach to religion and the natural world was among the
assumptions that he, like most of his tradition, simply took for granted.

Having adopted an essentially instrumentalist view of the natural world,
modern theologians have been poorly suited to challenge commercial society's
view of nature as a commodity to be conquered and exploited. Beyond the rather
weak reminder that Christians are called to be good stewards of creation, mainline
Christianity has given little resistance to a dominant commercial order that values
nature chiefly for its exchange value. For all of its concern with social justice,
modern Christianity has so accommodated itself to the dominant order that it
has become, as Christian essayist and poet Wendell Berry charges, "willy-nilly
the religion of the state and the economic status quo." For the most part, Berry
observes, modern Christianity has:

> stood silently by, while a predatory economy has ravaged the world, destroyed
> its natural beauty and health, divided and plundered its human communities
> and households. It has flown the flag and chanted the slogans of empire. It has
> assumed with the economists that "economic forces" automatically work for
> good, and has assumed with the industrialists and militarists that technology
> determines history.

Modern Christianity has equated progress with modernization and desperately sought to align itself with both. But this strategy of accommodation has
implicated liberal Christianity in the modern assault on the natural world, Berry
charges. If modern Christianity is to begin to take moral responsibility for its
complicity in the annihilation of nature, he contends, "then Christians, regardless
of their organizations, are going to have to interest themselves in economy—
which is to say, in nature and in work. They are going to have to give workable

---

39. Quoted in Richard Wightman Fox, *Reinhold Niebuhr: A Biography* (New York:
Pantheon Books, 1985), 145, 153.

answers to those who say we cannot live without this economy that is destroying us and our world, who see the murder of Creation as the only way of life."[40]

In the 1970s, theologians such as John B. Cobb Jr., H. Paul Santmire, and Joseph Sittler began to call attention to the urgency and seriousness of the environmental crisis.[41] In the 1980s, as new information about the dangers of ozone depletion, global warming, acid rain, deforestation, land and water pollution, and population growth produced a broader cultural awareness of the seriousness of the ecological crisis, numerous theologians joined Cobb, Santmire, and Sittler in seeking to rethink Christianity's theology of nature. This movement has generated a substantial ecotheological literature in recent years. Theologians such as Santmire, Dieter Hessel, Elizabeth Dodson Gray, George S. Hendry, and Jong-Sun Noh have described the nature-harming consequences of Christianity's typical insensitivity to nonhuman nature.[42] Ethical and political aspects of ecotheology have been developed by Gibson Winter, Wesley Granberg-Michaelson, Holmes Rolston III, Tom Regan, Carol Adams, and Larry Rasmussen. On a more popular level, Matthew Fox and Thomas Berry have developed creationist spiritualities that blend feminist, ecojustice, mystical, process, and traditional Christian themes.[43] Theologians such as Cobb, Santmire,

---

40. Wendell Berry, "Christianity and the Survival of Creation," *Cross Currents* 43 (Summer 1993), pp. 153, 162.

41. Cf. John B. Cobb, Jr., *Is It Too Late? A Theology of Ecology* (Beverly Hills, Calif.: Bruce Books, 1972); H. Paul Santmire, *Brother Earth: Nature, God, and Ecology in a Time of Crisis* (New York: Thomas Nelson, 1970); Joseph Sittler, *Essays on Nature and Grace* (Philadelphia: Fortress Press, 1972).

42. Cf. H. Paul Santmire, *The Travail of Nature: The Ambiguous Ecological Promise of Christian Theology* (Philadelphia: Fortress Press, 1985); Dieter T. Hessel, *For Creation's Sake: Preaching, Ecology, and Justice* (Philadelphia: Westminster/Geneva, 1985); Elizabeth Dodson-Gray, *Green Paradise Lost* (Wellesley, Mass.: Roundtable Press, 1981); George S. Hendry, *Theology of Nature* (Philadelphia: Westminster Press, 1980); Jong-Sun Noh, "The Effects on Korea of Un-Ecological Theology," in *Liberating Life: Contemporary Approaches to Ecological Theology*, ed. Charles Birch, William Eakin, and Jay B. McDaniel (Maryknoll, N.Y.: Orbis Books, 1990), 125–36.

43. Cf. Gibson Winter, *Liberating Creation: Foundations of Religious Social Ethics* (New York: Crossroad, 1981); Wesley Granberg-Michaelson, ed., *Tending the Garden: Essays on the Gospel and the Earth* (Grand Rapids: Eerdmans, 1987); Holmes Rolston III, *Environmental Ethics: Duties to and Values in the Natural World* (Philadelphia: Temple University Press, 1988); Tom Regan, *The Case for Animal Rights* (Berkeley: University of California Press, 1983); Larry Rasmussen, "Returning to Our Senses: The Theology of the Cross as a Theology for Eco-Justice," in *After Nature's Revolt: Eco-Justice and Theology*, ed. Dieter T. Hessel (Minneapolis: Fortress Press, 1992), 40–56; Carol J. Adams, *The Sexual Politics of Meat: A Feminist-Vegetarian Critical Theory* (New York: Continuum, 1991); Matthew Fox, *Original Blessing: A Primer in Creation Spirituality* (Santa Fe: Bear and Company, 1983); Fox, *The Coming of the Cosmic Christ* (San Francisco: Harper & Row, 1988); Fox, *Creation Spirituality: Liberating Gifts for the*

Sittler, Jürgen Moltmann, Jay McDaniel, and Douglas John Hall have sought to rethink the Christian doctrines of creation, stewardship, justice, and divine reality in light of the ecological crisis.[44] Important theological attempts to blend feminist and ecological perspectives have been offered by Ruether, Gray, and Sallie McFague.

McFague's writings have been especially influential in making the case for a heuristic ecofeminist theology that moves beyond traditional images and concepts of divine reality. She argues that a Christian theology informed by feminist, ecojustice, and peace concerns must displace the traditional Christian language of kingship and domination with alternative models of divine reality, especially those of mother, lover, and friend. "I am not suggesting that there are some sacred, permanent metaphors that can replace the royalist, triumphalist model," she explains, "but there may be a place to look for metaphors that goes even deeper than the political arena, from which most long-term models of the God-world relationship in the West have come." While politically grounded theologies are generally concerned with how to govern human life, a deeper theology would ask how human beings are able to live. Her images for expressing the human experience of love, including divine love, are drawn from the loving relationships of parent to child, lover to beloved, and friend to friend.[45] Her theology emphasizes God's indwelling immanence in the world without claiming that God's body is limited to the world. "God is not a solitary deity distant from and unrelated to the world, nor a God submerged into the world and undifferentiated from it," she explains. "Rather, God as mother, lover and friend of the world as God's body is both transcendent to the world (even as we are transcendent to our bodies) and profoundly immanent in the world (even as we are at one with our bodies)."[46]

At one level, the purpose of McFague's theology is to balance Christianity's transcendent monarchical models of divine reality with relational-immanental models, but the deeper purpose of her work is to develop a way of conceiving

---

Peoples of the Earth (San Francisco: Harper, 1990); Thomas Berry, *The Dream of the Earth* (San Francisco: Sierra Club Books, 1988).

44. Cf. Jürgen Moltmann, *God in Creation: A New Theology of Creation and the Spirit of God,* trans. Margaret Kohl (San Francisco: Harper & Row, 1985); Philip Hefner, "Nature's History as Our History: A Proposal for Spirituality," in *After Nature's Revolt,* ed. Dieter T. Hessel, 171–83; Jay McDaniel, *Of God and Pelicans: Theology of Reverence for Life* (Louisville: Westminster/John Knox Press, 1989); Douglas John Hall, *Imaging God: Dominion as Stewardship* (Grand Rapids: Eerdmans, 1986); Hall, *The Steward: A Biblical Symbol Comes of Age* (Grand Rapids: Eerdmans, 1990).

45. Sallie McFague, *Models of God: Theology for an Ecological, Nuclear Age* (Philadelphia: Fortress Press, 1987), 80–81, 91.

46. Ibid., 183.

God's transcendence in an immanental mode. Near the end of *Models of God,* she refers to the world as "our meeting place with God," noting that in this conception of the world, God's immanence is "universal" and God's transcendence is "worldly." If we see the world as God's body, she argues, then we will begin to apprehend the world as sacred space and movement: "God's immanence, then, being universal, undergirds a sensibility that is open to the world, both to other people and to other forms of life, as the way one meets God."[47]

In her subsequent major work, *The Body of God,* McFague elaborates what it means to perceive and confess that the world is our meeting place with God. Ecotheology is more deeply transformative than either political or psychological theologies, she contends, because its immanental organicist worldview revolutionizes the self-world and God-world dualities that Christian theism has traditionally presupposed. Her own ecofeminist theology rejects the God-world, self-world, nature-history, and male-female dualisms on which an alienated Christianity based its denigration of the natural world and the female sex.[48] It further rejects the anthropocentric assumption that only human beings are intrinsically valuable, while giving to human beings a new moral-religious vocation. "We have been *decentered* as the point and goal of creation and *recentered* as God's partners in helping creation to grow and prosper in our tiny part of God's body. A new place and vocation have been given to us," McFague declares. Christianity cannot save the world, she allows, but Christians have special contributions to make to God's world-body. As an incarnational religion, Christianity offers a theology of embodiment in which divine reality is constitutive of all being. "Christianity can also offer to the planetary agenda its vision of the liberation, healing, and inclusion of the oppressed, and in our day that must include vulnerable nature," she concludes. "Radical embodiment and radical inclusion of the outcast—these are not the only signs of the new creation, but they are essential ones."[49]

Just as feminist criticism demands deeper changes in religious consciousness and practice than the adoption of inclusive nonsexist language, so does the reality of the world's environmental crisis require theologians to move beyond traditional Christian appeals to the morality of good stewardship. Moltmann thus reconceives God as a nurturing Sanctifier who feels with and indwells all things, while bringing creation to its final Sabbath rest. Sittler emphasizes the Christian vision of the ever-gracious universal *Pantokrator* or redeeming Cosmic Christ. McFague appeals to the transformative power of imaging the world as God's body. Building

---

47. Ibid., 185.
48. Sallie McFague, *The Body of God: An Ecological Theology* (Minneapolis: Fortress Press, 1993), 65.
49. Ibid., 197–98, 207.

upon his earlier work in process theology, Cobb envisions God as an indwelling Creator Spirit who bestows value on all things and lures creation forward in its evolution. In language close to Cobb's, Ruether calls for an ecological spirituality that recognizes "the transcience of selves, the living interdependency of all things, and the value of the personal in communion."[50] The "living interdependency of all things" implies for her and for Cobb that divine reality is affected and shaped by all of the world's choices, goodness, evil, pain, and joy.

Ruether is not as committed to the language or metaphysics of process theology as Cobb, but her vision of the all-embracing interdependency of life draws upon the tradition of "dipolar theism" developed by Alfred North White-head, Charles Hartshorne, Bernard Meland, and Cobb.[51] Process theology distinguishes between the "primordial" and "consequent" natures of God, defining God's primordial nature as the total potentiality of all existing entities at all moments of their actualization. For each entity, the most life-enhancing option or choice is always made possible by its participation in God's primordial nature. Because each entity has its own subjectivity, however, it possesses the power to adapt to, actualize, or negate the life-enhancing aim of God's primordial nature. The gift of divine freedom makes it possible for subjective selves to choose evil. The God of process theology lures its subjects to make healthy, other-regarding, life-giving choices, always creating new possibilities to choose life, but the choice itself is never coerced. In process theology, the actualizations of the particular choices that *are* made are taken into the being of God. This processive divine reality-being is what process theology calls God's consequent nature. As Ruether explains, "The reality of God is thus shaped through interrelation with self-actualizing entities. God not only lures and offers new life, but also suffers, experiencing the pain of destructive choices as well as the pleasure of good choices."[52] For Cobb, this Whiteheadian vision provides not only the most compelling account of the origins and unity of consciousness but also the powerful and healing religious alternative to nature-harming, monarchical theisms.

Ruether appropriates much of this religious vision without investing any particular significance in its metaphysical categories. In the spirit of process theology, she accepts ecofeminist critiques of classical theism while rejecting

---

50. Rosemary Radford Ruether, *Gaia & God: An Ecofeminist Theology of Earth Healing* (San Francisco: HarperSanFrancisco, 1992), 251.

51. Cf. Alfred North Whitehead, *Process and Reality: An Essay in Cosmology* (New York: Free Press, 1978, c1929); Charles Hartshorne, *The Logic of Perfection: And Other Essays in Neoclassical Metaphysics* (LaSalle, Ill.: Open Court, 1962); John B. Cobb, Jr., and David Ray Griffin, *Process Theology: An Introductory Exposition* (Philadelphia: Westminster Press, 1976).

52. Ruether, *Gaia & God,* 246. Cf. Marjorie Suchocki, *God-Christ-Church: A Practical Guide to Process Theology* (New York: Crossroads, 1989).

the kind of ecofeminism that merely replaces a monotheistic, transcendent, male-identified, dominating faith with a religion that is multicentered, immanent, female-identified, and relational. "We need a more imaginative solution to these traditional oppositions than simply their reversal, something more like Nicholas of Cusa's paradoxical 'coincidence of opposites,' in which the 'absolute maximum' and the 'absolute minimum' are the same," she argues. Ruether notes that in modern physics the classical distinction between matter and energy has disappeared at the subatomic level; matter is conceived as energy moving in defined patterns of relationality:

> At the level of the "absolute minimum," the appearance of physical "stuff" disappears into a voidlike web of relationships, relationships in which the whole universe is finally interconnected and in which the observer also stands as part of the process. As we move below the "absolute minimum" of the tiniest particles into the dancing void of energy patterns that build up the "appearance" of solid objects on the macroscopic level, we also recognize that this is also the "absolute maximum," the matrix of all interconnections of the whole universe. This matrix of dancing energy operates with a "rationality," predictable patterns that result in a fixed number of possibilities. Thus what we have called "God," the "mind," or rational pattern holding all things together, and what we have called "matter," the "ground" of physical objects, come together. The disintegration of the many into infinitely small "bits," and the One, or unifying whole that connects all things together, coincide.[53]

Ecological theology connects the meaning of human living to these absolutely minimal and maximal worlds, "standing between the dancing void of energy" that underlies the atomic structure of all entities in the universe. To seek religious meaning in a possibly meaningless world, Ruether argues, is to commune with the universe as heart to heart, or between I and Thou. Human beings are connected to all living creatures past, present, and future through matter and consciousness and are thus linked to Gaia, the living and sacred earth-organism. To bear compassion for all living things is to break down the illusion of otherness with the power of spirit. Ruether writes:

> At this moment we can encounter the matrix of energy of the universe that sustains the dissolution and recomposition of matter as also a heart that knows us even as we are known. Is there also a consciousness that remembers and envisions and reconciles all things, as the process theologians believe? Surely, if we are kin to all things and offspring of the universe, then what has flowered in us as consciousness must also be reflected in that universe as well, in the ongoing creative Matrix of the whole.[54]

Ecotheologians thus call for new hymns and liturgies that awaken in human hearts an awareness of the deep kinship between humanity and the natural world.

---

53. Ruether, *Gaia & God,* 247–49.
54. Ibid., 252–53.

They argue not only for new ways of organizing the world, but new ways of perceiving the world and God.

Most ecotheologians caution that this does not mean that the imperative to organize the world differently is diminished. It is self-defeating to embrace McFague's claim about the transpolitical character of ecotheology in a way that undermines or diminishes the political struggle for justice. Berry's call for an ecological economics drives home the essential truism. If modern Christianity is to become part of the solution to the environmental crisis, it must show that there are alternatives to an economic order that is destroying creation. Though McFague's writings generally avoid the problems of oppression and maldistributed economic power, most of the movement's major theologians—especially Cobb, Ruether, and Moltmann—keep the struggle for economic alternatives at the center of ecotheological concern. Though he came rather late to this endeavor, it is Cobb who has made the most sustained effort to assess the problems of ecological economics.

John B. Cobb Jr. and Third-Way Economics

Having devoted his early career to process theology, Cobb was converted to environmentalism in 1969 by reading Paul Ehrlich's environmentalist potboiler, *The Population Bomb*. As he partially perceived even at the time, the book was alarmist and exaggerated. It used simplistic statistical arguments and projections to warn that the earth's growing population was rapidly outstripping its resource capacity to sustain life. Cobb recognized that the book's rhetoric and methodology were somewhat misleading, but he could not dismiss Ehrlich's fundamental argument that accelerating population and consumption pressures were feeding on each other and eroding the planet's natural resource carrying capacity. The book's Malthusian picture of an increasingly overburdened life system struck Cobb "with almost unbearable force" and converted him to environmentalism.[55]

It seemed to Cobb at the time that only a "new Christianity" could marshal the requisite spiritual forces to oppose the unsustainable exploitation of the world's natural resources. *Is It Too Late?* (1970) argued that neither classical Western theism nor any of the Eastern religions could provide the organic, ecological, politically activist faith that was needed to address the environmental crisis. In his view, process thought was uniquely suited to provide a nondualistic grounding

---

55. Cf. Paul Ehrlich, *The Population Bomb* (New York: Ballantine Books, 1968); cf. Ehrlich and A. H. Ehrlich, *On the Extinction of Species* (New York: Random House, 1981).

for religious concern and political engagement.[56] Christian process theology retains the Christian insistence on the linkage between personal spirituality and social ethics that Eastern religions lack. At the same time, process theology rejects the dualisms of history-nature, mind-matter, and God-world that ground traditional Christianity's nature-harming theism. At the heart of process theology is not a static concept of hypostatized being or Being Itself, but the assumption that dynamic process is more fundamental than being. Process theology conceives all reality, including divine reality, as interactive and dynamic. It offers a religious alternative to the hierarchical Christian conception of reality in which God stands at the apex of a pyramid that includes, in descending order, men, women, children, animals, plants, and minerals. Process theology offers an alternative to power-over theisms that sanction humanity's domination and unsustainable exploitation of the natural world. Cobb's important work *The Liberation of Life* (1981)—coauthored with biologist Charles Birch—elaborated these arguments with particular reference to issues in ethical theory and biology. "If the Spirit is the true Life within us, then God is that Life," the authors declared. "Somehow, somewhere, we trust Life will triumph even if life disappears from this planet. But much, of greatest value, that could have been will then never be. The human calling is to respond to Life here and now so that life on this planet may be liberated from the forces of death that now threaten it."[57]

The Liberation of Life concluded its extensive discussions of biological evolution, animal rights, biological engineering, and theology with a brief discussion of environmental economics. Drawing upon Herman Daly's pioneering work in "steady state" economic theory, Cobb and Birch made a plea for a "third way" economic strategy that rejected the pro-growth ideologies of the dominant socialist and market strategies. They called for sustainable strategies that were ecologically "capable of indefinite existence"—that is, capable of persisting for several hundred years.[58] Daly's vision of a just and ecologically sustainable economy gave ballast to their hope that a third way was attainable. Cobb and Birch noted that Daly's steady-state economy was not static; it presupposed a dynamic, ever-changing process of development. Moreover, they acknowledged that not all growth should be opposed; in much of the Third World, they allowed, production needed to be doubled "probably more than once" to attain decent

---

56. For Cobb's account of his conversion to environmentalism, see John B. Cobb, Jr., *Sustainability: Economics, Ecology, and Justice* (Maryknoll, N.Y.: Orbis Books, 1992), 1–3; and Cobb, "A Critical View of Inherited Theology," in *Theologians in Transition: The Christian Century "How My Mind Has Changed" Series*, ed. James M. Wall (New York: Crossroad, 1981), 74–81.

57. Charles Birch and John B. Cobb, Jr., *The Liberation of Life: From the Cell to the Community* (Cambridge: Cambridge University Press, 1981), 200–202.

58. Ibid., 239–40.

standards of living. Their hope was that Third World countries might pursue "a different sort of growth from that which the rich world has pursued," principally by shunning unsustainable technologies and by avoiding export-oriented strategies that made poor nations dependent upon the global market.

The Liberation of Life was longer on hope than hard economic analysis, however. The authors admitted that the religion of Life needed a more thoroughly elaborated economic perspective. Their call for a just and sustainable economics was based not so much upon a developed alternative as upon their utter certainty that some alternative was imperative. "From the perspective of the religion of Life it is obvious that the ideology of growth misunderstands the true nature of growth and aims at a monstrosity that will destroy life," they declared. The question was not whether human beings would find a sustainable alternative, but how they would find it. "It is not whether they reduce their consumption of oil. They will. It is not whether the use of oceanic fisheries and whales be limited. It will. It is not whether the existing manufacturing industry give way to something else. It will."[59] The question was whether societies would reach these limits through a catastrophe or sustainable transition. Cobb searched for hopeful signs that a sustainable transition could be made with minimal suffering and cultural upheaval. He emphasized that ecology was a multicentered, all-embracing social, ethical, political, religious, scientific, and economic cause. He warned that the environmental movement would make little progress, however, if it did not engender fundamental changes in the way that economic progress is typically conceived and pursued. Any serious attempt to address the world's ecological crisis has to privilege the economic question.

How should theologians view economic progress? Cobb's response to this question begins by ruling out the kind of neoliberal-capitalist model that neoconservatives such as Michael Novak and Peter Berger endorse, in which progress is equated with growth in gross national product and accumulation. Neoconservative theologians such as Stackhouse and McCann similarly assume that the purpose of economic activity is to maximize production and accumulation. Stackhouse and McCann's "Postcommunist Manifesto" asserts as a self-evident maxim that "creating wealth is the whole point of economic activity." If Christian ethics is to face up to this truism, they instruct, it will have to concern itself with the problems of "how to form corporations and manage them, how to find markets, how to develop technology, how to work with employees, and how to make profits for the common good." For Stackhouse and McCann, any Christian ethic that seeks to be relevant to the modern or postmodern world must therefore "labor in the vineyards of the world—even when the vineyards reach around the globe in new patterns of corporate capitalism." To face up to modernity is

59. Ibid., 253–64.

to accept and embrace the global capitalist system that modern transnational corporations are creating. Should American Christians finally learn how to appreciate the work of these corporations, the authors urge, they might "even learn to love them as we have learned to love our churches, neighborhoods, nations, schools and hospitals."[60]

But to Cobb, this prescription is exactly the problem. Instead of critiquing a dominant corporate capitalist order in which nature and social needs are subordinated to economic power, he observes, Stackhouse and McCann "simply accept that economy and the theoretical structure that justifies it." They repeat the neoclassical dogma that the purpose of economic activity is to maximize wealth, as though Christian ethics had nothing to say on the subject. In neoclassical theory, the purpose of economic activity is not to build sustainable communities but to acquire as many goods as possible for as little labor as possible. Whatever else may be said about this viewpoint, Cobb observes, it is not Christian anthropology or ethics. Neoclassical theory further assumes that capital is a nearly perfect substitute for land, in which "land" denotes the entire physical world. "But surely this is not the Christian doctrine of creation," Cobb remarks.[61]

Having swallowed neoclassical economic theory as a description of the way the world works, Stackhouse and McCann conclude that maximizing economic growth is a precondition for any realistic politics of the common good. They accept the neoclassical picture of the economy as an isolated system through which exchange value circulates between firms and households. They accept the neoclassical equation of economic progress with product growth. While lamenting that America is addicted to debt, dependent on foreign oil, and faced with "the peril of ecological disaster," they ignore the debt-driven, dependency-breeding, nature-harming character of the global capitalist system itself. In their view, a more efficient and morally sensitive capitalism will rectify the problems that corporate capitalism has created.

Cobb disputes their assumptions and conclusions. The environmental ravages of modern industrialism will not be solved by administering larger doses of the same medicine that created them, he argues. Though it is crucial to achieve sustainable economic welfare for all people, sustainable welfare is not achieved by maximizing general production because unlimited-growth strategies invariably create environmental problems that outstrip economic gains. In Cobb's view, it is better to promote sustainable economies that protect the environment than to finance environmental "repair" from the surplus earnings of nature-harming

---

60. Stackhouse and McCann, "A Postcommunist Manifesto," 46–47.

61. John B. Cobb, Jr., "Sustainable Community," *Christian Century* 108 (January 23, 1991), 81.

strategies. "Community is served far better by retaining community control over the economy than by first destroying community—as by factory closings—and then responding to the resulting social disruptions with special programs paid for by the extra product generated by the closings," he contends.[62]

The difference between general product growth and actual economic improvement is crucial to this argument. Unfortunately, the former concept is easily quantified, while the latter notion must isolate and measure particular factors of natural well-being that are impossible to quantify with certainty. Though the project is therefore inherently problematic, Cobb argues convincingly that some measure of sustainable economic welfare is necessary if economic policymakers are to distinguish between constructive and harmful growth. Working with Daly and Clifford Cobb, and drawing upon studies by Xenophon Zolotas, A. Myrick Freeman, and other economists, Cobb has therefore devised a highly complex index of national economic and social health. According to the calculations that Daly and the Cobbs have made, in the past twenty years American per capita gross national product has doubled while American sustainable economic welfare has made no improvement. Moreover, the trend in overall sustainable welfare since the late 1970s is downward. "Economic welfare has been deteriorating for a decade, largely as a result of growing income inequality, the exhaustion of resources, and the failure to invest adequately to sustain the economy in the future," the authors observe. Though each of these factors may be attacked separately, they are deeply interconnected. Cobb and Daly warn that the diminishing returns of oil extraction and the ripple effects of rising energy costs upon investment and worker productivity are particularly significant. "Reductions in the amount of energy and capital available per worker will lead to a long-term decline in worker productivity, though improved management may be able to counter that trend for short periods," they conclude. "As increasing competition lowers the returns to labor, and as returns to scarce capital increase, the income gap is likely to worsen if actions are not taken to improve equality."[63]

The trends are clear enough, with or without the particular numbers presented by the Cobb-Daly index of sustainable welfare. The global economy is rapidly generating massive levels of debt, structural dependency, accelerated inequality, and unsustainable environmental destruction. To continue to expand the globally integrated economy without regard for the social and environmental ravages of indiscriminating growth is to invite disaster:

> The whole world has become more and more dependent on a complex system administered by multinational finance and dependent on diminishing resources

---

62. Ibid., 81–82.

63. Herman E. Daly and John B. Cobb, Jr., with contributions by Clifford W. Cobb, *For the Common Good: Redirecting the Economy toward Community, the Environment, and a Sustainable Future* (Boston: Beacon Press, 1989), 401–55, quote on 455.

of energy whose use is environmentally destructive. Fewer and fewer communities will be able to participate in making the decisions that are determining their well-being, since more and more will be dependent on decisions made by those who control capital investments and whose professional commitment is maximization of profit, not well-being.[64]

As with the problem of economic justice, the problem of environmental destruction thus ultimately leads to the question of who controls the process of investment. Cobb's ecotheology opposes the increasing concentration of economic power in the hands of corporate multinational elites. It promotes worker ownership and greater democratic control over enterprise management, while rejecting the preoccupation with economic growth fostered by capitalism. Cobb asserts:

> As long as we collectively suppose that meeting economic needs and having full employment require a growing economy, we will collectively support policies that put greater and greater pressure on an already over-stressed environment. We will also continue to support policies whose results are greater and greater injustice, with the rich getting richer and the poor getting poorer both within each country and among the world's nations.[65]

Ecotheology thus refuses to accept that there is no third way between the statist and neoliberal models of economic development. Neoliberal strategies seek to overcome poverty by integrating poor nations, with minimal state economic planning, into the export-driven capitalist global market. To most neoconservatives, neoliberal strategies define what it means in the economic realm to face up to modernity.[66] Cobb curiously fails to challenge this claim to realism, but the irony of the neoliberal claim—even by capitalist definitions of realism and success—is important to note because this strategy has yet to yield a single example of successful economic modernization in the Two-Thirds World. The only poor countries to have entered the global market and economically "succeeded" thus far—in conventional economic terms—are east Asian nations characterized by high degrees of state economic planning and, for the most part, by repressive political regimes. Nations such as South Korea and Taiwan have achieved significant economic success through government-dominated forms of calculated economic dependence and, not insignificantly, through outright po-

---

64. Cobb, "Sustainable Community," 81–82.
65. Cobb, *Sustainability*, 5.
66. Cf. P. T. Bauer, *Equality, the Third World, and Economic Delusion* (Cambridge, Mass.: Harvard University Press, 1981); Lawrence E. Harrison, *Underdevelopment Is a State of Mind: The Latin American Case* (Lanham, Md.: Madison Books, 1985); W. W. Rostow, *The Stages of Economic Growth: A Non-Communist Manifesto* (Cambridge: Cambridge University Press, 1960); Michael Novak, *This Hemisphere of Liberty: A Philosophy of the Americas* (Washington, D.C.: American Enterprise Institute, 1990).

litical oppression. If the question is how to maximize export-oriented economic productivity, there is considerable evidence that east Asian state capitalism has a great deal to teach neoliberal theorists, World Bank economists, and American neoconservatives about what it means to face up to modernity.[67]

But ecological ethics poses a different question, asking what kind of economic development is sustainable over the long term. In the showcase examples of South Korea and Taiwan, this question is becoming unavoidably pertinent. Four decades of hyperindustrialization featuring heavy pesticide use and largely unregulated waste dumping have produced very high levels of agricultural contamination and air and water pollution in both countries, as well as elsewhere in east Asia. The agricultural and environmental ravages of South Korean and Taiwanese development increasingly present wrenching dilemmas for policymakers in both countries, who must continue to expand product growth or risk a debt-creating downturn that could trigger an economic collapse.[68] The notion that east Asian capitalism offers a replicable model for Two-Thirds World development assumes that the world economy can absorb and reward an ever-increasing number of export-oriented national economies and that the world's ecosystem can tolerate many Taiwans. Both assumptions fail the test of realism.

In the name of environmental realism, Cobb insists that third-way alternatives to the dominant neoliberal and statist strategies must be created. Both of the dominant strategies destroy community, neither supports family farming, and both create highly concentrated forms of economic power that disempower workers and communities. By contrast, he observes, "Family farming is a third way in agriculture over against collectives and agribusiness. Worker ownership or management of factories is a third way over against government or capitalist ownership and management. Import-substitution development differs from export-driven development without involving more bureaucratic control."[69] In the struggle to create third-way alternatives to environmental disaster, Cobb contends that Niebuhrian realism provides pragmatically indispensable, if ultimately insufficient, guidance.

67. Cf. Alice H. Amsden, "Third World Industrialization: 'Global Fordism' or a New Model?" *New Left Review* 182 (July/August 1990); Jung-en Woo, *Race to the Swift: State and Finance in Korean Industrialization* (New York: Columbia University Press, 1991); Peter A. Petri, "Korea's Export Niche: Origins and Prospects," *World Development* (January 1988), 47–68; Brian Kelly and Mark London, *The Four Little Dragons* (New York: Simon & Schuster, 1989).

68. Cf. Walden Bello and Stephanie Rosenfeld, "Dragons in Distress: The Crisis of the NICs," *World Policy Journal* 7 (Summer 1990), 443–47; Hla Myint, *Southeast Asia's Economy: Development Policies in the 1970s* (New York: Praeger, 1972), 58–72.

69. John B. Cobb, Jr., "Is There No Third Way?" *Christian Century* (January 27, 1993), 92.

"Niebuhr knew that the quest for justice in human affairs would not be consummated by the achievement of a just society," he explains. "There is no assurance that any amount of effort will lead to a society that is better than our own, and, even if it does, there is no assurance that the improvement will last."[70] The struggle for a better society can never attain more than highly limited victories, which are immediately contested and which inevitably create new forms of social evil. Moreover, moral suasion has quite limited force in the struggle to achieve even such limited gains as are attainable. Any Christian ethic that takes the environmental crisis seriously must enter the world of power politics, where competing group interests vie for power and other social goods. Christian environmentalists must learn these lessons from Niebuhrian realism, Cobb argues, if they are to make an impact on a society that is addicted to economic growth. The Niebuhrian ethic of limits and power politics is an indispensable resource to any Christian environmentalism that seriously seeks to change the system. At the same time, Niebuhrian realism is too self-limiting to provide the transformative social vision that is needed. "Since it accepts the existing structures of power, and since these structures are part of the total world system that moves toward catastrophe, Christian realism alone is not an adequate Christian response," Cobb contends. "It would be unfortunate if Christians became so immersed in a 'realistic' involvement in existing institutions that they could not respond creatively to the opportunity that may be offered to build different ones."[71]

The different economic vision that is needed would begin with the radical and commonsense maxim that there is such a thing as having enough. As Herman Daly remarks, "Once we have replaced the basic premise of 'more is better' with the much sounder axiom that 'enough is best,' the social and technical problems of moving to a steady state become solvable, perhaps even trivial. But *unless* the underlying growth paradigm and its supporting values are altered, all the technical prowess and manipulative cleverness in the world will not solve our problems and, in fact, will make them worse."[72] Long before Cobb turned to environmentalism, Daly was warning about the harmful consequences of "crackpot rigor" in the economics profession. He recalls that economics was once a branch of moral philosophy, but in the past century, economists have turned their discipline into a successful academic science by developing abstruse mathematical models "erected higher and higher above the shallow concrete foundation of fact." Modern economic theory thus avoids the moral aspects of economic behavior while it routinely analyzes even simple market activities in

---

70. Cobb, *Sustainability,* 11.
71. Ibid., 13.
72. Herman E. Daly, *Steady-State Economics,* ed. 2 (Washington, D.C.: Island Press, 1991, c1977), 2.

terms of Lagrangian multipliers and the calculus of variations. Daly charges that
this preoccupation with mathematizing their discipline at ever-higher levels of
abstraction is preventing mainstream economists from addressing society's interconnected moral, political, and economic problems. "The recognition that
there are problems of political economy that have no technical solution but do
have a moral solution goes very much against the grain of modern economic
theory," he observes. But the most pressing questions in political economy are
fundamentally moral. Economics is the last discipline that should seek to be
value-free, Daly argues. Throughout the 1970s and 1980s, he urged that until
economics returns to its moral and biophysical foundations, it will not help to
solve the environmental problems caused by the capitalist devotion to unlimited
growth.[73]

His classic work, *Steady-State Economics* (1977) developed his conception
of a dynamic equilibrium or steady-state economy, which Daly defined as "an
economy with constant stocks of people and artifacts, maintained at some desired
sufficient levels by low rates of maintenance 'throughput,' that is, by the lowest
feasible flows of matter and energy from the first stage of production (depletion
of low-entropy materials from the environment) to the last stage of consumption
(pollution of the environment with high-entropy wastes and exotic materials)."[74]
This normative conception is distinctive for its insistence on the physical nature
of the economy. If the economy is physical, Daly noted, it cannot grow forever.
Yet mainstream neoclassical economics pushes for unlimited growth as though
the earth has no limits. In the second edition of *Steady-State Economics* (1991),
Daly offers a homely metaphor to drive home the point. Neoclassical theory
regards economic activity as a circular flow of exchange value, while steady-
state theory defines economic activity as a linear throughput of matter-energy.
Mainstream economics thus ignores the heart of steady-state theory, Daly claims,
but without any recognition of the biophysical dimensions of economic activity,
it is impossible to relate the economy to the environment. As he explains:

> It is as if biology tried to understand animals only in terms of their circulatory
> system, with no recognition of the fact that they also have digestive tracts. The
> metabolic flow is not circular. The digestive tract firmly ties the animal to its
> environment at both ends. Without digestive tracts, animals would be self-
> contained perpetual motion machines. Likewise for an economy without an
> entropic throughput.[75]

The economic throughput consists primarily of the dimensions of scale and
allocation. But to find an optimal scale, Daly notes, ecological criteria are needed;

---

73. Ibid., 2–4.
74. Ibid., 17.
75. Ibid., 241.

to find an optimal distribution, moral criteria are needed. The market will not solve either problem in a way that is just or sustainable. For Daly, the question of scale is the deeper problem. He allows that under ideal conditions the market will produce a Pareto-optimal allocation for every scale. But even if ideal conditions could be attained and the market's allocation proved to be morally justifiable, the problem of scale would still overwhelm this (stupendously unlikely) achievement. An overloaded boat sinks even if the weight is optimally allocated, Daly observes. If the economic scale does not stay within the planet's ecological carrying capacity, the planet's life will die regardless of how well it has allocated its resources. "Economics has tried to reduce scale issues to matters of allocation (just get the prices right) and has thereby greatly obscured the relation between the economy and the environment," Daly remarks. "While an optimal allocation can result from the individualistic marketplace, the attainment of an optimal scale will require collective action by the community." He proposes that much confusion could be avoided if economists agreed to make "growth" refer only to the quantitative scale of the economy's physical dimensions while making "development" refer only to qualitative improvements. In this sense, he explains, steady-state economics promotes development without growth, just as the planet develops without growing. "Growth of the economic organism means larger jaws and a bigger digestive tract," he notes. "Development means more compete digestion and wiser purposes. Limits to growth do not imply limits to development."[76]

His claim that mainstream economics ignores environmental throughput issues is exaggerated. Economists have compiled a substantial literature on the economics of environmental destruction, waste, and protection. The telling fact about this rapidly expanding body of literature, however—as Daly observes— is that it has no place in the governing model of modern economic theory. Because neoclassical theory is based on a mechanistic diagram that charts the circular flow of exchange value, it can account for environmental costs only on the side, in a special category off the diagram called "externalities." In their major collaborative effort, *For the Common Good,* Daly and Cobb remark upon the function of this category in modern economic theory. "Whenever the abstracted-from elements of reality become too insistently evident in our experience, their existence is admitted by the category 'externality,' " they observe. "Externalities are ad hoc corrections introduced as needed to save appearances, like the epicycles of Ptolemaic astronomy." To call some theoretically unaccounted-for factor an "externality" is to acknowledge its existence without allowing it to challenge the operative neoclassical paradigm. Daly and Cobb allow that this is a reasonable way to dispose of minor issues and details. "But when vital issues (e.g., the

---

76. Ibid., 242–43.

capacity of the earth to support life) have to be classed as externalities, it is time to restructure basic concepts and start with a different set of abstractions that can embrace what was previously external," they declare.[77]

For the Common Good calls for an economics that places "externalities" such as carrying capacity at the center of attention. Much of the book repeats Daly's arguments against the mechanistic epistemology of neoclassical economics, the "misplaced concreteness" of much highly mathematized economic reasoning, and the illusions of unlimited-growth ideology. Citing a passage from Cobb's favorite philosopher, Daly argues that the Whiteheadian notion of misplaced concreteness aptly describes the central fault of modern economics. Because they fail to acknowledge the limitations of their abstract mathematical models, Daly argues, economists repeatedly draw unwarranted conclusions about concrete reality from their mathematical theories.[78] *For the Common Good* gives extensive attention to the problem, showing how standard economic reasoning routinely overlooks the importance of the natural environment and presents skewed understandings of the market, economic success, and human nature.[79]

Though Daly and Cobb differ somewhat on the utility of the phrase "sustainable development," they agree on the essential operational principles of sustainability. On the macro level, sustainability requires limits on human population that correlate with the earth's carrying capacity. "Sustainable development must deal with sufficiency as well as efficiency, and cannot avoid limiting scale," Daly remarks. In translating this macro principle to the micro level, three basic principles are pertinent. The first is that technological programs should increase efficiency rather than throughput. This objective requires limitations in the scale of resource throughput and, by implication, serious efforts to redistribute wealth and attain distributive social justice. The second principle concerns the development of nonrenewable resources. Daly argues that renewable resources should be exploited on a profit-maximizing, sustained-yield basis under which harvest rates do not exceed regeneration rates and waste emissions do not exceed the environment's renewable assimilation capacity. The third principle, concerning nonrenewable resources, allows that nonrenewable resources may be exploited, but only at a rate equal to the creation of renewable substitutes.[80]

Sustainable development thus requires national and international political policies that promote population control, a more just redistribution of wealth, and living on income. It calls policymakers to relinquish the cornucopian myth

77. Daly and Cobb, *For the Common Good*, 37.
78. Ibid., 36. See Daly's essay "A. N. Whitehead's Fallacy of Misplaced Concreteness: Examples from Economics," in *Steady-State Economics*, 280–87.
79. Daly and Cobb, *For the Common Good*, 44–117.
80. Daly, *Steady-State Economics*, 255–56.

of unlimited growth and face up to the limits on economic development imposed by a finite ecosystem. Daly muses that the vagueness of the phrase "sustainable development" has at least engendered substantial agreement "that it is both morally and economically wrong to treat the world as a business in liquidation," but Cobb is skeptical that "development" can acquire an ecological meaning. He insists that if the phrase is to be taken away from opportunists and reclaimed by serious environmentalists, it must be refashioned as a basically self-sufficient strategy called "sustainable community development."[81]

"The basic requirement is self-sufficiency," he asserts, arguing that all countries should make food self-sufficiency their top national priority on national and regional levels.[82] "It is my belief that people who feed themselves can begin the process of sustainable development from below," Cobb explains. "There is an appropriate technology that they can construct and employ to increase their productivity without long-term dependence on outside expertise." This appropriate technology would depend on solar energy instead of oil and would generate reinvestable economic surpluses without sacrificing subsistence. It would not sustain the privileges of current elites, "but it can support a tolerable life and a measure of hope for the vast majority."[83] Sustainable community development recovers a premodern moral perspective on development inasmuch as it returns to the premodern view that the economy should serve community needs.[84]

Cobb further contends that the essential precondition for genuine free trade can be attained only by countries that have achieved basic self-sufficiency; that is, only the achievement of essential self-sufficiency can put a nation into a situation in which it is free to trade or not. He emphasizes that this is very different from the dependency-breeding "freedom" of the capitalist global market in which poor nations try to compete with capitalist base powers by offering themselves as low-wage, tax-free, pollution-disregarding havens for corporate investment. "What is usually called free trade is really a system of bondage of all to the few multinational institutions that control the flow of capital and goods," he observes. This is not the kind of interdependence that Christian ethics should defend. Rather, the kind of world unity that Chistianity should endorse "is a community of diverse and self-reliant peoples, not a standardized pool of labor working for subsistence together with globally homogenized consumerism." As Cobb observes elsewhere, "free trade means that products manufactured by badly-paid workers, and with few costs associated with environmental protection, re-

---

81. John B. Cobb, Jr., "Sustainability and Community," *The Egg: An Eco-Justice Quarterly* (Summer 1992), 8; quote from Daly, *Steady-State Economics,* 248.

82. Cobb, *Sustainability,* 70.

83. Ibid., 47.

84. Cobb, "Sustainability and Community," 8.

enter the U.S. market to undercut goods made here, where manufacturers must meet higher standards."[85]

In pursuit of sustainable community development, Cobb supports a host of political and economic policies—some of them highly questionable—that aim to promote community-oriented ecological societies. He supports worker ownership and calls for government policies that promote worker and community-controlled cooperatives. He endorses Paolo Soleri's vision of architectural ecologies or "arcologies," in which urban centers feature large clusters of apartment buildings, schools, playgrounds, recreational facilities, hotels, shopping malls, and other businesses combined under one roof and housed on top of underground factories. Each arcology would be built as a fully integrated unit, with solar heating. Though arcologies would be designed with the aim of eliminating urban pollution and virtually eliminating energy costs, Cobb proposes that transportation between arcologies could be enhanced by national investments in high-speed rail and solar-powered vehicles. By creating relatively self-sufficient and democratically self-determined communities that minimize highway congestion, urban street traffic, and oil-driven technologies, he argues, modern cities could become safer, cleaner, and healthier places to live. In other words, they could become communities again.

Among other policy recommendations, Cobb calls for investments in soft energy hardware and other efficiency-maximizing technologies, development of high-yield perennial plants that do not damage topsoil, and government policies that support or promote family farming, redistribution of land and wealth, and population control. He and Daly make arguments for the institution of a negative income tax, a pollution tax, and the auctioning of depletion quotas, as well as arguments for abolishing corporate income taxes, transfering income taxes and welfare responsibilities to the states, and increasing state inheritance, sales, excise, and gasoline taxes. "We hope that over the years a combination of income and inheritance taxes, on the one hand, and social dividends, worker ownership of business, and guaranteed employment on the other, will reduce the spread of incomes from their present exaggerated range," they explain. "The goal for an economics of community is not equality, but limited inequality."[86]

Regarding trade policy, Cobb and Daly do not dispute the logic of neoclassical theory's principle of comparative advantage, which asserts that in a free market, both partners generally benefit from trading goods unless one of them trades on terms less favorable than its own internal cost ratios. The principle of comparative advantage is the heart of classical Adam Smith–David Ricardo economic theory and—with adjustments pertaining to imperfect competition and increasing returns

---

85. Cobb, *Sustainability,* 51; and "Sustainability and Community," 8.
86. Daly and Cobb, *For the Common Good,* 315–31, quote on 331.

to scale—comprises the creedal foundation of modern neoclassical theory. Though Cobb writes about trade issues with less regard for neoclassical theory than Daly, both affirm that most arguments for trade restrictions are self-serving and opposed to the national interest. Yet both also call for a stronger system of tariffs as well as incentives to promote internal competition. They argue that there is a legitimate case against free trade that Smith and Ricardo would have found compelling "had they lived in a world of free capital mobility, demographic explosion, ecological stress, and nation-states unwilling to cede any sovereignty to a world government."[87] In a world economy dominated by transnational corporations controlled by no government, poor countries are forced to compete by gambling their survival on world market prices for one or two exported commodities. They cannot feed themselves or pay for food imports without increasing exports—whatever the social or environmental costs. Yet they are exhorted by the economics establishment to bind themselves ever more deeply into a world trading system in which the power of monopoly capital sets the terms of trade. "To whatever extent individual nations follow the prescriptions of economists, they become dependent on a system of trade influenced, if not controlled, by this supranational economic power," Cobb and Daly observe. "Increasingly they must conform national policies to the desires of this economic power, for their economic survival depends on doing so."[88]

Cobb's tariff system would concentrate on the specific industrial and agricultural goods that self-sufficient societies need to produce at home. He would not impose tariffs on luxury, specialty, or other nonessential goods because his objective is not so much to reduce trade as to establish the preconditions of genuinely free trade. He argues that tariffs should be high enough to ensure that American goods can be produced profitably while yielding good wages, but not so high as to erode America's competitive efficiency. He would especially impose tariffs to protect America's declining manufacturing base and reduce American dependence on imports. "The operation of the free market, steered by tariffs, would lead to the industrial self-sufficiency that—along with a presupposed agricultural self-sufficiency—would make possible truly free trade," he contends.[89]

Cobb admits that some of these policy positions could be wrong. Whether any of them would work in ways that he and Daly hope for cannot be known. Some of them, such as Cobb's support for worker ownership, are commendable, though more problematic than he and Daly ever acknowledge. Some are too untried to have a track record. Some are highly questionable at best, such as the

---

87. Ibid., 210.
88. Ibid., 229.
89. Cobb, *Sustainability*, 70.

Cobb-Daly tax prescriptions. Some call for trade restrictions that have failed in the past. Cobb claims to recognize that protectionism undermines economic efficiency and that most protectionist arguments are reactionary and self-serving, yet he calls for dramatically expanded trade restrictions. As he concedes, his belief that a more equal, cooperative, community-oriented, and nature-sustaining social order can be created is fueled more by religious faith than by empirical evidence.

But it is also fueled by necessity. The world's ecosystem is being destroyed by commercial civilization; moreover, as Cobb observes, little can be done to avert an ecological catastrophe without bringing democratic accountability to the economic system. Only democratic political institutions can speak for the interests of all people, but modern societies are largely shaped, if not dominated, by undemocratic economic power. The ecological crisis thus ultimately reduces to the question whether democratic political power is to make the economy serve the common good or be controlled by concentrated economic interests. In Cobb's words, "The great need is that economic power be subordinated to political power."[90] Whatever else may be wrong with his specific proposals to restructure trade or promote community development, he is surely right that third-way alternatives will get nowhere without a new radical-democratic politics. Economic power can only be democratized by countervailing political power. Ecotheology has learned that much from Niebuhr.

For all of its concern with peace and justice issues, social Christianity has played only a small part in the environmentalist movement. Ecological theory and strategy have developed thus far in the United States largely without direct Christian influence. One symptom of this legacy is that when Christians today enter the ecological movement, they are frequently surprised to learn that the movement is bitterly divided over philosophy, strategy, tactics, and ideology. Humane Society activists emphasize humane treatment of animals, while animal rights ethicists such as Tom Regan go further in opposing all killing of animals for food or sport.[91] Deep ecologists such as Arne Naess, Dave Foreman, and Bill Devall, however, charge that animal rights environmentalism is merely sentimental. They argue that what is needed is appropriate reverence for the world's ecosystem and, especially, a massive reversion of much of the earth's land mass to wilderness.[92] Deep ecologists argue that human reverence should

---

90. Ibid., 49.

91. See Tom Regan, *The Case for Animal Rights* (Berkeley: University of California Press, 1983).

92. See Arne Naess, "Deep Ecology and Ultimate Premises," *Society and Nature* 1 (September-December 1992), 108–19; Dave Foreman, *Confessions of an Eco-Warrior* (New York: Harmony Books, 1991); Bill Devall and George Sessions, *Deep Ecology: Living as if Nature Mattered* (Salt Lake City: Peregrine Smith Books, 1985); Murray Bookchin and Dave Foreman, *Defending the Earth: A Dialogue between Murray Bookchin and Dave Foreman* (Boston: South End Press, 1991).

be paid to nature in all its brutality. For deep ecologists, as Cobb observes, it is "the loss of wildness that endangers the planet and also damages our own spiritual life."[93] Wildness should be celebrated rather than tamed or controlled to fit the standards of "civilization." Rather than apply the language of rights to animals or the environment, deep ecologists argue that human beings need to renounce moral categories altogether and stop ranking living things on any hierarchy of value.

These arguments have aroused bitter polemics and divisiveness in the green movement. Regan calls deep ecologists "eco-fascists," while proponents of another major perspective—social ecology—repeatedly denounce the "irrationalism" and "spiritualism" of deep ecologists. Social ecologists ranging from the anarchoconfederalist Murray Bookchin to neo-Marxist James O'Connor argue that the environmental crisis is essentially a by-product of modern government-supported modes of production and consumption. For them, economic exploitation is the chief cause of the environmental crisis and therefore must be the focus of environmental activism. As long as labor and land are treated primarily as commodities to be exchanged for capital gain, they contend, no moral, spiritual, or political movement will ever make more than small corrections in the margins of a self-destructing civilization. Bookchin has been especially critical of the spiritualizing trend in the environmentalist movement, arguing that his own philosophical naturalism provides a more rational and realistic basis for the movement. In his view, deep ecology spirituality and animal rights moralism distract attention from the essential work of the green movement, which is to create a new, decentralized, cooperative, nature-sustaining economic system. Like Howard Hawkins and other anarchocommunists, Bookchin carries on the refusenik-anarchist tradition of modern socialism, but with primary reference to ecological problems.[94]

Ecofeminism represents another major perspective in green politics. Reflecting its roots in the feminist, peace, and early environmentalist movements, ecofeminism typically blends the spiritual emphasis of deep ecology with the transformationist politics of social ecology. Without accepting deep ecology's thoroughgoing antispeciesism or the overpoliticized socialism or anarchocommunism of most social ecologists, ecofeminists such as Ruether and Gray appropriate central aspects of both traditions while insisting that ecological liberation

---

93. Cobb, *Sustainability*, 102.

94. See Murray Bookchin, "The Meaning of Confederalism," *Society and Nature* 1 (1993), 41–54; Bookchin, *Remaking Society* (Montreal: Black Rose Books, 1989); Bookchin, *The Philosophy of Social Ecology* (Montreal: Black Rose Books, 1990); Howard Hawkins, "Community Control, Workers' Control, and the Cooperative Commonwealth," *Society and Nature* 1 (1993), 55–85; James O'Connor, "Capitalism, Nature, Socialism," *Society and Nature* 1 (September-December 1992), 174–202.

must include liberation from male domination.[95] It is not enough to overcome anthropocentrism or create a postcapitalist society if male-female relations remain unchanged, they contend. Ecofeminism calls for the creation of a nature-cherishing and cooperative society that supports the liberation of female spirit.

Cobb's ecotheology draws upon all of these perspectives, but especially upon social ecology and ecofeminist arguments. He shares the deep ecology emphasis on spiritual transformation while rejecting its nondiscriminating nature worship and its failure to deal with socioeconomic issues. His religious and feminist commitments move him to argue that the socialist politics of social ecology is not enough; at the same time, he shares the social ecology insistence that the environmental crisis is primarily a by-product of modern growth-oriented economic systems that turn labor and nature into commodities. Without the development of third-way economic alternatives, he argues, no serious environmental progress is possible. He notes that the complexity and overwhelming immensity of the environmental crisis have moved others to create additional groupings in "the room beyond anthropocentrism," however. For example, followers of the Gaia hypothesis believe that the relation of the earth to its atmosphere is analogous to that of an organism to its environment. The earth itself is not a material object, in their view, but a living being or intelligent living being much like the earth goddess revered by the ancient Greeks—Gaia. Modern Gaia followers thus give reverence to the earth as a whole, while calling for an environmentalism that helps the goddess heal herself.

Another group in the room protests the lack of attention given to agriculture in the dominant forms of environmental activism. With the ongoing destruction of family farming by agribusiness monopolies, Cobb observes, the cultural habits and wisdom conducive to sustainable agriculture are being lost. None of the dominant forms of environmentalism pays nearly enough attention to the practical problem of how to create a culture of sustainable agriculture. Still other environmentalists protest against the highly ideological and theoretical character of most ecological discourse. They argue that the earth cannot wait for tens of millions of personal conversions to occur or for capitalism to disappear. The green imperative is to find solutions to the world's most pressing environmental problem, which is the nature-destroying use of nuclear and fossil fuels in producing energy. As Cobb notes, these activists generally contend that environmental activists must commit themselves to the marketplace. In their view, environmentalists need to show that new conservation technologies could become

---

95. See Rosemary Radford Ruether, *New Woman, New Earth: Sexist Ideologies and Human Liberation* (New York: Seabury Press, 1975); Elizabeth Dodson Gray, *Green Paradise Lost* (Wellesley, Mass.: Round Table Press, 1979); Gray, *Sacred Dimensions of Women's Experience* (Wellesley, Mass.: Round Table Press, 1988).

a huge growth industry and that utilities could make more money by conserving energy than by building new plants. The technology to provide energy at dramatically lower costs already exists. What it needs is an environmentalist movement that is willing to go into business.

The room beyond anthropocentrism contains an assortment of others, many of them recent converts to green politics, who are stunned to discover that something as nice-sounding as environmentalism could produce so much enmity and factionalism. There are not that many environmentalists to begin with, they protest. Is there no common ground on which these groups might unite? Is it conceivable that the various movements and factions within the green movement might begin to look past their differences to work together on matters of common urgency? For Cobb, Ruether, McFague, and most Christian environmentalists, these questions capsulize not only the hope for a new ecological movement, but also their vision of a possible Christian role within it. Though the debating points among environmentalists are often novel to Christians, the forms are usually familiar. Some groups focus on spiritual conversion, while others focus on changing social structures; some groups are deeply concerned with doctrine, while others are pragmatic; some are deeply politicized, while others avoid politics as much as possible. Liberal Christianity is not only familiar with these differences, Cobb observes, but has done better at making them mutually complementary. It is this kind of spirit that is needed in the room beyond anthropocentrism.

Christianity can make other kinds of contributions to green politics. Like liberal Protestantism, the environmentalist movement is mostly educated, white, and middle class—but the wider Christian church embraces all races and social classes. To a middle-class environmentalist movement that often seems more concerned about the fate of snail darters than about the welfare of vulnerable children, progressive Christianity brings a principled moral commitment to care for the poor and oppressed. Moreover, an ecologically sensitive Christianity brings to the movement a biblically grounded ethic of life that is not anthropocentric or animistic or nihilistic. In the Christian myth of creation, God sees that the creatures are good; they are valuable in themselves. When the creation is completed, God views the world as a whole and sees that it is good. "The implication is not only that species and their members are of value in themselves individually, but also that the total creation with all its complex patterns of interdependence has a value greater than the sum of its individual members," Cobb remarks.

Yet biblical teaching also affirms that human beings are not merely one species among others but are created in the image of God. In Christian teaching, human dominion over the earth is accepted as a fact of life for which human beings bear moral responsibility. "The question is not whether we should maintain it or relinquish it, as the deep ecologists favor," Cobb explains. "The question is how we should exercise it."[96] To wish the fact of human dominion away is to shirk moral responsibility for it. From a Christian perspective, humanity's moral responsibility for its unique powers of consciousness and cognition is not to be willed away but to be brought to the sacred project of saving, cherishing, and sustaining creation.

Modern Christianity brings a dismal legacy to this understanding of its moral responsibility. Having sought to identify itself with progress and modernization, mainline American Christianitity has, until recently, only rarely questioned the environmental costs of America's spectacularly successful venture in economic modernization. Having gained enormous material prosperity from the growth of its economic empire, American society is hardly disposed to accept that alternatives are necessary. The world's ecosystem cannot sustain an American-style affluence for more than a fourth of its population, but the world's remaining superpower is prepared to use its power to maintain this level of affluence. It is therefore in the United States that the ecological movement faces its most crucial struggle. As Cobb observes, most Americans are not culturally prepared to convert to sustainable development. "We have worshipped the great god Growth so long in theory and in practice that stable communities, rural or urban, have become rare," he notes. "Even those of us who recognize the need for community, prize our mobility. We may find it exciting to experiment with community living, but we have internalized the values of individualism too deeply to set them aside."[97]

Yet it is also in the United States that some of the largest and most promising experiments in sustainable development are occurring. The environmentalist movement in America has spawned a profusion of organizations, philosophies, policy initiatives, and community movements in recent years, many of them advanced by people who are new to political activism. In certain respects, Cobb observes, the atomizing fragmentation of modern American culture has actually enhanced environmental activism. "We have so embodied the values and ideologies of the modern world that traditional communities are too broken to inhibit us or to restrict our vision," he explains. "We are truly free to experiment. It is imperative that our own nation re-invent itself."[98] Cobb draws encouragement from the environmental activism of many young Americans who, while lacking any connection to traditional communities or religious traditions, are committed to the vision of sustainable community development. The spark for new experiments in ecocommunity life must come from them, he suggests.

---

96. Cobb, *Sustainability,* 108, 112.
97. Cobb, "Sustainability and Community," 9.
98. Ibid.

But the project of reinventing America must draw upon a wider diversity of moral sources than the deracinated idealism of experimental ecocommunities. If America is to become a community of communities dedicated to social justice and sustainable living, what are the sources or traditions of moral value that might inspire this countercultural project and enable it to gather strength? Is it to be assumed that America's religious and civic republican traditions no longer contribute to the progressive renewal of American society? Are Americans so drenched in the consumption-oriented culture of narcissism that their inherited moral languages have become unreal, unknown, or in any case unusable? Has the progressive communitarian spirit in American culture become so diminished that proponents of economic democracy and sustainable development must resort to year-zero social visions?

For environmentalists and other activists who lack any connection to inherited traditions of moral community or value, an affirmative answer to the last question is perhaps appropriate. From virtually any perspective, an affirmative verdict must be viewed as a plausible possibility. The cultural power of progressive Christian social teaching has been greatly diminished in a society that increasingly takes its moral and social values from the corporate-dominated commercial marketplace. It may be, as Cobb asserts, that the social Christian vision of a just and sustainable society can only be regenerated by experimental countercultural communities with no moral memory. The social mission of progressive Christianity at the end of the Christian century, however, is to regenerate communities of memory that keep alive the vision of a cooperative commonwealth. It is a project to which theologians such as Cobb, Ruether, McFague, Moltmann, West, and Bennett have devoted their lives and work. The social gospel dream of a Christian America cannot be redeemed in the language of the social gospelers. If progressive Christianity no longer speaks of Christianizing America, however, it continues in the spirit of the social gospel to forge new peacemaking, justice-seeking social movements that are infused with Christian influence.

The social gospelers proclaimed that America could become a commonwealth of freedom in which all social power is democratically accountable. This vision of a communitarian social democracy survives in the rhetoric and activism of innumerable religious, feminist, liberationist, antiwar, environmentalist, and other social movements today, though often in ways that preserve no memory of where it came from. In their efforts to make alliances with other groups to build a good society, Christians must seek to sustain not only the cultural habits and communites that sustain life but also the memories that remind them to care.

7 COMMUNITIES OF MEMORY
Social Christianity
after Christendom

IN THE MID-1980S, WHILE A TRIUMPHANT CONSERVATIVE ADMINISTRATION proclaimed that it was "morning in America," an assortment of mostly Left-leaning academics emerged to offer a quite different and seemingly novel portrait of America's condition. Communitarian social theorists such as Michael Sandel, Robert Bellah, William Sullivan, Michael Walzer, Amitai Etzioni, Benjamin Barber, Alasdair MacIntyre, Jean Bethke Elshtain, and James Fishkin criticized what they regarded as the defining characteristics of America's dominant political culture, including its egocentrism, its indifference to social and economic inequality, and its reverence for property rights. At the same time, communitarians took their distance from existing American liberalism, claiming that liberalism is overly preoccupied in its own way with individual rights and, especially, with the protection and extension of entitlement rights. They argued that neither of America's rights-based political traditions gives enough attention to the common good. Both traditions provide political sanction for policies that erode the connections between individuals and their families, communities, and nation. Both traditions rationalize the assaults of economic modernization on communities, mediating institutions, and the environment.[1]

Communitarianism was and is something new and something old. It calls for a new American political culture grounded in early American communitarian

---

1. See Michael Sandel, *Liberalism and the Limits of Justice* (Cambridge: Cambridge University Press, 1982); William Sullivan, *Reconstructing Public Philosophy* (Berkeley: University of California Press, 1982); Michael Walzer, *Spheres of Justice: A Defense of Pluralism and Equality* (New York: Basic Books, 1983); Benjamin Barber, *Strong Democracy* (Berkeley: University of California Press, 1984); Alasdair MacIntyre, *After Virtue: A Study in Moral Theory* (Notre Dame, Ind.: University of Notre Dame Press, 1984). For a more recent, movement-oriented work that popularizes these themes, see Amitai Etzioni, *The Spirit of Community: Rights, Responsibilities, and the Communitarian Agenda* (New York: Crown Publishers, 1993).

ideals. It rejects the liberal conception of politics, in which autonomous rights-bearing individuals pressure their representatives for benefits from the state. Communitarians resurrect John Dewey's understanding of democracy as a "great community" of shared values and his conception of politics as the project of continually re-creating the public. In political philosophy, Sandel's *Liberalism and the Limits of Justice* (1982) made a landmark critique of the liberal ideology of the "unencumbered self"; in theology, Stanley Hauerwas's *A Community of Character* (1981) and *The Peaceable Kingdom* (1983) argued that Christianity is (or should be) a distinctive, peacemaking, countercultural community faith.[2]

Habits of the Heart

The impact of one communitarian work of this period dwarfed all others, however. In 1985, Bellah and his colleagues—Sullivan, Richard Madsen, Ann Swidler, and Steven M. Tipton—published the national best-seller, *Habits of the Heart: Individualism and Commitment in American Life.* The book was fortuitously timed. In the wake of Ronald Reagan's massive electoral victory over the archetypal symbol of New Deal liberalism, Walter Mondale, the Bellah group countered that it was not morning in America. In their reading, America was wracked with massive problems of economic injustice, cultural fragmentation, and moral cynicism. The community-oriented biblical and civic republican languages of early American experience were being erased from America's cultural memory. American youth no longer knew or cared about the biblical sources of the American experiment, about John Winthrop's dream of a "city upon a hill," or about the modern Christian dream of a cooperative commonwealth. A new and largely unchurched American generation voted for Reagan and cheered his broadsides against liberalism, the welfare state, the feminist and peace movements, the mainline churches, and the unions. The dominant trend in American life, according to the Bellah group, was toward an increasingly atomized society that reduced all moral and social issues to the languages of possessive or expressive individualism. In national politics, the triumph of Reaganism symbolized this trend, just as Reagan himself mythologized it.

Habits of the Heart struck a cultural nerve. The book's portrait of an increasingly rootless and narcissistic American middle class was widely heralded as a telling critique of the loss of genuine community in American life. It was, to be sure, a book decidedly focused on the moral condition of professionally

---

2. See Stanley Hauerwas, *A Community of Character: Toward a Constructive Christian Social Ethic* (Notre Dame, Ind.: University of Notre Dame Press, 1981); and *The Peaceable Kingdom: A Primer in Christian Ethics* (Notre Dame, Ind.: University of Notre Dame Press, 1983).

oriented, middle-class, mostly white Americans. The book lauded Martin Luther King Jr. as an exemplar of America's best moral traditions but offered no account of the African American culture that produced him. It similarly took a bourgeois white liberal feminist perspective for granted without discussing feminism or the implications of its argument for feminism.[3] With all of its limitations in methodology and perspective, however, the book portrayed the eclipse of American moral community in ways that reflected upon most Americans. The process of cultural fragmentation that it described affects not only upwardly mobile white professionals.

For the Bellah group, the most telling symptom of America's loss of moral meaning is the erosion of its biblical and republican moral traditions. When pressed by the authors to explain the grounds on which their moral beliefs are based, many of the book's subjects gave remarkably thin or confused answers. Brian Palmer was the *Habits* prototype of the individualistic American whose moral sensibility is shaped by market society. Brian lived in California and explained that he liked California because "people by and large aren't bothered by other people's value systems as long as they don't infringe upon your own." The rule of thumb in California, he noted, "is that if you've got the money, honey, you can do your thing as long as your thing doesn't destroy someone else's property, or interrupt their sleep, or bother their privacy, that's fine. If you want to go in your house and smoke marijuana and shoot dope and get all screwed up, that's your business, but don't bring that out on the street, don't expose my children to it, just do your thing. That works out kind of neat."[4]

In a world of conflicting self-interests, Brian assumed that no one can say whether one value system is better or more humane than another. Given this assumption, he gave great importance to a single moral principle—the importance of honest communication. People can resolve their differences and learn to live with each other only through honest and open communication, he reasoned. This was the one moral value that modern people cannot do without. The Bellah group worried that Brian had already given away the store, however. They questioned his remaining article of faith and his ability to defend it. What makes integrity different from other moral values, they asked? If relativism devours every other

---

3. For essays that effectively criticize these limitations, see Vincent Harding, "Toward a Darkly Radiant Vision of America's Truth: A Letter of Concern, an Invitation to Re-Creation," and M. Elizabeth Albert, "In the Interest of the Public Good? New Questions for Feminism," both reprinted in *Community in America: The Challenge of Habits of the Heart,* ed. Charles H. Reynolds and Ralph V. Norman (Berkeley: University of California Press, 1988), 67–83, 84–96.

4. Robert N. Bellah, Richard Madsen, William M. Sullivan, Ann Swidler, and Steven M. Tipton, *Habits of the Heart: Individualism and Commitment in American Life* (Berkeley: University of California Press, 1985), 6–7.

value that he may have wanted to teach his children, what makes honesty so different?

Brian's education had educated him into skepticism, relativism, and ambivalence. Faced with a challenge to his only remaining moral principle, he did what he learned to do in school. He retreated. He was a nice person. The last thing he wanted to do was crowd someone's space. "I don't know," he replied. "It just is. It's just so basic. I don't want to be bothered with challenging that. It's part of me. I don't know where it came from, but it's very important." A moment's reflection about the basis of his personal morality brought further clarity. "I just find that I get more personal satisfaction from choosing course B over course A," he explained. "It makes me feel better about myself."[5]

Stripped of any framework or identity-forming narrative on which a language of moral value might be based or drawn, Brian fell back on his society's ethos of the sovereign consumer. Some choices yield more pleasant consequences than others. He had no sense of himself as someone who belongs to or is identified by any community transcending his private or family interests. *Habits* observed that Brian's case is increasingly common. Many Americans no longer take moral instruction from character-shaping communities of any kind. The religious and republican moral languages of America's past are being displaced by an individualistic pursuit of success or emotional satisfaction that places highly tenuous selves like Brian's at the center of a meaningless world.

Habits cautioned that this cultural process of deracination affects not only those, like Brian, who belong to no community. In modern America, an ethic of individualism provides the primary operative frame of moral reference even for many of those who identify with some religious, cultural, or political community. Mainline Christianity provides perhaps the most telling examples. American churches increasingly cater to the emotional needs of anxious, lonely, or stressed-out achievers, offering to provide undemanding communities of care for religious consumers. As *Habits* noted, much of modern mainline Christianity is primarily concerned with its therapeutic function. In taking the therapeutic option, modern Christianity builds upon a considerable American tradition of constructing the world out of the self. Thomas Jefferson delared, "I am a sect myself," and Thomas Paine said, "My mind is my church." When modern Americans declare themselves to be "spiritual, but not religious," or "religious, but not a church member," they echo a long American tradition of religious individualism that includes Emerson, Thoreau, and Whitman. Mainline American religion abets the triumph of this kind of individualism when it indulges the American tendency to conceive God as the self magnified.

---

5. Ibid., 8.

Habits of the Heart observed that two forms of individualism prevail over other moral perspectives in modern America. Utilitarian individualism exalts the self-reliant pursuit of material success, as expressed in the work ethic aphorisms of Benjamin Franklin's *Poor Richard's Almanac.* This ethic of self-interest was politicized in the nineteenth century—often without Franklin's republicanism—into the ideology of laissez-faire capitalism. In its nineteenth-century incarnation, American utilitarian individualism proclaimed that society is best served by maximizing the opportunities through which individuals pursue their self-interest. Nineteenth-century American utilitarianism was social Darwinist in its politics; it mythologized the industrious virtues of the self-made entrepreneur and conceived freedom as social power or access to privilege. By mid-century, it was America's dominant myth. *Habits* explained that the very success of this ideology set off a number of reactions to it, however: "A life devoted to the calculating pursuit of one's own material interest came to seem problematic for many Americans, some of them women, some of them clergymen, and some of them poets and writers."[6]

Franklin's success ethic left too little room for love, aesthetic feeling, and the hunger for meaning. American writers such as Emerson, Thoreau, and Nathaniel Hawthorne spurned the cramped Puritan ethic of self-control and material gain to pursue a deeper cultivation of the self. Expressive individualism is still individualistic—"I celebrate myself," Walt Whitman exulted—but it finds its reward in aesthetic appreciation, immediacy, and deeper personal relationships. Whitman epitomizes the expressivist reaction to America's dominant culture. "I loaf and invite my soul," he declared. If utilitarian individualism views freedom as social power—as a by-product of successful living—expressive individualism adds that genuine freedom requires psychic liberation. Whitman celebrated the soul of the unencumbered self and thus gave voice to a deeply American spiritual yearning. In late twentieth-century America, *Habits* observed, Americans are more dedicated than ever to material success, but this preoccupation is no longer constrained by the claims of strong moral traditions or communities. For many Americans, the religious and republican languages of America's past no longer provide a vital basis of moral identity. Americans increasingly compensate for the loss by resorting to therapeutic substitutes. Whitman's children are turning to psychotherapy and New Age spirituality. "The therapeutic attitude reinforces the traditional individualism of American culture, including the concept of utilitarian individuals maximizing their own interests, but stresses the concept of expressive individuals maximizing their experience of inner psychic goods," the Bellah group remarked.[7] Expressive and therapeutic individualism can make

6. Ibid., 33.
7. Ibid., 104.

American society less harsh, but not more just or sustainable. It cultivates deeper enrichments, but will never create the justice-making, other-regarding ethic that is needed.

What is needed is to renew America's morally generative communities of memory, especially its religious and activist communities. "We have committed what to the republican founders of our nation was the cardinal sin: we have put our own good, as individuals, as groups, as a nation, ahead of the common good," *Habits* declared. The authors observed that the biblical and republican traditions provide the same litmus test for assessing a society's moral health. The test is how society deals with the cluster of problems pertaining to wealth and poverty. Scripture repeatedly condemns inequality and oppression, taking the side of the poor against the principalities and powers that exploit them. Republican theory from Aristotle to the American founders has assumed that a free society can survive only if there is "a rough equality of condition, that extremes of wealth and poverty are incompatible with a republic."[8]

The Bellah group conceded that this fundamental moral conviction has always been contested in capitalist America. But with the erosion of America's religious and democratic traditions, they noted, the force of the biblical and republican ethic regarding distributive justice has seriously weakened in American political culture. Americans are willing to finance modest increases in welfare in prosperous times, but "when times are not so prosperous, we think that at least our own successful careers will save us and our families from failure and despair." In the face of overwhelming contrary evidence, Americans try to believe that poverty can be alleviated by the crumbs that fall from the tables of the rich. *Habits* observed that America's dominant commercial culture assiduously reinforces the private dream of being a star—of attaining enough success to permit one to stand apart from others, not have to worry about them, and perhaps look down on them. "And since we have believed in that dream for a long time and worked very hard to make it come true, it is hard for us to give it up, even though it contradicts another dream that we have—that of living in a society that would really be worth living in."[9]

A society worth living in would subordinate private interest to the common good, the authors urged. It would seek to reduce the punishments of failure and the rewards of success. It would resist the unrelenting capitalist drive to turn labor and nature into commodities. It would expand opportunities for socially useful work, partly by taking labor and nature out of the market. It would promote economic democracy by expanding the cooperative and community-development sectors. It would recognize that commercial society is at war not only with the

---

8. Ibid., 285.
9. Ibid.

world's natural ecology but also with its social ecology. *Habits* warned that the world's social ecology is being damaged not only by the assaults of modern civilization on the natural world or by the unparalleled horrors of modern war, genocide, and oppression made possible by modern technology but also by "the destruction of the subtle ties that bind human beings to one another, leaving them frightened and alone. It has been evident for some time that unless we begin to repair the damage to our social ecology, we will destroy ourselves long before natural ecological disaster has time to be realized."[10]

Sustainable development strategies therefore need to aim as much at renewing human communities as at repairing the natural world. To call for a new social ecology grounded in renewed religious and activist communities might appear to be "absurdly utopian, as a project to create a perfect society," the authors conceded. "But the transformation of which we speak is both necessary and modest. Without it, indeed, there may be very little future to think about at all." The new society that is needed will not be built by deracinated revolutionaries or year-zero utopians. If America is to build a future society worth living in, *Habits* suggested, it will have to build upon the long-held social Christian vision of a cooperative commonwealth.

Habits of the Heart thus reproduced the defining themes and tone of progressive Christianity. It extolled the same cooperative, community-oriented social virtues as the social gospelers. The book's arguments for economic democracy, socially useful work, and the need for a new social ecology were rooted in the social gospel tradition, as was its understanding of the moral meaning of biblical faith. In their subsequent work, *The Good Society* (1991), the Bellah group amplifies their programmatic argument for economic democracy, contending that "in a democratized economy it should be much clearer that the work each of us does is something we do *together* and *for each other* as much as by and for ourselves." A good society would limit the harshness of the labor market, expand the cooperative sector, and reduce "both the anxiety and the cynicism that are rampant in our present economic life," the authors claim. It would not sacrifice communities for economic growth, but would rather create the kind of society and culture in which people are secure enough to "form attachments, make commitments, and engage in activities that are good in themselves."[11]

Bellah-style communitarianism upholds the progressive Christian vision of a just and sustainable social order, it renews the social Christian theme that there is such a thing as having enough, it embraces the social Christian project of renewing America's biblical and democratic traditions, and it affirms the social

---

10. Ibid., 284.

11. Robert N. Bellah, Richard Madsen, William M. Sullivan, Ann Swidler, and Steven M. Tipton, *The Good Society* (New York: Alfred A. Knopf, 1991), 104–7.

Christian emphasis on sustaining communities of memory. It makes the case for a religiously inspired communitarian social democratic politics in language that is softer than Rauschenbusch's socialist rhetoric but harder-edged than Mathews's rhetoric of progressive idealism. Like the progressive Christian and Deweyan traditions with which they are linked, the Bellah group calls for a democratic community-sustaining politics that "would allow us to link interests with a conception of the common good."[12]

Communitarianism and the Social Gospel

For all of their emphasis on the importance of cultural memory, however, the Bellah group curiously fails to acknowledge their own multiple links to the social gospel tradition. *Habits of the Heart* and *The Good Society* make numerous references to Niebuhr, but both works discuss modern Christian ethics as though it began with Niebuhr. Like most contemporary Christian ethicists, the Bellah group has been strongly influenced by Niebuhr and is concerned to establish that their social vision passes Niebuhr's tests for realism. They appeal to Niebuhr's passion for justice, his commitment to democracy, his emphasis on the limits of politics, and his commitment to the Christian task of re-creating the public. They portray Niebuhr's work as an important corrective to Dewey's idealistic liberalism and imply that Niebuhr was right about the inevitability of social conflict and collective egotism. They do not question Niebuhr's harshly negative portrayal of the liberal-progressive stream of social Christianity. Yet for all of their favorable references to Niebuhr and their disregard for the social gospel tradition, the Bellah group is closer to the spirit of Rauschenbusch's progressivism than to Niebuhr's power politics reformism. To call for a democratized economic order or a new social ecology is to return to the very kind of social Christianity that Niebuhr sought to discredit. Niebuhr insisted that if reason is the servant of interest, it is useless to hope for a society that will "link interests with a conception of the common good." If politics is essentially about the struggle of competing interests for self-promoting power, he repeatedly lectured, it is useless and often counterproductive to hope that moral concern or religiously inspired good will might significantly advance the common good. In the social arena, Niebuhr taught, power can only be challenged by power.

Bellah-style communitarianism has absorbed these lessons deeply enough to understand that social Christianity cannot simply return to a pre-Niebuhrian progressivism. The social gospelers mistakenly thought that a cooperative commonwealth was literally achievable, partly because they refused to accept that group egotism is inevitable. Many liberation theologians have more recently

---

12. Bellah et al., *Habits of the Heart*, 287.

made the same mistake. If postmodern Christianity is to renew the social Christian ethic of the common good, it must begin with a Niebuhrian awareness that every social gain creates new forms of social evil. The inevitability of social evil and the complexity of the social factors in question preclude the possibility that "the good society" envisioned by the Bellah group and progressive Christianity might ever be attained. The very notion of a common good is finally impossible to define, given the unlimited amount of information that would have to be assessed, the multiplicity of perspectives upon it, and the continuous changes in circumstances that any ethic of the common good must address.

To relinquish the notion of a common good on these grounds, however, is to undercut the struggle for attainable gains toward a good society because it negates the elusive but formative vision of what is worth struggling for. To give up the search for a common good is to abandon the necessary vision of a just social order that inspires and shapes new struggles for attainable gains toward ecojustice. Without a social vision of a good society or a "new social ecology" that transcends the prevailing order, Christian ethics remains captive to the dominant order. Without an imaginative utopian dimension, social Christianity restricts itself to marginal reforms within the existing system. The borders of the possible remain untested. For the Bellah group, as for most progressive Christian ethicists, the social problems confronting America today require more than marginal reforms within the dominant order. Niebuhr's realism is not enough. By failing to address the differences between Niebuhr's form of social Christianity and the kind that they promote, however, the Bellah group obscures the discussion over the inheritance and future of social Christianity. The problem with Niebuhr is not only that his later work failed to challenge the structures or ethos of modern capitalist America. The deeper problem is that, despite his herculean efforts to salvage a public vocation for modern Christianity, the legacy of his lifework was to undermine much of the church's prophetic vocation in the public sphere.

Moral Man and Immoral Society drew the lines that are still at issue. Niebuhr's blast against liberal idealism repudiated the liberal Protestant belief that the ethos of a moral community can be insinuated into the public realm. Politics is not about morality or community, but about the distribution of power. In subsequent years, when pressed on the question, Niebuhr sometimes suggested that a pluralistic republic can hold together only if it is founded upon a tacit religious consensus in the private realm. Some basis of religious or moral value is necessary to keep a secular public order of rival interests from breaking into chaos.

Niebuhr's overriding commitment to pluralism prevented him from developing the implications of this vague sentiment, however. He preferred to reformulate the issue, arguing that Christian moral teaching compels Christians to struggle for justice in the public realm and that justice can be secured only through the intervention of a centralized secular state. Because the liberal Christian quest for a moralized politics of community is an illusion, the only recourse for a church that respects pluralism and cares about justice is to strengthen the capacity of the state to act as a secular moral guarantor.

This was the liberal faith in Niebuhr's time, which carried on the New Deal merger of liberalism and centralized power. It was an orthodoxy of recent vintage. For America's entire history before the Progressive movement, the party of democracy in American political life was the party of decentralized power, civic republicanism, and small-town populism. From Thomas Jefferson to the populists, American Democrats championed the values and interests of small towns, small businesses, farmers, laborers, and organic communities. They were opposed by the party of the nation—the party of the Federalists, then the Whigs, and finally the Republicans—who argued for the consolidation of the union and generally defended the values and interests of big business.

As Michael Sandel has recalled, the merger between democratic politics and concentrated power began shortly after the end of the Civil War, when the growth of large-scale enterprises and nationalized markets outstripped the decentralized political structures (and the decentralized economies) of early America.[13] In the early years of the twentieth century, progressives such as Rauschenbusch and Herbert Croly recognized that America's democratic tradition and institutions could survive only if American democracy made its peace with concentrated power. In order to defend democratic gains from the onslaught of concentrated economic power, the progressives began to argue that a consolidation of countervailing political power was necessary. What was needed was not only a centralization of government allied with a growing trade union movement but also a nationalization of politics. Croly wrote in 1909 that the nationalization of American political, economic, and social life was "an essentially formative and enlightening political transformation."[14] America would become more democratic only if it became more of a *nation* in its institutions and spirit.

The party of democracy would thus create a new political language in the twentieth century, turning liberalism into a form of democratic statism. As Sandel observes, this transition was consummated with the success of the New Deal, which effectively united liberalism and the national idea. In a society in which the civic republicanism of small-town, community-oriented America was no

---

13. Michael Sandel, "The Political Theory of the Procedural Republic," in *Reinhold Niebuhr Today,* ed. Richard John Neuhaus (Grand Rapids: Eerdmans, 1989), 28–29. See J.G.A. Pocock, *The Machiavellian Moment: Florentine Political Thought and the Atlantic Republican Tradition* (Princeton, N.J.: Princeton University Press, 1975); and Samuel Beer, "Liberalism and the National Idea," *The Public Interest* 5 (Fall 1966), 70–82.

14. Herbert Croly, *The Promise of American Life* (Indianapolis: Bobbs-Merrill, 1965), 270–73, quoted in Sandel, "The Political Theory of the Procedural Republic," 30.

longer a serious force, democrats would place their hopes in the politics of a nationalized liberalism. In a society increasingly shaped by the growth and power of corporate capitalism, the only viable politics of the common good would be a politics of the national republic.

These were the basic truisms of Niebuhr's later political life. They defined the positive side of his political realism. They shaped his understanding of Christianity's social mission. Realism recognized not only the depravity of human beings and the limitations of moral or political reformism but also the need to consolidate state power for the sake of relatively good ends. Throughout his later career, Niebuhr assumed that there were only three serious options for Western democracies: free market capitalism, state socialism, and welfare state capitalism. His insistence that these were the only choices was a realist theme. Though he supported the Delta Cooperative Farm movement in the late 1930s, there were never enough experiments in worker and community ownership for him to take these projects seriously as prototypes for an alternative politics.[15] He pointedly criticized those who sought to expand the cooperative sector, arguing that decentralized economic democracy approaches could never bring about the equality of power that was needed.[16] In the real world, there were few examples of cooperative ownership to cite and no reason to take them seriously as alternative examples of anything. Similarly, Niebuhr saw no pressing need for a theory of public virtue in a society in which the secular welfare state was creating a relatively just society. In Niebuhr's lifetime, the marriage between liberalism and state power achieved a degree of success that deflected seemingly nonutilitarian questions about the importance of community, the secularization of the public realm, the degradation of the democratic process, and the heightening maldistribution of economic power.

By the time he died in 1971, after several years of illness, Niebuhr recognized that he belonged to a bygone era of American politics and religion. The antiwar and countercultural movements of the 1960s challenged hierarchy at every turn and claimed that "liberalism" was part of the problem. Though liberals like Niebuhr opposed America's war in Vietnam, it was American liberalism that committed the United States to anticommunist containment in Vietnam. The New Left arose in the United States in part as a revolt against the corruption and cynicism of establishment liberal politics. For a new generation of radicals, Niebuhr's liberalism was too eager to wield power, too willing to compromise

---

15. On Niebuhr's support for the Delta Cooperative Farm experiment, see Ronald H. Stone, *Professor Reinhold Niebuhr* (Louisville: Westminster/John Knox Press, 1992), 111–12.

16. See Reinhold Niebuhr, "The Political Confusions of Dr. Kagawa," *Radical Religion* 1 (Winter 1936), 6–7.

with corporate and military power, and too inclined to identify its own interests with the common good. Radicals were the first to claim that liberalism was bankrupt.

In the succeeding generation, a coalition of conservatives, Right-wing populists, and neoconservatives produced a different, though not unrelated, litany of charges against liberalism. The Right-wing backlash of the 1970s and 1980s successfully associated liberalism in the national political consciousness with uncontrolled government spending, weakness in foreign policy, secular humanism, and lack of patriotism. The word itself was used only as an epithet in America's national political campaigns until 1992, when a Democratic presidential candidate made himself electable only after dissociating himself from his party's liberal past.

Numerous attempts were made throughout the 1970s and 1980s to imagine how Niebuhr would have responded to this many-sided crisis of liberalism. Conservatives, neoconservatives, centrists, unreconstructed liberals, neoliberals, social democrats, and others claimed Niebuhr for their position. The question whether Niebuhr would have turned Right, turned Left, or clung to a redefined vital center liberalism was pursued with energetic futility. A different form of the question is crucial for any post-Niebuhrian social Christianity, however. Besides those differences that reflect differences in context, how should a postmodern Christian ethic differ from the liberal realism that Niebuhr propounded? If Niebuhr's work was more than a series of improvised responses to the Great Depression, the fascist threat, the communist threat, and so on, which aspects of his highly influential approach need to be changed?

Chapter 3 compiled a substantial list. Niebuhr's theological ethics needed a theological groundwork that he never attempted to provide. Despite his heavy reliance on the language of myth and symbol, he gave virtually no attention to religious epistemology or to questions concerning method, language, and hermeneutics. His theology gave short shrift to the Christian mysteries of the divine trinity, the incarnation and resurrection of Christ, the work of the Spirit, and the church as the body of Christ. His antipathy for social gospel Christianity drove him to renounce the doctrine of the kingdom altogether. His preoccupation with the Cold War during his later career blunted his critical perspective toward America and impeded him from taking much interest in the Third World. His deep concern to find realistic approaches drove him to a status quo politics for much of his later career and made him overly cautious in his approach to racial justice. For all of his insistence on the determinative importance of power and interest, Niebuhr failed to recognize that his understandings of what was "real" or "realistic" reflected the social perspective of a privileged white male American academic. His insistence that reason is the servant of interest explained more about the "reality" defended by Christian realism than he acknowledged. His highly masculine rhetoric and his nearly exclusive emphasis on "man's" egotism and will to power produced a highly androcentric account of the religious and moral meaning of Christianity. For Niebuhr, Christianity was always centrally preoccupied with the human need for repentance and forgiveness before a righteous Judge. He had no interest in nonhuman nature at all. Moreover, his judgment that economic democracy is unrealistic caused him to avoid economic issues in his later work and thus made his writings unhelpful for those who pursue the question of how to democratize social and economic power.

These problems do not reduce to a single problematic or yield a single corrective. Niebuhr's religious vision was highly complex and multicentered, drawing upon a wide variety of religious, political, sociological, and existential sources. In 1939, he reported that his recent changes in theological perspective had come about "not so much through study as through the pressure of world events."[17] Throughout his career, his various shifts in position and perspective were driven by his distinctively passionate engagements with world political events, the world ecumenical movement, and other pressing movements and affairs. Theology in a postmodern mode can be no less contextual than Niebuhr but must appropriate a considerably more diverse variety of voices and perspectives than Niebuhr ever considered. If there is no single corrective to the problems that Niebuhrian theology bequeathed to social Christianity, however, there are two fundamental problems with his perspective that cannot be mitigated simply by taking up the issues he ignored or handled inadequately.

The crucial problems left by Niebuhr's work inhere in the core of his thought. The first is the patriarchal cast of his theology. Through all of the changes in his later politics and ethics, Niebuhr's conception of Christianity unfailingly privileged the language of sovereignty, repentance, and submission. The heart of Christianity, for him, was the promise of salvation from "man's" enslaving egotism through divine grace. This was not a promise of liberation or emancipation. For Niebuhr, the redemptive work of God's gift of grace was always to enable isolated egotists to surrender their prideful attempts to master their existence. God's redeeming love in the cross of Christ reconciled human beings to their finitude, weakness, abasement, and dependency but offered no promise of historical liberation from this condition. It is precisely against this conception of salvation—as submission to a divinely ordered condition of abasement and dependency—that feminist and other liberation theologies have arisen.

The second crucial problem with Niebuhr's legacy concerns his typically liberal-masculine cleavage between the private and public realms. Niebuhr's assumptions about theology's task in the modern world were conventionally

---

17. Reinhold Niebuhr, "Ten Years That Shook My World," *Christian Century* 56 (April 26, 1939), 546.

liberal. He believed that theologians must translate the moral, social, and even religious meaning of Christian faith into secular terms. This project would enable Christians to play a role in the political sphere and enable modern secular observers to make sense of Christian claims. Niebuhr jettisoned the language of original sin and the kingdom when these ideas obstructed his pragmatic ends. He eschewed other classical Christian doctrines that were too metaphysical or supernaturalist for his taste. For all of his brilliant and impassioned efforts to save a place for the churches in a secularized culture, however, it was Niebuhr who propounded an understanding of politics that kept the churches *as churches* out of the public arena.

Because politics is a struggle for power driven by interest and will to power, it was absurd and embarrassing to Niebuhr that the liberal churches of his time were wasting their influence and embarrassing themselves by seeking to moralize the public arena. Rauschenbusch used such terms as *Christianize, moralize,* and *democratize* interchangably. A generation after his death, liberal Christianity's grammar had been toned down, but the moralizing sentiments of the social gospel were still rampant. Niebuhr's assault on the illusions of liberal Christianity drove a wedge between the churches' moral identity and social mission. The social mission of the church would no longer be to transform the social order in the light of the biblical vision of freedom, justice, community, and peace. Niebuhrian realism assumed a more limited and self-limiting social mission than this, providing religious support for a secular liberal agenda that served the social struggle for freedom and justice.

This dichotomy between the church's moral identity and its social mission compromised the church's moral identity and helped to strip the public sphere of any language of moral value. The social gospel attempt to insinuate the ethos of a moral community into the public sphere was ridiculed as hopeless, sentimental, and confused. The public sphere was not the realm of moral value but the realm of interest and power. To accept this judgment on the futility of a communitarian politics was not only to strip the public sphere of its moral bearings but also to overload the private world of the family with moral and social burdens it cannot carry. These trends were inherent in the secularizing and commercializing logic of social and economic modernization. Niebuhr's realism tried to accommodate the modern world, partly by embracing the desacralized public square that modernity produced. Christian realism tried to save a place for the church by accepting the liberal bourgeois dichotomy between a virtue-producing private realm and an instrumental and technocratic public realm. But the practical effect of this strategy has been to reinforce the drift toward a cynical, self-absorbed, and morally uprooted society in which America's original biblical and republican moral languages have faded from cultural memory. For all of his success in keeping some form of the liberal Christian witness alive during his lifetime, Niebuhr's strategy left progressive Christianity without enough to say or do.

Stanley Hauerwas suggests that Niebuhr paid little attention to the church's social mission because his church was America. Those who criticize the loss of prophetic spirit in Niebuhr's later work typically misconstrue the nature of his work, Hauerwas contends, because they fail to grasp "that Niebuhr from beginning to end was involved in a stormy love affair with America."[18] Niebuhr was always more concerned with what America's domestic or foreign policy should be than with any distinctive perspective that the church might bring to political issues. While it is clear that Niebuhr's pro-Americanism eventually caused him to surrender much of the prophetic spirit of the social Christian tradition, Hauerwas argues, the more instructive truism for Christian ethics today is that Niebuhr's theological program carried out the crucial presuppositions of the social gospel, albeit in a more sophisticated and accommodationist form. "Under Niebuhr's influence, the agenda of Christian ethics became, for many, the attempt to develop those theological, moral, and social insights necessary to sustain the ambiguous task of achieving more relatively just societies," Hauerwas explains. "Although this would seem to indicate a decisive break with his social gospel forebears, in fact Niebuhr continued their most important theological and social presuppositions."[19]

Like the social gospelers, Niebuhr assumed that the chief task of Christian ethics in America is to inspire and guide Americans to make their nation a better society. Though he eschewed the social gospel equation of democracy and social regeneration, Niebuhr never doubted that Christian ethics must promote democracy. The social gospelers wanted to regenerate the church as a force for social justice and peace, but Niebuhr's realism made him uncomfortable with any conception of the church as a transformative agent in society. He was therefore left with a social gospel approach that lacked the social gospelers' faith in the regenerative social power and mission of the church. For Niebuhr, as for the social gospelers, the subject of Christian ethics was America, Hauerwas concludes: "They differed only on how nearly just such a society could be and the theological presupposition necessary to understand and sustain social involvement."[20]

---

18. Stanley Hauerwas, "On Keeping Theological Ethics Theological," in *Revisions: Changing Perspectives in Moral Philosophy,* ed. Stanley Hauerwas and Alasdair MacIntyre (Notre Dame, Ind.: University of Notre Dame Press, 1983), 39; reprinted in *Against the Nations: War and Survival in a Liberal Society,* ed. Stanley Hauerwas (Notre Dame, Ind.: University of Notre Dame Press, 1992), 23–50.

19. Ibid., 23–24.

20. Ibid., 24.

Stanley Hauerwas and the Kingdom

This conclusion provides the point of departure for Hauerwas's alternative Christian ethic. "The recent history of Christian ethics has largely been the story of the attempt to work out the set of problems bequeathed to us by the social gospel and the Niebuhrs," he observes.[21] But in his view, the social Christian tradition is not Christian enough to maintain the distinctive gospel faith. By committing the church to some variable form of an idealistic-realistic struggle for a good society, Hauerwas argues, social Christianity has blurred the church's distinctive religious identity and embraced the moral problems of Caesar. Modern social Christianity has been preoccupied with the Constantinian question of how to attain and exercise power in a morally responsible way. But this is not a Christian question, Hauerwas asserts. The question was unthinkable to pre-Constantinian Christianity, which never asked under what circumstances Christians should kill to serve a relative political good. Building upon the work of Mennonite theologian John Howard Yoder, Hauerwas argues that "something has already gone wrong when Christians think they can ask, 'What is the best form of society or government?' " Such a question could be asked in Christianity only after the church accepted Caesar as a member. "This question assumes that Christians should or do have social and political power so they can determine the ethos of society," Hauerwas observes. "That this assumption has long been with us does nothing to confirm its truth."[22]

He allows that not all modern Christian ethics derive from the Protestant social Christian tradition. Catholic moral theology features a distinctive form of natural law reasoning that blends biblical, patristic, classical, and modern elements within a casuistical framework.[23] The theocentric-neoorthodox tradition in modern American Protestantism emphasizes the relativity of human existence—including the relativity of all human conceptions of goodness, justice, and the divine will—in arguing that God alone deserves complete loyalty. For H. Richard Niebuhr and James Gustafson, the ineffable Maker of heaven and

21. Ibid., 27.

22. Stanley M. Hauerwas, "A Christian Critique of Christian America," in *Community in America,* ed. Charles H. Reynolds and Ralph V. Norman, 260; reprinted in Hauerwas, *Christian Existence Today: Essays on Church, World and Living in Between* (Durham, N.C.: Labyrinth Press, 1988), 171–90; see John Howard Yoder, *The Priestly Kingdom: Social Ethics as Gospel* (Notre Dame, Ind.: University of Notre Dame Press, 1984), 154.

23. See Timothy E. O'Connell, *Principles for a Catholic Morality* (New York: Seabury Press, 1978); David Hollenbach, *Justice, Peace, and Human Rights: American Catholic Social Ethics in a Pluralistic Context* (New York: Crossroad, 1988); Richard A. McCormick, *Notes on Moral Theology: 1965 through 1980* (Washington, D.C.: University Press of America, 1981).

earth is the absolute that relativizes all other claims to the good.[24] Hauerwas is respectful toward both of these traditions of modern Christian moral reasoning but argues that despite their particular virtues both approaches surrender the particularity of the gospel to a construct or methodology that seeks to establish common ground with unbelievers; that is, both of these traditions share the crucial failing of the social Christian tradition. Instead of emphasizing the particularity of Christian truth claims, modern mainline Christianity in its various prevailing forms has sought to accommodate itself to an increasingly secular culture, typically by translating religious claims into the purportedly more inclusive languages of philosophy or sociology. "Theologians and religious thinkers have largely sought to show that the modes of argument and conclusions reached by philosophical ethicists are no different from those reached by ethicists working with more explicit religious presuppositions," he observes. "The task of Christian ethics, both socially and philosophically, was not revision but accommodation."[25]

The pressure to translate religious truth into a nontheological idiom has been irresistible for theologians who seek to make Christianity relevant under the conditions of modernity. "But once such a translation is accomplished, it becomes very unclear why they need the theological idiom in the first place," Hauerwas notes.[26] The upshot is that modern theology has no work of its own to do but has sought rather to perpetuate itself by claiming linkages with non-Christian philosophical and sociopolitical perspectives. Having sought to convince unbelievers that Christianity still has some relevance in the modern world, theologians have reinforced the secular academic assumption that theology is a form of special pleading. "The more theologians seek to find the means to translate theological convictions into terms acceptable to the nonbeliever, the more they substantiate the view that theology has little of importance to say in the area of ethics," Hauerwas contends.[27] The inheritance of modern theology's strategy of accommodationist apologetics is that secular intellectuals feel no obligation to read theology.

"Christian theology attempted to deny the inherent historical and community-dependent nature of our moral convictions in the hopes that our 'ethics' might be universally persuasive," Hauerwas concludes. But it is precisely this preoccupation with finding common ground that modern Christianity needs to give up, in his view. Christianity is not a perennial philosophy, a world-embracing universal faith, or even a particular system of beliefs. The center of Christianity

---

24. See H. Richard Niebuhr, *Radical Monotheism and Western Culture* (New York: Harper & Brothers, 1943); James M. Gustafson, *Ethics from a Theocentric Perspective,* 2 vols. (Chicago: University of Chicago Press, 1981, 1984).

25. Hauerwas, "On Keeping Theological Ethics Theological," 31.

26. Ibid., 30.

27. Ibid., 31–32.

is not any particular belief about Jesus constructed by the church, nor is the purpose of Christian ethics to assume moral responsibility for organizing the world. The center of Christianity for Hauerwas is the community-forming way of Christ that inspires a new kind of corporate spiritual existence in an alien world. To say that the original Christians believed in God is true but uninteresting, Hauerwas explains. "What is interesting is that they thought that their belief in God as they had encountered him in Jesus required the formation of a community distinct from the world exactly because of the kind of God he was."[28]

Authentic Christianity is therefore necessarily narrative-dependent and community-oriented. It creates an embodied ethic that cannot be abstracted from the Christian community or translated into idioms shared by outsiders. "As Christians we believe we not only need a community, but a community of a particular kind to live well morally. We need a people who are capable of being faithful to a way of life, even when that way of life may be in conflict with what passes as 'morality' in the larger society," Hauerwas argues.[29] Christianity is the messianic community faith of those who inhabit the new aeon, the kingdom of God, in the face of the prevailing principalities and powers. In plainer terms, "Christianity is an invitation to be part of an alien people who make a difference because they see something that cannot otherwise be seen without Christ."[30]

Hauerwas cautions that his ecclesiology is not a form of sectarianism and does not advocate "withdrawal" from the world. "How can the church possibly withdraw when it by necessity must always find itself surrounded?" he asks. "There is no place to which it can withdraw. I am not asking the church to withdraw, but rather to give up the presumptions of Constantinian power, particularly when those take the form of liberal universalism."[31] To those who argue that this approach abandons the church's moral responsibility to keep society from disintegrating into chaos, he replies that there appears to be no shortage of liberal Constantinians who want to manage the world in a "good" way.[32] America's policy institutes and universities are bursting with people who believe they can make the world a better place if they attain power. It is not any part of the church's moral mission to reinforce this Constantinian disposition, Hauerwas argues. Constantinianism is a difficult habit for the church to break because modern Christians think they can do good by attaining power and because "all

---

28. Ibid., 34.

29. Ibid., 35.

30. Stanley Hauerwas and William H. Willimon, *Resident Aliens: Life in the Christian Colony* (Nashville: Abingdon Press, 1989), 24.

31. Stanley Hauerwas, *After Christendom? How the Church Is to Behave If Freedom, Justice, and a Christian Nation Are Bad Ideas* (Nashville: Abingdon Press, 1991), 18.

32. Hauerwas, "A Christian Critique of Christian America," 263.

our categories have been set by the church's establishment as a necessary part of Western civilization."[33]

But the church can attain power only by surrendering Christianity. It can make its peace with the war-making state only by compromising Christ's commands to love your enemies, do good to those who persecute you, resist not evil, and turn the other cheek. In seeking to make Christianity more relevant or palatable to the modern age, theologians such as Niebuhr surrendered the heart of Christian faith, Hauerwas charges. "Niebuhr's understanding of salvation was fundamentally individualistic, if not gnostic. Indeed, this has been a characteristic of most Protestant liberals, excepting Rauschenbusch," he argues.[34] Put differently, for all of his concern with politics, Niebuhr surrendered the heart of Christianity by depoliticizing Christology. "Jesus becomes salvation from the human condition and not the sanctifying possibility within history of a political alternative that is saving," Hauerwas explains. Niebuhr thus found in Christianity a useful mythology for "the task of reorienting the culture of our day," he observes, quoting Niebuhr, but the church's task is not to make Christianity the civil religion of America or the world. The church's mission is to live faithfully in the light of Christ's proleptic kingdom. "There's an important difference between what I mean by 'kingdom' and what Niebuhr means by it," he notes. "For Niebuhr the kingdom is always an ideal that stands over against any possible realization in history. What that means is that he doesn't have any concrete manifestation of God in history. He just has the ideal standing over against historical realities. And I don't know if you need Jesus for that project."[35]

Hauerwas calls for an ethic that needs and makes no sense without Jesus. Like Rauschenbusch and Morrison, he calls for a recovery of the biblical kingdom faith in which the reign of God is viewed not only as an ideal beyond or at the end of history but also as a new community-making social order within history. He is emphatic that without the reality of Christ's kingdom-inaugurating resurrection from the dead, there is no ethic of the kingdom and no point in rehabilitating Christianity. The kingdom is not merely an ethical or religious idea but a spiritual reality. Without the grounding Christian faith that Christ has inaugurated a new era within history, there is not enough reason to follow Christ, much less any reason to salvage Christian ethics. Niebuhr's discomfort with the language of Easter faith and the biblical theology of the kingdom epitomizes, for Hauerwas, the fatal problem with Christian realism. Niebuhr's work sought

---

33. Hauerwas, *After Christendom,* 18–19.

34. Stanley Hauerwas, "When the Politics of Jesus Makes a Difference," *Christian Century* 110 (October 13, 1993), 983.

35. Quoted by Paul T. Stallsworth, "The Story of an Encounter," in *Reinhold Niebuhr Today,* ed. Richard John Neuhaus (Grand Rapids: Eerdmans, 1989), 104, 114.

to salvage a social role for modern churches and provide a theological rationale for Christian involvement in modern culture without disputing the skepticism of modern culture toward Christianity's founding beliefs. For all of his immense influence and success in this project, he thus contributed greatly to the demise of social Christianity by defending it as a religious philosophy or mythology that served particular social purposes. Niebuhr reinforced the academic prejudice that Christian theology has no foundation and no work of its own to do. For Niebuhr, the "love perfectionist," nonviolent way of Christ was a serious option only for sectarians who opted out of the social struggle for justice. Hauerwas counters that the biblical ethic of nonviolence "is not an option for a few, but incumbent on all Christians who seek to live faithfully in the kingdom made possible by the life, death, and resurrection of Jesus." Nonviolence is not one among other possible implications of Christian existence, but "the hallmark of the Christian moral life."[36]

Hauerwas thus seeks to reground theological ethics in the kingdom-seeking spirit of early Christianity. If social Christianity is to become converted to this religious vision, he argues, it must unlearn many of its Niebuhrian lessons. "Niebuhr taught us how to think. He gave us the categories that we've thought with for years. But I've slowly tried to train myself out of thinking in those categories," Hauerwas relates. "That's a very hard task, because when you let someone set the problem, oftentimes you keep getting their answer. So the challenge is how not to let them set the problem anymore."[37] In his insistence on the eschatological-communal character of authentic Christian existence, Hauerwas has identified the key weaknesses in Niebuhr's legacy and much of the social Christian tradition. His work has sought to show why a theology that takes Easter faith and the presence of the kingdom seriously must reject Niebuhr's categories. The spiritual reality confessed by Christian faith transcends the mundane reality of Christian realism.

But Hauerwas's version of this project internalizes certain Niebuhrian lessons only too well. Like the social gospelers, he calls for a recovery of the biblical ethic of the kingdom. He emphasizes the differences between a Constantinian ethic and a kingdom ethic, virtually repeating the central arguments of Morrison's *The Social Gospel and the Christian Cultus.* Like Morrison and Rauschenbusch, he contends that the presence of the eschatological kingdom radically changes the context in which Christian existence flourishes and in which Christian moral thinking should occur. He observes that the political achievement of the Enlightenment "has been to create people who believe it necessary to kill others

36. Hauerwas, *The Peaceable Kingdom,* xvi.
37. Quoted by Stallsworth, "The Story of an Encounter," 103.

in the interest of something called 'the nation,' " while the identity and loyalty of Christians belong to the kingdom.[38]

These are familiar themes to the progressive stream of social Christianity, but Hauerwas's version of the kingdom ethic strips Christianity of much of its social meaning. He claims that the social mission of the church does not include efforts to create a better government or social order. It does not include making alliances with non-Christians to struggle for social justice. In this area, Niebuhr's realism defines reality for Hauerwas. For Niebuhr, the mistake of the social gospelers was to enter the social struggle for justice armed only with moral idealism. The social gospelers had little sense of the inevitable brutality and evil of politics. Though some of them grasped that the struggle for social justice is fundamentally a struggle for power, none of them comprehended that all struggles for power, including their own, were inevitably fueled by egotism, hubris, and idolatry. Their attempts to recover the social meaning of Christian faith were thus fatally misconceived. They committed the church to a project of social regeneration that was itself morally corrupting. In their concern to "give the progressive movement a soul," the social gospelers misconstrued not only the love perfectionism of Christianity but also the demands of justice.

Hauerwas accepts this Niebuhrian reading of the social gospel tradition while rejecting Niebuhr's alternative to it. The social gospelers "never doubted the uniqueness of the American experience nor entertained any critical doubt about the achievement of the American ideal," he observes. "The only question was how to bring the economic institutions of American life under the same spirit of cooperation that our political institutions had already achieved."[39] In his reading, both of the dominant versions of modern social Christianity thus distorted Christianity. The social gospelers recovered the kingdom idea, but reduced the kingdom to their own futile idealistic politics; Niebuhr exposed the confusions of the social gospelers, but replaced them with a religious ethic that cut the heart out of Christianity. Both strategies evaded the strongly eschatological character of the gospel. But to recover the kingdom ethic, Hauerwas insists, is precisely to give up the social Christian hope of making the world a better place through moral effort or effective planning or some combination of love-inspired power politics. "The task of the Christian people is not to seek to control history, but to be faithful to the mode of life of the peaceable kingdom," he declares. "Such a people can never lose hope in the reality of that kingdom, but they must surely also learn to be patient. For they must often endure injustice that might appear to be quickly eliminated through violence."[40] The Christian calling is not to be

---

38. Hauerwas, *After Christendom*, 33.
39. Hauerwas, "On Keeping Theological Ethics Theological," 22.
40. Hauerwas, *The Peaceable Kingdom*, 106.

effective or successful, but to be faithful to the community-creating, kingdom-seeking way of Christ.

For Hauerwas, this is not a way that centers on questions about what the church should do in the struggle for racial, sexual, international, or economic justice. As he explains, "once such questions are made central for determining ✓ an agenda for a social ethic we feel the pull of natural law as an essential feature of Christian ethics. For to accomplish justice, to work for a more nearly free and equitable social order requires cooperation with non-Christians."[41] This commitment inevitably generates an agenda that compromises the church's identity and moral purpose. But the church is not called to attain and defend social justice, Hauerwas contends; rather, the church is called to be a faithful manifestation of the peaceable kingdom in the world; that is, "the church does not have a social ethic; the church is a social ethic."[42] The point of Christian ethics is not so much to do anything in particular, but to be something particular. Moreover, the kingdom ethic does not require the church to be a culture-renouncing sect removed from the world, but to be a confessing colony of believers who give witness to the presence of a new aeon in the midst of a dying world order. "The church need not feel caught between the false Niebuhrian dilemma of whether to be in or out of the world, politically responsible or introspectively irresponsible," Hauerwas argues. "Alas, our greatest tragedies occurred because the church was all too willing to serve the world. The church need not worry about whether to be in the world. The church's only concern is *how* to be in the world, in what form, for what purpose."[43] The Christian social mission is thus to create a kingdom-indwelling community in the world that worships and follows Christ in all things.

But what about the Scriptural command to seek justice and attain it? What about the biblical command to "establish justice in the gate" (Amos 5:15) and "execute justice one with another" (Jer. 7:5)? Is the way of Christ not summarized in Jesus' call to serve the poor, proclaim release to the captives, and set at liberty those who are oppressed (Luke 4:18-19)? Does it not include observing "the weightier matters of the law: justice and mercy and faith" (Matt. 23:23)? In the gospels, Jesus distinguishes between justice and mercy and calls his followers to pour themselves out in faith for both justice and mercy. It is not merely a communal ethic, for the nations shall be judged according to whether they have fed the hungry, given welcome to strangers, and given care to the sick, the destitute, and those in prison (Matt. 25:31-46). Hauerwas repeatedly laments that modern Christianity is preoccupied with social justice—"If there is anything

41. Ibid., 99.
42. Ibid.
43. Hauerwas and Willimon, *Resident Aliens*, 43.

Christians agree about today it is that our faith is one that does justice" he complains—but this is surely the aspect of modern social Christianity that holds the strongest biblical warrant.[44]

At a conference on the legacy of Niebuhr's theological ethics, the evangelical-social Christian theologian Ronald Sider pressed Hauerwas to acknowledge that, in a different way from Niebuhr's, his theology also failed the biblical tests of a kingdom ethic. "Why don't you say the following, Stan?" Sider offered. " 'The core of the gospel is the good news of the kingdom. The kingdom involves a new community which is a new social order that will be completed at the eschaton. Then the whole created order will be truly transformed.' " The unavoidable implication of this confession is that God cares about the right ordering of the world, Sider observed. "Furthermore, whenever we erect even modest signs of positive political change, we're moving things a little bit in the way in which they'll finally be completed. So of course Christians are concerned with the right ordering of the world." These are biblical truisms, Sider implied. How could Hauerwas deny that following Christ has something to do with caring about the right ordering of the world when the New Testament repeatedly proclaims that it does?

"Because when people say that, they always become Constantinian," Hauerwas immediately replied. "They want you to play the game of responsibility. Aha, they say, you're not being responsible! But, because of Niebuhr, responsibility carries a whole set of presumptions that I don't want to accept."[45] Having bought the Niebuhrian assumption that one can live the kingdom ethic or promote justice but not do both, Hauerwas concludes that justice "is a bad idea for Christians."[46] He calls for a social Christianity that renounces moral responsibility for the common good.[47] As he observes, to accept responsibility for the right ordering of society is to take on a more confounding, emotionally draining, and overwhelming task than the social gospelers ever imagined. Niebuhr remarked near the end of his life that if Rauschenbusch had lived to see the inheritance of the First World War, it would have broken his heart. Niebuhr's theology provided an alternative language for a church that still believed it had a mission to make the social order just, but which could not credibly view itself as a transforming agent for Christianizing the social order.

---

44. Hauerwas, *After Christendom,* 45.

45. Quoted by Stallsworth, "The Story of an Encounter," 113–14.

46. See Hauerwas, *After Christendom,* 45–68; Hauerwas, "Should Christians Talk So Much about Justice?" *Books and Religion* 14 (May/June, 1986); Hauerwas, "On the Right to Be Tribal," *Christian Scholars Review* 16 (March 1987), 238–41.

47. For Hauerwas's response to the charge that the church on which his ethic depends does not exist, see Stanley Hauerwas, "The Testament of Friends," in *How My Mind Has Changed,* ed. James M. Wall and David Heim (Grand Rapids: Eerdmans, 1991), 4–5.

That is, Niebuhr relinquished a transformationist view of the church's social purpose in favor of a view that assimilated the church into the dominant order. In the language of H. Richard Niebuhr's classic *Christ and Culture,* Reinhold Niebuhr gave up the social gospel "Christ the transformer of culture" perspective in favor of a dialectical "Christ and culture in paradox" position that also included elements of the outright accommodationist "Christ of culture" model.[48] Breaking with the social gospel faith that the church is called to transform society into the kingdom of God, Niebuhr went back—in his reckoning—to Luther and Augustine, contending that liberal Christianity read too much of its utopian progressivism into the question of what it means to follow Christ. Modern Christian social ethics has oscillated for the most part between these transformationist and assimilationist approaches, but Hauerwas chooses the third main option—isolation.

It is a distinctive kind of isolationism, which shares more with activist strains of the Mennonite and Brethren traditions than with traditional Christian sectarianism. The faithful confessing church is not a sect, he insists, but a countercultural colony living within and among a pagan world. The faithful church does not withdraw from the world; it lives out its distinctive communal existence within the world and in witness to it. Building on Yoder's ecclesiology, Hauerwas makes a strong claim that the church is called to be faithful to its identity as the living manifestation of the peaceable kingdom. For him, however, as for Yoder, this calling precludes any acceptance of a moral responsibility to work with non-Christians to create a just social order in a pagan world.

This insistence on dichotomizing the world between Christians and pagans marks the essential difference in spirit between Hauerwas's theology and progressive social Christianity. For the social gospelers, as for contemporary liberationists and ecofeminists, the moral core of Christianity compels cooperative efforts with unbelievers, in whom the Spirit also dwells. Hauerwas's emphasis on the Christian–non-Christian dichotomy produces an unacceptable position regarding the Christian struggle for a just social order, as well as a way of speaking about non-Christians that smacks of religious arrogance. The premodern church that dichotomized the world into these categories believed that all other religions are false, that Christ is the only way to salvation, and, therefore, that only Christians can escape eternal damnation. Modern Christianity cannot pretend to aspire to this worldview or seek to rescue some aspect of it for other purposes. To believe in the reality of the indwelling kingdom of Christ does not require that one regard the rest of the world as unregenerate or deprived of grace. Hauerwas gives short shrift to those who press him on the question. "That's a

---

48. See H. Richard Niebuhr, *Christ and Culture* (New York: Harper & Brothers, 1951).

liberal question," he abruptly told me at a conference. "You're worried about non-Christians because you're a liberal."[49]

The progressive Christianity with which I *do* identify takes more from Rauschenbusch than from Hauerwas in this area. It is inspired and reshaped by liberationist movements that Hauerwas spurns. In a historical context in which confessional accommodation is the norm and Hauerwas's communitarian pacifism offers an important alternative to what remains of Christendom, the rebirth of social gospel hope in the various liberationist, ecofeminist, and progressive Christian movements offers another alternative. When Gustavo Gutiérrez taught at Union Theological Seminary, in 1977 and 1978, he read Rauschenbusch for the first time and exhorted his North American students to resume Rauschenbusch's work. To take this recommendation to heart is to infuse American Christianity with the spirit of the social gospel in new forms.

Though Hauerwas's isolationism is influential among Christian ethicists, it does not have a large following in mainline churches, where the debate generally focuses on whether America's highly assimilated religious communities can or should become agents of social transformation. With the rise of liberationist and other progressive social theologies in the past generation, virtually all of the mainline churches have produced strong social action agencies and networks that outstrip the social gospel ministries that Morrison described in the 1930s. The establishment of numerous peace and ecojustice units and the positions on social issues taken by American churches in recent years have also heightened the tensions described by Morrison between liberal clergy and a generally more conservative laity. Morrison worried in the 1930s that a cultural-religious-political gulf had opened between a clerical generation influenced by social Christian theology and a larger group of laity who thought that ministers should stick to individualistic religion. Today neoconservatives and conservative evangelicals claim that American church leaders are abusing their power by promoting liberation theology.[50] In the 1980s, the pastoral letters of the American Catholic bishops on peacemaking and economic justice and the United Methodist Council of Bishops statement *In Defense of Creation* drew the most fire from conservatives, but virtually all of the mainline churches issued statements that strongly criticized American social injustice and militarism. The Left-Right split observed by Morrison intensified with the rise of theological currents that challenged not

---

49. Quotations from discussion session at American Academy of Religion national conference, Anaheim, California, November 1989.

50. See Stanley Atkins and Theodore McConnell, eds., *Churches on the Wrong Road* (Chicago: Regnery Gateway, 1986); Edward Norman, *Christianity and the World Order* (Oxford: Oxford University Press, 1979); Ronald Nash, ed., *Liberation Theology* (Milford, Mich.: Mott Media, 1984).

only American injustice but also the American empire.[51] As John C. Bennett observed, "The forward-looking social activism of the Social Gospel is with us again, but in a much more radical form."[52] Under the influence of liberation theology, many Christians have since concluded that American Christianity is too compromised by its desire for a respectable role in American society. In the ongoing debate between the church's various assimilationist and transformationist perspectives, American mainline Christianity has come to resemble exactly the cultural battleground that Morrison predicted, in which two variable theologies with profoundly different worldviews struggle for the soul of the church.

In the intellectual arena, transformationist theologies have clearly gained the upper hand in the generation since Niebuhr. Liberationist perspectives permeate contemporary Christian theological discussion as deeply as the social gospel infused liberal Christianity in the 1930s. Major theologians such as Ruether, Moltmann, Metz, Gutiérrez, Míguez Bonino, Cox, Cone, and Schüssler Fiorenza conceive the church's social role in liberationist or transformationist terms. The problem for those who are committed to a transformationist view of the church's social mission, however, is that liberation theology has flourished in the United States primarily in the classroom. As Morrison observed about an earlier form of social Christianity, it is primarily a preacher's gospel—or a theologian's gospel. For all of its influence in academe, liberation theology has not significantly influenced the religious outlook of most American churchgoers, who remain only dimly aware of its existence or its possible influence over their pastors.

Culture Religion and American Christianity

Morrison observed in 1948 that a distinctive but mostly unarticulated form of culture religion was becoming pervasive in American Christianity. This religious worldview was not taken from any theologian but consisted of a kind of folk religion that endorsed individualism, popular piety, and the American way of life. In Morrison's view, the religious worldview of most American Protestants

---

51. See National Conference of Catholic Bishops, *The Challenge of Peace: God's Promise and Our Response* (Washington, D.C.: U.S. Catholic Conference, 1983); National Conference of Catholic Bishops, *Economic Justice for All* (Washington, D.C.: U.S. Catholic Conference, 1986); United Methodist Council of Bishops, *In Defense of Creation: The Nuclear Crisis and a Just Peace* (Nashville: Graded Press, 1986); United Church Board for Homeland Ministries, *The Churches Speak: Findings 1986–1987, UCC Soundings Project* (New York: United Church of Christ, 1988); General Assembly Presbyterian Church (USA), *Peacemaking: The Believer's Calling* (New York: Office of the General Assembly, 1980).

52. John C. Bennett, "Christian Responsibility in a Time That Calls for Revolutionary Change," in *Marxism and Radical Religion: Essays toward a Revolutionary Humanism*, ed. John C. Raines and Thomas Dean (Philadelphia: Temple University Press, 1970), 50.

was too thoroughly accommodated to American commercial society for most Protestants to sanction any challenge to the ethos or arrangements of American society. Because of its sycophantic relationship to modern culture, modern Protestantism was losing its vitality. It had no dynamic of its own and no stomach for conflict. Morrison warned that mainline Protestantism was spiritually enervated and socially compromised. It did not instill in its members any commitment to a faith or way of life that challenged the dominant American order but turned the gospel into a blend of religious therapy, cultural piety, and middle-class American values.

Can Protestantism Win America? was written at a time when mainline Protestant membership rolls and church participation were still high enough to make the book's title not seem ridiculous. More recently, after two decades of steady decline in mainline church membership and participation, the central claims of Morrison's manifesto have been confirmed with instructive consistency in a series of sociological studies conducted by Dean Hoge, Wade Clark Roof and William McKinney, Robert Wuthnow, Benton Johnson, and others. Building upon Dean M. Kelley's influential 1972 study, *Why Conservative Churches Are Growing,* Roof and McKinney have confirmed Kelley's thesis that the most exclusivist and antiecumenical religious communities in America are growing; the more moderately exclusive denominations are neither growing nor shrinking, while witnessing some erosion in weekly participation; and the more liberal religious communities are absorbing serious losses. Kelley predicted that communities such as the Black Muslims, Jehovah's Witnesses, Churches of Christ, Orthodox Jews, and Seventh-Day Adventists would continue to grow in the 1970s and 1980s; that the Southern Baptist, Roman Catholic, and Orthodox churches would hold steady with some erosion; and that the liberal Protestant, Baptist, Episcopal, Presbyterian, Methodist, and Congregational churches would continue to shrink.[53] In 1979, Hoge and David A. Roozen confirmed these trends, noting that the churches suffering the worst membership losses were those that supported individualism and pluralism in belief, held the highest socioeconomic status, and were most affirming of American culture.[54] As Roof and McKinney later observed, these are defining characteristics of American liberal Protestantism. "Identification with the American Way especially lies at the core of this tradition," they remark. "Almost all of the churches that retained distance from the culture by encouraging distinctive life-styles and beliefs grew; those most

---

53. Dean M. Kelley, *Why Conservative Churches Are Growing* (New York: Harper & Row, 1972), 88–90.

54. Dean R. Hoge and David A. Roozen, *Understanding Church Growth and Decline, 1950–1978* (New York: Pilgrim Press, 1979).

immersed in the culture and only vaguely identifiable in terms of their own features suffered declines."[55]

The persistence of this cultural trend in the 1980s moved Roof and McKinney to elaborate on the Kelley-Hoge explanations for it. The fundamental problem with the liberal churches is that they are "very much captive to middle-class values" and therefore lacking in any capacity to sustain a strong transcendent vision, they observe. "So wedded were the liberal, mainline churches to the dominant culture that their beliefs, values, and behavior were virtually indistinguishable from the culture." Quoting Sidney Ahlstrom, Roof and McKinney note that Protestant neoorthodoxy tried to place a "layer of dogmatic asphalt" over the enervated culture faith of modern Protestantism, but this maneuver only warded off the impending crisis for a short time. "The old liberal synthesis of religion and culture was itself in crisis, and unable any longer to forge a meaningful vision of modern life," they observe.[56]

Having accommodated themselves so thoroughly to the dominant culture, the mainline churches no longer engage American culture with energy or conviction. They are no longer communities at all, but "religious audiences" with very weak group bonds. Liberal Protestantism has lost its inner core and its public voice, Roof and McKinney conclude. "Having made more accommodations to modernity than any other major religious tradition, liberal Protestantism shows many signs of tired blood: levels of orthodox belief are low, doubt and uncertainty in matters of faith common, knowledge of the Scriptures exceedingly low. A loss of morale and mission shows up in both its public demeanor and its corporate life."[57]

This picture of the state of mainline American religion is generally confirmed by Wuthnow, who emphasizes the role that narrow interest groups play in modern denominations, and by the team of Johnson, Hoge, and Donald Luidens, who argue that the crisis of liberal Protestantism is fundamentally a crisis of belief. Wuthnow observes that many Americans choose their religious community not on the basis of theological identification or family history but because it addresses a single therapeutic, political, or family interest. Church members expect to participate in special interest groups for only a limited period, he notes, "and their participation is restricted mainly to the specialized goals with which the

---

55. Wade Clark Roof and William McKinney, *American Mainline Religion: Its Changing Shape and Future* (New Brunswick, N.J.: Rutgers University Press, 1987), 20–21.

56. Ibid., 22; Sidney E. Ahlstrom, "The Radical Turn in Theology and Ethics: Why It Occurred in the 1960s," *Annals of the American Academy of Political and Social Science* 387 (January 1970), 1–13.

57. Ibid., 86.

group is concerned."[58] This trend toward interest group religion turns church membership into a commodity and virtually negates the function of the church as a character-shaping or culture-forming institution.

The Johnson, Hoge, and Luidens study of American Presbyterianism confirms the trends identified by the past generation of sociological research, while casting doubt upon various sociological explanations for them. Focusing on the religious beliefs of America's postwar baby-boom generation, they report that while many baby-boomers have left the church, very few have left because they found the church too liberal or conservative in either theology or politics. Few of them appear to be aware of the church's positions on social issues, the amount of their formal education has no discernible bearing on their religious attitudes or choices, and very few of them are actively searching for an alternative church or faith. "We have found no evidence that a substantial portion of these people are deeply concerned with religious questions or have explored a variety of religious options," the authors conclude. "In short, our baby boom drop-outs did not leave the Presbyterian church in search of salvation or enlightenment; they left because religion itself had become low on their list of personal priorities." They hold Jesus in high esteem and occasionally wonder about eternal life, "but they do not consider it necessary to attend church in order to nourish what faith they have."

But what about those who remain active in the church? The authors coin the phrase "lay liberalism" to describe the salad bar approach to religion taken by most church-going Presbyterian baby-boomers. Nearly all respondents who believe that Jesus is the only way to salvation are active in the church, the authors note, but this group represents a small minority among Presbyterians. Most Presbyterians (and probably most mainliners) subscribe to lay liberalism, which is "liberal" because it rejects the view that Christianity is the only true religion and "lay" because it bears little relationship to any contemporary academic theological system. "Lay liberalism does borrow from the views of certain dead intellectuals, but it is largely a homemade product, a kind of modern-age folk religion," the authors explain.[59] Modern Presbyterians report that they "prefer" Christianity because they are comfortable with it, they definitely do not believe in hell, and they strongly believe in the existence of a universal moral code that is common to all religions. They are hard-put to offer a religious reason why anyone should become a Christian, much less a Presbyterian. In contrast to

---

58. Robert Wuthnow, *The Restructuring of American Religion: Society and Faith since World War II* (Princeton, N.J.: Princeton University Press, 1988), 124.

59. Benton Johnson, Dean R. Hoge, and Donald A. Luidens, "Mainline Churches: The Real Reason for Decline," *First Things* 31 (March 1993), 15. See Hoge, Johnson, and Luidens, *Vanishing Boundaries: The Religion of Protestant Baby Boomers* (Louisville: Westminster/John Knox Press, 1994).

fundamentalists, who view their faith as a serious community-forming system of belief, lay liberals view Christianity as a set of conjectures concerning religious matters. "It supports honesty and other moral virtues, and it encourages tolerance and civility in a pluralistic society, but it does not inspire the kind of conviction that creates strong religious communities," the authors conclude.[60]

For anyone who is committed to the renewal of American social Christianity, these studies of mainline American religion are disturbing at best. Like *Habits of the Heart,* they portray American society as deeply privatistic and uprooted, but the depiction of these cultural traits within America's "communities of memory" seems to undermine the Bellah group's hope that American churches might become transformative agents in American society. Like *Habits of the Heart,* these studies unfortunately pay little attention to the black churches or African American culture, but like *Habits,* this approach also yields an instructive picture of the state of America's majority culture. Mainline churches once played an essential role in bolstering the dominant commercial order, but today, while still aspiring to political influence, the churches have become a refuge from the nihilism and predatory individualism unleashed by commercial society. Having long accommodated themselves to the American way, they are impeded by their own history and therapeutic ethos from renewing themselves as genuine religious communities. The studies repeatedly show that mainline churchgoers generally lack a deep or coherent faith, they expect to be catered to, they do not expect to be asked to do anything, they feel little commitment to each other as participants in something greater than themselves, and they consider social mission activities to be optional. Most mainliners view the church simply as a voluntary association. According to a 1990 Lilly Foundation–Search Institute study, 72 percent of adult mainline church members report that they have never met with others to promote social change; 52 percent have never given any time to helping the poor, hungry, and sick; and 78 percent have never engaged in any activity that promotes social justice.[61]

Mainline organizational structures typically reinforce this pattern of voluntarism and weak communal identity. Rather than organize themselves as organic, cooperative communities in which each part of the church is accountable to the others, most mainline churches are organized hierarchically and segmented into a bewildering variety of specialized areas and projects, usually with little connection between different levels and areas. This structural fragmentation breeds not only a pattern of voluntarism and overspecialization but also issue

---

60. Ibid., 16.
61. Lilly Foundation and Search Institute, *Effective Christian Education,* 1990, 26; cited in Audrey R. Chapman, *Faith, Power, and Politics: Political Ministry in Mainline Churches* (New York: Pilgrim Press, 1991), 110.

proliferation. Church agencies produce reams of policy statements and reports that are targeted toward selected segments of the church but that reflect little community input and have little impact on local congregations. The segmentation of American denominations inevitably pits various program agencies against each other as separate fiefdoms and undercuts the impact of national church statements within local congregations.

Having inherited a self-image as the religious foundation of American culture, the mainline churches have presumed the right to an insider strategy. Having bought the liberal notion that politics is about the struggle of interest groups for power, they have used their resources to build an elaborate infrastructure of lobbying organizations, policy committees, and information networks, seeking to influence American government by practicing interest group politics. Most mainline denominations maintain offices in Washington, D.C., that monitor legislative developments, lobby on Capitol Hill, organize advocacy seminars, and publish various legislative updates and policy statements. Like the Americans for Democratic Action and the Environmental Defense League, the churches use their newsletter subscriber lists and other contacts to mobilize support for particular legislative measures, typically with policy memos that are indistinguishable from bulletins issued by other liberal interest groups. Rather than devote their resources to outsider strategies that build religious communities and other grassroots organizations from below, the churches typically use their prestige, their inside contacts, and their formidable membership base to pressure the state for legislation that promotes mainline interests and moral beliefs.

The problem with this strategy is symptomatic of the problem with liberal Christianity. Instead of focusing their energies on developing strong religious communities that are truly religious and genuinely communities, the mainline churches have sought to minimize their differences with the dominant secular culture in order to salvage some influence within it. Much of their work in this area has been socially beneficial. Most lobbying organizations represent single-issue constituencies that practice a narrowly self-interested politics. As Allen Hertzke has shown, the mainline churches represent wider constituencies than most lobbying interests, and, unlike most lobbies, the churches devote more of their lobbying efforts to the public good than to issues that advance their own material interests. Because the mainline churches are committed to giving a voice to groups with little power in American society, they are sometimes able to use their power to provoke the political establishment to address pressing social needs; that is, the lobbying efforts of mainline church groups are often as effective as any other liberal interest group, and sometimes more so.[62]

---

62. Allen D. Hertzke, *Representing God in Washington: The Role of Religious Lobbies in the American Polity* (Knoxville: University of Tennessee Press, 1988), 111–206.

The problem with the churches' insider legislative orientation is not therefore that they make ineffective or inappropriate lobbying groups, but that this orientation is devitalizing to the churches as distinctively inspired religious communities. It produces a highly compromised politics and a watered-down theology. As Audrey Chapman observes, "the advocacy initiatives of these churches have been rendered generally reactive and captive to the secular Washington agenda, the dynamics of interest-group lobbying, and an unimaginative incremental issue approach."[63] By working so assiduously to make themselves relevant to a secular culture, the churches have been driven to adopt a highly secular rhetoric and agenda. Instead of challenging the dominant order from the perspective of a prophetic faith, the adoption of an insider strategy inevitably conforms the church to the culture and power structure of the dominant order. Instead of building religious communities that highlight the differences between the way of Christ and the American way, mainline Christianity continues to offer various forms of culture religion to diminishing "religious audiences." Chapman notes that mainline Christianity has therefore "become synonymous with lack of serious commitment, with the church imaged as a voluntary association catering to individual members rather than as a community dedicated to partnership with a God of peace, justice, and compassion."[64]

James Gustafson and the Church as Participant

The liberal churches thus find themselves in a bind. They cannot arrest their declining fortunes by returning to some form of fundamentalism. They cannot begin to pretend that the Bible is inerrant or that only Christians will escape eternal damnation. At the same time, despite its seriously eroding membership base, liberal Protestantism does provide the kind of inclusive, culture-affirming, individualistic religion that millions of Americans clearly want. Many mainliners are already exposed to as much community and religious fervor in their churches as they can stand. While belonging to a church that has accommodated much of its identity to the dominant culture, they experience the church as dangerously idealistic. Their participation in the church already pushes them to the edge of their idealism. It is the church that prods them to question the materialism and amorality of commercial society. The liberal churches cannot become more intentional, countercultural, or religious without alienating the critical mass of their existing membership base. For this reason especially, it is true, as Harlan Beckley argues, that the social gospel vision of the church as a culture-

---

63. Chapman, *Faith, Power, and Politics,* 107.
64. Ibid., 110.

transforming moral community is not a viable possibility for the mainline churches as presently constituted.

Yet Beckley gives too much religious significance to this sociological conclusion. Building upon Gustafson's image of the church as a participatory "community of moral discourse," he explicitly gives up the social gospel idea of the church as a socially regenerative manifestation of the kingdom in society. Beckley urges that the church as "participant" can play an educative role in the dominant culture and cooperate with other groups that strive for social justice, but he insists that the church must not regard itself "or any other collective agent, as a force for redemption in which divine justice is fully immanent."[65] The most that a highly assimilated American church can strive to become is a pluralistic moral community that cooperates with other groups to define and achieve attainable gains toward justice. The participant church insinuates itself into the dominant culture to bring to light as much of the Christian moral vision as is attainable within it.

This is a plausible and attractive strategic vision for "really existing mainline Protestantism." It seeks to maximize the church's justice-making efforts while acknowledging that mainline Protestantism is unavoidably part of the dominant order. It seeks to renew the church's identity as a teaching community while acknowledging that the church is limited, divided, and often wrong. Beckley's understanding of the church as a participatory moral community offers a compelling model of how an assimilated but progressive social Christianity might view its role in the public square. In seeking to develop an ecclesiological vision that is more realistic than the social gospel, however, Beckley gives up the New Testament notion of the church as the kingdom-prefiguring body of Christ. In seeking to present Gustafson's participant model as a superior alternative to the social theologies of Rauschenbusch and Niebuhr, Beckley also exaggerates Gustafson's break from transformationist understandings of the church's social mission.

For Gustafson, the model of the church as participant includes a transformative social function. The church as participant is distinct from the prophetic Christ-against-culture model of the church, which views the kingdom in apocalyptic terms and insists on absolute obedience to an absolute will of God. It is also distinct from the preservationist Christ-of-culture model of the church, which views the kingdom in historically immanent terms and calls for faithful responsibility to "traditional, practical, and proved values." The participant model is a dialectical notion for Gustafson, which is distinct from the prophetic and

---

65. Harlan Beckley, *Passion for Justice: Retrieving the Legacies of Walter Rauschenbusch, John A. Ryan, and Reinhold Niebuhr* (Louisville: Westminster/John Knox Press, 1992), 381.

preserver models of the church while drawing upon elements of both of these alternative ideal types. "The participant is wedded neither to the condemnation of the existing state of affairs, nor to whole-hearted support to them," he explains. The participant theologian brings the resources of Christian theology and tradition to the relative, ambiguous, but religiously necessary task of serving the common good.[66]

"The participant is one partner among many in the human conversation that will give some determination to the ways in which men use their technical and political powers, their resources and talents in the development of history and society toward humane ends," Gustafson remarks. While the participant theologian addresses social issues from a religiously informed perspective, he or she does not regard this perspective as revealed truth. "He neither stands with and for God announcing the failings of man, nor stands with and for God defending the achievements of society and culture," he explains. The participant theologian conceives God neither as the wrathful judge of prophetic theologies nor as the establisher of immutable order portrayed by preservationist theologies. In the participant perspective, God is the active presence or energy in history to which a faithful church responds. God is the innermost ground and ultimate future of the world who guides historical events, "but not as an inexorable process." Citing process theology and the work of Catholic theologian Karl Rahner as examples of this perspective, Gustafson contends that the participant theologian "becomes a participant in the creativity that leads to the future that is open with many possibilities for man."[67]

This sounds like culture religion, but Gustafson's elaboration of participant theology is explicitly transformationist and kingdom-oriented. Participant theology views Christ as the transformer of culture "rather than its radical critic or its defender." Christ calls the church neither to isolate itself from the world nor to assimilate into the dominant culture, Gustafson asserts. "He knows and feels the pain and suffering of the world in which the hungry remain unfed, the oppressed remain shackled in the chains of indifferent and tyrannical social orders. He knows the potentialities for a fairer and more loving pattern of human relationships that remain unrealized because of the defensiveness and greed of those in control." Participant Christianity thus brings the compassion and idealism of Christ into the dominant culture in order to bring the world "to the claims of God's perfect reign, his kingdom."[68]

---

66. James M. Gustafson, *Theology and Christian Ethics* (Philadelphia: Pilgrim Press, 1974), 82–84.

67. Ibid., 85–86.

68. Ibid., 88. For Gustafson's theological reflections on Christ as Creator, Redeemer, Sanctifier, Justifier, Pattern, and Moral Teacher, see James M. Gustafson, *Christ and the Moral Life* (New York: Harper & Row, 1968).

Gustafson observes that participant Christianity does not defend a kingdom that already exists because it recognizes that any outright identification of the kingdom with any historical institution or ideology is idolatry. "Rather, the participant is a member of a kingdom whose full reality is not perfectly manifest, yet whose power is at work in the actions of men that are in accord with its reality," he argues. The kingdom provides followers of Christ with a regenerative vision of the egalitarian, cooperative, peaceable social order that is worth struggling for. Moreover, the participant theologian does not shy away from drawing inferences about necessary political action from this vision of the kingdom. Faithfulness requires a willingness to run the risk of being wrong and a willingness to confess one's mistakes, Gustafson concludes:

> Like the American theologians of the social gospel, he will hazard the opinion that social ethical correlates of the coming kingdom can be determined. Thus, the kingdom toward which he is oriented suggests that oppression must give way to human freedom, concentration of wealth to distributive economic justice, concentrations of power to the participation of the powerless in the determination of their lives, the ways of war to the insurance of peace, deprivation of opportunities to the availability of education, health benefits, and other blessings of abundance.

The participant church thus serves the glory of God by living out the ethic of the kingdom, "striving toward the order of life that brings a greater measure of justice and love, peace and reconciliation, health and welfare."[69]

Making allowances for Gustafson's prefeminist language, this is a theological perspective that proclaims the heart of progressive social Christian faith. It embraces a transformationist understanding of the kingdom while importantly emphasizing that all attempts to understand the implications of Christian moral teaching are partial and subject to error. It refuses to identify the kingdom with any existing institution or ideology but insists that Christians must attempt in unavoidably fallible ways to draw concrete moral and political imperatives from the kingdom ethic. It cautions that the reign of God does not exist but affirms that it is partially prefigured in the communities of those who follow Christ. If there is any sense in which Gustafson's participant theology falls short of a transformationist Christian social perspective, it is only that he does not press the implications of his affirmation that the kingdom is partially manifest in history. He does not pursue the biblical notion of the body of Christ as an eschatological community gathered in the new aeon of the Spirit because he fears that this kind of language leads to sectarian understandings of history.

---

69. Ibid., 91–92, 95.

The Kingdom of Christ

Church history provides ample warrant for this fear. If the pressing danger of participant theology is accommodationism, as Beckley concedes, the chief danger of embracing an eschatological ecclesiology is that it can be taken to sanction a Christ-against-culture absolutism and religious sectarianism. But there is no reason why an eschatological kingdom-prefiguring Christianity must fall into some kind of ghettoizing absolutism or separatism. In the New Testament, the peace of Christ is an eschatological presence. It is disclosed not only at the edge of history or beyond history, but in the new aeon of the partially manifest reign of God. Yoder explains that the aeons of the kingdom and human history are not distinct periods of time but exist simultaneously: "They differ rather in nature or in direction; one points backwards to human history outside of (before) Christ; the other points forward to the fullness of the Kingdom of God, of which it is a foretaste. Each aeon has a social manifestation: the former in the 'world,' the latter in the body of Christ."[70]

If the church is not merely the body of Christians that awaits the kingdom, but the partial manifestation of the kingdom as the body of the resurrected Christ, it cannot regard the way of Christ as an ethic for an age yet to come. As Hauerwas remarks, the church in the biblical understanding *is* a social ethic. At the same time, against Hauerwas, this cannot mean that the biblical command to create a just social order is relativized, because, as liberationist Jon Sobrino explains, the ethic of the kingdom requires "action directed toward structurally transforming society in the direction of the reign of God by doing justice to the poor and oppressed majorities, so that they obtain life and historical salvation."[71] In Scripture, the crucial sign of the presence of the kingdom is that justice is brought to the poor and oppressed.

The church of the kingdom does not seek to attain or accommodate political power but seeks to incarnate the way of Christ and transform society into Christ's reign of justice and peace. It does not worry about finding a respectable place in society, but lives by its own dynamic. Yoder observes, "The real issue is not whether Jesus can make sense in a world far from Galilee, but whether—when he meets us in our world, as he does in fact—we want to follow him."[72] A Christian community that accepts this call to follow Christ will relate to the dominant order in a way that more closely resembles the witness of the historic peace churches than the culture religion of mainline Protestantism, but it will

---

70. John Howard Yoder, *The Original Revolution* (Scottdale, Pa.: Herald Press, 1971), 58.

71. Jon Sobrino, *Spirituality of Liberation: Toward Political Holiness,* trans. Robert R. Barr (Maryknoll, N.Y.: Orbis Books, 1988), 80.

72. Yoder, *The Priestly Kingdom,* 62.

not reduce the moral meaning of Christianity to any principle pertaining to moral absolutism, renunciation of power, or communal life. The kingdom ethic is not ethical fundamentalism. It should not equate the kingdom with a particular socioeconomic system (as Rauschenbusch did), make absolute pacifism the test of the kingdom (as Hauerwas and Yoder often seem to do), or sacralize any other principle or ideology with divine sanction. Gustafson's emphasis on this point is crucial. The church of the kingdom seeks always to discern what it means for Christian communities to follow Christ in new historical contexts, assuming that the church is called in the Spirit to prefigure a new society and emancipate the poor and oppressed.

This ecclesiological vision forms the basis of numerous koinonia groups, religious communities, and congregations within existing mainline Protestantism and Catholicism. It could conceivably form the basis for a new denominational or ecumenical grouping. As Morrison observed, the structures of modern American denominationalism are not only anachronistic for the faiths that live within them but also stifle the possibility of creating more vital religious forms. In either case, whether or not a significant realignment in American Christianity is a plausible possibility, the kingdom ethic does not provide a plausible ecclesiological vision if its religious inspiration is not true or not embraced as truth. Despite its compelling words about the importance, utility, and social necessity of religious communities of memory, this is the critical point at which *Habits of the Heart* shies away from its subject. The Bellah group laments that the biblical language of justice, community, solidarity, and the common good is being lost in commercial society. They call for a renewal of the kind of progressive religion that plays a morally regenerative role in American culture.

But they carefully avoid the religious claims that generate the Christian moral language that they seek to renew. They criticize the predominant consumerist understanding of freedom, for example, comparing it unfavorably to the morally prescriptive conception of freedom taught by Christianity. Consumer society loses its sense of the moral character of freedom when it reduces freedom to the morally neutral capacity to make choices among maximal possibilities, they suggest. The morally impoverished idea of freedom that predominates in commercial society is thus, for them, a symptom of a wide-ranging cultural degeneration under which the individualistic market has become not only the unchallenged model of economic life but also the model of social and moral existence.

In Christian ethics, freedom is never morally neutral but is always constitutive of the good. It is not the morally neutral capacity to choose between morally righteous and harmful means, because harmful choices are not made in freedom, but rather reflect the condition of moral bondage. To want to hurt or cheat someone is not to be free but to live in bondage to sin. In Christianity, freedom is liberation from sin, bondage, and oppression. Freedom is the desire and capacity to do the good. The Bellah group implicitly urges that American society needs to recover this understanding of the moral character of freedom. But the Christian understanding of freedom is not simply an alternative moral idea or tradition; it is the product of a distinctive spiritual experience of Christ as the truth that sets us free. In Christianity, freedom is the spiritual experience of salvation from sin and death. It is not true or real apart from the saving reality of Christ's death and resurrection.

Habits of the Heart stops short of this confessional center. It clings to the language and perspective of sociology. It comes close to dealing with moral issues prescriptively, while steering clear of theology. But in a Christian context, morality follows from religious claims. It is not separable from Christian theology, but rather reflects the ethical meaning of religious experiences and commitments. To argue that a renewal of progressive Christianity would be a good thing for American society is therefore not to make a particularly strong claim, unless Christianity can make a stronger claim to truth.

Social Christianity since the generation of Rauschenbusch and Mathews has often downplayed the question of religious truth. Mathews took a thoroughly historicist approach to religious claims and often reduced his own apologetic to the claim that progressive Christianity is good for America; Rauschenbusch rarely mentioned the resurrection of Christ; Niebuhr regarded the basic symbols of Christian faith (with the partial exception of the cross) as essentially myths. Christian ethicists have too often assumed that the crisis of modern Christianity can be resolved if Christianity can be translated into a sufficiently compelling social vision. At a time when large numbers of Americans have no religious background at all, this assumption is more untenable than ever. Christianity must be more than the underpinning of an attractive social philosophy or politics if it is to become a living faith for unchurched religious seekers.

The Next Generation

At the same time, it is a mistake to write off modern Christianity as a progressive social force. Whenever I am told by friends in secular progressive organizations that the churches are dying or that social Christianity is "used up" as a regenerative political force, I always think, compared to what? There are more Methodists in Cleveland than members of any national Left organization in the United States. For all of their losses between 1965 and 1985, American liberal Protestant churches still number more than 25 million members, while the Catholic church claims 58 million members and the growing, socially conscious African American churches contain nearly 20 million members. More than any comparable social institution in American life, the mainline churches have diversified beyond their ethnic families of origin to reflect the diversity of American society. Moreover, the social ministries of these churches, such as Church World Service and the various denominational relief agencies, still outstrip the secular progressive organizations with which they are typically allied. Those who participate in the peace fellowships, relief agencies, urban ministries, and justice organizations sponsored by the churches have already chosen the outlet for their idealism. Most of them are not looking for the large Leftist movement or political party that secular Leftists yearn for. Mainline Christianity is far from the soul in the socialist movement that Rauschenbusch hoped it would become, but it is still the largest part of America's organized progressive political constituency.[73]

"Like all the rest of us, the Church will get salvation by finding the purpose of its existence outside of itself, in the Kingdom of God, the perfect life of the race," Rauschenbusch wrote in *Christianizing the Social Order:*

> We do not want less religion; we want more; but it must be a religion that gets its orientation from the Kingdom of God. To concentrate our efforts on personal salvation, as orthodoxy has done, or on soul culture, as liberalism has done, comes close to refined selfishness. All of us who have been trained in egotistic religion need a conversion to Christian Christianity, even if we are bishops or theological professors. Seek ye first the Kingdom of God and God's righteousness, and the salvation of your souls will be added to you.[74]

That is the spirit of progressive social Christianity. To seek the kingdom in the political sphere is to embrace the tridimensional social vision of liberty, equality, and community, Rauschenbusch argued, but in a country "where people only understand individualism," social Christianity is constantly pressed to defend the values of equality and community. To Rauschenbusch, the project of working for a cooperative commonwealth was ultimately a matter of faith, to be carried on regardless of the political, cultural, or economic obstacles to it.

At the same time, it is crucial that the next generation of social Christians not share the illusions of their forerunners about their own power or purposes. The idea that liberal Christianity can reorganize the world has been a defining social Christian illusion. If Hauerwas takes the point too far and thus abdicates Christian moral responsibility to struggle for a just society, it is nonetheless a Christian truism, as he claims, that Christians are not called to run the world. The kingdom to which Christians belong and owe their loyalty is partially prefigured in the world; it calls Christians to bring the transforming virtues of love, peace, and justice into the world; it calls Christians to join sides with the poor and oppressed to attain justice; but it does not make political success the criterion

---

73. Cf. Kenneth B. Bedell, ed., *Yearbook of American & Canadian Churches 1993* (Nashville: Abingdon Press, 1993).

74. Walter Rauschenbusch, *Christianizing the Social Order* (New York: Macmillan, 1919, c1912), 464--65.

of its action or seek power over the social order. The social ethic of the way of Christ is an ethic of faithfulness to the prophetic biblical ideals of freedom, equality, community, and redemptive love. It calls the body of Christ to be a moral community that incarnates these ideals in the world and lives faithfully by them. It seeks to bring sustainable justice and peace to the world but does not live by the world's tests for worthwhile activity.

Whether or not the triumph of corporate capitalism nullifies the possibility of creating an egalitarian democratic society, the Christian imperative to struggle for whatever gains toward social justice as may be attainable is not negated. Rauschenbusch tried to wed Christianity to what he believed was a world-conquering movement for democratic socialism. The social Christianity that is needed would eschew his historical optimism and his identification of the kingdom with particular social movements while sharing his motivating faith that the church must take sides with the poor and oppressed to democratize social and economic power. As he often remarked, the limits of attainable justice cannot be known or realized unless they are struggled for. The church that does not struggle for "things not seen" betrays the hope of the poor and oppressed. Liberation theology is therefore crucial to any future social Christianity because it brings to Christianity the perspectives of those who have no choice but to struggle for a just social order. As Rauschenbusch also observed, social Christianity cannot go far on the strength of middle-class idealism. It needs the perspectives and solidarity of communities from the "underside of history," who will not settle for less than justice.

No one knows whether America's current experiments in ecojustice and economic democracy can create new possibilities in a society driven by seemingly uncontrollable economic forces. No one can say for certain that worker and social ownership will bring about greater equality, that environmental catastrophe will be averted, or that the movements for racial and gender equality have any reasonable chance of success in a world economy that destroys nature and community. But the necessity of struggling for equality and sustainable community is utterly certain. The future belongs to God, and after all our efforts to change the world are finished, it is God who will make something new in the world out of our strivings for sustainable justice and peace.

At the heart of modern capitalist economics is the idea of infinite accumulation. At the heart of Christian social teaching, however, is a strong conception of distributive justice and the related notion that there is such a thing as having enough. The prevailing American preoccupation with piling up money and material possessions is spiritually deadening. The readiness to defend ill-begotten privileges with force is immoral. The prevailing view of nature as a commodity to be conquered and exploited degrades the sacredness of creation. These themes have marked Christian ethics at its best. Figures such as Rauschenbusch and

Temple were powerful advocates for progressive Christianity, partly because their minds were rooted in the biblical and spiritual wisdom of the past, partly because they were alive to new challenges and horizons for the church, and partly because they believed that Christianity has an important social mission. If liberal Christianity is to regain its public voice, it must recover this spirit.

Index